Edvantage Scien

AP Chemistry 2

St. Andrew's College

Development Team

Authors

Cheri Smith
Yale Secondary
School District 34 Abbotsford

Gary Davidson
School District 22 Vernon

Megan Ryan
Walnut Grove Secondary
School District 35 Langley

Chris Toth
St. Thomas More Collegiate
Burnaby, British Columbia

Program Consultant
Lionel Sandner
Edvantage Interactive

MW01708718

COPIES OF THIS BOOK MAY BE
OBTAINED BY CONTACTING:

Edvantage Interactive

E-MAIL:
info@edvantageinteractive.com

TOLL-FREE FAX:
866.275.0564

TOLL-FREE CALL:
866.422.7310

EDVANTAGE
INTERACTIVE

AP Chemistry 2: St. Andrew's College

Copyright © 2019, Edvantage Interactive

All rights reserved. No part of this publication may be reproduced or transmitted in any form or by any means, or stored in a database or retrieval system, without the prior written permission of Edvantage Interactive.

ISBN 978-1-77430-035-0

Care has been taken to trace ownership of copyright material contained in this text. The publishers will gladly accept any information that will enable them to rectify any reference or credit in subsequent printings.

Vice-President of Marketing: *Don Franklin*
Director of Publishing: *Yvonne Van Ruskenveld*
Design and Production: *Donna Lindenberg, Paula Gaube*
Editorial Assistance: *Rhys Sandner*
Proofreading: *Eva van Emden*

The AP Units at the beginning of each chapter are quoted from *AP Chemistry: Course and Exam Description*, revised edition, effective Fall 2019, published by the College Board, New York, NY. Advanced Placement, AP, and College Board are registered trademarks of the College Board.

QR Code — What Is This?

The image to the right is called a QR code. It's similar to bar codes on various products and contains information that can be useful to you. Each QR code in this book provides you with online support to help you learn the course material. For example, find a question with a QR code beside it. If you scan that code, you'll see the answer to the question explained in a video created by an author of this book.

You can scan a QR code using an Internet-enabled mobile device. The program to scan QR codes is free and available at your phone's app store. Scanning the QR code above will give you a short overview of how to use the codes in the book to help you study.

Note: We recommend that you scan QR codes only when your phone is connected to a WiFi network. Depending on your mobile data plan, charges may apply if you access the information over the cellular network. If you are not sure how to do this, please contact your phone provider or us at info@edvantageinteractive.com

Contents

AP Chemistry 2

EDVANTAGE INTERACTIVE

© Edvantage Interactive 2019

Welcome to AP Chemistry 2

AP Chemistry 2 is a print and digital resource for classroom and independent study, aligned with the AP curriculum. You, the student, have two core components — this write-in textbook or WorkText and, to provide mobile functionality, an interactive Online Study Guide.

AP Chemistry 2 WorkText

What is a WorkText?

A WorkText is a write-in textbook. Not just a workbook, a write-in **textbook**.

Like the vast majority of students, you will read for content, underline, highlight, take notes, answer the questions — all in this book. **Your book**.

Use it as a textbook, workbook, notebook, AND study guide. It's also a great reference book for post secondary studies.

Make it your own personal WorkText.

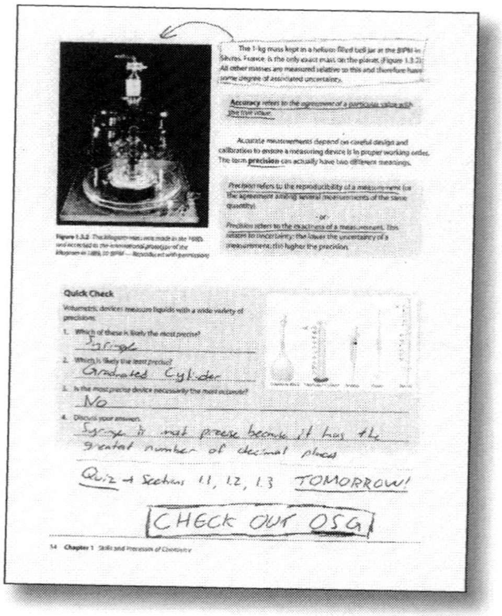

Why a write-in textbook?

Reading is an extremely active and personal process.

Research has shown that physically interacting with your text by writing margin notes and highlighting key passages results in better comprehension and retention.

Use your own experiences and prior knowledge to make meaning, not take meaning, from text.

How to make this book work for you:

1. Scan each section and check out the shaded areas and bolded terms.
2. Do the Warm Ups to activate prior knowledge.
3. Take notes as required by highlights and adding teacher comments and notes.
4. Use Quick Check sections to find out where you are in your learning.
5. Do the Review Questions and write down the answers. Scan the **QR codes** or go to the **Online Study Guide** to see YouTube-like video worked solutions by *AP Chemistry 2* authors.
6. Try the **Online Study Guide** for online quizzes, PowerPoints, and more videos.
7. Follow the six steps above to be successful.

For more information on how to purchase your own personal copy
info@edvantageinteractive.com

 © Edvantage Interactive 2019

AP Chemistry 2 Online Study Guide (OSG)

What is an Online Study Guide?

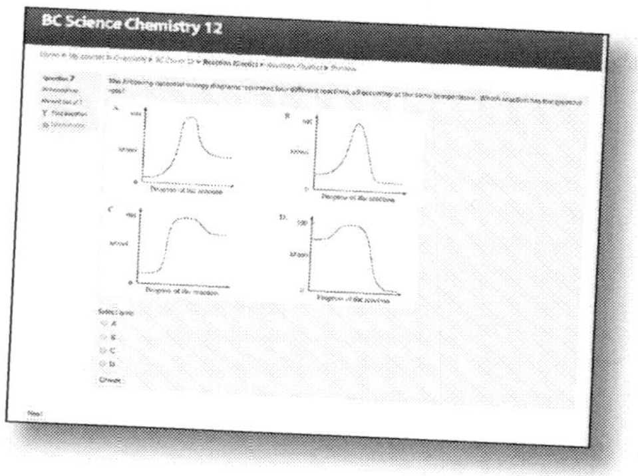

It's an interactive, personalized, digital, mobile study guide to support the WorkText.

The **Online Study Guide** or OSG, provides access to online quizzes, PowerPoint notes, and video worked solutions.

Need extra questions, sample tests, a summary of your notes, worked solutions to some of the review questions? It's all here!

Access it where you want, when you want.

Make it your own personal mobile study guide.

What's in the Online Study Guide?

- Online quizzes, multiple choice questions, exam-like tests with instant feedback
- PowerPoint notes: Key idea summary and student study notes from the textbook
- Video worked solutions: Select video worked solutions from the WorkText

Scan this code for a quick tour of the OSG

If you have a smart phone or tablet, scan the QR code to the right to find out more.
Color e-reader WorkText version available.

Where is the Online Study Guide located?

www.edvantagescience.com

Should I use the Online Study Guide?

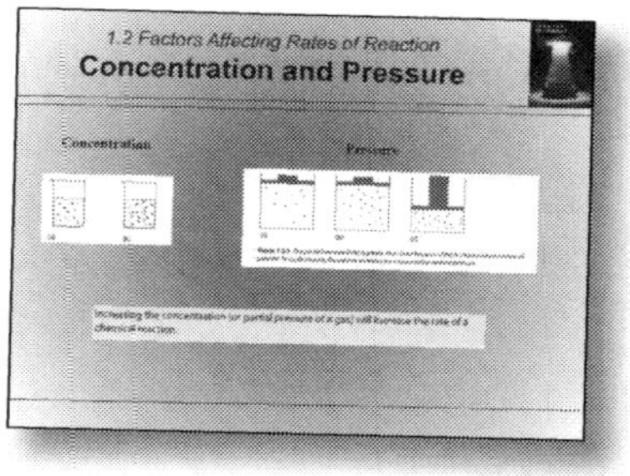

YES... if you want to do your best in this course.
The OSG is directly LINKED to the activities and content in the WorkText.
The OSG helps you learn what is taught in class.

If your school does not have access to the Online Study Guide and you'd like more information — info@edvantageinteractive.com

1 Reaction Kinetics

This chapter focuses on the following AP Unit from the College Board:

Unit 5: Kinetics

By the end of this chapter, you should be able to do the following:

- Demonstrate awareness that reactions occur at differing rates
- Experimentally determine rate of a reaction
- Demonstrate knowledge of collision theory
- Describe the energies associated with reactants becoming products
- Apply collision theory to explain how reaction rates can be changed
- Analyze the reaction mechanism for a reacting system
- Represent graphically the energy changes associated with catalyzed and uncatalyzed reactions
- Describe the uses of specific catalysts in a variety of situations

By the end of this chapter, you should know the meaning of these **key terms**:

- activated complex
- activation energy
- bimolecular
- catalyst
- catalytic converter
- collision theory
- ΔH notation
- elementary processes
- endothermic
- enthalpy
- enzymes
- exothermic
- heterogeneous catalysts
- homogeneous catalysts
- initial rate
- integrated rate law
- KE distribution curve
- kinetic energy (KE),
- metalloenzymes
- molecularity
- overall order
- potential energy (PE)
- product
- rate-determining step
- reactant
- reaction intermediate
- reaction mechanism
- reaction rate
- successful collision
- termolecular
- thermochemical equation

External tanks of liquid oxygen and hydrogen fuel react to create the energy needed to launch a rocket carrying the space shuttle.

1.1 Measuring the Rate of Chemical Reactions

Warm Up

In previous Science courses, you were introduced to the concept of rate of change in the position of an object as it moves. You learned that this is the object's velocity. If we don't consider the object's direction, we might use the more general terms, "speed" or "rate." Velocity is a vector quantity while speed is a scalar quantity. When dealing with chemical reactions, we need not concern ourselves with vectors.

Assume a vehicle moves the following distances over the stated periods of time as it travels from Anaheim into Los Angeles:

Distance Travelled (km)	Time (min)
0	0
22	20.0
62	50.0
117	90.0
125	100.0

What is the average velocity (rate) of the car (over the entire time period)?

(a) in km/min ____________________

(b) in km/h ____________________

(c) Why do we refer to this as an *average* rate?

____

____

(d) A unit of __________ is always placed in the denominator when calculating rate.

Measuring Reaction Rate

Chemical reactions involve the conversion of reactants with a particular set of properties into products with a whole new set of properties.

Chemical kinetics is the investigation of the rate at which these reactions occur and the factors that affect them.

If you consider familiar reactions like the explosion of a firecracker, the metabolism of the lunch you ate today and the rusting of your bicycle, it is evident that chemical reactions occur at a wide variety of rates (Figure 1.1.1).

Time for reaction: < 1 s — several hours — weeks to many months

Figure 1.1.1 *An explosion, food digestion, and rusting metal all involve chemical reactions but at very different rates.*

Reaction rates may be determined by observing either the disappearance of a reactant or the appearance of a product. Deciding exactly what to measure can be a tricky business. There are several things the chemist needs to consider:

- Is there a measurable property associated with the change in quantity of a reactant or product you might use to determine the rate?

 © Edvantage Interactive 2019

- Exactly how might you measure the quantity of reactant or product in the laboratory?
- Finally, what units would be associated with the quantity you measure and consequently, what units will represent the reaction rate?

Once these questions have been answered, it is simply a matter of determining the rate using the following equation:

$$\text{average reaction rate} = \frac{\text{change in a measurable quantity of a chemical species}}{\text{change in time}}$$

Experimentally, it turns out that, for most reactions, the rate is greatest at the beginning of the reaction and decreases as the reaction continues. Because the rate changes as a reaction proceeds, reaction rates are generally expressed as averages over a particular time period. As reactants are being consumed during a reaction, the forward rate might be thought of as having a negative value. However, we generally report the rate as an absolute or positive value.

Quick Check

Thionyl chloride is a reactive compound used in a variety of organic synthesis reactions. Due to its potential to release dangerous gases explosively on contact with water, it is controlled under the Chemical Weapons Convention in the United States. It can be decomposed in solution with an organic solvent according to the reaction:

$SO_2Cl_2(soln) \rightarrow SO_2(g) + Cl_2(g)$

Removal of small samples called aliquots and titration of these samples as the reaction proceeds produces the data given in the table on the next page.

Note: Ideally, a reaction should be *monitored* as it proceeds without interference. In a technique such as this, it is critical to remove as small an aliquot as possible so that the sampling's interference with the subject reaction is minimal. It is also important to complete the titration as quickly as possible because the reaction, of course, continues to occur within the sample. Nonetheless, removal and sampling of small aliquots is one technique for monitoring the rate of a chemical reaction.

Use the grid provided on this page to produce a graph of concentration of thionyl chloride versus time.

$[SO_2Cl_2]$ (mol/L)	Time (seconds)
0.200	0
0.160	100.
0.127	200.
0.100	300.
0.080	400.
0.067	500.
0.060	600.

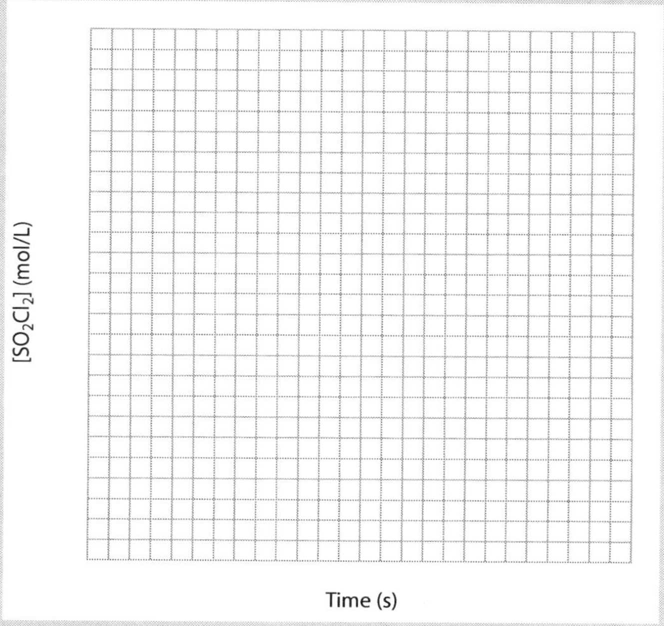

(Quick Check continued on next page)

Quick Check *(continued)*

1. What would the slope of this graph ($\Delta[SO_2Cl_2]/\Delta time$) represent?

2. How does the slope of the graph change as time passes?

3. What does this indicate about the reaction rate?

4. What is the average rate of decomposition of thionyl choride?

5. How does the rate at 500 s compare to the rate at 300 s?

6. Suggest a way to determine the rate at the particular times mentioned in question 5. The rates at those particular instants are called **instantaneous rates**.

7. Calculate the instantaneous rates of reaction at 500 s and 300 s (if you're unsure of how to do this, ask a classmate or your teacher).

Reaction Measuring Techniques

The technique used to measure the change in the quantity of reactant or product varies greatly depending on the reaction involved and the available apparatus. In many cases, the reactant or product involved in a reaction may be measured directly. As in the Quick Check above, the concentration of a reactant in solution may be determined from time to time as the reaction proceeds by the titration of an aliquot of the reacting species. If a gas is being formed or consumed in a closed system, a manometer may be used to measure the change in pressure (Figure 1.1.2(a)). Gas production might also be measured using a pneumatic trough and a gas volume measuring tube called a eudiometer (Figure 1.1.2(b)). Of course, if a gas is leaving an open system, there will be a change in mass that could easily be measured using a balance.

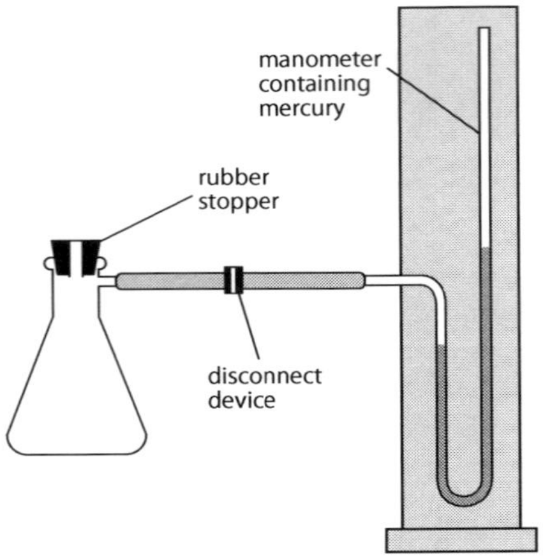

(a) A manometer measures the partial pressure of a gas formed in a reaction

Figure 1.1.2 *A manometer (a) and a eudiometer (b) are two different devices that can be used to measure the production of a gas from a reaction in a closed system.*

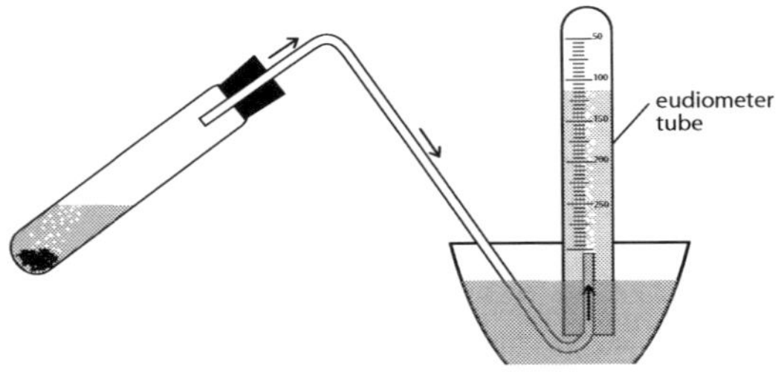

(b) A eudiometer measures the volume of gas produced during a reaction.

© Edvantage Interactive 2019

If the amount of a reactant or a product can't be monitored directly, a chemist can monitor some property of the reacting mixture that correlates in a known manner with the quantity of a reactant or a product. If a reaction is occurring in aqueous solution, the solution's color and pH (acidity) are properties that might indicate the quantity of reactant or product present.

A pH electrode is one type of ion selective electrode (ISE) that can be used to measure acidity. The concentrations of many types of ions can be measured with different ISEs. The ion's concentration correlates with the charge that builds up as the ion diffuses across the ISE's membrane. It is simplest if only one chemical involved in the reaction affects the monitored property. If the property is influenced by more than one chemical, then their relative influences must be known. Reactions involving color changes may be colorimetrically analyzed using a spectrophotometer.

Sample Problem 1.1.1 — Determining the Rate of a Reaction in the Laboratory

State five different methods for measuring the rate of the reaction of an iron nail in concentrated hydrochloric acid.

What to Think About	How to Do It
1. Begin by writing a balanced chemical equation. It is very important to consider the states (and any colors) of all species.	$Fe(s) + 2HCl(aq) \rightarrow FeCl_2(aq) + H_2(g)$ colorless (HCl) — yellow-orange color (like rust) ($FeCl_2$)
2. Decide if there is a property associated with the quantity of reactant consumed or product produced that you might measure to monitor the reaction rate.	The first species, Fe(s) is a solid that will be consumed during the reaction.
3. Decide exactly how you might measure this property and what unit would be associated with it.	A balance could be used to determine the mass of the iron before and after the reaction was completed. The time would also need to be recorded. The resulting rate of reaction would be recorded in units of g Fe used/unit of time.

4. A repeat of the same steps would reveal more than five different ways to determine the rate of this particular reaction. Other answers might include:

$\frac{\Delta[HCl]}{time}$	$\frac{\Delta pH}{time}$	$\frac{\Delta Vol\ H_2}{time}$	$\frac{\Delta P_{(H_2)}}{time}$	$\frac{\Delta mass_{H_2}}{time}$
titrate	pH meter	eudiometer	manometer	balance (open system)
M/s	pH units/s	mL/s	kPa/s	g/s

Practice Problems 1.1.1 — Determining the Rate of a Reaction in the Laboratory

1. Indicate two methods for determining the rate of each of the following reactions:
   (a) $Cu(s) + 2\ AgNO_3(aq) \rightarrow Cu(NO_3)_2(aq) + 2\ Ag(s)$ (Cu^{2+} ions are blue.)

   (b) $PCl_5(g) \rightarrow PCl_3(g) + Cl_2(g)$

   (c) $CaCO_3(s) \rightarrow CaO(s) + CO_2(g)$

   (d) $H_2SO_4(aq) + Ba(OH)_2(aq) \rightarrow BaSO_4(s) + 2\ H_2O(l)$

2. Why would volume of water **not** be an acceptable answer for question 1(d) above?

3. Why would concentration of copper metal, [Cu(*s*)], **not** be an acceptable answer for question 1(a) above?

Calculating Reaction Rate

Once the chemist has decided what quantity of a particular chemical species to measure, he or she may begin to gather data. These data may be used to calculate the rate of the chemical reaction. Data may be presented graphically to monitor the rate throughout the entire reaction, or initial and final data may be used to determine the reaction's average rate as indicated earlier.

$$\text{average reaction rate} = \frac{\Delta\ \text{measurable quantity of a chemical species}}{\Delta\ \text{time}}$$

As chemistry often involves the application of a balanced chemical equation, it is possible to convert from the rate of one reacting species to another by the simple application of a **mole ratio**.

Sample Problem 1.1.2 — Calculating Average Rate from Laboratory Data

A paraffin candle ($C_{28}H_{58}$) is placed in a petri dish on an electronic balance and combusted for a period of 15.0 min. The accompanying data is collected.

(a) Calculate the average rate of combustion of the paraffin over the entire 15 min period.
(b) Calculate the average rate of formation of water vapor for the same period.
(c) Note the mass loss in each 3.0 min time increment. Comment on the rate of combustion of the candle during the entire trial. Suggest a reason why the rate of this reaction isn't greatest at the beginning, with a steady decrease as time passes.
(d) Why don't the mass values drop in a completely constant fashion?

Time (min)	Mass (g)
0	180.00
3.0	178.00
6.0	175.98
9.0	173.99
12.0	172.00
15.0	170.01

Continued opposite

 © Edvantage Interactive 2019

Sample Problem 1.1.2 (*Continued*)

What to Think About	How to Do It
1. Write a balanced chemical equation. Hydrocarbon combustion always involves reaction with oxygen to form water vapor and carbon dioxide.	$2\ C_{28}H_{58}(s) + 85\ O_2(g) \rightarrow 56\ CO_2(g) + 58\ H_2O(g)$
2. Think about the system carefully. Consider the balanced equation. What is causing the loss of mass?	In this case, all mass loss is due to the combusted paraffin. This paraffin is converted into two different gases: carbon dioxide and water vapor.
Question (a) 3. Apply the equation with appropriate significant figures to calculate the rate. Note that the rate is a negative value as paraffin is lost. To simplify things, reactant and product rates are often expressed as absolute values. Consequently they appear positive.	$\frac{170.01\text{ g} - 180.00\text{ g}}{15.0\text{ min} - 0\text{ min}} = -0.666\text{ g/min}$
Question (b) 4. Now apply appropriate molar masses along with the mole ratio to convert the rate of consumption of paraffin to the rate of formation of water vapor as follows: mass paraffin (per minute) → moles paraffin → moles water vapor → mass water vapor (per min)	$\frac{0.666\text{ g } C_{28}H_{58}}{\text{min}} \times \frac{1\text{ mol } C_{28}H_{58}}{394.0\text{ g } C_{28}H_{58}}$ $\times \frac{58\text{ mol } H_2O}{2\text{ mol } C_{28}H_{58}} \times \frac{18.0\text{ g } H_2O}{1\text{ mol } H_2O}$ $= 0.882\text{ g } H_2O/\text{min}$
Question (c) 5. Notice the mass loss in each 3.0 min time increment recorded in the table.	The rate of consumption of paraffin seems to be nearly constant. This may be due to the $[O_2]$ being very plentiful and so essentially constant. As well, the quantity of molten paraffin at the reacting surface stays constant through the entire reaction. As this reaction proceeds, there is no decrease in [reactants] to lead to a decrease in reaction rate.
Question (d) 6. Explain why the mass values do not drop in a completely constant fashion.	There is some variation in rate. This is due to the expected uncertainty associated with all measuring devices (in this case, the balance).

Practice Problems 1.1.2 — Calculating Average Rate

1. A piece of zinc metal is placed into a beaker containing an aqueous solution of hydrochloric acid. The volume of hydrogen gas formed is measured by water displacement in a eudiometer every 30.0 s. The volume is converted to STP conditions and recorded.
   (a) Determine the average rate of consumption of zinc metal over the entire 150.0 s in units of g/min.

Volume H_2 (STP) (mL)	0	15.0	21.0	24.0	25.0	25.0
Time (seconds)	0	30.0	60.0	90.0	120.0	150.0

   (b) When is the reaction rate the greatest?

   (c) What is the rate from 120.0 to 150.0 s?

   (d) Assuming there is still a small bit of zinc left in the beaker, how would you explain the rate at this point?

2. A 3.45 g piece of marble ($CaCO_3$) is weighed and dropped into a beaker containing 1.00 L of hydrochloric acid. The marble is completely gone 4.50 min later. Calculate the average rate of reaction of HCl in mol/L/s. Note that the volume of the system remains at 1.00 L through the entire reaction.

Using Rate as a Conversion Factor

A **derived unit** is a unit that consists of two or more other units. A quantity expressed with a derived unit may be used to convert a unit that measures one thing into a unit that measures something else completely. One of the most common examples is the use of a rate to convert between distance and time.

The keys to this type of problem are:
- determining which form of the conversion factor to use, and
- deciding where to start.

Sample Problem 1.1.3 — Using Rate as a Conversion Factor

A popular organic chemistry demonstration is the dehydration of sucrose, $C_{12}H_{22}O_{11}$, using sulfuric acid to catalyze the dehydration. The acid is required for the reaction, but it is still present once the reaction is complete, primarily in its intact form and partially as dissolved sulfur oxides in the water formed. Because of this, it does not appear at all in the reaction. The product is a large carbon cylinder standing in a small puddle of water as follows: $C_{12}H_{22}O_{11}(s) \rightarrow 11\ H_2O(g) + 12\ C(s)$. Due to the exothermicity of the reaction, much of the water is released as steam, some of which contains dissolved oxides of sulfur. Ask your teacher to perform the demonstration for you, ideally in a fume hood.

Given a rate of decomposition of sucrose of 0.825 mol/min, how many grams of C(*s*) could be formed in 30.0 s?

Continued opposite

 © Edvantage Interactive 2019

Sample Problem 1.1.3 (*Continued*)

What to Think About

1. You need to know *where you are going* in order to determine *how to get there.*

   In this problem, you want to determine the mass of carbon in *grams*. Essentially, the question is: Do you use the rate as is or do you take the reciprocal? As time needs to be cancelled, use the rate as is. Once you have determined the need to convert time into mass, consider which form of the conversion factor to use.

2. Now design a "plan" for the "conversion route," using the rate, the mole ratio, and the molar mass.

How to Do It

As your answer contains one unit, begin with a number having one unit, in this case the time.

time → moles sucrose → moles carbon → mass of carbon

$$30.0\ s \times \frac{1\ min}{60\ s} \times \frac{0.825\ mol\ C_{12}H_{22}O_{11}}{1\ min} \times \frac{12\ mol\ C}{1\ mol\ C_{12}H_{22}O_{11}} \times \frac{12.0\ g\ C}{1\ mol\ C}$$

$= 59.4\ g\ C$

Practice Problems 1.1.3 — Using Rate as a Conversion Factor

1. Ozone is an important component of the atmosphere that protects us from the ultraviolet rays of the Sun. Certain pollutants encourage the following decomposition of ozone: $2\ O_3(g) \rightarrow 3\ O_2(g)$, at a rate of 6.5×10^{-4} M O_3/s. How many molecules of O_2 gas are formed in each liter of atmosphere every day by this process? (As this problem provides a rate in units of mol/L/s and requires molecules/L as an answer, we can simply leave the unit "L" in the denominator the entire time.)

2. Propane gas combusts in camp stoves to produce energy to heat your dinner. How long would it take to produce 6.75 L of CO_2 gas measured at STP? Assume the gas is combusted at a rate of 1.10 g C_3H_8/min. Begin by writing a balanced equation for the combustion of C_3H_8.

3. A 2.65 g sample of calcium metal is placed into water. The metal is completely consumed in 25.0 s. Assuming the density of water is 1.00 g/mL at the reaction temperature, how long would it take to consume 5.00 mL of water as it converts into calcium hydroxide and hydrogen gas?

1.1 Activity: Summarizing a Concept in Kinetics

Question
How can you summarize the methods that are useful for measuring the rate of a chemical reaction?

Background
As you're moving through any course in senior high school or university, it is very useful to summarize the concepts you learn into "chunks" of material. These summary notes may take the form of bulleted points or tables or charts.

Procedure
1. Use the outline provided below to organize what you've learned about methods that are useful for measuring the rates of various chemical reactions.
2. For each method, provide a balanced chemical equation for a reaction that could be measured using that method. Do not repeat equations that were already used in this section of the book. Your textbook and the Internet may be helpful for finding examples if you're having trouble recalling the major reaction types.
3. The first row has been completed as an example of what is expected. Note that the same property may be used multiple times (for example, with different states of species).

Property	State of Species	Apparatus Used	Units	Sample Reaction
Mass	solid	balance	g/min	$2\ K(s) + 2\ H_2O(l) \rightarrow 2\ KOH(aq) + H_2(g)$
Mass	gas			
Volume				
Concentration				
pH				
Color				
Pressure				
Conductivity				

Results and Discussion
1. You will find it extremely helpful to produce similar formats to help you summarize material for study in the remaining sections of this course. Dedicate a section of your notebook for these summary notes and refer to them from time to time to help you prepare for your unit and final examinations.

© Edvantage Interactive 2019

1.1 Review Questions

1. Give three reasons why the distance-time data in the Warm Up at the beginning of this section is so different from the property-time data collected for a typical chemical reaction.

2. Consider the following reaction, which could be done in either flask, using any of the equipment shown:

   $6\,Cu(s) + 8\,HNO_3(aq) + O_2(g) \rightarrow 6\,CuNO_3(aq) + 4\,H_2O(l) + 2\,NO_2(g)$

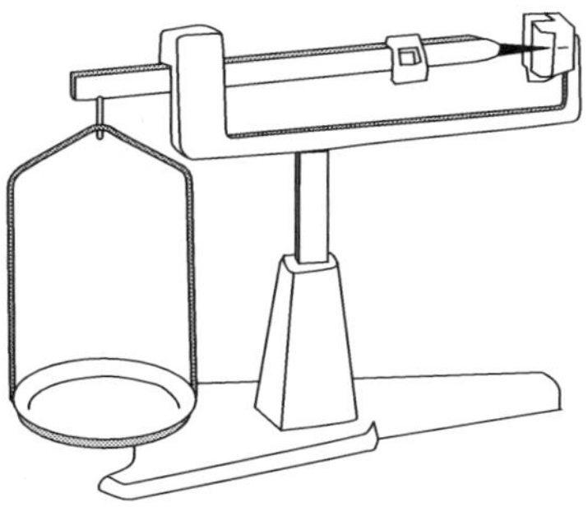

   (a) If 5.00 g of copper solid is completely reacted in 250.0 mL of excess nitric acid in 7.00 min at STP, calculate the rate of the reaction in:

   (i) g Cu/min (ii) g NO_2/min (iii) mol HNO_3/min

   (b) Assume the reaction continues at this average rate for 10.0 min total time. Determine the final:

   (i) mL NO_2 formed at STP (ii) molarity of $CuNO_3$

   (c) Describe SIX ways you might measure the reaction rate. Include the equipment required, measurements made and units for the rate. You may use a labeled diagram.

3. Consider the graph for the following reaction:
$CaCO_3(s) + 2\ HCl(aq) \rightarrow CaCl_2(aq) + CO_2(g) + H_2O(l)$

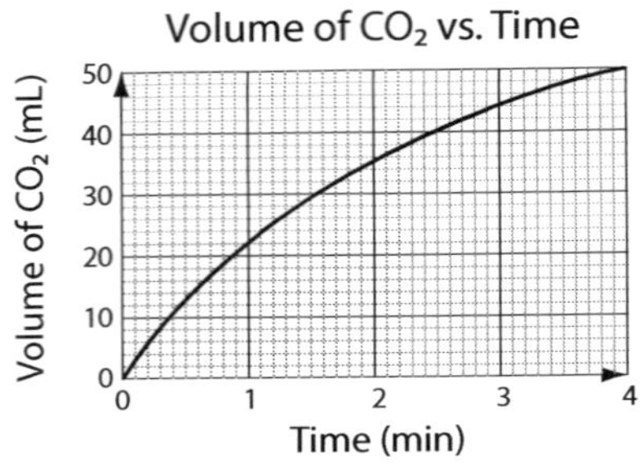

Recall the discussion of the *instantaneous rate* earlier in this section.

(a) Determine the instantaneous rate at the following times:
(i) an instant after 0 min (This is the *initial rate*.)

(ii) 1 min

(iv) 4 min

(b) How do these rates compare? What do you suppose causes this pattern?

4. Here is a table indicating the volume of gas collected as a disk of strontium metal reacts in a solution of hydrochloric acid for 1 min.
$Sr(s) + 2\ HCl(aq) \rightarrow SrCl_2(aq) + H_2(g)$

Time (seconds)	Volume of Hydrogen at STP (mL)
0	0
10.0	22.0
20.0	40.0
30.0	55.0
40.0	65.0
50.0	72.0
60.0	72.0

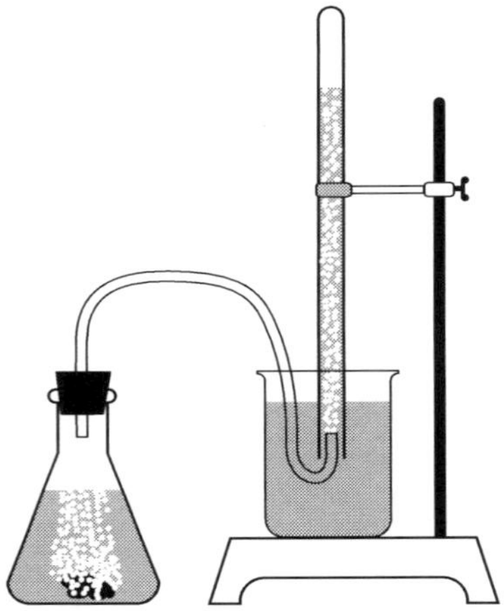

(a) Calculate the average rate of reaction in moles of HCl consumed/second over the first 50.0 s.

© Edvantage Interactive 2019

(b) Calculate the mass of strontium consumed in this 50.0 s period.

(c) Why did the volume of gas collected decrease in each increment until 50.0 s?

(d) Why did the volume of gas remain unchanged from 50.0 s to 60.0 s?

5. The spectrophotometer works by shining a single wavelength of light through a sample of a colored solution. A photocell detects the amount of light that passes through the solution as **% transmittance** and the amount of light that does not pass through as the **absorbance**. The more concentrated the solution, the darker the color. Dark color leads to a lower percentage of light transmitted and thus a higher absorbance. There is a direct relationship between absorbance and the concentration of a colored solution. The "calibration curve" (actually a straight line) below was created using solutions of *known* $Cu(NO_3)_2$ concentration.

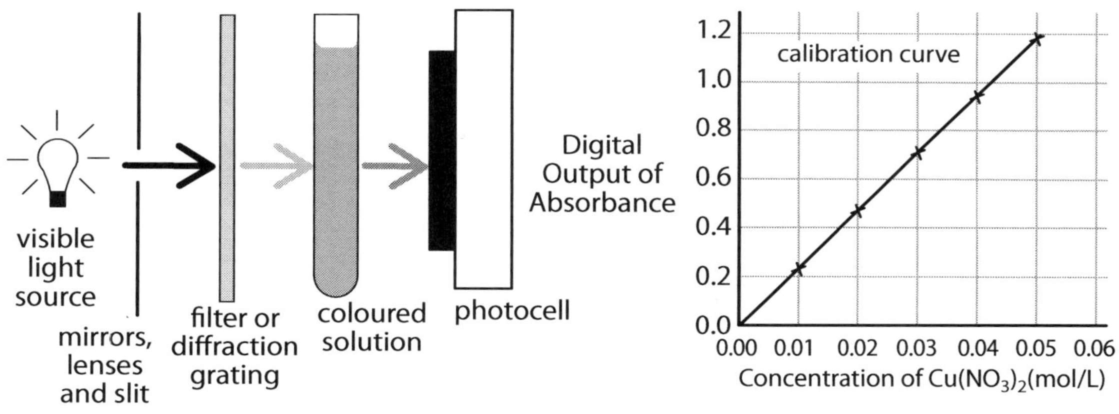

A simplified diagram of a colorimeter

A copper sample was reacted with 250 mL of nitric acid by the following reaction:

$3\,Cu(s) + 8\,HNO_3(aq) \rightarrow 3\,Cu(NO_3)_2(aq) + 2\,NO(g) + 4\,H_2O(l)$

As the reaction proceeded, small aliquots were removed and placed in a cuvette (the special test tube used to hold a sample in the spectrophotometer). The cuvettes were then placed in the instrument and the absorbances were recorded as follows:

Time (seconds)	Absorbances (no unit)	Concentration of Copper(II) Ion (mol/L)
0	0	0 mol/L
20.	0.40	
40.	0.70	
60.	0.90	
80.	1.00	

Find the absorbances on the standard graph and record the corresponding concentrations of the copper(II) ions (equal to the concentration of $Cu(NO_3)_2$) in the table.

(a) Calculate the average rate of the reaction from time 0 s to 80. s in units of M of $HNO_3(aq)$/s.

(b) What mass of Cu(*s*) will be consumed during the 80. s trial?

(c) What will you observe in the main reaction flask as the reaction proceeds?

 © Edvantage Interactive 2019

1.2 Factors Affecting Rates of Reaction

Warm Up

Compare the following reactions. Circle the one with the greatest reaction rate. Indicate what is causing the rate to be greater in each case.

(a) Solid marble chips (calcium carbonate) reacting with 3.0 M hydrochloric acid at room temperature produces calcium chloride solution, water and carbon dioxide gas.

____

(b) Glow sticks contain two chemicals, one of which is held in a breakable capsule that floats inside the other. Once the capsule is broken, a reaction occurs that produces energy in the form of light. This is called chemiluminescence. Glow sticks are placed in different temperature water baths.

____

(c) Alkali metals react with water to form a basic solution and hydrogen gas. Sometimes the reaction is so exothermic, the hydrogen gas bursts into flame.

____

Factors Affecting Reaction Rate

In the previous section, we discovered that reactions tend to slow down as they proceed. What might cause this phenomenon? What is true about a reacting system when it contains lots of reactants? Consideration of this question leads us to recognize there are more particles available to react when a reaction first starts. Intuition tells us in order for a reaction to occur, the reacting particles must contact each other. If this is so, anything that results in an increased frequency of particle contact must make a reaction occur faster.

The three factors of surface area, concentration, and temperature may all be manipulated to increase the frequency with which particles come together. Two of these factors were dealt with in the Warm Up. Part (c) of the Warm Up demonstrates the periodic trend in reactivity moving down the alkali metal family. Different chemicals inherently react at different rates so the nature of the reactants affects reaction rate. Finally, you may recall from Science 10 that a chemical species called a *catalyst* may be used to increase the rate of a reaction. We will consider each of these five factors in turn.

Surface Area

Most reactions in the lab are carried out in solution or in the gas phase. In these states, the reactants are able to intermingle on the molecular or atomic level and contact each other easily. When reactants are present in different states in a reacting system, we say the reaction is **heterogeneous.** Most heterogeneous systems involve the reaction of a *solid* with a solution or a gas. In a heterogeneous reaction, the reactants are able to come into contact with each other only where they meet at the interface between the two phases. The size of the area of contact determines the rate of the reaction. Decreasing the size of the pieces of solid reactant will increase the area of contact (Figure 1.2.1).

Increasing the surface area of a solid will increase the rate of a heterogeneous reaction.

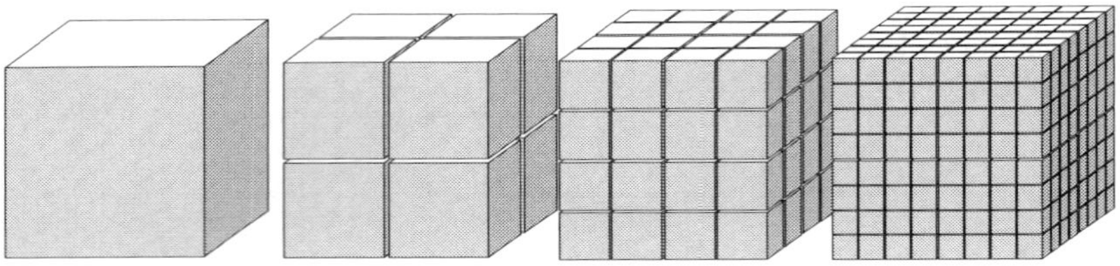

Figure 1.2.1 *Increasing the number of pieces leads to a significant increase in the surface area.*

Concentration (Pressure)

The rates of all reactions are affected by the concentrations of the dissolved or gaseous reactants. When more solute is placed in the same volume of solvent, the solution's concentration is increased (Figure 1.2.2).

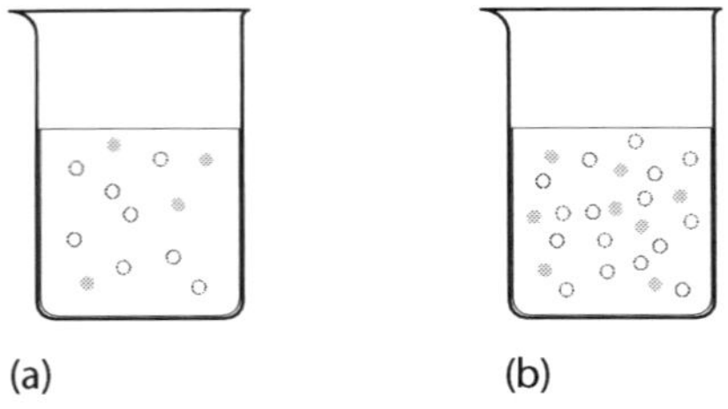

Figure 1.2.2 *Solution (b) contains twice the number of solute particles in the same volume as solution (a). The opportunity for particle contact is doubled in solution (b).*

When more gas particles are placed in the same volume of a container, the **partial pressure** of the gas has increased. In Figure 1.2.3, container (b) has twice as many gas particles in the same volume as container (a). This, of course, means the concentration has been doubled. We might also say the *partial pressure* of the gas has doubled. In container (c), the piston has been lowered to half the volume. The result is another doubling of concentration (and pressure).

© Edvantage Interactive 2019

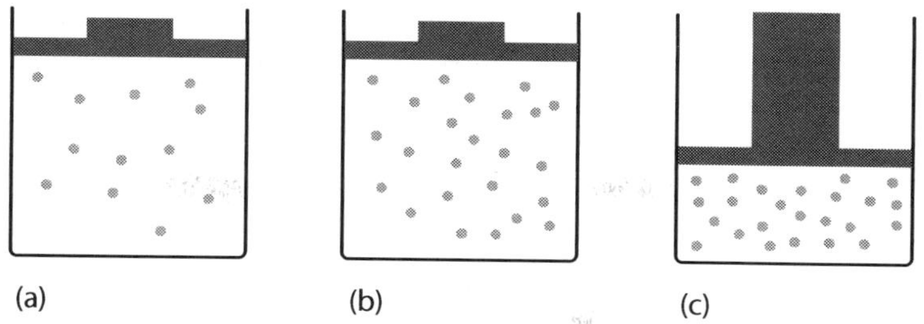

Figure 1.2.3 *The partial pressure in (b) is greater than in (a) because of the increased concentration of particles. In (c), decreasing the volume increases the concentration and the pressure.*

Increasing the concentration (or partial pressure of a gas) will increase the rate of a chemical reaction.

Always remember the concentration of pure solids and liquids cannot be increased because adding more substance increases both the moles and the liters, so the molarity or moles per liter remains constant. Also remember that crushing or breaking a solid will increase its surface area. However it is impossible to cut a piece of liquid or gas into smaller bits. The surface area of liquids can be increased by spreading them over a larger area.

Temperature

Recall the qualitative relationship between temperature and kinetic energy. Mathematically speaking, KE = $3/2RT$ where R is a constant having the value 8.31 J/mol K, and T is the Kelvin temperature. From this relationship, we see that temperature and kinetic energy are directly related to one another. If the temperature is doubled, the kinetic energy is doubled (as long as the temperature is expressed in units of Kelvin).

An increase in temperature will lead to particles striking one another more frequently. However, we now see that it will also result in the particles striking one another with more energy. In other words, an increase in temperature means that the same particles are travelling faster. As a consequence, they hit each other more frequently and more forcefully. As a result, *temperature is the most significant factor* that affects reaction rate.

Within any substance there is a "normal" distribution of kinetic energies among the particles that make up the system due to their random collisions. Such a distribution might be graphed as shown in Figure 1.2.4.

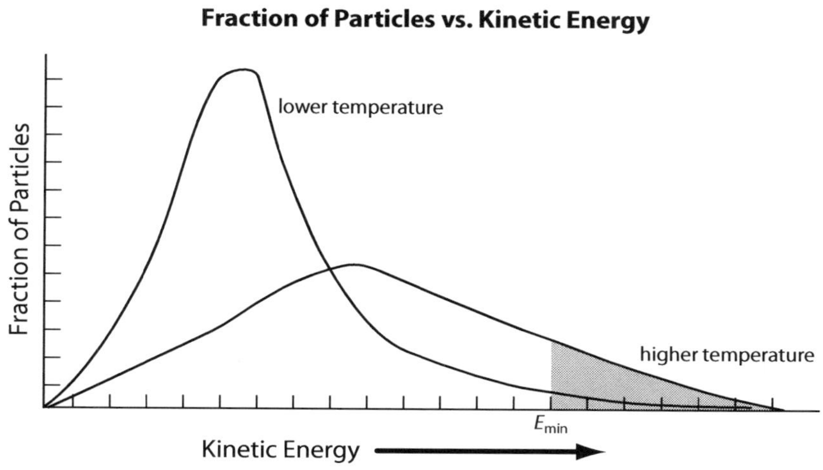

Figure 1.2.4 *Kinetic energy shows a "normal" distribution at both lower and higher temperatures.*

Note that some of the particles have very little energy and others have a lot. The *x*-axis value associated with the peak of the curve indicates the kinetic energy of most of the particles. The second curve indicates how the distribution would change if the temperature were increased. The area under the curves represents the total number of particles and therefore should be the same for both curves. The gray area represents the particles that have sufficient energy to *collide successfully* and produce a product. Notice that this has increased with an increase in temperature. A common generalization is that an increase of 10°C will double reaction rate. This is true for some reactions around room temperature.

Increasing temperature will increase the rate of a reaction for *two* reasons: *more frequent* and *more forceful* collisions.

The Nature of Reactants

Fundamental differences in chemical reactivity are a major factor in determining the rate of a chemical reaction. For instance, zinc metal oxidizes quickly when exposed to air and moisture, while iron reacts much more slowly under the same conditions. For this reason, zinc is used to protect the integrity of the iron beneath it in galvanized nails.

Generally reactions between simple monoatomic ions such as Ag^+ and Cl^- are almost instantaneous. This is due to ions being extremely mobile, in close proximity to one another, having opposite charges, and requiring no bond rearrangement to react. However, more complicated ionic species such as CH_3COO^- react more slowly than those that are monoatomic.

In general, differences in chemical reactivity can be attributed to factors that affect the breaking and forming of chemical bonds. Ionization energy, electronegativity, ionic and molecular polarity, size, and complexity of structure are some of these factors. The state of the reacting species may also play a role.

In general, at room temperature the rate of (*aq*) reactants > (*g*) > (*l*) > (*s*).

Precipitation occurs quickly between ions in solution. In Figure 1.2.5(a), the AgCl forms as a heavy, white precipitate the instant the silver ions contact the chloride in solution. In (b), the $AgCH_3COO$ precipitate is less heavy and forms over a period of 10 s to 20 s. The complex structure of the acetate ion makes it more difficult to achieve the correct orientation to bond successfully.

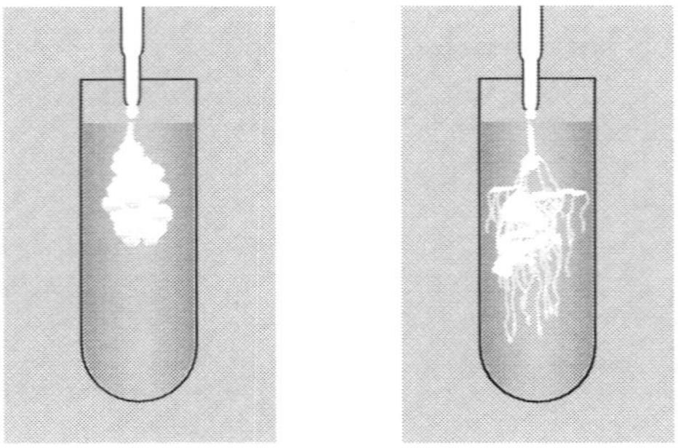

(a) (b)

Figure 1.2.5 *(a) AgCl quickly forms a precipitate. (b) $AgCH_3COO$ forms a precipitate more slowly.*

© **Edvantage Interactive 2019**

Presence of a Catalyst

Catalysts are substances that increase the rates of chemical reactions without being used up. Because they remain in the same quantity and form when a reaction is completed, the formulas of catalysts are not included in the chemical reaction. Sometimes the formula is shown above the arrow between the reactants and products like this:

$$2\ H_2O_2(l) \xrightarrow{MnO_2} 2\ H_2O(l) + O_2(g)$$

What actually happens is that catalysts are consumed during an intermediate step in a reaction and regenerated in a later step. The catalysts most familiar to you are probably the enzymes produced by living organisms as they catalyze digestive and other biochemical processes in our bodies. The reaction depicted in graduated cylinders in Figure 1.2.6 is the catalyzed decomposition of hydrogen peroxide as shown in the equation above. In addition to the H_2O_2, there is a bit of dish soap and some dye in the cylinders so the oxygen gas bubbles through the soap solution and produces foam. This demonstration is often called "elephant toothpaste." Note that the cylinder in (b) contained 30% hydrogen peroxide while the cylinder in (a) was only 6%, so the effect of concentration was demonstrated in addition to the catalytic effect.

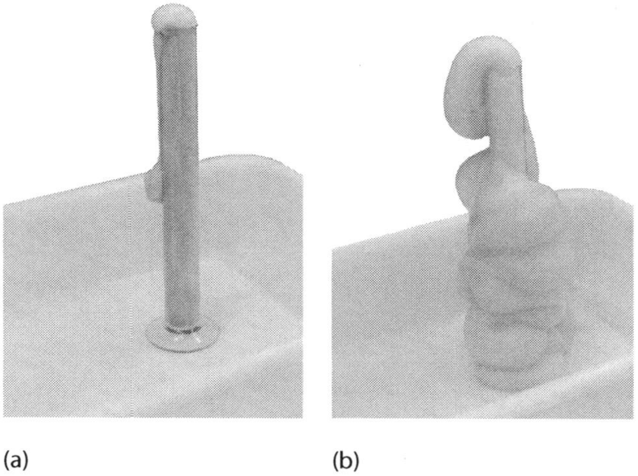

Figure 1.2.6 *"Elephant toothpaste" is produced through a catalytic reaction. The concentration of H_2O_2 is greater in (b) than in (a).*

> A catalyst increases reaction rate without itself being consumed or altered.

An **inhibitor** is a species that reduces the rate of a chemical reaction by combining with a reactant to stop it from reacting in its usual way. A number of pharmaceuticals are inhibitors. Drugs that act through inhibition are called *antagonists*.

Sample Problem 1.2.1 — Factors Affecting Reaction Rate

Which of the following reactions is faster at room temperature?

(a) $H_2(g) + I_2(s) \rightarrow 2\ HI(g)$ (b) $Ba^{2+}(aq) + SO_4^{2-}(aq) \rightarrow BaSO_4(s)$

List two ways to increase the rate of each reaction.

What to Think About	How to Do It
1. First consider the nature of the reactants.	The reactant states lead us to believe that reaction (b) involving aqueous species would be the fastest.
2. To increase the rate of reaction (a), start by recognizing this is a heterogeneous reaction. This means that, in addition to the usual factors, surface area can be considered.	• Increase surface area of iodine solid. • Increase temperature. • Increase concentration of hydrogen gas. • Increase partial pressure of hydrogen gas (decrease container volume). • Add an appropriate catalyst.
3. To increase the rate of reaction of the homogeneous reaction in (b), apply all the usual factors except surface area. *Note that you must be specific when mentioning the factors.* For example, what species' concentration will be increased?	• Increase temperature. • Increase concentration of either or both reactant ions (Ba^{2+} and/or SO_4^{2-}). • Add an appropriate catalyst.

1.2 Activity: Graphic Depiction of Factors Affecting Reaction Rates

Question

How do concentration, surface area, and temperature affect reaction rate?

Background

Four trials were carried out in which a chunk of zinc was reacted with hydrochloric acid under four different sets of conditions. In all four trials, the chunk of zinc was of equal mass. The data collected indicate that varying factors have a significant impact on reaction rate. These data can be represented in tabular and graphical form.

The reaction was allowed to proceed for the same time period in each trial. In all four trials, the gas was collected in a eudiometer using the apparatus shown below.

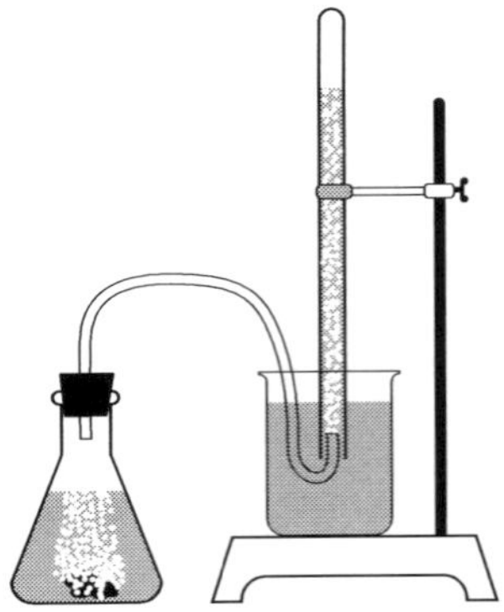

Time (s)	Trial 1 25°C, 1 M HCl (mL)	Trial 2 50°C, 1 M HCl (mL)	Trial 3 25°C, 2 M HCl (mL)	Trial 4 25°C, 1 M HCl, zinc powder (mL)
0	0	0	0	0
30.	12	34	20	26
60.	19	56	34	44
90.	24	65	44	57
120.	27	65	51	65
150.	29	65	54	65

Procedure

1. Use the following grid to graph all four sets of data. Vary colors for each trial line.

Results and Discussion

© Edvantage Interactive 2019

1. Write a balanced equation for the reaction that was studied.

2. Rank the conditions from those producing the fastest to slowest reaction rates. What factor influences reaction rate the most? Which factor is second most effective? Which factor has the least influence on the rate?

3. Calculate the average reaction rate in mL H_2/min for each trial. Use the time required to collect the maximum amount of hydrogen gas formed (e.g., the time for trial 2 will be 90. s). Place the rates on the graphed lines.

4. How many milligrams of zinc were used in 1.50 min for each trial? Assume a molar volume for $H_2(g)$ of 24.5 L/mol. (This is for SATP conditions or 25°C and 101.3 kPa or the pressure at sea level.) For the 50°C trial, use 26.5 L/mol.

5. What error is introduced by the assumption in question 4? Would the actual mass of Zn be larger or smaller than that calculated? Explain.

1.2 Review Questions

1. Identify the four factors that affect the rate of any reaction. Give a brief explanation as to how each one applies. Which of these factors can be altered to change the rate of a particular chemical reaction?

2. Identify the one factor that affects only the rate of heterogeneous reactions. Explain why it does not affect homogeneous reaction rates.

3. Use the Internet to find examples of catalysts that do the following:
   (a) Convert oxides of nitrogen into harmless nitrogen gas in the catalytic converter of an automobile.

   (b) Increase the rate of the Haber process to make ammonia.

   (c) Found on disinfectant discs to clean contact lenses.

   (d) Found in green plants to assist in photosynthesis.

4. How would each of the following changes affect the rate of decomposition of a marble statue due to acid rain? Begin by writing the equation for the reaction between marble (calcium carbonate) and nitric acid below.

   (a) The concentration of the acid is increased.

   (b) Erosion due to wind and weathering increases the surface area on the surface of the statue.

   (c) The statue is cooled in cold winter weather.

   (d) The partial pressure of carbon dioxide gas in the atmosphere is increased due to greenhouse gases.

5. (a) At room temperature, catalyzed decomposition of methanoic acid, HCOOH, produced 80.0 mL of carbon monoxide gas in 1.00 min once the volume was adjusted to STP conditions. The other product was water. Calculate the average rate of decomposition of methanoic acid in moles per minute.

 © Edvantage Interactive 2019

(b) Give general (approximate) answers for the following:

(i) How long would you expect the production of 40.0 mL of gas to take?

(ii) How long would you expect the production of 80.0 mL to take without a catalyst?

(iii) How long would you expect the production of 80.0 mL of gas to take at 10°C above the experimental conditions?

6. Answer the questions below for each of the following reactions:

(i) $C(s) + O_2(g) \rightarrow CO_2(g)$

(ii) $Pb^{2+}(aq) + 2\,I^-(aq) \rightarrow PbI_2(s)$

(iii) $Mg(s) + CuCl_2(aq) \rightarrow MgCl_2(aq) + Cu(s)$

(a) Indicate whether you think it would be fast or slow if performed at room temperature. Then rank the three reactions from fastest to slowest.

(b) List which of the five factors could be used to increase the rate of each reaction.

7. Rank the diagrams below in order of expected reaction rate for this reaction:
$G(g) + B(g) \rightarrow GB(g)$
where G = gray, B = black and GB is the product. Explain your ranking. Assume the same temperature in all three reacting systems.

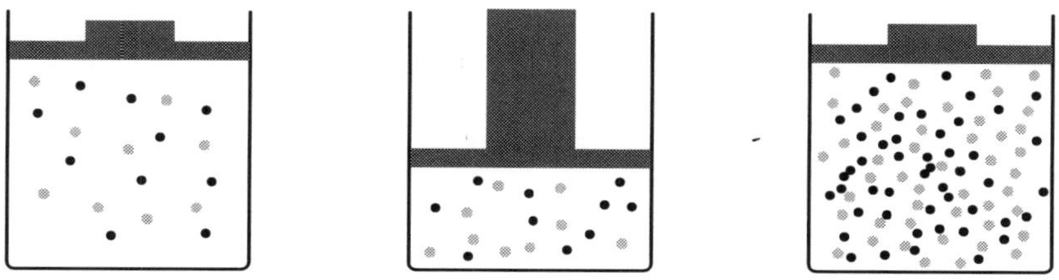

(a) (b) (c)

1.3 Collision Theory

Warm Up

Consider a hypothetical reaction between two gas particles, A and B, to form AB according to the reaction, $A(g) + B(g) \rightarrow AB(g)$. Determine the total number of possible distinct collisions that could occur between the A particles and the B particles in each situation shown in the diagram below. Let □ represent A and ● represent B. Draw arrows from each A particle to each B particle in turn to help you track each possible collision. The third case is done as an example for you.

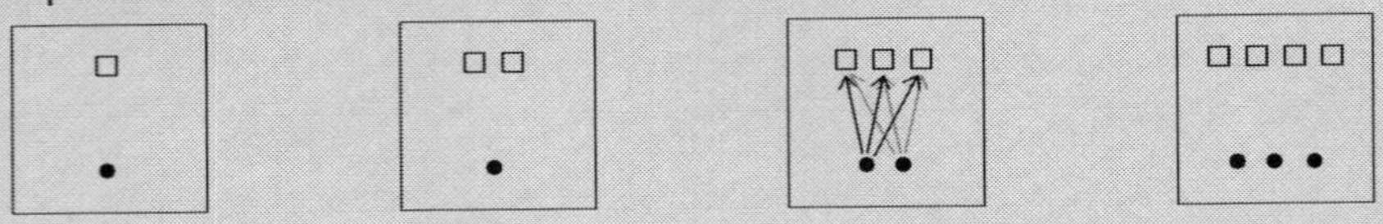

Total possible collisions: ______ ______ ___6___ ______

What is the relationship between the number of A and B particles and the total number of distinct collisions possible?

___

What might this relationship indicate regarding the rate of a reaction between A and B?

___

Collisions and Concentrations

From our study of the factors affecting reaction rates, it seems obvious that a successful reaction requires the reacting particles to collide with one another. The series of diagrams in the Warm Up above show that the more particles of reactant species present in a reacting system, the more collisions can occur between them in a particular period of time. Careful examination of the situations described in the Warm Up reveals that the number of possible collisions between the reactant molecules, A and B, is simply equal to the product of the number of molecules of each type present. That is:

number of A × number of B = total possible collisions between A and B

The number of particles per unit volume may be expressed as a concentration. In the example, all of the particles are in the same volume so we can think of the number of particles of each type as representing their concentrations. From this, we can infer that the concentration of the particles colliding must be related to the rate. These two statements allow us to represent the relationship discovered in the Warm Up as follows.

The rate of a reaction is directly proportional to the product of the concentrations of the reactants.

When two variables are directly proportional to one another there is a constant that relates the two. In other words, multiplying one variable by a constant value will always give you the other variable. We call this multiplier a *proportionality constant*. In science, proportionality constants are commonly represented by the letter *k*.

The slope of any straight-line graph is a proportionality constant. Applying this concept to the relationship discovered in the Warm Up results in the following.

$$\text{reaction rate} = k[A]^x[B]^y$$

 © Edvantage Interactive 2019

The relationship above is called a **rate law**. The proportionality constant in this case is called a **rate constant**. Every reaction has its own unique rate law and its own unique rate constant. For many reactions, the exponents, x and y, are each equal to 1. The values of x and y are called **reactant orders**. In this section, we will focus on reactions that are first order with respect to all reactants. In other words, both $x = 1$ and $y = 1$. Be aware, however, that there are reactions involving second and even third order reactants. Clearly, the higher the order of a particular reactant, the more a change in the concentration of that reactant affects the reaction rate.

Quick Check

1. Write the general form for a rate law in which two reactants, C and D, react together. Assume the reaction is first order for each reactant. Explain what the rate law means.

2. Assume a reaction occurs by this rate law: rate = k[A]. How would the rate be affected by each of the following changes in concentration?
   (a) [A] is doubled.

   (b) [A] is halved.

3. Assume a gaseous reaction occurs by this rate law: rate = k[A][B]. How would the rate be affected if the volume of the container were halved?

4. How is the rate of a reaction affected by increasing the temperature? What part of the rate law must be affected by changing temperature?

A Distribution of Collisions

When reacting particles collide with one another, each collision is unique in its energy and direction. If you've ever played a game of billiards, snooker, or 8-ball, you're familiar with the transfer of energy from the shooter's arm to the pool stick to the cue ball to the ball being shot. Only when the shooter sends the cue ball directly into the ball being shot with a controlled amount of strength are the momentum and direction of the ball easily predictable.

This control is required in a "direct shot" or in a classic "bank shot" where, much like a beam of reflected light, the angle of incidence equals the angle of reflection (Figure 1.3.1(a)). Bank shots may be necessary when an opponent's balls are blocking a clear shot. In most cases, however, collisions between the cue ball, the ball being shot, and other balls on the table are different in direction and amount of energy transferred (Figure 1.3.1(b)). Skillful players may intentionally play "shape" or put "English" on the ball to manipulate the direction and the amount of energy transfer involved in collisions.

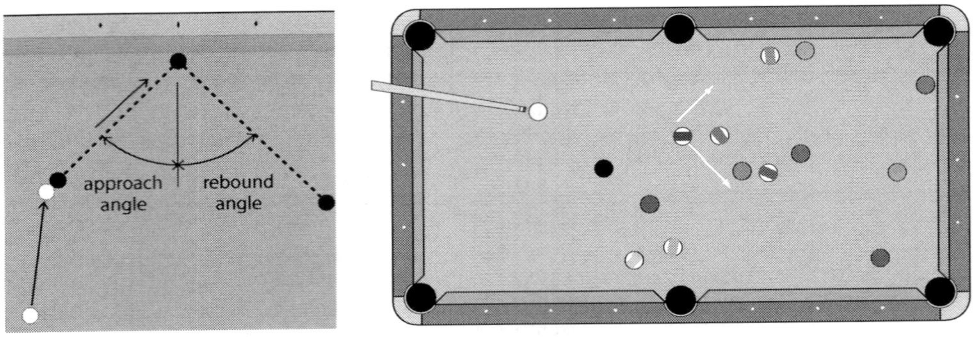

(a) (b)

Figure 1.3.1 *(a) A bank shot involves predictable collisions. (b) Skilled players determine exactly what type of collision is required for the shot they need to make.*

The break at the start of the game is probably the best model of the distribution of collision energies involved between the reacting particles in a chemical reaction (Figure 1.3.2). Some of the particles move quickly and collide directly with others to transfer a great deal of energy. Others barely move at all or collide with a glancing angle that transfers very little energy. In addition, we must remember that real reactant collisions occur in three dimensions, while our pool table model is good for two dimensions only (Figure 1.3.3).

Figure 1.3.2 *The break at the start of a game provides a large distribution of collision energies.*

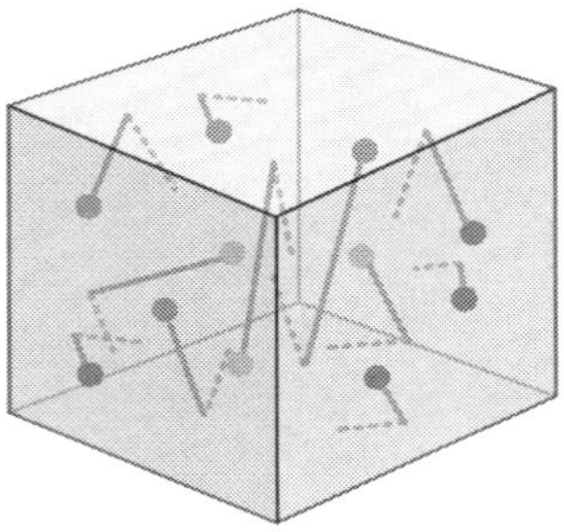

Figure 1.3.3 *The collisions occurring between species in a chemical reaction occur in three dimensions.*

Collision Theory

Regardless of the fact that the energy of particle collisions is distributed in a regular way, the rate of a reaction actually depends on *two* considerations.

Collision theory states that reaction rates depend upon:
- the number of collisions per unit time, and
- the fraction of these collisions that succeed in producing products.

Requirements for Effective Collisions

A mixture of hydrogen and oxygen gas may sit indefinitely inside a balloon at room temperature without undergoing any apparent reaction regardless of concentrations. Addition of a small amount of energy such as a spark to the system, however, causes the gases to react violently and exothermically. How can this phenomenon be explained?

In 1 mol of gas under standard conditions, there are more than 10^{32} collisions occurring each second. If the rate of collisions per second were equal to the rate of reaction, every reaction would be extremely rapid. Since most gaseous reactions are slow, it is evident that only a small fraction of the total collisions effectively result in the conversion of reactants to products.

© Edvantage Interactive 2019

Quick Check

Consider the factors affecting reaction rate that you studied in the previous section.

1. Which of these factors do you think increase reaction rate by increasing the number of collisions per unit time?

   ____

2. Which of the factors do you think increase reaction rate by increasing the fraction of collisions that succeed in producing products?

   ____

3. Do you think any of the factors increase *both* the number of collisions per unit time and the fraction of successful collisions? If so, which one(s)?

   ____

As discussed earlier, the tremendous number of collisions in a reacting sample results in a wide range of velocities and kinetic energies. Only a small percentage of the molecules in a given sample have sufficient kinetic energy to react.

The minimum kinetic energy that the reacting species must have in order to react is called the **activation energy** or E_a of the reaction.

Only collisions between particles having the threshold energy of E_a are energetic enough to overcome the repulsive forces between the electron clouds of the reacting molecules and to weaken or break bonds, resulting in a reaction. Most gaseous reactions have relatively high E_a values; hence reactions like the one between hydrogen and oxygen gas do not occur at room temperature.

Reactions often occur in a series of steps called a reaction mechanism. Energy is required to break bonds and energy is released during the formation of bonds. The activation energy of a reaction often reflects the difference between these energies during the early steps of the reaction mechanism. As bond energies are a characteristic of a particular chemical species, the only thing that can change the activation energy of a reaction is to change its reaction mechanism. This is precisely what occurs when a reaction is catalyzed.

A kinetic energy distribution diagram was shown for a sample of matter at two different temperatures. Figure 1.3.4 shows a similar pair of energy distributions at two different temperatures. It also shows two different activation energies. E_{a2} represents the activation energy without a catalyst present. E_{a1} represents a lowered activation energy that results in the presence of a catalyst. Note that in both cases, with and without a catalyst, the number of particles capable of colliding effectively (as represented by the shaded area under the curve) increases at the higher temperature.

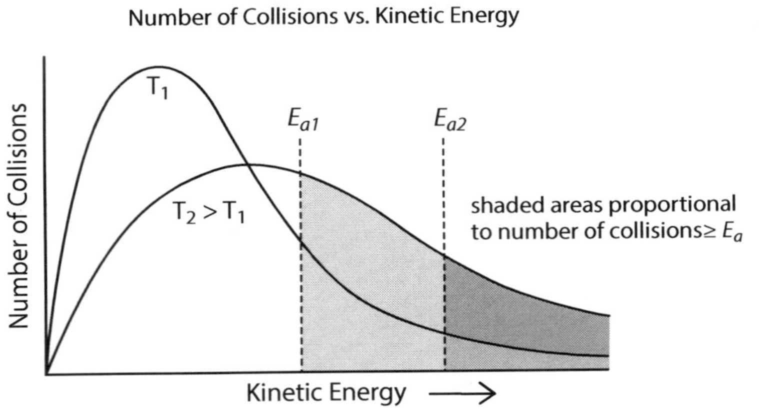

Figure 1.3.4 *With higher temperatures, the number of effective collisions increases.*

It turns out there is one further factor that complicates collision theory even more. Collisions possessing the activation energy don't always result in reaction. Even very high-energy collisions may not be effective unless the molecules are properly oriented toward one another.

In addition to attaining E_a, the *geometric shape* and the *collision geometry* of reacting particles must also be favorable for a successful collision to occur.

Consider the reaction $CO(g) + NO_2(g) \rightarrow CO_2(g) + NO(g)$

Figure 1.3.5 shows two different ways the reactants CO and NO_2 could collide. Here we see a successful collision followed by an unsuccessful collision between carbon monoxide and nitrogen dioxide in an attempt to form carbon dioxide and nitrogen monoxide. No matter how energetic the collision, it will only succeed when the molecules are oriented properly with respect to each other. For the CO molecule to become CO_2, the oxygen from the NO_2 molecule must collide with the carbon atom in the CO molecule so that a bond can form.

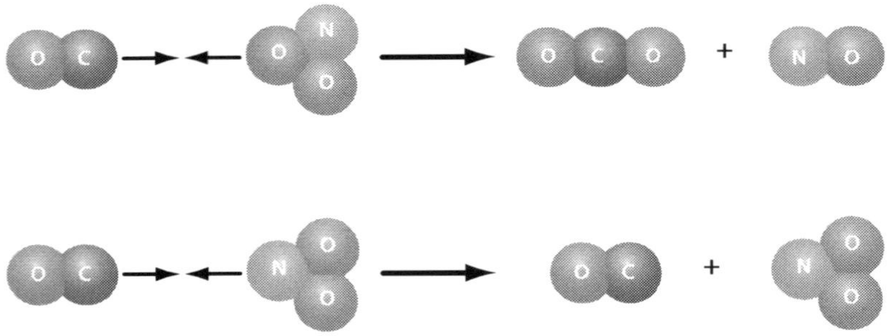

Figure 1.3.5 *The top collision is successful because the molecules are oriented so that the carbon and oxygen atoms can bond to form CO_2.*

Collision Theory and Factors Affecting Reaction Rate

Increased temperature, concentration, and surface area all increase the frequency of collisions leading to an increase in reaction rate. The presence of a catalyst and increased temperature both increase the fraction of collisions that are successful.

 © Edvantage Interactive 2019

Sample Problem 1.3.1 — Collision Theory

Study the following data for 1 mol of reactants at two different temperatures. $T_1 < T_2$.

	Temperature 1	Temperature 2
Frequency of collisions:	$1.5 \times 10^{32}\ s^{-1}$	$3.0 \times 10^{32}\ s^{-1}$
% of collisions > E_a:	10%	30%

(a) How many collisions exceed activation energy per second at each temperature?

(b) How many times greater is the reaction rate at temperature 2 than temperature 1? (Assume the percent of collisions with correct geometry is the same at both temperatures.)

(c) If the frequency of collisions was only doubled by increasing the temperature from T_1 to T_2, why is the rate increased by a factor of six?

What to Think About	How to Do It
1. Multiply the percentage by the frequency at each temperature.	$0.10(1.5 \times 10^{32}\ s^{-1}) = 1.5 \times 10^{31}\ s^{-1}$ at T_1 $0.30(3.0 \times 10^{32}\ s^{-1}) = 9.0 \times 10^{31}\ s^{-1}$ at T_2
2. Divide the result for T_2 by the result for T_1.	$\frac{9.0 \times 10^{31}\ s^{-1}}{1.5 \times 10^{31}\ s^{-1}} = 6.0 \times$ greater
3. Decide what, in addition to collision frequency, must be influenced by reaction temperature.	Increasing reaction temperature increases the energy of collisions as well as collision frequency.

Practice Problems 1.3.1 — Collision Theory

1. For slow reactions, at temperatures near 25°C, an increase of 10°C will approximately double the number of collisions that have enough energy to react. At temperatures much higher than that, increasing temperature leads to smaller and smaller increases in the number of successful collisions. In the graph below, the area under the kinetic energy distribution curve represents the total number of collisions.
   (a) Assume the curve shown represents the kinetic energy distribution for a sample of collisions at room temperature. Add a curve to represent the kinetic energy distribution for a sample of collisions at 10°C above room temperature.
   (b) Add a second curve to represent the kinetic energy distribution for a sample of collisions at a temperature 100°C above curve (a).
   (c) Add a third curve for a temperature 10°C above curve (b).

Number of Collisions vs. Energy

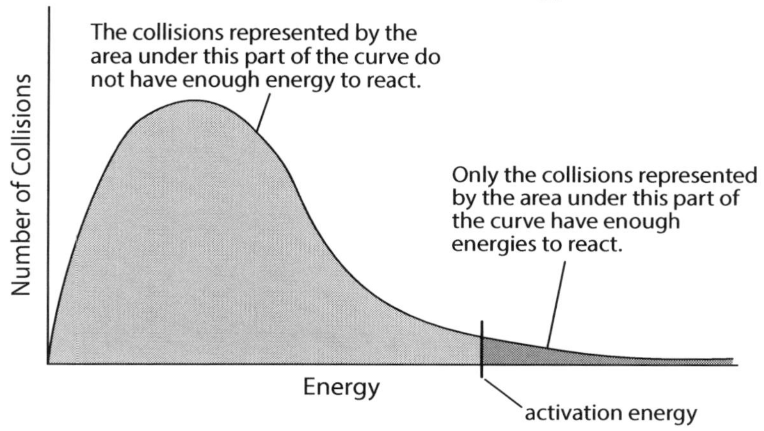

Continued on the next page

Practice Problems 1.3.1 *(Continued)*

2. At higher temperature ranges, that is, for reactions already occurring at a high rate, most of the collisions already possess E_a. Hence, an increase in temperature increases the rate primarily because of the increased frequency of collisions. Although the particles hit each other harder and with more energy, this is not really relevant because they have already achieved E_a. Complete the following table for a reacting particle sample.

Temperature	**100°C**	**300°C**
Frequency of collisions	$2.00 \times 10^{15}\ s^{-1}$	$3.00 \times 10^{15}\ s^{-1}$
Force of collisions (% possessing E_a)	95.0%	97.0%
Frequency of collisions possessing activation energy		

(a) How many times greater is the percentage of collisions possessing Ea at 300°C than at 100°C?

(b) How many times greater is the frequency of collisions at 300°C than at 100°C?

(c) How many times greater is the frequency of collisions possessing Ea at 300°C than at 100°C?

(d) The data in the table shows that at higher temperatures the increase in rate is almost entirely due to what?

(e) Why might increasing the force of collisions eventually produce less successful reactions?

 © Edvantage Interactive 2019

1.3 Activity: Tracking a Collision

Question

How is a single reactant particle affected by a variety of factors that impact the rate of a chemical reaction?

Background

A variety of factors may affect the rate of a chemical reaction. These factors include the nature of the reactants, the concentration of the reactants, their surface area, temperature, and the presence of a catalyst.

Procedure

1. The diagrams below represent snapshots taken within a nanosecond of the "life" of an ordinary gas particle. None of these particles reacts during this time, but they do a lot of colliding. Follow the pathway of an individual reactant particle as several of the factors affecting reaction rates are changed. Each time the particle changes direction it has collided with either another particle or the walls of the container.
2. While the temperature remains constant, the concentration of the reacting particle is doubled in each frame from (a) to (b) to (c).

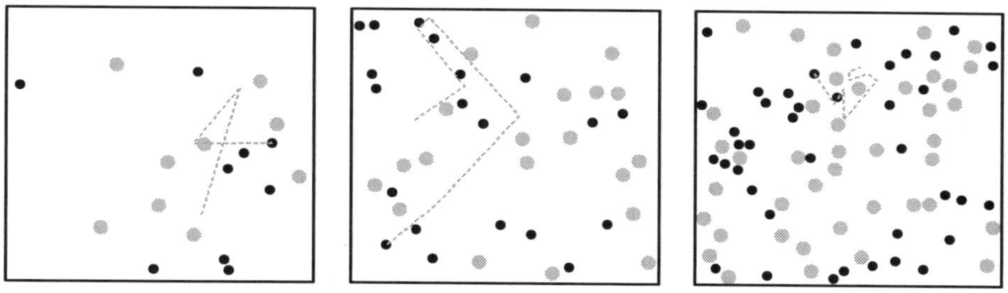

(a) (b) (c)

3. The temperature of the reaction system is increased from 25°C to 35°C to 45°C.

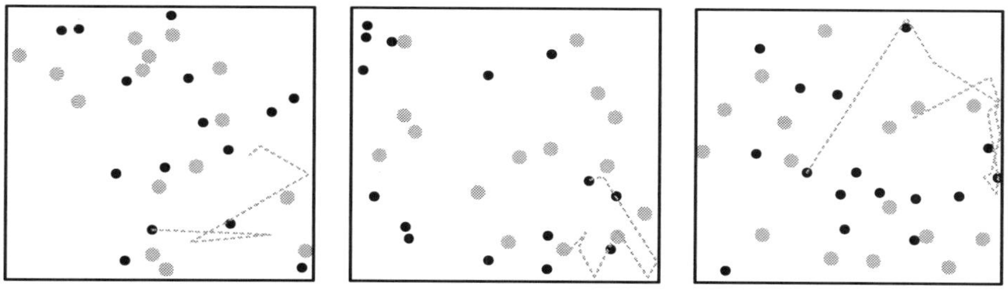

(a) (b) (c)

4. The volume of the reaction system is decreased by approximately half from (a) to (b) and again to (c), causing the pressure to approximately double each time. Assume the temperature remains constant.

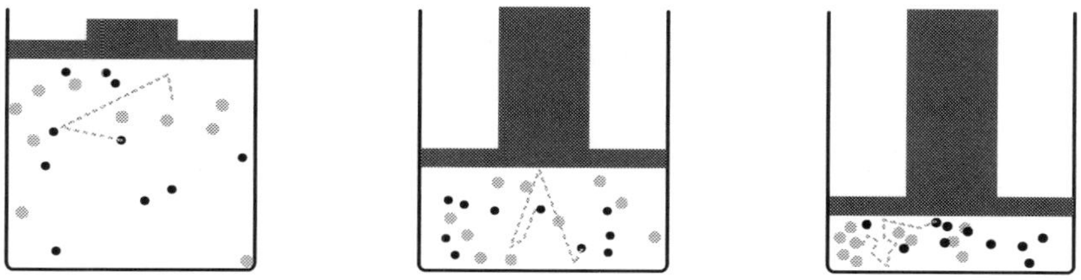

(a) (b) (c)

Results and Discussion

1. Complete the following table by indicating the number of collisions experienced by each reacting particle.

The Number of Collisions per Unit of Time	Snapshot (a)	Snapshot (b)	Snapshot (c)
Snapshot series 1 (effect of concentration)			
Snapshot series 2 (effect of temperature)			
Snapshot series 3 (effect of volume/pressure)			

2. Which two of the three factors shown produce the most similar effect on the rate of a chemical reaction?

3. One of the three factors will increase reaction rate more than the other two. Which factor is this?

4. Why would this factor have more of an impact on reaction rate than the other two?

5. Reaction rates are increased by collisions occurring more frequently and by collisions occurring more effectively. Which of these two things would be impacted by:
   (a) the addition of a catalyst to a reaction system?

   (b) increasing the surface area in a heterogeneous reaction?

© Edvantage Interactive 2019

1.3 Review Questions

1. List the two things that affect the rates of all chemical reactions according to collision theory.

2. What are the two requirements for a collision to be successful?

3. One chunk of zinc is left whole and another is cut into pieces as shown. Both samples of zinc are reacted in an equal volume of 6.0 mol/L aqueous hydrochloric acid.

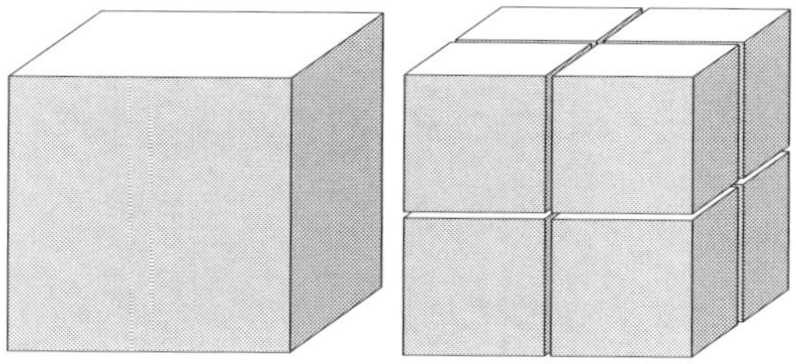

(a) Assuming the surface area of the first zinc sample is 6.00 cm^2, what is the surface area of the second sample of zinc?

(b) Compare the frequency of collisions between the hydrochloric acid and the single piece of zinc with those between the acid and the cut sample of zinc.

(c) Assuming the average rate of reaction for the single piece of zinc with the acid is 1.20×10^{-3} mol Zn/min, calculate the rate of reaction for the cut sample of zinc.

(d) Assuming this rate is maintained for a period of 4.50 min, how many milliliters of hydrogen gas would be collected at STP?

4. A reaction between ammonium ions and nitrite ions has the following rate law:

$$\text{rate} = k[NH_4^+][NO_2^-]$$

Assume the rate of formation of the salt is 3.10×10^{-3} mol/L/s. Note that the units may also be expressed as mol/L s. The reaction is performed in aqueous solution at room temperature.

(a) What rate of reaction would result if the $[NH_4^+]$ was tripled and the $[NO_2^-]$ was halved?

(b) Determine the reaction rate if the $[NH_4^+]$ was unchanged and the $[NO_2^-]$ was increased by a factor of four?

(c) If the $[NH_4^+]$ and the $[NO_2^-]$ were unchanged, but the rate increased to 6.40×10^{-3} mol/L s, what must have happened to the reacting system?

(d) What would the new reaction rate be if enough water were added to double the overall volume?

5. A student reacts ground marble chips, $CaCO_3(s)$, with hydrochloric acid, $HCl(aq)$, in an open beaker at constant temperature.

(a) In terms of collision theory, explain what will happen to the rate of the reaction as it proceeds from the beginning to completion.

(b) Sketch a graph of volume of $CO_2(g)$ vs. time to show the formation of product with time as the reaction proceeds.

© Edvantage Interactive 2019

6. Consider the following three experiments, each involving the same mass of zinc and the same volume of acid at the same temperature. Rank the three in order from fastest to slowest, and explain your ranking using collision theory.

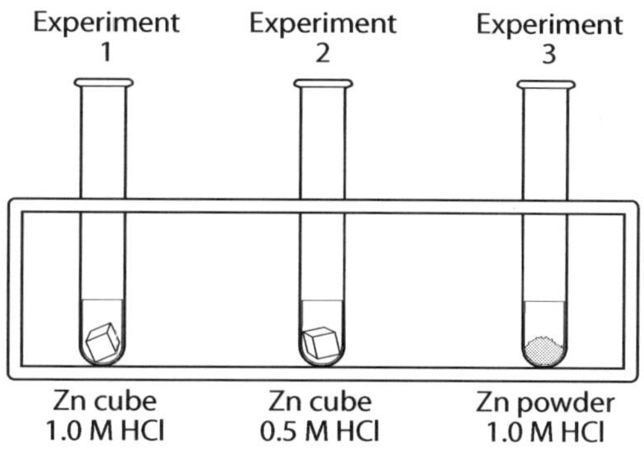

7. Is the following collision likely to produce Cl_2 and NO_2 assuming the collision occurs with sufficient energy? If not, redraw the particles in such a way that a successful collision would be likely.

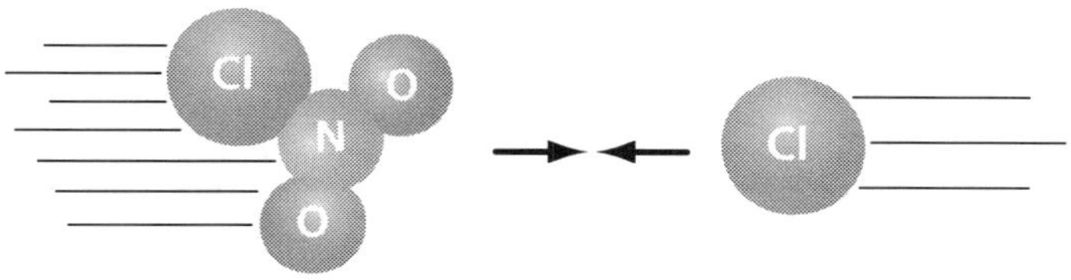

8. Use collision theory to explain each of the following.
   (a) Food found in camps half way up Mount Everest is still edible once thawed.

   (b) Campers react magnesium shavings with oxygen to start fires.

   (c) A thin layer of platinum in a vehicle's exhaust system converts oxides of nitrogen into non-toxic nitrogen gas.

1.4 Determining Rate Laws from Experimental Data

Warm Up

In the previous section we introduced the concept of a *rate law*. Rate laws express rates of reaction in the following form: reaction rate = $k[A]^x[B]^y$, where [A] and [B] represent the concentrations of the reactants, and *x* and *y* represent the orders with respect to reactants A and B.

The following diagrams represent systems of gaseous reactants A (symbolized by **O**) and B (symbolized by ■) at a fixed temperature and volume. The equation for the reaction is $A(g) + B(g) \rightarrow C(g)$.

The rate law equation uses only the reactant concentrations, so we did not depict the presence of the product C in these diagrammatic representations. Below the containers, we have provided the instantaneous rate of reaction for each system in units of mol/L of C produced per second.

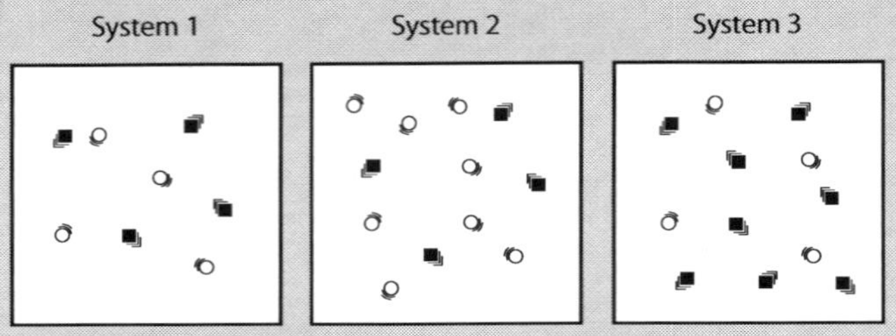

Rate = 0.010 mol/L/s 0.020 mol/L/s 0.040 mol/L/s

1. By what factor did the concentration of A (**O**) change from System 1 to 2?

____

2. How did this affect the reaction rate?

____

3. By what factor did the concentration of B (■) change from System 1 to 3?

____

4. How did this affect the reaction rate?

____

5. Complete the following expression:

   rate = $k[A]^{*}[B]^{*}$

Determining an Initial Reaction Rate

In an earlier section, we discussed methods of determining rates of chemical reactions. and we determined both the average and instantaneous rates of reaction from a graph of data we collected for the decomposition of thionyl chloride. We call the instantaneous rate determined at the very beginning of a reaction the **initial rate** (Figure 1.4.1).

© Edvantage Interactive 2019

Concentration of Product vs. Time

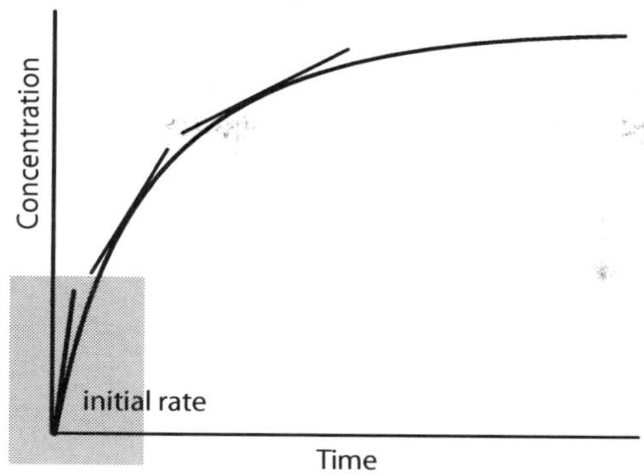

Figure 1.4.1 *The slope of a tangent line drawn to the curve at the beginning of a reaction is greater than that of any other tangent. This slope gives the initial rate of a reaction.*

As predicted by collision theory, the initial rate of a reaction depends on the concentration of the reactants present. Increasing the number of reactant particles in a particular volume leads to more frequent collisions between particles, which usually increases the reaction rate. Performing multiple trials with different concentrations of reactants shows how varying the reactant concentration affects the rate of a reaction (Figure 1.4.2).

Concentration of Product vs. Time

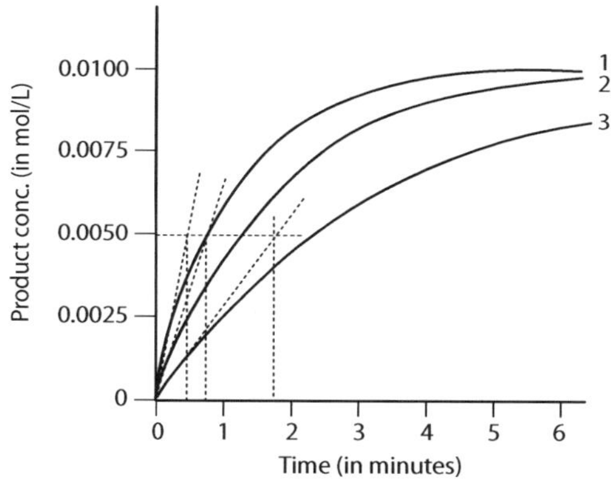

Figure 1.4.2 *The graph shows the relationship between concentration and time for three different initial reactant concentrations. Trial 1 has the greatest initial reactant concentration. The reaction rate increases from Trial 3 to 2 to 1. We determine the initial rate of each reaction from the slope of the tangent at the beginning of the reaction.*

Determining Reaction Orders

We can summarize data from a series of trials such as those shown in the Warm Up in a tabular form. If we assume that each **O** represents 1.00 mmol of A, and each ■ represents 1.00 mmol of B, all of which are contained in a 1.00 L container, the table would look like Table 1.4.1.

Table 1.4.1 *Data Table for Three Trials*

Trial Number	Initial Rate (mol/L/s)	Initial [A] (mol/L)	Initial [B] (mol/L)
1	0.010	0.00400	0.00400
2	0.020	0.00800	0.00400
3	0.040	0.00400	0.00800

From Trial 1 to 2, we double [A] and hold [B] constant. The result is a doubling of the reaction rate. This implies that the rate is directly proportional to the [A], and the process is first order with respect to A. We can demonstrate the relationship mathematically by setting up a ratio of the rate laws for the two trials:

$$\frac{\text{rate 2}}{\text{rate 1}} = \frac{k[A]^x[B]^y}{k[A]^x[B]^y} \text{ thus } \frac{0.020 \text{ mol/L/s}}{0.010 \text{ mol/L/s}} = \frac{\cancel{k}(0.00800 \text{ mol/L})^x(\cancel{0.00400} \text{ mol/L})^y}{\cancel{k}(0.00400 \text{ mol/L})^x(\cancel{0.00400} \text{ mol/L})^y}$$

or $2 = 2^x$ so $x = 1$ *(first order with respect to A)*

From Trial 1 to 3, [A] is constant, while [B] doubles. The result is a quadrupling of the reaction rate. This implies an exponential relationship between the reaction rate and [B] in which the rate is proportional to the [B] squared, and the process is second order with respect to B. Setting up a ratio of the rate laws for these two trials gives:

$$\frac{\text{rate 3}}{\text{rate 1}} = \frac{k[A]^x[B]^y}{k[A]^x[B]^y} \text{ thus } \frac{0.040 \text{ mol/L/s}}{0.010 \text{ mol/L/s}} = \frac{\cancel{k}(\cancel{0.00400 \text{ mol/L}})^x(0.00800 \text{ mol/L})^y}{\cancel{k}(\cancel{0.00400 \text{ mol/L}})^x(0.00400 \text{ mol/L})^y}$$

or $4 = 2^y$ so $y = 2$ *(second order with respect to B)*

The data indicates the following rate law:

reaction rate = $k[A][B]^2$

The **overall order** for a reaction is the sum of the orders with respect to each reactant; hence, in this case, the overall reaction order is 1 + 2 = 3 or third order.

Determining the Rate Constant

Once we have determined the orders with respect to each of the individual reactants, we can determine the numerical rate constant by substituting the rate and concentration values from any of the trials. In the example from the Warm Up, the rate law is: reaction rate = $k[A][B]^2$.

Therefore, the rate constant, $k = \frac{\text{reaction rate}}{[A][B]^2}$

Substitution of the values from Trial 1 in the table gives

$$k = \frac{0.010 \cancel{\text{mol/L}}\text{/s}}{(0.00400 \cancel{\text{mol/L}})(0.00400 \text{ mol/L})^2} = 1.6 \times 10^5 \text{ L}^2\text{mol}^{-2}\text{s}^{-1}$$

We determine the units for the rate constant by canceling the units in the substituted equation. As the overall orders for reactions become larger, the units for rate constants become more complex. We observe a general pattern for the rate constant units as shown in Table 1.4.2.

Table 1.4.2 *Pattern of Rate Constants from Zero to nth Order*

Zero Order	First Order	Second Order	*n*th Order (n >1)
$\frac{M}{s}$	$\frac{1}{s}$	$\frac{1}{M \cdot s}$	$\frac{1}{M^{n-1} \cdot s}$

The magnitude of rate constants varies from one reaction to another. However, for a particular reaction, the value of the rate constant changes only if the temperature changes. In an actual experiment, the process of substitution to determine the numerical value of the rate constant (k) would be repeated for each trial and all values would be averaged.

 © Edvantage Interactive 2019

Sample Problem 1.4.1 — Determining a Rate Law from Experimental Data

Bromate and bromide ions react in acidic solution to form bromine:

$$BrO_3^-(aq) + 5\,Br^-(aq) + 6\,H^+(aq) \rightarrow 3\,Br_2(l) + 3\,H_2O(l)$$

Use the data from this table to determine the rate law expression and the rate constant for the reaction.

Run	$[BrO_3^-]_{initial}$ (mol/L)	$[Br^-]_{initial}$ (mol/L)	$[H^+]_{initial}$ (mol/L)	Initial Rate (mol/L·s)
1	0.10	0.10	0.10	0.00080
2	0.20	0.10	0.10	0.00160
3	0.20	0.20	0.10	0.00320
4	0.10	0.10	0.20	0.00320

What to Think About

1. Identify two trials for which the concentration of only one reactant changes.

2. Set up a ratio to compare these two trials to one another. The value of the exponent that makes the ratio of the concentration change equal the ratio of the rates is the order with respect to the reactant for which the concentration changes between the two trials.

3. Repeat, comparing trials for which the concentration of a different reactant changes while the concentration of all other reactants remains constant.

4. Repeat this process for all reactants.
Note that once the order of a particular species is known, we can calculate the order with respect to another reactant even if the concentration of the reactant with the known order changes. We substitute the value of the known order into the equation and attribute the changes in reaction rate to two different concentration changes.

5. Substitute the values for Trial 1 into the rate law and solve for the rate constant, *k*.

How to Do It

$$\frac{\text{rate }2}{\text{rate }1} = \frac{\cancel{k}(0.20)^x\cancel{(0.10)^y}\cancel{(0.10)^z}}{\cancel{k}(0.10)^x\cancel{(0.10)^y}\cancel{(0.10)^z}} = \frac{0.00160\ \cancel{M/s}}{0.00080\ \cancel{M/s}}$$

hence $2^x = 2$; therefore $x = 1$

$$\frac{\text{rate }3}{\text{rate }2} = \frac{\cancel{k(0.20)^x}(0.20)^y\cancel{(0.10)^z}}{\cancel{k(0.20)^x}(0.10)^y\cancel{(0.10)^z}} = \frac{0.00320\ \cancel{M/s}}{0.00160\ \cancel{M/s}}$$

hence $2^y = 2$; therefore $y = 1$

$$\frac{\text{rate }4}{\text{rate }1} = \frac{\cancel{k(0.10)^x}\cancel{(0.10)^y}(0.20)^z}{\cancel{k(0.10)^x}\cancel{(0.10)^y}(0.10)^z} = \frac{0.00320\ \cancel{M/s}}{0.00080\ \cancel{M/s}}$$

hence $2^z = 4$; therefore $z = 2$

$$\text{rate} = k[BrO_3^-][Br^-][H^+]^2$$

$$k = \frac{\text{rate}}{[BrO_3^-][Br^-][H^+]^2}$$

$$k = \frac{0.00080\ \cancel{mol/L}\cdot s}{(0.10\ \cancel{mol/L})(0.10\ mol/L)(0.10\ mol/L)^2}$$

$$k = 8.0\ L^3mol^{-3}s^{-1}$$

Practice Problems 1.4.1 — Determining Rate Laws from Experimental Data

1. Use the information in the table below to write the rate-law expression for the reaction, and explain how you obtained your answer. Determine the rate constant with units.

   $2\ NO(g) + O_2(g) \rightarrow 2\ NO_2(g)$

Experiment Number	Initial $[O_2]$ ($mol{\cdot}L^{-1}$)	Initial [NO] ($mol{\cdot}L^{-1}$)	Initial Rate of Formation of NO_2 ($mol{\cdot}L^{-1}{\cdot}s^{-1}$)
1	0.0010	0.0010	x
2	0.0010	0.0020	$2x$
3	0.0020	0.0010	$2x$
4	0.0020	0.0020	$4x$

2. Consider an imaginary reaction: $2\ X + Y \rightarrow Z$. Determine the rate law and the rate constant, with units, from the experimental data in the table below.

Initial Rate of Formation of Z ($mol{\cdot}L^{-1}{\cdot}s^{-1}$)	Initial $[X]_o$ ($mol{\cdot}L^{-1}$)	Initial $[Y]_o$ ($mol{\cdot}L^{-1}$)
7.0×10^{-4}	0.20	0.10
1.4×10^{-3}	0.40	0.20
2.8×10^{-3}	0.40	0.40
4.2×10^{-3}	0.60	0.60

3. The following systems represent gaseous reactants A (symbolized by **O**) and B (symbolized by ■) at a fixed temperature and volume. The equation for the reaction is $A(g) + B(g) \rightarrow C(g)$.

   Assume the rate law for the reaction is: rate = $k[A][B]^3$

   System 1 represents a reaction with a rate of 0.010 mol/L/s. Complete the diagrams for the other systems as follows:

   (a) Adding enough particles of A **O**) to System 2 to represent a system that would react with an initial rate of 0.020 mol/L/s.

   (b) Adding enough particles of B (■) to System 3 to represent a system that would react with an initial rate of 0.080 mol/L/s.

System 1 System 2 System 3

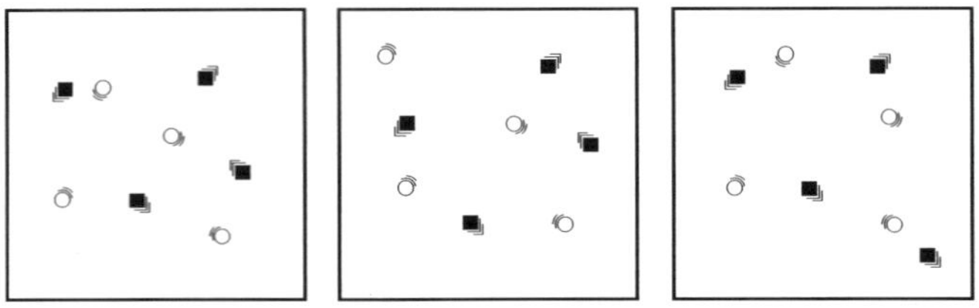

Rate = 0.010 mol/L/s 0.020 mol/L/s 0.080 mol/L/s

© Edvantage Interactive 2019

Determining a Rate Law from Laboratory Data

In summary, to determine a rate law for a reaction, we start by measuring the initial rate of reaction for at least two trials while varying the concentration of one of the reacting species and keeping the concentrations of the other reactants constant. We continue the experimental analysis by continuing to perform comparison trials varying the concentration of each reacting species while keeping the concentrations of the other reactants constant until we collect enough data to determine the rate law (Figure 1.4.3). Once we have determined the general rate law expression, we can calculate the rate constant by algebraic substitution.

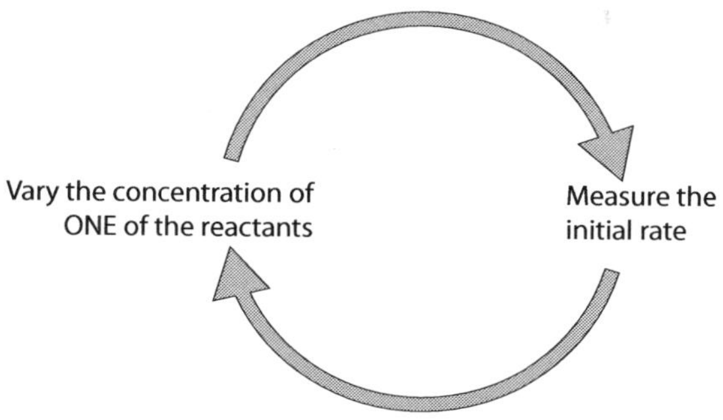

Figure 1.4.3 *A cycle to determine rate laws from experimental data. Continue this cycle until the orders with respect to all reactants have been determined.*

1.4 Review Questions

1. Consider the hypothetical reaction: X + Y → Z and the following data:

Initial Rate of Appearance of Z (mol/L/s)	$[X]_0$ (mol/L)	$[Y]_0$ (mol/L)
0.053	0.05	0.25
0.127	0.10	0.15
1.02	0.20	0.30
0.254	0.10	0.30
0.509	0.20	0.15

(a) Use the data in the table to determine the rate law for the reaction.

(b) Determine the value of the rate constant with units.

(c) Determine the initial rate of appearance of Z when the concentration of X is 0.15 mol/L and that of Y is 0.20 mol/L.

2. Nitrosyl fluoride, NO_2F, can be made by reacting NO_2 and F_2 gases as follows:

$$2\ NO_2(g) + F_2(g) \rightarrow 2\ NO_2F(g)$$

The following table represents data collected for the rate of formation of nitrosyl fluoride at room temperature. Recall that mol L^{-1} is equivalent to mol/L.

$[NO_2]_0$ (mol·L^{-1})	$[F_2]_0$ (mol·L^{-1})	Rate (mol·L^{-1}·s^{-1})
0.00100	0.00100	4.00×10^{-5}
0.00100	0.00300	1.20×10^{-4}
0.00500	0.00300	6.00×10^{-4}
0.00500	0.00500	1.00×10^{-3}

(a) Use the data in the table to determine the rate law for the reaction.

(b) Calculate the rate constant at room temperature. Include appropriate units.

© **Edvantage Interactive 2019**

3. The following trials were performed during the kinetic study of an oxidation-reduction reaction:

$$2\,MnO_4^-(aq) + 5\,H_2C_2O_4(aq) + 6\,H^+(aq) \rightarrow 2\,Mn^{2+}(aq) + 10\,CO_2(g) + 8\,H_2O(l)$$

$[MnO_4^-]_{initial}$ (mol/L)	$[H_2C_2O_4]_{initial}$ (mol/L)	$[H^+]_{initial}$ (mol/L)	Initial Rate of Formation of Mn^{2+} (mol/L/s)
1.0×10^{-3}	1.0×10^{-3}	1.0	2.0×10^{-4}
2.0×10^{-3}	1.0×10^{-3}	1.0	8.0×10^{-4}
2.0×10^{-3}	2.0×10^{-3}	1.0	1.6×10^{-3}
2.0×10^{-3}	2.0×10^{-3}	2.0	1.6×10^{-3}

(a) Use the data in the table for the initial rates of formation of the manganese(II) ion to determine the rate law and the rate constant for the redox reaction.

(b) By what factor would the initial reaction rate change if the concentrations of all three reactants doubled?

(c) By what factor would the initial reaction rate change if the volume of the reaction system doubled due to the addition of distilled water?

4. The equation for a general reaction is: $2\,A(g) + 2\,B(g) \rightarrow C(g) + 2\,D(g)$. The initial rate of formation of C is determined in four trials with various initial concentrations of reactants as shown in the table.

Trial Number	Initial [A] ($mol{\cdot}L^{-1}$)	Initial [B] ($mol{\cdot}L^{-1}$)	Initial Reaction Rate ($mol{\cdot}L^{-1}{\cdot}s^{-1}$)
1	0.100	0.100	4.00×10^{-5}
2	0.200	0.100	1.60×10^{-4}
3	0.100	0.200	4.00×10^{-5}
4	0.300	0.200	?

(a) Determine the rate law for the reaction.

(b) Determine the rate constant with units.

(c) Calculate the initial reaction rate for Trial 4.

5. The table below provides data obtained under lab conditions for the reaction:

$$2\ MnO_4^{2-} + H_3IO_6^{2-} \rightarrow 2\ MnO_4^{-} + IO_3^{-} + 3\ OH^{-}$$

The experimental trials involved measuring the initial rate of formation of the iodate (IO_3^-) ion with varying initial concentrations of reactants.

Experimental Trial	$[MnO_4^{2-}]_0$ (mol·L^{-1})	$[H_3IO_6^{2-}]_0$ (mol·L^{-1})	Initial Rate (*M*/min)
1	1.6×10^{-4}	3.1×10^{-4}	2.6×10^{-6}
2	6.4×10^{-4}	3.1×10^{-4}	4.2×10^{-5}
3	1.6×10^{-4}	6.2×10^{-4}	2.6×10^{-6}
4	3.2×10^{-4}	3.1×10^{-4}	?
5	?	6.2×10^{-4}	2.3×10^{-5}

(a) Determine the rate law for the reaction.

(b) Calculate the rate constant with units.

(c) What is the initial rate of formation of IO_3^- ion for Trial 4?

(d) What is the required initial concentration of MnO_4^{2-} ion for Trial 5?

(e) What is the initial rate of formation of MnO_4^- ion for Trial 1?

6. The equation for the bromination of acetone in acidic solution is:

$$CH_3COCH_3(aq) + Br_2(aq) \rightarrow CH_3COCH_2Br(aq) + H^+(aq) + Br^-(aq)$$

The following data were collected in four trials by varying the concentration of reactants and measuring the initial rate of disappearance of aqueous bromine ($Br_2(aq)$).

Trial Number	$[CH_3COCH_3]_o$ (*M*)	$[Br_2]_o$ (*M*)	$[H^+]_o$ (*M*)	Initial Rate (*M*/s)
1	0.30	0.050	0.050	5.7×10^{-5}
2	0.30	0.100	0.050	5.7×10^{-5}
3	0.30	0.100	0.100	1.4×10^{-4}
4	0.40	0.050	0.200	3.2×10^{-4}

Determine the rate law and the rate constant (with appropriate units) for the acidic bromination of acetone.

© Edvantage Interactive 2019

1.5 Integrated Rate Equations

Warm Up

Graph the following data using the grids provided.

Time (s)	Concentration (mol/L)	ln Concentration	1/Concentration (L/mol)
0	0.500		
10	0.197		
20	0.078		
30	0.031		
40	0.012		
50	0.005		

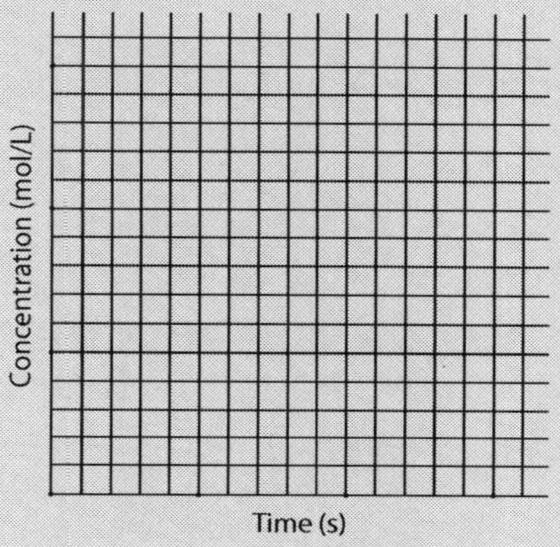

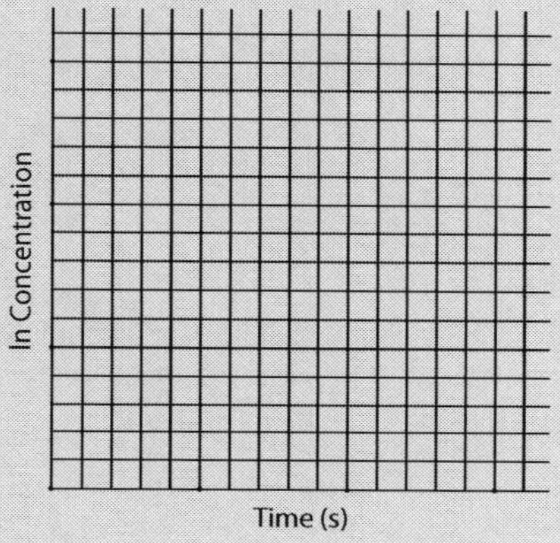

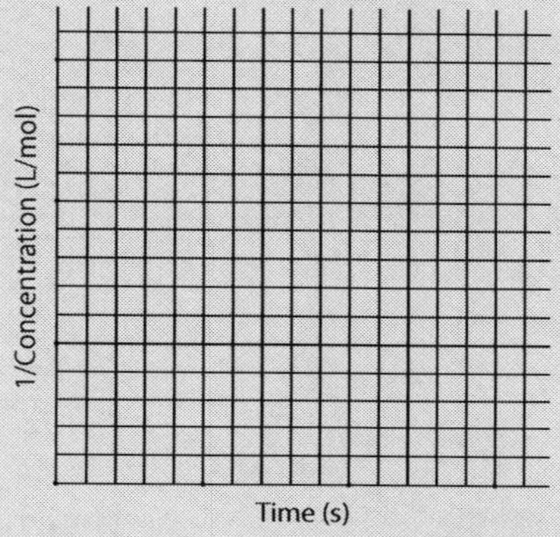

1. Which set of data gives represents a direct relationship?

   ____

2. What type of relationship do the other sets of data represent?

   ____

3. Determine the equation for the straight-line graph.

Integrating Rate Laws — Relating Concentration to Time

In the previous section we learned how to determine the rate law for a chemical reaction by comparing experimentally determined initial rates with concentrations of reactants. Measuring the initial rate of a reaction involves determining small changes in the concentration of a reactant or product during a very short time interval. It can be difficult to obtain sufficiently precise experimental data for such small changes. An alternative is to use an **integrated rate law**, which expresses the *concentration of a species directly as a function of time*. For a *simple rate expression* (also called a *differential rate expression*), calculus provides the math to calculate a corresponding integrated rate law. In deducing the rate law from experimental data, we can analyze the integrated rate laws for zero-, first-, and second-order reactions to determine which equation fits the data.

Using Calculus to Derive Integrated Rate Equations

If you have taken a calculus course this year, you may already know how to find a derivative. A derivative function is an equation that defines a rate of change. In the kinetics unit, we determined the rate of change of some measurable property during a chemical reaction over a period of time (e.g., the change in concentration of a reactant or product over time). Solving for an antiderivative is the reverse operation of finding a derivative. For integration calculations, we determine antiderivatives over the endpoints of an interval. In kinetics, we consider the interval from time zero to a time, *t*. Over this interval, we are interested in how an initial concentration, C_0 changes to a new concentration, *C*.

Some antiderivatives are fairly easy to express and others are more challenging. The following table shows three functions, *f*(*x*), the antiderivatives of these functions, *F*(*x*), and the integrals of these functions between two points, x_2 and x_1, where a is a constant.

Table 1.5.1 *Applying Calculus to Derive Integrated Rate Equations*

Function *f*(*x*)	Antiderivative *F*(*x*)	Integral $\int_{x_1}^{x_2} f(x)\,dx$
a	ax	$ax_2 - ax_1$
$1/x = x^{-1}$ $(x>0)$	$\ln x$	$(\ln x_2 - \ln x_1) = \ln (x_2/x_1)$
$1/x^2 = x^{-2}$	$-1/x = -x^{-1}$	$-(1/x_2 - 1/x_1)$

You will not be required to produce derivatives, antiderivatives, or integrals as part of this Chemistry course. However, the following discussion will help you understand the derivation of three important integrated rate equations in Chemistry.

First-Order Rate Laws

Dinitrogen pentoxide decomposes as follows: $N_2O_5(g) \rightarrow 2\ NO_2(g) + \frac{1}{2}\ O_2(g)$. From experimental data, scientists determined the rate law for this reaction follows first-order kinetics, expressed as follows:

$$\text{rate} = \frac{-\Delta[N_2O_5]}{\Delta t} = \frac{-d[N_2O_5]}{dt} = k[N_2O_5]$$

The negative sign indicates the decrease in reactant concentration. A derivative is a rate of change, hence we replace the symbol Δ, which means "change in," by *d*. Replacement of $[N_2O_5]$ with *C* (for concentration) gives the following equation for the change in concentration as a function of time:

$$\textbf{First-order reaction: } \frac{dC}{dt} = -kC$$

Multiplying both sides by *dt* and dividing both sides by *C* results in: $(1/C)dC = -kdt$

Referencing Table 1.5.1 shows that integration from an initial concentration C_0 at time = 0 to a concentration *C* at time = *t* appears as follows:

$$\int_{C_0}^{C} \frac{1}{C} dC = -k\int_0^t dt$$

This gives $\ln C - \ln C_0 = -kt$, which we can also express as

$$\ln \frac{C}{C_0} = -kt$$

 © Edvantage Interactive 2019

The linear $y = mx + b$ equation of this first-order integrated rate equation becomes:

$\ln C = -kt + \ln C_0$

Integrated first-order rate equation: $\ln C = -kt + \ln C_0$ **or** $\ln \frac{C}{C_0} = -kt$

Sample Problem 1.5.1(a) — Calculating the Time Required to Reach a Desired Concentration

Dinitrogen pentoxide is the unstable anhydride of nitric acid that decomposes by first-order kinetics into nitrogen dioxide and oxygen gas, as shown earlier in this section. The rate law is rate = $k[N_2O_5]$. The rate constant for the reaction is $6.22 \times 10^{-4}\ s^{-1}$ at 45°C. If the initial concentration of N_2O_5 is 0.500 mol/L, how long will it take for the concentration to drop to 0.0500 mol/L?

What to Think About	How to Do It
1. Determine the order for the reaction.	The question states that the reaction is first order. The exponent in the rate law ($r = k[N_2O_5]$) is a 1 and the units for the rate constant are also consistent with a first-order rate law. The units of the rate constant of first-order reactions are always the reciprocal of a unit of time (in this case the unit is s^{-1}).
2. Substitute into the integrated rate equation for a first-order reaction. Take care not to drop the negative sign. Be sure to substitute the values of *C* and C_0 correctly.	Since $\ln(C/C_0) = -kt$, $t = \dfrac{\ln(C/C_0)}{-k}$ $t = \dfrac{\ln(0.0500\ M/0.500\ M)}{-6.22 \times 10^{-4}\ s^{-1}} = 3.70 \times 10^3\ s$

Sample Problem 1.5.1(b) — Calculating the Concentration of a Reactant After a Given Period of Time

If the initial concentration of N_2O_5 is 0.250 mol/L at 45°C, what is the concentration after exactly 1 h?

What to Think About	How to Do It
1. The previous example indicates that the decomposition reaction is first order. Use the integrated rate equation for a first-order reaction to solve for ln *C*.	$\ln C = -kt + \ln C_0$ $= -6.22 \times 10^{-4}\ s^{-1}(3600\ s) + \ln 0.250\ mol/L$ $= -3.62$
2. Use the inverse ln function, or e^x to determine the concentration. Take care not to drop the negative sign.	$C = \text{antiln} -3.62 = e^{-3.62}$ $= 0.0266\ mol/L$

Practice Problems 1.5.1 — Relating Concentrations and Time in First-order reactions

1. What is the rate constant for a first-order reaction with an initial reactant concentration of 0.300 mol/L if, after 158 s, the concentration is 0.200 mol/L?

2. The reaction in question 1 occurs at the same temperature with an initial reactant concentration of 1.50 mol/L. What is the reactant's concentration 2.75 min later?

3. The reaction in question 1 reacts for 5.00 min at the same temperature until the reactant concentration drops to 0.0100 mol/L. What was the reactant's initial concentration?

Second-Order Rate Laws

Another oxide of nitrogen, nitrogen dioxide, decomposes as follows:

$$2\,NO_2(g) \rightarrow 2\,NO(g) + O_2(g)$$

From experimental data, scientists determined that this reaction is second order with respect to the concentration of NO_2. Hence the following is true:

$$\text{rate} = \frac{-d[NO_2]}{dt} = k[NO_2]^2$$

Replacing $[NO_2]$ with the more general symbol C:

$$\textbf{Second-order reaction: } \frac{dC}{dt} = -kC^2$$

Algebraic manipulation of the second-order rate expression results in

$$\frac{1}{C^2}dC = -kdt$$

Integrating from an initial concentration, C_0 at time = 0 to C at time = t gives:

$$\int_{C_0}^{C} \frac{1}{C^2}dC = -k\int_0^t dt$$

This becomes: $-1/C + 1/C_0 = -kt$ or in the format of the linear equation ($y = mx + b$): $1/C = kt + 1/C_0$.

$$\textbf{Integrated second-order rate equation: } \frac{1}{C} = kt + \frac{1}{C_0}$$

© Edvantage Interactive 2019

Sample Problem 1.5.1 — Calculating Concentration after a Given Period of Time for a Second-Order Reaction

Nitrosyl chloride, NOCl, is a corrosive orange gas that intensely irritates membranes in the human body, including eyes and skin. It decomposes slowly to form the gases NO and Cl_2 by second-order reaction kinetics with a rate constant, $k = 0.020$ L/mol·s. Given an initial concentration of 0.450 mol/L, what concentration of NOCl will remain after 40.0 h of decomposition?

What to Think About	How to Do It
1. Determine the reaction order.	The reaction is second order as stated in the question. A second-order rate law is also consistent with the units of the rate constant. The units of the product of reciprocal molarity and reciprocal time indicate a second-order reaction.
2. Substitute into the integrated rate equation for a second-order reaction.	$1/C = kt + 1/C_0$ $1/C = 0.020 \text{ L mol}^{-1} \text{ s}^{-1} \times (40.0 \text{ h} \times 3600 \text{ s}/1 \text{ h}) + 1/0.450 \text{ mol/L}$ $= 2882$ L/mol
3. Apply algebra to solve for *C*.	Thus $C = (2882 \text{ L/mol})^{-1}$ $= 3.5 \times 10^{-4}$ mol/L

Practice Problems 1.5.1 — Relating Concentrations and Time in Second-Order Reactions

1. Refer to the reaction in the Sample Problem above and determine how long it will take for a sample of NOCl with an initial concentration of 0.038 mol/L to drop to 0.012 mol/L.

2. Pharmacokinetics is the study of how the body takes up, distributes, and eliminates drugs. The elimination of a newly designed medical drug from the body follows second-order kinetics. The drug is called Zippidy Eh. Its molar mass is 122.0 g/mol. The rate constant for the elimination process is 2.4 L mol^{-1} min^{-1}. If the initial dose of Zippidy Eh is 250 mg for a 70 kg patient with a blood volume of 4.8 L, what mass of the drug will remain 12 h after ingestion?

Zero-Order Rate Equations

Most reactions involving a single reactant follow either first- or second-order kinetics. However, zero-order kinetics with respect to a reactant are possible. In first- and second-order reactions, the rate of reaction is fastest at the beginning of the reaction when the concentration of the reactant is the greatest. In zero-order reactions, the reaction rate is constant throughout the reaction and is independent of the reaction concentration.

Zero-order reaction: $\frac{dC}{dt} = kC^{0} = k(1) = k$

For a zero-order reaction, the rate does not depend on concentration. Only temperature or the presence of a catalyst can affect the rate of a zero-order reaction.

Integrated zero-order rate equation: $C = -kt + C_0$

Zero-order reactions are common when reactions occur in the presence of a heterogeneous enzyme. Exposing the surface of the enzyme provides a lower activation energy pathway for the reaction. The reaction's rate depends on the enzyme's available surface area rather than the concentration of the reactant.

Graphical Method for Distinguishing Orders of Reactions

In the previous section, we used an algebraic method to determine reaction order using given initial rates and reactant concentrations. In the laboratory, initial rates are not easily determined. In fact, some kinetics experiments use the reciprocal of time as an indicator of initial reaction rate since these two values are directly proportional. One way to study a reaction's rate is by collecting changes in concentration values as a function of time. Graphing these data allows us to determine which of the integrated rate equations plots as a straight line.

First-order reactions are more common than zero- or second-order reactions. In a first-order reaction, a plot of C versus time looks like the graphs in Figure 1.5.1. The tangent line is steepest at the beginning of the reaction when the rate is the greatest. Plotting ln C versus time gives a straight line with a negative slope. The absolute value of the slope is equal to the rate constant. The value of the *rate constant must always be positive*. The *y*-intercept is equal to ln C_0. The reciprocal of concentration versus time gives a parabolic shape with an upward curve (Figure 1.5.1).

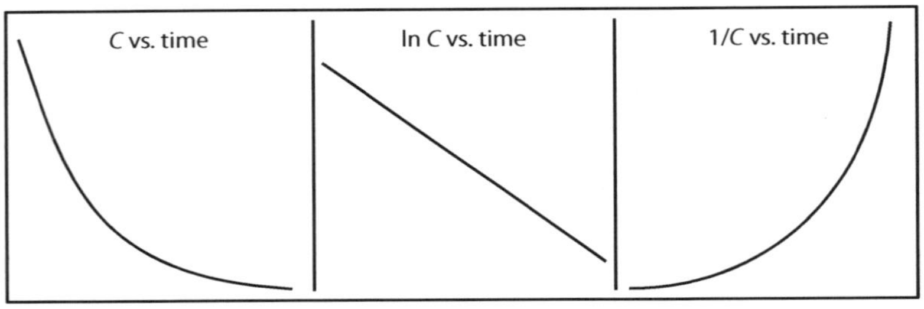

Figure 1.5.1 *Typical graphs for a first-order reaction*

A plot of C versus time for a second-order reaction produces a curve similar to that of a plot of C versus time for a first-order reaction. The ln C-versus-time plot of a second-order reaction produces a graph that is slightly less curved than the C-versus-time plot. Unlike the curve produced for a first-order reaction, a plot of the reciprocal of C versus time for second-order reactions gives a straight line with a positive slope. The slope of this line is equal to the rate constant. The *y*-intercept is equal to $1/C_0$ (Figure 1.5.2).

 © Edvantage Interactive 2019

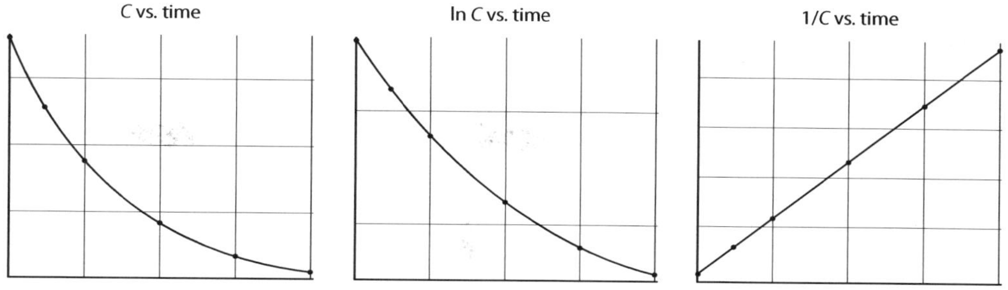

Figure 1.5.2 *Typical graphs for a second-order reaction*

The relationship between C and time for a zero-order reaction is simply a straight-line graph with a negative slope. The absolute value of the slope is equal to the rate constant for the reaction. For zero-order reactions, the ln C-versus-time relationship is a convex curve with increasingly steep negatively sloped tangents and the $1/C$-versus-time plot is a concave curve with increasingly steep positively sloped tangents (Figure 1.5.3).

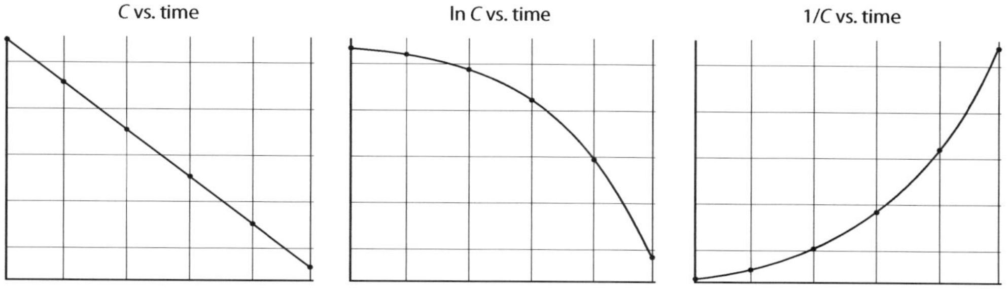

Figure 1.5.3 *Typical graphs for a zero-order reaction*

Straight-line integrated rate equations:

zero order: $C = -kt + C_0$

first order: $\ln C = -kt + \ln C_0$

second order: $\frac{1}{C} = kt + \frac{1}{C_0}$

Sample Problem 1.5.3 — Graphical Analysis of Integrated Rate Equations

Nitrosyl bromide is a reddish brown gas that decomposes into nitrogen monoxide and bromine:

$$2\ NOBr(g) \rightarrow 2\ NO(g) + Br_2(g)$$

Complete the following table of experimental data for the decomposition. Plot three graphs to determine whether the reaction is zero, first, or second order with respect to NOBr. Write the rate law expression and determine the rate constant with units.

Time (s)	[NOBr] (mol/L)	ln [NOBr]	1/[NOBr] (L/mol)
0.00	0.0100		
2.00	0.0071		
4.00	0.0055		
6.00	0.0045		
8.00	0.0038		
10.00	0.0033		

Continued

Sample Problem 1.5.3 *(Continued)*

What to Think About

1. Complete the data table for the missing columns.
2. Plot graphs of:
   [NOBr] vs. time
   ln [NOBr] vs. time
   1/[NOBr] vs. time
3. The [NOBr] vs. time graph is curved. This indicates the decomposition is not zero order.
4. The ln [NOBr] vs. time graph is also curved, indicating the decomposition is not first order.
5. You may have predicted that the reciprocal plot would be a straight line by examining the changes every 2 s. Both [NOBr] and ln [NOBr] decrease most rapidly at the beginning of the reaction, while 1/[NOBr] increases by about 40 M^{-1} in each 2 s increment.
6. Determine the rate constant by finding the slope of the straight-line graph.

How to Do It

Time (s)	ln [NOBr]	1/[NOBr] (M^{-1})
0.00	−4.61	100.
2.00	−4.95	141
4.00	−5.20	182
6.00	−5.40	222
8.00	−5.57	263
10.00	−5.71	303

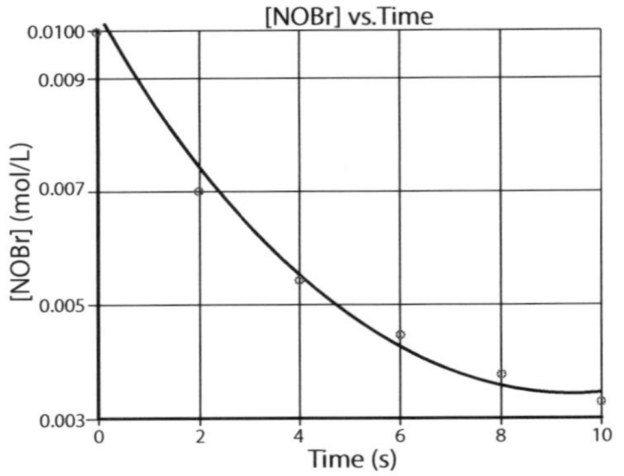

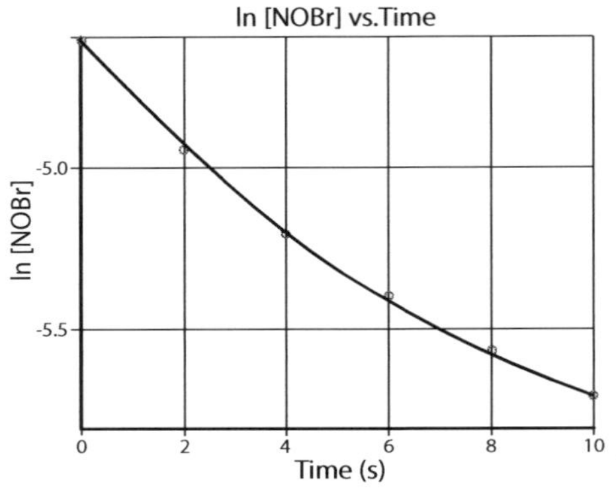

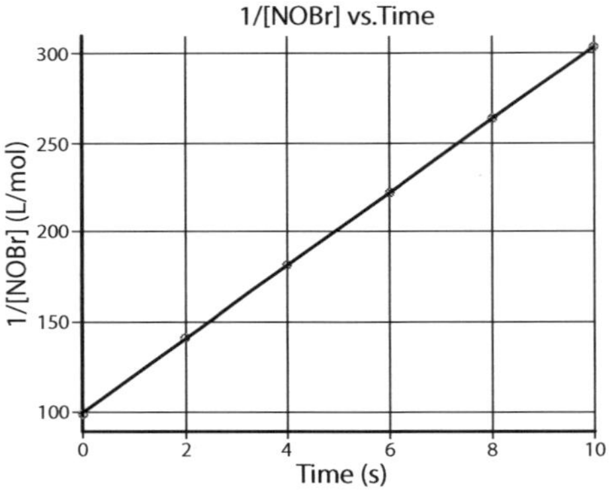

The 1/[NOBr] vs. time graph produces a straight line; hence, the decomposition is a second-order reaction.

rate = $k[NOBr]^2$

The straight-linegraph-shows a slope = k

= the rate constant

= 20.L/mol•s

 © Edvantage Interactive 2019

Practice Problems 1.5.3 — Graphic Analysis of Integrated Rate Equations

1. We can use **pseudo integrated rate analysis** when a reaction involves more than one reactant. We use a large excess of one of the reactants to manipulate the system so that the change in the concentration of the excess reactant is negligible. The value of the concentration of the excess reactant is subsumed into the rate constant because it barely changes and is therefore constant within the margin of error. We determine the order with respect to the species that is present in a very small concentration. We refer to the absolute value of the slope of the straight line plot as the **pseudo rate constant, *k′*** (*k* prime). We determine the actual rate constant by dividing *k′* by the [excess].
A student collected the following data during a laboratory study of the substitution reaction:
$(CH_3)_3CBr + OH^- \rightarrow (CH_3)_3COH + Br^-$ with a large excess of OH^-.

Time (s)	$[(CH_3)_3CBr]$ mol/L	ln $[(CH_3)_3CBr]$	$1/[(CH_3)_3CBr]$ L $mol^{-1}s^{-1}$
0	0.100		
30	0.074		
60	0.055		
90	0.041		

Draw graphs of $[(CH_3)_3CBr]$ vs. time, ln $[(CH_3)_3CBr]$ vs. time, and $1/[(CH_3)_3CBr]$ vs. time. Is the substitution reaction zero, first, or second order with respect to $(CH_3)_3CBr$? What is the value of the pseudo rate constant with units?

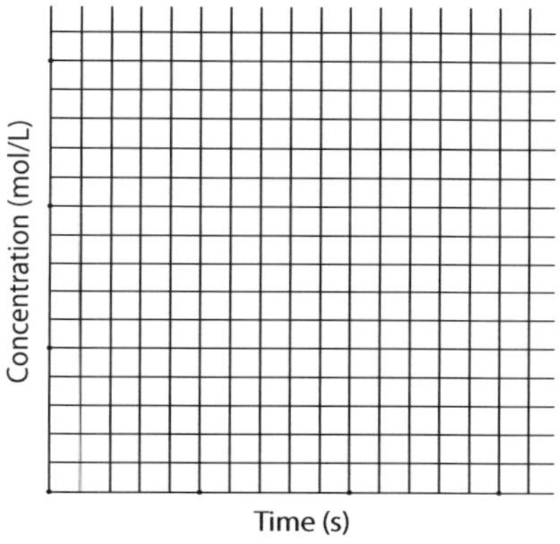

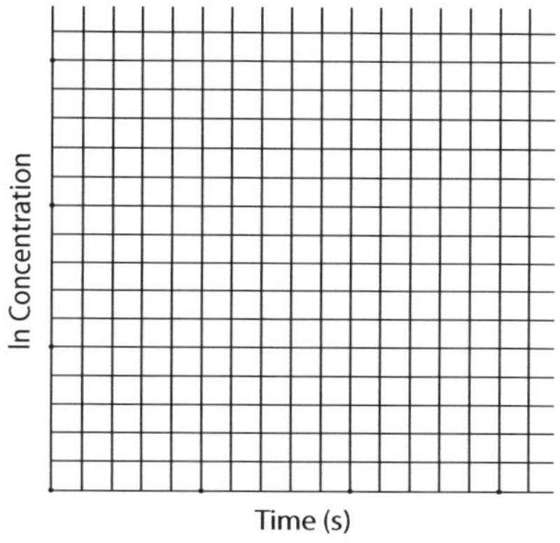

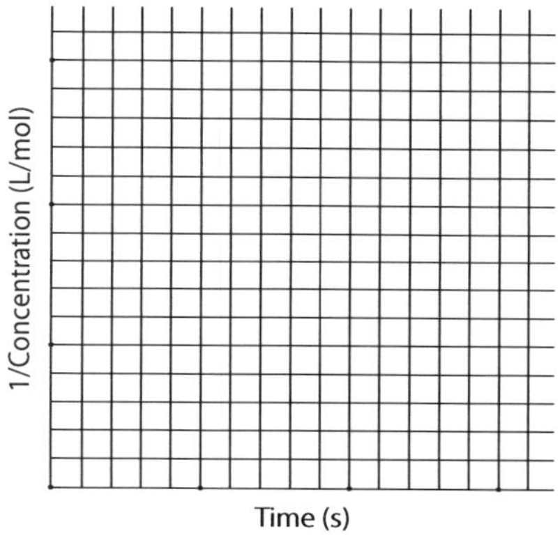

2. Nitrogen dioxide decomposes as indicated in the following equation:

$$2\ NO_2(g) \rightarrow 2\ NO(g) + O_2(g)$$

A student collected the following data for the decomposition at an elevated temperature.

Time (s)	$[NO_2]$ (mol/L)	ln $[NO_2]$	$1/[NO_2]$ (L/mol·s)
0	0.0100		
50.	0.0079		
100.	0.0065		
200.	0.0048		
300.	0.0038		
400.	0.0032		

(a) Draw three graphs and determine the rate law expression and the rate constant with units for the decomposition of nitrogen dioxide.

Continued

Practice Problems 1.5.3 *(Continued)*

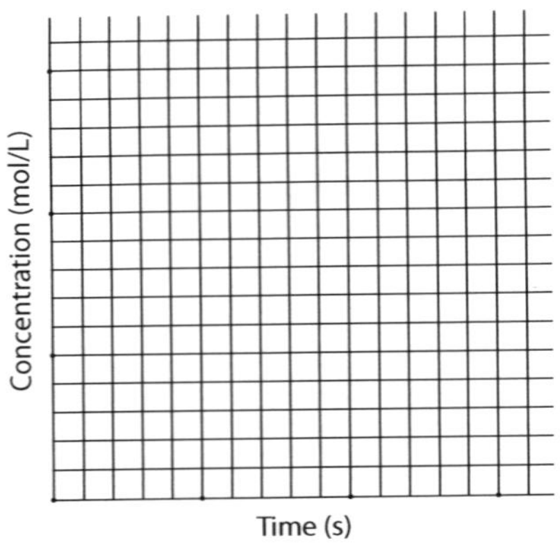

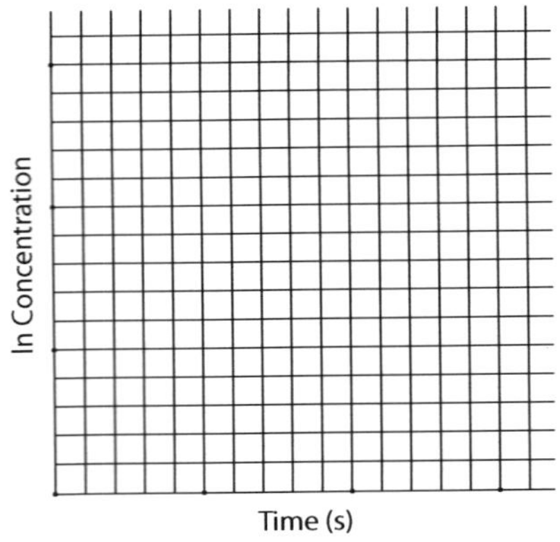

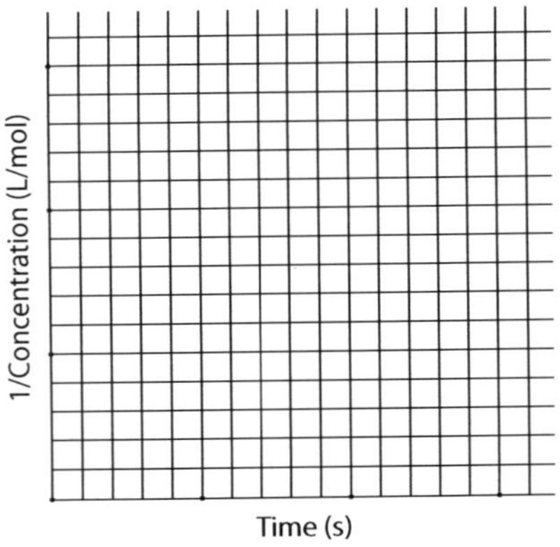

(b) How would the straight-line graph change (in general) if:
   (i) the initial concentration of the nitrogen dioxide were increased?

   (ii) the temperature of the decomposition were elevated?

Half-Life

The magnitude of the rate constant k is a good indication of the speed of a chemical reaction. The larger the magnitude of the rate constant, the greater the rate of a reaction. The *half-life of a reaction* is another useful measure of the rate of a reaction (Figure 1.5.4). You may have heard about half-lives in an earlier course in science, most likely associated with nuclear radiation.

The **half-life ($t_{1/2}$)** of a reaction is the time it takes for one-half of a reactant to be consumed in a chemical reaction.

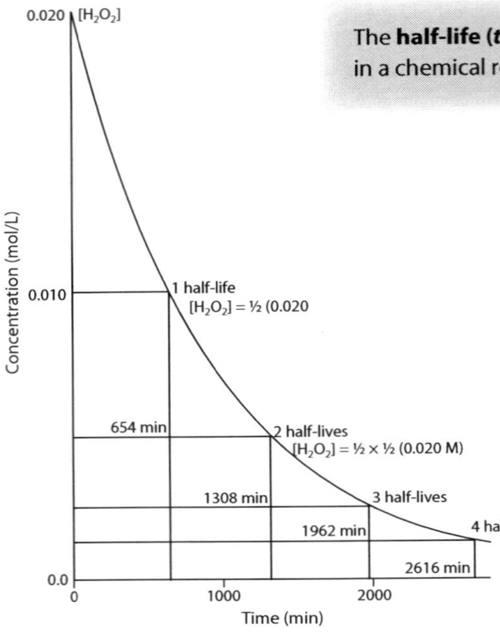

Figure 1.5.4 *A graph of the concentration of hydrogen peroxide against time shows the $[H_2O_2]$ dropping to one-half of its previous concentration every 654 min.*

To derive an equation for the half-life of a reaction, substitute $1/2C_0$ for C in the integrated rate equation and solve for time. For example, in a first-order integrated rate equation:

$$\ln(1/2C_0) = -kt_{1/2} + \ln C_0$$

Subtracting $\ln C_0$ from both sides of the equation gives:

$$\ln(1/2C_0) - \ln C_0 = -kt_{1/2}$$

Applying the logarithm quotient rule gives:

$$\ln[1/2C_0/C_0] = -kt_{1/2}$$

Cancelling C_0/C_0 gives:

$$\ln(1/2) = -kt_{1/2}$$

Finally, multiplying both sides by −1 gives:

$$\ln 2 = kt_{1/2}$$

For a first-order reaction: $t_{1/2} = \ln 2/k = 0.693/k$ and $k = \ln 2/t_{1/2} = 0.693/t_{1/2}$

© Edvantage Interactive 2019

Sample Problem 1.5.4 — Half-life of a First-Order Reaction

The rate constant for the catalyzed isomerization of *cis*-2-butene gas to produce trans-2-butene gas is 0.00693 s^{-1}.

cis-2-butene   *trans*-2-butene

(a) What is the half-life of the reaction?
(b) What fraction of the original *cis*-2-butene sample remains 5.00 min after the reaction begins?
(c) If the original [*cis*-2-butene] were 3.45 mol/L, what concentration remains 7.00 min after the reaction begins?

What to Think About	How to Do It
1. Determine the order of the reaction so that you can apply the correct equations to calculate the half-life. A rate constant unit of reciprocal time is typical of a first-order reaction.	(a) For a first-order reaction: $t_{1/2} = \ln 2/k$ Thus $t_{1/2} = 0.693/0.00693\ s^{-1}$ $= 100.\ s$
2. Convert 5.00 min to seconds.	(b) 5.00 min x 60 s/1 min = 300. s This is equivalent to the time required for the reaction to go through three half-lives. The fraction of the original sample remaining after 3 half-lives is calculated by dividing by 2 three times: $1 \rightarrow 1/2 \rightarrow 1/4 \rightarrow$ 1/8 remains
3. The time of 7.00 min does not divide by a whole number of half-lives. Using the integrated rate equation for first-order reactions, calculate the final concentration.	(c) $\ln C = -kt + \ln C_0$ $= -0.00693\ s^{-1}(7.00\ min \times 60\ s/1\ min)$ $+ \ln 3.45\ mol/L$ $= -0.00693\ s^{-1}(420.\ s) + 1.24$ $= -1.67$
The answer to (c) is slightly less than 1/16 (3.45 M) as it should be since 7.00 min is just over four half lives.	Finally, $C = e^{-1.67} = 0.188$ mol/L

Practice Problems 1.5.4 — Half-Life of a First-Order Reaction

1. The rate constant for the first order conversion of cyclopropane to propene in a laboratory is $9.0 \times 10^{-4}\ \text{min}^{-1}$.
   (a) What is the half-life of the reaction?

   (b) Assuming the initial concentration of the cyclopropane is 1.50 mol/L, what concentration will remain after 51.2 h?

2. The half-life for the decomposition of N_2O_5 under laboratory conditions is 2.0 min.
   (a) What is the rate constant for the reaction under these conditions?

   (b) What is the concentration of N_2O_5 270 s after the reaction starts, assuming an initial concentration of 0.180 mol/L?

   (c) How much time does it take for the concentration of N_2O_5 to drop from 0.180 mol/L to 0.100 mol/L?

Second-Order Half-Life Equations

Second-order half-life equations are derived in a similar way. The second-order integrated rate equation is $1/C = kt + 1/C_0$, which can be rearranged to:

$$1/C - 1/C_0 = kt$$

Setting $t = t_{1/2}$ and $C = 1/2C_0$ gives:

$$2/C_0 - 1/C_0 = kt_{1/2}$$

Solving for $t_{1/2}$ gives:

$$t_{1/2} = 1/kC_0$$

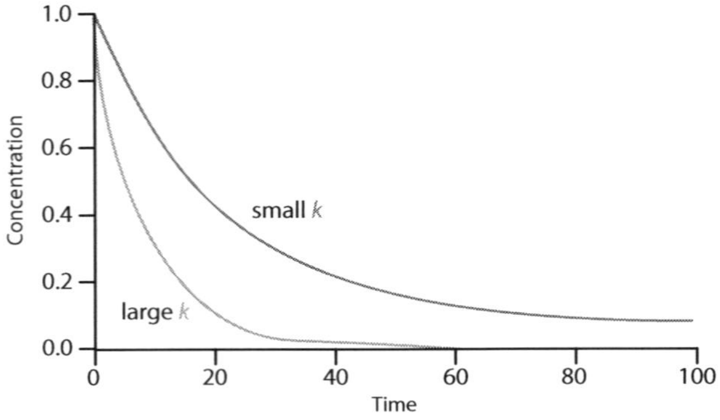

Figure 1.5.5 *Faster reactions have larger rate constants.*

For both first- and second-order reactions, $t_{1/2}$ is inversely proportional to k. This makes sense because the larger the value of k, the faster the reaction (Figure 1.5.5). The faster the reaction, the shorter the time required to consume half of the reactant.

The half-life for a second-order reaction is also inversely proportional to the initial concentration of the reactant. This means the smaller the C_0, the longer the $t_{1/2}$. Each successive half-life is double the length of the previous one.

© Edvantage Interactive 2019

For a *second-order reaction:* $t_{½} = \dfrac{1}{kC_0}$

Each successive $t_{1/2}$ is double the length of the previous $t_{1/2}$.

For a zero-order reaction, substituting $1/2C_0$ for C_0 and solving for *t* in the integrated rate equation demonstrates that the half-life is inversely proportional to *k*, but is directly related to the initial concentration of the reactant. As with first- and second-order reactions, a larger rate constant, *k*, means a faster reaction and a shorter half-life. A lower initial reactant concentration also leads to a shorter half-life. For zero-order reactions, each successive half-life is half the previous one (Figure 1.5.6).

For a *zero-order reaction:* $t_{½} = \dfrac{C_0}{2k}$

Each successive $t_{1/2}$ is half the length of the previous $t_{1/2}$.

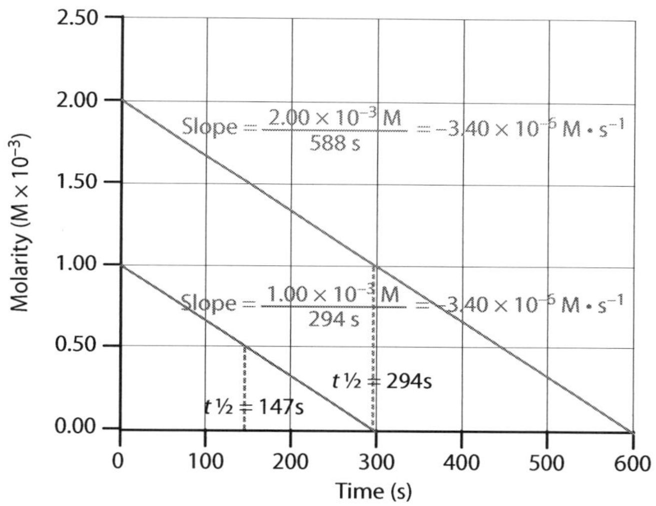

Figure 1.5.6 *A zero-order reaction gives a straight line with a negative slope when we plot concentration against time. A second plot shows that when we halve the reactant concentration, the half-life is also halved. The slope remains the same for both plots. The absolute value of the slope is equal to the rate constant k, which is the same for all reactant concentrations. (Note that the slope is also equal to the rate, which is constant for a zero-order reaction.)*

Sample Problem 1.5.5 — Half-Life of a Second-Order Reaction

Earlier in this section, we determined that nitrosyl bromide, NOBr, decomposes via second-order kinetics with a rate constant of 20. L/mol·s under a particular set of laboratory conditions.

(a) What is the half-life for nitrosyl bromide?

(b) How long would it take the concentration of nitrosyl bromide to drop from 0.0100 mol/L to 0.0025 mol/L?

What to Think About	How to Do It
1. Determine the order of the reaction so that you can apply the correct equation to calculate the half-life. The units for the rate constant are (L/mol·s) and units of reciprocal molarity, reciprocal time are typical of a second-order reaction.	(a) For a second-order reaction: $t_{1/2} = 1/kC_0$ $t_{1/2} = \dfrac{1}{20.\ \cancel{L}/\cancel{mol}\cdot s\,(0.0100\ \cancel{mol}/\cancel{L})}$ $= 1/0.20\ s^{-1} = 5.0\ s$
2. Remember that each successive half-life is twice the previous.	(b) Because 0.0025 mol/L is 1/4 of 0.0100 mol/L, 2 half-lives are required. $5.0 + 2(5.0) = 5.0 + 10.0 = 15.0\ s$

Practice Problems 1.5.5 — Half-life of Second and Zero-Order Reactions

1. The reaction $2\ HI(g) \rightarrow H_2(g) + I_2(g)$ has the rate law, rate = $k[HI]^2$, with $k = 0.0796\ L\ mol^{-1}s^{-1}$ at 500°C.

   (a) What is the half-life for this reaction when the initial concentration is 0.100 mol/L?

   (b) What is the concentration after 375 s if the initial concentration is 0.100 mol/L?

2. If the half-life of a reaction is independent of the initial concentration of the reactants, what do you know about the reaction?

 © Edvantage Interactive 2019

Table 1.5.1 *Summary of Integrated Rate Laws and Half-Lives*

Order in C	Rate Law	Integrated Form $y = mx + b$	Rate Constant (k) Units	Straight Line Plot	Half-life $t_{½}$	Graph
Zero order (n=0)	rate = $kC^0 = k$	$C_t = -kt + C_0$	$\frac{\text{M}}{\text{s}}$	C_t vs. t (slope = $-k$)	$t_{½} = \frac{C_0}{2k}$	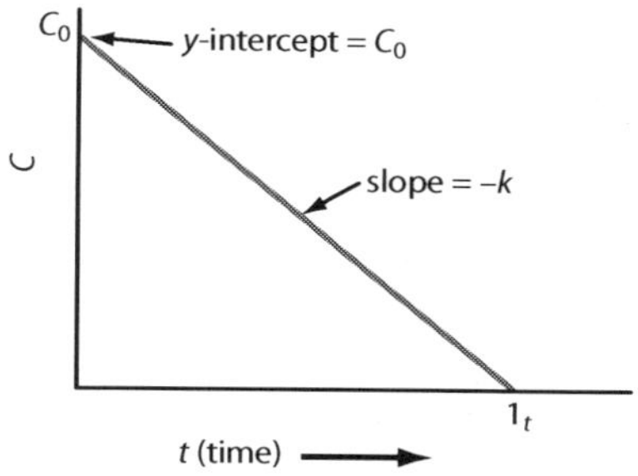
First order (n=1)	rate = kC^1	$\ln C_t = -kt + \ln C_0$	$\frac{1}{\text{s}}$	$\ln C_t$ vs. t (slope = $-k$)	$t_{½} = \frac{\ln 2}{k} = \frac{0.693}{k}$	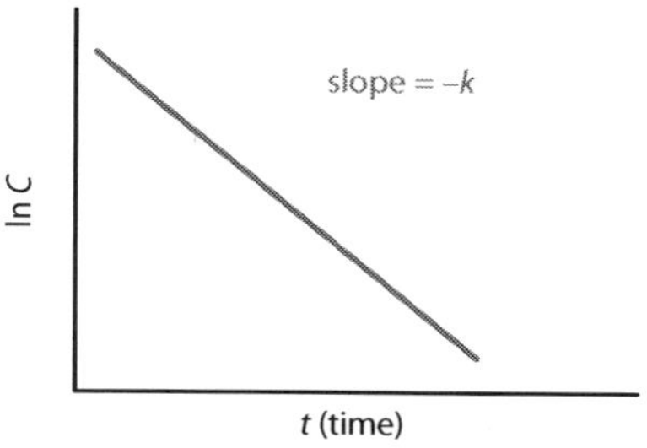
Second order (n=2)	rate = kC^2	$\frac{1}{C_t} = kt + \frac{1}{C_0}$	$\frac{1}{\text{M} \cdot \text{s}}$	$\frac{1}{C_t}$ vs. t (slope = k)	$t_{½} = \frac{1}{kC_0}$	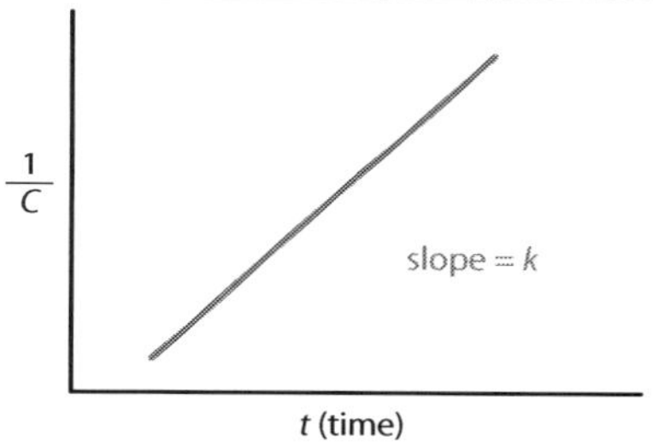
nth order	rate = kC^n	$\frac{1}{C^{(n-1)}} = (n-1)kt + \frac{1}{C_0^{(n-1)}}$	$\frac{1}{\text{M}^{(n-1)} \cdot \text{s}}$	$\frac{1}{C_t^{(n-1)}}$ vs. t (slope = $(n-1)k$)	$t_{½} = \frac{2^{(n-1)}-1}{(n-1)kC_0^{(n-1)}}$	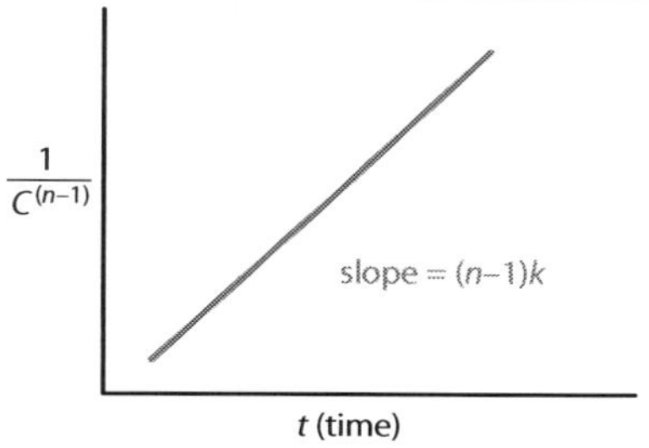

1.5 Review Questions

1. (a) What happens to each of the following as time passes for a first-order reaction?
   (i) rate of reaction

   (ii) rate constant

   (iii) half-life

   (b) Answer question (a) for a zero-order reaction.
   (i) rate of reaction

   (ii) rate constant

   (iii) half-life

   (c) Answer question (a) for a second-order reaction.
   (i) rate of reaction

   (ii) rate constant

   (iii) half-life

2. The rate constant of a first-order reaction is $4.03 \times 10^{-3}\ s^{-1}$. What concentration of reactant remains after 74.6 s assuming an initial concentration of 0.300 mol/L?

3. The reaction $2\ B \rightarrow C + A$ is a second-order reaction, and the rate constant is 0.15 L/mol·min. If the initial concentration of B is 2.00 mol/L, what is the concentration of B after 45 min?

4. A zero-order reaction has $k = 0.0025$ mol/L/s for the disappearance of A. What is the concentration of A after 35 s if the initial concentration is 0.50 mol/L?

5. In 17.5% w/w HCl, the complex ion $Ru(NH_3)_6^{3+}$ decomposes to a variety of products. The reaction is first order in $[Ru(NH_3)_6^{3+}]$ and has a half-life of 14 h at 25°C.
   (a) What is the rate constant for this reaction?

   (b) Under these conditions, how long will it take for the $[Ru(NH_3)_6^{3+}]$ to decrease to 6.25% of its initial value?

© Edvantage Interactive 2019

6. What is the rate constant in s^{-1} for a first-order reaction with an initial concentration of 0.600 mol/L if, after 142 s, the concentration is 0.444 mol/L?

7. What is the half-life in seconds for a second-order reaction with the rate constant $k = 2.74 \times 10^{-1}$ L $mol^{-1}s^{-1}$ if the initial reactant concentration is 0.500 mol/L?

8. Compare the two graphs shown here, focusing on lines (a), (b), and (c), which represent plots for various experimental trials run for the same first-order reaction under different conditions.

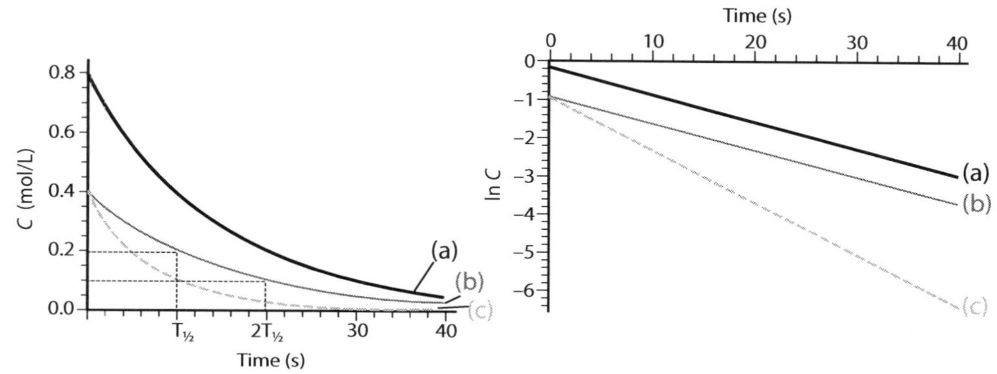

(a) What condition was changed from trial (a) to trial (b)?

(b) What effect did the change have? Explain your answer.

(c) What was not affected by the change? Justify your answer.

(d) What condition was changed from trial (b) to trial (c)? Be specific.

(e) Give two things about the reaction that this change impacted. Justify your answers.

9. Compare the two graphs shown here, focusing on lines (a), (b), and (c), which represent plots for the same second-order reaction under different conditions.

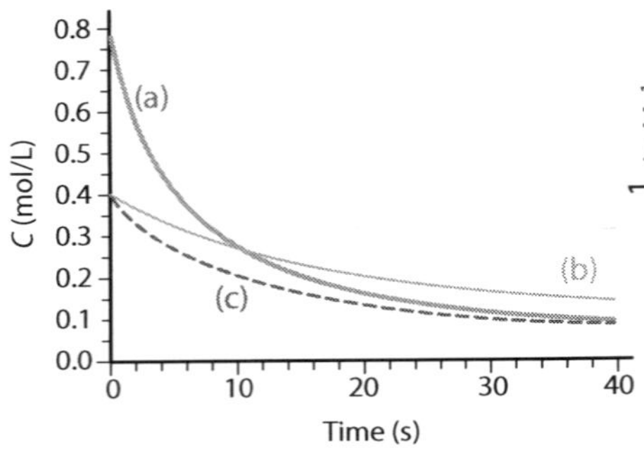

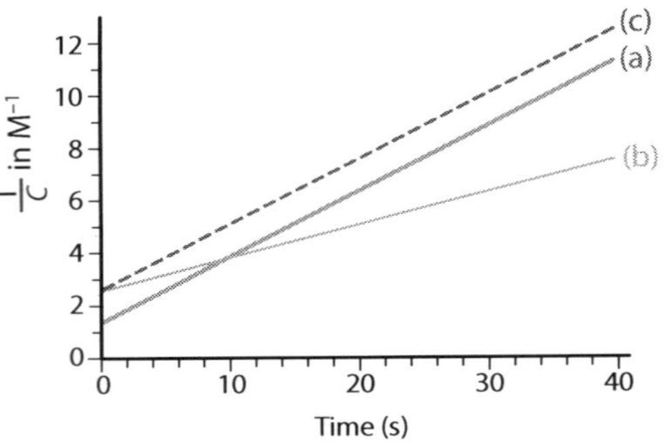

(a) What condition was changed from trial (a) to trial (b)?

(b) What effect did the change have? Explain your answer.

(c) What was not affected by the change? Justify your answer.

(d) What condition was changed from trial (b) to trial (c)? Be specific.

(e) Give two effects the change had on the reaction? Justify your answers.

10. The decomposition of aqueous sucrose to form the isomers glucose and fructose is a common organic reaction, which requires a strong acid catalyst: $C_{12}H_{22}O_{11}(aq) + H_2O(l) \rightarrow 2\ C_6H_{12}O_6(aq)$. The following data were collected during the process:

Time (min)	$[C_{12}H_{22}O_{11}]$ (mol/L)
0	0.316
39	0.274
80	0.238
140	0.190
210	0.146

Use the following grids to plot three separate graphs of $[C_{12}H_{22}O_{11}]$, ln $[C_{12}H_{22}O_{11}]$, and 1/[$C_{12}H_{22}O_{11}$] against time to determine the reaction order.

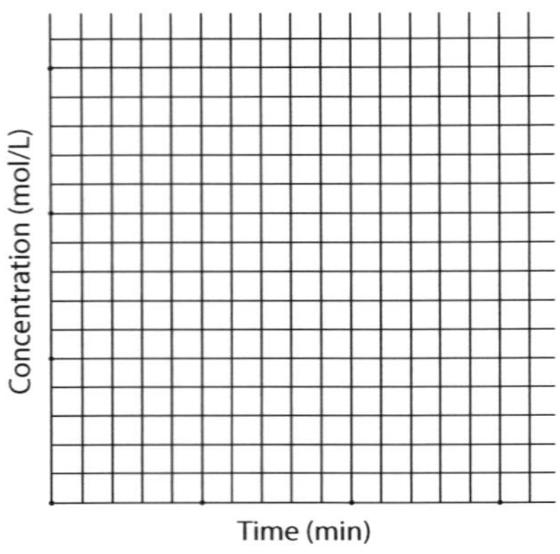

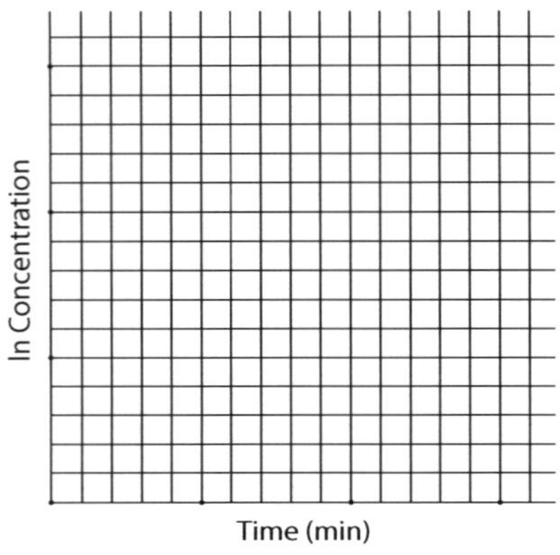

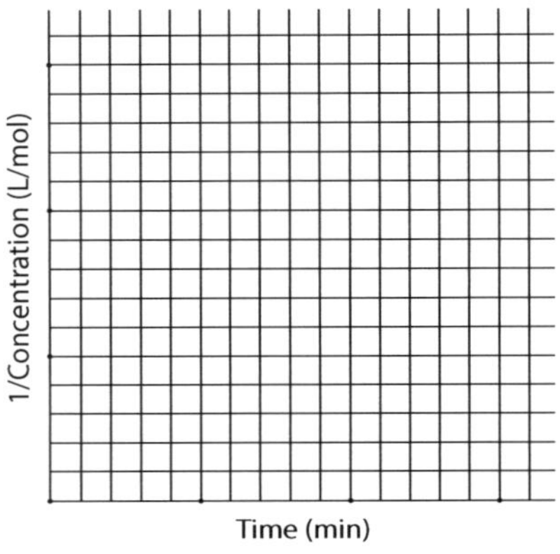

 © Edvantage Interactive 2019

(a) Write the rate law expression in its general form (water should not be included).

(b) Determine the rate constant with units.

(c) Determine the half-life.

(d) If we performed a new trial with an initial concentration of sucrose of 0.400 mol/L, what concentration would remain after 4.00 h has passed?

11. Methyl isonitrile isomerizes to acetonitrile: $CH_3NC(g) \rightarrow CH_3CN(g)$ at 215°C.
The following data were collected during the process:

Time (s)	$[CH_3NC]$ (mol/L)
2000	0.0110
5000	0.0059
8000	0.0031
12000	0.0014
15000	0.0007

Use the following grids to plot three separate graphs of $[CH_3NC]$, ln $[CH_3NC]$, and $1/[CH_3NC]$ against time to determine the reaction order.

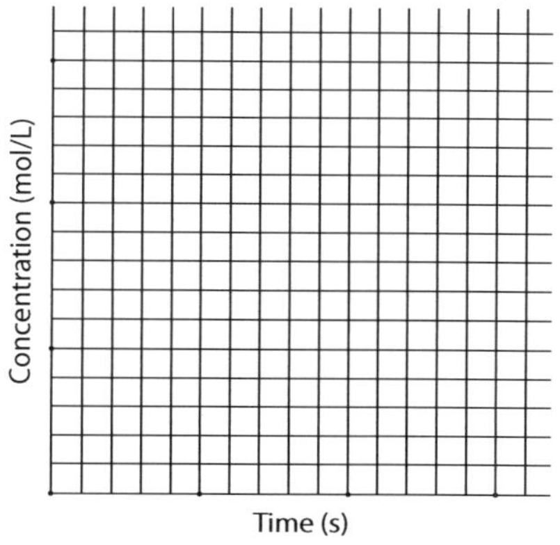

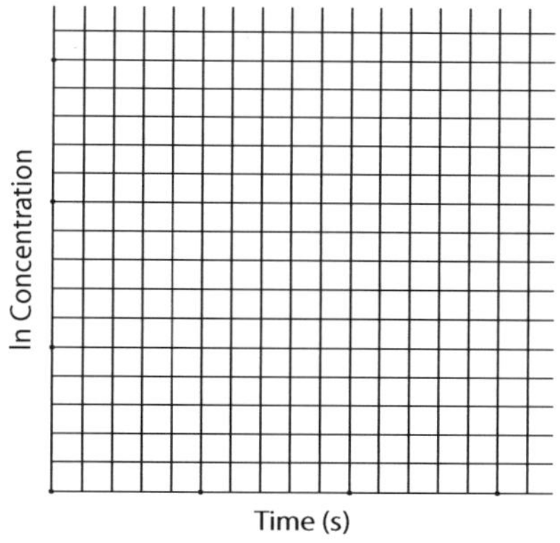

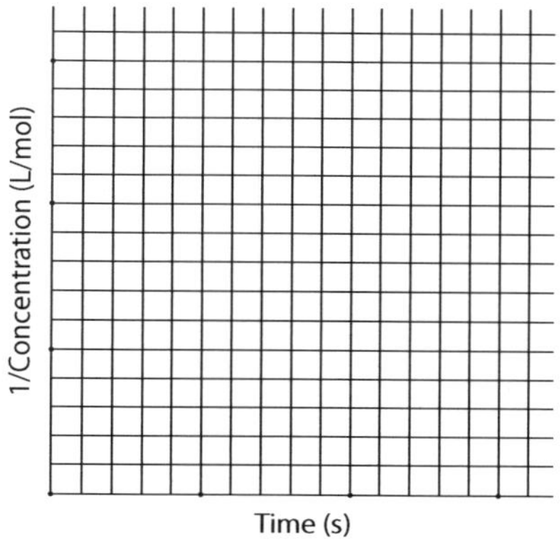

(a) Write the rate law expression in its general form.

(b) Determine the rate constant.

(c) Determine the half-life.

(d) Assuming the process continues, what concentration of methyl isonitrile would we expect after 5.00 h?

12. (a) What is the rate constant for a second-order reaction with an initial reactant concentration of 0.300 mol/L if after 158 s, the concentration is 0.200 mol/L?

(b) What is the half-life of this reaction?

13. Tritium decays by a first-order process that has a half-life of 12.5 y. How many years will it take to reduce the radioactivity of a tritium sample to 15% of its original value?

14. A zero-order reaction has a rate constant $k = 0.025$ mol/L/s for the disappearance of reactant, A.
(a) What is the half-life of this process?

(b) What will be the concentration of A after 15 s if the initial concentration is 0.50 mol/L?

15. The half-life is 22.7 s for the first-order conversion of cyclobutane to ethylene, $C_4H_8(g) \rightarrow 2\,C_2H_4(g)$, at a constant temperature. How much time, in seconds, does it take for the partial pressure of cyclobutane to decrease from 100.0 mmHg to 10.0 mmHg?

© Edvantage Interactive 2019

1.6 Potential Energy Diagrams

Warm Up

Complete the following table by placing a checkmark in the appropriate energy change column for each chemical change classification listed.

Reaction Type	Endothermic	Exothermic
Most synthesis (combination) reactions		
Most decomposition reactions		
Neutralization reactions		
Combustion reactions		

Sources of Energy

Fuels such as natural gas, wood, coal, and gasoline provide us with energy. Recall that most of this energy is stored as chemical potential energy that can be converted into heat. The amount of potential energy available depends upon the position of the subatomic particles making up a chemical sample and the composition of the sample. While the absolute potential energy content of a system is not really important, a change in potential energy content often is. We use conversions of chemical energy to other energy forms to do work for us, such as heating our homes and moving our vehicles. Because chemical energy is most commonly converted to heat, we use the symbol, ΔH to symbolize a change in energy available as heat. The symbol is sometimes read as "delta *H*" or an enthalpy change.

Enthalpy is potential energy that may be evolved (given off) or absorbed as heat.

All sorts of processes, both physical and chemical, have an enthalpy change associated with them. A general change in enthalpy is symbolized as ΔH. Combustion reactions have a large enthalpy change and are frequently used for energy production:

$$C_3H_8(g) + 5\ O_2(g) \rightarrow 3\ CO_2(g) + 4\ H_2O(l) \qquad \Delta H_{combustion} = -2221\ \text{kJ/mol}$$

What causes the enthalpy stored in reactants to differ from that in the products of a physical or chemical change? What exactly is responsible for producing the ΔH value? The answer is the chemical bonds.

The Energy of Chemical Bonds

Suppose your textbook has fallen off your desk to the floor. When you lift it back to the desktop, you give the text potential energy. The gravitational potential energy your text now has in its position on the desktop could easily be converted into mechanical and sound energy should it happen to fall again.

In a similar way, the electrons in the atoms of the molecules of any substance have potential energy. Think of the negative electrons as being pulled away from the positive nucleus of their atom. If it were not for their high velocity, they would certainly rush toward and smash directly into the nucleus of their atom, much like your textbook falling to the floor. By virtue of the position of the negative electrons in an atom relative to the positive nucleus and the other nuclei nearby in a molecule, the electrons (and the protons in the nuclei) have potential energy. This is the chemical potential energy called **bond energy.**

Bond *breaking* requires energy *input*, while bond *forming* results in energy *release*.

Figure 1.6.1 *Energy is required to break bonds.*

It's fairly intuitive that breaking something requires energy. For a karate master to break a board, he must certainly apply energy. Similarly, breaking chemical bonds requires energy. This energy is used to overcome the electrostatic forces that bind atoms or ions together. It should follow from this that bond formation must result in a more stable situation in which energy is released.

If more energy is absorbed as bonds break than is released as bonds form during a chemical change, there will always be a net absorption of energy. As energy is required to break bonds, there will be a gain in enthalpy. Reactions such as these will have a positive ΔH value and are called **endothermic** reactions.

The energy absorbed to break bonds is greater than the energy released during bond formation in an *endothermic* reaction. Therefore, they have *positive* ΔH *values*.

If, on the other hand, more energy is released as bonds are formed than is absorbed as they are broken during a chemical change, there will always be a net release of energy. Hence, there will be a decrease in enthalpy content. Reactions such as these will have a negative ΔH value and are called **exothermic reactions**.

More energy is released during bond formation than is absorbed during bond breaking in an *exothermic* reaction. Therefore, they have *negative* ΔH *values*.

Recall there are two ways to express the ΔH value associated with a chemical reaction.

A *thermochemical equation* includes the energy change as an integral part of the chemical equation, while ΔH *notation* requires the energy change to be written after the equation following a "$\Delta H =$" symbol.

Quick Check

Given the following ΔH values, write a balanced thermochemical equation and an equation using ΔH notation with the smallest possible whole number coefficients for each of the following chemical changes. Note: These units imply that the energy released or absorbed is for *1 mol* of the reacting species. The first one is done as an example.

1. $\Delta H_{synthesis}$ of $NH_3(g) = -46.1$ kJ/molNH_3

   Thermochemical equation: $N_2(g) + 3\ H_2(g) \rightarrow 2\ NH_3(g) + 92.2$ kJ/mol$_{rxn}$

   ΔH notation: $N_2(g) + 3\ H_2(g) \rightarrow 2\ NH_3(g) \quad \Delta H = -92.2$ kJ/mol$_{rxn}$

2. $\Delta H_{combustion}$ of $C_2H_6(g) = -1428.5$ kJ/molC_2H_6

3. $\Delta H_{decomposition}$ of $HBr(g) = 36.1$ kJ/molHBr

© Edvantage Interactive 2019

Transition State Theory

If we could examine reacting molecules coming together in a collision at a molecular level, we would see them slow down as their electron clouds repel one another. At some point, they would collide and then fly apart. If a reaction occurs during a collision, the particles that separate are chemically different from those that collide. When collision geometry is favorable and the colliding molecules have a kinetic energy at least equal to E_a, they interact to a form a high-energy, unstable, transitory configuration of atoms called an **activated complex**. This unstable complex will decompose and form new, lower-energy, more stable products.

As the reacting molecules collide, their electron cloud repulsions cause the reactant bonds to stretch and weaken. As reactant bonds break, kinetic energy is transformed into potential energy. At the same time, new bonds are forming between the atoms of the product. This process evolves energy as the newly formed bonds shorten and strengthen. The activated complex forms when potential energy is at a maximum and kinetic energy is minimized. The energy conversions and mechanics of bond breaking and forming are very complex and occur extremely rapidly (in less than a nanosecond or 10^{-9} s). The easiest way to follow these changes is to use a visual profile of the energy changes that occur during a collision. Figure 1.6.2 shows how the following reactions proceeds:

$$H_2(g) + I_2(g) \rightleftharpoons 2\ HI(g)$$

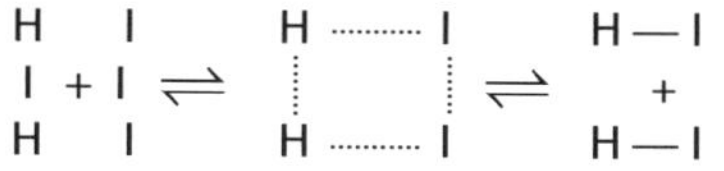

Figure 1.6.2 *H_2 and I_2 bonds break (KE→PE) as HI bonds form (PE→KE). The activated complex H_2I_2 exists for less than a nanosecond between these two processes*

Potential Energy Profiles

A **potential energy diagram** is a graphical representation of the energy changes that take place during a chemical reaction. The enthalpy changes can be followed along the vertical axis, which measures potential energy in kJ/mol. The horizontal axis is called by a variety of names such as the "reaction coordinate" or the "progress of reaction." It is critical to remember it is *not* a time axis. We are simply following the energy profile as the reaction proceeds from reactants to activated complex formation to products. Increasing the rate of the reaction will *not* change the length of this axis.

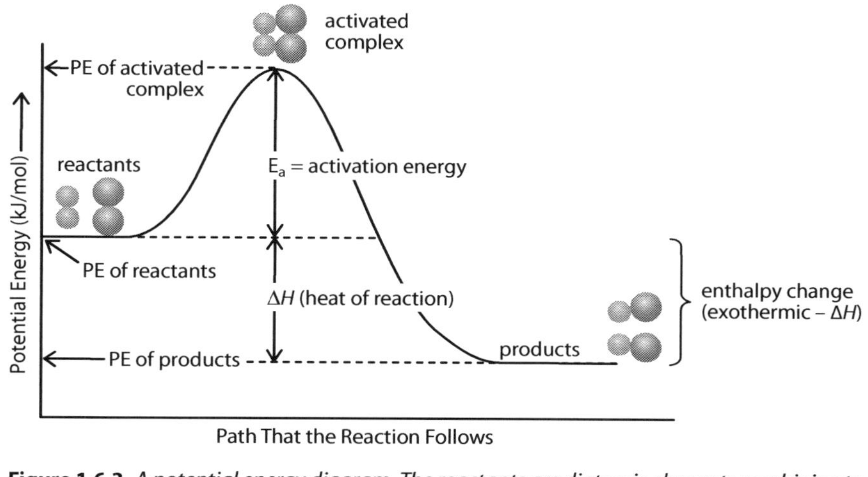

Figure 1.6.3 *A potential energy diagram. The reactants are diatomic elements combining to form an activated complex, which decomposes to form two product molecules.*

The activation energy, E_a, is the difference between the potential energy of the activated complex and the total potential energy of the separated reactant molecules. It represents the amount of energy the reactant molecules must gain to form an activated complex.
Thus $E_a = PE_{\text{activated complex}} - PE_{\text{reactants}}$

It is important to be aware that the net energy evolved or absorbed during the reaction is independent of the activation energy. If the potential energy (enthalpy) of the products is less than that of the reactants, the reaction is exothermic. Such is the case in Figure 1.6.3 above. On the other hand, if the products have more potential energy than the reactants, the reaction must be endothermic.

The enthalpy change (ΔH) is the difference between the total potential energy of the products and the total potential energy of the reactants.
Thus $\Delta H = PE_{products} - PE_{reactants}$

While altering factors such as concentration, surface area, or temperature will affect the rate of a chemical reaction, they will *not* affect the appearance of a potential energy diagram. This should make sense if we think of the diagram as a profile of potential bond energies (or enthalpies) per mole. While increasing the concentration of a reactant supplies more bonds, and consequently more bond energy, it also supplies more moles, so the energy *per mole* does not change. Changing temperature changes reaction rate, but it has no effect on the potential energy of the reactant or product bonds.

Sample Problem 1.6.1(a) — Reading an Energy Profile

Read the following potential energy diagram and answer the questions.

1. Is the reaction endothermic or exothermic?
2. What is the activation energy of the reaction?
3. What is the potential energy of the activated complex?
4. What is the ΔH for this reaction?

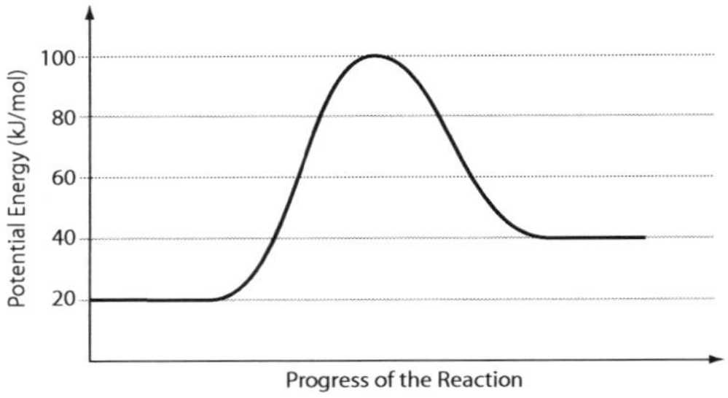

What to Think About	How to Do It
1. Check if the products or the reactants have more PE.	The products have more PE than the reactants. The reaction must be endothermic.
2. Consider the activation energy. The activation energy is the difference between the PE of the activated complex and the reactants.	$E_a = PE_{AC} - PE_{react}$ $= 100 - 20 = 80$ kJ/mol
3. Do not confuse the potential energy of the activated complex with the E_a. Activation energy is *always positive*.	$PE_{AC} = 100$ kJ/mol
4. Note endothermicity or exothermicity to ensure the sign is correct. This is an essential step.	$\Delta H = PE_{prod} - PE_{react}$ $= 40 - 20 = +20$ kJ/mol

Reversible Reactions

Many chemical reactions are reversible under certain conditions. This should be easy to accept if you think about a simple combination reaction being reversed to cause decomposition. The potential energy diagrams for a reaction pair such as these are simply mirror images of one another. Consider the combination of diatomic molecules A_2 and B_2 to form two AB molecules and the decomposition of two AB molecules to form diatomic A_2 and B_2. The potential energy profiles for these reactions would appear as shown in Figure 1.6.4.

 © Edvantage Interactive 2019

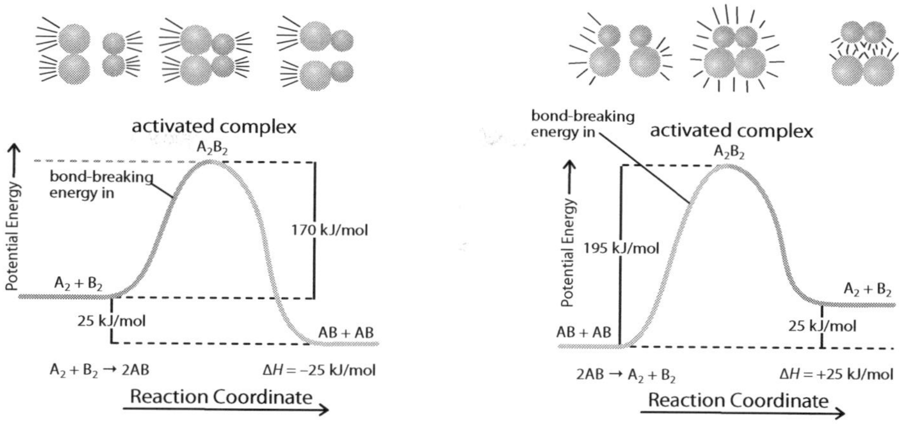

Figure 1.6.4 *The exothermic combination reaction's profile is simply the reverse of that for the endothermic decomposition reaction.*

Notice that the first potential energy diagram could be read in reverse to give the same measurements provided by the second diagram. Whether A_2 and B_2 are reactants or products, their potential bond energy or enthalpy is the same. The same could be said for two AB molecules. As a consequence, the decomposition reaction's ΔH value can be read as +20 kJ/mol from either Figure 1.6.4 or by reading Figure 1.6.3 in reverse (from right to left).

Sample Problem 1.6.1(b) — Reading a Reversible Energy Profile

Read the potential energy diagram for a reversible reaction and answer the questions.

1. Which reaction, forward or reverse, is exothermic?
2. Give ΔH for the forward reaction and the reverse reaction.
3. Give E_a for the forward reaction and the reverse reaction.
4. Give the potential energy for the activated complex. How does this value compare for the forward and reverse reactions? Explain

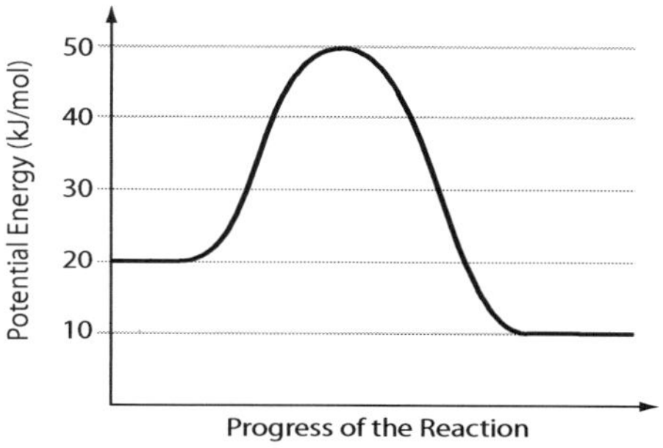

What to Think About

1. Check if the products or the reactants have more PE. Exothermic reactions have $PE_{prod} < PE_{reactants}$.
2. Identify the sign of the ΔH. We know the forward ΔH is $-\Delta H$ because this is an exothermic reaction. The reverse ΔH must be $+\Delta H$ as the reactants become products and vice versa.
3. Recall the definition of E_a. Do not confuse it with the PE of the activated complex. When determining E_a for the reverse reaction, the reactants become the products.
4. Remember that the complex is the same aggregation (collection and arrangement) of atoms whether formed by the reactants or the products.

How to Do It

The forward reaction is exothermic.

$\Delta H_{forward} = PE_{prod} - PE_{react} = 10 - 20 = -10$ kJ/mol

$\Delta H_{reverse} = PE_{prod} - PE_{react} = 20 - 10 = +10$ kJ/mol

$E_{a\,(forward)} = PE_{AC} - PE_{react} = 50 - 20 = 30$ kJ/mol

$E_{a\,(reverse)} = PE_{AC} - PE_{react} = 50 - 10 = 40$ kJ/mol

$PE_{AC} = 50$ kJ/mol for forward and reverse reaction as the same atoms are assembled in the same way and hence have the same potential bond energy (enthalpy) in both cases.

Practice Problems 1.6.1 — Reading a Reversible Energy Profile

1. Answer the following questions about this potential energy diagram:

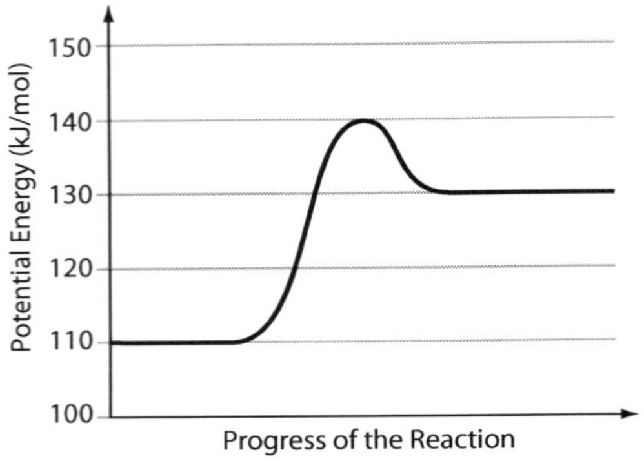

   (a) Is the forward reaction exothermic or endothermic?

   (b) Indicate the following values for the forward reaction:

      (i) activation energy

      (ii) enthalpy change

      (iii) potential energy of the products

      (iv) potential energy of the activated complex

2. Indicate the meaning of each of the measured values, I through IV, on the following potential energy diagram.

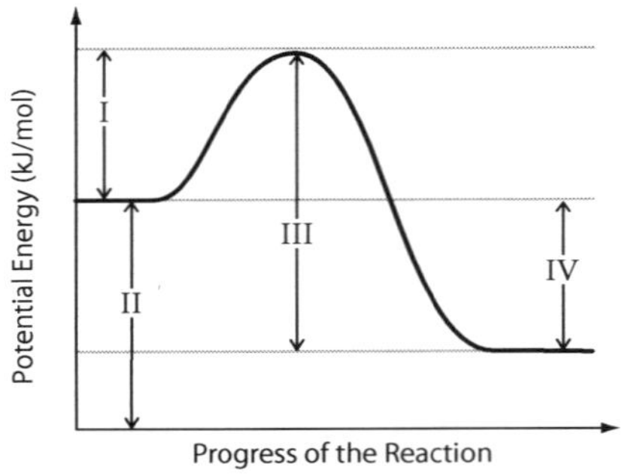

Summary for Reversible Diagrams

In summary, we see that for a reversible potential energy diagram the following points are always true:

- ΔH for the forward and reverse reactions have the *same magnitude* and *opposite signs*.
- E_a is always smaller for the exothermic reaction.
- Altering temperature, pressure, concentration, or surface area will have *no effect* on a potential energy diagram. There is only one thing that will alter a diagram and that is discussed below.

© Edvantage Interactive 2019

Activation Energy and Catalysis

An increase in temperature or concentration allows many more collisions to attain activation energy and hence react successfully. Increasing temperature may, in some situations, cause the decomposition of reactants before they can react. Increased temperature may also cause the formation of unwanted side products. Fortunately, since the great Swedish chemist Berzelius, scientists have been aware of catalysts that may increase the rate of a reaction without raising the temperature.

In general, catalysts provide an alternate reaction pathway in which a different, lower-energy activated complex can form. Reaction pathways are called *mechanisms*.

> Catalysts provide an *additional reaction mechanism* with a *lower activation energy*, which results in an *increased reaction rate*. The catalyst is *neither consumed nor changed* following the reaction.

Catalysts reduce the activation energy to the same extent for both the forward and the reverse reaction in a reversible reaction. Consequently both forward and reverse reaction rates are increased by the same amount.

Catalysts must be consumed in one step of a reaction mechanism and be regenerated in a later step. This is why they are neither consumed, nor changed as a chemical reaction occurs. A consequence of this is that more than one activated complex is formed. This leads to more than one "peak" in the potential energy diagram for most catalyzed reactions. Occasionally textbooks show a single peak in the catalyzed pathway on a potential energy diagram. In those cases, the diagram is simply showing a *net* or *overall* reduced energy pathway produced by the use of the catalyst.

> Potential energy profiles for catalyzed reactions will usually involve the formation of more than one activated complex and hence more than one "peak" in the diagram.

The calculation of the activation energy for a multiple peak diagram such as Figure 1.6.5 is simply the difference between the highest energy activated complex and the reactants.

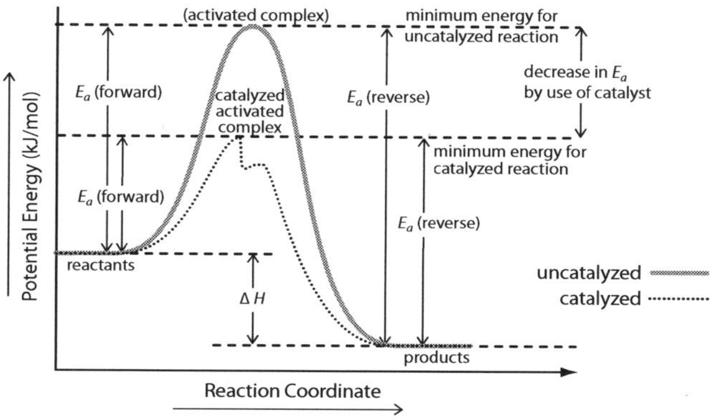

Figure 1.6.5 *The presence of a catalyst actually changes the energy profile to a lower activation energy pathway.*

Quick Check

Study the following potential energy diagrams for two independent reactions.

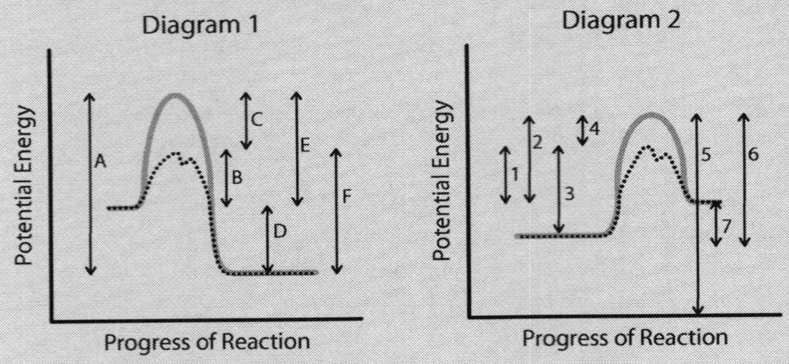

1. For diagram 1, indicate what each of the measurements shown by the lettered arrows represents. A is completed for you as an example.
2. From diagram 2, indicate the number that *represents* the same measurement in diagram 1. A is completed for you as an example.

A. Reverse uncatalyzed activation energy. $E_{a(\text{reverse uncatalyzed})}$ is #2 in diagram 2.

B.

C.

D.

E.

F.

 © Edvantage Interactive 2019

1.6 Activity: Comparing and Contrasting Concepts in Kinetics

Question

How can you compare and contrast endothermic and exothermic processes?

Background

For this activity, you will use the method of "compare and contrast" to create a table that could become part of your summary notes for this section.

Procedure

1. Use the outline provided below to organize what you've learned about endothermic and exothermic reactions.
2. The first row has been completed as an example of what is expected. Note that there may be many other comparisons and contrasts (or similarities and differences) that you can add to your table. Don't feel limited to only those lines where clues have been provided.

Characteristic	Endothermic	Exothermic
Sensation	Feels cold	Feels hot
Sign of ΔH		
Change in enthalpy		
PE ←→ KE transformation		
Sample thermochemical equation		
Sample equation using ΔH		
Bond energy comparisons		
Energy involved in breaking vs. forming bonds		
Sample PE diagram		

Results and Discussion

You will find it very helpful to produce similar charts to help you summarize material for study in the remaining sections of this course. Add these to the dedicated section of your notebook for summary notes and refer to them from time to time to help you in preparing for your unit and final examinations.

1.6 Review Questions

1. Given the following ΔH values, write a balanced thermochemical equation and an equation using ΔH notation with the smallest possible whole number coefficients for each of the chemical changes given below.
   (a) The replacement of iron in thermite, $Fe_2O_3(s)$, by aluminum $\Delta H = -852$ kJ/molFe_2O_3

   (b) The formation of $Ca(OH)_2(s)$ from its elements $\Delta H = -986$ kJ/mol$Ca(OH)_2$

   (c) The decomposition of $H_2O(l)$ into its elements $\Delta H = +286$ kJ/molH_2O

2. Study the graphs shown below.
   (a) Draw a vertical line on the first graph to represent E_a. Place the line so that about 10% of the particles in the reacting sample have enough energy to react.

   (b) Explain what these graphs indicate about the reacting particles.

   (c) What does this say about an endothermic reaction compared to an exothermic one?

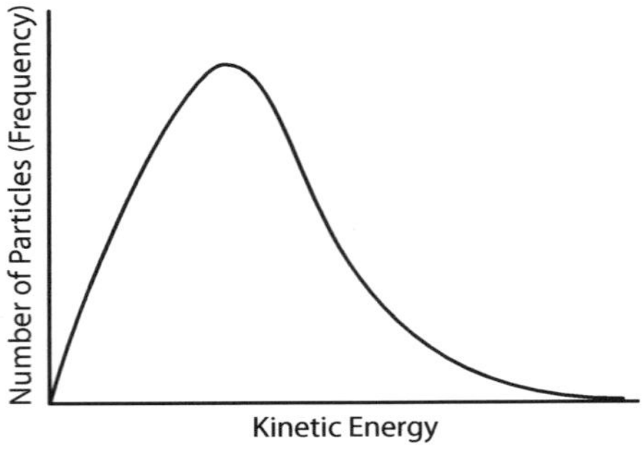

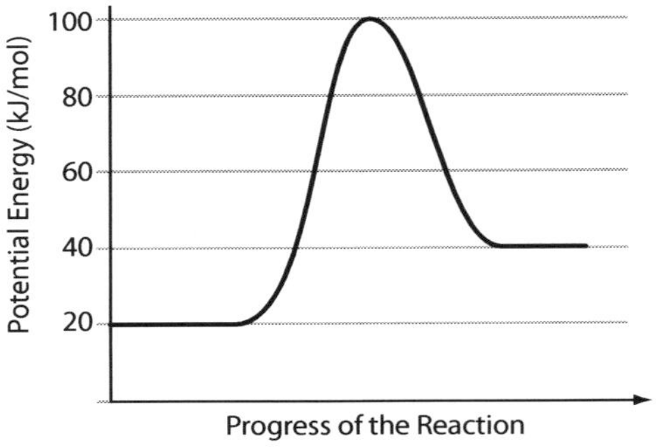

3. For a hypothetical reaction, $XY(g) \rightleftharpoons X(g) + Y(g)$ $\Delta H = 35$ kJ/mol. For the reverse reaction, $E_a = 25$ kJ/mol.

© Edvantage Interactive 2019

(a) Sketch a potential energy diagram for this reaction (label general values as given).

(b) What is the activation energy for the forward reaction?

(c) What is ΔH for the reverse reaction?

4. Study the potential energy diagram shown below.

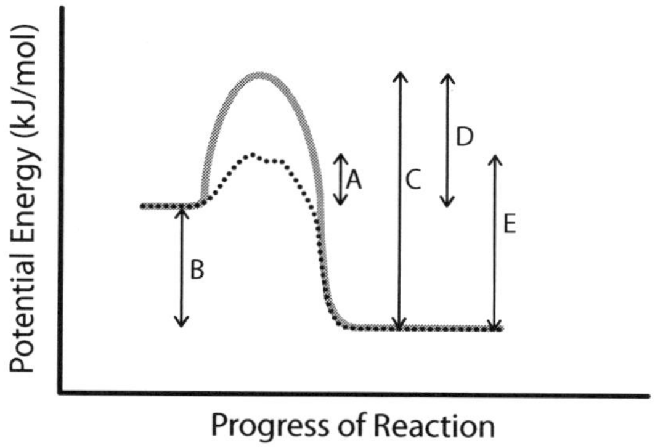

(a) Indicate what each of the letters (A through E) represents.

A.

B.

C.

D.

E.

(b) Is this reaction endothermic or exothermic?

(c) How would the diagram be affected if the reacting system were heated?

5. Examine the following potential energy diagram for this reaction:
   $Q + S \rightarrow T$

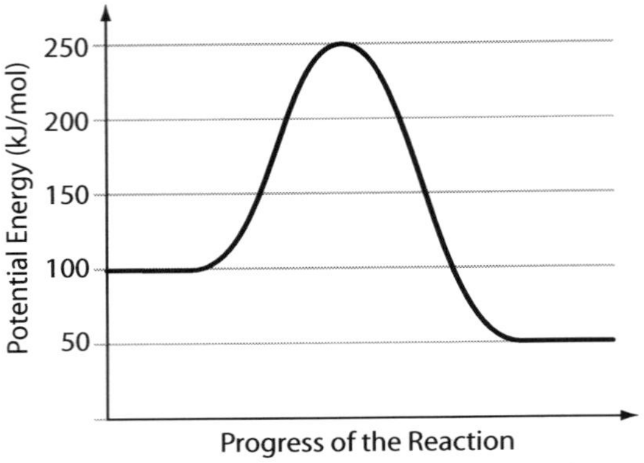

   (a) Determine ΔH for the reaction.

   (b) Write the thermochemical equation for the reaction.

   (c) Rewrite the equation in ΔH notation.

   (d) Classify the reaction as exothermic or endothermic.

   (e) Determine the E_a of the reaction.

6. Why are exothermic reactions usually self-sustaining. In other words, why do they continue once supplied with activation energy? Use the burning of a pile of driftwood as an example.

7. Fill in the blanks for an EXOthermic reaction: The energy released during bond forming is ____________ than the energy required for bond ____________. As a result, there is a net ____________ of energy. The bonds formed have ____________ potential energy than the ____________ bonds did.
8. How would a PE diagram for a *fast* reaction compare to a PE diagram for a *slow* reaction? Explain.

© Edvantage Interactive 2019

9. (a) As two reactant particles approach one another for a collision, what happens to their kinetic energy? Why?

(b) What happens to their potential energy? Why?

(c) What happens to their total energy (sum of potential and kinetic)?

(d) Complete the following graph:

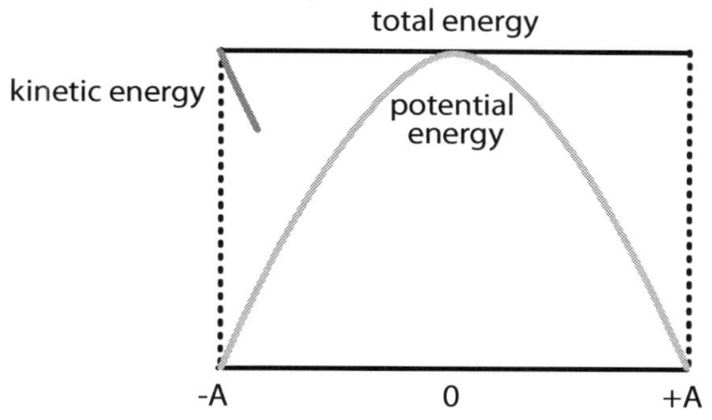

10. Study the following potential energy diagram.

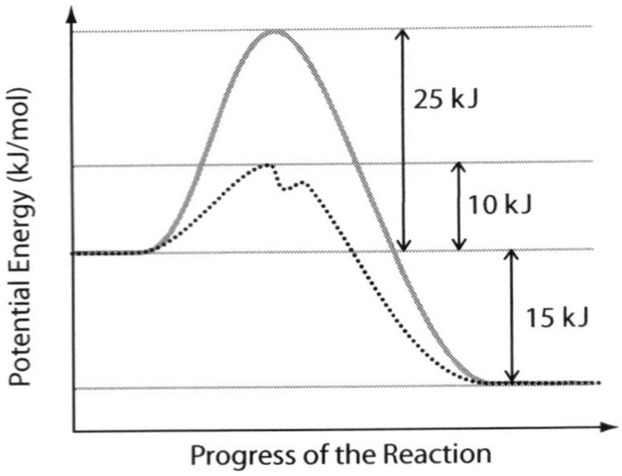

(a) Is this reaction endothermic or exothermic?

(b) What is E_a for the catalyzed pathway?

(c) What is E_a for the uncatalyzed pathway?

(d) What is ΔH for this reaction? How does this value change with a catalyst?

(e) How much lower is the potential energy of the activated complex with a catalyst?

(f) How does this affect the reaction rate?

© Edvantage Interactive 2019

1.7 Reaction Mechanisms, Catalysis, and Rate Laws

Warm Up

Study the following series of molecular collisions representing the catalyzed decomposition of formic acid.

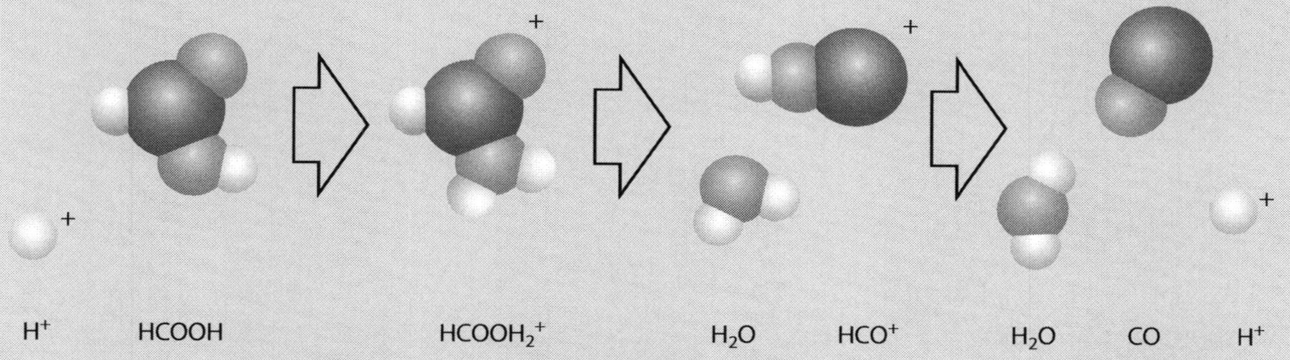

1. How many reactions are shown in the series above? ____________

2. In the format provided below question 3, write the balanced chemical equation for each reaction in the series. As it is a product of the overall series of collisions, the H_2O produced in the second step should *not* be shown as a reactant *or* product in the *third* step.

3. Algebraically sum the three equations to give the overall reaction. (Species that appear as reactants in one step and products in another should be cancelled.) What is the overall reaction once the three steps have been added together?

Step 1: →

Step 2: →

Step 3: →

Overall Reaction: →

Reaction Mechanisms

A balanced equation for a chemical reaction shows us what substances are present before and after the reaction. Unfortunately, it tells us nothing about the detailed steps occurring at the molecular level in between. Studies have shown that most reactions occur by a series of steps called the reaction mechanism. The individual steps in such a series are called **elementary processes.** These steps are themselves individual *balanced* chemical reactions that may be added together algebraically to give the overall balanced chemical equation.

A **reaction mechanism** is a series of steps that may be added together to give an overall chemical reaction.

Successful collisions require sufficient energy and appropriate orientation. As a consequence, the simultaneous collision of more than two reactant molecules with good geometry and E_a is highly unlikely. It's not surprising then that reactions having more than two reactant particles almost always involve more than one step in their reaction mechanism.

As mentioned above, each step in a reaction mechanism is called an elementary process. The **molecularity** of each elementary process is defined as the number of reactant species that must collide to produce the reaction indicated by that step. A reaction involving one molecule only is called a **unimolecular** step. A reaction involving the collision of two species is called a **bimolecular** step, and a reaction involving three species is called a **termolecular** step. Termolecular steps are extremely rare.

Quick Check

1. Why are termolecular steps extremely rare?

    ____

2. Indicate the molecularity of each of the following reactions.

    (a) $NO(g) + Br_2(g) \rightarrow NOBr_2(g)$ ____________________

    (b) $HCOOH(aq) \rightarrow H_2O(l) + CO(g)$ ____________________

    (c) $2\ NO(g) + Cl_2(g) \rightarrow 2\ NOCl(g)$ ____________________

3. An overall reaction is the sum of two or more elementary processes. Is each reaction above likely to be an elementary process or an overall reaction?

    ____

Species Identification: Intermediates and Catalysts

Since we can't actually *see* reacting particles colliding, flying apart, and reassembling, the mechanisms we use to describe chemical reactions are really just theoretical models. Chemists determine these models by altering the concentration of species involved in the mechanism and examining the effects these alterations produce. Computer models are also very useful in understanding mechanisms.

In any multi-step reaction mechanism the first collision, or decomposition of an energized reactant, always produces some product that is consumed in a later step of the mechanism. Such a species is called a reaction intermediate.

An **intermediate** is a species that is formed in one step and consumed in a subsequent step and so does not appear in the overall reaction.

As was described briefly in earlier sections, a catalyst functions by "providing an alternate, lower-energy pathway" for a reaction to follow. We now know this "alternate pathway" is actually a different reaction mechanism. In essence, most catalysts function by allowing the assembly of a different, lower-energy activated complex than would have formed if the catalyst was not present. Since catalysts are present before and after a reaction is complete, they must be used to facilitate the formation of the lower-energy activated complex in one step and then be reformed in some later step.

Catalysts in biological systems are referred to as **enzymes**. Enzymes are proteins that have an *active site*. This active site is exposed to assist a biological reaction in one step of a mechanism so an *enzyme-substrate* complex can form. Once the substrate reacts, the complex comes apart and the enzyme is regenerated for use again (Figure 1.7.1).

A *catalyst* is consumed in one step and regenerated in a subsequent or later step.

© Edvantage Interactive 2019

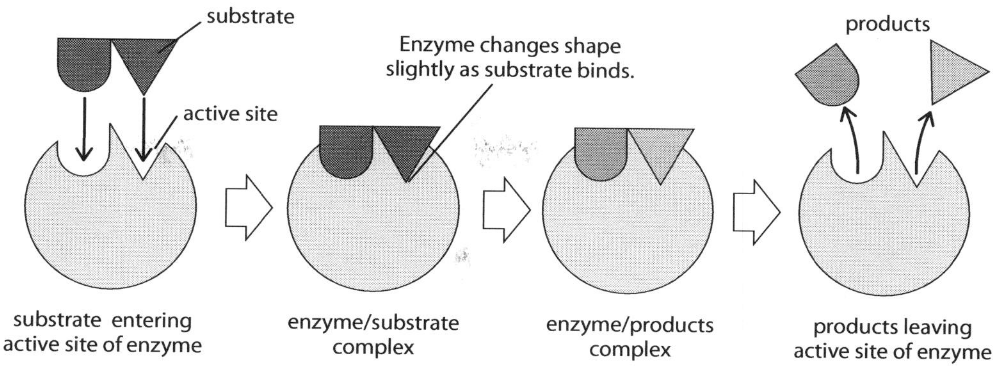

Figure 1.7.1 *Notice that the catalyst (in this case the enzyme) is consumed and then regenerated in its original form.*

Reaction Mechanisms and Potential Energy Diagrams

Despite the fact that many reactions involve only two reactant particles, studies show that the majority of chemical changes occur by mechanisms that involve at least two steps. Often one step is much slower than the other(s). The overall reaction rate cannot exceed the rate of the slowest elementary process. Because this slow step limits the overall reaction rate it is called the **rate-determining step**. A variety of conditions may cause a particular step to limit the overall reaction rate. These include the step having:

- complex collision geometry
- a high activation energy
- low concentrations of reactants
- a termolecular collision

A good analogy for this concept occurred back in the days before the invention of textbooks and even before collating copy machines were available. In those days, teachers had to assemble pages of students' notes by hand and staple them together individually. If several teachers were teaching the same course, they might get together with each taking on a portion of the job. One teacher would pull the pages off the copier and pass them to another who would assemble the pages in the correct order. Another would tap each pile on the table to make sure the edges were all aligned. Finally, a fourth teacher would staple the pile together. Which of these jobs would be the rate-determining step? Would it increase the rate of the job if a math teacher were asked to assist with passing the papers from the copier or tapping or stapling them? Clearly the assembler is the rate-determining step in such a job. Calling in a math teacher to assist with passing papers would have no effect on the overall rate at all. In fact, it might only serve to annoy the assembler.

As the analogy implies, adding reactants that appear in the non-rate-determining steps of a mechanism will have no effect on the reaction rate. To increase the rate of a reaction, it is necessary to increase the concentration of the reactants that appear in the rate-determining step.

The slowest elementary process in a reaction mechanism determines the overall reaction rate and is called the *rate-determining step.*

Each step in a reaction mechanism involves different chemical species with different bonding arrangements and hence different potential energies or enthalpies. Each step also has its own *rate constant* and its own *activation energy*, depending on the activated complex formed for that step. As a consequence, the potential energy diagram for a particular reaction will have the same number of *peaks,* as there are *steps* in the reaction mechanism.

Calculation of the activation energy for a multi-step reaction mechanism can be confusing. The activation energy for any particular step is simply the potential energy change from the reactants for an elementary process to the activated complex for that process. Consequently, the rate-determining step is the step with the highest activation energy. This value, however, is *not necessarily* the overall activation energy for the reaction. Rather, the overall activation energy is the difference between the potential energy of the activated complex with the highest energy and the potential energy of the reactants for the reaction as a whole.

E_a for a reaction with a multi-step mechanism is equal to

$$PE_{\text{highest energy activated complex}} - PE_{\text{reactants}}$$

As an example, consider the potential energy profile for the reaction in the Warm Up. Figure 1.7.2 and Figure 1.7.3 are for the uncatalyzed reaction followed by the catalyzed reaction. In Figure 1.7.2, a methanoic acid molecule (HCOOH) is energized and forms an activated complex by shifting a hydrogen ion. The energized molecule then decomposes into water and carbon monoxide. This occurs in a single step.

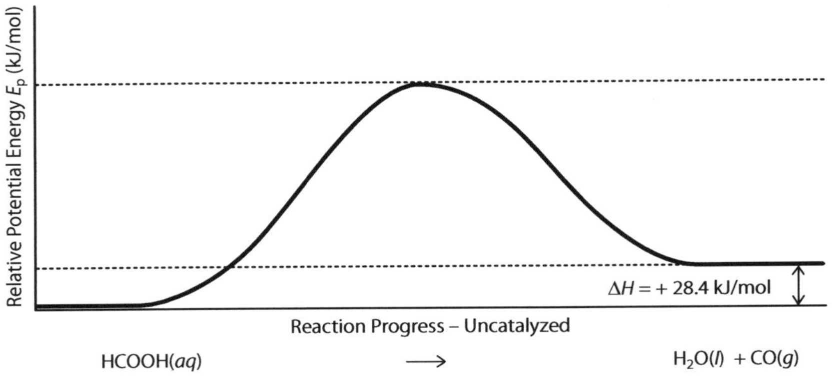

Figure 1.7.2 *A methanoic acid molecule (HCOOH) forms water and carbon monoxide in a single step.*

Notice that Figure 1.7.3 has three "peaks" corresponding to the three steps in the catalyzed reaction mechanism. The rate-determining step is the second one. This step would also determine E_a for the overall reaction. The enthalpy change or ΔH value is unaffected by catalysis as the reactants and products remain the same.

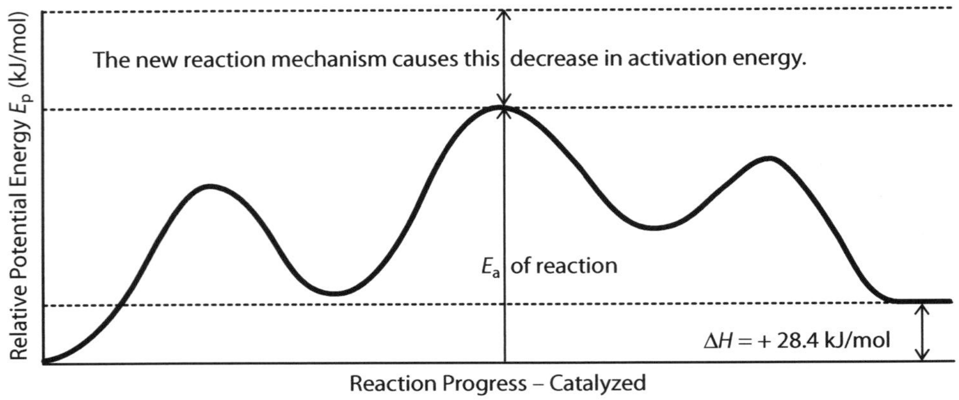

Figure 1.7.3 *This diagram shows the three peaks representing the three steps in a catalyzed reaction.*

 © **Edvantage Interactive 2019**

Sample Problem 1.7.1 — Identifying Intermediates and Catalysts in a Mechanism

Use the reaction mechanism produced in the Warm Up for this section to identify reaction intermediates and catalysts.

What to Think About	How to Do It
1. To describe the reaction mechanism, write three reactions for the reactants listed on the left side of each arrow to form the products on the right. As water was an overall product, do not include it as a reactant or product in step 3.	$H^+ + HCOOH \rightarrow HCOOH_2^+$ $HCOOH_2^+ \rightarrow H_2O + HCO^+$ $HCO^+ \rightarrow CO + H^+$
2. Sum the three steps algebraically to give the overall reaction. Cancel species appearing on both sides of the arrows. Identify species based on the definitions in the grey boxes above.	$HCOOH \rightarrow H_2O + CO$
3. Intermediates appear as *products* first *(on the right side)* and as *reactants* later *(on the left side)*. Identify them by drawing a slash from the upper right to the lower left through intermediates.	Intermediates include: $HCOOH_2^+$ and HCO^+ ions.
4. Catalysts are consumed, so they appear as *reactants* first *(left)* and *products* later *(right)*, as they are regenerated. Identify catalysts by drawing a slash from the upper left to the lower right through them.	There is only one catalyst (as is typically the case). It is homogeneous and is in solution in this case. Specifically the catalyst is the H^+ ion.

Practice Problems 1.7.1 — Identifying Intermediates and Catalysts in a Mechanism

For each of the following reaction mechanisms, determine the overall reaction and identify all catalysts and intermediates (some may not have catalysts). Then sketch a potential energy diagram for the reaction. Indicate E_a for the overall reaction. A numerical value is *not* expected.

1. $O_3(g) \rightarrow O_2(g) + O(g)$ (slow)

   $O(g) + O_3(g) \rightarrow 2\,O_2(g)$ (ΔH value for entire reaction = –284.6 kJ/mol)

2. Palladium catalyzes the hydrogenation of ethene (commonly called ethylene) in a reaction having a ΔH value of –136.9 kJ/mol. The mechanism is as follows.

$$H_2(g) + 2\,Pd(s) \rightleftharpoons 2\,Pd\text{-}H(s)$$
$$C_2H_4(g) + Pd\text{-}H(s) \rightarrow C_2H_5\text{-}Pd(s) \quad \text{(slowest step)}$$
$$C_2H_5\text{-}Pd(s) + Pd\text{-}H(s) \rightarrow C_2H_6(g) + 2\,Pd(s)$$

Continued

Practice Problems 1.7.1 (*Continued*)

3. A "chain reaction" often involves *free radical* halogen or hydrogen atoms. These are atoms with an unpaired electron. Free radicals are high energy, unstable, and therefore very reactive. The formation of two free radical atoms in the first step of this mechanism makes the first step the rate-determining one. The first step in a chain mechanism is called the *initiation step*. The second step, however, has the highest energy activated complex. The overall reaction is slightly exothermic.

$Cl_2(g) \rightarrow Cl(g) + Cl(g)$	initiation step
$(CH_4(g) + Cl(g) \rightarrow CH_3Cl(g) + H(g) \times 2$	propagation steps
$H(g) + H(g) \rightarrow H_2(g)$	termination step

Heterogeneous Catalysts

Catalysts may be classified as one of two types, heterogeneous or homogeneous. **Heterogeneous catalysts** are those in which reactions are limited to their surface area only. Most heterogeneous catalysts are solids. The most common are transition metals such as platinum or nickel. Catalysts of this type undergo *adsorption* of reactants onto their surface. The catalyst energizes the reactants and holds them in a position that allows easy interaction between them and other reacting species. Figure 1.7.4 describes the function of a typical heterogeneous metal catalyst in an addition reaction involving ethene (ethylene), a component of natural gas and hydrogen.

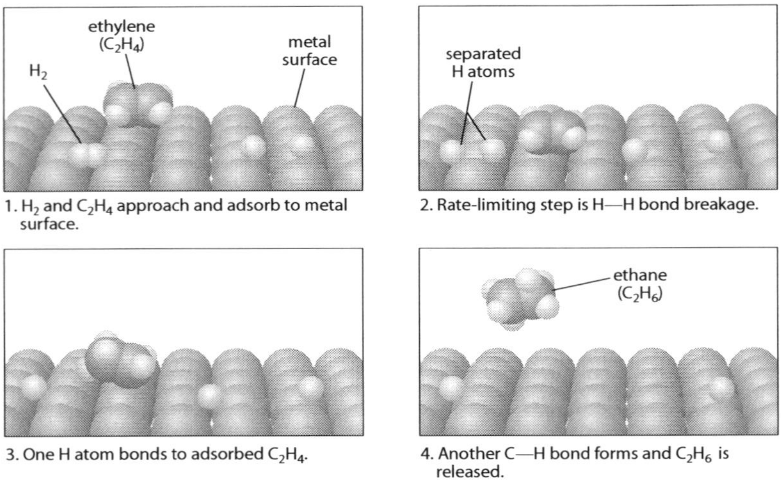

Figure 1.7.4 *This process reduces the double bond in $CH_2CH_2(g)$ to a single bond in $CH_3CH_3(g)$ by addition of $H_2(g)$*

© Edvantage Interactive 2019

Heterogeneous catalysis also occurs inside the exhaust system of our automobiles. A device called a **catalytic converter** activates several oxidation and/or reduction reactions. These transform harmful pollutants such as carbon monoxide, a variety of hydrocarbons, and nitrogen oxides into harmless carbon dioxide, water, and nitrogen gas. The converter contains a series of honeycomb-patterned channels lined with the catalyst, platinum (Figure 1.7.5). A number of other transition metals may function as catalysts in a catalytic converter.

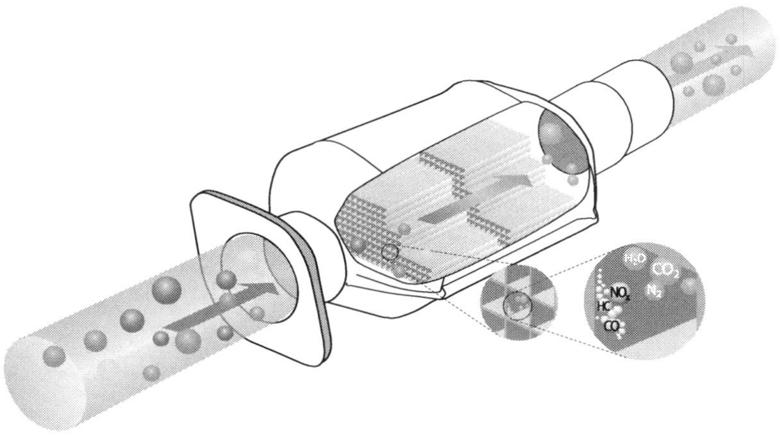

Figure 1.7.5 *Vehicles with properly functioning catalytic converters nearly always pass emissions tests.*

Homogeneous Catalysts

Many reactions are catalyzed by the presence of an acid. In such a case, the hydrogen ions from the acid react with and somehow modify the structure of a reactant to make it more susceptible to reaction with another reagent. The decomposition of methanoic acid using an acid catalyst is shown in the Warm Up and the Sample Problem 1.7.1 in this section. Catalysts such as this, which exist in the same phase as the rest of the reaction system, are sometimes called **homogeneous catalysts**.

One of the most important catalysts in the world is the enzyme, *nitrogenase*. Nitrogenase catalyzes the life-sustaining process of nitrogen fixation. Microorganisms convert the nitrogen in animal waste and dead plants and animals into $N_2(g)$, which is returned to the atmosphere. For the food chain to be sustained, however, there must be a means of converting atmospheric nitrogen back into a form plants can use. This process is called *nitrogen fixation*. The fixing of nitrogen involves the high activation energy reduction of elemental nitrogen into ammonia. Sometimes atmospheric lightning can provide the energy. Bacteria that live in the root nodules of certain plants carry out most of the nitrogen fixation. These bacteria contain **metalloenzymes** that are particularly useful for catalyzing oxidation and in this case, reduction, reactions. Nitrogenase contains an iron-molybedenum-sulfur cofactor in its structure. A cofactor, sometimes called a coenzyme, is a secondary substance that is required for an enzyme to function properly.

Reaction Mechanisms and Rate Laws

A valid reaction mechanism for a particular chemical reaction must fit these criteria:

1. The elementary steps must algebraically sum to the overall balanced equation.
2. Each elementary step is most commonly unimolecular or bimolecular. The chances of more than two particles colliding at once with sufficient energy and proper geometry are infinitesimally small.
3. The reaction mechanism must correlate with the rate law. The steps involved in correlating a mechanism with a rate law are outlined below.

There are four steps involved in the deduction of a rate law from a reaction mechanism:

1. Locate the *rate-determining step.*

As indicated earlier in this section, the *rate-determining step* is the slowest elementary process in the reaction mechanism and determines the overall reaction rate. This step is labeled "slow" or "rate determining."

2. Write a temporary *rate law expression.*

The temporary rate law expression uses the reactants in the rate-determining step and their molecularity. The coefficients for each reactant (the reactant *molecularity*) become the exponents of that reactant's concentration in the temporary rate law (the *order* with respect to that reactant).

3. Write an *equilibrium expression* or a *"fast-forward reversible" expression.*

The *double arrow* in the equation indicates that an elementary step is in equilibrium.

4. Use the expression to *substitute for appropriate species* in the temporary rate law.

As the final rate law is determined experimentally, it must ONLY contain reactant species (or in rare cases, a catalyst) that a chemist can manipulate directly. This means we must substitute actual reactants for intermediates or products that appear in the temporary rate law. We can algebraically manipulate the equilibrium expression to allow substitutions to occur.

Sample Problem 1.7.2 — Deducing a Rate Law from a Mechanism

The reaction of nitrogen monoxide and chlorine gas occurs via the following two step mechanism:

fast-forward reversible: $NO(g) + Cl_2(g) \rightleftharpoons NOCl_2(g)$ (step 1)

slow: $NOCl_2(g) + NO(g) \rightarrow 2\,NOCl(g)$ (step 2)

overall reaction: $2\,NO(g) + Cl_2(g) \rightarrow 2\,NOCl(g)$

Determine the rate law for the overall reaction.

What to Think About	How to Do It
1. Step 2 in the given mechanism is rate determining and the coefficients of both species in this step are 1's. Consequently both of these species are first order in the *temporary rate law*.	The temporary rate law based on the slow step in the given mechanism is $\text{rate} = k'[NOCl_2][NO]$ Note: The rate constant is also temporary and so is shown as k' ("k prime").
2. Write an expression for the *equilibrium* or *fast-forward reversible* step. The first elementary step is an equilibrium, as indicated by the presence of the double arrow.	The equilibrium expression for the reaction in the first elementary step is: $K_{eq} = \frac{[NOCl_2]}{[NO][Cl_2]}$ According to the K_{eq} expression above, $[NOCl_2] = K_{eq}[NO][Cl_2]$

Continued

Sample Problem 1.7.2 *(Continued)*

3. Substitute the $[NOCl_2]$ in the temporary rate law since it is an intermediate and does not appear in the overall reaction. The product of two constants such as $k' \times K_{eq}$ is equal to a new constant, in this case, the overall rate constant, k.

Substitute this expression into the temporary rate law to give:

$rate = k'K_{eq}[NO][Cl_2][NO]$

This rate law simplifies to:

$rate = k[NO]^2[Cl_2]$

Practice Problems 1.7.2 — Deducing a Rate Law from a Mechanism

1. The reaction of the iodide ion and the hypochlorite ion is an oxidation-reduction reaction occurring in basic solution:

$$I^-(aq) + OCl^-(aq) \rightarrow IO^-(aq) + Cl^-(aq) \quad (basic)$$

The three-step mechanism is represented as follows:

fast-forward reversible: $OCl^-(aq) + H_2O(l) \rightleftharpoons HOCl(aq) + OH^-(aq)$

rate-determining step: $I^-(aq) + HOCl(aq) \rightarrow HIO(aq) + Cl^-(aq)$

$HIO(aq) + OH^-(aq) \rightarrow H_2O(l) + IO^-(aq)$

(a) Show how the above steps combine mathematically to give the overall reaction. Identify all *intermediates* and *catalysts*. (Show work directly on the mechanism provided.)

(b) Show that the mechanism provided gives the rate law: $rate = k[I^-][OCl^-][OH^-]^{-1}$
(Note: Because this *redox* reaction is occurring in a basic solution, $[OH^-]$ can appear in the rate law expression.)

Continued

Practice Problems 1.7.2 *(Continued)*

2. Although fractional orders are rare, they can occur. Consider the following overall equation for a substitution reaction to form carbon tetrachloride from chloroform:

$$Cl_2(g) + CHCl_3(g) \rightarrow CCl_4(g) + HCl(g)$$

Here are the three elementary steps in the mechanism:

fast-forward reversible reaction: $Cl_2(g) \rightleftharpoons 2\,Cl(g)$

slow reaction: $Cl(g) + CHCl_3(g) \rightarrow HCl(g) + CCl_3(g)$

fast reaction: $Cl(g) + CCl_3(g) \rightarrow CCl_4(g)$

(a) Show how the reactants and products of the elementary steps cancel to produce the overall reaction.

(b) Identify any *intermediates or catalysts*. (Show work for parts (a) and (b) on the steps provided above.)

(c) Determine the overall rate law for the reaction.

Equation Coefficients and Rate Law Exponents

It is impossible to deduce a reaction mechanism from an equation alone. The rate law provides guidance as to what occurs on the pathway between the reactants and products. It helps us determine what is formed and consumed during the mechanism for a reaction. Rate laws are determined experimentally. They relate the rate of a reaction to the concentration of the reactants. Rate laws help us determine whether the equation for an overall reaction represents an elementary process, and if it does not, rate laws help us deduce a reaction mechanism.

If the coefficients in an equation match the exponents in a rate law, the reaction *may* consist of *one step*. However, if they do *not*, there is no doubt that the reaction *must* consist of more than one step. Information such as this can be helpful in determining the relationship between a rate law and a reaction mechanism.

 © Edvantage Interactive 2019

1.7 Activity: A Molecular View Of a Reaction Mechanism

Question

How can you determine the mechanism for a reaction given a "molecular view"?

Background

Two series of "snapshots" of a reacting system taken several microseconds apart are available for viewing. The first set is of an uncatalyzed reaction. The second set is of the same reaction, but it is catalyzed.

Uncatalyzed reaction: Reactants are B + G; Product is BG.

Snapshot 1

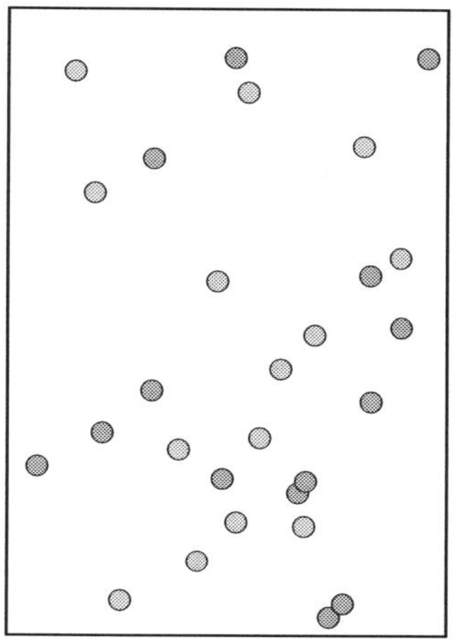

Snapshot 2

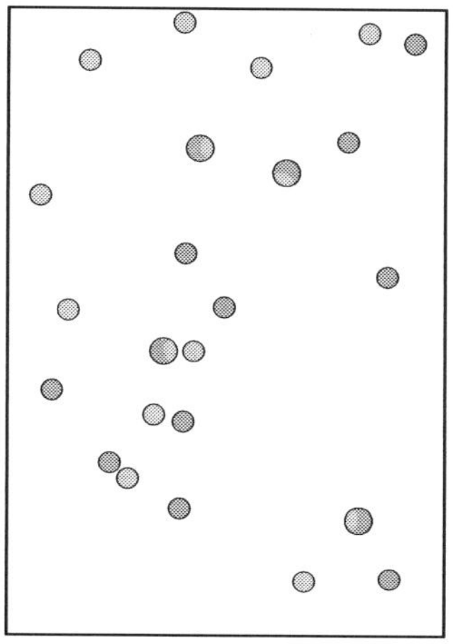

Snapshot 3

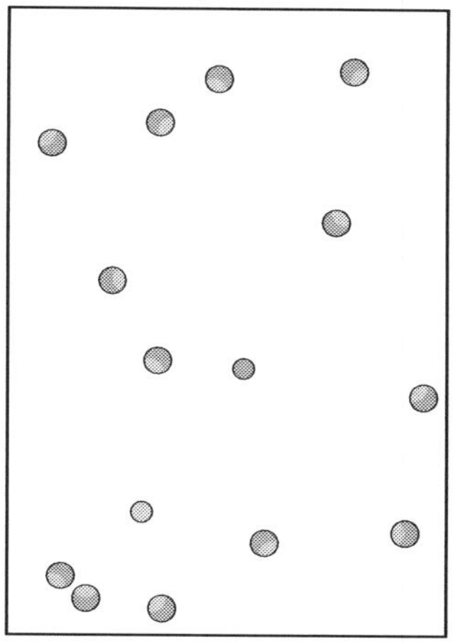

Catalyzed reaction: Reactants are the same as above. Catalyst R added.

Snapshot 1

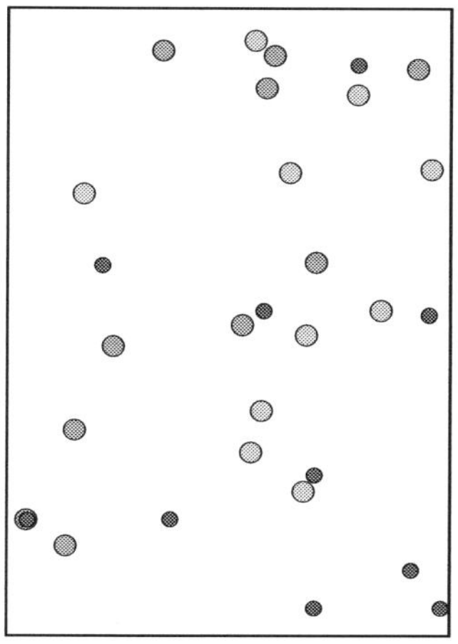

Snapshot 2

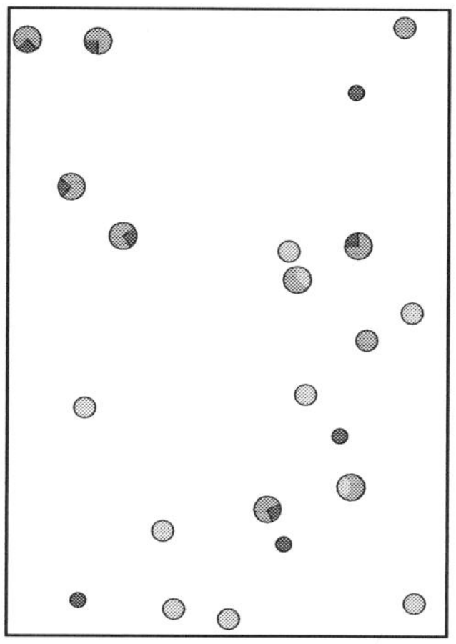

Snapshot 3

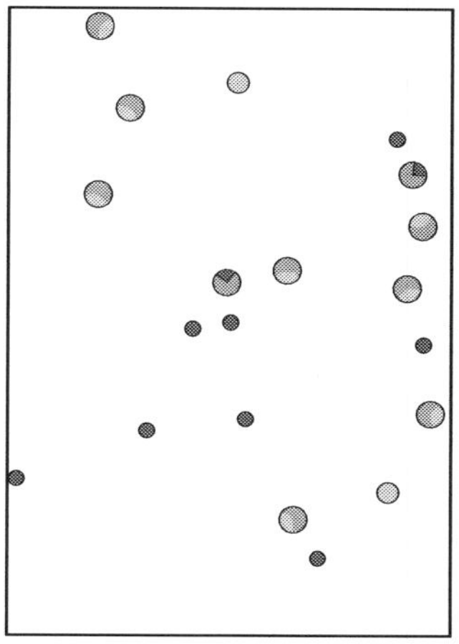

Procedure

1. Determine an equation that represents the uncatalyzed reaction.

2. Determine the reactions that represent the two-step mechanism for the catalyzed reaction.

   Step 1:

   Step 2:

   Overall Reaction:

Results and Discussion

1. Show how steps 1 and 2 sum to give the overall catalyzed reaction.

2. How does the overall reaction compare with the uncatalyzed reaction?

3. Identify the catalyst in the mechanism.

4. Identify any and all intermediates in the mechanism.

5. How would the time passed from snapshots 1 through 3 in the catalyzed series compare with the time for the uncatalyzed series?

6. Assume the second step in the catalyzed series is rate-determining. How would the time passed between snapshots 1 and 2 compare to the time passed between snapshots 2 and 3?

7. For the catalyzed reaction, how would the addition of more B affect the overall reaction rate? More G? Explain your answers.

© Edvantage Interactive 2019

1.7 Review Questions

1. What is a reaction mechanism?

2. What is a rate-determining step?

3. How do chemists determine reaction mechanisms?

4. Indicate whether each of the following reactions involves heterogeneous or homogeneous catalysis:

(a) $H_2(g) + CH_2CH_2(g) \xrightarrow{Pt(s)} CH_3CH_3(g)$ hydrogenation of ethylene

(b) Chlorofluorocarbons (CFCs) catalyze the conversion of ozone ($O_3(g)$) to oxygen gas (O_2).

$2\,O_3(g) \xrightarrow{CFC(g)} 3\,O_2(g)$

(c) Manganese(IV) oxide catalyzes the decomposition of hydrogen peroxide.

$2\,H_2O_2(aq) \xrightarrow{MnO_2(s)} 2\,H_2O(l) + O_2(g)$

5. The oxygen produced by the decomposition of hydrogen peroxide may be used to clean a variety of items from contact lenses to dentures. The decomposition may be initiated by the addition of small disks. Study the following mechanism:

1st: $H_2O_2(aq) + I^-(aq) \rightarrow H_2O(l) + IO^-(aq)$ slow

2nd: $H_2O_2(aq) + IO^-(aq) \rightarrow H_2O(l) + O_2(g) + I^-(aq)$ fast

Overall reaction:

(a) Determine the overall reaction.

(b) Identify any intermediate(s) present.

(c) What is the material contained on the disks?

6. Examine the following potential energy diagram and use it to construct a reaction mechanism. Show each step and the overall reaction. Label the rate-determining step.

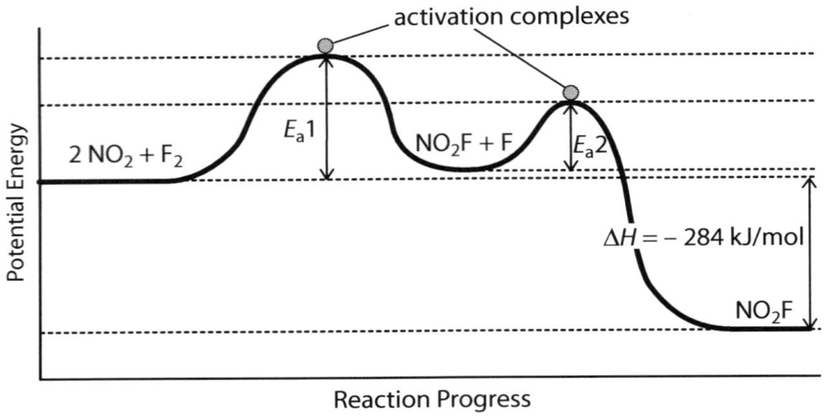

7. Look at the PE diagram shown here and answers the questions below. Write your answers at the end of each question.

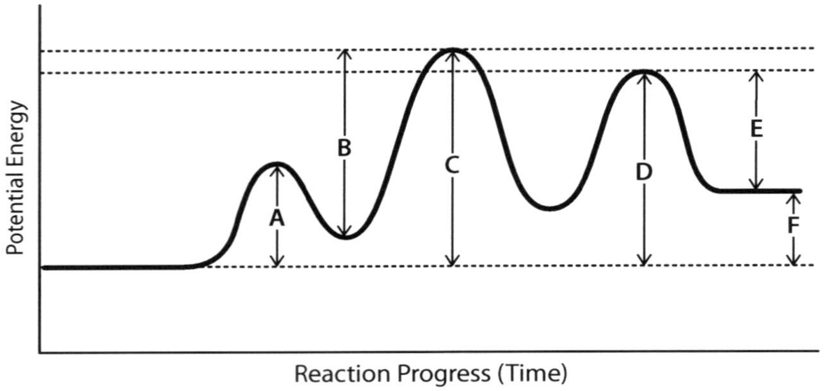

(a) How many steps are in the reaction represented by this potential energy profile?

(b) Which step is rate determining?

(c) What arrow represents E_a for the forward reaction?

(d) What arrow represents E_a for the rate-determining step?

(e) What arrow represents ΔH for the reaction?

(f) Is this an endo- or exothermic reaction?

© Edvantage Interactive 2019

8. The reaction, $CO(g) + NO_2(g) \rightarrow CO_2(g) + NO(g)$ may occur by either of the following two mechanisms:

Mechanism 1: Step 1: $2\ NO_2(g) \rightarrow NO_3(g) + NO(g)$ slow

Step 2: ________________________ fast

Reaction:

Mechanism 2: Step 1: $2\ NO_2(g) \rightarrow N_2O_4(g)$ fast

Step 2: ________________________ slow

Reaction:

(a) Fill the reaction in and use it to discern the missing step 2 for each mechanism.

(b) Experimental data shows that increasing the [CO] has *no effect* on the overall reaction rate. Based on these data, which mechanism must be correct?

9. Consider the reaction: $4\ HBr(g) + O_2(g) \rightarrow 2\ H_2O(g) + 2\ Br_2(g)$ + heat

(a) Does this reaction represent an elementary process? Explain

(b) Propose a reaction mechanism for the overall reaction, given the following clues: There are two intermediates in the reaction. The first to form is HOOBr(g) and the second is HOBr(g).

(c) Experimental data show that a change in [HBr] has the same effect on the rate of the reaction as an identical change in $[O_2]$. What is the rate-determining step?

(d) Sketch a potential energy profile for the reaction. Recall that two identical steps involving the same potential bond energies will be shown as the *same step* in a potential energy diagram.

10. Sketch a potential energy diagram for the following reversible reaction:

$$\text{heat} + 2\text{ A} + 2\text{ B} \rightleftharpoons 3\text{ C}$$

Be sure to label the axes. Indicate the following features on the diagram:

(a) reverse activation energy

(b) ΔH

(c) potential energy of activated complex

(d) use a dotted line to represent the pathway for a catalyzed reaction

11. Consider the following mechanism for a chemical reaction.

Step 1: $2\text{ NO}(g) \rightleftharpoons N_2O_2(g)$ *fast-forward reversible*

Step 2: $N_2O_2(g) + O_2(g) \rightarrow 2\text{ NO}_2(g)$ *slow*

(a) Determine the overall reaction. Indicate any catalysts or intermediates.

(b) Determine the rate law for the overall reaction.

© Edvantage Interactive 2019

12. A hypothetical reaction, $2\,A + B \rightarrow C + D$, has the rate law, rate = k [A][B].
Your teacher proposes the following three reaction mechanisms for the reaction. Which of these mechanisms is consistent with the rate law ? Consider and address each mechanism in turn and justify your choice.

Mechanism 1: $A + B \rightleftharpoons C + M$ *fast-forward reversible*
$M + A \rightarrow D$ *slow*

Mechanism 2: $B \rightleftharpoons M$ *fast-forward reversible*
$M + A \rightarrow C + X$ *slow*
$A + X \rightarrow D$ *fast*

Mechanism 3: $A + B \rightleftharpoons M$ *fast-forward reversible*
$M + A \rightarrow C + X$ *slow*
$X \rightarrow D$ *fast*

13. The reaction of NO and O_2 gases likely occurs according to the following mechanism.
Step 1: $NO(g) + O_2(g) \rightleftharpoons NO_3(g)$ *fast-forward reversible*
Step 2: $NO_3(g) + NO(g) \rightarrow 2\,NO_2(g)$ *slow*

(a) Show how the two steps combine to give the overall reaction.

(b) Determine the rate law for the overall reaction.

14. You propose the following three-step mechanism for a reaction. The second step is rate determining.

$NH_3(aq) + OBr^-(aq) \rightleftharpoons NH_2Br(aq) + OH^-(aq)$

$NH_2Br(aq) + NH_3(aq) \rightarrow N_2H_5^+(aq) + Br^-(aq)$

$N_2H_5^+(aq) + OH^-(aq) \rightarrow N_2H_4(aq) + H_2O(l)$

(a) Show how the three steps combine to give the overall reaction.

(b) Identify any catalysts and/or intermediates.

(c) Determine the rate law predicted by this mechanism.

© **Edvantage Interactive 2019**

2 Chemical Equilibrium

This chapter focuses on the following AP Units from the College Board:

Unit 5: Kinetics

Unit 7: Equilibrium

By the end of this chapter, you should be able to do the following:

- Explain the concept of chemical equilibrium with reference to reacting systems
- Predict, with reference to entropy and enthalpy, whether reacting systems will reach equilibrium
- Apply Le Châtelier's principle to the shifting of equilibrium
- Apply the concept of equilibrium to a commercial or industrial process
- Draw conclusions from the equilibrium constant expression
- Perform calculations to evaluate the changes in the value of K_{eq} and in concentrations of substances within an equilibrium system

By the end of this chapter, you should know the meaning of these **key terms**:

- chemical equilibrium
- closed system
- dynamic equilibrium
- enthalpy
- entropy
- equilibrium concentration
- equilibrium constant expression
- equilibrium shift
- Haber process
- heterogeneous reaction
- homogeneous reaction
- ICE table
- K_{eq}
- Le Châtelier's principle
- macroscopic properties
- open system
- PE diagram

When the number of shoppers travelling between the two floors on the escalators is equal, the crowd has reached equilibrium.

2.1 Introduction to Dynamic Equilibrium

Warm Up

Every weekday from 7 a.m. to 9 a.m. a large volume of traffic flows into New York as people who live in the surrounding communities drive to work.

1. Are there any cars leaving New York between 7 a.m. and 9 a.m.?

   ____

2. Explain how the number of cars in New York remains relatively constant between 10 a.m. to 2 p.m. when cars are still entering the city.

   ____
   ____

3. The number of cars in New York decreases between 3 p.m. and 7 p.m. Describe the traffic flow during this period.

   ____

Defining Chemical Equilibrium

Many chemical reactions are reversible. For example a decomposition reaction is the reverse of a synthesis reaction. This reversibility of chemical reactions facilitates an important phenomenon known as chemical equilibrium.

Chemical equilibrium exists when the forward rate of a chemical reaction equals its reverse rate.

Chemical equilibria are said to be *dynamic*, which means they are active. In chemical equilibria, the forward and reverse reactions continue to occur. This contrasts with a *static* equilibrium of forces, such as the equal and opposite forces acting on a weight hanging motionless on the end of a string. In a chemical equilibrium, each reactant is being "put back" by the reverse reaction at the same rate that it is being "used up" by the forward reaction and vice versa for each product. Note that the rate at which one chemical is being consumed and produced is not necessarily the same as the rate at which another chemical is being consumed and produced. The consumption and production ratios are provided by the coefficients in the balanced chemical equation. The example below describes the synthesis and decomposition of water. The equation shows that hydrogen is consumed and produced at twice the rate in moles per second that oxygen is.

$$2\,H_2(g) + O_2(g) \rightleftharpoons 2\,H_2O(g)$$

© Edvantage Interactive 2019

Sample Problem 2.1.1 — Determining Equivalent Reaction Rates at Equilibrium

NO_2 is being consumed at a rate of 0.031 mol/s in the equilibrium below. How many moles of N_2O_4 are being consumed each second?

$$2\ NO_2(g) \rightleftharpoons N_2O_4(g)$$

What to Think About	How to Do It
1. Recall that, at equilibrium, the rate of any chemical's consumption equals the rate of its production. Therefore, NO_2 is also being produced at 0.031 mol/s.	$0.031\ \frac{\text{mol } NO_2}{\text{s}} \times \frac{1\ \text{mol } N_2O_4}{2\ \text{mol } NO_2} = \frac{0.016\ \text{mol } N_2O_4}{\text{s}}$
2. Look at the coefficients.	The coefficients in the balanced equation indicate that 1 mol of N_2O_4 is consumed for each 2 mol of NO_2 produced.

Practice Problems 2.1.1 — Determining Equivalent Reaction Rates at Equilibrium

SO_2 and O_2 are placed in a sealed flask where they react to produce SO_3. When equilibrium is achieved, SO_3 is being produced at a rate of 0.0082 mol/s.

$$2\ SO_2(g) + O_2(g) \rightleftharpoons 2\ SO_3(g)$$

1. How many moles of SO_3 are being consumed each second?

2. How many moles of O_2 are being produced each second?

3. How many grams of O_2 are being consumed each second?

Recognizing Chemical Equilibrium

How do chemists recognize a chemical equilibrium? There are three criteria for a system to be at chemical equilibrium. It must:

1. have constant **macroscopic** properties. Macroscopic properties are those that are large enough to be measured or observed with the unaided eye.
2. be closed.
3. shift when conditions change.

1. Constancy of Macroscopic Properties

A system at equilibrium has constant macroscopic properties such as color, pH, temperature, and pressure because the amount of each reactant and product remains constant. Each chemical is being produced (put back) at the same rate that it is being consumed (removed). There is no macroscopic activity in a system at equilibrium because the continuing forward and reverse reactions are not observable because we cannot see atoms or molecules. Minor unobservable fluctuations in rates and concentrations are presumed to occur in equilibria since reaction rates are dependent on random collisions between reactant species. Another notable characteristic of equilibria is that they are self-perpetuating because the forward and the reverse reactions continuously supply each other with reactants.

2. Closed System

A system is **closed** if no chemicals are entering or leaving the defined system. If a system's properties are constant but the system is open then it is a **steady state** rather than an equilibrium (Figure 2.1.1). In a steady state, components enter and leave the system at the same rate rather than going back and forth within an equilibrium system. A steady state exists when the water level behind a dam stays constant because water is flowing into the lake behind the dam, at the same rate that it is flowing through the dam.

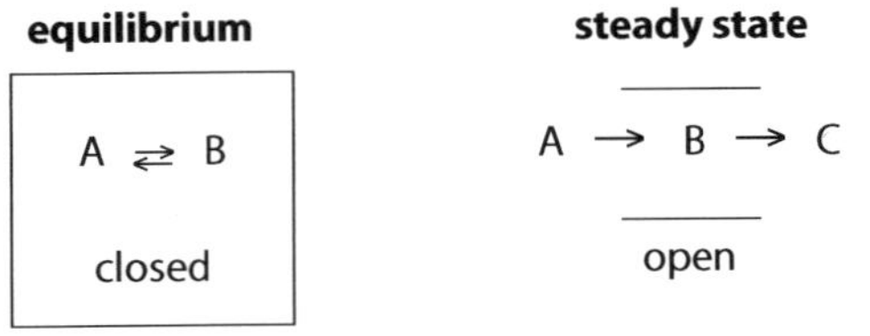

Figure 2.1.1 *Equilibrium occurs only in a closed system. In an open system, steady state can be reached, but not equilibrium.*

A reaction occurring in aqueous solution may only achieve equilibrium if all the reactant particles, product particles, and solvent water molecules remain in the solution. If an equilibrium system is temporarily disrupted by opening it and removing chemicals, the remaining chemicals will re-establish equilibrium if the system is closed again. Chemicals could be removed in a disruption, for example, if a chemical in the aqueous equilibrium is precipitated out or evaporates.

For a system to be at equilibrium, it must be closed and at a constant temperature (constancy of macroscopic properties). The intent of these conditions is to hold the amount of matter and energy constant within the system. For a system to be at a constant temperature it must be at thermal equilibrium with its surroundings, meaning that kinetic energy must be entering and leaving the system at the same rate.

3. A Shift due to Changed Conditions

The world is full of closed systems at constant temperatures in which nothing appears to be happening. In the vast majority of these, there really is nothing happening. They are just chemical mixtures. Equilibrium exists in only a small percentage of those systems that meet the first two criteria. Just as a child might poke a snake to see if it's alive, chemists "poke" chemical systems by changing their conditions. A change in temperature usually forces an equilibrium to reveal itself by causing a change or a *shift* in the amounts of reactants and products. When the solution's original temperature is restored, so are the original amounts. The equilibrium shifts back. If the reaction is photoactivated, it will respond to a change in lighting conditions rather than a change in temperature.

Quick Check

1. Why are chemical equilibria referred to as dynamic? ______________________________

2. List three criteria that must be satisfied for chemical equilibrium to exist.

   ______________________________ ______________________________

   ____

3. What is a closed chemical system? ______________________________

4. What is a macroscopic property? ______________________________

 © Edvantage Interactive 2019

How Equilibrium Is Established

Recall that as a reaction proceeds, reactant concentrations fall. Hence, the forward rate of the reaction (r_f) decreases. In a closed system, the product concentrations rise at the same time as the reactant concentrations are falling. Hence, the reverse rate of the reaction (r_r) increases. This continues until $r_r = r_f$ and equilibrium is established (Figure 2.1.2).

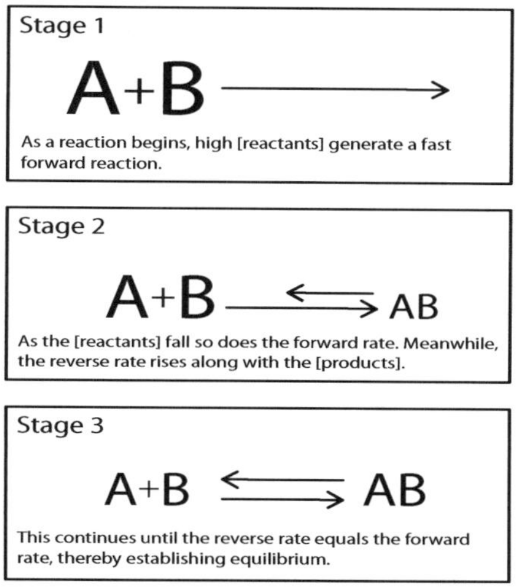

Figure 2.1.2 *Diagrammatic representation of chemical equilibrium being established*

Figure 2.1.3 shows equilibrium being achieved at about $t = 7$ s when the reactant and product concentrations become constant. It is important to note that the concentrations of reactants are not equal to the concentration of products at equilibrium. Only the forward and reverse reaction *rates* are equal.

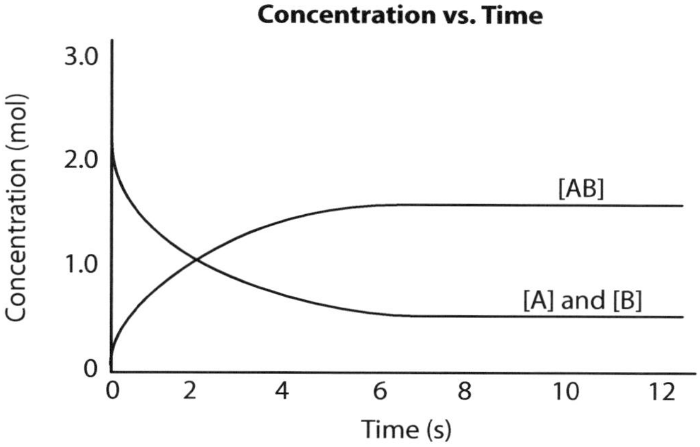

Figure 2.1.3 *This graph shows what happens with reactant and product concentrations as a function of time as equilibrium is established.*

Quick Check

Is each question below true or false? Place T or F in the places provided.

1. The reactant concentrations always equal the product concentrations at equilibrium. ________
2. When approaching equilibrium, [reactants] decreases while the [products] increases. ________
3. The [reactants] hold steady at equilibrium. ________
4. Before achieving equilibrium, the forward rate (r_f) is less than the reverse rate (r_r). ________

2.1 Activity: A Mathematical Model of Dynamic Equilibrium That Makes Cents

Question

Can we use a model to demonstrate how an equilibrium develops?

Background

Chemical equilibrium exists when each reactant and product is being consumed at the same rate that it is being produced. Chemical species are represented by pennies in this model with heads representing reactants and tails representing products.

Procedure

1. Perform this activity in groups of 2 to 4 students. Each group requires 32 pennies and one six-sided die.
2. Begin by placing all 32 pennies on your desk with their head side up.
3. Each round represents 1 s of reaction time. Reactants (heads) have a 50.0% (1/2) chance of turning into products (tails) each round. Products (tails) have a 16.7% (1/6) chance of turning into reactants (heads) each round. For each round:
   (a) For each head: Simply flip the coin to see whether it remains a head or changes to a tail. This means that in round 1 you flip all 32 coins.
   (b) For each tail: Roll a die and only turn the coin over if you roll a 6.

   Note: Although the reactant and product species would actually be mixed, it is easier to keep track of your heads and tails if you put them in separate groups after each round.
4. Use the table and graph provided below to record the number of reactant and product species present after each round. Draw the reactant's and product's plots using different colored pencils.

Time (Round) (s)	No. of Reactant Species (Heads)	No. of Product Species (Tails)
0	32	0
1		
2		
3		
4		
5		
6		
7		
8		
9		

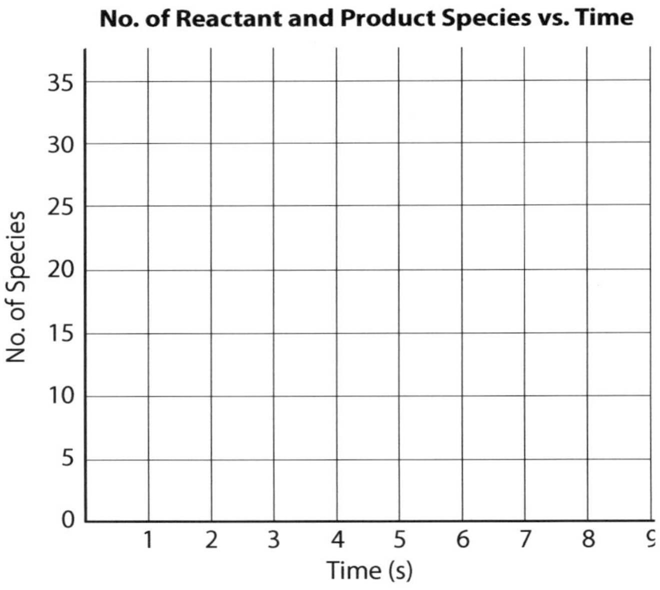

 © Edvantage Interactive 2019

Results and Discussion

1. What does turning over a coin represent in this model?

2. Approximately one-half of the reactants are converted into products each second while only about one-sixth of the products are converted into reactants each second. Identify two possible reasons for the reverse reaction being more difficult to complete than the forward reaction.

3. Why should the percentage of tails that react (turn over) actually increase as the number of tails increases?

2.1 Review Questions

1. Identify each of the following as being either an *equilibrium* or a *steady state*:
   (a) As bees go back and forth from their hive to a flowerbed, the number of bees inside the hive and at the flowerbed remains constant.

   (b) Despite people checking in and out of a motel each day, the number of guests registered at the motel each night remains constant.

   (c) During a basketball game, team members are frequently being substituted in and out of the game. There are always five players on the floor and seven players on the bench.

   (d) Two new students enroll in your chemistry class each day because they hear from their friends how interesting the class is. Unfortunately two students also withdraw each day.

   (e) Shoppers at the Hotel California Mall can never leave (but it's a lovely place). Shoppers travel back and forth on escalators between the mall's two levels though the number of shoppers on each level never changes.

2. An equilibrium exists when a reaction's forward rate equals its reverse rate. Answer the questions below for the following equilibrium:

$$2\ NO(g) + Cl_2(g) \rightleftharpoons 2\ NOCl(g)$$

   (a) Do the moles of NO consumed per second equal the moles of NO produced per second?

   (b) Do the moles of NO consumed per second equal the moles of NOCl consumed per second?

   (c) Do the moles of NOCl produced per second equal the moles of Cl_2 consumed per second?

   (d) Do the grams of NO consumed per second equal the grams of NO produced per second?

   (e) Do the grams of NO consumed per second equal the grams of NOCl consumed per second?

© Edvantage Interactive 2019

3. $H_2(g)$ is being consumed at a rate of 0.012 mol/s in the following equilibrium:

$$N_2(g) + 3\,H_2(g) \rightleftharpoons 2\,NH_3(g)$$

(a) How many moles of N_2 are being produced and consumed each second?

(b) How many grams of NH_3 are being produced and consumed each second?

4. Melting and evaporating are physical changes, not chemical changes, but changes of physical state can also form dynamic equilibria.

(a) An ice cube floats in a water bath held at 0°C. The size of the ice cube remains constant because the ice is melting at the same rate as the water is freezing. Describe and explain what you would observe if the temperature of the water bath was increased slightly.

(b) The water level in a flask drops as water evaporates from it. The flask is then closed using a rubber stopper. The water level continues to drop for a while but eventually holds steady. Explain why the water level is no longer falling. (Has the evaporation stopped?)

5. A chemist observes a closed system at a constant temperature in which no macroscopic changes are occurring. To determine whether or not the system is at equilibrium, the chemist increases its temperature and notes a change in the properties of the system. Can you be sure that this system is at equilibrium? Explain your answer.

6. Nobel laureate (prize winner) Ilya Prigogine coined the term *dissipative structures* for systems such as candle flames that are in steady state. The chemical reaction for burning one type of wax is:

$$C_{25}H_{52}(g) + 38\,O_2(g) \rightarrow 25\,CO_2(g) + 26\,H_2O(g)$$

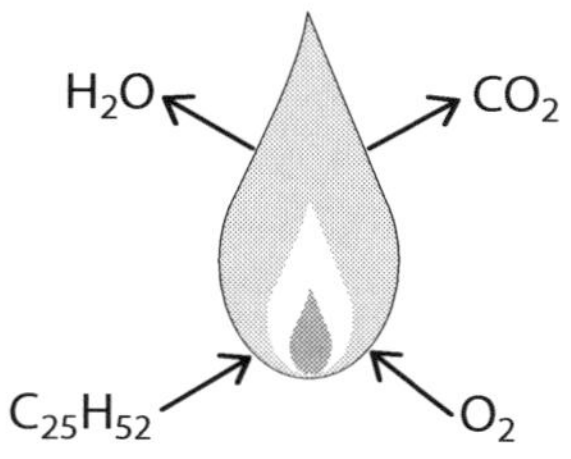

A continuous reaction occurs in a flame. The amount of each reactant and product in the flame remains relatively constant as reactants are continuously drawn in to replace those consumed and the products continuously dissipate into the surrounding air.

(a) How is this situation like an equilibrium?

(b) How is this situation different from an equilibrium?

Fascinate your friends by blowing out a candle flame and then re-igniting the evaporating paraffin gas by placing a lit match a couple centimeters above the wick. Try it!

7. Clock reactions are often used to demonstrate the effect of concentration and temperature on reaction rates. The distinctive aspect of clock reactions is a long delay followed by a sudden appearance of product. This peculiar behavior frequently results from a cyclic mechanism. Consider the mechanism of the iodine clock reaction below:

Step 1 $3\,HSO_3^- + IO_3^- \rightarrow I^- + 3\,H^+ + 3\,SO_4^{2-}$

Step 2 $10\,I^- + 12\,H^+ + 2\,IO_3^- \rightarrow 6\,I_2 + 6\,H_2O$

Step 3 $I_2 + H_2O + HSO_3^- \rightarrow 2\,I^- + 3\,H^+ + SO_4^{2-}$

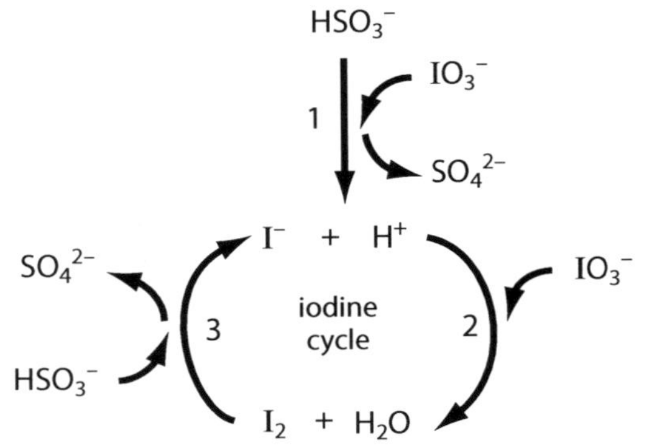

Why is the two-step iodine cycle at the end of this mechanism not at equilibrium even when the two steps are proceeding at the same rate?

8. When considering equilibria, chemists sometimes forget that the forward and reverse reactions may occur through a series of steps. Consider the following reaction mechanism approaching equilibrium:

Step 1:	$2\,NO + H_2 \rightarrow N_2 + H_2O_2$
Step 2:	$H_2O_2 + H_2 \rightarrow 2\,H_2O$
Overall:	$2\,NO + 2\,H_2 \rightarrow N_2 + 2\,H_2O$

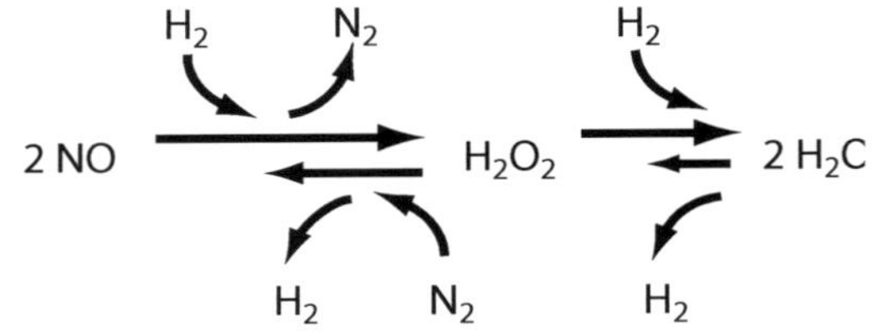

If a reaction is at equilibrium, every step in its mechanism must be at equilibrium. When the above reaction establishes equilibrium, how do you know that:

(a) step 1 must be at equilibrium?

(b) step 2 must be at equilibrium?

 © **Edvantage Interactive 2019**

9. A chemical reaction achieves equilibrium 20 s after it is initiated. Plot and label the forward reaction rate and the reverse reaction rate as a function of time from $t = 0$ s (initiation) until $t = 30$ s. (Caution: This is **not** the same kind of plot as in Figure 2.1.3. Here you are plotting the rate as a function of time whereas in Figure 2.1.3, we plotted the concentration of reactants and products as a function of time.)

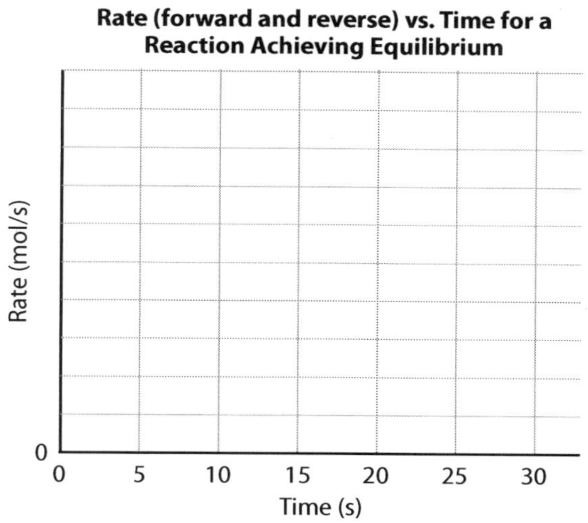

10. Nitrogen dioxide gas is placed in a sealed flask.

$2\ NO_2(g) \rightarrow N_2O_4(g)$

orange colorless

(a) What would you see as the reaction approaches equilibrium?

(b) Describe the change in the concentrations of reactants and products as the reaction approaches equilibrium.

(c) Describe the change in the forward and reverse rates as the reaction approaches equilibrium.

11. A system at equilibrium has all of its reactants suddenly removed. Describe how the system would restore equilibrium in terms of its forward and reverse reaction rates and its reactant and product concentrations.

2.2 Le Châtelier's Principle

Warm Up

Consider the following equilibrium: $2\ SO_2(g) + O_2(g) \rightleftharpoons 2\ SO_3(g)$

1. What is equal at equilibrium?

   ____

2. What would happen to the forward rate if some O_2 were removed from this equilibrium?

   ____

3. Explain why, in terms of collision theory.

   ____

4. Would the reaction still be at equilibrium at this point?

   ____

Equilibria Response to Adding or Removing Chemicals

In 1888, the French chemist Henry Le Châtelier wrote, "Every change of one of the factors of an equilibrium occasions a rearrangement of the system in such a direction that the factor in question experiences a change in a sense opposite to the original change." Le Châtelier's principle has since been expressed in many different ways that are fortunately easier to understand than Le Châtelier's own wording.

> **Le Châtelier's principle**: An equilibrium system subjected to a stress will shift to partially alleviate the stress and restore equilibrium.

In other words, when an equilibrium system is disrupted, it will shift its reactant and product concentrations, changing one into the other, to reduce the disruption and re-establish equilibrium. Le Châtelier's principle allows chemists to predict what will happen to an equilibrium's reactant and product concentrations when its conditions change.

> When a quantity of reactant or product is added to an equilibrium system, the system will shift to remove *some* of the added chemical.
>
> When a quantity of reactant or product is removed from an equilibrium system, the system will shift to replace *some* of the removed chemical.

An **equilibrium system** is a reacting system that is at or approaching equilibrium. When we change the concentration of a reactant or a product, we "stress" the equilibrium system by temporarily destroying the equilibrium condition. When a system responds by changing some reactants into products, the response is referred to as a "**shift right**" because the products are on the right side of a chemical equation. When a system responds by changing some products into reactants, the response is called a "**shift left**."

 © Edvantage Interactive 2019

Sample Problem 2.2.1(a) — Predicting How an Equilibrium System Will Respond to the Addition of Reactant or Product

Some HI is added to the system below. In what direction will the system shift to restore equilibrium? When equilibrium is restored, how will the concentration of each substance compare to its concentration before the HI was added?

$$H_2(g) + I_2(g) \rightleftharpoons 2\ HI(g)$$

What to Think About	How to Do It
1. Using Le Châtelier's principle, determine that the system will shift to remove some of the added HI.	The system must *shift left* (toward reactants) to consume some of the added HI.
2. Infer from Le Châtelier's principle that the shift left produces H_2 and I_2. Note that Le Châtelier's principle doesn't explicitly state what happens to the concentrations of H_2 and I_2, but you can infer what happens from your understanding of the principle	Since not all of the added HI will be removed, the [HI] will increase. The $[H_2]$ and $[I_2]$ will also increase

How does a chemist remove chemicals from an equilibrium system? Obviously you can't simply reach in and pick some ions or molecules out. Chemists usually remove one chemical by reacting it with another. The reaction that removes the chemical might also arrive at equilibrium. We'll discuss this situation in later chapters.

Students often state that a stressed equilibrium system "*tries to* restore equilibrium" or "*tries to* remove some of the added chemical." As Yoda of *Star Wars* says, "Do or do not. There is no try." A stressed system doesn't *try to* restore equilibrium; it *does* restore equilibrium. When a reactant or product is added to an equilibrium system, it doesn't *try to* remove some of the added chemical; it *does* remove some of the added chemical.

Sample Problem 2.2.1(b) — Predicting How an Equilibrium System Will Respond to the Removal of Reactant or Product

Some solid calcium hydroxide is in equilibrium with a saturated solution of its ions.

$$Ca(OH)_2(s) \rightleftharpoons Ca^{2+}(aq) + 2\ OH^-(aq)$$

This is a solubility equilibrium. The rate of dissolving equals the rate of recrystallizing. Some OH^- is removed by adding some hydrochloric acid to the solution. (The H^+ in the acid neutralizes some OH^- to produce H_2O.) In what direction will the equilibrium shift? When equilibrium is restored, how will the calcium ion and the hydroxide ion concentrations compare to their concentrations before the acid was added?

What to Think About	How to Do It
1. Using Le Châtelier's principle, determine that the system will shift to replace some of the removed OH^-.	The system must shift right (towards products) to replace some of the removed OH^-.
2. Determine the effect of the shift right. The shift right also produces some Ca^{2+} and causes more of the $Ca(OH)_2(s)$ to dissolve.	Since not all of the removed OH^- is replaced, the $[OH^-]$ will decrease. The $[Ca^{2+}]$ will increase.

Practice Problems 2.2.1 — Predicting How an Equilibrium System Will Respond to the Addition or Removal of Reactant or Product

Use the following system for questions 1 and 2:

$Fe^{3+}(aq) + SCN^-(aq) \rightleftharpoons FeSCN^{2+}(aq)$

1. (a) What does Le Châtelier's principle say will occur if some $Fe(NO_3)_3$ is added to the system? ($Fe(NO_3)_3$ dissociates into independent Fe^{3+} and NO_3^- ions in solution.)

   (b) In what direction will the system shift?

   (c) When equilibrium is restored, how will the concentration of each substance compare to its concentration before the $Fe(NO_3)_3$ was added?

2. (a) What does Le Châtelier's principle say will occur if some sodium biphosphate is added to the system? (The HPO_4^{2-} ion reacts with the Fe^{3+} ion to produce $FeHPO_4^+$.)

   (b) In what direction will the system shift?

   (c) When equilibrium is restored, how will the concentration of each substance compare to its concentration before the sodium biphosphate was added?

3. Look at the graph below. At t_1 more H_2 was suddenly added to the closed system as shown. Equilibrium was re-established at t_2. Complete the plots to show how the system would respond.

Concentration vs. Time for $H_2(g) + I_2(g) \rightleftharpoons 2\,HI(g)$

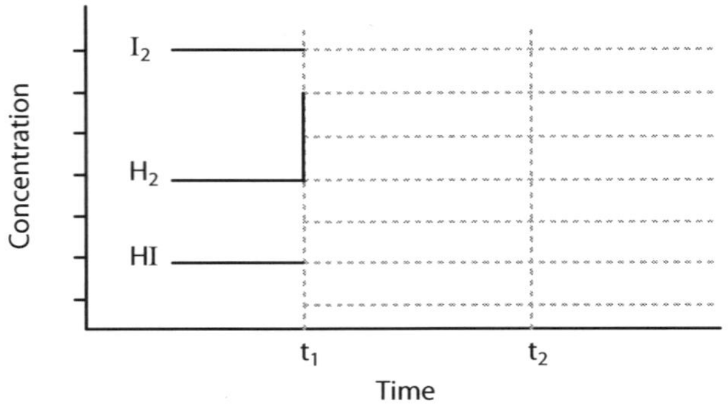

 © Edvantage Interactive 2019

The Shift Mechanism: Effects of Stress on Forward and Reverse Reaction Rates

Le Châtelier's principle describes how an equilibrium system responds to a stress without offering any explanation of the response. The explanation is related to the effect of the stress on the equilibrium's forward and reverse reaction rates. To an equilibrium system, a **stress** is any action that has a different effect on the forward reaction rate than it does on the reverse reaction rate, thus disrupting the equilibrium. In other words, a disrupted or stressed equilibrium system is no longer at equilibrium because its forward and reverse reaction rates are not equal.

Sample Problem 2.2.2(a) — Describing the Shift Mechanism

Explain in terms of forward and reverse reaction rates how the following equilibrium system would respond to adding some iron(III) chloride. ($FeCl_3$ dissociates into independent Fe^{3+} and Cl^- ions in solution.)

$$Fe^{3+}(aq) + SCN^-(aq) \rightleftharpoons FeSCN^{2+}(aq)$$

What to Think About	How to Do It
1. Determine the immediate effect of the stress on the forward and/or reverse reaction rates	Adding some Fe^{3+} increases the forward reaction rate (r_f).
2. Decide if this results in a net forward or net reverse reaction.	This results in a net forward reaction, also known as a shift right.

The system in Sample Problem 2.2.2(a) would re-equilibrate in the same manner that it established equilibrium in the first place. Figure 2.2.1(a) shows the rates when the system is initially at equilibrium (E_i), when the system is stressed (S), and when the system restores equilibrium (E_f). The net forward reaction would cause the reactant concentrations and the forward rate (r_f) to decrease, while the product concentrations and the reverse rate (r_r) increase, until r_f once again equals r_r.

The graph in Figure 2.2.1(b) is the more traditional way of depicting the same information shown in the arrow diagram in (a). In (b), the solid line represents the forward rate and the dotted line represents the reverse rate.

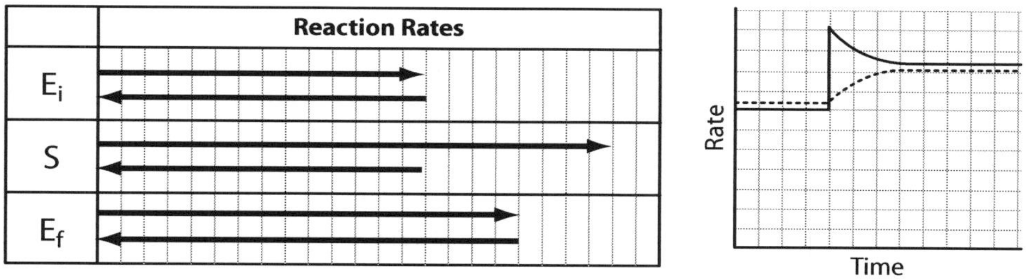

(a) (b)

Figure 2.2.1 *Two different ways of representing a reaction in a diagram*

Sample Problem 2.2.2(b) — Describing the Shift Mechanism

Explain in terms of forward and reverse reaction rates how the following reaction would respond to removing some SO_2.

$$2\,SO_2(g) + O_2(g) \rightleftharpoons 2\,SO_3(g)$$

What to Think About	How to Do It
1. Determine the immediate effect of the stress on the forward and/or reverse reaction rates.	Removing some SO_2 decreases the forward reaction rate (r_f).
2. Decide if this results in a net forward or net reverse reaction.	This results in a net reverse reaction, also known as a shift left.

The kinetics diagram on the right illustrates the rates at the initial equilibrium, at the time of the stress, and when equilibrium is restored. Note that the rates are lower when equilibrium is restored than they were at the initial equilibrium. This is logical since some chemical was removed from the system.

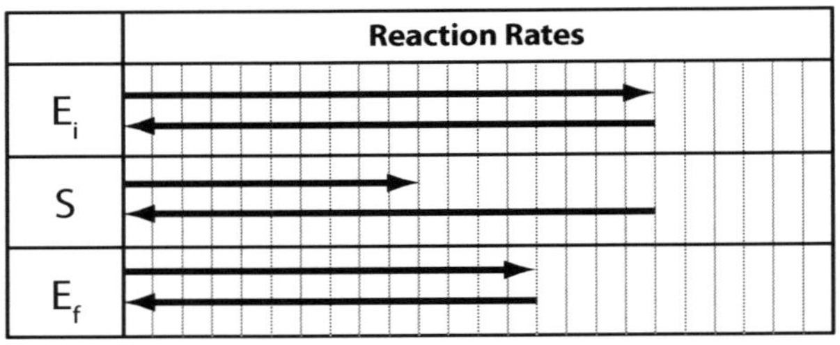

Practice Problems 2.2.2 — Describing the Shift Mechanism

Consider the following equilibrium system:

$$2\,NOCl(g) \rightleftharpoons 2\,NO(g) + Cl_2(g)$$

1. Explain in terms of forward and reverse reaction rates how the equilibrium would respond to each of the following changes.
   (a) adding some NO
   (b) removing some Cl_2
   (c) removing some NOCl

2. Show how the forward and the reverse reaction rates respond to a sudden addition of NO to the system at t_1. Use a solid line for the forward rate and a dotted line for the reverse rate. The system re-equilibrates at t_2. The arrow diagram on the right of the graph is another way of depicting the same information. You may use it to do your rough work.

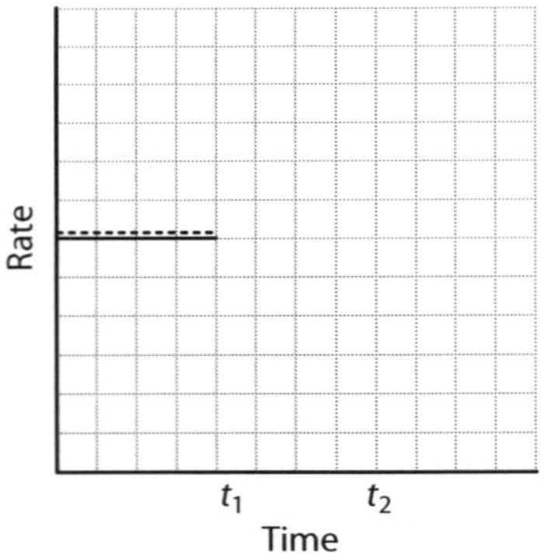

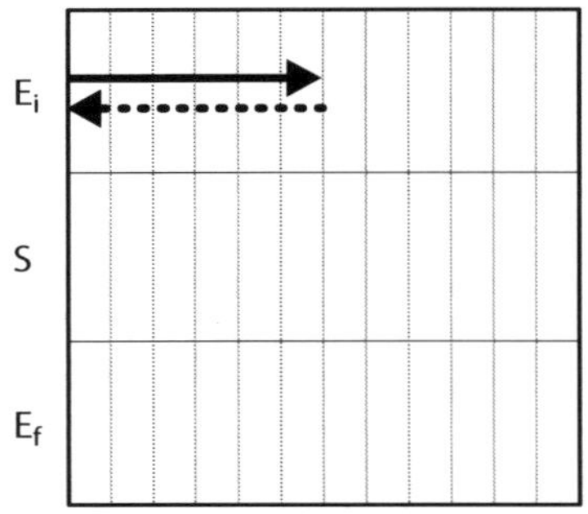

© Edvantage Interactive 2019

Changing Surface Area and Adding Catalysts

In heterogeneous reactions, an increase in surface area increases the forward and reverse rates equally since both forward and reverse reactions occur at the same surface. Adding more solid or crushing the solid present at equilibrium therefore has no effect on the equilibrium concentrations of the reactants and products in solution. When the initial reactants have a greater surface area, the system reaches equilibrium sooner. Likewise, adding a catalyst increases the forward and reverse rates equally and therefore has no effect on the position of the equilibrium. When a catalyst is added to the initial reactants, the system reaches equilibrium sooner.

The Equilibrium Position

The phrase **equilibrium position** refers to the relative concentrations of reactants and products at equilibrium and is usually expressed as percent yield. In previous years, you learned that percent yield is the amount of a product formed or recovered as a percentage of what the complete reaction will theoretically produce.

$$\textbf{percent yield} = \frac{\text{actual yield}}{\text{theoretical yield}} \times 100$$

An equilibrium system with an increased percent yield is said to have an equilibrium position farther to the right. "The equilibrium *position* shifted right" translates to: "the system has a greater percent yield than it had at the previous equilibrium." It is important to make a distinction between the equilibrium system shifting in response to a stress (as described by Le Châtelier's principle) and the equilibrium position shifting as a possible result. When you lose your balance snowboarding, you shift your weight to regain your balance. Sometimes you also shift your balance farther forward or backward on your board. Likewise, when an equilibrium system shifts to remove some of an added chemical or to replace some of a removed chemical, the system may "overshoot" or "undershoot" the original equilibrium position, depending on the circumstance. Consider the following equilibrium:

$$\underset{\text{yellow}}{HP(aq)} \rightleftharpoons H^+(aq) + \underset{\text{blue}}{P^-(aq)}$$

A green solution indicates equal concentrations of HP and P^- and therefore a 50% yield. If some yellow HP is added to a green equilibrium mixture, the *system will shift right* to remove some of the added HP. However, when equilibrium is restored, the solution is still yellow so we know that *the equilibrium position has shifted left.*

The expression "products are favored" is sometimes used to describe an equilibrium system. Be careful making inferences from this expression. Let's examine what the phrase does and, perhaps more importantly, does not mean. Products are *favored* when the equilibrium has a greater than 50 percent yield. This means that more than half of the limiting reactant has been converted into product.

percent yield ●————————|————————●

0% 50% 100%

favors reactants favors product(s)

Without knowing which reactant is limiting, you cannot infer that any reactant or product has a higher or lower concentration than any other reactant or product solely from the products being favored. For example:

$$H_3BO_3(aq) + CN^-(aq) \rightleftharpoons H_2BO_3^-(aq) + HCN(aq)$$

Even though products are favored in the above equilibrium, the [HCN] may be less than the [CN^-] if the CN^- is in excess. Likewise, the [HCN] may be less than the [H_3BO_3] if the H_3BO_3 is in excess. Furthermore, a reasonable excess of either reactant ensures that the total [reactants] will be greater than the total [products] even though the products are favored.

© Edvantage Interactive 2019

Quick Check

1. State Le Châtelier's principle in your own words.

 ____

 ____

2. According to Le Châtelier's principle, how will an equilibrium respond when a quantity of product is removed?

 ____

3. How is a stress to an equilibrium system defined?

 ____

4. How does adding a catalyst affect an equilibrium's forward and reverse reaction rates?

 ____

5. A chemist dissolves NaHSO3 in a solution of HNO2. The following equilibrium is established with reactants being favored:
 $HSO_3^-(aq) + HNO_2(aq) \rightleftharpoons H_2SO_3(aq) + NO_2^-(aq)$
 True or False? We can infer from this that $[HNO_2] > [H_2SO_3]$. __________

2.2 Activity: How an Equilibrium System "Copes" With Stress

Question

Can we use our mathematical model to demonstrate how an equilibrium system "copes" with having some reactant added?

Background

Le Châtelier's principle states that any equilibrium system subjected to a stress will restore equilibrium by partially counteracting the stress. Let's test this principle by adding some reactant to the equilibrium we established in the 2.1 Activity.

Procedure

1. Perform this activity in groups of two to four students. Each group requires 48 pennies.
2. Begin by recreating the equilibrium you achieved in the 2.1 Activity by placing 32 pennies on your desk, 8 with their "head" side up and 24 with their "tail" side up.
3. Each round represents 1 s of reaction time. Reactants (heads) have a 50.0% (1/2) chance of turning into products (tails) each round. Products (tails) have a 16.7% (1/6) chance of turning into reactants (heads) each round. For each round:
 (i) For each head: Simply flip the coin to see whether it remains a head or changes to a tail.
 (ii) For each tail: Roll a die and only turn the coin over if you roll a 6.
4. After two rounds, add 16 heads to the reacting mixture and then continue the activity as before until equilibrium has been restored.

Continued opposite

 © Edvantage Interactive 2019

5. Use the table and graph provided below to record the number of reactant and product species present after each round. Draw the reactant's plot and the product's plot with different-colored pencils.

Time (Round) (s)	No. of Reactant Species (Heads)	No. of Product Species (Tails)
0	8	24
1		
2	+ 16 =	
3		
4		
5		
6		
7		
8		
9		

No. of Reactant and Product Species vs. Time

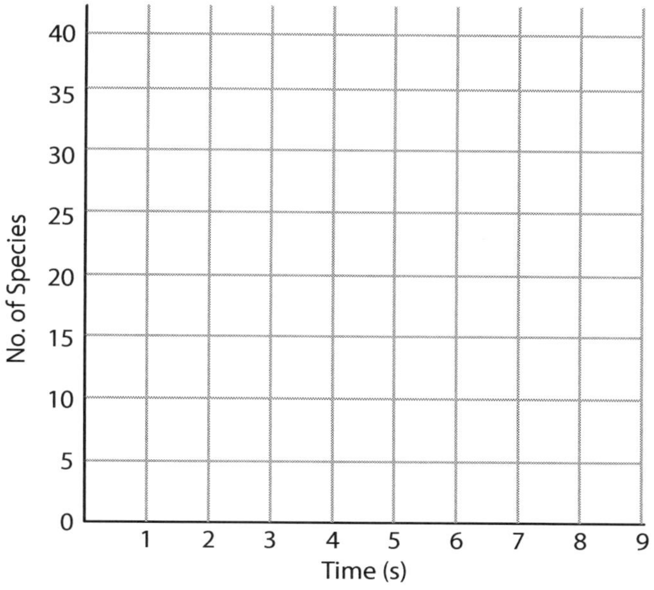

Results and Discussion

1. According to Le Châtelier's principle, the number of heads present when equilibrium is restored could be as few as ________ or as many as ________. Explain.

2. How many heads were present when equilibrium was re-established? ________

2.2 Review Questions

1. Consider the following equilibrium system: $2\ NO(g) + Cl_2(g) \rightleftharpoons 2\ NOCl(g)$

   (a) What does Le Châtelier's principle say will occur if some NO is added to the system?

   (b) In which direction will this system shift in response to the stress?

   (c) Compare the $[Cl_2]$ when equilibrium is reestablished to its concentration before the NO was added.

2. Consider the following equilibrium system: $2\ NO(g) + O_2(g) \rightleftharpoons 2\ NO_2(g)$

   (a) Explain in terms of forward and reverse reaction rates how the system responds to removing some O_2.

   (b) Compare the rates of the forward and reverse reactions when equilibrium is reestablished with the rates before some O_2 was removed.

3. Silver nitrate is added to the equilibrium system:
   $Ag(S_2O_3)_2^{3-}(aq) \rightleftharpoons Ag^+(aq) + 2\ S_2O_3^{2-}(aq)$

   When equilibrium is restored, how will each ion's concentration compare with its concentration before the silver nitrate was added? Explain how you arrived at your answer.

4. Cholesterol is a component of cell membranes and a building block for hormones such as estrogen and testosterone. About 80% of the body's cholesterol is produced by the liver, while the rest comes directly from our diet. There are two forms of cholesterol: a "good" form (HDL) that helps lubricate blood vessels and a "bad" form (LDL) that deposits on the inside of artery walls where it can restrict blood flow. Suppose these two forms could be converted from one to the other via the following "equilibrium" reaction:
   $LDL + X \rightleftharpoons HDL + Y$

   (a) Briefly explain why a drug that removes the bad cholesterol (LDL) would not be completely effective (i.e., it would have a bad side-effect).

   (b) Referring to the above equilibrium, how could a drug company effectively treat people with too high an LDL:HDL ratio?

© Edvantage Interactive 2019

5. Sulfur dioxide is an important compound in wines, where it acts as an antimicrobial and antioxidant to protect the wine from spoiling. The following equilibrium exists in wines:
$SO_2(aq) + H_2O(l) \rightleftharpoons H^+(aq) + HSO_3^-(aq)$
State whether a winemaker should increase the wine's pH (by removing H^+) or decrease the wine's pH (by adding H^+) to shift the equilibrium toward the active SO_2?

6. Complete the following table using the words "decrease," "same," or "increase" to indicate how the equilibrium concentrations are affected by the stated stress. "Increase" means that when equilibrium is restored, the chemical's concentration is greater than it was before the stress.

$$2\,NH_3(g) \rightleftharpoons N_2(g) + 3\,H_2(g)$$

		Add NH_3	**Remove some H_2**	**Add N_2**
Equilibrium Concentration	N_2			
	H_2			
	NH_3			

7. $HP \rightleftharpoons H^+ + P^-$

HP: red
P^-: yellow

The above equilibrium system appears orange due to equal concentrations of HP and P^-.
(a) What action will shift the equilibrium so the solution turns red?

(b) What could be done to shift the equilibrium so the solution turns yellow?

8. Hemoglobin is the protein in red blood cells that transports oxygen to cells throughout your body. Each hemoglobin (Hb) molecule attaches to four oxygen molecules:
$Hb(aq) + 4\,O_2(aq) \rightleftharpoons Hb(O_2)_4(aq)$

In which direction does the above equilibrium shift in each of the following situations:
(a) At high elevations the air pressure is lowered reducing the $[O_2]$ in the blood.

(b) At high altitude, climbers sometimes breathe pressurized oxygen from a tank to increase the $[O_2]$ in the blood.

(c) People who live at higher altitudes produce more hemoglobin.

(d) Carbon monoxide poisoning occurs when carbon monoxide molecules bind to hemoglobin instead of oxygen molecules. Carboxyhemoglobin is even redder than oxyhemoglobin; therefore, one symptom of carbon monoxide poisoning is a flushed face.

9. Explain why neither adding a catalyst nor increasing the surface area of S(*s*) stresses the following equilibrium, even though each of these actions increases the forward reaction rate.

$2\ S(s) + 3\ O_2(g) \rightleftharpoons 2\ SO_3(g)$

10. The following equilibrium exists in an aqueous solution of copper(II) chloride:

$CuCl_4^{2-}(aq) + 4\ H_2O(l) \rightleftharpoons Cu(H_2O)_4^{2+}(aq) + 4\ Cl^-(aq)$

green — blue

(a) Some Cl^- is removed by adding some silver nitrate to the solution. The Ag^+ in the silver nitrate precipitates with the Cl^- to produce AgCl(*s*). In what direction will the equilibrium shift?

(b) If the initial equilibrium mixture was blue, what would you observe as a sodium chloride solution was added dropwise to the equilibrium mixture?

11. At t_1 some CO was suddenly removed from the closed system shown below. Equilibrium was reestablished at t_2. Complete the plots to show how the system would respond.

$Ni(s) + 4\ CO(g) \rightleftharpoons Ni(CO)_4(g)$

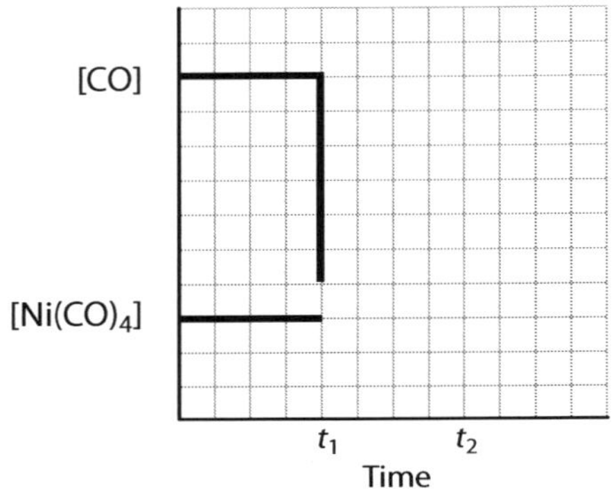

12. Show how the forward and reverse reaction rates respond to having some HOCl suddenly removed from the following system at t_1.

$H_2O(g) + Cl_2O(g) \rightleftharpoons 2\ HOCl(g)$

Use a solid line for the forward rate and a dotted line for the reverse rate. The system re-equilibrates at t_2. The arrow diagram on the right is another way of displaying the same information. You may use it to do your rough work.

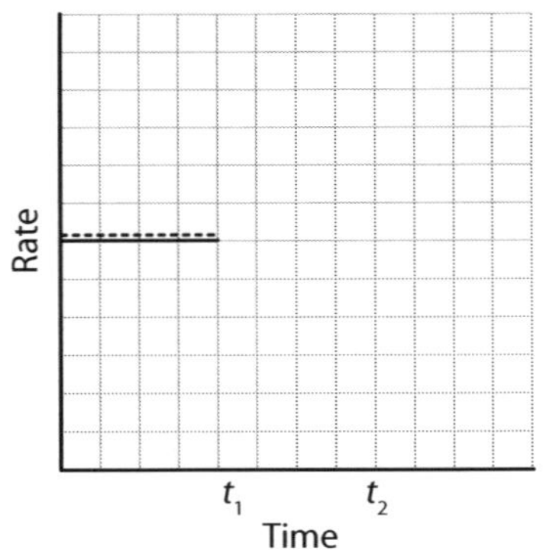

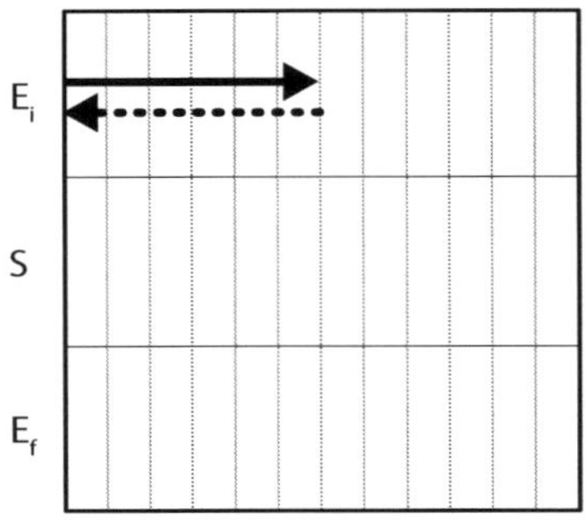

© Edvantage Interactive 2019

13. Equilibria are often linked through one chemical common to both. Even two equilibria coupled together present an interesting dynamic.

Equilibrium 1

$$Cu^{2+} + 4\,NH_3 \rightleftharpoons Cu(NH_3)_4^{2+}$$

$$+$$

$$4\,H^+$$

Equilibrium 2 $\upharpoonleft\downharpoonright$

$$4\,NH_4^+$$

How would the $[Cu^{2+}]$ be affected by adding some H^+ to this coupled system? Briefly explain using Le Châtelier's principle.

14. Silver acetate has a low solubility in water. A small amount of solid silver acetate is in equilibrium with a saturated solution of its ions.

Equilibrium 1

$$AgCH_3COO(s) \rightleftharpoons Ag^+(aq) + CH_3COO^-(aq)$$

$$+$$

$$H^+(aq)$$

Equilibrium 2 $\upharpoonleft\downharpoonright$

$$CH_3COOH(aq)$$

What would you observe occurring in the beaker as $H^+(aq)$ is added dropwise to the solution? Briefly explain using Le Châtelier's principle.

15. Consider the following equilibrium:

$$2\,NO(g) + O_2(g) \rightleftharpoons 2\,NO_2(g)$$

Describe how [NO] could be greater than the $[NO_2]$ despite the products being favored at equilibrium.

16. Because few natural systems are closed, many of nature's reversible reactions are perpetually "chasing after" equilibrium. In *At Home in the Universe*, the author, Stuart Kauffman, describes living systems as "persistently displaced from chemical equilibrium." Describe one way to ensure that a reversible reaction never achieves equilibrium.

2.3 How Equilibria Respond to Volume and Temperature Changes

Warm Up

1. What is the scientific meaning of *pressure*?

   ____

2. To increase gas pressure, we ______________ the gas into less space.

3. What is temperature a measure of?

   ____

4. An increase in temperature increases the rate of reactions because the molecules collide more ______________ and ______________.

How Equilibria Respond to Volume Changes

We've described and explained how equilibria respond to changing the concentration of a single reactant or product. The concentrations of all the reactants and products can be changed simultaneously by changing the volume of the reacting system. The volume of a gaseous system can be changed by compressing or decompressing it. The volume of an aqueous system can be changed by evaporating water from it or by diluting it. A change in volume changes all the reactants' and products' concentrations.

It isn't possible for a shift to partially restore all the chemicals' concentrations but some equilibria can shift to partially restore the total or combined concentration of the chemicals. For example, if an aqueous equilibrium is diluted then all the chemical concentrations are decreased. A shift can't increase the concentrations of chemicals on both sides of the equation but some equilibria can increase the total chemical concentration by shifting to the side of the equation with the greater number of particles. Le Châtelier views this situation from the perspective of pressure.

> Equilibria respond to volume changes by shifting to relieve some of the added pressure or to replace some of the lost pressure.

You are probably familiar with the concept of gas pressure, but you may not be familiar with the concept of solute (osmotic) pressure. A detailed discussion of osmosis and osmotic pressure is not required here. You need only know that osmotic pressure is to dissolved particles what gas pressure is to gas particles. In 1901, the Dutch chemist Jacobus van't Hoff discovered that dissolved particles in an aqueous solution behave just like gas particles in a container. The relationship between the concentration, temperature, and pressure is the same for gas particles and dissolved particles. Van't Hoff won the first Nobel Prize in chemistry for his work on osmotic pressure and chemical equilibrium. Just as a gas's pressure is proportional to its concentration of gas particles, an aqueous solution's osmotic pressure is proportional to its concentration of solute particles. Decompressing a gas lowers its gas pressure. Diluting a solute lowers its osmotic pressure.

Chemists sometimes refer to the partial pressure of a gas. **Partial pressure** is the gas's part of the total gas pressure or the pressure exerted by this gas alone in a mixture of gases. The sum of the partial pressures equals the total pressure of the gas mixture. A gas's partial pressure is proportional to its concentration. The same concepts and principles apply to solutes and their partial osmotic pressures.

© Edvantage Interactive 2019

Consider the following equilibrium:

$H_2(g) + F_2(g) \rightleftharpoons 2\,HF(g)$

This equilibrium doesn't respond to a volume change. It cannot partially restore the pressure by shifting in either direction since there are the same number of gas particles on each side of the equation.

Quick Check

1. According to Le Châtelier's principle, how will an equilibrium respond to being compressed?

____

2. What is *partial pressure*?

____

3. According to Le Châtelier's principle, how will an aqueous equilibrium respond to being diluted?

____

Sample Problem 2.3.1(a) — Predicting How an Equilibrium Will Respond to a Decrease in Volume

The system described by the equation below is compressed. In what direction will the system shift to restore equilibrium? When equilibrium is restored, how will the number of each type of molecule and the concentration of each substance compare to those before the system was compressed?

$$PCl_3(g) + Cl_2(g) \rightleftharpoons PCl_5(g)$$

What to Think About

1. Recall that Le Châtelier's principle says the system will shift to relieve *some* of the added pressure.
2. Consider the effect the stress has on the system to determine the number of each type of molecule. The stress changed the amount of space that the particles move around in, not the number of particles. Only the system's response to the stress changes the number of particles. The forward reaction converts two molecules into one molecule. Thus a shift right reduces the total number of particles and the pressure of the system.
3. Determine the effect of compression on the concentrations of the substances in the system. The situation regarding concentration is illustrated below:

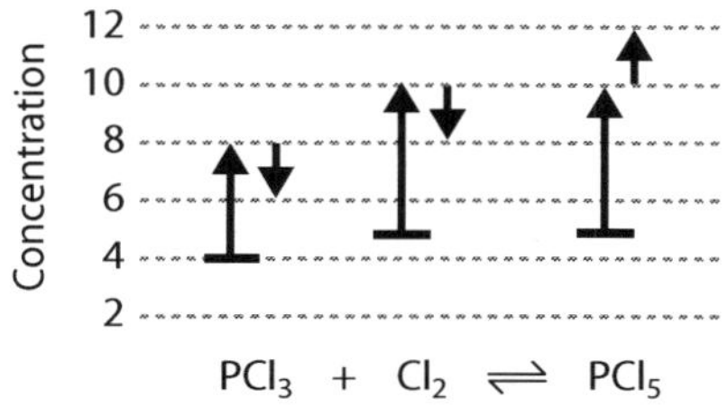

In this diagram, all the original concentrations are doubled by the compression so the volume must have been halved.

How to Do It

The system must shift right to reduce the pressure.

The number of PCl_5 molecules will increase, while the number of PCl_3 and Cl_2 molecules will decrease.

Because the system was compressed, every substance has a higher concentration or partial pressure at the new equilibrium than it did at the initial equilibrium.

(Although the shift can't reduce all the chemicals' concentrations or partial pressures, it is reducing most of them (2/3) by shifting to the right. The result is that some of the added pressure is relieved.)

Sample Problem 2.3.1(b) — Predicting How an Equilibrium Will Respond to an Increase in Volume

The system below is diluted. In what direction will the system shift to restore equilibrium? When equilibrium is restored, how will the number of each type of particle and the concentration of each species compare to those before the system was diluted?

$$H^+(aq) + NO_2^-(aq) \rightleftharpoons HNO_2(aq)$$

What to Think About

1. Recall that Le Châtelier's principle says that equilibrium will be restored by replacing *some* of the lost osmotic pressure.
2. Consider the effect the stress has on the system to determine the number of each type of molecule. Only the system's response to the stress, not the stress itself, changes the number of particles. The reverse reaction converts one particle into two particles thus a shift left increases the total number of particles and the osmotic pressure of the system.
3. Determine the effect of dilution on the concentrations of the substances in the system. The situation regarding concentration is illustrated below:

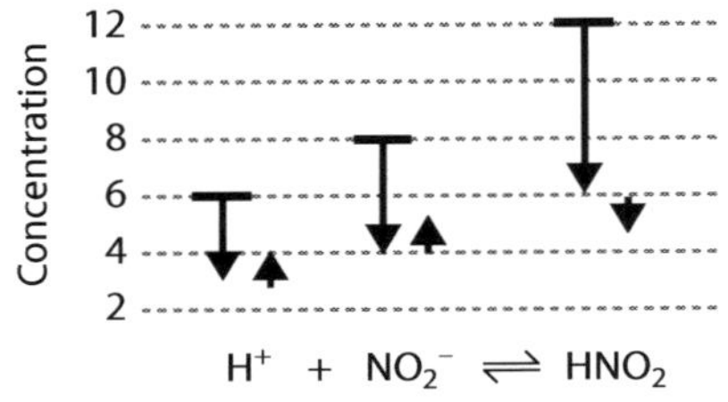

In this diagram, all the original concentrations are halved by the dilution so the volume must have been doubled.

How to Do It

The system must shift left to increase the pressure.

The number of HNO_2 molecules will decrease while the number of H^+ and NO_2^- ions will increase.

Because the system was diluted, every substance has a lower concentration at the new equilibrium than it did at the initial equilibrium.

Practice Problems 2.3.1 — Predicting How an Equilibrium Will Respond to a Volume Change

1. The system below is compressed:

   $2\,NOCl(g) \rightleftharpoons 2\,NO(g) + Cl_2(g)$

   In what direction will the system shift to restore equilibrium? When equilibrium is restored, how will the number of each type of molecule and the concentration of each substance compare to those before the system was compressed?

2. The system below is diluted:

   $Ag(S_2O_3)_2^{3-}(aq) \rightleftharpoons Ag^+(aq) + 2\,S_2O_3^{2-}(aq)$

   In what direction will the system shift to restore equilibrium? When equilibrium is restored, how will the number of each type of particle and the concentration of each species compare to those before the system was diluted?

Continued opposite

 © Edvantage Interactive 2019

Practice Problems 2.3.1 — *Continued*

3. The volume of the system below is decreased:

   $CO_2(g) + H_2(g) \rightleftharpoons CO(g) + H_2O(g)$

   Will the equilibrium system respond? Explain.

The Shift Mechanism: The Effect of Volume Change on Forward and/or Reverse Reaction Rates

For an explanation of what causes this shift, we must once again turn to chemical kinetics. When the volume of an equilibrium system changes, all the reactant and product concentrations change proportionately. Nevertheless, the forward and reverse reaction rates may change by different amounts. In doing so, they become unequal. From Le Châtelier's predictions, we can infer the following:

> The direction (forward or reverse) that has the greater sum of gaseous or aqueous reactant coefficients is the more sensitive of the two directions to volume changes.

By "more sensitive," we mean that a volume change will decrease or increase the rate of that direction more than that of the opposite direction. At equilibrium, the relationship between concentration and the reaction rate depends only on the coefficients in the balanced equation. For example, consider the following system:

$Fe^{3+}(aq) + SCN^{-}(aq) \rightleftharpoons FeSCN^{2+}(aq)$

Diluting this aqueous system decreases its forward rate more than its reverse rate because the sum of the reactant coefficients for the forward reaction is 2 whereas the lone reactant coefficient for the reverse reaction is only 1. If the sum of gaseous or aqueous reactant coefficients equals the sum of the gaseous or aqueous product coefficients then the equilibrium is not stressed by volume changes. This is because any volume change will have the same effect on the forward and reverse rates. For example, consider the following system:

$H_2(g) + F_2(g) \rightleftharpoons 2\,HF(g)$

Compressing this gaseous system increases its forward and reverse rates equally and therefore does not disrupt the equilibrium.

The only external factors that affect reaction rates are the reactant concentrations and temperature. A pressure change only stresses an equilibrium if the pressure change reflects a change in the reactant and product concentrations. The pressure of an equilibrium system can be changed without changing its concentrations by, for example, adding an inert gas to the system. Since this pressure change does not reflect any change of reactant or product concentrations, it does not affect the equilibrium.

Sample Problem 2.3.2(a) — Describing the Shift Mechanism for a Decrease in Volume

Explain in terms of forward and reverse reaction rates how the equilibrium system below would respond to a decrease in volume.

$$2\,SO_2(g) + O_2(g) \rightleftharpoons 2\,SO_3(g)$$

What to Think About	How to Do It
1. Determine the immediate effect of the stress on the forward and/or reverse reaction rates.	Compressing the system increases the forward rate (r_f) more than the reverse rate (r_r).
2. Decide if this would result in a net forward or net reverse reaction.	This results in a net forward reaction, also known as a shift right.

The arrow diagram on the right illustrates the rates at the initial equilibrium, at the time of the stress, and when equilibrium is restored.

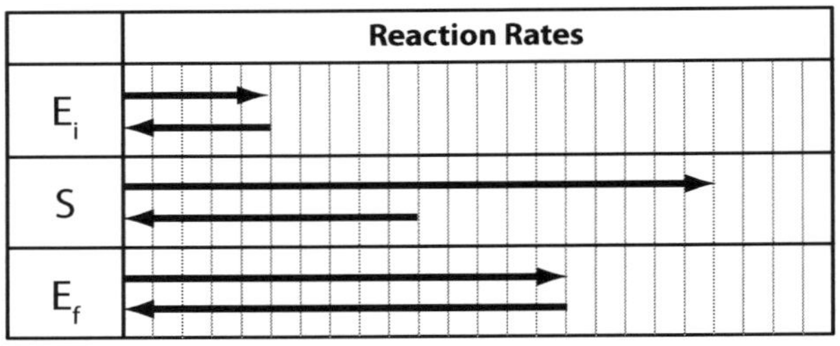

Sample Problem 2.3.2(b) — Describing the Shift Mechanism for a Volume Change

Explain in terms of forward and reverse reaction rates how the equilibrium system below would respond to being diluted.

$$H^+(aq) + SO_4^{2-}(aq) \rightleftharpoons HSO_4^-(aq)$$

What to Think About	How to Do It
1. Determine the immediate effect of the stress on the forward and/or reverse reaction rates.	Diluting the system decreases the forward rate (r_f) more than the reverse rate (r_r).
2. Decide if this would result in a net forward or net reverse reaction.	This results in a net reverse reaction, also known as a shift left.

The arrow diagram on the right illustrates the rates at the initial equilibrium, at the time of the stress, and when equilibrium is restored.

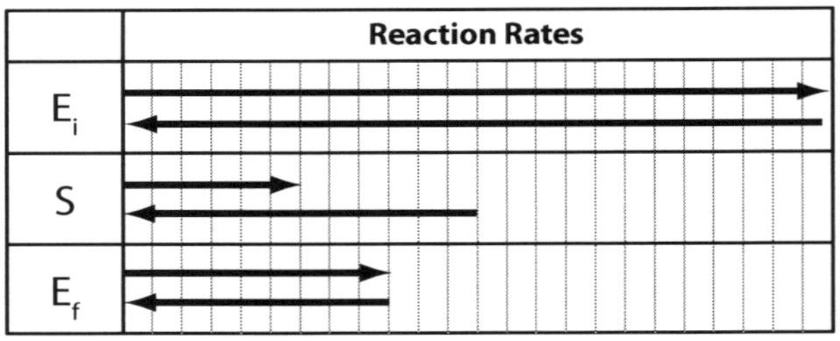

 © Edvantage Interactive 2019

Practice Problems 2.3.2 — Describing the Shift Mechanism for Changes in Volume

1. Explain in terms of forward and reverse reaction rates how the equilibrium system below would respond to a decrease in volume. $2\ NOCl(g) \rightleftharpoons 2\ NO(g) + Cl_2(g)$

2. Explain in terms of forward and reverse reaction rates how the equilibrium system below would respond to being diluted.
$Ag(S_2O_3)_2^{3-}(aq) \rightleftharpoons Ag^+(aq) + 2\ S_2O_3^{2-}(aq)$

3. Show how the forward and reverse reaction rates respond to a sudden compression of the system at t_1. Use a solid line for the forward rate and a dotted line for the reverse rate. The system restores equilibrium at t_2. The arrow diagram on the right is another way of depicting the same information. You may use it to do your rough work.
$2\ SO_2(g) + O_2(g) \rightleftharpoons 2\ SO_3(g)$

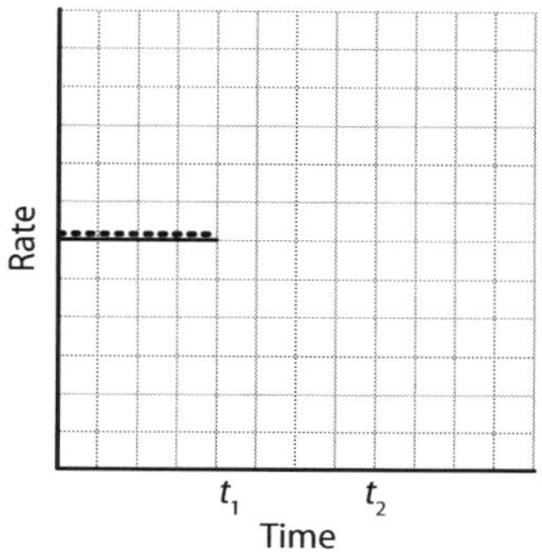

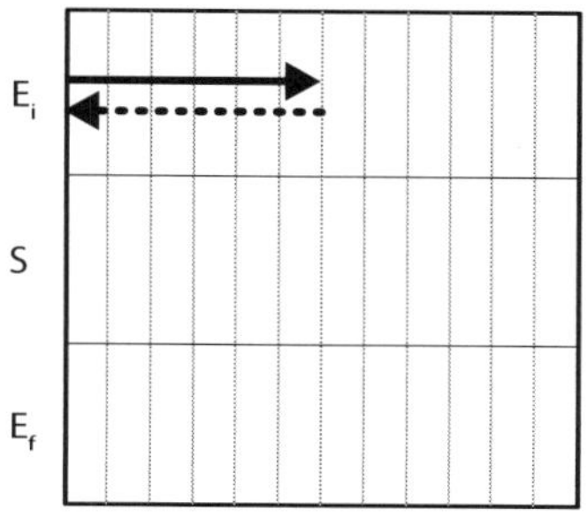

How Equilibria Respond to Temperature Changes

Le Châtelier's principle states the following:

Equilibria respond to changing temperatures by shifting to remove some of the added kinetic energy or to replace some of the removed kinetic energy.

Sample Problem 2.3.3(a) — Predicting How an Equilibrium Will Respond to an Increase in Temperature

The system below is heated. In what direction will the system shift to restore equilibrium? When equilibrium is restored, how will the concentration of each species compare to its concentration before the system was heated?

$N_2(g) + O_2(g) \rightleftharpoons 2\ NO(g) \qquad \Delta H = 181\ kJ/mol$

What to Think About	How to Do It
1. Recall that Le Châtelier's principle says the system will shift to remove *some* of the added kinetic energy and cool itself.	The system must shift right (in the endothermic direction) to convert some of the added KE into PE.
2. Determine the effect of heating on the concentrations of the substances in the system. Note that 2 NO molecules are formed for each N_2 and O_2 molecule that react.	The $[N_2]$ and $[O_2]$ will decrease and the [NO] will increase.

Note that ΔH can be included as part of a thermochemical equation:

$N_2(g) + O_2(g) + 181\ \text{kJ} \rightleftharpoons 2\ NO(g)$

In that case, the kinetic energy can be treated just as though it were a chemical. Adding O_2 would cause a shift to the right to remove some of the added O_2. Likewise, adding kinetic energy causes a shift to the right to remove some of the added kinetic energy.

Sample Problem 2.3.3(b) — Predicting How an Equilibrium Will Respond to a Decrease in Temperature

The system below is cooled. In what direction will the system shift to restore equilibrium? When equilibrium is restored, how will the concentration of each species compare to its concentration before the system was cooled?

$$N_2(g) + O_2(g) \rightleftharpoons 2\ NO(g) \qquad \Delta H = 181\ \text{kJ/mol}$$

What to Think About	How to Do It
1. Recall that Le Châtelier's principle says the system will shift to replace *some* of the lost kinetic energy and warm itself.	The system must shift left (in the exothermic direction) to convert some PE into KE.
2. Determine the effect of cooling on the concentrations of the substances in the system. Note that 2 NO molecules are consumed for each N_2 and O_2 molecule formed.	The [NO] will decrease. The $[N_2]$ and $[O_2]$ will increase.

Practice Problems 2.3.3 — Predicting How an Equilibrium Will Respond to a Temperature Change

1. The system below is heated. In what direction will the system shift to restore equilibrium? When equilibrium is restored, how will the concentration of each species compare to its concentration before the system was heated?

$$2\ SO_2(g) + O_2(g) \rightleftharpoons 2\ SO_3(g) \qquad \Delta H = -198\ \text{kJ/mol}$$

2. The system below is cooled. In what direction will the system shift to restore equilibrium? When equilibrium is restored, how will the concentration of each species compare to its concentration before the system was cooled?

$$H_2(g) + I_2(g) \rightleftharpoons 2\ HI(g) + 17\ \text{kJ/mol}$$

Effects of Volume and Temperature Changes on the Equilibrium Position

Figure 2.3.1 depicts the situation described in Sample Problem 2.3.3(b) above. When the stress is a sudden concentration or volume change it appears as a spike(s) on plots of concentrations versus time. Temperature changes do not appear on these plots so the system responds to an invisible stress. Another difference is that concentration changes, both individual and those resulting from volume changes, can be very sudden. However, the temperature of a system, particularly an aqueous system, cannot change rapidly. This means that chemical systems begin responding while the temperature is still changing. In other words, the response begins before the stress is complete.

© Edvantage Interactive 2019

Neither volume nor temperature change itself changes the percent yield so a system's response to these stresses shifts its equilibrium position in the same direction that the system shifted in response to the stress.

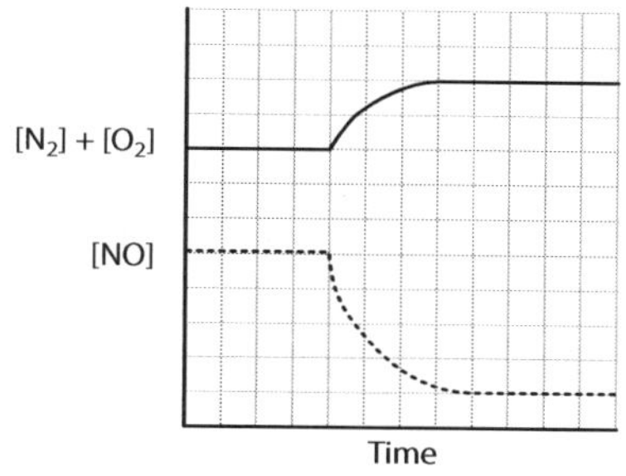

Figure 2.3.1 *Changes in concentration show up in the graph but the temperature change doesn't.*

Pressure-Temperature Relationships

Increasing the temperature of gases in a closed container increases their pressure. The temperature change itself affects the equilibrium. However, the resulting pressure change is irrelevant to the equilibrium because it does not reflect a change of concentrations. The same cannot be said for the reverse.

When a gas is compressed, its temperature rises because some of the particles' potential energy converts to kinetic energy as the particles are forced closer together. The temperature change resulting from compressing or decompressing a gas mixture does affect its equilibrium. In questions where a gaseous equilibrium is compressed or decompressed, assume that its temperature was held constant unless otherwise stated. Such a stipulation allows you to deal with only one variable at a time.

The Shift Mechanism: The Effect of Temperature Change on Forward and Reverse Reaction Rates

If the collision geometry requirements are the same for the forward and reverse reactions, then their rates depend solely on the frequency of collisions possessing the activation energy. The forward and reverse reaction rates are equal at equilibrium. Therefore the frequency of collisions possessing the activation energy must be the same for the forward and reverse reactions. The percentage of the area under a collision energy distribution curve that is at or beyond the activation energy (E_a) represents the percentage of collisions having enough energy to react.

For an endothermic reaction, like that represented in Figure 2.3.2 and Figure 2.3.3, the forward reaction has a lower percentage of collisions with the activation energy needed than the reverse reaction does. The forward reaction must therefore have a greater frequency of collisions to achieve the same frequency of successful collisions as the reverse reaction. For example, 4% of the forward reaction's 800 collisions per second and 20% of the reverse reaction's 160 collisions per second would both equal 32 successful collisions per second. For an endothermic reaction, a higher concentration of reactants is therefore required to generate the same rate as a lower concentration of products because a lower percentage of the reactant collisions are successful.

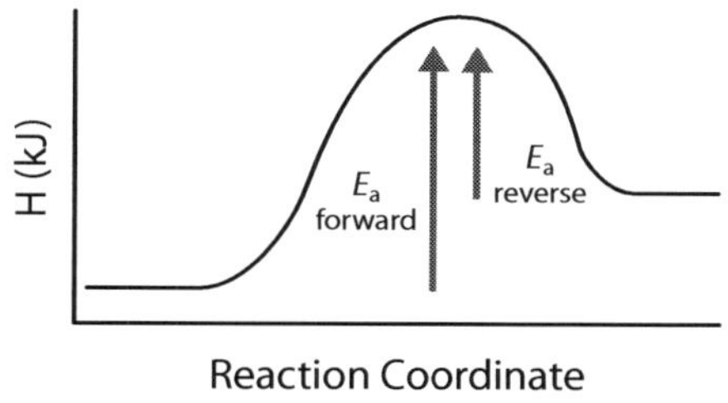

Figure 2.3.2 *Potential energy diagram.*

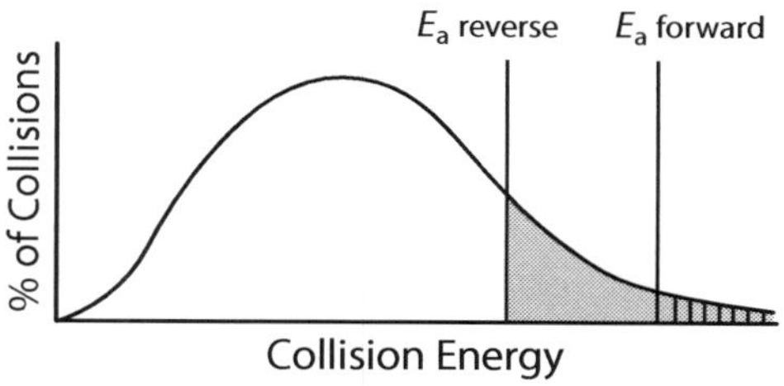

Figure 2.3.3 *Collision energy diagram*

Increases in temperature cause a shift in the endothermic direction because they increase the rate of the endothermic direction more than they increase the rate of the exothermic direction. The endothermic direction has the harder task due to its higher activation energy so it benefits more from the assistance provided by the increased temperature. Likewise, decreases in temperature cause a shift in the exothermic direction because they decrease the rate of the endothermic direction more than they decrease the rate of the exothermic direction. The endothermic direction is hindered more than the exothermic direction by the decreased temperature.

An equilibrium's endothermic direction is more sensitive to temperature changes than its exothermic direction due to the endothermic direction's greater activation energy.

Sample Problem 2.3.4(a) — Describing the Shift Mechanism for an Increase in Temperature

Explain in terms of forward and reverse reaction rates how the system below would respond to being heated.

$$N_2(g) + O_2(g) \rightleftharpoons 2\ NO(g) \qquad \Delta H = 181\ \text{kJ/mol}$$

What to Think About	How to Do It
1. Determine the immediate effect of the stress on the forward and/or reverse reaction rates.	Heating the system increases the forward rate (r_f) more than the reverse rate (r_r).
2. Decide if this would result in a net forward or net reverse reaction.	This results in a net forward reaction, also known as a shift right.

The arrow diagram on the right illustrates the rates at the initial equilibrium, at the time of the stress, and when equilibrium is restored.

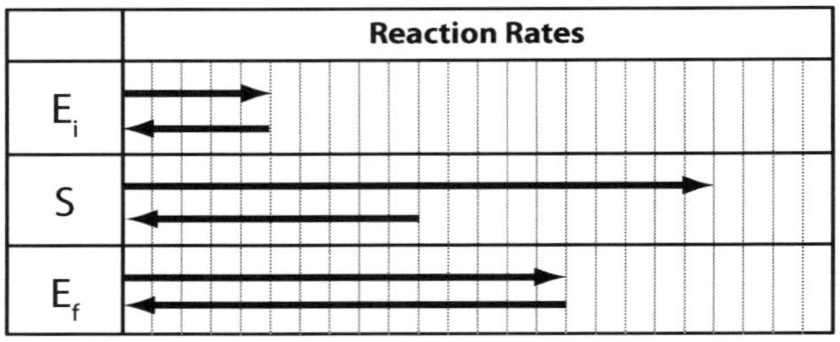

Sample Problem 2.3.4(b) — Describing the Shift Mechanism for a Decrease in Temperature

Explain in terms of forward and reverse reaction rates how the system below would respond to being cooled.

$$N_2(g) + O_2(g) \rightleftharpoons 2\ NO(g) \qquad \Delta H = 181\ \text{kJ/mol}$$

What to Think About	How to Do It
1. Determine the immediate effect of the stress on the forward and/or reverse reaction rates?	Cooling the system decreases the forward rate (r_f) more than the reverse rate (r_r).
2. Decide if this would result in a net forward or net reverse reaction.	This results in a net reverse reaction, also known as a shift left.

The arrow diagram on the right illustrates the rates at the initial equilibrium, at the time of the stress, and when equilibrium is restored.

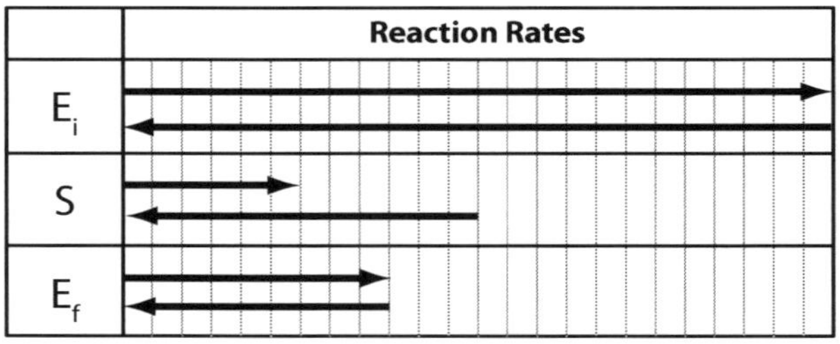

 © Edvantage Interactive 2019

Practice Problems 2.3.4 — Describing the Shift Mechanism for Changes in Temperature

1. Explain in terms of forward and reverse reaction rates how the system below would respond to being heated.

$$2\ SO_2(g) + O_2(g) \rightleftharpoons 2\ SO_3(g) \qquad \Delta H = -198\ kJ/mol$$

2. Explain in terms of forward and reverse reaction rates how the system below would respond to being cooled.

$$2\ Cl_2(g) + 2\ H_2O(g) + 113\ kJ/mol \rightleftharpoons 4\ HCl(g) + O_2(g)$$

3. Show how the forward and reverse reaction rates in the system below would respond to a temperature increase at t_1. Use a solid line for the forward rate and a dotted line for the reverse rate. The system restores equilibrium at t_2. The arrow diagram on the right is another way of depicting the same information. You may use it to do your rough work.

$$2\ NCl_3(g) \rightleftharpoons N_2(g) + 3\ Cl_2(g) \qquad \Delta H = -460\ kJ/mol$$

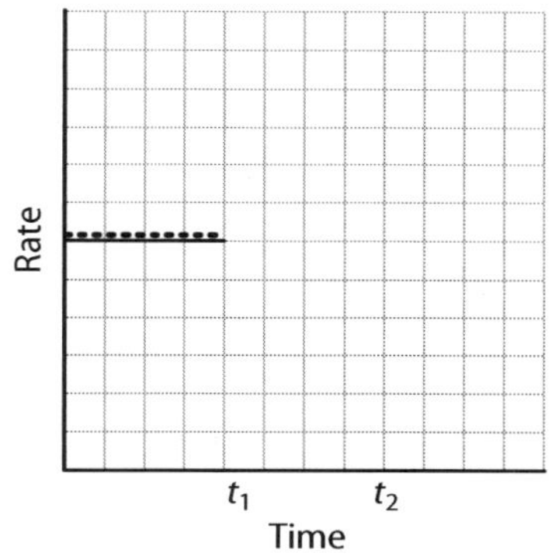

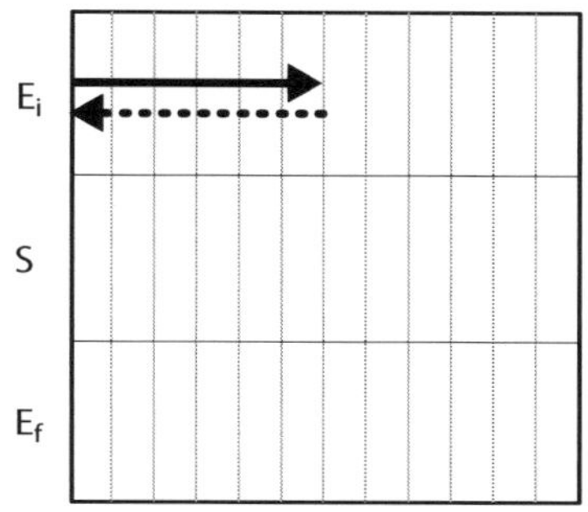

The Haber-Bosch Process

Almost all of the world's ammonia is produced via the Haber-Bosch process and almost all of our inorganic nitrogen compounds are produced from this ammonia. More than 100 million tonnes of ammonia with a value in excess of $600 million are produced annually. About 80% of the world's ammonia is used to produce fertilizers. Other products include explosives, plastics, fibres, and dyes.

German chemist Fritz Haber developed the equipment and procedures for producing ammonia (NH_3) from its constituent elements (N_2 and H_2) in 1910. In 1918, he received the Nobel Prize in chemistry for this accomplishment. In 1931, another German chemist, Carl Bosch, won the Nobel Prize in chemistry, in part for transforming the process to an industrial scale. The balanced equation and enthalpy for the reaction are:

$$N_2(g) + 3\ H_2(g) \rightleftharpoons 2\ NH_3(g) \qquad \Delta H = -92.4\ kJ/mol$$

Process Production Rate and Temperature Considerations

Consider the plight of a chemist who wants to produce NH_3 in his or her laboratory by allowing a single set of reactants to achieve equilibrium within a closed container. The percent yield and the reaction rate both need to be considered in choosing the optimal temperature. Lower temperatures produce higher percent yields of NH_3 at equilibrium since lower temperatures shift this equilibrium toward products. However, at lower temperatures the reaction proceeds at slower rates in both forward and reverse directions. Therefore it takes longer to produce any given amount of product. In other words, a higher temperature generates a faster forward rate but sustains it for a much shorter time period, both because the reaction rate is faster and the percent yield is less. To use a racing analogy, at higher temperatures the reaction runs faster toward a closer finish line (lower % yield).

Reactions proceeding at lower temperatures will eventually produce the amount produced at higher temperatures and then just keep rumbling along. This is the chemical version of the familiar tale of the tortoise versus the hare. Maximum productivity might be achieved by initially establishing equilibrium at a high temperature and then shifting the equilibrium toward products by lowering the temperature. Using a catalyst allows chemists to increase the reaction rate at a lower temperature that produces a higher percent yield.

For the Haber-Bosch process, lower temperatures produce a higher percent yield but at a lower rate.

The chemical industry does not produce ammonia by allowing single sets of reactants to establish equilibria within closed containers. As the reacting mixture is cycled and recycled through a Haber reactor, N_2 and H_2 are continuously fed in at one location while NH_3 is continuously liquefied and removed at another. The ammonia can be selectively removed because hydrogen bonding between NH_3 molecules causes them to condense at a higher temperature than hydrogen and nitrogen. The temperatures in the reactor are adjusted to maximize the concentration of NH_3, when and where it is extracted. The forward rate is kept high by replacing the consumed reactants while the reverse rate is kept low by removing product. Percent yield ceases to be a consideration if the system doesn't achieve equilibrium.

An industrial chemist must strike a compromise between the increased rate provided by a greater temperature and the increased cost to produce it. The reaction rate is also increased by using a catalyst. The "bottom line" for industry is its annual profit, not its annual production of ammonia. A plant strives to generate the greatest possible amount of ammonia for the lowest possible cost. The industry is obviously influenced by a tremendous number of commercial and economic factors as well as chemical factors.

Process Production Rate and Pressure Considerations

Higher pressures generate faster rates and push the reaction toward a higher percent yield.

According to Le Châtelier's principle, the system partially relieves the increased pressure by shifting right as the forward reaction converts four molecules into two. Compressing the gases also raises their temperature. High compression systems are expensive to build and to operate. Most Haber reactors operate at about 3.5×10^4 kPa. The increased yield at this pressure more than compensates for the higher construction and operation costs.

Quick Check

1. Name the chemical produced by the Haber-Bosch process.

   ____

2. What increases the rate of the Haber-Bosch process without decreasing its percent yield?

   ____

2.3 Activity: Dealing With Pressure

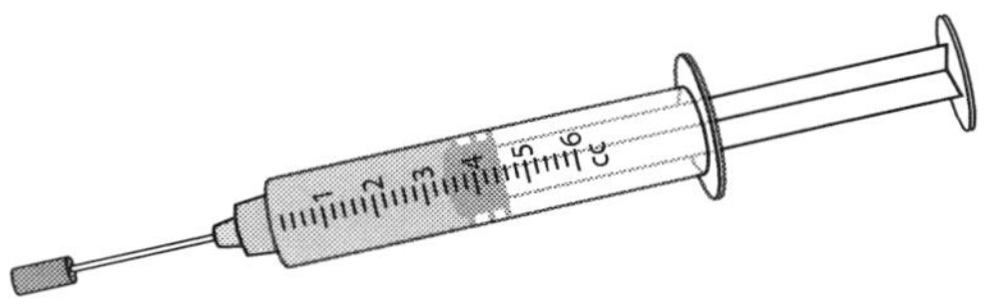

Question

What will a gaseous equilibrium mixture look like at the molecular level as it responds to being compressed?

Background

An equilibrium mixture of colorless dinitrogen tetroxide, $N_2O_4(g)$, and orange nitrogen dioxide, $NO_2(g)$, forms when nitric acid is poured over copper. When this equilibrium mixture is compressed in a plugged syringe, the mixture becomes darker orange as a result of concentrating the NO_2 molecules. Within seconds the mixture's color changes slightly, yet unmistakeably, as the equilibrium shifts in response to the stress.

$$\underset{\text{colorless}}{N_2O_4(g)} + \text{energy} \rightleftharpoons \underset{\text{orange}}{2\ NO_2(g)}$$

Procedure

1. The three diagrams below represent the tube in a syringe. Complete the third diagram by drawing in a possible number of NO_2 and N_2O_4 molecules after the system has responded to the stress and restored equilibrium.
2. Color in the circles underneath each syringe to indicate how pale or dark orange the gas would appear.

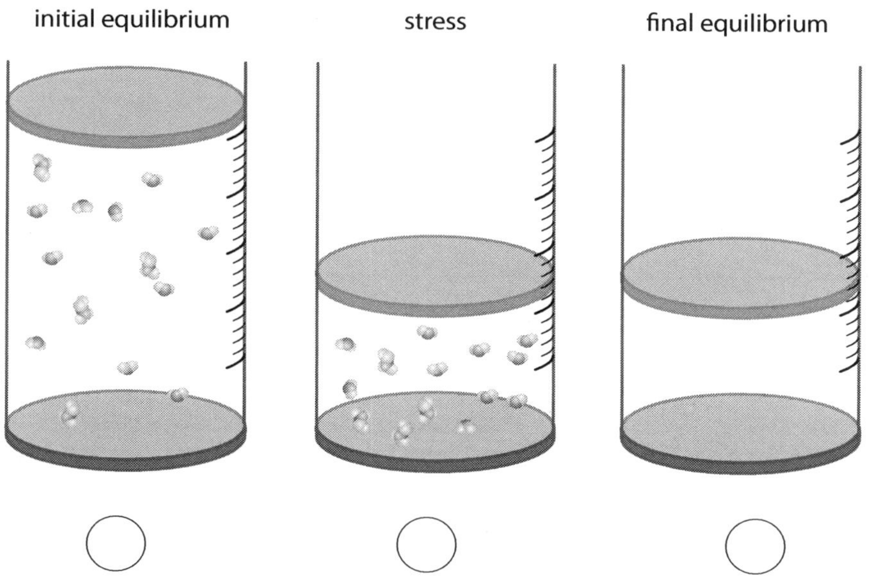

Results and Discussion

1. In response to the compression, the number of NO_2 molecules ______________ and the number of N_2O_4 molecules ______________.

2. Describe the molecules' behavior when the reaction in the syringe is at equilibrium.

3. How would the color of the equilibrium mixture change when the syringe is plunged into an ice bath? Explain.

2.3 Review Questions

1. Consider the following equilibrium: $Fe^{3+}(aq) + SCN^-(aq) \rightleftharpoons FeSCN^{2+}(aq)$
   (a) In which direction will the system shift if it is diluted? Explain your answer in terms of Le Châtelier's principle.

   (b) Compare the number and the concentration of SCN^- ions when equilibrium is restored to their number and concentration before the system was diluted.

2. Explain *in terms of forward and reverse reaction rates* how this system responds to an increase in volume.

$$PCl_5(g) \rightleftharpoons PCl_3(g) + Cl_2(g)$$

3. In which direction does the following equilibrium shift when the gas mixture is compressed? Explain using Le Châtelier's principle *and* in terms of forward and reverse reaction rates.

$$2\,C(s) + O_2(g) \rightleftharpoons 2\,CO(g)$$

4. Describe a situation when equilibrium concentrations change but no stress occurs.

5. Complete the following plots. The system is at equilibrium prior to t_1. At t_1 the volume of the system is suddenly doubled. The system responds to this stress between t_1 and t_2 until it re-equilibrates at t_2.

$$N_2O_4(g) \rightleftharpoons 2\,NO_2(g)$$

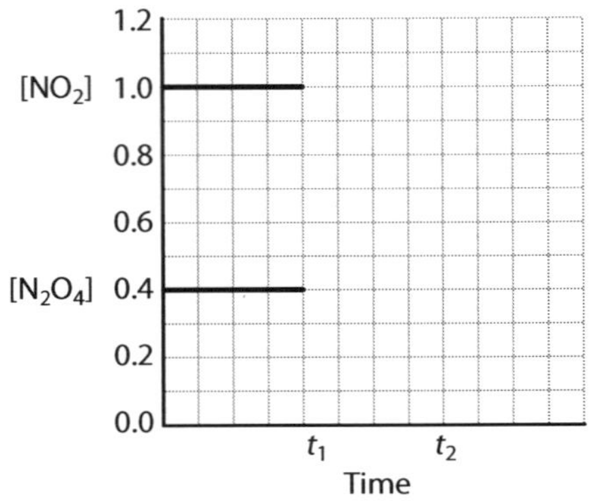

© Edvantage Interactive 2019

6. Show how the forward and reverse reaction rates respond to a sudden increase in the volume of the system at t_1. Use a solid line for the forward rate and a dotted line for the reverse rate. The system restores equilibrium at t_2. The arrow diagram on the right is another way of depicting the same information. You may use it to do your rough work.

$$N_2O_4(g) \rightleftharpoons 2\,NO_2(g)$$

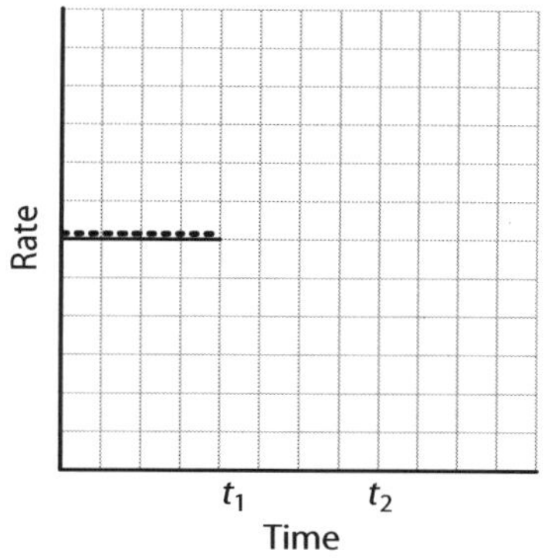

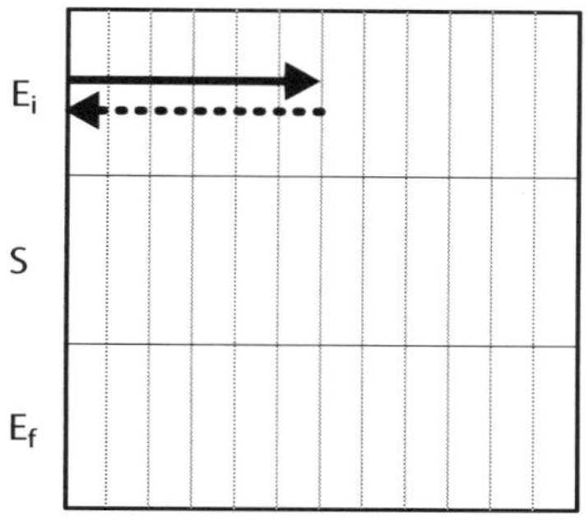

7. The solubility of a substance is its highest possible concentration at a given temperature. Any further solid added to the solution will remain undissolved in equilibrium with the dissolved state. Dissolving sodium sulfate in water is exothermic.

$$Na_2SO_4(s) \rightleftharpoons 2\,Na^+(aq) + SO_4^{2-}(aq) + \text{heat}$$

State whether sodium sulfate will be less soluble or more soluble when the temperature of the solution is increased. Explain.

8. In which direction will the following equilibrium system shift when it is heated?

$$2\,SO_3(g) + 192\text{ kJ/mol} \rightleftharpoons 2\,SO_2(g) + O_2(g)$$

Provide two ways to arrive at this answer.

9. Complete the following plots. The system below is at equilibrium prior to t_1. The system is suddenly cooled at t_1. The system responds to this stress between t_1 and t_2 until it re-equilibrates at t_2.

$$N_2O_4(g) + 57\text{ kJ} \rightleftharpoons 2\,NO_2(g)$$

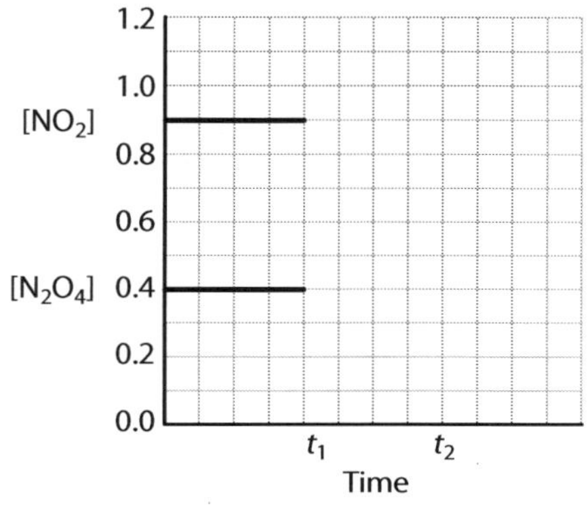

10. Show how the forward and reverse reaction rates respond to a sudden increase in the temperature of the system below at t_1. Use a solid line for the forward rate and a dotted line for the reverse rate. The system restores equilibrium at t_2. The arrow diagram on the right is another way of depicting the same information. You may use it to do your rough work.

$$Ni(s) + 4\ CO(g) \rightleftharpoons Ni(CO)_4(g) \qquad \Delta H = -603\ kJ/mol$$

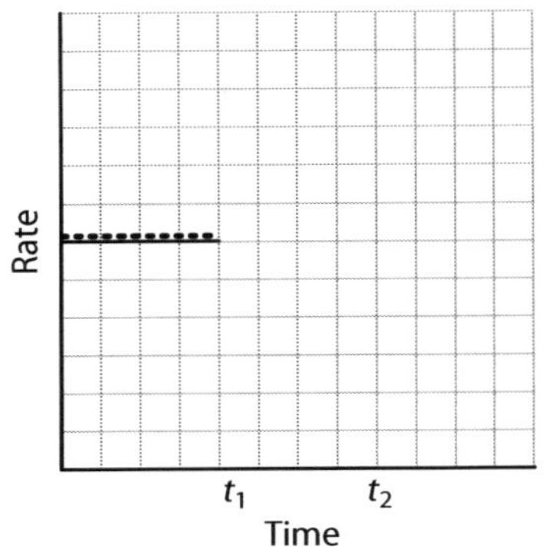

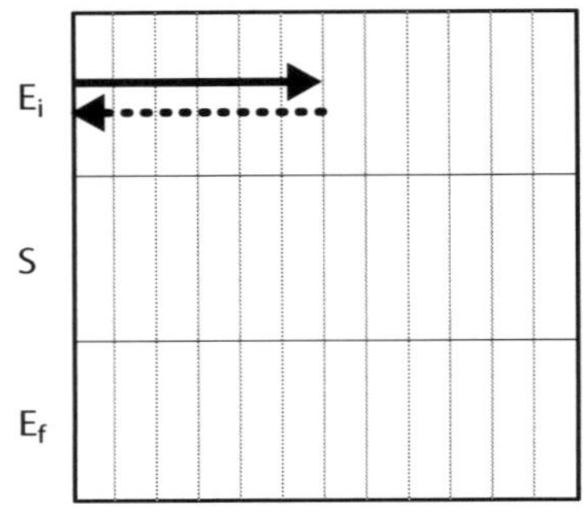

11. $Co(H_2O)_6^{2+}(aq) + 2\ Cl^-(aq) \rightleftharpoons Co(H_2O)_4Cl_2(aq) + 2\ H_2O(l)$
pink purple

A flask containing the above equilibrium turns from purple to pink when cooled. State whether the forward reaction is endothermic or exothermic. Explain how you arrived at your answer.

12. $A + B \rightleftharpoons AB + 16.8\ kJ/mol$

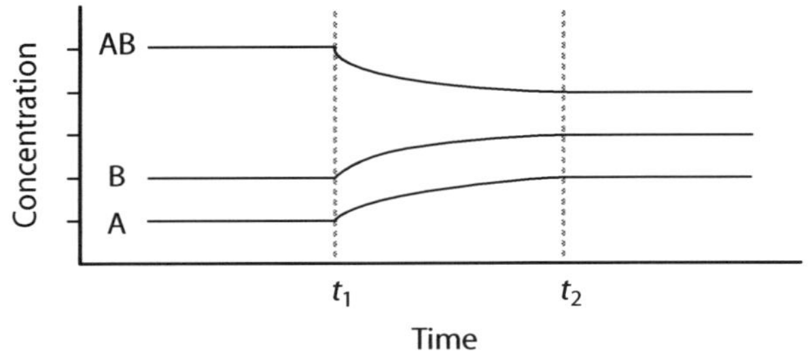

(a) In which direction is the equilibrium system shifting?

(b) What specifically was done to this system at t_1?

 © Edvantage Interactive 2019

13. Explain *in terms of forward and reverse reaction rates* how the equilibrium below responds to a decrease in temperature:

$$N_2(g) + 3\,H_2(g) \rightleftharpoons 2\,NH_3(g) \qquad \Delta H = -92.4 \text{ kJ/mol}$$

14. Why is an equilibrium's endothermic direction more sensitive to temperature changes than its exothermic direction?

15. What conditions of temperature and pressure favor products in the following reaction:

$$PCl_5(g) \rightleftharpoons PCl_3(g) + Cl_2(g) \qquad \Delta H = 238 \text{ kJ/mol}$$

16. Briefly describe the conflicting factors that chemists face when choosing a temperature to perform the Haber-Bosch process.

17. Consider the system below. When equilibrium is restored, how will the number of each type of molecule and the concentration of each substance compare to those before the stress was introduced? Complete the following table using the words "decrease," "same," or "increase."

$$2\,NH_3(g) \rightleftharpoons N_2(g) + 3\,H_2(g) \qquad \Delta H = 92.4 \text{ kJ/mol}$$

		Decrease Volume	**Decrease Temperature**
Equilibrium concentration	N_2		
	H_2		
	NH_3		
Equilibrium number	N_2		
	H_2		
	NH_3		

18. The graph below shows how forward and reverse reaction rates change as an exothermic reaction goes from initiation to equilibrium. Plot the forward and reverse reaction rates for the same reaction at a higher temperature.

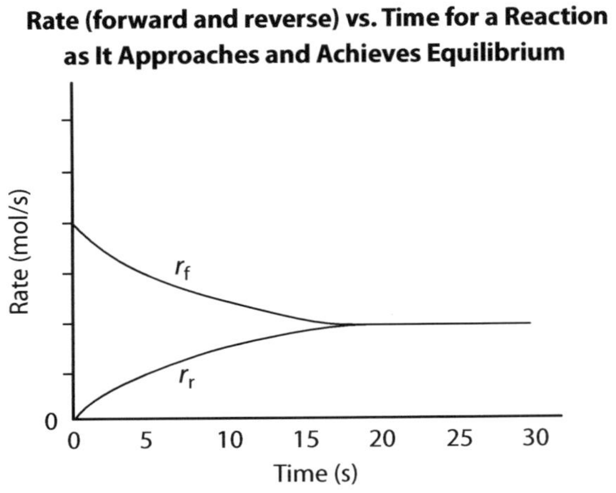

19. Nitric acid is produced commercially by the Ostwald process. The first step of the Ostwald process is:

$$4\,NH_3(g) + 5\,O_2(g) \rightleftharpoons 4\,NO(g) + 6\,H_2O(g) + \text{energy}$$

In which direction will the above system shift in the following situations:

(a) Some NO is added.

(b) Some NH_3 is removed.

(c) The pressure of the system is decreased by increasing the volume.

(d) The temperature of the system is decreased.

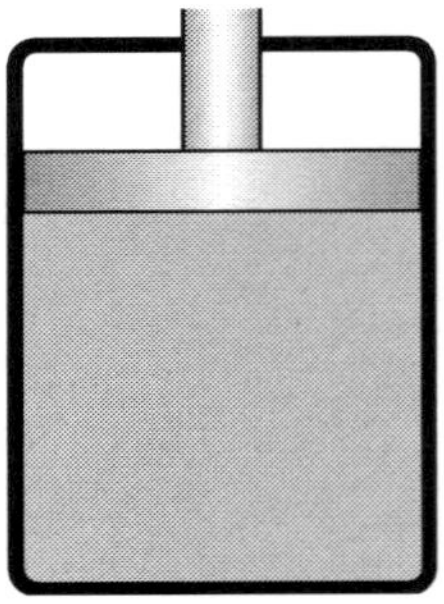

20. A piston supported by gas trapped in a cylinder is a fixed pressure apparatus. As long as the gas in the cylinder is supporting the same piston then its pressure must be constant because it is exerting the same force over the same bottom surface of the piston. If the piston weighs more, then the fixed pressure is greater. Consider the following equilibrium system trapped in a cylinder:

$$PCl_5(g) \rightleftharpoons PCl_3(g) + Cl_2(g)$$

(a) In which direction will the system shift when some weight is added to the piston?

(b) How would this shift affect the apparatus?

© Edvantage Interactive 2019

21. Complete the following review table.

$N_2(g) + 3\ H_2(g) \rightleftharpoons 2\ NH_3(g) \quad \Delta H = -92.4$ kJ/mol				
Stress	**Le Châtelier Predicts**		**Chemical Kinetics Explains**	
	Response	**Shift**	**Effect**	**Net Rx**
Add H_2	some of the added H_2 removed			
Add NH_3		left		
Remove N_2			r_f decreases	
Decrease volume (compress)				net forward rx
Decrease temperature			r_r decreases more than r_f	

22. Holding the temperature and pressure constant when a reactant or product is added to an equilibrium system is easier said than done. Some SO_3 is added to the following system. Its temperature and pressure are *not* fixed.

$$2\ SO_2(g) + O_2(g) \rightleftharpoons 2\ SO_3(g) + 198 \text{ kJ/mol}$$

(a) In which direction will the system shift in response to the added SO_3?

(b) In which direction will the system shift in response to the small change in pressure resulting from the added SO_3?

(c) In which direction will the system shift in response to the small change in temperature resulting from the increased pressure?

(d) In which direction will the system's shift in response to the change in temperature resulting from the system's shift to the added SO_3?

2.4 Entropy Change versus Enthalpy Change

Warm Up

Everything around you can be perceived as being in a relative state of organization or disorganization. For each picture below, check the box that applies.

☐ organized
☐ disorganized

☐ organized
☐ disorganized

☐ organized
☐ disorganized

☐ organized
☐ disorganized

☐ organized
☐ disorganized

☐ organized
☐ disorganized

☐ organized
☐ disorganized

☐ organized
☐ disorganized

What Is Entropy?

Entropy is the amount of thermal energy in a closed system that is not available to do work. The entropy of a substance or a system correlates with its state of disorganization or randomness. This has become most chemists' working definition of the term. Chemists think of **entropy** as a substance's or system's state of disorganization or randomness. Every form of matter and every particle, except a fundamental particle, is a relationship of its components and thus has an entropy or degree of disorder that can be measured. Scientists use the letter *S* as the symbol for entropy. Standard molar entropies are expressed in joules per mole per kelvin (J/K·mol).

Scientists view a more organized — lower entropy — system as one with fewer available variations or fewer *degrees of freedom*. In other words, a more organized state is a more "fixed" state. Simpler things have lower entropies because they have fewer possible configurations or **microstates**. Likewise, more systematic or patterned arrangements have lower entropies because they are more distinctive. There are many more ways your clothes can be strewn around your room than there are ways they can be hung in your closet.

Chemical Systems and Entropy

Atoms are organizations of subatomic particles; molecules are organizations of atoms; and molecular substances are organizations of molecules. A molecular substance's entropy is a function of its intramolecular (within molecules) relationships and its intermolecular (between molecules) relationships. The third law of thermodynamics states that a perfect crystal at 0 kelvin has 0 entropy.

For elements of the same state within a family, the higher the element's atomic number is, the greater its entropy. More electrons provide more variability in positions. For example, the entropies of the noble gases increase as you move down the periodic table (Table 2.4.1).

Table 2.4.1 *Standard Entropies (S°) of the Noble Gases*

Noble Gas	He	Ne	Ar	Kr	Xe
S° (J/mol·K)	126	147	155	164	170

© Edvantage Interactive 2019

Likewise, the heavier and more complex a molecule is, the greater its compound's entropy. As well as having more atoms (each with its own variability), more complex molecules have more possible rotational and vibrational orientations. This is exemplified by the entropies of nitrogen oxides (Table 2.4.2).

Table 2.4.2 *Standard Entropies (S°) of Some Nitrogen Oxides*

Substance	$NO(g)$	$N_2O(g)$	$N_2O_4(g)$	$N_2O_5(g)$
S° (J/mol·K)	211	220	304	356

The entropy of a substance is strongly dependent on its temperature. As particles gain kinetic energy, their motion becomes increasingly chaotic. The physical state or phase of a substance affects its entropy as illustrated by the standard entropies of different phases of molecular iodine shown in Table 2.4.3. Entropy increases from solid to liquid to gas. Particle motion (whether individual atoms or molecules) in the gas state is almost completely random. Particle motion in the liquid state is limited to within the body of the liquid but the particles can still slip past one another thereby allowing many different permutations (orders) of the same particles. The order of the particles is fixed in the solid state, thereby leaving only vibrational motion to provide for different possible inter-particle configurations.

Table 2.4.3 *Standard Entropies (S°) of Different Phases of Molecular Iodine*

Substance	$I_2(s)$	$I_2(aq)$	$I_2(g)$
S° (J/mol·K)	116	137	261

Quick Check

1. How do chemists define "entropy"?

____

2. State the third law of thermodynamics.

____

3. Which of these two elements has greater entropy: Ag(*s*) or Cu(*s*)? Explain.

____

4. Which of these two compounds has greater entropy: water, $H_2O(l)$, or hydrogen peroxide, $H_2O_2(l)$? Explain.

____

Chemical Reactions and Entropy Change

A chemical equation alone does not contain enough information for you to reliably determine whether entropy increases or decreases during the reaction. This can only be determined with certainty by comparing the standard entropies of the reactants and products. The standard entropies are included in the examples below to verify each example's claim regarding entropy change. Standard entropies are commonly available in chemical handbooks and are in the Appendix. Entropy problems in this course are therefore restricted to reactions having entropy changes that conform to the general characteristics described here.

1. Entropy Changes in Reactions Involving Gases

Combining particles reduces their number but increases their complexity. The reduced number of particles usually decreases entropy more than the increased complexity increases it.

Entropy usually decreases when gas particles combine into fewer particles.

The entropy of gases is considerably greater than the entropy of solids or liquids. For this reason, the entropy change in reactions involving gases is usually dominated by the increasing or decreasing moles of gas.

In the synthesis of water from its elements, entropy decreases as three gas molecules are organized into two.

$$2\,H_2(g) + O_2(g) \rightarrow 2\,H_2O(g)$$
$$2(131) + 205 \;>\; 2(189) \quad \text{J/K·mol}$$

Solids typically decompose by releasing a gas. Entropy increases in the following example as zero gas molecules are converted into one. The standard entropies show that entropy increases mainly because a gas is produced.

$$CaCO_3(s) \rightarrow CaO(s) + CO_2(g)$$
$$93 \;<\; 40 + 214 \quad \text{J/K·mol}$$

Despite the following reaction being a synthesis reaction, entropy increases because one gas molecule becomes two.

$$2\,C(s) + O_2(g) \rightarrow 2\,CO(g)$$
$$2(5.7) + 205 \;<\; 2(197.6) \quad \text{J/K·mol}$$

If the number of gas molecules doesn't change during the reaction then count the number of atoms that are part of gas molecules. Entropy decreases in the following example as there are 9 atoms (3 CO_2) in reactant gas molecules and only 6 atoms (3 CO) in product gas molecules.

$$2\,Fe(s) + 3\,CO_2(g) \rightarrow Fe_2O_3(s) + 3\,CO(g)$$
$$2(27.3) + 3(213.6) \;>\; 87.4 + 3(197.6) \quad \text{J/K·mol}$$

Recall the caution given in the opening paragraph of this subsection. The standard entropies show that entropy increases in the following synthesis reaction despite six gas molecules combining into four. The phosphorus atoms changing from the solid state to the gas state in a compound with hydrogen has a greater influence on the entropy than the reduced number of gas particles.

$$P_4(s) + 6\,H_2(g) \rightarrow 4\,PH_3(g)$$
$$44 + 6(131) \;<\; 4(210) \quad \text{J/K·mol}$$

2. Chemical Changes

What if a reaction the number of gas molecules doesn't change during a reaction and neither does the number of atoms that are part of gas molecules? In such cases, it may be evident whether entropy is decreasing or increasing by examining whether atoms of the same element are becoming less or more disordered.

A group of items has less entropy when the common items are grouped together. Hanging your white shirts separately from your colored shirts is more organized than any arrangement that combines the two together (Figure 2.4.1). In the example below, nitrogen and oxygen atoms have less entropy when the "like" atoms are combined together than when the "unlike" atoms are combined.

$$N_2(g) + O_2(g) \rightarrow 2\,NO(g)$$
$$191.5 + 205 \;<\; 2(210.7) \quad \text{J/K·mol}$$

© Edvantage Interactive 2019

Figure 2.4.1 *A lower-entropy arrangement of shirts*

Recall that a state's entropy increases with the number of ways it can be achieved or expressed. There is only one way to combine two nitrogen atoms ($^aN^bN$) where the superscripts "a" and "b" tag or distinguish the two atoms. Likewise, there is also only one way to combine two oxygen atoms ($^aO^bO$). On the other hand, there are two ways of combining the two nitrogen atoms with the two oxygen atoms to form NO ($^aN^aO$ & $^bN^bO$ or $^aN^bO$ & $^bN^aO$). Since the product condition has more variations (more microstates), it represents the less ordered system and therefore the one with greater entropy.

Entropy increases when common items split up to form or be part of more groups. In the example below, entropy increases as the oxygen atoms go from being in the same molecule (CO_2) to being in two molecules (CO and H_2O).

$$CO_2(g) + H_2(g) \rightarrow CO(g) + H_2O(g)$$
$$213.6 + 130.6 < 197.6 + 188.7 \quad J/K\cdot mol$$

Sample Problems 2.4.1 — Predicting by Inspection Whether Entropy Increases or Decreases

Predict whether entropy increases or decreases in each of the following and provide your reasoning:

(a) $PCl_3(g) + Cl_2(g) \rightarrow PCl_5(g)$ (b) $Fe_2O_3(s) + 3\,H_2(g) \rightarrow 2\,Fe(s) + 3\,H_2O(g)$

What to Think About	How to Do It
For both problems, consider (in usual order of importance) the following: 1. Changes in the number of gas particles	(a) Entropy decreases because two gas molecules combine into one.
2. Reorganization of atoms of the same element	(b) Entropy increases because there are only six atoms in the reactant gas molecules and there are nine atoms in the product gas molecules..

Practice Problems 2.4.1 — Predicting by Inspection Whether Entropy Increases or Decreases

Predict whether entropy increases or decreases in each of the following and provide your reasoning

1. $2\,FeO(s) \rightarrow 2\,Fe(s) + O_2(g)$

2. $S_8(s) + 8\,O_2(g) \rightarrow 8\,SO_2(g)$

3. $H_2O(s) \rightarrow H_2O(l)$

Natural Thermodynamic Drives

Two thermodynamic "drives" influence an equilibrium's position:

1. the drive toward decreasing enthalpy
2. the drive toward increasing entropy or disorder

Figure 2.4.2 *When the car moves, the book will fall into a more stable position.*

1. The Drive Toward Decreasing Enthalpy

Objects naturally adopt the lowest energy state available to them. This is illustrated by placing a book on its edge in the trunk of a car (Figure 2.4.2). Nobody would expect the book to remain in this position after the car had moved. A slight jostle causes the book to adopt a more stable orientation as it falls onto its face. The book lowers its gravitational potential energy as its center of mass moves closer to Earth. The jostle plays the role of the activation energy in this analogy. This principle applies to all objects including molecules, atoms, and subatomic particles. It is responsible for atoms forming stronger bonding associations with lower potential energy. In other words, chemical reactions tend to proceed in the exothermic direction.

For example, consider this reaction: $N_2(g) + 2\ O_2(g) + 68\ \text{kJ/mol} \rightarrow 2\ NO_2(g)$

The tendency toward decreasing enthalpy (energy) pushes this reaction in the exothermic direction toward reactants (Figure 2.4.3).

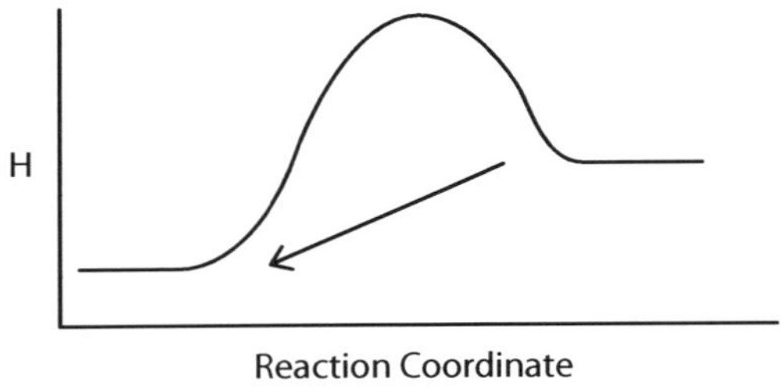

Figure 2.4.3 *Chemical reactions tend to proceed in the exothermic direction.*

2. The Drive Toward Increasing Entropy

Randomly moving objects such as liquid and gas molecules become disorganized when left on their own. It takes work to collect such objects and to keep them organized. Diffusion is an example of the tendency of objects toward disorder. Diffusion is the self-movement of chemicals from an area of greater concentration to an area of lesser concentration. If you open a bottle of perfume, its molecules will rapidly diffuse throughout the room. This tendency toward increasing entropy applies to chemical changes as well as to physical processes.

Enthalpy, Entropy, and Equilibrium

Chemical reactions are driven toward minimum or decreasing enthalpy and maximum or increasing entropy. If both drives are toward products then the reaction, having no opposition, will achieve an equilibrium position far to the right. If both drives are toward reactants, the forward reaction barely gets going before establishing equilibrium with a position far to the left. From a thermodynamic perspective, equilibria with a "reasonable" proportion of both reactants and products develop as a compromise between the two drives when they oppose each other.

> If the drive toward increasing entropy opposes the drive toward decreasing enthalpy, an equilibrium will develop with a "reasonable" proportion of both reactants and products.

Consider the following two examples:

$2\ CO_2(g) + 566\ \text{kJ/mol} \rightarrow 2\ CO(g) + O_2(g)$	$2\ H_2(g) + O_2(g) \rightarrow 2\ H_2O(g) + 483.6\ \text{kJ/mol}$
Decreasing enthalpy favors reactants. ←	Decreasing enthalpy favors products. →
→ Increasing entropy favors products.	← Increasing entropy favors reactants.

 © Edvantage Interactive 2019

Figure 2.4.4 *The low enthalpy–low entropy option for water's movement*

The movement of rainwater is a good thermodynamic model of equilibrium. Water flows downhill and also seeps outward. Consider how rain distributes itself on a street. Some water covers the street but some also collects in the gutters and into puddles (Figure 2.4.4). The puddles and gutters are the low enthalpy–low entropy option while the street surface is the high enthalpy–high entropy option.

Figure 2.4.5 shows the four possible enthalpy-entropy combinations that could occur in a chemical reaction. Both the enthalpy and entropy could increase, they could both decrease, or one could increase and one could decrease. Although Figure 2.4.5 nicely lays out every possible thermodynamic scenario for reactions, there is absolutely no benefit to memorizing it. The thermodynamic drives themselves can easily be applied to any reaction rather than applying a table derived from them.

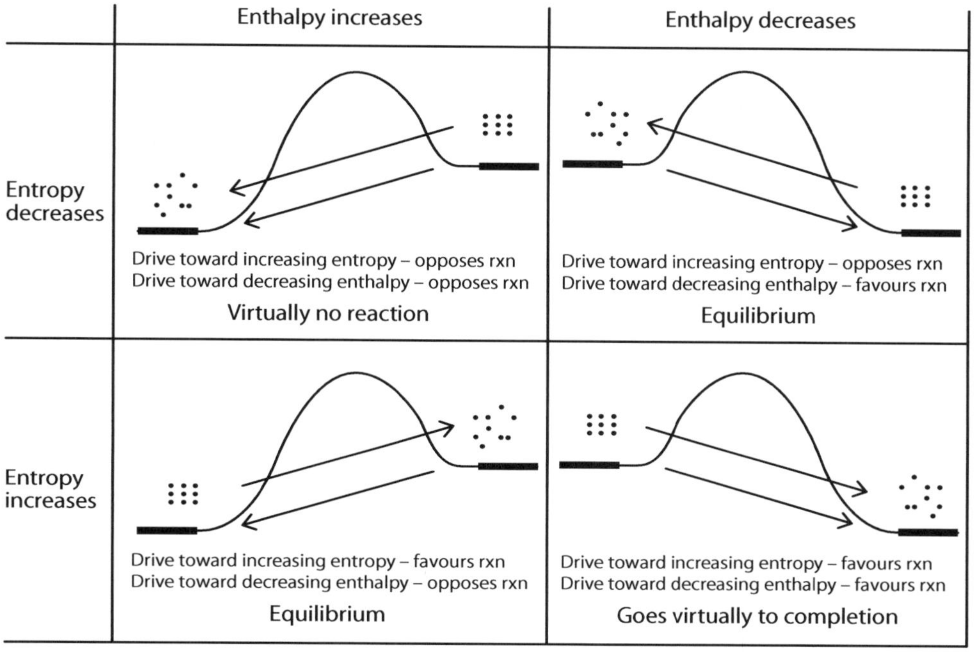

Figure 2.4.5 *The four thermodynamic categories of chemical reactions*

Why does a reaction not go entirely to completion when both drives are toward products? Maximum entropy is achieved just short of the completed reaction because even if the entropy of the products is much greater than the entropy of the reactants, a mixture containing a very small proportion of reactants will have a greater entropy than products alone. Chemists may say that such a reaction "goes to completion" because the equilibrium mixture consists of very nearly pure products.

Likewise, even if both drives are toward reactants, a mixture containing a very small proportion of products will still have greater entropy than the reactants alone. Chemists may say that such a reaction "does not occur" because the equilibrium mixture consists of very nearly pure reactants.

The relationship between enthalpy, entropy, and equilibrium facilitates a popular series of questions where students are directly or indirectly provided with two of these features of a reaction and asked for the third.

Enthalpy, Entropy, and Spontaneity

The spontaneity of a reaction is frequently a concern for chemists. A **spontaneous process** is one that happens "on its own" with no outside intervention.

> Chemical systems move spontaneously toward equilibrium.

Sample Problem 2.4.2(a) — Predicting an Equilibrium's Position from Its Thermodynamics

State whether the following reaction will achieve *equilibrium* (with a reasonable proportion of reactants and products), go nearly to *completion*, or virtually *not occur*.

$$N_2(g) + 3\,H_2(g) \rightarrow 2\,NH_3(g) \quad \Delta H = -92 \text{ kJ/mol}$$

What to Think About

1. Consider the two thermodynamic drives:
   - The drive toward increasing entropy is toward reactants.
   - The drive toward decreasing enthalpy is toward products.

How to Do It

Since the two drives are opposing each other, the reaction will achieve equilibrium with a reasonable proportion of reactants and products.

Sample Problem 2.4.2(b) — Predicting an Equilibrium's Thermodynamics from Its Position

The following equilibrium has a reasonable proportion of reactants and products. State whether the forward reaction is endothermic or exothermic.

$$C(s) + H_2O(g) \rightleftharpoons H_2(g) + CO(g)$$

What to Think About

1. Determine from the equilibrium position whether the drives are opposed, both toward reactants, or both toward products.
2. By inspection, determine whether entropy is increasing or decreasing.
3. Decide whether the reaction is endothermic or exothermic from steps 1 and 2.

How to Do It

The two thermodynamic drives are opposed because the reaction establishes equilibrium with a reasonable proportion of reactants and products.

Entropy is increasing as one gas molecule reacts to produce two gas molecules.

The drives are opposed and the drive toward increasing entropy is toward products. Therefore the drive toward decreasing enthalpy must be toward reactants: the reaction is endothermic.

Practice Problems 2.4.2 — Predicting an Equilibrium's Position from Its Thermodynamics or Vice Versa

1. State whether the following reaction will achieve *equilibrium* (with a reasonable proportion of reactants and products), go nearly to *completion*, or almost *not occur*. $3\,O_2(g) \rightleftharpoons 2\,O_3(g)$ $\Delta H = +285$ kJ/mol

2. The following reaction establishes equilibrium with a reasonable proportion of reactants and products. State whether this reaction is endothermic or exothermic. $CO(g) + H_2O(g) \rightleftharpoons CO_2(g) + H_2(g)$

3. The following equilibrium has a reasonable proportion of reactants and products. State whether entropy increases or decreases during the forward reaction. $CH_2O(g) + O_2(g) \rightleftharpoons CO_2(g) + H_2O(g)$ $\Delta H = -518$ kJ/mol

 © Edvantage Interactive 2019

The system's entropy change and enthalpy change both play a role in determining whether or not a reaction is spontaneous. You will learn much more about this in later chemistry courses. Do not confuse whether it's going to happen (spontaneity) with when it's going to happen (how quickly the final condition will be achieved). A spontaneous reaction can occur at a tediously slow rate. Nails spontaneously rust and diamonds spontaneously turns into graphite. Spontaneity is a thermodynamic function and depends only on the conditions at the start and the end of the process. Rate is a kinetic function and depends on the path taken between the two. The situation is loosely analogous to children telling their parents that they will take out the kitchen garbage but when this will occur is an entirely different matter.

2.4 Activity: Imitating Disorder

Question

Can you place some black dots in a matrix so that they appear to your classmates to be randomly distributed?

Background

When people attempt to randomize objects in space or time, they tend to err toward an even distribution. Let's see if you and your classmates can identify which of each other's two matrices contains the set of dots that are actually randomly distributed.

Procedure

1. Attempt to randomly distribute 12 dots within the squares of one of the two matrices below. You may place more than one dot within a square.
2. Randomly place a single dot *in the other matrix* by rolling a pair of dice twice to determine the row and column to place the dot in (e.g., a 1-1 roll would place the dot in the upper left hand corner of the matrix). Repeat this technique 11 more times to produce a matrix that actually contains 12 randomly distributed dots.

	1	2	3	4	5	6
1						
2						
3						
4						
5						
6						

	1	2	3	4	5	6
1						
2						
3						
4						
5						
6						

3. Exchange books with 10 classmates. Each time, attempt to identify which of your classmate's two matrices contains the set of dots that are actually randomly distributed.

Continued on next page

2.4 Activity: *Continued*

Results and Discussion

1. Keep a record (𝍸) in the table below of how many of your classmates chose correctly and how many times you chose correctly.

Your Guesses	
Correct	**Incorrect**

Your Classmates' Guesses	
Correct	**Incorrect**

If a person can't tell the difference between the two matrices then there is still a 50% chance that the person will choose the correct matrix. There is only a 17% probability that 7 or more of the 10 people could pick the correct (random) matrix by chance. If this happens, we'll declare your fake "busted." Likewise, if you can correctly identify the random distribution 7 out of 10 times then we'll declare you "randomly gifted."

Each trial tests two things: a person's ability to fake a random distribution and another person's ability to spot the fake. Correctly spotting the random distribution could indicate a "poor" fake or a "good" spotter.

2. Look around the room at your classmates' results and comment on whether there is a relationship between people who are good at faking random patterns and people who are good at recognizing random patterns.

 © Edvantage Interactive 2019

2.4 Review Questions

1. Which substance in each of the following pairs would likely have the greater entropy? Explain.
   (a) $Br_2(l)$ or $Br_2(g)$

   (b) $SO_3(g)$ or $SO_2(g)$

   (c) $Sn(s)$ or $Pb(s)$

2. For each of the following state whether entropy is increasing or decreasing and briefly state your reasoning.
   (a) $2\ NH_3(g) \rightarrow N_2(g) + 3\ H_2(g)$

   (b) $NOCl_2(g) + NO(g) \rightarrow 2\ NOCl(g)$

   (c) $4\ Fe(s) + 3\ O_2(g) \rightarrow 2\ Fe_2O_3(s)$

   (d) $H_2(g) + Cl_2(g) \rightarrow 2\ HCl(g)$

   (e) $WO_3(s) + 3\ H_2(g) \rightarrow W(s) + 3\ H_2O(g)$

3. State whether each of the following reactions will achieve *equilibrium* with a reasonable amount of reactants and products, go almost to *completion*, or virtually *not occur*.
   (a) $4\ NH_3(g) + 5\ O_2(g) \rightarrow 4\ NO(g) + 6\ H_2O(g)$ $\Delta H = -907.2$ kJ/mol

   (b) $N_2(g) + 2\ O_2(g) \rightarrow 2\ NO_2(g)$ $\Delta H = +68$ kJ/mol

   (c) $PCl_3(g) + Cl_2(g) \rightarrow PCl_5(g)$ $\Delta H = -92.5$ kJ/mol

   (d) $S(s) + O_2(g) \rightarrow SO_2(g)$ $\Delta H = -297$ kJ/mol

4. For the following reaction, state whether the forward reaction is endothermic or exothermic, given that the two thermodynamic drives are opposed to each other. Explain your reasoning.
   $CaCO_3(s) \rightleftharpoons CaO(s) + CO_2(g)$

5. Describe the thermodynamics of a reaction that establishes equilibrium so far toward reactants that it is said to virtually not occur.

6. The following equilibrium has a reasonable proportion of reactants and products. State whether entropy is increasing or decreasing during the forward reaction. Explain your reasoning.
$CO_2(g) + NO(g) \rightleftharpoons NO_2(g) + CO(g) \quad \Delta H = +82$ kJ/mol

7. Given that equilibrium is established with a reasonable proportion of reactants and products, in what direction will the system shift when the temperature is decreased? Explain your reasoning.
$2\,SO_2(g) + O_2(g) \rightleftharpoons 2\,SO_3(g)$

8. Why does a reaction that has both thermodynamic drives toward products (the drive toward increasing entropy and the drive toward decreasing enthalpy) not go entirely to completion?

© Edvantage Interactive 2019

2.5 The Equilibrium Constant

Warm Up

A **constant** is a specific piece of information that does not change value, possibly within a set of described parameters. You have already used many constants in your science and mathematics classes. Some constants simply relate one system of measurement to another. For example, there are 2.54 cm in an inch.

1. Pi (π) is a mathematical constant that relates the circumference of a circle to its radius. What is the approximate value of pi?

   ____

2. The speed of light (c) in a vacuum is a physical constant with a value of 3.00×10^8 m/s. What famous formula of Albert Einstein's uses the speed of light to relate energy to mass?

   ____

3. State the name, symbol, and value of a chemical constant that provides the number of items in a mole of anything.

   ____

4. Why is it important to scientists to have accurate constants?

   ____

Deriving the Equilibrium Expression

Figure 2.5.1 provides the forward and reverse rate equations for the following reaction at equilibrium:

$$H_2(g) + I_2(g) \rightleftharpoons 2\,HI(g)$$

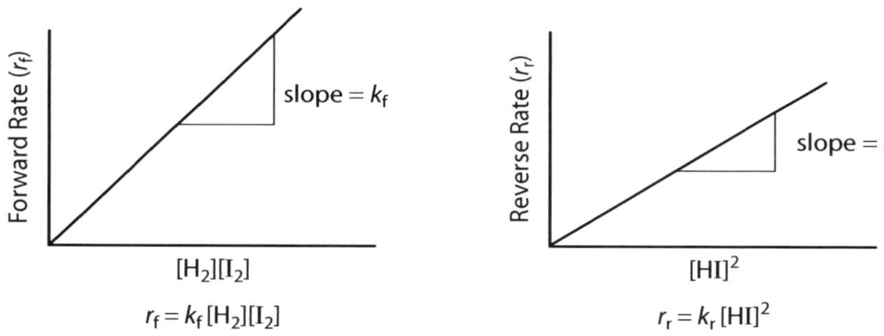

Figure 2.5.1 *Forward and reverse reaction rates for the equation above*

At equilibrium: $r_f = r_r$

Therefore: $k_f[H_2][I_2] = k_r[HI]^2$

Rearranging to isolate the constants we get:

$$\frac{k_f}{k_r} = \frac{[HI]^2}{[H_2][I_2]}$$

A constant divided by another constant equals a third constant. In this case $k_f \div k_r$ provides a constant that chemists call the equilibrium constant, K_{eq}.

Therefore: $K_{eq} = \dfrac{[HI]^2}{[H_2][I_2]}$

Regardless of the initial concentrations of reactants and possibly products, when equilibrium is achieved and the equilibrium concentrations are substituted into this expression, the calculated value will always be the same at any given temperature. Since the rate constants k_f and k_r are temperature dependent, so too is the equilibrium constant, K_{eq}, that can be derived from them. This relationship is the mathematical "hook" we needed to quantify our understanding and descriptions of equilibrium. It provides chemists and chemical engineers with the ability to predict the concentrations that will be present when equilibrium is achieved.

The **equilibrium expression** refers to *the formula* for the equilibrium constant in terms of the equilibrium concentrations of reactants and products. The **equilibrium constant** refers to *the numerical value* provided by the equilibrium expression. The units of equilibrium constants vary too much from equation to equation to be useful and are therefore not required for this course.

> The *equilibrium law* states that for the general equation:
>
> $$p\,A + q\,B \rightleftharpoons r\,C + s\,D$$
>
> $$K_{eq} = \frac{[C]^r[D]^s}{[A]^p[B]^q}$$
>
> where *p*, *q*, *r*, and *s* are the coefficients in the balanced chemical equation.

The equilibrium law is valid for both single-step equilibria and multiple-step equilibria. In other words, the equilibrium expression and constant are independent of the reaction mechanism. Consider the following reaction mechanism:

Step 1	$NO_2 + F_2 \rightleftharpoons NO_2F + \cancel{F}$
Step 2	$\cancel{F} + NO_2 \rightleftharpoons NO_2F$
Net reaction	$2\,NO_2 + F_2 \rightleftharpoons 2\,NO_2F$

If the reaction is at equilibrium, then step 1 must be at equilibrium to maintain the reactants at a constant concentration. Step 2 must be at equilibrium to maintain the products at a constant concentration. The equilibrium expression for the overall reaction can be derived from the equilibrium expressions for each individual step:

$$K_{eq1} = \frac{[NO_2F][F]}{[NO_2][F_2]} \qquad K_{eq2} = \frac{[NO_2F]}{[F][NO_2]}$$

$$K_{eq1} \times K_{eq2} = \frac{[NO_2F][\cancel{F}]}{[NO_2][F_2]} \times \frac{[NO_2F]}{[\cancel{F}][NO_2]} = \frac{[NO_2F]^2}{[NO_2]^2[F_2]} = K_{eq}$$

The most common and reliable means of determining a reaction's equilibrium constant is to simply substitute equilibrium concentrations into the equilibrium expression.

Sample Problem 2.5.1 — Determining K_{eq} from the Equilibrium Concentrations

For the following equation, 0.19 mol NO_2 and 0.64 mol N_2O_4 are found at equilibrium in a 250 mL flask at 92°C.

$$2\,NO_2(g) \rightleftharpoons N_2O_4(g)$$

What is the equilibrium constant for this reaction at 92°C?

What to Think About	How to Do It
1. Write the equilibrium expression for the reaction. As indicated by the notation [ ], K_{eq} values are determined using molar concentrations so it is important to consider the units provided for the reacting species (moles or M) and the container size if the concentrations need to be calculated.	$K_{eq} = \frac{[N_2O_4]}{[NO_2]^2}$
2. Substitute the equilibrium concentrations into the expression.	$K_{eq} = \frac{(0.64 \text{ mol}/0.25 \text{ L})}{(0.19 \text{ mol}/0.25 \text{ L})^2} = 4.4$

© Edvantage Interactive 2019

Practice Problems 2.5.1 — Determining K_{eq} from the Equilibrium Concentrations

1. The following gases are at equilibrium in a flask at 423°C: 4.56×10^{-3} M H_2, 7.4×10^{-4} M I_2, and 1.35×10^{-2} M HI. What is the equilibrium constant for the reaction at this temperature?

   $2\ HI(g) \rightleftharpoons H_2(g) + I_2(g)$

2. A quantity of 3.88×10^{-3} M NO_2 is at equilibrium with 1.73×10^{-4} M N_2O_4 at 60°C.

   $2\ NO_2(g) \rightleftharpoons N_2O_4(g)$

   (a) What is the equilibrium constant for the reaction at 60°C?

   (b) State whether this reaction is endothermic or exothermic by comparing the equilibrium constant for this reaction at 60°C to the constant at 92°C provided in the preceding sample problem. Explain your reasoning.

3. As a slight variation on this type of problem, you could be asked to determine an equilibrium concentration from the K_{eq} and the other equilibrium concentrations. For example, 0.14 M NH_3 is at equilibrium with 0.020 M N_2 at 225°C. What is the equilibrium concentration of H_2 in the reacting mixture?

   $N_2(g) + 3\ H_2(g) \rightleftharpoons 2\ NH_3(g)$ $\qquad K_{eq} = 1.7 \times 10^2$ at 225°C

What Does a Bigger Equilibrium Constant Mean?

Recall our derivation of K_{eq}. For the equilibrium system, $H_2(g) + I_2(g) \rightleftharpoons 2\ HI(g)$:

$$\frac{k_f}{k_r} = \frac{[HI]^2}{[H_2][I_2]} = K_{eq} \qquad \text{but } \frac{k_r}{k_f}\text{, which equals } \frac{[H_2][I_2]}{[HI]^2}\text{, is also a constant.}$$

Presumably, chemists chose the numerical value provided by the first expression, $[HI]^2/[H_2][I_2]$ to be K_{eq} because the product concentration is in its numerator and the reactant concentrations are in its denominator. This means that the size of the equilibrium constant indicates the extent of the reaction's progress towards products.

> The further a given reaction progresses to the right to achieve equilibrium, the greater its equilibrium constant will be.

This appeals to us because it is consistent with the number line, which also has numbers increasing from left to right. Here we are combining the chemical equation metaphor that changing from reactants to products is proceeding to the right with the number line metaphor that proceeding to the right is increasing in numerical value.

Knowing what a bigger equilibrium constant *does not mean* is perhaps just as important as knowing what it *does mean*. Chemists must be careful not to attempt to infer too much from equilibrium constants. The following two points outline important information about interpreting equilibrium constants:

1. It is impossible to infer anything about an equilibrium's position solely from its equilibrium constant. An equilibrium's position depends on the initial reactant concentrations as well as the equilibrium constant. A given reaction therefore has a wide range of equilibrium positions that result from the same equilibrium constant. Consider the following equilibrium:

   $CH_3COOH(aq) \rightleftharpoons H^+(aq) + CH_3COO^-(aq)$ $\qquad K_{eq} = 1.8 \times 10^{-5}$

   If the initial concentration of CH_3COOH is 1.0 M then there will be a 0.42% yield at equilibrium, but if its initial concentration is 1.0×10^{-6} M then there will be a 95% yield at equilibrium. From Le Châtelier's perspective, diluting the system causes a shift to the right to partially restore the osmotic pressure.

2. Even with the same initial reactant concentrations, it is difficult to make meaningful comparisons between the equilibrium constants of different equilibria unless their expressions have identical forms. The following two equilibria have radically different percent yields even when they have the same equilibrium constant (at different temperatures) and the same initial reactant concentrations. The first equilibrium can have a greater K_{eq} than the second one and still have a lower percent yield.

   $Ni(CO)_4(g) \rightleftharpoons Ni(s) + 4\ CO(g)$ $\qquad K_{eq} = 1$

   When the initial $[Ni(CO)_4] = 1.0$ M there is a 23% yield at equilibrium.

   $2\ NO(g) \rightleftharpoons N_2(g) + O_2(g)$ $\qquad K_{eq} = 1$

   When the initial [NO] = 1.0 M there is an 83% yield at equilibrium.

Does an Equilibrium Constant Change When the Equilibrium System Shifts?

When an equilibrium is stressed by changing concentration(s), the new concentrations will not provide the equilibrium constant when plugged into the equilibrium expression. The equilibrium will shift to restore a set of concentrations that once again provide the equilibrium constant. It is after all, a constant.

On the other hand, the shift caused by a temperature change makes all the product concentrations increase and all the reactant concentrations decrease or vice versa so it must change the equilibrium constant. Equilibrium constants are temperature dependent. A shift to the right in response to a temperature change causes the equilibrium constant to increase. A shift to the left in response to a temperature change causes the equilibrium constant to decrease.

Changing the temperature is the only way to change a chemical equation's equilibrium constant.

When a temperature change causes an equilibrium system to shift to the right, its [products] increase and its [reactants] decrease; therefore its equilibrium position also shifts to the right. Conversely, when a temperature change causes an equilibrium system to shift to the left, its [reactants] increase and its [products] decrease; therefore its equilibrium position also shifts to the left.

Table 2.5.1 *The Effect of Stresses on the Equilibrium System, Position, and Constant*

$2\ SO_2(g) + O_2(g) \rightleftharpoons 2\ SO_3(g)$		$\Delta H = -198$ kJ/mol	
Stress	**Equilibrium System**	**Equilibrium Position**	**Equilibrium Constant**
Add reactant	shifts right	may shift left or right	no change
Decrease volume	shifts right	shifts right	no change
Decrease temperature	shifts right	shifts right	increases

 © Edvantage Interactive 2019

Quick Check

1. Consider the following equilibrium: $Ag^+(aq) + 2\ NH_3(aq) \rightleftharpoons Ag(NH_3)_2^+(aq)$
   (a) In what direction will the system shift if some ammonia (NH_3) is added to it? __________
   (b) How will this affect the equilibrium constant? ______________________________
2. Consider the following equilibrium: $PCl_5(g) + 92.5\ kJ \rightleftharpoons PCl_3(g) + Cl_2(g)$
   A decrease in temperature will cause the equilibrium system to shift ________________
   causing its percent yield to ________________ and its equilibrium constant to ________________.
3. Consider the following equilibrium: $C_2H_2(g) + 3\ H_2(g) \rightleftharpoons 2\ CH_4(g)$ $K_{eq} = 0.36$
   True or False? We know that reactants are favored in this reaction because $K_{eq} < 1$. ________

No Liquids or Solids in Equilibrium Expressions

Chemicals in liquid or solid states are not included in equilibrium expressions.

For example, the equilibrium formed when common salt dissolves in water is:

$$NaCl(s) \rightleftharpoons Na^+(aq) + Cl^-(aq)$$

Its equilibrium expression is simply: $K_{eq} = [Na^+][Cl^-]$

While the term *concentration* normally refers to the amount of one chemical per unit volume of a mixture, it is sometimes used to describe how concentrated particles of pure matter are. For example, [pure $H_2O(l)$] = 55.6 M. However, the *concentration* of a pure solid or liquid is fixed by its density while the concentration of a solute is not. Regardless, this is a heterogeneous reaction, and it is the surface area of the NaCl that affects the reaction rate, not its concentration. So why is the surface area of the salt not part of the equilibrium expression? Increasing the surface area by grinding the salt or by adding more salt increases the rate of dissolving but does not affect the equilibrium concentrations because the rate of recrystallizing increases equally.

Although our example was a physical equilibrium, this principle holds true for heterogeneous chemical equilibria as well. A solid's surface area, although affecting the rate at which equilibrium is achieved, does not affect the equilibrium position. Solids therefore do not appear in equilibrium expressions. Likewise, adding or removing solids from an equilibrium affects the forward and reverse rates equally and therefore does not cause a shift.

The same logic applies to pure liquids involved in heterogeneous reactions but liquids involved as solvents are not included for a different reason. For example:

$$Cr_2O_7^{2-}(aq) + H_2O(l) \rightleftharpoons 2\ H^+(aq) + 2\ CrO_4^{2-}(aq)$$

$$K_{eq} = \frac{[H^+]^2[CrO_4^{2-}]^2}{[Cr_2O_7^{2-}]}$$

The $[H_2O(l)]$ is not included in any equilibrium expression. In the above chemical equation, water is a reactant and a solvent for the reactant and product ions. Since water's concentration is nearly constant, we omit it from equilibrium expressions.

There is one situation where liquids appear in equilibrium expressions. When there is more than one liquid in the chemical equation, the liquids dilute each other so these chemicals are included in the equilibrium expression.

Quick Check

Write the equilibrium expression for the following reactions:

1. $B_2H_6(g) + 3\,O_2(g) \rightleftharpoons B_2O_3(s) + 3\,H_2O(g)$ ______________________

2. $4\,HCl(g) + O_2(g) \rightleftharpoons 2\,Cl_2(g) + 2\,H_2O(g)$ ______________________

3. $H_2(g) + Br_2(l) \rightleftharpoons 2\,HBr(g)$ ______________________

4. $CaCO_3(s) \rightleftharpoons Ca^{2+}(aq) + CO_3^{2-}(aq)$ ______________________

The Equilibrium Constant and the Form of the Chemical Equation

The form in which a chemical equation is written affects its K_{eq} expression and constant. To avoid possible ambiguity, chemists should provide the chemical equation with the K_{eq} value.

$$H_2(g) + ½\,O_2(g) \rightleftharpoons H_2O(g)$$

At a particular temperature, 2.0 mol H_2, 4.0 mol O_2, and 12.0 mol H_2O are discovered at equilibrium in a 1.0 L flask.

$$K_{eq} = \frac{[H_2O]}{[H_2][O_2]^{½}} = \frac{12.0}{(2.0)(4.0)^{½}} = 3.0$$

The same reaction has a different equilibrium expression and a different constant when the coefficients in its equation are doubled:

$$2\,H_2(g) + O_2(g) \rightleftharpoons 2\,H_2O(g)$$

$$K_{eq} = \frac{[H_2O]^2}{[H_2]^2[O_2]} = \frac{(12.0)^2}{(2.0)^2(4.0)} = 9.0$$

The exact same equilibrium concentrations, when substituted into the new expression, provide a value that is the square of the original chemical equation's constant. Doubling a chemical equation's coefficients has the effect of squaring its K_{eq}. This is reasonable since the coefficients in the chemical equation appear as powers in the equilibrium expression.

Reversing a chemical equation has the effect of inverting its equilibrium expression and constant. The K_{eq} for any reaction is the reciprocal of the K_{eq} for its reverse reaction. Reversing the original equation we get:

$$H_2O(g) \rightleftharpoons H_2(g) + ½\,O_2(g)$$

$$K_{eq} = \frac{[H_2][O_2]^{½}}{[H_2O]} = \frac{(2.0)(4.0)^{½}}{12.0} = 0.33$$

Quick Check

$2\,HI(g) \rightleftharpoons H_2(g) + I_2(g)$ $\quad K_{eq} = 0.018$ at 423°C

1. What is the K_{eq} at 423°C of $H_2(g) + I_2(g) \rightleftharpoons 2\,HI(g)$? ____________

2. What is the K_{eq} at 423°C of $HI(g) \rightleftharpoons ½\,H_2(g) + ½\,I_2(g)$? ____________

3. What is the K_{eq} at 423°C of $½\,H_2(g) + ½\,I_2(g) \rightleftharpoons HI(g)$? ____________

 © Edvantage Interactive 2019

The Reaction Quotient

The numerical value derived when *any* set of reactant and product concentrations is plugged into an equilibrium expression is called the **trial K_{eq}** or the **reaction quotient, Q**. This value tells chemists whether a reaction is at equilibrium and, if not, the direction that the reaction will proceed or shift to achieve equilibrium. If the trial K_{eq} is less than the actual K_{eq} then the reaction must proceed to the right to achieve equilibrium. The reaction quotient's numerator must increase and its denominator decrease until the quotient itself has risen to equal the equilibrium constant. If the trial K_{eq} is greater than the actual K_{eq} then the reaction must proceed to the left to achieve equilibrium. The reaction quotient's numerator must decrease and its denominator increase until the quotient itself has dropped to equal the equilibrium constant.

Sample Problem 2.5.2 — Determining the Direction a System Will Proceed to Achieve Equilibrium, Given its Reactant and Product Concentrations

The following gases are introduced into a closed flask: 0.057 M SO_2, 0.057 M O_2, and 0.12 M SO_3. In which direction will the reaction proceed to establish equilibrium?

$$2\,SO_2(g) + O_2(g) \rightleftharpoons 2\,SO_3(g) \qquad K_{eq} = 85$$

What to Think About	How to Do It
1. Write the equilibrium expression for the reaction provided.	$\text{Trial } K_{eq} = \dfrac{[SO_3]^2}{[SO_2]^2[O_2]}$
2. Substitute the concentrations into the equilibrium expression and solve for the trial K_{eq}. Compare the trial K_{eq} to the actual K_{eq}.	$= \dfrac{(0.12)^2}{(0.057)^2\,0.057} = 78 < 85$
3. Note that, by shifting to the right, the $[SO_3]$ will rise while the $[SO_2]$ and $[O_2]$ fall, causing the trial K_{eq} to increase toward 85 and the establishment or restoration of equilibrium.	Therefore this reaction must proceed or shift to the right to achieve equilibrium.

Practice Problems 2.5.2 — Determining the Direction a System Will Proceed to Achieve Equilibrium, Given its Reactant and Product Concentrations

1. The industrial synthesis of hydrogen involves the reaction of steam and methane to produce *synthesis gas*, a mixture of hydrogen and carbon monoxide.
   $CH_4(g) + H_2O(g) \rightleftharpoons CO(g) + 3\ H_2(g)$ $\qquad K_{eq} = 4.7$ at 1127°C
   A mixture at 1127°C contains 0.045 M H_2O, 0.025 M CH_4, 0.10 M CO, and 0.30 M H_2. In which direction will the reaction proceed to establish equilibrium?

2. The following gases are introduced into a closed 0.50 L flask: 1.5 mol NO_2 and 4.0 mol N_2O_4. In which direction will the reaction proceed to achieve equilibrium?
   $2\ NO_2(g) \rightleftharpoons N_2O_4(g)$ $\quad K_{eq} = 0.940$.

3. In a container, 0.10 M H^+ and 0.10 M SO_4^{2-} exist in equilibrium with 0.83 M HSO_4^-. A buffer is added that increases the concentration of both the bisulfate and sulfate ions by 0.10 M. What happens to the [HSO_4^-] as equilibrium is restored?
   $HSO_4^-(aq) \rightleftharpoons H^+(aq) + SO_4^{2-}(aq)$

Reactants or Products?

It is awkward to call some chemicals "reactants" and others "products" if they are all present when the reaction starts. It is nevertheless convenient to use these terms so chemists write the chemical equation with the chemicals on the left side of the arrow being called the reactants and those on the right side of the arrow being called the products. Which direction the equation is written and therefore which chemicals are called reactants and which chemicals are called products is arbitrary. Of course, once decided, reversing the equation would invert the equilibrium expression and provide a K_{eq} that is the reciprocal of the original one.

An Addendum to Le Châtelier's Principle

Le Châtelier's principle of *partially* alleviating a stress is based on more than one chemical concentration being involved in the equilibrium process. When an equilibrium removes some of an added chemical, other chemicals' concentrations also change along with it. The changing concentrations of these others essentially prevent the stressed chemical from reaching its original equilibrium concentration before equilibrium is re-established. Consider the following hypothetical equilibrium's response to the stress of adding some A.

$$A + B \rightleftharpoons AB$$

If all the added A were removed (by reacting it with B to form AB) then the forward rate would be less than it was at the original equilibrium (due to the decreased [B]) but the reverse rate would be greater than at the original equilibrium (due to the increased [AB]). To re-establish equilibrium the forward rate must be greater than it was at the original equilibrium and therefore all the added A cannot be removed.

Some heterogeneous chemical reactions and physical processes involve only one chemical concentration. When such a system is stressed by changing that concentration, equilibrium is not re-established until the entire stress is removed and the original concentration restored.

© Edvantage Interactive 2019

Equilibria that have only one chemical concentration in their equilibrium expression *completely* alleviate any stress that changes that concentration.

For example, any stress that changes the concentration of the lone gaseous product in the following equilibria will be completely, rather than partially, alleviated.

- Water evaporating and condensing in a closed vessel
  $H_2O(l) \rightleftharpoons H_2O(g)$ $K_{eq} = [H_2O(g)]$
- Calcium carbonate decomposing and synthesizing within a closed vessel
  $CaCO_3(s) \rightleftharpoons CaO(s) + CO_2(g)$ $K_{eq} = [CO_2]$

These equilibrium expressions have only one chemical concentration in them. As this implies, this value is constant at a given temperature. When these systems are stressed by removing some of this chemical, the entire loss must be replaced to restore the reaction quotient back to that of the equilibrium constant.

Quick Check

State whether each of the following equilibria would partially or completely alleviate a stress that changes a reactant's or product's concentration.

1. $CoCl_2(s) + 6\,H_2O(g) \rightleftharpoons CoCl_2 \cdot 6\,H_2O(s)$ ______________________
2. $NH_4Cl(s) \rightleftharpoons NH_3(g) + HCl(g)$ ______________________
3. $CO_2(g) + NaOH(s) \rightleftharpoons NaHCO_3(s)$ ______________________

2.5 Activity: What's My Constant?

Question

How can you determine the mathematical relationship that is common to three sets of numbers? Of course, it's a lot easier to discover the relationship when you know that one actually exists!

Background

Do you think that you could have reasoned or recognized that different sets of equilibrium concentrations have a common mathematical relationship? The Norwegian chemists Cato Maximilian Guldberg and Peter Waage proposed the equilibrium law in 1864 after observing many different sets of equilibrium concentrations.

Procedure

Each set of numbers in the table below satisfies the formula A – B + C = 5.

Set	A	B	C
1	10	6	1
2	3	1	3
3	– 4	2	11

A – B + C = 5 ______________________

Continued on next page

2.5 Activity: *Continued*

1. Each set of numbers in the table below can also be substituted into a common formula yielding a constant. Determine that formula.

Set	A	B	C
1	18	3	9
2	6	22	2
3	5	10	15

Easy

____

2. Repeat procedure step 1 for each table below.

Set	A	B	C
1	3	4	20
2	5	37	3
3	14	24	88

Challenging

____

Set	A	B	C
1	7	13	20
2	0	5	9
3	3	10	33

Really Hard

____

Results and Discussion

1. Briefly describe the method(s) you used to determine the expression for each collection of data.

2. How successful were you and your colleagues at this task?

3. Why do you not need anyone to mark this activity to know whether or not you were successful?

© Edvantage Interactive 2019

2.5 Review Questions

1. At a given temperature the forward and reverse rate equations for the following reaction are as shown (the units for the rate constants are left out for simplicity):

   $2\ N_2O_5(g) \rightleftharpoons 2\ N_2O_4(g) + O_2(g)$

   $r_f = 2.7 \times 10^{-3}\ [N_2O_5]^2$ $\qquad r_r = 4.3 \times 10^{-2}\ [N_2O_4]^2[O_2]$

   Derive the equilibrium constant, K_{eq}, for this reaction at this temperature.

2. A student claims that the coefficients in balanced chemical equations provide the ratio of the chemicals present at equilibrium? For example, consider the following equation.

   $2\ NO(g) + Cl_2(g) \rightleftharpoons 2\ NOCl(g)$

   The student asserts that the equation tells us that the ratio of the equilibrium concentrations will be 2 NO: 1 Cl_2: 2 NOCl. Is the student correct? If not, what do the coefficients represent?

3. Write the equilibrium expression for each of the following:

   (a) $HNO_2\ (aq) \rightleftharpoons H^+(aq) + NO_2^-(aq)$

   (b) $2\ SO_3(g) \rightleftharpoons 2\ SO_2(g) + O_2(g)$

   (c) $4\ NH_3(g) + 5\ O_2(g) \rightleftharpoons 4\ NO(g) + 6\ H_2O(g)$

4. A 2.0 L flask contains 0.38 mol $CH_4(g)$, 0.59 mol $C_2H_2(g)$, and 1.4 mol $H_2(g)$ at equilibrium. Calculate the equilibrium constant, K_{eq}, for the reaction:

   $2\ CH_4(g) \rightleftharpoons C_2H_2(g) + 3\ H_2(g)$

5. A cylinder contains 0.12 M $COBr_2$, 0.060 M CO, and 0.080 M Br_2 at equilibrium. The volume of the cylinder is suddenly doubled.

$COBr_2(g) \rightleftharpoons CO(g) + Br_2(g)$

(a) What is the molar concentration of each gas immediately after the volume of the cylinder is doubled?

(b) Explain, in terms of Le Châtelier's principle, why the system shifts right to restore equilibrium.

(c) The system re-equilibrates by converting 0.010 M $COBr_2$ into CO and Br_2. Verify that the original equilibrium concentrations and the re-established equilibrium concentrations provide the same value when substituted into the reaction's equilibrium expression.

6. A closed flask contains 0.65 mol/L N_2 and 0.85 mol/L H_2 at equilibrium. What is the $[NH_3]$?

$N_2(g) + 3\,H_2(g) \rightleftharpoons 2\,NH_3(g) \qquad K_{eq} = 0.017$

7. A 1.0 L flask is injected simultaneously with 4.0 mol N_2, 3.0 mol H_2, and 8.0 mol NH_3. In what direction will the reaction proceed to achieve equilibrium? Show your mathematical reasoning.

$N_2(g) + 3\,H_2(g) \rightleftharpoons 2\,NH_3(g) \qquad K_{eq} = 1.0$

8. Write the equilibrium expression for each of the following:

(a) $Fe(s) + 2\,H^+(aq) \rightleftharpoons H_2(g) + Fe^{2+}(aq)$

(b) $2\,I^-(aq) + Cl_2(aq) \rightleftharpoons I_2(s) + 2\,Cl^-(aq)$

(c) $CaO(s) + CO_2(g) \rightleftharpoons CaCO_3(s)$

© Edvantage Interactive 2019

(d) $CO_2(g) \rightleftharpoons CO_2(aq)$ (Include each chemical's phase in the equilibrium expression.)

(e) $2\ Na_2O(s) \rightleftharpoons 4\ Na(l) + O_2(g)$

9. Write the chemical equation and the equilibrium expression for the equilibrium that develops when:
   (a) Gaseous chlorine dissolves in water.

   (b) Gaseous carbon tetrachloride decomposes into solid carbon and chlorine gas.

   (c) Solid magnesium oxide reacts with sulfur dioxide gas and oxygen gas to produce solid magnesium sulfate.

10. $2\ NOCl(g) \rightleftharpoons 2\ NO(g) + Cl_2(g)$ $K_{eq} = 8.0 \times 10^{-2}$ at 462°C
    For each of the following, what is the K_{eq} at 462°C?
    (a) $NOCl(g) \rightleftharpoons NO(g) + ½\ Cl_2(g)$

    (b) $2\ NO(g) + Cl_2(g) \rightleftharpoons 2\ NOCl(g)$

    (c) $NO(g) + ½\ Cl_2(g) \rightleftharpoons NOCl(g)$

11. How would each of the following stresses affect the equilibrium constant, K_{eq}, for:

$2\ CO(g) + O_2(g) \rightleftharpoons 2\ CO_2(g)$ $\Delta H = -31$ kJ/mol

(a) Add some $CO_2(g)$?

(b) Decrease the volume of the reaction vessel (at a constant temperature)?

(c) Increase the temperature?

(d) Add a catalyst?

12. Can you infer that reactants are favored in the reaction below because $K_{eq} < 1$? Explain.

$C(s) + H_2O(g) \rightleftharpoons CO(g) + H_2(g)$ $K_{eq} = 0.16$

13. Consider the following two equilibria:

(a) $2\ SO_3(g) \rightleftharpoons 2\ SO_2(g) + O_2(g)$ $K_{eq} = 0.25$

(b) $PCl_5(g) \rightleftharpoons PCl_3(g) + Cl_2(g)$ $K_{eq} = 0.50$

Given that their initial reactant concentrations are equal, can you infer from their equilibrium constants that the first equilibrium has a lower percent yield than the second equilibrium? Explain.

14. Consider the following equilibrium:

$2\ KClO_3(s) \rightleftharpoons 2\ KCl(s) + 3\ O_2(g)$ $\Delta H = 56$ kJ/mol

Compare the $[O_2]$ when equilibrium is re-established to its concentration before:

(a) some $KClO_3(s)$ is added.

(b) some $O_2(g)$ is removed.

(c) the temperature is decreased.

 © Edvantage Interactive 2019

2.6 Equilibrium Problems

Warm Up

Chemists use a simple table called an **ICE table** to help solve equilibrium problems. ICE is an acronym for **I**nitial concentration, **C**hange in concentration, and **E**quilibrium concentration. All the units are molarity (M). ICE tables are like Sudoku for chemists and are fun to solve!

The following ICE table shows a system that initially had 3.0 M N_2 and an unknown concentration of Cl_2. In the system, 2.0 M of the N_2 was consumed before achieving equilibrium. Complete the ICE table to determine the initial concentration of Cl_2. The steps following the table will assist you if you need help.

$K_{eq} = 0.128$	$N_2(g)$ +	$3\,Cl_2(g)$ $\rightleftharpoons$	$2\,NCl_3(g)$
I	3.0	?	0
C	– 2.0		
E			

1. Solve for the equilibrium concentration (E) of N_2. 3.0 – 2.0 = ?
2. Solve for the change of concentration (C) of Cl_2 and NCl_3 using the coefficients in the balanced chemical equation.
3. Solve for the equilibrium concentration (E) of NCl_3.
4. Solve for the equilibrium concentration (E) of Cl_2 using K_{eq}.
5. Solve for the initial concentration (I) of Cl_2.

Solving Equilibrium Problems

There are three related values in any chemical system that develops an equilibrium:
- the equilibrium constant
- the initial concentrations
- the equilibrium concentrations

In equilibrium problems, you will be given two of these values and asked to determine the third. The only two chemical concepts used to solve equilibrium problems are:
- reaction stoichiometry — the mole ratio in which the reactants are consumed and the products are formed
- the equilibrium law — the relationship between the equilibrium constant and any set of equilibrium concentrations

Determining K_{eq} from Initial Concentrations and One Equilibrium Concentration

The coefficients in a balanced chemical equation provide the mole ratios in which the reactants are consumed and the products are formed. Thus, if you know how much the concentration of one chemical changed in reaching equilibrium, you can easily determine how much the others have changed. The C in the ICE table stands for *change* but it can also remind you to pay attention to the *coefficients*.

It's important as well to pay attention to the units provided and requested in equilibrium problems. In this type of problem, you may be given the number of moles and liters, thus requiring you to calculate the molar concentrations, or you may have the molarity provided directly.

Sample Problem 2.6.1 — Determining K_{eq} from Initial Concentrations and One Equilibrium Concentration

A student placed 7.00 mol NH_3 in a 0.500 L flask. At equilibrium, 6.2 M N_2 was found in the flask. What is the equilibrium constant, K_{eq}, for this reaction?

$$2\,NH_3(g) \rightleftharpoons N_2(g) + 3\,H_2(g)$$

What to Think About

1. Draw an ICE table and fill in the information provided in the question.

$$\frac{7.00\text{ mol}}{0.500\text{ L}} = 14.0\text{ M}$$

How to Do It

	$2\,NH_3(g)$ ⇌	$N_2(g)$	+ $3\,H_2(g)$
I	14.0	0	0
C			
E		6.2	

2. Use the coefficients in the balanced chemical equation to relate (in the C row) the moles of reactant consumed to the moles of each product formed.
For every 2 mol of NH_3 that are consumed, 1 mol of N_2 and 3 mol of H_2 are produced.

	$2\,NH_3(g)$ ⇌	$N_2(g)$	+ $3\,H_2(g)$
I	14.0	0	0
C	−12.4	+ 6.2	+ 18.6
E		6.2	

3. Do the math.

	$2\,NH_3(g)$ ⇌	$N_2(g)$	+ $3\,H_2(g)$
I	14.0	0	0
C	−12.4	+ 6.2	+ 18.6
E	1.6	6.2	18.6

4. Calculate K_{eq} using the equilibrium expression and concentrations.
Exercise caution indicating your final answer to the appropriate degree of certainty. ICE tables involve subtraction and addition. In subtraction and addition, the answer must be rounded to the number of decimal places that the least precise piece of data is rounded to.

$$K_{eq} = \frac{[N_2][H_2]^3}{[NH_3]^2} = \frac{(6.2)(18.6)^3}{(1.6)^2} = 1.6 \times 10^4$$

Practice Problems 2.6.1 — Determining K_{eq} from Initial Concentrations and One Equilibrium Concentration

1. The following gases were placed in a 4.00 L flask: 8.00 mol N_2 and 10.00 mol H_2. After equilibrium was achieved, 1.20 M NH_3 was found in the flask. Complete the ICE table below and determine the equilibrium constant, K_{eq}.

	$N_2(g)$ +	$3\,H_2(g)$ ⇌	$2\,NH_3(g)$
I			
C			
E			

Continued opposite

 © Edvantage Interactive 2019

Practice Problems 2.6.1 — *Continued*

2. Equal volumes of 1.60 M Ag^+ and 2.60 M $S_2O_3^{2-}$ were mixed. The $[Ag(S_2O_3)_2^{3-}]$ at equilibrium was 0.35 M. Complete the ICE table below and determine K_{eq}. (Reminder: Whenever you mix aqueous solutions, there is a dilution effect. Mixing equal volumes doubles the solution's volume and halves the concentration of both solutes.)

	$Ag^+(aq)$ +	$2\,S_2O_3^{2-}(aq)$ $\rightleftharpoons$	$Ag(S_2O_3)_2^{3-}(aq)$
I			
C			
E			

3. A sample of 6.0 g of carbon was placed in a 1.0 L flask containing 1.4 mol O_2. When equilibrium is established, 1.2 g of carbon remains. Determine K_{eq}. (Note: Because carbon is a solid it is crossed out in the ICE table but the moles of carbon consumed must be calculated — outside the ICE table — to determine the equilibrium concentrations of O_2 and CO.)

	$2\,C(s)$ +	$O_2(g)$ $\rightleftharpoons$	$2\,CO(g)$
I			
C			
E			

Determining Equilibrium Concentrations from K_{eq} and the Initial Concentrations

The equilibrium law provides chemists with the ability to predict the concentrations that will be present when equilibrium is achieved from any initial set of concentrations. This includes determining the concentrations that will be reached when a stressed system restores equilibrium. In re-equilibration problems, the initial concentrations are created by stressing a previous equilibrium. Such calculations will allow you to verify Le Châtelier's principle.

Chemists solve this type of problem algebraically. There are no questions in this course that require the quadratic equation or synthetic division to obtain the answer. The course is limited, in problems of this type, to perfect squares or to solving by trial and error.

Sample Problem 2.6.2(a) — Determining Equilibrium Concentrations from K_{eq} and the Initial Concentrations

The following gases are injected into a 1.00 L flask: 1.20 mol of $H_2(g)$ and 1.20 mol of $F_2(g)$. What will the concentration of HF be when equilibrium is achieved? (Note: There is no dilution effect when gases are mixed because the mixture's volume isn't increased. Injecting another gas into the same flask is possible because there is so much space between gas particles.)

$$H_2(g) + F_2(g) \rightleftharpoons 2\,HF(g) \qquad K_{eq} = 2.50$$

What to Think About / How to Do It

1. Draw an ICE table and fill in the information provided in the question.

	$H_2(g)$ +	$F_2(g)$ ⇌	$2\,HF(g)$
I	1.20	1.20	0
C			
E			

2. Set up an algebraic solution using the coefficients in the balanced chemical equation to relate the moles of reactants consumed to each other and to the moles of the product formed.
For every *x* moles of H_2 and F_2 that are consumed, 2*x* moles of HF are produced.

	$H_2(g)$ +	$F_2(g)$ ⇌	$2\,HF(g)$
I	1.20	1.20	0
C	−x	−x	+2x
E			

3. Complete the ICE table.

	$H_2(g)$ +	$F_2(g)$ ⇌	$2\,HF(g)$
I	1.20	1.20	0
C	−x	−x	+2x
E	1.20 − x	1.20 − x	2x

4. Solve for *x* using the equilibrium expression and constant:

$$K_{eq} = \frac{[HF]^2}{[H_2][F_2]} = \frac{(2x)^2}{(1.20 - x)^2} = 2.50$$

(i) Find the square root of each side.

$$\frac{2x}{1.20 - x} = (2.50)^{1/2} = 1.58$$

(ii) Multiply each side by 1.20 – *x*.
(iii) Expand.
(iv) Add 1.58*x* to both sides.
(v) Divide each side by 3.58.

$$2x = 1.58\,(1.20 - x)$$
$$2x = 1.896 - 1.58x$$
$$3.58x = 1.896$$
$$x = 0.530\text{ M}$$

5. Don't forget to answer the question!
How could you check your answer?

$$[HF]_{eq} = 2x = 2(0.530\text{ M}) = 1.06\text{ M}$$

© Edvantage Interactive 2019

Sample Problem 2.6.2(b) — Determining Equilibrium Concentrations from K_{eq} and the Initial Concentrations

A 3.00 L flask contains 6.00 M H_2, 6.00 M Cl_2, and 3.00 M HCl at equilibrium. An additional 15 mol of HCl is injected into the flask. What is $[Cl_2]$ when equilibrium is re-established?

$$H_2(g) + Cl_2(g) \rightleftharpoons 2\,HCl(g)$$

What to Think About

1. Draw an ICE table and fill in the information provided in the question.
   E_o = original equilibrium
   E_f = final (re-established) equilibrium

   Adding $\frac{15.0\text{ mol}}{3.00\text{ L}}$ increases the [HCl] by 5.00 M.

2. Le Châtelier predicts that the system will shift to the left to remove some of the added HCl.
   For every *x* moles of H_2 and Cl_2 that are produced in the shift, 2*x* moles of HCl are consumed.

3. Complete the ICE table.

4. Calculate K_{eq} by substituting the original equilibrium concentrations into the equilibrium expression.

5. Solve for *x* using the equilibrium expression and constant and by taking the square root of each side.

   Note that this value corroborates our qualitative prediction based on Le Châtelier's principle. The system re-establishes equilibrium by removing only 4 M of the added 5 M HCl.

6. Don't forget to answer the question!

7. Check your answer by substituting your value for *x* back into the equilibrium expression.

How to Do It

	$H_2(g)$	$+\ Cl_2(g)$	$\rightleftharpoons 2\,HCl(g)$
E_o	**6.00**	**6.00**	**3.00**
I	**6.00**	**6.00**	**8.00**
C			
E_f			

	$H_2(g)$	$+\ Cl_2(g)$	$\rightleftharpoons 2\,HCl(g)$
E_o	6.00	6.00	3.00
I	6.00	6.00	8.00
C	**+x**	**+x**	**−2x**
E_f	**6.00 + x**	**6.00 + x**	**8.00 − 2x**

$$K_{eq} = \frac{[HCl]^2}{[H_2][Cl_2]} = \frac{(3.00)^2}{(6.00)^2} = 0.250$$

$$K_{eq} = \frac{[HCl]^2}{[H_2][Cl_2]} = \frac{(8.00 - 2x)^2}{(6.00 + x)^2} = 0.250$$

$$\frac{8.00 - 2x}{6.00 + x} = (0.250)^{1/2} = 0.500$$

$$x = 2.00\text{ M}$$

$[Cl_2]$ when equilibrium is restored is:
6.00 M + *x* = 6.00 M + 2.00 M = 8.00 M

$\frac{(8.00 - 4.00)^2}{(6.00 + 2.00)^2}$ does indeed equal 0.250.

Practice Problems 2.6.2 — Determining the Equilibrium Concentrations from K_{eq} and the Initial Concentrations

1. In the lab, 4.5 mol of HCl(*g*) are pumped into a 3.00 L flask and heated to 80°C. How many moles of Cl_2 will be found in the flask after equilibrium is established? K_{eq} at 80°C = 0.36

	$2\,HCl(g)$ ⇌	$H_2(g)$ +	$Cl_2(g)$
I			
C			
E			

2. As part of an experiment, 4.00 mol H_2, 4.00 mol C_2N_2, and 8.00 mol HCN are injected into a 2.00 L flask where they establish equilibrium. What is the $[C_2N_2]$ when equilibrium is achieved? $K_{eq} = 5.00$

	$H_2(g)$ +	$C_2N_2(g)$ ⇌	$2\,HCN(g)$
I			
C			
E			

3. The table below shows the molarity of three gases at equilibrium. The concentration of HCl is then decreased as shown. What is the [HCl] when equilibrium is re-established?

	$H_2(g)$ +	$Cl_2(g)$ ⇌	$2\,HCl(g)$
E_o	6.00	6.00	12.0
I	6.00	6.00	5.00
C			
E_f			

© Edvantage Interactive 2019

Determining Initial Concentrations from K_{eq} and the Equilibrium Concentrations

Determining past conditions from present ones is perhaps even more remarkable than predicting future conditions. In solving the previous type of problem, we predicted a future event by determining the concentrations that will be reached at equilibrium from the system's initial concentration. In solving the type of problem covered in this section, we will do exactly the opposite as we travel back into the past to determine what initial concentrations would have resulted in the current equilibrium concentrations. We've outlined one method of solving this type of problem below but many variations exist.

Sample Problem 2.6.3 — Determining Initial Concentrations from K_{eq} and the Equilibrium Concentrations

Some CH_3OH was injected into a flask where it established equilibrium with a [CO] = 0.15 M. What was the initial concentration of CH_3OH?

$$CH_3OH(g) \rightleftharpoons 2\,H_2(g) + CO(g) \qquad K_{eq} = 0.040$$

What to Think About

How to Do It

1. Draw an ICE table and fill in the information provided in the question.

	$CH_3OH(g)$ $\rightleftharpoons$	$2\,H_2(g)$ +	$CO(g)$
I	x	0	0
C			
E			0.15

2. Use the coefficients in the balanced chemical equation to relate the moles of reactant consumed to the moles of each product formed.
For each mole of CH_3OH that is consumed, 2 mol of H_2 and 1 mol of CO are produced.

	$CH_3OH(g)$ $\rightleftharpoons$	$2\,H_2(g)$ +	$CO(g)$
I	x	0	0
C	−0.15	+0.30	+0.15
E			0.15

3. Complete the ICE table.

	$CH_3OH(g)$ $\rightleftharpoons$	$2\,H_2(g)$ +	$CO(g)$
I	x	0	0
C	−0.15	+0.30	+0.15
E	x − 0.15	0.30	0.15

4. Solve for *x* using the equilibrium expression and constant.

$$K_{eq} = \frac{[H_2]^2[CO]}{[CH_3OH]} = \frac{(0.30)^2(0.15)}{x - 0.15} = 0.040$$

$$\frac{(0.30)^2(0.15)}{0.040} = x - 0.15$$

$$x = 0.49\ M$$

Practice Problems 2.6.3 — Determining Initial Concentrations from K_{eq} and the Equilibrium Concentrations

1. NiS reacted with O_2 in a 2.0 L flask. When equilibrium was achieved 0.36 mol of SO_2 were found in the flask. What was the original $[O_2]$ in the flask? $K_{eq} = 0.30$

	$2\ NiS(s)$ +	$3\ O_2(g) \rightleftharpoons$	$2\ SO_2(g)$ +	$2\ NiO(s)$
I				
C				
E				

2. Some HI is pumped into a flask. At equilibrium, the [HI] = 0.60 mol/L. What was the initial [HI]? $K_{eq} = 0.25$

	$2\ HI(g) \rightleftharpoons$	$H_2(g)$ +	$I_2(g)$
I			
C			
E			

3. Some SO_2 and O_2 are injected into a flask. At equilibrium, the $[SO_2] = 0.050$ M and the $[O_2] = 0.040$ M. What was the initial $[O_2]$? $K_{eq} = 100$

	$2\ SO_2(g)$ +	$O_2(g) \rightleftharpoons$	$2\ SO_3(g)$
I			
C			
E			

© Edvantage Interactive 2019

The Equilibrium Constant and Partial Pressures

The equilibrium position of a reaction is characterized by a mathematical value often referred to as the **mass action expression**. For the reaction:

$$dD + eE \rightleftharpoons fF + gG$$

where D, E, F, and G represent chemical formulas, and *d*, *e*, *f*, and *g* are coefficients, the mass action expression is:

$$\frac{(aF)^f(aG)^g}{(aD)^d(aE)^e}$$

where *a* stands for the *activity* of each of the species in the equation.

The activity of a chemical species may be represented by its concentration (e.g., [F]) in the case of species present in solution or as gases, or by its partial pressure (e.g., P_F) in the case of a reaction where all species are present as gases. If the activities are represented by concentrations and the system is at equilibrium, the mass action expression is called an equilibrium constant K_c. If, however, the activities are represented by partial pressures and the system is at equilibrium, the expression is still called an equilibrium constant, but it is represented by K_p. To summarize:

$$K_c = \frac{[F]^f[G]^g}{[D]^d[E]^e} \qquad K_p = \frac{[P_F]^f[P_G]^g}{[P_D]^d[P_E]^e}$$

Note: K_p should always be *calculated* using partial pressures in *atmospheres*.

The numerical values of K_c and K_p are usually different. Their relationship becomes clear if you remember the ideal gas law, which states that $PV = nRT$. Rearrangement of the ideal gas law shows:

Concentration, $C = n/V$ and $n/V = P/RT$, hence $C = P/RT$, thus $P = CRT$

Substitution of *CRT* for *P* into the K_p expression above allows you to derive the relationship between K_p and K_c as follows:

$$\mathbf{K_p = K_c(RT)^{\Delta n}}$$

Because K_p is determined using partial pressures in atmospheres, it follows that the ideal gas constant value, *R* equals 0.08206 L·atm/mol·K. Additionally,

T = temperature in K, and
$\Delta n = (f + g) - (d + e)$ (the difference in the sums of the coefficients for the *gaseous* reactants and products)

Sample Problem 2.6.4 — Conversion Between K_c and K_p

The Haber process for the formation of ammonia establishes equilibrium at 498 K. Under these circumstances, $[N_2] = 0.020$ mol/L, $[H_2] = 0.18$ mol/L, and $[NH_3] = 0.14$ mol/L. Determine the numerical value of K_c and K_p.

What to Think About	How to Do It
1. Determine the balanced chemical equation that describes the equilibrium.	$N_2(g) + 3\,H_2(g) \rightleftharpoons 2\,NH_3(g)$
2. Write an appropriate K_c expression for the equation.	$K_c = \frac{[NH_3]^2}{[N_2][H_2]^3} = \frac{(0.14)^2}{(0.020)(0.18)^3} = 170$
3. Substitute concentrations and solve for K_c.	
4. Determine Δn and substitute into the appropriate equation to determine K_p. (Be sure to apply the exponent Δn to the *entire product* of $R \times T$. Also take care with the *sign* of Δn and substitution of the correct R value.)	$\Delta n = 2 - (1 + 3) = -2 \quad K_p = K_c(RT)^{\Delta n}$ $= 170(0.08206\ \text{L atm/mol K} \times 498\ \text{K})^{-2}$ $= 170 \times 0.000599 = 0.10$ Notice that NO units are included in a K_c or K_p value.

Practice Problems 2.6.4 — Conversion Between K_c and K_p

1. Given the equilibrium quantities stated below each species, determine K_p for the following reactions at a fixed temperature:

   (a) $N_2O_4(g) \rightleftharpoons 2\,NO_2(g)$
   2.71 atm — 0.600 atm

   (b) $CaCO_3(s) \rightleftharpoons CaO(s) + CO_2(g)$
   15.6 g/L — 0.02 g/L — 1.04 atm

2. Given the equilibrium partial pressures stated below each species, and the K_p value at a fixed temperature, determine the missing partial pressure.

   (a) $2\,NO(g) + O_2(g) \rightleftharpoons 2\,NO_2(g) \quad K_p = 1.6 \times 10^{12}$
   6.5×10^{-5} atm — 4.5×10^{-5} atm — ?

   (b) $N_2O_4(g) \rightleftharpoons 2\,NO_2(g) \quad K_p = 0.715$
   ? — 15.8 atm

3. At 500.°C, the reaction between N_2 and H_2 to form ammonia has a $K_p = 1.5 \times 10^{-5}$. What is the numerical value of K_c for this reaction?

4. For which of the following reactions would $K_p = K_c$? Explain your choice.

   (a) $N_2(g) + O_2(g) \rightleftharpoons 2\,NO(g)$

   (b) $2\,NO(g) + O_2(g) \rightleftharpoons 2\,NO_2(g)$

© Edvantage Interactive 2019

2.6 Activity: Visualizing Equilibria

Question

How could you determine an equilibrium system's constant if you were able to count the number of molecules present at equilibrium?

Background

The amount of each reactant and product remains constant at equilibrium because each chemical is being produced at the same rate that it is being consumed. The diagrams below represent the interconversion of A (dark) molecules and B (light) molecules:

$$\text{A (dark)} \rightleftharpoons \text{B (light)}$$

Procedure

1. Each row of drawings represents a separate trial that results in equilibrium. Answer the questions below about the trials.

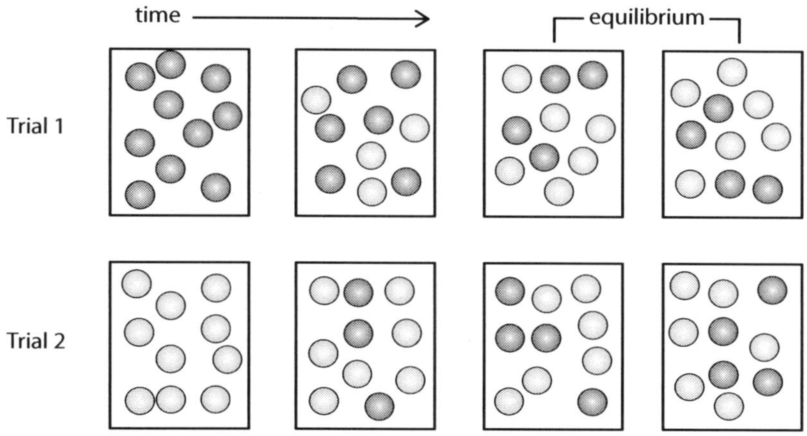

Results and Discussion

1. State a property of chemical equilibrium that is evident by observing trials 1 and 2.

2. What is the equilibrium constant for A $\rightleftharpoons$ B? The container could be any volume because the volumes cancel in this particular equilibrium expression.

3. In another trial, 20 A molecules and 50 B molecules were counted in a reaction vessel. How many A molecules will there be in the vessel when equilibrium is established?

4. After equilibrium was established in trial 2, the temperature was decreased. When equilibrium was restored, there were 7 A molecules and 3 B molecules in the container. State whether A $\rightleftharpoons$ B is exothermic or endothermic.

2.6 Review Questions

1. Complete the following ICE tables.

(a)

	$2\,CH_4(g) \rightleftharpoons$	$C_2H_2(g)$ +	$3\,H_2(g)$
I	6.0	0	0
C			
E		1.5	

(b)

	$N_2(g)$ +	$3\,H_2(g) \rightleftharpoons$	$2\,NH_3(g)$
I		5.0	0
C			
E	2.0		1.0

2. During an experiment, 3.0 mol of NO_2 are injected into a 1.0 L flask at 55°C. At equilibrium, the flask contains 1.2 mol of N_2O_4.

   $2\,NO_2(g) \rightleftharpoons N_2O_4(g)$

   (a) What is the $[NO_2]$ at equilibrium?

   (b) What is K_{eq} for this reaction at 55°C?

3. Equal volumes of 3.60 M A^{2+} and 6.80 M B^- are mixed. After the reaction, equilibrium is established with $[B^-] = 0.40$ M.

   $A^{2+}(aq) + 3B^-(aq) \rightleftharpoons AB_3^-(aq)$

   (a) What is the $[A^{2+}]$ at equilibrium?

   (b) Determine K_{eq}.

© Edvantage Interactive 2019

4. Complete the following ICE tables:

(a)

$K_{eq} = 1.20$	$H_2(g)$ +	$C_2N_2(g)$ ⇌	$2\ HCN(g)$
I			0
C			
E	5.0	1.5	

(b)

$K_{eq} = 1.20$	$H_2(g)$ +	$C_2N_2(g)$ ⇌	$2\ HCN(g)$
I	5.4		0
C			
E			3.6

5. The interconversion of the structural isomers glyceraldehyde-3-phospate (G3P) and dihydroxyacetone phosphate (DHAP) is a biochemical equilibrium that occurs during the breakdown of glucose in our cells. What will their concentrations be at equilibrium if the initial concentration of each isomer is 0.020 M?

G3P(*aq*) ⇌ DHAP(*aq*) $K_{eq} = 19$

6. A 1.00 L flask is injected with 0.600 mol of each of the following four gases: H_2, CO_2, H_2O, and CO.

$H_2(g) + CO_2(g) \rightleftharpoons H_2O(g) + CO(g)$ $K_{eq} = 1.69$

(a) What is the $[H_2]$ at equilibrium?

(b) What is the [CO] at equilibrium?

7. A 500 mL flask is injected with 0.72 mol of C_2N_2 and 0.72 mol of H_2. What will the [HCN] be when the system reaches equilibrium?

$H_2(g) + C_2N_2(g) \rightleftharpoons 2\ HCN(g)$ $K_{eq} = 1.20$

8. A 1.0 L flask containing 4.0 mol of H_2 and a 1.0 L flask containing 4.0 mol of F_2 are connected by a valve. The valve is opened to allow the gases to mix in the 2.0 L combined volume.

$H_2(g) + F_2(g) \rightleftharpoons 2\,HF(g)$ $\qquad K_{eq} = 121$

How many moles of H_2 will be present in the system when it equilibrates?

9. A 250 mL flask containing 1.0 g of excess BN(*s*) is injected with 0.21 mol of $Cl_2(g)$.

$2\,BN(s) + 3\,Cl_2(g) \rightleftharpoons 2\,BCl_3(g) + N_2(g)$ $\qquad K_{eq} = 0.045$

(a) What will the $[BCl_3]$ equal when the system attains equilibrium? (Hint: The math is a bit trickier on this one; you need to take the cube root of each side.)

(b) Would the reaction achieve equilibrium if the flask initially contained 1.0 g of BN(s)? Support your answer with calculations.

10. A flask is injected with 0.60 M C_2H_2 and 0.60 M H_2. Determine the $[H_2]$ at equilibrium by trial and error. Lower the $[C_2H_2]$ and the $[H_2]$ and raise the $[CH_4]$ in appropriate increments until you find a set of concentrations that provides the K_{eq} value when substituted into the equilibrium expression.

$2\,CH_4(g) \rightleftharpoons C_2H_2(g) + 3\,H_2(g)$ $\quad K_{eq} = 2.8$

11. In a 2.00 L flask, 3.00 M H_2, 3.00 M Cl_2, and 7.50 M HCl coexist at equilibrium. A student removes 7.00 mol of HCl from the flask.

(a) What would the concentration of each gas be when equilibrium re-establishes?

	$H_2(g)$ +	$Cl_2(g)$ $\rightleftharpoons$	$2\,HCl(g)$
E_o			
I			
C			
E_f			

 © Edvantage Interactive 2019

(b) Describe how the system's response is consistent with Le Châtelier's principle.

12. A 200.0 mL solution of 0.10 M Fe^{3+}, 0.10 M SCN^-, and 1.8 M $FeSCN^{2+}$ is at equilibrium. The solution is diluted by adding water up to 500.0 mL. Complete the ICE table below and show the algebraic equation that would allow you to solve for the ion concentrations when equilibrium is restored. Do **NOT** solve for *x*.

	$Fe^{3+}(aq)$ +	$SCN^-(aq)$ $\rightleftharpoons$	$FeSCN^{2+}(aq)$
E_o	0.10	0.10	1.8
I			
C			
E_f			

13. In a 500.0 mL flask, 2.5 mol of H_2, 2.5 mol of Br_2, and 5.0 mol of HBr coexist at equilibrium. At 35 s, 2.5 mol of Br_2 is injected into the flask, and the system re-establishes equilibrium at 55 s. Use three different-colored plots on the graph below to show how the concentration of each chemical changes during this period. (This question can be solved algebraically without using the quadratic formula despite not providing a perfect square.)

$H_2(g) + Br_2(g) \rightleftharpoons 2\,HBr(g)$

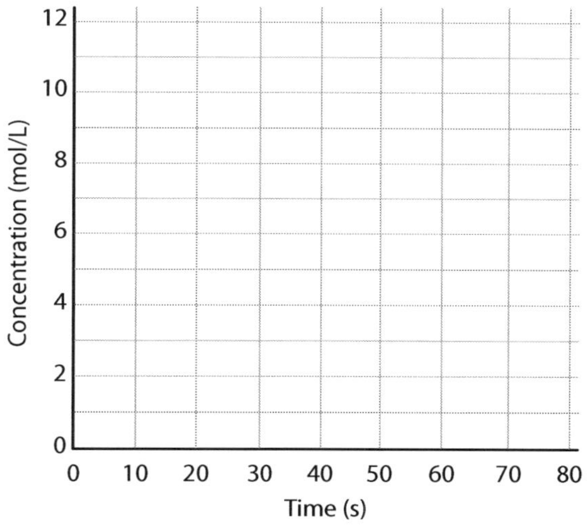

14. Some SO_3 is injected into a 500 mL flask. At equilibrium the $[O_2] = 1.80$ M.

$2\,SO_3(g) \rightleftharpoons 2\,SO_2(g) + O_2(g)$ $\qquad K_{eq} = 3.83 \times 10^{-2}$

(a) What is the $[SO_3]$ at equilibrium?

(b) How many moles of SO_3 were originally injected into the flask?

15. Equal quantities of $H_2(g)$ and $I_2(g)$ are pumped into a flask. At equilibrium the [HI] = 1.0 M. What was the initial $[H_2]$?

$H_2(g) + I_2(g) \rightleftharpoons 2\,HI(g)$ $\qquad K_{eq} = 4.0$

16. Some PCl_5 is pumped into a 500 mL flask. The $[PCl_3] = 1.50$ M at equilibrium. What was the initial $[PCl_5]$?

$PCl_5(g) \rightleftharpoons PCl_3(g) + Cl_2(g)$ $\qquad K_{eq} = 2.14$

17. A reaction mixture contains 0.24 mol of NO, 0.10 mol of O_2, and 1.20 mol of NO_2 at equilibrium in a 1.0 L container. How many moles of O_2 would need to be added to the mixture to increase the amount of NO_2 to 1.30 mol when equilibrium is re-established?

$2\,NO(g) + O_2(g) \rightleftharpoons 2\,NO_2(g)$

18. Write the K_p expression for each of the following equations:

(a) $PCl_5(g) \rightleftharpoons PCl_3(g) + Cl_2(g)$

(b) $P_4(s) + 5\,O_2(g) \rightleftharpoons 2\,P_2O_5(g)$

(c) $CO_2(g) + CaO(s) \rightleftharpoons CaCO_3(s)$

© Edvantage Interactive 2019

19. Calculate K_p for the equilibria in Review Questions 4, 6, and 7 in the previous section. Assume SATP conditions.
Review Question 4:

Review Question 6:

Review Question 7:

20. Consider the following reaction:
$2\ SO_2(g) + O_2(g) \rightleftharpoons 2\ SO_3(g)$ $K_p = 0.14$ at 625°C

If a reaction vessel is filled with SO_3 at a partial pressure of 0.10 atm and 0.20 atm each of SO_2 and O_2 gas, is the reaction at equilibrium? If not, in which direction does it proceed to reach equilibrium?

21. The following graph represents partial pressure vs. time for the reaction between A and B gas to form C gas. Gas A is present in excess. Assume SATP conditions.

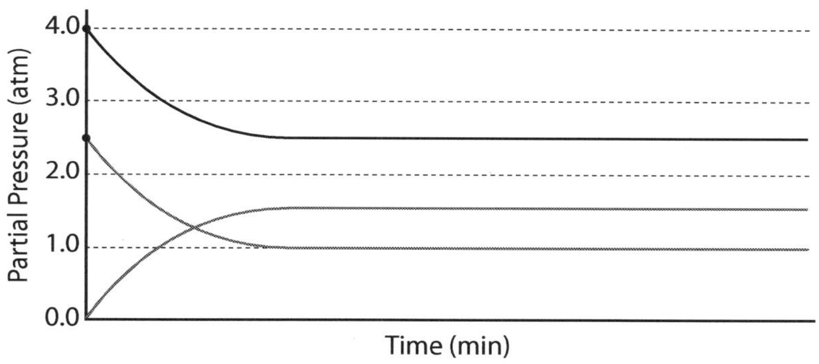

(a) Write a balanced chemical equation for the equilibrium in the question.

(b) Write the equilibrium expression K_p for the reaction.

(c) Calculate the numerical value for K_p for this reaction.

(d) Calculate the numerical value for K_c for this reaction.

22. In a container, 1.00 mol of N_2 and 3.00 mol of H_2 are mixed together to produce ammonia. At equilibrium, the total pressure of the system is 1.8×10^6 Pa and the mixture contains only 50% of the N_2 that was present originally. Calculate K_p for this reaction at this temperature.

23. A lab technician places 0.300 atm of SO_2, 0.400 atm O_2, and 0.020 atm of SO_3 into a 10.0 L bulb. Once equilibrium is established, the partial pressure of SO_3 is found to be 0.140 atm. What is the value of K_p for the reaction under these conditions?

24. $PCl_5(g)$ decomposes into $PCl_3(g)$ and $Cl_2(g)$. A pure sample of phosphorus pentachloride is placed into an evacuated 1.00 L glass bulb. The temperature remains constant while the pure sample decomposes as shown below:

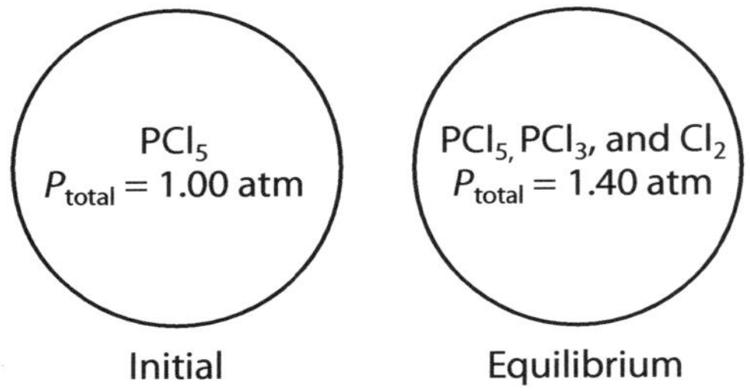

(a) Explain why the pressure increases in the container as the reaction reaches equilibrium.

(b) Determine the partial pressure of each gas when the system reaches equilibrium.

(c) Calculate K_p for the equilibrium system.

(d) If the decomposition were to go to completion, what would the total pressure be in the system?

© Edvantage Interactive 2019

3 Thermodynamics

This chapter focuses on the following AP Units from the College Board:

Unit 6: Thermodynamics
Unit 9: Applications of Thermodynamics.

By the end of this chapter, you should be able to do the following:

- Use representations and models to predict the sign and relative magnitude of the entropy change associated with chemical or physical processes
- Predict, either quantitatively or qualitatively, whether or not a physical or chemical process is thermodynamically favored by determination of the signs of both $\Delta H°$ and $\Delta S°$, and calculation or estimation of $\Delta G°$ when needed
- Determine whether a chemical or physical process is thermodynamically favorable by calculating the change in standard Gibbs free energy
- Explain why a thermodynamically favored chemical reaction may not produce large amounts of product based on consideration of both initial conditions and kinetic effects, or why a thermodynamically unfavored chemical reaction can produce large amounts of product for certain sets of initial conditions

By the end of this chapter, you should know the meaning of these **key terms**:

- endergonic
- exergonic
- Gibbs free energy
- microstates
- positional disorder
- second law of thermodynamics
- thermal disorder
- thermodynamically favorable
- third law of thermodynamics

Thermodynamics is the study of heat and temperature and their relation to energy and work. It includes concepts such as entropy and pressure.

3.1 Entropy — A Quantitative Treatment

Warm Up

In the chapter on Entropy Change versus Enthalpy Change) we dealt with the impact of ΔS and ΔH on spontaneity. we also know that heat flows from a region of high energy to a region of low energy. This might lead to the conclusion that spontaneous change must be exothermic.

1. Consider the following change occurring at room temperature:

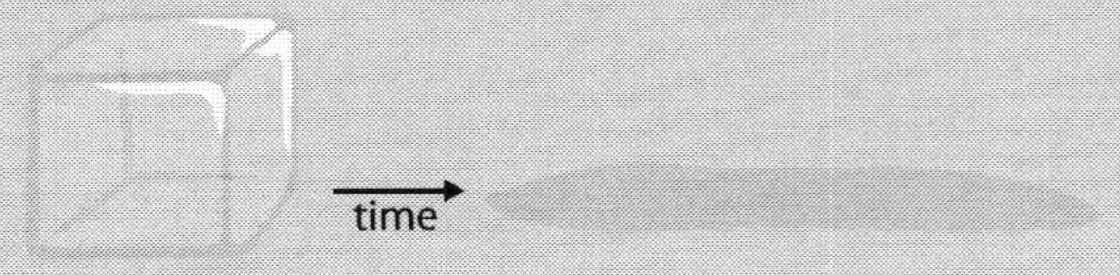

   (a) Is this change spontaneous (did it occur without outside intervention)? _______
   (b) Is this process endothermic or exothermic? _______________
   (c) What is the sign of ΔH? _______

2. Consider the change at a molecular level:

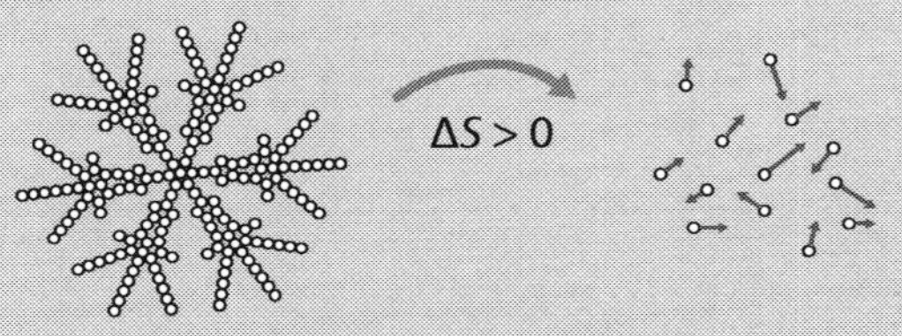

   (a) What is the sign for ΔS? _______
   (b) Is this process enthalpy driven or entropy driven? _____________

   Explain. ____

   ____

The First Law of Thermodynamics

Energy is conserved — never created or destroyed. When energy is released by an exothermic change, the potential energy stored in chemical bonds is converted to kinetic energy, which is the energy of motion of atoms and molecules. As the kinetic energy of the atoms and molecules in the system and the surroundings increases, the temperature rises. Sometimes we speak of exothermic changes as "giving off heat." Heat is the energy transferred between a system and its surroundings.

Spontaneous Change

When thermodynamicists say that a reaction is spontaneous, they mean that the reaction will occur without any outside intervention. They do not mean the reaction occurs rapidly. We studied the rate or speed of a reaction in Unit 1: Reaction Kinetics.

In contrast, a non-spontaneous event can continue only as long as it receives some sort of outside assistance. All non-spontaneous events occur at the expense of spontaneous ones. They can occur only when some spontaneous change occurs first.

© Edvantage Interactive 2019

Enthalpy and Spontaneity

When a change lowers the potential energy of a system, it tends to occur spontaneously. Fuels evolve heat as they combust to form H_2O and CO_2 and convert the potential energy in the bonds of the reactants to heat. Since a change that lowers the potential energy of a system is exothermic, we can say that exothermic changes have a tendency to occur spontaneously.

While many spontaneous changes are indeed exothermic, there are common examples of spontaneous endothermic changes including the melting of ice, the vaporization of water, and the dissolving of most salts in water to form aqueous solutions. Since each of these events is both endothermic AND spontaneous, they must have some other factor in common that allows them to overcome the unfavorable energy change. Careful examination shows that in each of these events, there is an increase in the randomness or disorder of the system. These observations led to the development of the **second law of thermodynamics**.

Figure 3.1.1 *Every spontaneous process increases the entropy of the universe.*

> **Second law of thermodynamics:** The entropy of the universe increases with every spontaneous process.

Quick Check

1. Use qualitative reasoning to decide which of the two options in each of these examples will occur spontaneously:

   (a) A mole of ice at 0°C *or* a mole of liquid water at the same temperature

   ____

   (b) Solid sodium chloride in the bottom of a bucket of water *or* a solution of the salt in water

   ____

   (c) A collection of jigsaw pieces *or* the completed puzzle

   ____

   (d) One kilogram of raw rubber *or* 1 kg of vulcanized rubber (Vulcanized rubber is rubber that is polymerized into long chains; vulcanized rubber is used to make tires.)

   ____

   (e) A pack of cards arranged in suits *or* a pack of cards that is randomly shuffled

   ____

The Boltzmann Equation

Ludwig Boltzmann, a famous physicist, studied fluid mechanics in the late 1800s. During this time, Boltzmann determined the probability that a group of particles might occupy a particular set of positions in space at any particular time. These sets of positions are referred to as **microstates**. It has been suggested that this term, microstates (states), may have led to the symbol ***S*** being selected to represent entropy. Boltzmann noted that entropy is directly proportional to the natural log of the number of microstates available. In 1872, Boltzmann derived his famous equation to represent entropy:

$$\boldsymbol{S = k_B \ln W}$$

where S = entropy

k_B = Boltzmann's constant = $R/N_A = \dfrac{8.314 \text{ L·kPa/mol·K}}{6.02 \times 10^{23} \text{ mol}^{-1}} = 1.38 \times 10^{-23}$ J/K

W = number of microstates

In a pure crystal at absolute zero (0 K), the particles orient themselves in only one possible microstate. At absolute zero, the entropy is $S = 1.38 \times 10^{-23}$ J/K (ln 1). Since the natural log of 1 = 0, the *entropy of a pure crystal at 0 K equals zero*. This is the **third law of thermodynamics**.

Third law of thermodynamics: The entropy of a *pure crystal* at absolute zero is zero ($S = 1.38 \times 10^{-23}$ J/K × ln (1) = 0).

We know that increasing the number of electrons in an element or increasing the number of atoms in a molecule leads to an increase in entropy. More electrons or atoms mean more possible microstates and therefore a higher entropy according to the Boltzmann equation.

Dependence of Entropy on Temperature

The second law of thermodynamics states "the entropy of the universe increases with every spontaneous change." The "universe" is the *system* plus the *surroundings* and the entropy of a system is a quantitative measure of the disorder or randomness within a system. There are two kinds of disorder in a system: **positional disorder**, depending on the arrangement of particles (molecules and atoms) in space, and **thermal disorder**, depending on how the total energy is distributed among all the particles. The more random the distribution of particles in space, the higher the entropy. The more randomly energy is distributed among the particles, the greater the entropy.

Table 3.1.1 shows all possible arrangements for two identical particles among three relative energy levels. The most likely total energy is 2 kJ. Maximizing thermal disorder does not necessarily lead to maximum overall energy.

Table 3.1.1 *All possible two-particle arrangements among three relative energy levels*

Energy Level	Particle Arrangements					
2 kJ			X		X	XX
1 kJ		X		XX	X	
0 kJ	XX	X	X			
Total energy	0 kJ	1 kJ	2 kJ	2 kJ	3 kJ	4 kJ

Adding heat to a system results in greater disorder and, therefore, greater entropy. The entropy increase is directly proportional to the amount of heat added. However, the increase in entropy is more significant when we add heat to a system at a lower temperature where little disorder exists, rather than at high temperature where there is already substantial disorder. For a given quantity of heat, the entropy change is inversely proportional to the temperature at which we add the heat. Thus entropy can be determined as:

$$\Delta S_{surroundings} = \frac{q}{T} = \frac{-\Delta H}{T}$$

The equation above shows that entropy has units of energy divided by temperature (J/K). If an entropy change is being calculated for a particular quantity of material undergoing a physical or chemical change, the units may be J/K·mol.

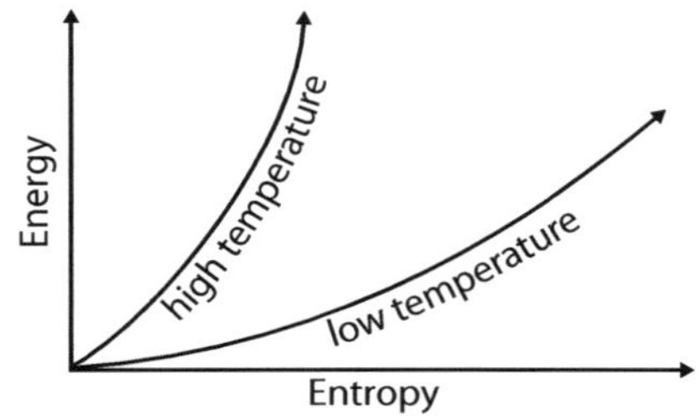

Figure 3.1.2 *The change in entropy (ΔS) is most noticeable at a low temperature.*

© Edvantage Interactive 2019

Quick Check

1. When 1.0 mole of steam condenses to form 1.0 mole of liquid water at 100.0° C, 40.7 kJ of heat is released. What is ΔS for the surroundings?

2. Select the example with greater entropy in each case.

   (a) $F_2(g)$ or $Cl_2(g)$

   (b) $CO_2(g)$ or $CO(g)$

   (c)

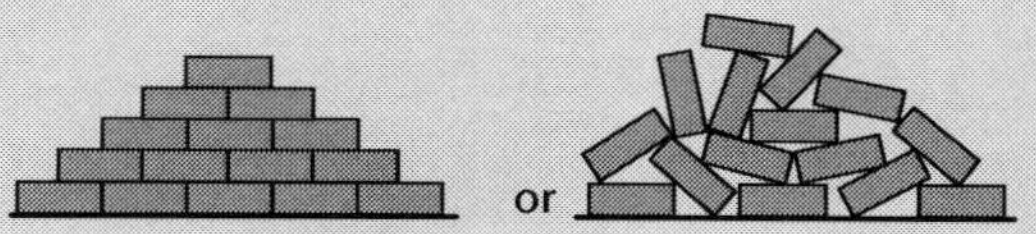

Entropy Is a State Function

We know the third law of thermodynamics states that at absolute zero, the entropy of a pure crystal is equal to zero joules. Mathematically, we can state:

$$S = 0 \text{ J when } W = 1 \text{ at } T = 0 \text{ K}$$

Because we know the point at which entropy has a value of 0 J, it is possible to determine the actual amount of entropy that a substance possesses at temperatures above 0 K. If we determine the entropy of 1 mole of a substance at a temperature of 298 K (25°C) and a pressure of 1 atm, we call it the standard entropy or $S°$. Tables of standard entropies are available, similar to the tables of standard enthalpies of formation used in AP 1. These values are listed in Table A8 in the appendix at the back of this book. (Notice that the standard entropy values of pure elements in their standard states are *not* equal to zero because standard entropy values are not recorded at 0 K.) Once we know the entropies of a variety of substances we can calculate the standard entropy change, or $\Delta S°$, for chemical reactions in the same way as we calculated $\Delta H°$ earlier.

Entropy is a state function — it is not pathway dependent. Therefore, we can use the same logic as that of a Hess's law type of calculation to determine the entropy change for a given chemical reaction. It is important to note that like enthalpy, entropy is an extensive property — it depends on the amount of substance present. This means that the number of moles of all species in the reaction must be taken into account. Hence:

$$\Delta S°_{\text{reaction}} = \sum nS°_{\text{products}} - \sum nS°_{\text{reactants}}$$

Recall that for a process to be spontaneous, there must be an overall increase in the entropy of the universe. If the entropy change of the universe is negative, the process is non-spontaneous. A spontaneous entropy change is positive or in the reverse direction of non-spontaneous change.

Sample Problem 3.1.1 — Quantifying Entropy Change

Urea (from urine) hydrolyzes slowly in the presence of water to produce ammonia and carbon dioxide.

$$CO(NH_2)_2(aq) + H_2O(l) \rightarrow CO_2(g) + 2\,NH_3(g)$$

What is the standard entropy change, for this reaction when 1 mol of urea reacts with water? Is the process spontaneous? The standard entropies for reactants and products are:

Substance	$S°$ (J mol^{-1} K^{-1})	Substance	$S°$ (J mol^{-1} K^{-1})
$CO(NH_2)_2(aq)$	173.7	$CO_2(g)$	213.8
$H_2O(l)$	70.0	$NH_3(g)$	192.8

What to Think About

1. Calculate the change in entropy using the equation:

   $\Delta S°_{rxn} = \sum nS°_{products} - \sum nS°_{reactants}$

2. After determining the stoichiometrically correct entropy values, substitute and solve.

3. Does the answer make sense?
   One mole of aqueous substance and 1 mole of liquid form *3 moles of gas*.

4. What does the answer mean?

How to Do It

Determine $S°$ values for all reactants and products. These are listed in the table given above in this example.

$\left[\frac{1\ \text{mol}\ CO_2}{\text{mol rxn}} \times \frac{213.8\ \text{J}}{\text{mol K}} + \frac{2\ \text{mol}\ NH_3}{\text{mol rxn}} \times \frac{192.8\ \text{J}}{\text{mol K}}\right] -$

$\left[\frac{1\ \text{mol}\ CO(NH_2)_2}{\text{mol rxn}} \times \frac{173.7\ \text{J}}{\text{mol K}} + \frac{1\ \text{mol}\ H_2O}{\text{mol rxn}} \times \frac{70.0\ \text{J}}{\text{mol K}}\right]$

$= 599.4 - 243.7 = 355.7\ \text{J/mol}_{rxn}\cdot\text{K}$

The number of microstates (W) has increased. So we expect a positive ΔS value. ✓

A positive ΔS value is indicative of a spontaneous change

Practice Problems 3.1.1 — Quantifying Entropy Change

1. Use qualitative reasoning (no calculations are necessary) to predict whether the entropy change in each of the following processes is positive or negative. Does the entropy change of the system favor spontaneous change or not?
   (a) The evaporation of 1 mole of rubbing alcohol

   (b) $2\,Ca(s) + O_2(g) \rightarrow 2\,CaO(s)$

   (c) $XeF_4(g) \rightarrow Xe(g) + 2\,F_2(g)$

   (d) The dilution of an aqueous solution of lime Kool-Aid

2. Use the standard entropy table in Table A8 in the appendix at the back of this book to calculate the standard entropy change for each of the following reactions. Is the reaction thermodynamically favorable (spontaneous) based on the $\Delta S°$ value?
   (a) $CaO(s) + 2\,HCl(g) \rightarrow CaCl_2(s) + H_2O(l)$

   (b) $C_2H_4(g) + H_2(g) \rightarrow C_2H_6(g)$

© Edvantage Interactive 2019

3.1 Review Questions

1. Predict the sign you would expect for $\Delta S°$ in each of the following processes. Give a short explanation of why you think it is (+) or (–). Do NOT do any calculations.
   (a) Blowing up a building

   (b) Organizing a stack of files in alphabetical order

   (c) $AgCl(s) \rightarrow Ag^+(aq) + Cl^-(aq)$

   (d) $2\,H_2(g) + O_2\,(g) \rightarrow 2\,H_2O(l)$

   (e) $Na(s) + ½\,Cl_2(g) \rightarrow NaCl(s)$

   (f) Removing medication from bottles and organizing the pills by the day in "blister packs"

2. Predict the sign of $\Delta S°$ you would expect for each of the following changes. Give a short explanation of why you think it is (+) or (–). Do NOT do any calculations.

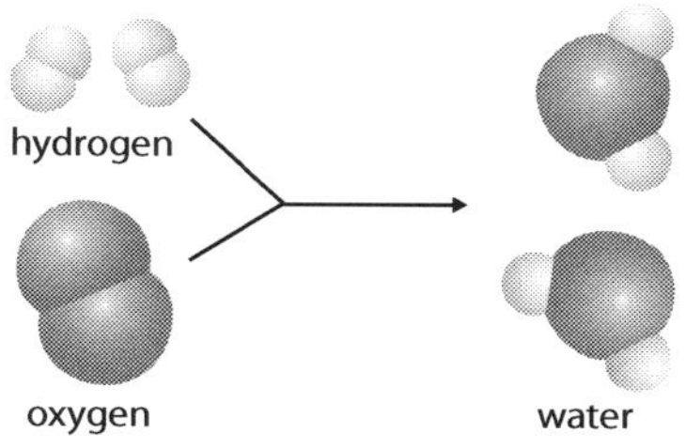

(a)

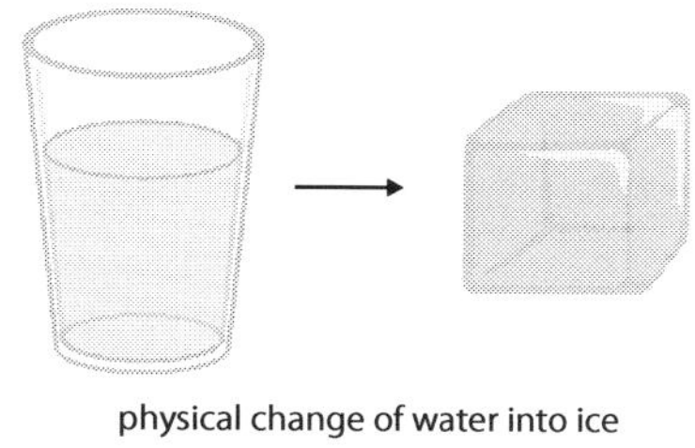

(b)

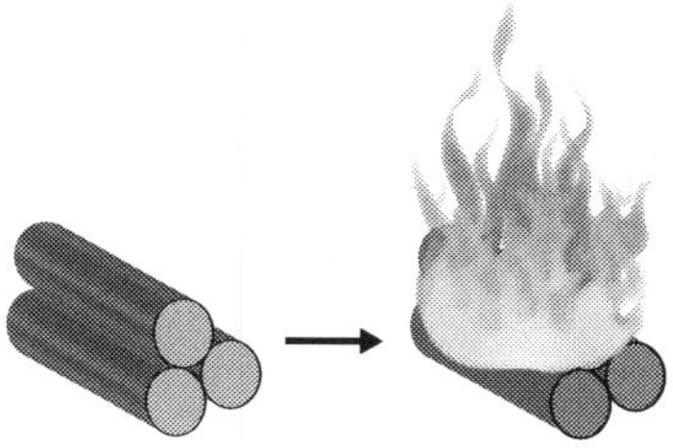
(c)

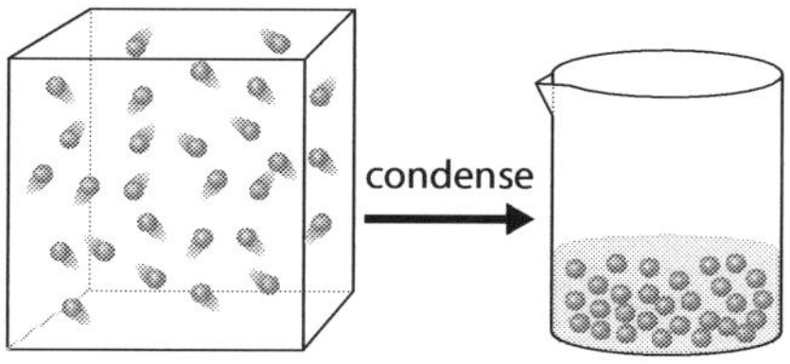

(d)

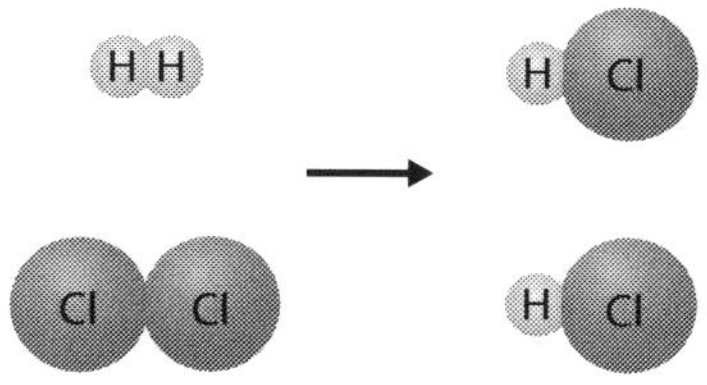

(e)

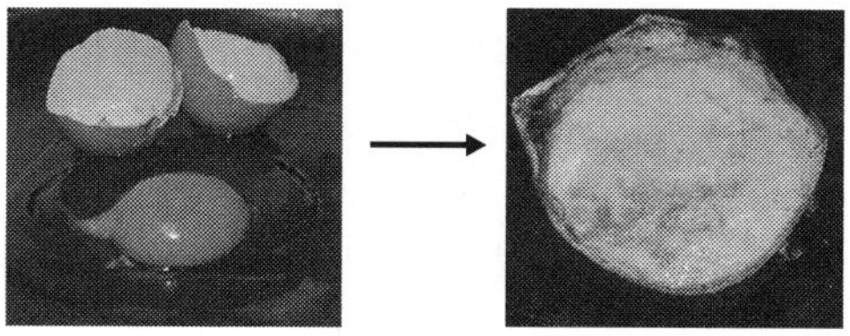
(f)

3. The boiling point of chloroform ($CHCl_3$) is 61.7°C. The enthalpy of vaporization is 31.4 kJ/mol. Calculate the entropy of vaporization. Does the sign for entropy of vaporization make sense? Explain.

4. (a) What is the normal boiling point for formic acid, HCOOH?
Given: $\Delta H_f^\circ = -424.72$ kJ/mol for liquid HCOOH and −379.1 kJ/mol for gaseous HCOOH
$S^\circ = 128.95$ J/mol K for liquid HCOOH and 251.0 J/mol K for gaseous HCOOH

(b) Based on the calculated boiling point, in what state does formic acid exist at room temperature? Explain.

5. The normal boiling point of water is 100.0°C, and its molar enthalpy of vaporization is 40.7 kJ/mol. What is the change in entropy in the system in J/K when 39.3 g of steam at 1 atm condenses to a liquid at the normal boiling point? Does the sign for the value you calculate make sense? Explain.

6. Iodine is an unusual element that sublimes under standard conditions. If the ΔS°_{subl} of iodine is 145 J/mol K and the ΔH°_{subl} of iodine is 62 kJ/mol, what is the standard sublimation temperature for iodine?

7. Consider the following addition reaction: $C_2H_2(g) + 2\ H_2(g) \rightarrow C_2H_6(g)$
The following data is known for this reaction:

Substance	S° (J/mol K)	ΔH_f (kJ/mol)
$C_2H_2(g)$	200.9	226.7
$H_2(g)$	130.7	0
$C_2H_6(g)$	????	−84.7

(a) If the value of ΔS° for the reaction is −232.7 J/mol K, calculate the value of S° for C_2H_6 gas.

(b) Calculate the enthalpy change ΔH° for the reaction.

© Edvantage Interactive 2019

(c) Assume that Boltzmann's equation applies when the system is in equilibrium. What is the temperature at this point (use the non-SI unit of °C)?

8. Consider the following reaction: $2\ H_2S(g) + SO_2(g) \rightarrow 3\ S(s) + 2\ H_2O(g)$

(a) Predict the sign of $\Delta S°$ for the reaction at 298 K. Explain the basis of your prediction.

(b) Calculate the actual value of $\Delta S°$ for the reaction. Assume the sulfur produced is the *rhombic* form. Does your calculation justify your prediction? Explain.

9. The combustion of methanol is described by the following equation:

$$2\ CH_3OH(l) + 3\ O_2(g) \rightarrow 4\ H_2O(l) + 2\ CO_2(g)$$

The value of $\Delta S°$ for this reaction is –38.6 cal/mol K at 25°C. One calorie is the energy required to warm 1 g of water by 1°C. One calorie is equivalent to 4.18 J.
Data collected for this reaction:

Reaction Species	**$\Delta H_f°$ (kcal/mol) at SATP**	**$S°$ (cal/mol K) at SATP**
$CH_3OH(l)$	–57.0	30.3
$H_2O(l)$	–68.3	16.7
$CO_2(g)$	–94.0	51.1

Calculate the standard absolute entropy $S°$ per mole of $O_2(g)$. Convert this value to units of J/mol K.

10. Use the values in Table A8 in the appendix to calculate $\Delta S°$ for each of the following equations. (It is important to use the values in the appendix because entropy values may differ slightly from one source to another. It is important to refer to the recommended source for reference values to ensure consistency in answers.)

(a) $H_2(g) + ½ O_2(g) \rightarrow H_2O(g)$

(b) $3 O_2(g) \rightarrow 2 O_3(g)$

(c) $CH_4(g) + 2 O_2(g) \rightarrow CO_2(g) + 2 H_2O(g)$

(d) $P_4O_{10}(s) + 6 H_2O(l) \rightarrow 4 H_3PO_4(s)$
(Given $S°$ for solid phosphoric acid = 110.54 J/mol K.)

(e) The complete combustion of octane in gasoline

© Edvantage Interactive 2019

3.2 Gibbs Free Energy

Warm Up

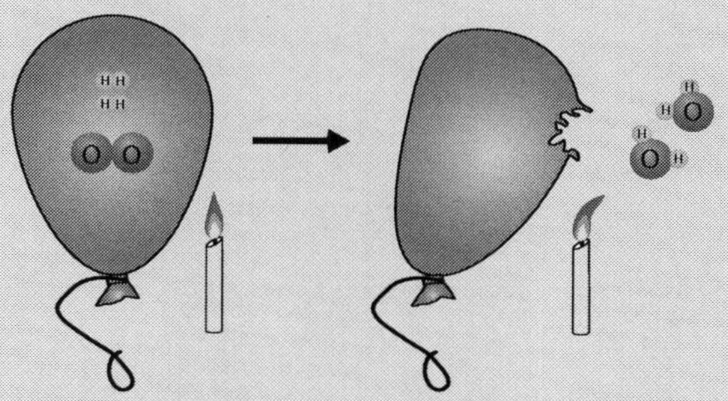

1. Write a balanced chemical equation (including phase subscripts) for the reaction shown in the diagram.

2. Use the values in Table A8 in the appendix at the back of this book to calculate ΔH_{rxn} and ΔS_{rxn} for the reaction.

3. What is the function of the candle in this process?

____

4. Is this spontaneous process *enthalpy driven* or *entropy driven*? Explain.

____

____

Free Energy — Enthalpy and Entropy Combine

We have now seen that two factors — enthalpy and entropy — determine whether or not a physical or chemical event is spontaneous or thermodynamically favorable. Sometimes these two factors work together. For example, when a stone wall crumbles, its enthalpy decreases and its entropy increases. Since a decrease in enthalpy and an increase in entropy both favor a spontaneous change, the two factors complement one another. In other situations, the effects of enthalpy and entropy are in opposition. Such is the case in the melting of ice, the vaporization of water and even the formation of water from its elements as in the Warm Up.

When enthalpy and entropy effects oppose one another, the overall reaction spontaneity is less obvious. We can determine the net effect of the two factors through another thermodynamic quantity called **Gibbs free energy, *G***, named after Josiah Willard Gibbs (1839–1903), a U.S. scientist (Figure 3.2.1). Gibbs free energy is defined as: $G = H - TS$. For a chemical or physical *change* at constant temperature and pressure, the equation becomes:

$$\Delta G = \Delta H - T\Delta S$$

A change is spontaneous only if it is accompanied by a decrease in free energy. In other words, ΔG must be negative for a spontaneous change. A spontaneous change is also termed a **thermodynamically favorable** change.

Figure 3.2.1 *American scientist Josiah Willard Gibbs*

> Spontaneous change must be accompanied by a decrease in free energy. That is, ΔG must be *NEGATIVE* for a spontaneous change.

Table 3.2.1 shows the effects of positive and negative values of ΔH and ΔS on ΔG. The table shows the importance of the absolute temperature in determining whether a change will occur spontaneously. Temperature is important in cases where ΔH and ΔS have the same signs.

Table 3.2.1 *Impact of ΔH and ΔS at various temperatures on the thermodynamic favorability (spontaneity) of chemical reactions*

ΔH	ΔS	ΔG	Reaction Characteristics	Examples
–	+	Always negative	Reaction is spontaneous at all temperatures; reverse reaction is always non-spontaneous.	$2\,O_3(g) \rightarrow 3O_2(g)$
+	–	Always positive	Reaction is non-spontaneous at all temperatures; reverse reaction occurs spontaneously.	$3\,O_2(g) \rightarrow 2\,O_3(g)$
–	–	Negative at low temps; positive at high temps	Reaction is spontaneous at low temperatures and becomes non-spontaneous as temperature is raised.	$CaO(s) + CO_2(g) \rightarrow CaCO_3(s)$
+	+	Positive at low temps; negative at high temps	Reaction is non-spontaneous at low temperatures but becomes spontaneous as temperature is raised.	$CaCO_3(s) \rightarrow CaO(s) + CO_2(g)$

Reactions that occur with a free energy decrease in the system are **exergonic**. Those that occur with a free energy increase are **endergonic**.

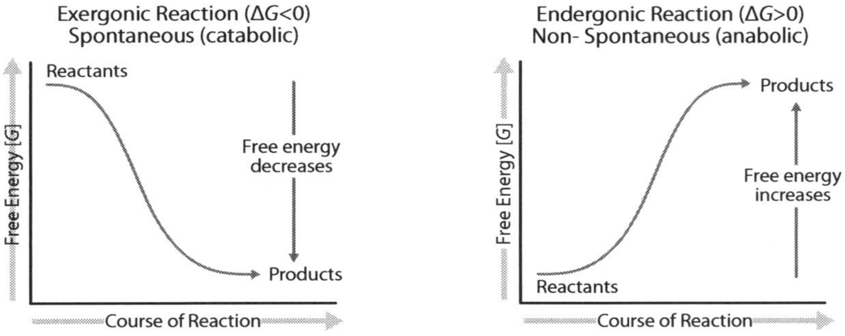

Figure 3.2.2 *Exergonic (left) and endergonic reactions*

The terms *exergonic* and *endergonic* are most commonly applied in biological contexts (Figure 3.2.2). Catabolic processes break down large proteins and lipids into amino and fatty acids producing many small molecules, each resulting in a large number of bond formations. These catabolic processes are exergonic. Anabolic processes form biological macromolecules following a multitude of bond breakages. Anabolic processes are endergonic. Essentially, *anabolic processes* are "powered" by *catabolic processes* during the metabolic processes that occur in our bodies. When one reaction is "powered" by another, the reactions are said to be **coupled**.

 © Edvantage Interactive 2019

Free Energy and Maximum Work

Spontaneous chemical reactions perform useful work. The burning of fuels in heat engines, chemical reactions in batteries, and the catabolic portion of metabolism within our bodies are all spontaneous processes that produce useful work. We cannot harness all of the energy released when spontaneous chemical reactions occur. Some energy is lost as heat. Engineers seek to maximize the efficiency of converting chemical energy to work and to minimize the amount of energy transferred unproductively to the environment as heat.

Is there a limit to the amount of energy in a reaction that can be harnessed as useful work? The maximum amount of energy we can harness from a reaction, as work is equal to ΔG. This is the energy that is not lost as heat and is *therefore free* (or available) to be used for work. By determining the value of ΔG, we can find out whether or not a given reaction will be an effective source of energy. By comparing the actual work derived from a given system with the ΔG value for the reactions involved, we can measure the efficiency of the system.

Free Energy and Equilibrium

Reactions with a negative free energy change are spontaneous (thermodynamically favorable), while those with a positive free energy change are non-spontaneous. (The reverse reaction is spontaneous.) When the value of ΔG is equal to zero, the reaction is at equilibrium. Recall that when at equilibrium the forward and reverse reactions occur at equal rates. A system is at equilibrium during a state change.

For the state change, $H_2O(l) \rightleftharpoons H_2O(s)$, equilibrium exists at 0°C and atmospheric pressure. Above 0°C, only liquid water can exist, and below 0°C, all the liquid will freeze to form ice. This gives us an interesting relationship between ΔH and ΔS.

$$\Delta G = 0 = \Delta H - T\Delta S$$

Therefore at equilibrium, $\Delta H = T\Delta S$; and

$$\Delta S_{system} = \frac{\Delta H}{T}$$

Thus, if we know ΔH and ΔS, we can calculate the temperature at which equilibrium will occur. This is the temperature at which a state change occurs.

Quick Check

1. For the process $Br_2(l) \rightleftharpoons Br_2(g)$, $\Delta H = +31.0$ kJ/mol and $\Delta S = 92.9$ J/mol K.
   (a) Explain why a (+) value for the enthalpy change is reasonable for this process.

   ____

   ____

   (b) Why would we expect the entropy change to be (+) for this process?

   ____

   (c) Assuming that ΔH and ΔS are temperature independent, calculate the temperature at which $Br_2(l)$ will be in equilibrium with $Br_2(g)$. Give the answer in °C.

   (d) What property does this temperature represent for bromine?

   ____

Standard Free Energies

About the same time the American Josiah Gibbs derived the free energy equation, German physicist Hermann von Helmholtz deduced the same thing. For this reason, the Gibbs-Helmholtz equation is a common name for $\Delta G = \Delta H - T\Delta S$. The equation is valid under all temperature, pressure, and concentration conditions. We will begin by restricting all of our calculations to standard conditions of pressure (1 atm) and concentration (1 *M*, where it applies). In other words, we will use the equation in the form (See Figure 3.2.3).

$$\Delta G° = \Delta H° - T\Delta S$$

Where $\Delta G°$ is the standard free energy change (determined at 1 atm, 1 *M*), $\Delta H°$ is the standard enthalpy change calculated from reference values, $\Delta S°$ is the standard entropy change calculated from reference values, and *T* is the Kelvin temperature.

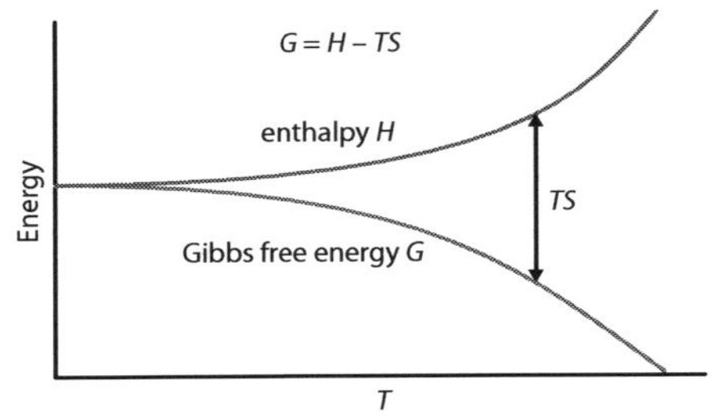

Figure 3.2.3 *This graph of energy vs. temperature shows that the difference between enthalpy (H) and free energy (G) is equal to TS. The graph shows that as the temperature increases, the difference between these two forms of energy becomes larger.*

Since enthalpy and entropy are state functions, it follows that Gibbs free energy is also a state function. We can use Hess's law and we can calculate standard free energies of formation as follows:

$$\Delta G° = \sum n\Delta G°_{prod} - \sum n\Delta G°_{react}$$

Note: $\Delta G°_f = 0$ for an element in its normal state at 25°C and 1 atm.

 © Edvantage Interactive 2019

Sample Problem 3.2.1(a) — Using the Gibbs-Helmholtz Equation to Calculate a Free Energy Change at Standard Temperature

For the process $NaCl(s) \rightarrow Na^{+}(aq) + Cl^{-}(aq)$, use the tables in Table A8 in the appendix at the back of this book to calculate:

(a) $\Delta H°$

(b) $\Delta S°$

(c) Use the values from (a) and (b) to calculate $\Delta G°$.

(d) According to your results, is this a spontaneous process?

What to Think About

1. As $\Delta H°$ is a state function, calculate it using the equation introduced in AP 1. The $\Delta H_f°$ values are listed in Table A8 in the appendix.

   Notice that while *elements in their standard states have $\Delta H_f°$ values of 0 kJ/mol*, this is *not* the case for ions in solution.

2. We use a similar process to determine $\Delta S°$, also a state function.

   Absolute entropy values of formation $S_f°$ are in Table A8 in the appendix.

3. Instructions indicate that you should calculate $\Delta G°$ using the answers to (a) and (b). Use the Gibbs- Helmholtz equation.

   It is important to ensure that the ***units are consistent*** *throughout the equation.* In other words, you must convert $\Delta S°$ to kJ/K mol before substituting the values into the Gibbs equation.

   In general, if a question requiring the Gibbs Equation does *not provide* a specific *temperature*, assume ***SATP conditions (or T = 25°C = 298 K) apply***. The presence of the ° symbol, however, does **not** restrict all calculations to a temperature of 25°C.

4. A (–) ΔG value indicates spontaneity (also called ***thermodynamic favorability***) though the magnitude is not very large.

How to Do It

a) $\Delta H°_{(overall)} = \Sigma n \Delta H°_{f(prod)} - \Sigma n \Delta H°_{f(react)}$

$\Delta H_f°$ for $Na^{+}(aq)$ = –240.12 kJ/mol

$\Delta H_f°$ for $Cl^{-}(aq)$ = –167.16 kJ/mol

$\Delta H_f°$ for NaCl(s) = –411.15 kJ/mol

$$\Delta H° = \left[\frac{1 \text{ mol } Na^+}{\text{mol rxn}}\left(\frac{-240.12 \text{ kJ}}{\text{mol } Na^+}\right) + \frac{1 \text{ mol } Cl^-}{\text{mol rxn}}\left(\frac{-167.16 \text{ kJ}}{\text{mol } Cl^-}\right)\right] - \left[\frac{1 \text{ mol NaCl}}{\text{mol rxn}}\left(\frac{-411.15 \text{ kJ}}{\text{mol NaCl}}\right)\right] = 3.87 \text{ kJ/mol rxn}$$

(b) $\Delta S° = \Sigma n S°_{prod} - \Sigma n S°_{react}$

$S_f°$ for $Na^{+}(aq)$ = 59.0 J/K mol

$S_f°$ for $Cl^{-}(aq)$ = 56.5 J/K mol

$S_f°$ for NaCl(s) = 72.13 J/K mol

$$\Delta S° = \left[\frac{1 \text{ mol } Na^+}{\text{mol rxn}}\left(\frac{0.0590 \text{ kJ}}{\text{K mol } Na^+}\right) + \frac{1 \text{ mol } Cl^-}{\text{mol rxn}}\left(\frac{0.0565 \text{ kJ}}{\text{K mol } Cl^-}\right)\right] - \left[\frac{1 \text{ mol NaCl}}{\text{mol rxn}}\left(\frac{0.07213 \text{ kJ}}{\text{K mol NaCl}}\right)\right] = 0.04337 \text{ kJ/K mol rxn}$$

(c) $\Delta G° = \Delta H° - T\Delta S°$

$$\Delta G° = 3.87 \frac{\text{kJ}}{\text{mol}_{rxn}} - 298 \text{ K}\left(\frac{0.04337 \text{ kJ}}{\text{K mol}_{rxn}}\right)$$

$$= -9.05 \text{ kJ/mol}_{rxn}$$

(d) The dissolving of the salt has a (–) ΔG value meaning it is spontaneous as would be expected for dissolving a salt at room temperature.

In fact, endothermicity and an increased number of microstates also make sense for the dissolving process. This process is entropy driven.

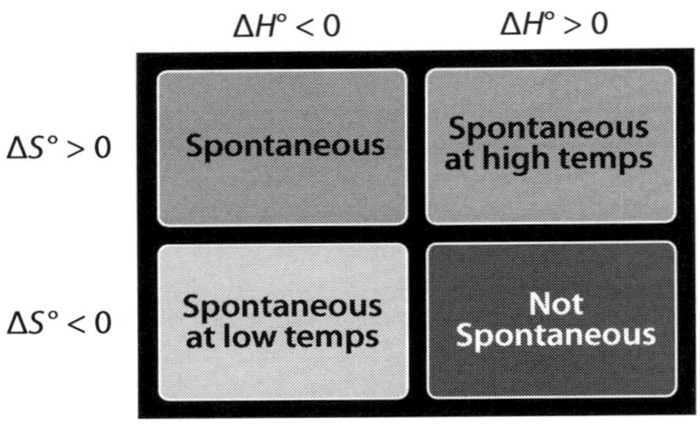

Figure 3.2.4 *Examination of the equation, $\Delta G° = \Delta H° - T\Delta S°$, shows that if $\Delta H°$ and $\Delta S°$ share the same sign, temperature will determine spontaneity. The temperature at which $\Delta H°$ and the term $T\Delta S°$ are equal is the temperature at which equilibrium will occur. "High" and "low" temperatures are relative and refer to temperatures above or below the equilibrium T value.*

It is significant that $\Delta S°$ values are usually very small compared to $\Delta H°$. Only multiplication by T causes subtraction of the $T\Delta S°$ term from $\Delta H°$ to have a significant impact on the value of $\Delta G°$. In an example such as the dissolving of table salt, both $\Delta H°$ and $\Delta S°$ are positive. This dissolution process is spontaneous only when the temperature is large enough to allow subtraction of the $T\Delta S°$ term from $\Delta H°$ to result in a negative $\Delta G°$.

The values of standard free energies of formation of pure compounds and elements and aqueous ions are listed in Table A8 in the appendix. As is the case for the $S°$ and $\Delta H_f°$ values in the appendix, standard conditions for $\Delta G_f°$ are 25°C and 1 atm.

Sample Problem 3.2.1(b) — Using Free Energies of Formation to Calculate a Free Energy Change at Standard Temperature

For the process $NaCl(s) \rightarrow Na^+(aq) + Cl^-(aq)$, use the tables in Table A8 in the appendix to calculate:

(a) $\Delta G°$

(b) According to your results in (a), is this a spontaneous process?

What to Think About

1. As $\Delta G°$ is a state function, calculate the value using the equation introduced earlier in this section. The $\Delta G_f°$ values are listed in Table A8 in the appendix.

   As with $\Delta H°_f$ values, ***elements in their standard states have $\Delta G_f°$ values of 0 kJ/mol***. This is *not* the case for ions in solution.

   The value calculated for $\Delta G°$ using reference values and the state function equation is very close to the value calculated using the Gibbs-Helmholtz equation. Using the state function algorithm to calculate $\Delta H°$ and $\Delta S°$ values introduces further approximations due to rounding to appropriate significant figures. This leads to differences between the two calculated values.

2. A (–) ΔG value indicates spontaneity even though the magnitude is not very large.

How to Do It

(a) $\Delta G° = \Sigma n\Delta G°_{(prod)} - \Sigma n\Delta G°_{(react)}$

$\Delta G_f°$ for $Na^+(aq)$ = -261.91 kJ/mol

$\Delta G_f°$ for $Cl^-(aq)$ = -131.23 kJ/mol

$\Delta G_f°$ for NaCl(s) = -384.12 kJ/mol

$$\Delta G° = \left[\frac{1\ \text{mol Na}^+}{\text{mol rxn}}\left(\frac{-261.91\ \text{kJ}}{\text{mol Na}^+}\right) + \frac{1\ \text{mol Cl}^-}{\text{mol rxn}}\left(\frac{-131.23\ \text{kJ}}{\text{mol Cl}^-}\right)\right]$$

$$\left[\frac{1\ \text{mol NaCl}}{\text{mol rxn}}\left(\frac{-384.12\ \text{kJ}}{\text{mol NaCl}}\right)\right] = -9.02\ \text{kJ/mol rxn}$$

b) This is a spontaneous process. This makes sense for the dissolving of a salt at room temperature. We know that virtually all salts dissolve spontaneously at room temperature. This is generally entropy driven. It is interesting that the dissolving of NaCl is very nearly at equilibrium under SATP conditions.

 © Edvantage Interactive 2019

Practice Problems 3.2.1 — Using the Gibbs-Helmholtz Equation and Free Energies of Formation to Calculate a Free Energy Change at Standard Temperature

1. Use the ΔG_f° values in Table A8 in the appendix to calculate ΔG°_{comb} for the combustion of ethanol under SATP conditions.

2. Calculate the maximum work available from the oxidation of 1 mole of octane at 25°C and 1 atm. Use the ΔH_f° and the S_f° values from Table A8 in the appendix along with the Gibbs-Helmholtz equation.

3. Calculate ΔG°_{rxn} for the reaction of $N_2(g) + O_2(g) \rightarrow 2\ NO(g)$. Do the calculation *two* ways. First by determining ΔH_f°, then ΔS_f° followed by the Gibbs-Helmholtz equation. Then use the ΔG_f° values and see how the values compare.

Calculation of Free Energy at Non-Standard Temperatures

ΔG° is the most temperature dependent of the thermodynamic functions. We can use the Gibbs-Helmholtz equation to calculate ΔG° at temperatures other than 25°C. To do this, we neglect the variations of ΔH° and ΔS° with temperature because they are relatively temperature independent quantities compared to ΔG°.

> ΔH° is essentially independent of temperature and the variations of ΔS° with temperature are ordinarily very small — entropy is most dependent on temperature near absolute zero. Near room temperature, variations in ΔS° are negligible.

In other words, we take the values of ΔH° and ΔS° from the tables and simply insert them into the Gibbs-Helmholtz equation using the appropriate value of T (in Kelvin degrees) to calculate ΔG°.

Sample Problem 3.2.2 — Using the the Gibbs-Helmholtz Equation to Calculate a Free Energy Change at Non-Standard Temperatures

Calculate $\Delta G°$ for the reaction $Cu(s) + H_2O(g) \rightarrow CuO(s) + H_2(g)$ at a temperature of 227.0°C.

What to Think About

1. As the temperature is non-standard, you must use the Gibbs-Helmholtz equation to solve the problem.
2. Use reference tables to determine the $\Delta H°$ and $\Delta S°$ values of each compound or element in the reaction first.
3. Calculate the overall enthalpy change for the reaction.
4. Evaluate the sign of the enthalpy value and its significance.
5. Calculate the overall entropy change for the reaction
6. Consider the sign of the overall entropy change of the reaction and its significance.
7. Finally, use the Gibbs-Helmholtz equation to calculate $\Delta G°$ at a temperature of 227.0 °C, but first convert the temperature to Kelvin degrees.

How to Do It

$\Delta H°_{(overall)} = \Sigma n\Delta H°_{f(prod)} - \Sigma n\Delta H°_{f(react)}$

$\Delta H°_f$ for $CuO(s)$ = −157.3 kJ/mol

$\Delta H°_f$ for $H_2(g)$ = 0 kJ/mol

$\Delta H°_f$ for $Cu(s)$ = 0 kJ/mol

$\Delta H°_f$ for $H_2O(g)$ = −241.82 kJ/mol

$$\Delta H° = \left[\frac{1\ \text{mol CuO}}{\text{mol rxn}}\left(\frac{-157.3\ \text{kJ}}{\text{mol CuO}}\right) + \frac{1\ \text{mol }H_2}{\text{mol rxn}}\left(\frac{0\ \text{kJ}}{\text{mol }H_2}\right)\right] - \left[\frac{1\ \text{mol Cu}}{\text{mol rxn}}\left(\frac{0\ \text{kJ}}{\text{mol Cu}}\right) + \frac{1\ \text{mol }H_2O}{\text{mol rxn}}\left(\frac{-241.82\ \text{kJ}}{1\ \text{mol rxn}}\right)\right]$$

$= 84.5\ \text{kJ/mol}_{rxn}$

A slightly endothermic process

$\Delta S° = \Sigma nS°_{(prod)} - \Sigma nS°_{(react)}$

$S°_f$ for $CuO(s)$ = 42.63 J/K mol

$S°_f$ for $H_2(g)$ = 130.68 J/K mol

$S°_f$ for $Cu(s)$ = 33.15 J/K mol

$S°_f$ for $H_2O(g)$ = 188.83 J/K mol

$$\Delta S° = \left[\frac{1\ \text{mol CuO}}{\text{mol rxn}}\left(\frac{42.63\ \text{kJ}}{\text{K mol CuO}}\right) + \frac{1\ \text{mol }H_2}{\text{mol rxn}}\left(\frac{130.68\ \text{kJ}}{\text{K mol }H_2}\right)\right] - \left[\frac{1\ \text{mol Cu}}{\text{mol rxn}}\left(\frac{33.15\ \text{kJ}}{\text{K mol Cu}}\right) + \frac{1\ \text{mol }H_2O}{\text{mol rxn}}\left(\frac{188.83\ \text{kJ}}{\text{K mol rxn}}\right)\right]$$

$= -48.67\ \text{kJ/mol}_{rxn}\ \text{K}$

A (−) value for ΔS makes sense as the O atoms have moved from a gaseous compound to a solid compound. Additionally the H has moved from gaseous water where it was combined with oxygen to pure gaseous hydrogen.

$227\ °\text{C}\left(\frac{1\ \text{K}}{1\ °\text{C}}\right) + 273\ \text{K} = 500.\ \text{K}$

$\Delta G° = \Delta H° - T\Delta S°$

$\Delta G° = 84.5\ \frac{\text{kJ}}{\text{mol}_{rxn}} - 500.\ \text{K}\left(\frac{-0.04867\ \text{kJ}}{\text{K mol}_{rxn}}\right)$

$= 108.8\ \text{kJ/mol}_{rxn}$

Note that the (+) $\Delta G°$ value indicates a non-spontaneous reaction. The (+) $\Delta H°$ and the (−) $\Delta S°$ both favor a non-spontaneous reaction. Hence this reaction would be non-spontaneous under any temperature conditions.

© Edvantage Interactive 2019

Practice Problems 3.2.2 — Using the Gibbs-Helmholtz Equation to Calculate a Free Energy Change at Non-Standard Temperatures

1. The mineral calcite decomposes according to the following reaction:

   $CaCO_3(s) \rightarrow CaO(s) + CO_2(g)$ in which $\Delta H° = 178.3\ kJ/mol_{rxn}$ and $\Delta S° = 160.6\ J/mol_{rxn}\ K$.

   (a) Calculate $\Delta G°$ at 750.0°C.

   (b) Calculate $\Delta G°$ at 950.0°C.

   (c) Does the reaction become more or less spontaneous (thermodynamically favorable) as temperature increases?

Experimental Manipulation of the Gibbs-Helmholtz Free Energy Equation

We can arrange the equation, $G = H - TS$ to the form $G = -ST + H$. A plot of G vs. T will be a straight line with a slope of $-S$ and a y-intercept of H. Various experiments may be set up to study the variables in the Gibbs-Helmholtz equation. These experiments produce graphs such as those shown in Figure 3.2.5.

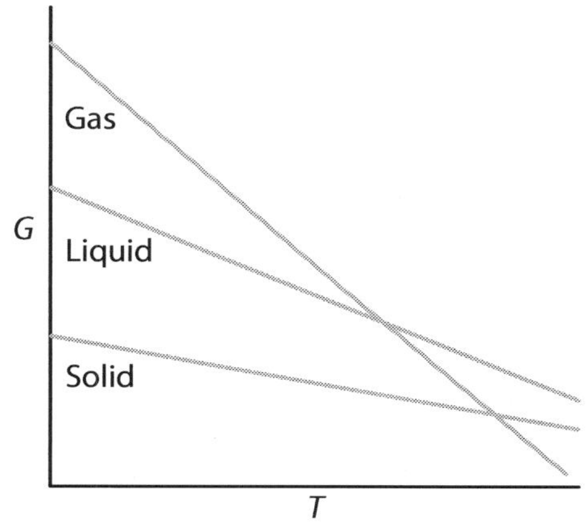

Figure 3.2.5 *The graph above shows that free energy (G) varies with temperature (T).*

Since all chemical species have a positive value for entropy, G decreases with an increase in temperature (at constant pressure and state). Gases have far greater entropy than liquids, which have greater entropy than solids. Figure 3.2.5 shows the free energies of gases are more temperature dependent than liquids, which are more temperature sensitive than solids.

The direct measurement of free energy is not easily accomplished. In the next section, we will apply our understanding of equilibrium to a more detailed investigation of free energy and how it varies with temperature.

3.2 Review Questions

1. (a) What two factors, other than temperature, influence the spontaneity of a process?

   (b) Describe each factor.

   (c) What sign is associated with spontaneity for each factor?

2. Complete the following table for the equation: $\Delta G° = \Delta H° - T\Delta S°$.

Sign of $\Delta H°$	Sign of $\Delta S°$	Temperature	Sign of $\Delta G°$	Spontaneous /Non-Spontaneous
–	+	low		
–	+	high		
+	–	low		
+	–	high		
–	–		–	
+	+			spontaneous
–	–	high		
+	+		+	

3. Examine the representation of ice melting and water condensing on a glass of ice water. Consider circled areas A and B.

Circle A:

(i) What are the signs of $\Delta H°$ and $\Delta S°$ for this process? Explain your answers.

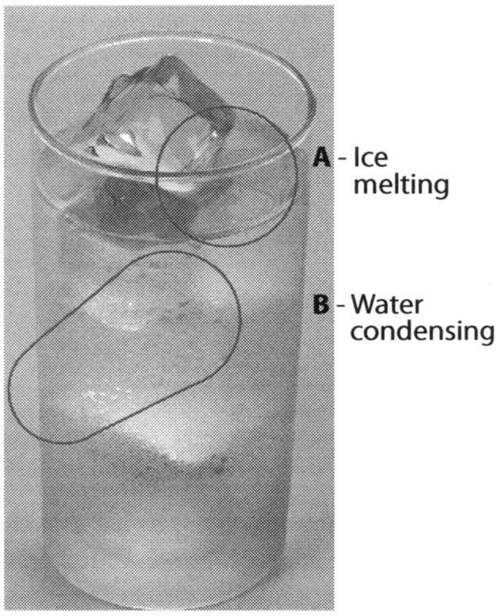

(ii) Is this process spontaneous at all temperatures, only low temperatures, only high temperatures or never? Explain.

Circle B:

(i) What are the signs of $\Delta H°$ and $\Delta S°$ for this process? Explain your answers.

(ii) Is this process spontaneous at all temperatures, only low temperatures, only high temperatures or never? Explain.

© Edvantage Interactive 2019

4. $\Delta H°$ is –196.1 kJ/mol$_{rxn}$ for the following representation of a reaction of $H_2O_2(l)$.

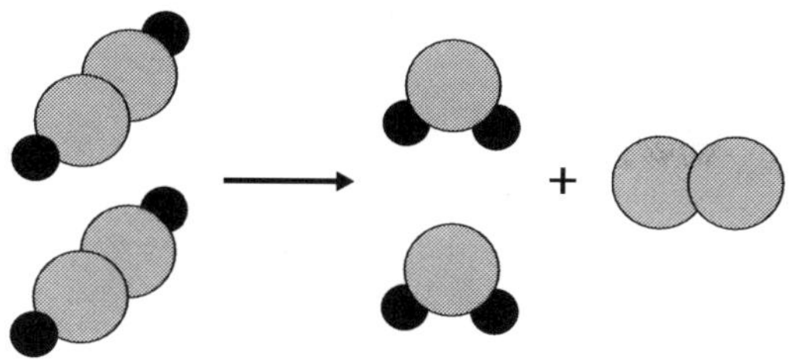

(a) What are the signs of $\Delta S°$ and $\Delta G°$ for the reaction? Explain.

(b) Is the process spontaneous at all temperatures, only low temperatures, only high temperatures or never? Explain.

5. (a) Use the representation below to produce a balanced chemical equation. Use the lowest possible whole number coefficients in your equation.

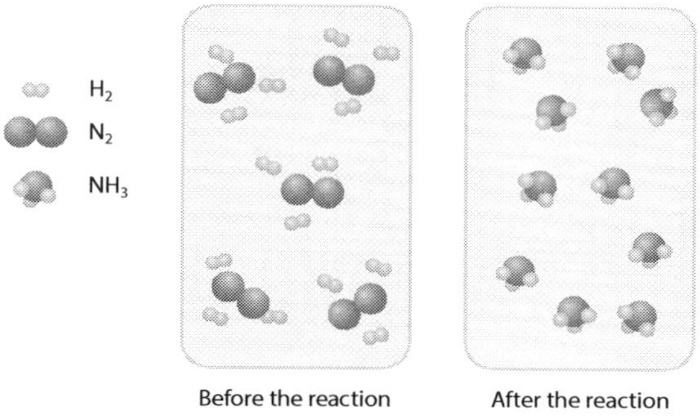

(b) Use Table A8 in the appendix to calculate $\Delta H°_{rxn}$ for the reaction. Show your work.

(c) Predict the *sign* of $\Delta S°_{rxn}$ for the reaction (do not calculate).

(d) Is this process spontaneous at all temperatures, only low temperatures, only high temperatures or never? Explain.

(e) Determine the temperature (in °C) at which the spontaneity of this reaction changes.

6. Shiny silver iodine crystals are deposited on the surface of ice placed into a test tube filled with purple iodine vapor.

(a) Write a balanced chemical equation to describe the process pictured here.

(b) Use Table A8 in the appendix to calculate the sublimation temperature (same as the deposition temperature) for iodine.

7. Consider the following reaction: $2\,O_3(g) \rightarrow 3\,O_2(g)$. $\Delta H° = -285.4$ kJ/mol$_{rxn}$.
(a) Predict the signs for $\Delta S°_{rxn}$ and $\Delta G°_{rxn}$ and the spontaneity of the reaction (no calculations required).

(b) Use values from Table A8 in the appendix to calculate $\Delta S°_{rxn}$ and $\Delta G°_{rxn}$ and to determine the accuracy of your prediction.

8. Calculate $\Delta G°_{rxn}$ for each of the following reactions using Table A8 in the appendix.
(a) $NH_3(g) + HCl(g) \rightarrow NH_4Cl(s)$

(b) $AgNO_3(aq) + NaI(aq) \rightarrow AgI(s) + NaNO_3(aq)$ (Hint: Use the net ionic equation.)

(c) $P_4O_{10}(s) + H_2O(l) \rightarrow H_3PO_4(l)$ (Hint: The reaction is unbalanced.)

9. Government requirements in the United States and Canada state that fuels should contain a "renewable" component. Fermentation of glucose isolated from a variety of garden products such as sugar cane, beets, and corn produces ethanol. Producers can add ethanol to gasoline to fulfill the renewable fuel requirement. Here is the fermentation reaction for glucose:
$C_6H_{12}O_6(s) \rightarrow 2\,C_2H_5OH(l) + 2\,CO_2(g)$

 © Edvantage Interactive 2019

Calculate:

(a) $\Delta H°$

(b) $\Delta S°$

(c) $\Delta G°$

(d) Under what temperature conditions does this reaction occur spontaneously? Justify.

(e) How might this impact the economic feasibility of producing renewable fuels in this way?

10. In low concentrations, phosgene is a colorless to pale yellow cloud with the pleasant odor of freshly cut hay. In higher concentrations, phosgene becomes a choking agent toxic to the pulmonary system. Armies used phosgene to kill hundreds of people during the World War 1. Carbon monoxide and chlorine combine to form phosgene, $COCl_2(g)$.

(a) Calculate $\Delta S°_{rxn}$ given that $\Delta H° = -220.$ kJ/mol_{rxn} and $\Delta G° = -206$ kJ/mol_{rxn} at 25 °C.

(b) The (–)$\Delta G°$ value means the production of the war gas is spontaneous under SATP conditions. Considering the signs of $\Delta S°$ and $\Delta H°$, what temperature conditions should further favor the spontaneous production of phosgene?

(c) Assuming the temperature effects on $\Delta S°$ and $\Delta H°$ are negligible, calculate $\Delta G°$ at 435°C. Is the reaction spontaneous at this higher temperature?

3.3 Pressure, Equilibrium, and Free Energy

Warm Up

In this activity, you will determine if entropy is increased or decreased when you stretch a balloon. Your determination will help you complete the ΔS cells in the table below.

- Stretch a balloon (or a thick rubber band) by pulling and relaxing multiple times.
- Hold the balloon against your upper lip or forehead during a stretch. Keep it in contact with your face while letting the balloon relax slowly.

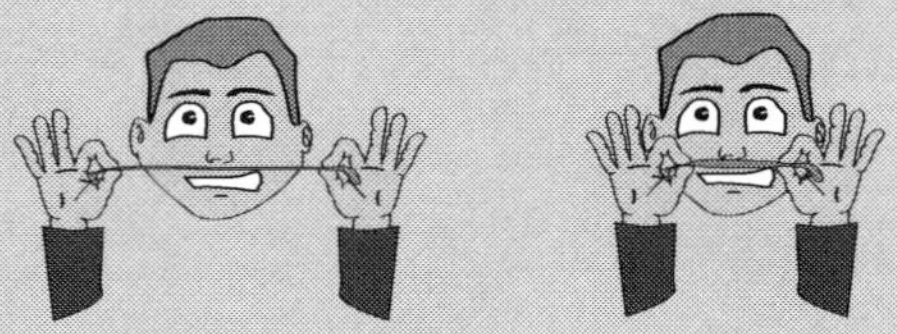

1. What do you feel when the balloon is stretched? When it is relaxed?

___

2. Complete the ΔH portion of the data table below using + or – signs.

	ΔH	ΔG	ΔS	**Representation**
Stretched				
Relaxed				

3. Does the balloon stretch or relax *spontaneously*? Stretch the balloon and let go of the both ends simultaneously to find out.

___

4. Complete the ΔG portion of the table.
5. What MUST the sign of ΔS be? Indicate in the table above.
6. Is the relaxation of the balloon *enthalpy* or *entropy driven*?

___

7. Draw a molecular representation to show how the chains of molecules must align themselves when you stretch the balloon and when you relax it. (Rubber is a polymer, which consists of long chains of repeating chemical units called *monomers*.)
8. Do the sign of ΔS and the drawings of chain alignment representation portions of your table agree? Why or why not?

___

___

© Edvantage Interactive 2019

Dependence of Free Energy on Pressure

The entropy of 1 mole of a gas in a 20.0 L container is larger than the entropy of 1 mole of the same gas in a 10.0 L container. There are more microstates for the gas or ways for the molecules of the gas to arrange themselves in the space in a larger volume. If the entropy of a gas depends on the volume and consequently the pressure, then the free energy of the gas must also depend on these two factors. Experimentally, it can be seen that:

$$G = G^\circ + RT \ln P$$

where G° is the free energy of a gas sample at 1 atm pressure, and G is the free energy of the gas at some pressure P. R is 8.314 J/mol·K, and T is the temperature in Kelvin degrees.

How does the free energy change for a reaction depend upon pressure?

Methane "burns" in oxygen to form carbon dioxide and water:

$$CH_4(g) + 2\,O_2(g) \rightleftharpoons CO_2(g) + 2\,H_2O(g)$$

For this reaction:

$$\Delta G = G_{CO_2} + 2\,G_{H_2O} - G_{CH_4} - 2\,G_{O_2} \text{ (under non-standard conditions)}$$

If we use $G = G^\circ + RT \ln P$ for each component:

$$\Delta G = (G^\circ_{CO_2} + RT \ln P_{CO_2}) + 2(G^\circ_{H_2O} + RT \ln P_{H_2O}) - (G^\circ_{CH_4} + RT \ln P_{CH_4})$$
$$- 2(G^\circ_{O_2} + RT \ln P_{O_2})$$

Collecting all the G° terms and all the $RT \ln P$ terms:

$$\Delta G = G^\circ_{CO_2} + 2\,G^\circ_{H_2O} - G^\circ_{CH_4} - 2\,G^\circ_{O_2} + RT\,(\ln P_{CO_2} + 2 \ln P_{H_2O} - \ln P_{CH_4} - 2 \ln P_{O_2})$$

Since $\Delta G^\circ = G^\circ_{CO_2} + 2\,G^\circ_{H_2O} - G^\circ_{CH_4} - 2\,G^\circ_{O_2}$ and $2 \ln x = \ln x^2$

We have $\Delta G = \Delta G^\circ + RT\,(\ln P_{CO_2} + \ln P^2_{H_2O} - \ln P_{CH_4} - \ln P^2_{O_2})$

Applying log rules: $\ln a + \ln b = \ln (a \cdot b)$ and $\ln c - \ln d = \ln (c/d)$,

we end up with $\Delta G = G^\circ + RT \ln \left[\dfrac{(P_{CO_2})(P^2_{H_2O})}{(P_{CH_4})(P^2_{O_2})}\right]$

The expression in square brackets is the reaction quotient Q.

You do not need to be able to derive this equation. We provide the mathematical justification for those who want to understand how the reaction quotient appears in the equation when we consider a change in the Gibbs free energy of a reaction. For any reaction *with species present at non-standard pressures*:

$$\Delta G = \Delta G^\circ + RT \ln Q$$

You can calculate ΔG° for a reaction from reference values of free energies of formation of reactants and products. Using ΔG° and Q, you can determine ΔG.

The sign of ΔG allows you to predict whether the reaction will proceed spontaneously forward (– sign) or reverse (+ sign) to reach equilibrium. If a reaction mixture is at equilibrium ΔG will be 0.

Sample Problem 3.3.1 — Calculation and Use of ΔG

Consider the reaction:

$$2\ NO_2(g) \rightleftharpoons N_2O_4(g) \qquad \Delta G^\circ = -5.39\ \text{kJ/mol}_{rxn} \text{ at } 25°C$$

A mixture contains NO_2 with a partial pressure of 0.10 atm and N_2O_4 with a partial pressure of 0.20 atm. Use ΔG to determine whether the gas mixture is at equilibrium. If it is not, in which direction will the reaction proceed?

What to Think About	How to Do It
1. The pressures are not 1 atm and the question asks for the value of ΔG as opposed to $\Delta G°$, so the equation required is: $\Delta G = \Delta G° + RT \ln Q$	Determine the reaction quotient Q by placing the partial pressure of the product over the partial pressure of the reactant and raising the pressure of each species to the power of its coefficient: $Q = \frac{P_{N_2O_4}}{P^2_{NO_2}} = \frac{0.20\text{ atm}}{(0.10\text{ atm})^2} = 20$
2. The temperature must be expressed in Kelvin degrees.	$25°C \times \frac{1\text{ K}}{1°C} + 273\text{ K} = 298\text{ K}$
3. The value of the gas constant must have units of energy. Recall: $\frac{0.08206\text{ L·atm}}{\text{mol·K}} \times \frac{101.3\text{ J}}{\text{L·atm}} = 8.31 \frac{\text{J}}{\text{mol·K}}$ (or more precisely 8.314)	If K were given in the question, a comparison of Q to K would predict the reaction's preferred direction. However, K is not given, hence
4. Be sure the $G°$ and R units are *the same* (both kJ or both J).	$\Delta G = \Delta G° + RT \ln Q$ $= -5.39 \frac{\text{kJ}}{\text{mol}_{rxn}} + \left(0.008314 \frac{\text{kJ}}{\text{mol·K}} \times 298\text{ K} \times \ln(20.)\right)$ $= -5.39\text{ kJ/mol}_{rxn} + 7.42\text{ kJ/mol}$ $= 2.03\text{ kJ/mol}_{rxn}$ or 2.0 kJ/mol_{rxn} A non-zero ΔG value indicates the system is not at equilibrium.
5. Be sure to carry the correct signs through the entire calculation.	The system is NOT at equilibrium. Because the sign of ΔG is **positive**, the reaction will proceed in the reverse direction (to the LEFT) to reach equilibrium.

 © Edvantage Interactive 2019

Practice Problems 3.3.1 — Calculation and Use of ΔG

1. What is the value for Gibbs free energy in the production of ammonia from nitrogen and hydrogen: $N_2(g) + 3\,H_2(g) \rightleftharpoons 2\,NH_3(g)$, if the pressure of all three gases is 2.00 atm and the temperature is 23°C? Begin by determining $\Delta G°$ for this reaction using the reference values from Table A8 in the appendix.

2. $\Delta G°$ for the reaction $H_2(g) + I_2(g) \rightleftharpoons 2\,HI(g)$ is 2.60 kJ/mol$_{rxn}$ at 25°C. Calculate ΔG and predict the direction in which the reaction proceeds spontaneously if the initial pressures are 7.0 atm, 3.0 atm, and 3.50 atm for H_2, I_2, and HI respectively.

3. Methanol, a common gasoline additive is also present as a component in windshield washer solution. A common method for synthesis of this alcohol is to react carbon monoxide with hydrogen gas:

$$CO(g) + 2\,H_2(g) \rightleftharpoons CH_3OH(l)$$

Calculate ΔG for this reaction at 25°C when 2.5 atm of carbon monoxide and 1.5 atm of hydrogen gases react to form liquid methanol. Begin by determining $\Delta G°$ for this reaction using the reference values from Table A8 in the appendix.

Free Energy and the Equilibrium Constant

The relationship between the reaction quotient and free energy is:

$$\Delta G = \Delta G° + RT \ln Q$$

At equilibrium, $\Delta G = 0$. The reaction mixture has reached a minimum free energy. Also at equilibrium, $Q = K_{eq}$, so the reaction quotient is equal to the equilibrium constant.

Then, at equilibrium, $\Delta G = \Delta G° + RT \ln Q$

becomes $0 = \Delta G° + RT \ln K$

Thus, $\boldsymbol{\Delta G° = -RT \ln K}$

With this expression, we can use the reference values of $\Delta G°_f$ to calculate $\Delta G°$ for a reaction and then calculate K.

Note 1: Some references prefer to deal with logs to the base 10, rather than natural logs to the base e. In that case, since 2.303 log x = ln x, the above expression becomes:

$$\Delta G° = -2.303\ RT \log K$$

Note 2: Usually the change in Gibbs free energy at equilibrium is calculated from the partial pressures of the reagents in a reaction such as the oxidation of methane gas, so the equilibrium constant is actually K_p. However, occasionally the change in Gibbs free energy at equilibrium may refer to K_c in situations such as low solubility salt equilibria (K_{sp}) or weak acids (K_a).

Using $\Delta G°$ and K to Predict Reaction Direction

There are three possible situations when calculating the change in Gibbs free energy at equilibrium:
1. If $\Delta G°$ is negative, ln K must be positive. This means that K is greater than 1 and the reaction proceeds spontaneously (is thermodynamically favorable) in the forward direction.
2. If $\Delta G°$ is positive, ln K must be negative. This means that K is less than 1 and the reverse reaction is spontaneous.
3. If $\Delta G° = 0$, ln $K = 0$. The reaction is at equilibrium.

If $\Delta G°$ is a large negative number, K will be much greater than one. This means that the forward reaction will go virtually to completion. Conversely, if $\Delta G°$ is a large positive number, K will be a tiny fraction, much less than 1, and the reverse reaction will go nearly to completion. Table 3.3.1 summarizes these relationships.

Table 3.3.1 *$\Delta G°$, K, and Reaction Direction*

$\Delta G°$ negative	$K > 1$	spontaneous reaction
$\Delta G°$ = zero	$K = 1$	at equilibrium
$\Delta G°$ positive	$K < 1$	reverse reaction is spontaneous
$\Delta G° <<< 0$	K very BIG	spontaneous to near completion
$\Delta G° >>> 0$	K nearly 0	reverse reaction to near completion

Sample Problem 3.3.2(a) — Calculating $\Delta G°$ from K Values

The equilibrium constant K for the reaction $PCl_3(g) + Cl_2(g) \rightleftharpoons PCl_5(g)$ is 24.0 at 250.°C. Calculate $\Delta G°$. Is the reaction spontaneous in the forward or reverse direction?

What to Think About	How to Do It
1. Convert the temperature to Kelvin degrees.	$250.°C \times \frac{1\ K}{1°C} + 273\ K = 523\ K$
2. Use the equation $\Delta G° = -RT \ln K$ to calculate $\Delta G°$.	$\Delta G° = -RT \ln K$ $= -8.314 \frac{J}{mol \cdot K} \times 523\ K \times \ln(24.0)$
3. It is critical to use the appropriate R value and to carry the negative sign that precedes the equation through each step in the equation.	$= -13\ 800\ J/mol_{rxn}$ $= -13.8\ kJ/mol_{rxn}$
4. If $K > 1$, $\Delta G°$ must be *negative*.	The forward reaction is spontaneous.

 © Edvantage Interactive 2019

Sample Problem 3.3.2(b) — Conversion of $\Delta G°$ to K

Phosphorus pentachloride decomposes as follows: $PCl_5(g) \rightleftharpoons PCl_3(g) + Cl_2(g)$.
$\Delta G° = 26.5$ kJ/mol$_{rxn}$ at 227°C. Calculate the equilibrium constant, *K*. Does the reaction favor products or reactants under these conditions?

What to Think About	How to Do It
1. Convert the temperature to Kelvin degrees.	$227°C \times \frac{1\ K}{1°C} + 273\ K = 500.\ K$
2. As $\Delta G°$ and *K* are in the question, use the equation $\Delta G° = -RT \ln K$.	$\Delta G° = -RT \ln K$ so $\ln K = \frac{-\Delta G°}{RT}$
3. It is critical to use the appropriate *R* value and to carry the *negative sign* that precedes the equation throughout the calculations.	hence, $K = e^{\frac{G°}{-RT}}$ where $\frac{\Delta G°}{-RT} = \frac{26.5\ kJ/mol_{rxn}}{-0.008314\ \frac{kJ}{mol \cdot K} \times 500.\ K} = -6.37$
4. Make sure the energy units for $\Delta G°$ and *R* agree.	Thus $K = e^{-6.37} = 1.70 \times 10^{-3}$

Practice Problems 3.3.2 — Conversions of $\Delta G°$ to K and K to $\Delta G°$

1. The pollutant gas nitrogen monoxide forms from nitrogen and oxygen gas according to the following equation: $N_2(g) + O_2(g) \rightleftharpoons 2\ NO(g)$. *K* is only 8.44×10^{-3} at 2500°C. Calculate $\Delta G°$. Is the reaction spontaneous in the forward or the reverse direction?

2. (a) Calculate *K* for a reaction at 25°C that has a $\Delta G°$ value of –35.0 kJ/mol$_{rxn}$.

   (b) Repeat the calculation at the same temperature for a reaction with $\Delta G°$ equal to +35.0 kJ/mol$_{rxn}$.

   (c) Compare the *K* values and what they mean for these two reactions.

Variations in Total Free Energy for Reversible Reactions

In an *exergonic* reaction (one in which $\Delta G°$ *is negative*) the products (point 2 in Figure 3.3.1(a)) have less free energy and are more stable than the reactants (point 1 in Figure 3.3.1(a)). The difference between these two points (2 – 1) is $\Delta G°$. All points between 1 and 2 correspond to various mixtures of the reactants and products present as the reaction proceeds. The difference between point 1 (in the forward direction) or point 2 (in the reverse direction) and any point on the curve is ΔG. The mixture of reactants and products present at the *minimum* of the curve (point 3) has the *least free energy* and is the *most stable* of all. This represents the *equilibrium mixture.*

At any point on the curve, a comparison of the *reaction quotient Q* to the *equilibrium constant K* indicates the *direction* in which the reaction must proceed *to reach equilibrium*. This will always be the direction that is *downhill* in a free energy diagram! For an exergonic reaction, because $\Delta G°$ *is negative, K must be* > *1* so the *equilibrium mixture will always contain more products than reactants.*

In an *endergonic* reaction (one in which $\Delta G°$ *is positive*) the products (point 2 in Figure 3.3.1(b)) will have more free energy than the reactants (point 1 in Figure 3.3.1(b)). In this case, *K* < *1* and the standard reaction is *reactant favored*, resulting in an equilibrium mixture containing more reactants than products.

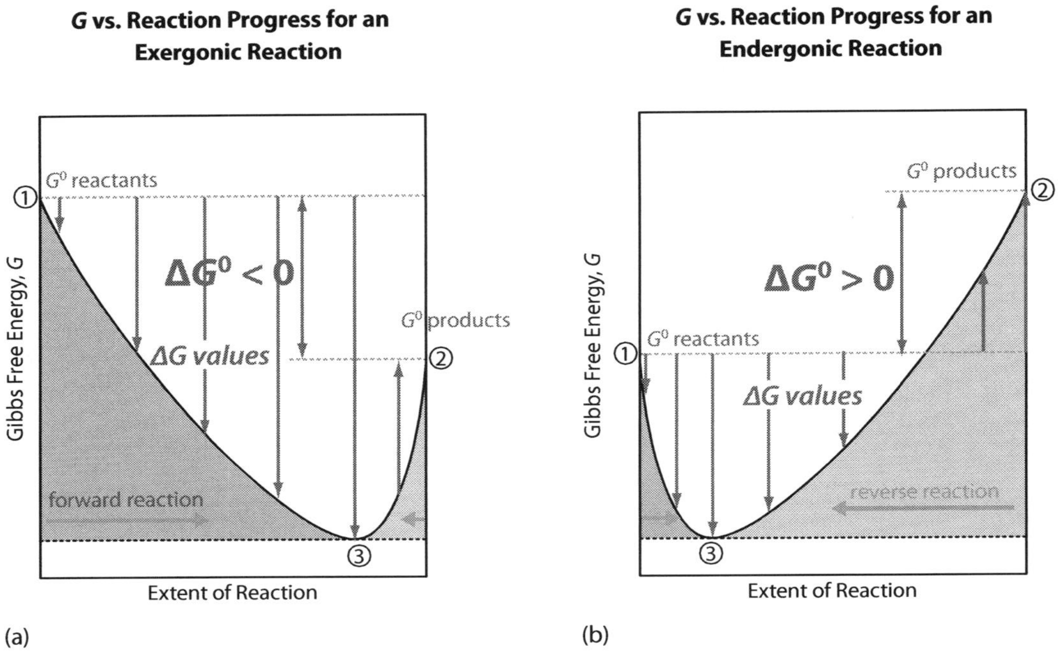

Figure 3.3.1 *Free energy changes during the course of an exergonic and an endergonic reaction at constant temperature.*

 © Edvantage Interactive 2019

3.3 Review Questions

1. Calculate ΔG° for the conversion of oxygen to ozone:

   $3\ O_2(g) \rightleftharpoons 2\ O_3(g)$ at 25°C given that $K = 2.50 \times 10^{-29}$

2. Consider the reaction: $MgCO_3(s) \rightleftharpoons MgO(s) + CO_2(g)$

   (a) Is the forward reaction spontaneous at room temperature (25°C)? Give a mathematical justification.

   (b) Is the reaction driven by enthalpy, entropy, both, or neither? Give a mathematical justification.

   (c) What is the value of K at 25°C?

   (d) At what temperature does the direction of the spontaneous reaction change?

   (e) Does high temperature make the reaction more or less spontaneous in the forward direction? Include a full explanation.

3. Methane, $CH_4(g)$, is the main component of natural gas. When the barrel of a Bunsen burner is wide open, more oxygen ($O_2(g)$) is available for the combustion of the methane. The products are entirely $CO_2(g)$ and $H_2O(g)$. When the barrel is nearly closed, the products are $CO_2(g)$ and some $H_2O(l)$.

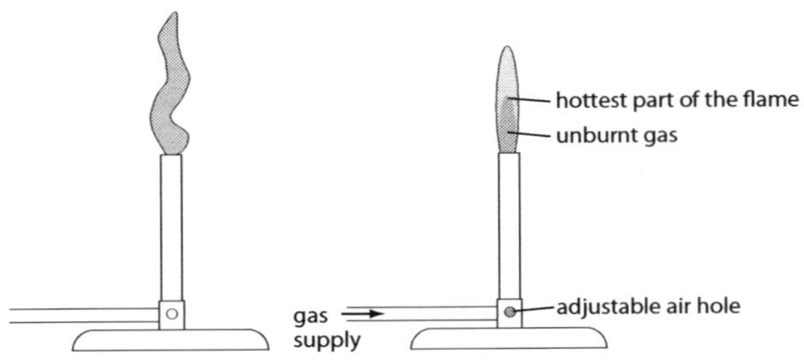

(a) Calculate $\Delta G°$ at 25°C for each reaction.

(b) Calculate K for each reaction.

(c) Which burner adjustment gives a hotter flame?

(d) Why does opening the barrel on the burner force a more complete combustion?

4. Use the reference values for ΔH_f° and $S°$ from Table A8 in the appendix to calculate $\Delta H°$, $\Delta S°$, and $\Delta G°$ for the reaction:

$CO(g) + H_2O(g) \rightleftharpoons CO_2(g) + H_2(g)$ at 25°C.

(a) $\Delta H°$ (Show all work completely.)

(b) $\Delta S°$ (Show all work completely.)

(c) $\Delta G°$ (Use the Gibbs-Helmholtz equation with a temperature of 25°C.)

 © Edvantage Interactive 2019

(d) Calculate the equilibrium constant K for this reaction at 25°C.

(e) Calculate the equilibrium constant K for this reaction at 225°C.

(f) Using your answers to parts (d) and (e), determine whether this reaction is exo- or endothermic? Justify your answer. Does this response agree with the answer to part (a)?

5. Consider what each of the following graphs represent.

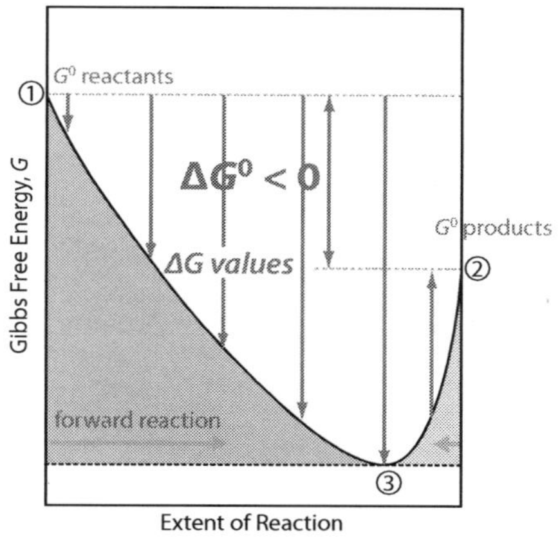

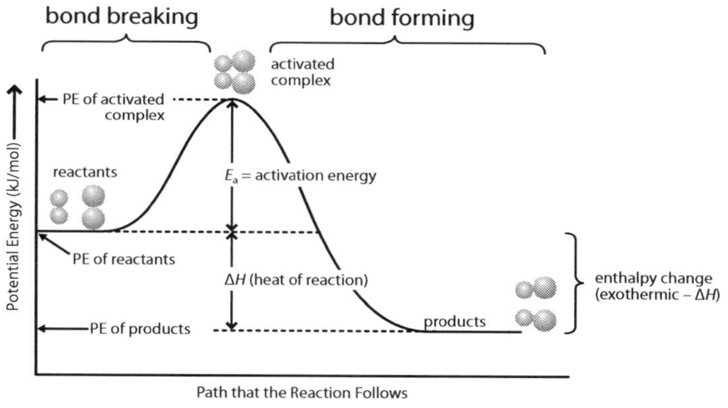

(a) How are the graphs similar? Be specific.

(b) How are the graphs different? Be specific.

6. Consider the following representations of a physical and a chemical change. Answer each question for A and B.

A. A physical change

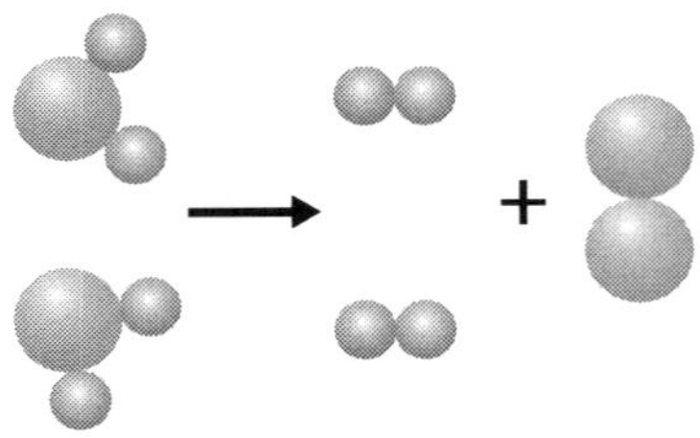

B. A chemical change

(a) What is the sign of $\Delta H°$?

(b) What is the sign of $\Delta S°$?

(c) How does the sign of $\Delta G°$ vary with temperature?

7. Consider the following reaction:

$N_2O_4(g) \rightleftharpoons 2\ NO_2(g)$

(a) Calculate $\Delta G°$.

(b) Examine the following molecular representation. Assume each molecule exerts a partial pressure of 0.010 atm at 25°C. Calculate ΔG.

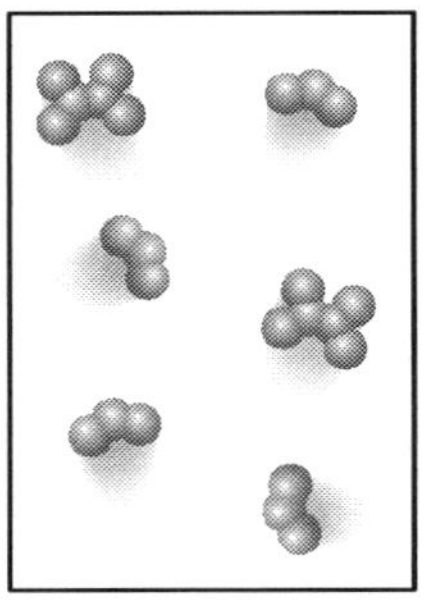

(c) In general, how would the representation change if the system were to achieve equilibrium?

© Edvantage Interactive 2019

8. Consider the following reaction at 25°C.

$$2\ NO(g) + O_2(g) \rightleftharpoons 2\ NO_2(g) \quad \Delta G° = -71.2\ kJ/mol_{rxn}$$

(a) Calculate ΔG under the following conditions:

$P_{NO} = 0.0500$ atm $\quad P_{O_2} = 0.0500$ atm $\quad P_{NO_2} = 0.100$ atm

(b) Is the reaction more or less spontaneous under these pressure conditions?

9. (a) Given ΔG = -5.44 kJ/mol, calculate ΔG at 298 K for the reaction $2\ ICl(g) \rightleftharpoons I_2(g) + Cl_2(g)$ in a mixture containing the following partial pressures:

$P_{ICl} = 2.0$ atm $\quad P_{I_2} = 0.0020$ atm $\quad P_{Cl_2} = 0.0020$ atm

(Remember: I_2 is normally a solid under standard conditions.)

(b) Is this reaction more or less spontaneous under these conditions than under standard conditions?

10. At 25°C, acetic acid, CH_3COOH, ionizes in water to form hydrogen and acetate ions. The acid is quite weak and has a small equilibrium constant, K_a, of 1.8×10^{-5}. $CH_3COOH(aq) \rightleftharpoons H^+(aq) + CH_3COO^-(aq)$

(a) Calculate $\Delta G°$ for the ionization of acetic acid.

(b) Calculate ΔG for the reaction if $[CH_3COOH] = 0.10$ mol/L, $[H^+] = 9.5 \times 10^{-5}$ mol/L, and $[CH_3COO^-] = 9.5 \times 10^{-5}$ mol/L.

(c) Compare the spontaneity of ionization under the conditions in part (b) to those under standard conditions.

© Edvantage Interactive 2019

4 Solubility Equilibrium

This chapter focuses on the following AP Units from the College Board:

Unit 1: Atomic Structure and Properties

Unit 4: Chemical Reactions

Unit 7: Equilibrium.

By the end of this chapter, you should be able to do the following:

- Determine the solubility of a compound in aqueous solution
- Describe a saturated solution as an equilibrium system
- Determine the concentration of ions in a solution
- Determine the relative solubility of a substance, given solubility tables
- Apply solubility rules to analyze the composition of solutions
- Formulate equilibrium constant expressions for various saturated solutions
- Perform calculations involving solubility equilibrium concepts
- Devise a method for determining the concentration of a specific ion

By the end of this chapter, you should know the meaning of these **key terms**:

- aqueous solution
- common ion
- complete ionic equation
- dissociation equation
- electrical conductivity
- formula equation
- hard water
- ionic solution
- K_{sp}
- molecular solution
- net ionic equation
- precipitate
- relative solubility
- saturated solution
- solubility equilibrium

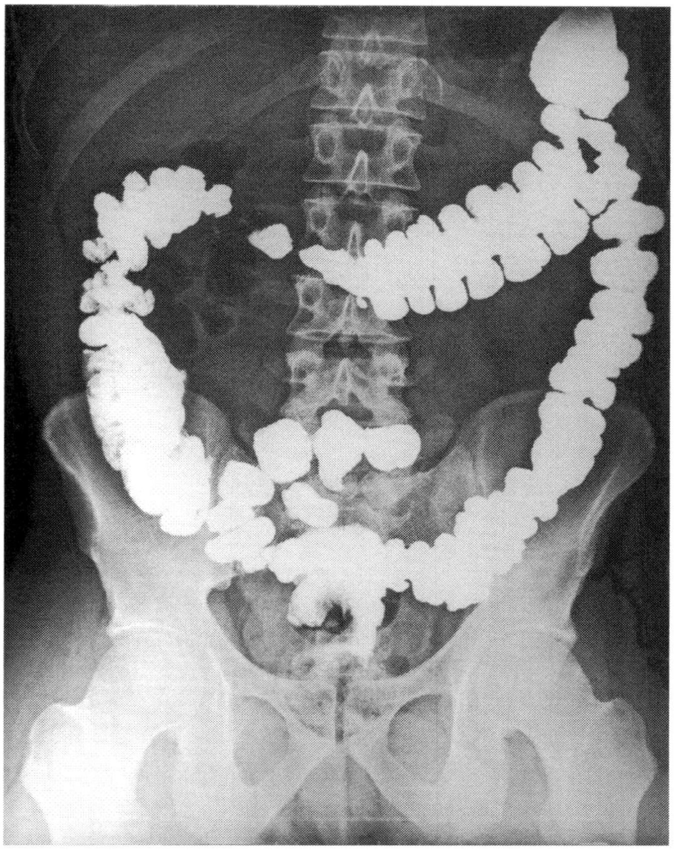

A patient must ingest a solution of barium sulfate for the large intestine (shown here) to be visible on an X-ray. The small solubility product, or K_{sp}, of $BaSO_4$ means humans can safely ingest the suspension.

4.1 The Concept of Solubility

Warm Up

1. Classify solutions of the following solutes as ionic or molecular by putting a checkmark in the appropriate column.

	Ionic	Molecular
Potassium phosphate		
Xenon hexafluoride		
Phosphoric acid		
Sulfur dioxide		
Ammonium sulfide		

2. Describe a simple test and its results to determine whether a solute is ionic or molecular.

____

____

Electrical Conductivity

You have learned about different types of solutes and solvents, and how they interact with each other. In this chapter, we will concern ourselves with aqueous solutions only. These are solutions where the solvent is water. Let's review some concepts from previous chemistry courses:

- An **electrolyte** solution conducts electricity. A weak electrolyte solution does not conduct electricity well. A non-electrolyte solution does not conduct electricity at all.
- Electrical conductivity requires the presence of ions in solution. The more ions present, the greater the electrical conductivity.

Ionic compounds are made up of metal and non-metal ions. Metal ions are called **cations** and non-metal ions are called **anions**. Note that the ammonium ion is a cation even though it contains only non-metal atoms.

Salts are ionic compounds. Examples of salts include NaCl, $(NH_4)_2SO_4$, AgCl, FeC_2O_4, and $Al_2(CrO_4)_3$. Salts differ in their abilities to dissolve in water. For example, NaCl is quite soluble in water, but AgCl is only slightly soluble in water. You will learn how to compare the relative solubilities of salts in the next section in more detail. All salts dissolve in water to produce electrolyte solutions. Salts that dissolve well in water can produce solutions with high ion concentrations, so these salts are called strong electrolytes.

Molecular compounds are made up of non-metal atoms and do not form ions. Most exist as individual molecules. A few form networks of connected molecules that appear crystalline in their solid states. Organic compounds are molecular. Examples of molecular substances are SO_2, Cl_2, and CH_3OH. Molecular solutes do not form ions in water. When a molecular compound dissolves, its molecules enter the solution intact.

Some compounds, even though they appear molecular, do form ions. Recall from that solutions of acids are ionic to varying degrees. Strong acids completely ionize in solution. Strong acids include

 © Edvantage Interactive 2019

HCl, HBr, HI, HNO_3, H_2SO_4, and $HClO_4$. A solution of 1.0 M HCl actually does not contain any HCl molecules; it contains 1.0 M H^+ ions and 1.0 M Cl^- ions. Weak acids are able to form ions, but only to a limited extent. Even high concentrations of weak acids have very low ion concentrations and thus weak acids are also weak electrolytes. Examples of weak acids include CH_3COOH, H_3PO_4, HF, H_2CO_3, and HNO_2. You will learn later in this course how to determine whether an acid is strong or weak.

Quick Check

1. Are all salt solutions strong electrolytes? Explain.

____

2. Classify the following as ionic or molecular in solution:
   (a) octane — a substance in gasoline: C_8H_{18} ____________________
   (b) trisodium phosphate — a common cleaner: Na_3PO_4 ____________________
   (c) chalk — calcium carbonate ____________________
   (d) sulfur dioxide — a pollutant from heavy industry ____________________
   (e) hydrochloric acid — the acid present in your stomach ____________________

3. The SI unit for electrical conductivity is siemens (S). A student tests the electrical conductivity of carbon tetrachloride, tap water, and seawater. The results are tabulated below. Identify samples A, B, and C. (Note: The unit mS stands for millisiemens.)

	Electrical Conductivity (mS)	Identity of Sample
Sample A	0.0005	
Sample B	0	
Sample C	4.8	

Concentrations of Ions in Solution

Water is a polar covalent solvent. Each water molecule contains a molecular dipole resulting from the polar H–O bonds, as shown in Figure 4.1.1.

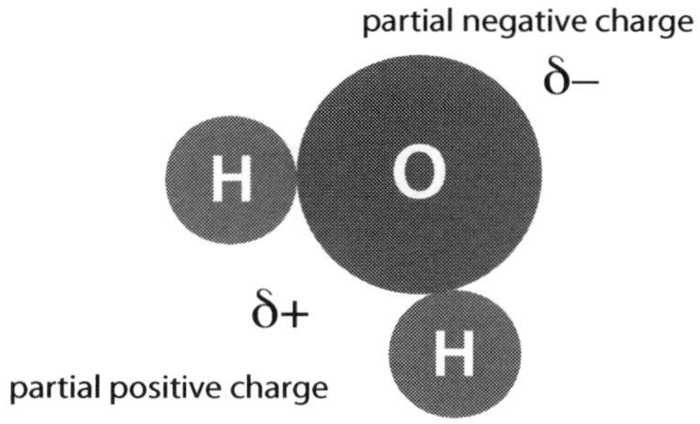

Figure 4.1.1 *A water molecule has polar H–O bonds.*

When an ionic compound dissolves in water, the water molecules attract and separate the anions and cations in the solute. For example, when NaCl(*s*) dissolves in water, the Na^+ cations are attracted to the negative dipoles on the oxygen atoms of water (Figure 4.1.2). The Cl^- anions are attracted to the positive dipoles on the hydrogen atoms of water. The process of separating the positive and negative ions in solution is called **dissociation.** We can write a dissociation equation to represent this process:

$$NaCl(aq) \rightarrow Na^+(aq) + Cl^-(aq)$$

If the salt were Na_3PO_4 instead, the dissociation equation would be:

$$Na_3PO_4(aq) \rightarrow 3\ Na^+(aq) + PO_4^{3-}(aq)$$

Notice that the dissociation equation is balanced for both numbers of atoms and charge.

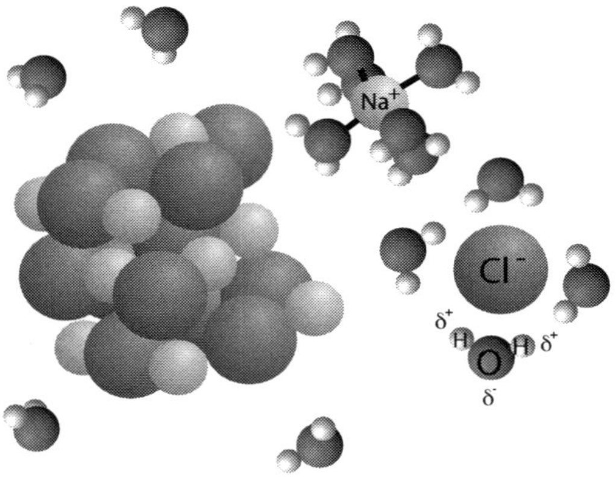

Figure 4.1.2 *NaCl dissociates in water.*

Quick Check

Write dissociation equations for the following aqueous solutions:

1. calcium chloride

2. ammonium oxalate

3. sodium phosphate

 © Edvantage Interactive 2019

Calculating the Molarity of a Solution

When a solute dissolves in water, the concentration of ions is proportional to the concentration of the solution formed. You know how to calculate the molarity of a solution. Consider the addition of 2.3 g of $CaCl_2$ to water to produce 500. mL of solution. We can calculate the concentration of the $CaCl_2$ solution:

$$[CaCl_2] = \frac{2.3\ \cancel{g}}{0.500\ L} \times \frac{1\ mol}{111.1\ \cancel{g}} = 0.041\ M$$

From the dissociation equation, we use the mole ratio to determine the concentration of each ion in the solution:

$$CaCl_2(aq) \rightarrow Ca^{2+}(aq) + 2\ Cl^-(aq)$$
$$0.041\ M \qquad 0.041\ M \qquad 0.082\ M$$

For each formula unit of $CaCl_2$ that dissociates, one calcium ion and two chloride ions are formed. The $[Ca^{2+}] = 0.041$ M, the $[Cl^-] = 0.082$ M, and the total ion concentration is 0.124 M.

Quick Check

1. Calculate the concentration of each ion in solution, and then the total ion concentration. Begin by writing a dissociation equation for each.
   (a) 0.45 M sodium oxalate

   (b) 2.5 M aluminum chloride

2. Which solution would have the greater conductivity: 1.0 M LiOH or 0.8 M $CaCl_2$? Support your answer with calculations.

3. Solid aluminum bromide was dissolved in water to form 100. mL of solution. If the resulting $[Br^-] = 0.15$ M, what is the $[Al^{3+}]$ in solution ?

Accounting for Dilution and Dissociation

When two solutions are mixed together, each is diluted by the other. The following sample problem describes how to account for both the dilution of the solution and the dissociation of the solutes to form ions.

Sample Problem 4.1.1 — Calculating Ion Concentrations

Calculate the concentration of each ion in a solution formed when 25 mL of 0.50 M $MgCl_2$ is mixed with 10. mL of 0.60 M $AlCl_3$.

What to Think About	How to Do It
1. When one solution is added to another solution, both are diluted. First calculate the diluted concentrations of each, recognizing that the final volume of the solution is 25 mL + 10. mL = 35 mL.	$[MgCl_2] = \frac{0.50 \text{ mol}}{1 \text{ L}} \times \frac{0.025 \text{ L}}{0.035 \text{ L}} = 0.36 \text{ M}$ $[AlCl_3] = \frac{0.60 \text{ mol}}{1 \text{ L}} \times \frac{0.010 \text{ L}}{0.035 \text{ L}} = 0.17 \text{ M}$
2. Write dissociation equations for each solution and calculate the concentration of ions in each.	$MgCl_2(aq) \rightarrow Mg^{2+}(aq) + 2\,Cl^-(aq)$ 0.36 M 0.36 M 0.72 M $AlCl_3(aq) \rightarrow Al^{3+}(aq) + 3\,Cl^-(aq)$ 0.17 M 0.17 M 0.51 M
3. Ions that are present in both solutions have a total concentration calculated by adding their individual concentrations together.	$[Cl^-] = 0.72 \text{ M} + 0.51 \text{ M} = 1.23 \text{ M}$ $[Mg^{2+}] = 0.36 \text{ M}$ $[Al^{3+}] = 0.17 \text{ M}$

Practice Problems 4.1.1 — Calculating Ion Concentrations

1. Calculate the concentration of all ions in the following solutions:
   (a) 0.35 g of ammonium phosphate dissolved in 650. mL of solution

   (b) A solution formed when 15 mL of 6.0 M HCl is added to 20. mL water

2. What mass of aluminum sulfate must be dissolved in 250. mL of solution to result in $[SO_4^{2-}] = 0.45$ M ?

3. What are the ion concentrations in a solution made by mixing 55 mL of 0.22 M ammonium sulfate with 25 mL of 0.45 M ammonium sulfide?

© Edvantage Interactive 2019

Saturated Solutions and Solubility

To make a solution, we dissolve some solute in a solvent. If we continue to add solute, we will get to a point where no more solute will dissolve. At this point, the solution is **saturated**. In a saturated solution, there must be undissolved solid present. When a precipitate is formed, the solution is saturated with the ions that form that precipitate.

> The **solubility** of a substance is the amount of solute required to make a certain volume of saturated solution. It is the maximum amount of solute that can be dissolved in a particular volume of solution.

Recall that the solubility of most salts increases with temperature. For this reason, solubilities are determined at different temperatures. You will learn later in this section that the solubility of a salt also depends on other ions that might be present in the solution.

There are many possible units for solubility:

- molarity or mol/L for molar solubility
- g/mL
- ppm (parts per million)
- g solute/100. g solvent

In this course, we will use mainly molarity and g/mL.

Sample Problems 4.1.2 — Converting Between Units of Solubility

1. Calculate the molar solubility of lead(II) sulfate, if 500. mL of saturated solution contains 0.020 g of lead(II) sulfate.
2. The molar solubility of lead(II) chloride is 0.014 M at 25°C. What is the solubility in g/mL?

What to Think About	How to Do It
1. Molar solubility is measured in mol/L. Use the molar mass of $PbSO_4$ to convert between grams and moles.	$[PbSO_4] = \frac{0.020\ g}{0.500\ L} \times \frac{1\ mol}{303.4\ g} = 1.3 \times 10^{-4}\ M$
2. To convert between mass and moles, use the molar mass of $PbCl_2$.	$\frac{0.014\ mol}{1000.\ mL} \times \frac{278.3\ g}{1\ mol} = 3.9 \times 10^{-3}\ g/mL$

Practice Problems 4.1.2 — Converting Between Units of Solubility

1. The solubility of MnS is 4.7×10^{-6} g/mL. Calculate its molar solubility.

2. The solubility of lead(II) iodate is 4.5×10^{-5} M. What mass of lead(II) iodate is dissolved in 300. mL of saturated solution?

3. Calcium carbonate is commonly found in eggshells and rock formations. A student evaporates 100. mL of saturated solution and 7.1×10^{-4} g remains. What is its molar solubility?

Equilibrium in Solutions

As stated earlier, a saturated solution must contain some undissolved solute. An equilibrium exists between the undissolved solid and dissolved ions. The equilibrium in a saturated solution of lead(II) chloride can be represented by the following equation:

$$PbCl_2(s) \rightleftharpoons Pb^{2+}(aq) + 2\ Cl^-(aq)$$

Notice that the solid is on the left of the equation. Practise writing the equilibrium present in a saturated solution by always placing the solid as a reactant. The equation for the equilibrium is balanced for both number of atoms and charge. As in all equilibrium systems, the forward reaction rate (dissociation or dissolving) and reverse reaction rate (crystallization) are equal. If this equilibrium were established by adding solid $PbCl_2$ to water, the $[Pb^{2+}]$ and $[Cl^-]$ would be related to each other in a 1:2 mole ratio. That means that the $[Cl^-]$ would be twice the $[Pb^{2+}]$ in solution.

Quick Check

Write the equations to represent the equilibrium present in a saturated solution of each of the following.

1. zinc carbonate

2. aluminum hyroxide

3. iron(III) sulfide

© Edvantage Interactive 2019

4.1 Activity: A Solubility Crossword

Question

How can you construct a crossword to define vocabulary terms?

Background

Chemists use very precise vocabulary to describe concepts. A solid understanding of the meaning of these words is essential to understanding the concepts.

Procedure

1. Construct a crossword puzzle containing the following vocabulary terms:

anion	ionization	soluble
cation	molarity	solute
conductivity	molecular	solution
dissociation	precipitate	solvent
electrolyte	saturated	unsaturated
ionic	solubility	

2. Your clue for each term must be in your own words.

Results and Discussion

1. Exchange your crossword with your partners.
2. Complete your partner's crossword.
3. Were there terms that you found difficult to define? If they were, compile a list of these terms separately, and for each, identify examples that illustrate the meaning of the term.

4.1 Review Questions

1. Give three examples for each of the following:
   (a) strong electrolytes

   (b) non-electrolytes

2. Compare the electrical conductivity of 1.0 M $HClO_4$ to that of 1.0 M H_3PO_4. Explain your reasoning.

3. Write dissociation equations for the following in aqueous solution. Ensure that your equations are balanced for both number of atoms and charge.

   (a) magnesium perchlorate

   (b) calcium dichromate

   (c) copper(II) acetate

   (d) manganese(II) thiocyanate

   (e) aluminum binoxalate

   (f) barium hydroxide octahydrate

4. Barium sulfate is used in medicine as a radiopaque contrast material. Patients drink a suspension of barium sulfate to coat their gastrointestinal tract. The surface of the tissue being studied is then highly visible under X-ray or CT scan. Radiologists can better see disease or trauma internally using this method. What is the molar solubility of barium sulfate if a saturated solution contains 0.0012 g dissolved in 500. mL of solution?

© Edvantage Interactive 2019

5. Calcium carbonate is used to treat calcium deficiencies in the body. Your body needs calcium to build and maintain healthy bones. What mass of calcium carbonate is required to produce 250. mL of solution with a calcium ion concentration of 7.1×10^{-5} M ?

6. Sodium dichromate is used in the production of chromic acid; a common etching agent. Calculate the concentration of each ion in a solution of sodium dichromate prepared by dissolving 0.50 g in 150. mL of solution.

7. Solutions of magnesium chloride and sodium chloride are mixed to make brine commonly used to keep roads from becoming slippery because of ice. The brine solution lowers the freezing point of water by up to 10°C. A brine solution is made by mixing 60. L of 5.0 M sodium chloride with 30. L of 2.4 M magnesium chloride. Calculate the concentration of each ion in this solution.

8. Describe how you would prepare 1.0 L of a saturated solution of sodium chloride.

9. Write the equation for the equilibrium present in saturated solutions of the following:
   (a) silver bromate

   (b) aluminum chromate

   (c) magnesium hydroxide

   (d) lead(II) sulfate

   (e) copper(II) phosphate

4.2 Qualitative Analysis — Identifying Unknown Ions

Warm Up

1. The solubility of silver chloride is 1.4×10^{-3} g/L at room temperature. Calculate its molar solubility.

2. The solubility of sodium chloride is 359 g/L at room temperature. Calculate its molar solubility.

3. We define a salt as soluble if its solubility is greater than 0.1 M. Classify NaCl and AgCl as being soluble or having low solubility.

   NaCl ____________________ AgCl ____________________

Precipitate Formation

Salts have different abilities to dissolve in water. When a salt is added to water, it will dissolve if the attraction of the cation and anion to each other is overcome or replaced by an attraction of the ions to a polar water molecule. For example, when NaCl is placed in water, the attraction of the Na^+ cation to the Cl^- anion is replaced. The cation is attracted to the negative dipole on the oxygen atom of the water molecule. The anion is attracted to the positive dipole on the hydrogen atoms of water. Because the ions are attracted to the solvent, dissociation occurs. However, when a salt such as AgCl is placed in water, the Ag^+ cation is more strongly attracted to the Cl^- anion. That attraction can only be slightly overcome by an attraction to water molecules, so most of the AgCl solute remains undissociated. When only a small amount of solute dissolves, we say the solute has *low solubility*. Note that AgCl is not *insoluble*; a small amount of AgCl will dissolve.

A solubility table like Table 4.2.1 on the next page can be used to help predict which salts will be soluble or have a low solubility in water.

How to Use a Solubility Table

Make note of the following points related to Table 4.2.1:

- The term *soluble* means that more than 0.1 mol of salt will dissolve in 1.0 L of solution. *Low solubility* means that less than 0.1 mol of salt will dissolve in 1.0 L of solution. It does **not** mean that the salt does not dissolve.
- Because the solubility of a salt changes with temperature, the terms *soluble* and *low solubility* refer to amounts of solute that dissolve at room temperature.
- Alkali metal ions are listed at the top of the table, and are simply referred to as "alkali ions" farther down the table.
- Salts with alkali ions or ammonium ion are soluble.
- Acids are soluble.
- Salts with nitrate ion are soluble.
- Salts containing phosphates, sulfites, and carbonates usually have low solubility (except for alkali and ammonium salts)

To use this table, simply find the anion present in the salt and then read across to identify the cation with which it is *soluble* or has *low solubility*.

 © Edvantage Interactive 2019

Table 4.2.1 *Solubility of Common Compounds in Water*

Note: In this table, soluble means > 0.1 mol/L at 25°C.

Negative Ions (Anions)	Positive Ions (Cations)	Solubility of Compounds
All	Alkali ions: Li^+, Na^+, K^+, Rb^+, Cs^+, Fr^+	Soluble
All	Hydrogen ion: H^+	Soluble
All	Ammonium ion: NH_4^+	Soluble
Nitrate: NO_3^-	All	Soluble
Chloride: Cl^- Or Bromide: Br^- Or Iodide: I^-	All others	Soluble
	Ag^+, Pb^{2+}, Cu^+	Low solubility
Sulfate: SO_4^{2-}	All others	Soluble
	Ag^+, Ca^{2+}, Sr^{2+}, Ba^{2+}, Pb^{2+}	Low solubility
Sulfide: S^{2-}	Alkali ions, H^+, NH_4^+, Be^{2+}, Mg^{2+}, Ca^{2+}, Sr^{2+}, Ba^{2+}	Soluble
	All others	Low solubility
Hydroxide: OH^-	Alkali ions, H^+, NH_4^+, Sr^{2+}	Soluble
	All others	Low solubility
Phosphate: PO_4^{3-} Or Carbonate: CO_3^{2-} Or Sulfite: SO_3^{2-}	Alkali ions, H^+, NH_4^+	Soluble
	All others	Low solubility

Sample Problem 4.2.1 — Predicting the Solubility of Salts Using the Solubility Table

Classify the following salts as being "soluble" or having "low solubility."

1. copper(II) chloride
2. aluminum hydroxide
3. sodium phosphate

What to Think About

1. Identify the formula as $CuCl_2$. The anion is Cl^-. The cation is Cu^{2+}. From the table, Cl^- is soluble with Cu^{2+}. (Be careful to note which copper ion you have, as Cl^- has a low solubility with Cu^+.)

2. Identify the formula as $Al(OH)_3$. The anion is OH^-. The cation is Al^{3+}, which falls into the "all others" category on the table. OH^- has low solubility with Al^{3+}.

3. Identify the formula as Na_3PO_4. The anion is PO_4^{3-}. The cation is Na^+. From the table, PO_4^{3-} is soluble with Na^+. (A sodium ion is an alkali ion.)

How to Do It

Copper(II) chloride is soluble.

Aluminum hydroxide has low solubility.

Sodium phosphate is soluble.

Practice Problems 4.2.1 — Predicting the Solubility of Salts Using the Solubility Table

1. Classify the following salts as being soluble or having low solubility in water:

   (a) calcium sulfate ______________________________

   (b) iron(II) sulfide ______________________________

   (c) strontium hydroxide ______________________________

   (d) zinc bromide ______________________________

   (e) cesium sulfite ______________________________

   (f) potassium chromate ______________________________

2. Write the formula for the following:

   (a) a salt containing carbonate that is soluble

   (b) a salt containing sulfate with low solubility

   (c) a cation that forms a salt with low solubility with both chloride and sulfate ions

   (d) an anion that forms soluble salts with all cations

3. A student is given a sample of a solution that is either magnesium nitrate or strontium nitrate. When a few drops of a solution of sodium hydroxide is added to the sample, no precipitate forms. Does the sample contain magnesium nitrate or strontium nitrate? Explain your reasoning.

Equations Representing Precipitate Reactions

Three types of chemical equations are used to represent a double replacement or metathesis reaction. Let's use the reaction between solutions of potassium iodide and lead(II) nitrate to illustrate the three types of equations.

A **formula equation** shows the chemical formulas of the compounds and their states. You would use the solubility table to identify the product with the low solubility.

$$2\ KI(aq) + Pb(NO_3)_2(aq) \rightarrow 2\ KNO_3(aq) + PbI_2(s)$$

When writing ionic equations, you must carefully identify all soluble ionic compounds and any strong acids. These species must be shown in their dissociated or ionized forms. All other substances appear in an ionic equation in the same format as they do in a formula equation.

In a **complete ionic equation**, the soluble salts are represented in their dissociated form. Because the precipitate has low solubility, it is not shown dissociated. This makes sense when you consider that the precipitate forms very few ions in solution.

$$2\ K^+(aq) + 2\ I^-(aq) + Pb^{2+}(aq) + 2\ NO_3^-(aq) \rightarrow 2\ K^+(aq) + 2\ NO_3^-(aq) + PbI_2(s)$$

In a **net ionic equation**, only the ions that take part in the reaction appear. Ions that are the same on both sides of the equation are called **spectator ions**. Spectator ions are much like spectators at a sports event. They only watch the event; they do not take part in its outcome. Spectator ions are not included in a net ionic equation.

$$Pb^{2+}(aq) + 2\ I^-(aq) \rightarrow PbI_2(s)$$

 © Edvantage Interactive 2019

Quick Check

1. Write the formula for the precipitate that forms when the following solutions are mixed.

   (a) BaS and $MgSO_4$

   (b) NH_4OH and $FeBr_2$

   (c) H_3PO_4 and $ZnCl_2$

   (d) K_2CO_3 and $CrSO_4$

   (e) MnI_2 and $Sr(OH)_2$

2. Write a formula equation, complete ionic equation, and net ionic equation for the following reactions.

   (a) Solutions of strontium hydroxide and silver nitrate are mixed.

   (b) Solutions of magnesium sulfide and zinc chloride are mixed.

   (c) Solutions of sodium carbonate and barium sulfide are mixed.

Qualitative Analysis

Qualitative analysis refers to any procedure that can be used to help identify unknown ions in solution. There are many different qualitative analysis methods. Simply looking at a colored solution can help identify ions present. For example, solutions containing copper(II) ions are blue. Chromates can be yellow, and dichromates are orange. Permanganate is a deep purple color, and nickel(II) is light green.

Flame tests are another method to identify ions. A sample of the solution is placed in a flame. Depending on the ions present, the flame may change color. Copper(II) ions turn the flame a blue-green, whereas lithium ions turn the flame red and barium ions make it green. Atomic absorption spectroscopy makes use of this property. Samples are vaporized and passed through a flame. The instrument records the quantity of energy or wavelength that is absorbed by the atoms to give off particular spectra.

One important method of testing a sample for the presence of unknown ions involves adding a reagent to the sample to selectively precipitate ions. The color of the precipitate is often indicative of the ion present. For example, you have probably seen the bright yellow precipitate $PbI_2(s)$. Additionally, the amount of precipitate formed or the speed at which the precipitate forms can also help identify ions. By applying the solubility rules you have learned, you can develop a qualitative analysis scheme to determine the identity of ions in a solution. Your scheme should list steps, including the compounds that you are adding to precipitate one ion at a time and how you will remove the precipitate from the solution.

Sample Problem 4.2.2 — Selective Precipitation

A solution may contain the ions Ca^{2+}, Sr^{2+}, and Zn^{2+}. How would you precipitate the ions out of solution individually?

What to Think About	How to Do It
1. Since these are all cations, add an anion that will only precipitate one of these cations. Add compounds containing the anion of choice. Moving down the anions on the solubility table, NO_3^- and Cl^- will not precipitate any of the ions. SO_4^{2-} will precipitate both Ca^{2+} and Sr^{2+}. You need an anion that only precipitates one of the cations, so SO_4^{2-} won't work. S^{2-} will precipitate only the Zn^{2+}, so this is a good place to start. Remove the *least* soluble ion first.	S^{2-} precipitates only the Zn^{2+}.
2. To add S^{2-} ions, choose a soluble compound that will contain a significant amount of ions. Compounds containing alkali ions are soluble. The formation of a precipitate when Na_2S is added confirms the presence of Zn^{2+}.	A good source of S^{2-} ions would be Na_2S. First add a solution of Na_2S to the sample.
3. Remove the precipitate.	Remove the precipitate of ZnS by filtration or centrifugation.
4. Only $Ca^{2+}$and Sr^{2+} remain in solution. OH^- ions will precipitate Ca^{2+} but not Sr^{2+}. Choose a source of OH^- ions.	NaOH is a good source of OH^- ions. Add a solution of NaOH.
5. Remove the precipitate.	Filter out the precipitate of $Ca(OH)_2$.
6. Only Sr^{2+} ions remain in solution. Precipitate this by adding CO_3^{2-}, SO_4^{2-}, or PO_4^{3-}.	Na_2SO_4 is a good source of SO_4^{2-} ions. Finally add a solution of Na_2SO_4. Filter out the precipitate of $SrSO_4$.

Using Tables and Flow Charts

It may help you to organize your thoughts by constructing a table similar to the one below. Use an X to show no precipitate, and a √ to show a precipitate forming. Once the precipitate is formed, consider that cation removed from solution.

	S^{2-}	OH^-	SO_4^{2-}
Zn^{2+}	√	X	X
Ca^{2+}	removed	√	X
Sr^{2+}	removed	removed	√

A flow chart like the one in Figure 4.2.1 can also be used.

 © Edvantage Interactive 2019

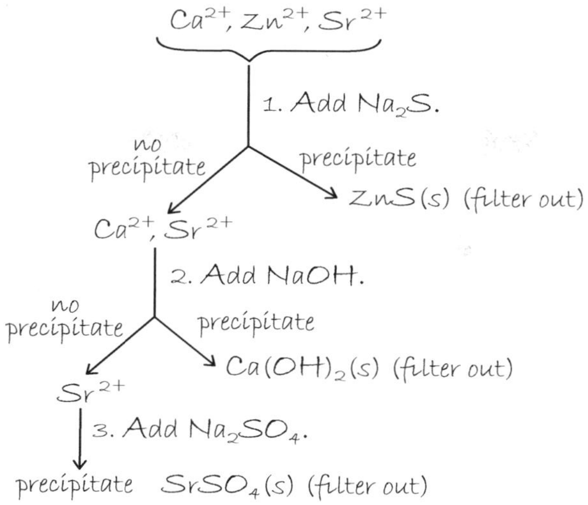

Figure 4.2.1 *A flow chart like this can help you show the process for removing iions from solution.*

Practice Problems 4.2.2 — Selective Precipitation

1. Describe a process to individually remove the ions Ag^+, Ba^{2+}, and Be^{2+} from a solution. Be sure to list the compounds that you add in order, and the method of removing the precipitate. You may wish to use a flow chart.

2. Describe a process to individually remove the ions Br^-, SO_4^{2-}, and S^{2-} from a solution. Be sure to list the compounds that you add in order, and the method of removing the precipitate.

3. Describe a process to individually remove the ions OH^-, PO_4^{3-}, and S^{2-} from a solution. Be sure to list the compounds that you add in order, and the method of removing the precipitate.

Identifying Precipitates

While the formation of a precipitate may identify an ion, sometimes the precipitate may have more than one possible identity. There may be more than one ion present in solution that could be responsible for the precipitate. You can see this on the solubility table.

Consider a solution that may contain Cl^- and I^-. From the solubility table, we can see that the addition of Ag^+ ions would precipitate both anions, but due to the similarity in their colors we would be unable to conclude if the precipitate was AgCl, AgI, or both AgCl and AgI. Another part of qualitative analysis involves adding reagents to dissolve precipitates. In our example, if we added a concentrated solution of NH_3 (at least 6 M) to our precipitates, the AgCl would redissolve and the AgI would not. The following equation represents the formation of the silver diammine ion when AgCl dissolves:

$$AgCl(s) + 2\ NH_3(aq) \rightarrow Ag(NH_3)_2^+(aq) + Cl^-(aq)$$

Other common precipitates that can be easily dissolved are carbonates. The addition of a strong acid, such as HCl will cause the carbonate precipitate to dissolve, forming water and carbon dioxide:

$$BaCO_3(s) + 2\ H^+(aq) \rightarrow CO_2(g) + H_2O(l) + Ba^{2+}(aq)$$

Quick Check

1. List three properties that can be used to determine the identity of ions in solution.

____

2. Consider a solution that may contain Pb^{2+}, Ag^+, and Cu^{2+}. Devise a qualitative analysis scheme to confirm the presence of each ion in solution. Remove each ion individually from solution.

3. A solution contains carbonate and phosphate ions. How could you remove these two ions individually from solution?

 © Edvantage Interactive 2019

Hard Water

The term *hard water* refers to the presence of Ca^{2+}, Mg^{2+}, and/or Fe^{2+} ions in water at relatively high concentrations. Water without these ions is called *soft water*. There are significant amounts of limestone ($CaCO_3$) and dolomite ($CaMg(CO_3)_2$) in the soil in many parts of the world. When CO_2 from the atmosphere dissolves in water from streams or rain, this solution dissolves limestone:

$$CaCO_3(s) + CO_2(aq) + H_2O(g) \rightarrow Ca^{2+}(aq) + 2\ HCO_3^-(aq)$$

The presence of the Ca^{2+} ions in the water supply poses hazards for municipal water systems and homes. As water is heated, the CO_2 is driven off as a gas, reforming a "scale" of $CaCO_3$ in water heaters, pipes, kettles, and boilers. This results in lowering the efficiency of heating systems and in extreme cases, blocking water pipes.

$$Ca^{2+}(aq) + 2\ HCO_3^-(aq) + \text{heat} \rightarrow \underset{\text{scale}}{CaCO_3(s)} + CO_2(g) + H_2O(g)$$

Soaps also react with Ca^{2+} and Mg^{2+} ions to form soap scum that is commonly visible on bathtubs and laundered clothes. Some laundry detergents contain water softeners to prevent the build up of scum on clothes. Shampoos have lathering agents for producing a rich foam when you wash your hair. Washing your hair in an area with hard water significantly reduces the ability of shampoo to lather.

$$Ca^{2+}(aq) + 2\ \underset{\text{soap}}{NaC_{17}H_{35}COO(aq)} \rightarrow \underset{\text{soap scum}}{Ca(C_{17}H_{35}COO)_2(s)} + 2\ Na^+(aq)$$

Municipal water treatment for hard water often includes the addition of CaO or Na_2CO_3 to underground water reservoirs to precipitate out Ca^{2+} and Mg^{2+} ions. Some home treatment systems use ion exchange resins that attract $Ca^{2+}$and Mg^{2+} to the resin surface and release Na^+ ions (Figure 4.2.2). The system can be "recharged" by flooding it with NaCl to replenish the Na^+ ions on the resin and release the $Ca^{2+}$and Mg^{2+} ions.

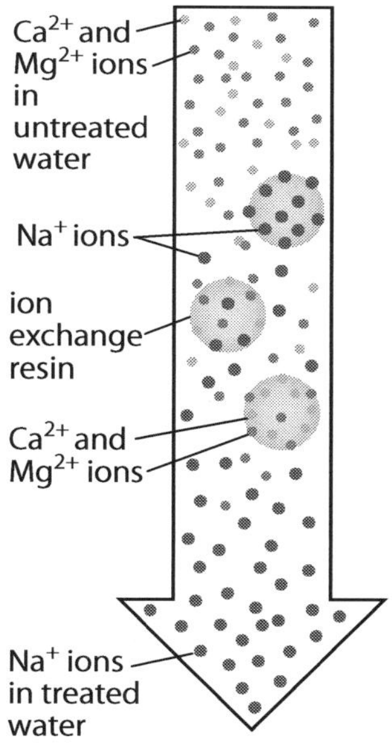

Figure 4.2.2 *Ion exchange treatment for hard water*

4.2 Activity: Using Titration to Calculate the Unknown $[Cl^-]$ In A Sample of Seawater

Question

What is the concentration of Cl^- in seawater?

Background

Titration is an analytical method used to determine the unknown amount of a substance in a sample by reacting it with a measured amount of another substance. You will become more familiar with titration in the acid-base and redox chapters later in this textbook.

Seawater contains a significant amount of salts, largely sodium chloride. In this activity, a sample of seawater is titrated against a standardized solution of silver nitrate. The silver ions cause the chloride ions in the seawater to form a white precipitate. The concentration of chloride ion can be determined by measuring the amount of silver ions required to completely precipitate out the chloride ion. An indicator of potassium chromate is used. When almost all of the chloride ions in the sample have precipitated, any added silver ion will react with the chromate ion, causing a red precipitate to form. The equivalence point is reached once the solution begins to turn reddish.

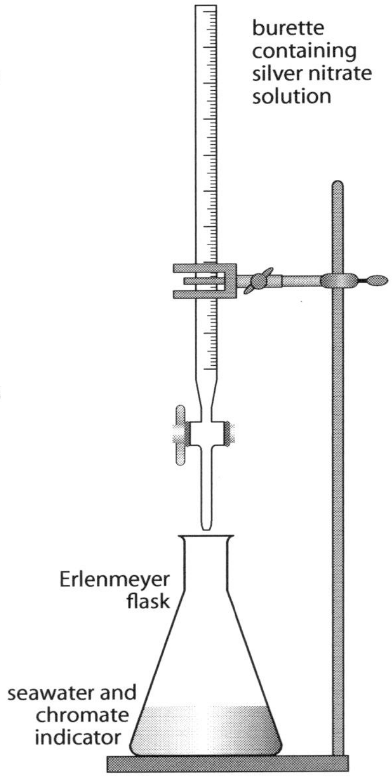

Procedure

1. A 25.0 mL sample of seawater was diluted to 250. mL. From this diluted solution, a 25.0 mL sample was measured out and placed in the Erlenmeyer flask.
2. A few drops of potassium chromate were added to the flask to act as an indicator.
3. A burette was filled with 0.100 M silver nitrate solution. An initial burette reading was taken. The silver nitrate solution was slowly added to the flask. A white precipitate formed. After a few more drops of silver nitrate were added, the precipitate turned a reddish color. At this point, no more silver nitrate was added. A final burette reading was recorded.
4. Procedure steps 1 to 3 were repeated in two more trials, and the data below was recorded.

	Trial 1	Trial 2	Trial 3
Initial burette reading (mL)	0.00	14.70	28.60
Final burette reading (mL)	14.70	28.60	42.35
Volume $AgNO_3$ added (mL)			
Average volume $AgNO_3$ used (mL)			

5. Complete the data table above by subtracting the initial volume from the final volume in each trial to determine the volume of silver nitrate added.
6. The average volume of silver nitrate added is calculated by taking the average of the closest two trials. Calculate the average volume of silver nitrate added, and record it in the data table.

 © Edvantage Interactive 2019

Results and Discussion

1. Write a balanced net ionic equation that represents the reaction between silver ion and chloride ion.

2. Calculate the moles of silver nitrate reacted in the titration using the average volume and concentration of the silver nitrate.

3. Using the mole ratio from the balanced net ionic equation, calculate the moles of chloride ion present in the sample.

4. Using the volume of the *diluted* sample and the moles of chloride calculated above, calculate the concentration of chloride ion in the diluted sample.

5. Calculate the concentration of chloride ion in the original sample of seawater.

6. The level of salt in seawater varies across the planet. The average amount of chloride ion in seawater is 21.2 g/L. How does your sample compare?

7. Silver ions will form a precipitate with both chloride and chromate ions. Use a reference book to look up the solubility of $AgCl$ and Ag_2CrO_4. Calculate the concentration of Ag^+ in a saturated solution of each. Use this information to explain why $AgCl$ precipitates before Ag_2CrO_4.

4.2 Review Questions

1. Classify the following solutes as soluble or low solubility according to the solubility table (Table 4.2.1):
   (a) Rb_2SO_3

   (b) Al_2S_3

   (c) CuI

   (d) ammonium sulfate

   (e) chromium(III) nitrate

   (f) potassium oxalate

2. According to the solubility table, silver sulfate has a low solubility. In a saturated solution of silver sulfate, are silver and sulfate ions present in solution? Explain.

3. The solubility of silver acetate is 11.1 g/L at 25°C. According to the solubility table, would silver acetate be classified as being soluble or of low solubility?

4. Describe the difference between a formula equation, a complete ionic equation, and a net ionic equation. How are they similar? Different?

5. What is a spectator ion? Give an example of a cation and an anion that are common spectator ions in precipitate reactions.

6. Write a balanced formula equation, complete ionic equation, and net ionic equation for each of the following reactions:

   (a) $(NH_4)_2S(aq) + FeSO_4(aq) \rightarrow$

   (b) $H_2SO_3(aq) + CaCl_2(aq) \rightarrow$

   (c) copper(II) sulfate and calcium sulfide $\rightarrow$

© Edvantage Interactive 2019

7. Explain why it would be difficult to separate the ions Na^+ and K^+ in solution using precipitation.

8. A solution contains Cr^{3+}, Ca^{2+}, and Mg^{2+} ions. Describe a method to remove each ion individually from solution. Be sure to state the compound you would add and how you would remove the precipitate from solution. For each reaction that occurs, write a net ionic equation.

9. A solution contains PO_4^{3-}, Cl^-, and S^{2-} ions. Describe a method to remove each ion individually from solution. Be sure to state the compound you would add and how you would remove the precipitate from solution. For each reaction that occurs, write a net ionic equation.

10. Why are compounds containing nitrates used to test for anions?

11. Give two examples where re-dissolving is necessary to separate two precipitates.

12. A solution of Na_2CO_3 is added to a solution of $AgNO_3$.
   (a) Write the net ionic equation for this reaction.

   (b) Two different reagents will dissolve the precipitate formed. Write a net ionic equation for each reaction in which the precipitate dissolves.

13. (a) Define *hard water* and *scale*.

   (b) Scale can be removed by adding a solution of HCl to the water. Write a formula equation, complete ionic equation, and net ionic equation for this reaction.

   (c) Suggest a substance that could be added to water to remove both Ca^{2+} and Mg^{2+} from solution.

   (d) Explain why adding a water softener to your washing machine when doing laundry improves the cleaning job on your clothes.

© Edvantage Interactive 2019

4.3 The Solubility Product Constant K_{sp}

Warm Up

1. Define each of the following terms:
   (a) solubility

   ____

   (b) product (the mathematical definition)

   ____

   (c) constant

   ____

2. The solubility of lead(II) chloride is 4.4 g/L at a particular temperature.
   (a) Write a balanced dissociation equation for lead(II) chloride.

   (b) Calculate the molar solubility of lead(II) chloride at this temperature.

   (c) Calculate the concentration of each ion in a saturated solution of lead(II) chloride.

The Solubility Product Constant

Recall that some chemical systems establish an equilibrium. For such systems, you learned how to write an equilibrium constant expression, K_{eq}.

In a saturated solution, an equilibrium is established between the dissolving and recrystallization of a salt. Consider a saturated solution of $PbCl_2$. We can represent this equilibrium using the following dissociation equation:

$$PbCl_2(s) \rightleftharpoons Pb^{2+}(aq) + 2\ Cl^-(aq)$$

Notice that the solid appears on the reactant side of the equation and the ions on the product side. Recalling that solids do not appear in the K_{eq} expression, for this equilibrium

$$K_{eq} = [Pb^{2+}][Cl^-]^2$$

This is a special type of equilibrium, so it is given its own equilibrium constant type: K_{sp}.

$K_{sp} = [Pb^{2+}][Cl^-]^2$ where K_{sp} stands for the **solubility product constant**

In the Warm Up at the beginning of this section, you defined solubility as the maximum amount of solute that can be dissolved in a particular volume of solution. You defined a product as a mathematical answer derived from multiplication. Therefore, the *solubility product* is the value obtained when the maximum concentrations of ions are multiplied together. This is different from simply the solubility. As solubility depends on temperature, so does the value of K_{sp}.

The molar solubility of a substance is the molar concentration of solute in a saturated solution.

The solubility product constant (K_{sp}) is the *product* of the ion concentrations in a saturated solution raised to the power of the coefficients in the equilibrium.

Obviously, as the solubility of a substance increases, so does the concentration of ions. It follows that the value of K_{sp} also increases.

Quick Check

1. Write an equation to represent the equilibrium present in saturated solutions of the following:
   (a) strontium carbonate

   (b) magnesium hydroxide

   (c) calcium phosphate

2. For each of the equilibria above, write the corresponding K_{sp} expression next to it.

3. Explain the difference between the solubility and the solubility product constant of strontium carbonate.

   ____

   ____

Calculating the K_{sp} From Solubility

The solubility of a substance differs from its solubility product constant, but they are related, and we can calculate one from the other. *When solving any K_{sp} type problem, it is wise to start by writing the equilibrium equation for the saturated solution and then the K_{sp} expression.*

 © Edvantage Interactive 2019

Sample Problem 4.3.1(a) — Calculating K_{sp} from Solubility

The molar solubility of $CaSO_4$ is 8.4×10^{-3} M at a particular temperature. Calculate its K_{sp}.

What to Think About	How to Do It
1. Write an equation representing the equilibrium in a saturated solution.	$CaSO_4(s) \rightleftharpoons Ca^{2+}(aq) + SO_4^{2-}(aq)$ 8.4×10^{-3} M　8.4×10^{-3} M　8.4×10^{-3} M
2. Write the corresponding K_{sp} expression.	$K_{sp} = [Ca^{2+}][SO_4^{2-}]$
3. The solubility of $CaSO_4$ is given in mol/L. Fill in the concentrations of each ion in the equation.	
4. Substitute the concentrations of ions into the K_{sp} expression.	$K_{sp} = [8.4 \times 10^{-3}][8.4 \times 10^{-3}]$ $= 7.1 \times 10^{-5}$

Sample Problem 4.3.1(b) — Calculating K_{sp} from Solubility

The solubility of lead(II) chloride is 4.4 g/L at a particular temperature. Calculate its K_{sp}.

What to Think About	How to Do It
1. The formula is $PbCl_2$. Write an equation representing the equilibrium present in a saturated solution.	$PbCl_2(s) \rightleftharpoons Pb^{2+}(aq) + 2\,Cl^-(aq)$
2. Write the corresponding K_{sp} expression.	$K_{sp} = [Pb^{2+}][Cl^-]^2$
3. In order to calculate K_{sp}, the molarities of Pb^{2+} and Cl^- must be known. Calculate the concentration of each ion from the solubility given.	$[PbCl_2] = \frac{4.4\ \text{g}}{1\ \text{L}} \times \frac{1\ \text{mol}}{278.3\ \text{g}} = 0.016$ M so $[Pb^{2+}] = 0.016$ M and $[Cl^-] = 0.032$ M
4. Substitute the concentrations of ions into the K_{sp} expression.	$K_{sp} = [0.016][0.032]^2$ $= 1.6 \times 10^{-5}$

Practice Problems 4.3.1 — Calculating K_{sp} from Solubility

1. Calculate the K_{sp} for each of the following.
   (a) $CaCO_3$ has a solubility of 6.1×10^{-5} M.

   (b) $Mn(OH)_2$ has a solubility of 3.6×10^{-5} M.

   (c) The solubility of barium chromate is 2.8×10^{-3} g/L.

   (d) The solubility of silver oxalate is 0.033 g/L.

2. A student prepares a saturated solution by dissolving 5.5×10^{-5} mol of $Mg(OH)_2$ in 500. mL of solution. Calculate the K_{sp} of $Mg(OH)_2$.

3. A student evaporated 150. mL of a saturated solution of MgC_2O_4. If 0.16 g of solute remains, calculate the K_{sp}.

 © Edvantage Interactive 2019

Calculating Solubility From K_{sp}

Chemists can calculate the solubility of a substance from its K_{sp}. The K_{sp} values of some salts are listed in Table 4.3.1. Note that these values are for saturated solutions at 25°C.

It is very important to understand that the K_{sp} value is NOT a concentration. It is the *product* of the ion concentrations in a saturated solution raised to the power of their coefficients from the balanced dissociation equation.

Table 4.3.1 *Solubility Product Constants at 25°C*

Name	Formula	K_{sp}
Barium carbonate	$BaCO_3$	2.6×10^{-9}
Barium chromate	$BaCrO_4$	1.2×10^{-10}
Barium sulfate	$BaSO_4$	1.1×10^{-10}
Calcium carbonate	$CaCO_3$	5.0×10^{-9}
Calcium oxalate	CaC_2O_4	2.3×10^{-9}
Calcium sulfate	$CaSO_4$	7.1×10^{-5}
Copper(I) iodide	CuI	1.3×10^{-12}
Copper(II) iodate	$Cu(IO_3)_2$	6.9×10^{-8}
Copper(II) sulfide	CuS	6.0×10^{-37}
Iron(II) hydroxide	$Fe(OH)_2$	4.9×10^{-17}
Iron(II) sulfide	FeS	6.0×10^{-19}
Iron(III) hydroxide	$Fe(OH)_3$	2.6×10^{-39}
Lead(II) bromide	$PbBr_2$	6.6×10^{-6}
Lead(II) chloride	$PbCl_2$	1.2×10^{-5}
Lead(II) iodate	$Pb(IO_3)_2$	3.7×10^{-13}
Lead(II) iodide	PbI_2	8.5×10^{-9}
Lead(II) sulfate	$PbSO_4$	1.8×10^{-8}
Magnesium carbonate	$MgCO_3$	6.8×10^{-6}
Magnesium hydroxide	$Mg(OH)_2$	5.6×10^{-12}
Silver bromate	$AgBrO_3$	5.3×10^{-5}
Silver bromide	AgBr	5.4×10^{-13}
Silver carbonate	Ag_2CO_3	8.5×10^{-12}
Silver chloride	AgCl	1.8×10^{-10}
Silver chromate	Ag_2CrO_4	1.1×10^{-12}
Silver iodate	$AgIO_3$	3.2×10^{-8}
Silver iodide	AgI	8.5×10^{-17}
Strontium carbonate	$SrCO_3$	5.6×10^{-10}
Strontium fluoride	SrF_2	4.3×10^{-9}
Strontium sulfate	$SrSO_4$	3.4×10^{-7}
Zinc sulfide	ZnS	2.0×10^{-25}

Sample Problem 4.3.2(a) — Calculating Solubility from K_{sp}

Calculate the molar solubility of iron(II) hydroxide from its K_{sp}.

What to Think About	How to Do It
1. The formula is $Fe(OH)_2$. Write an equation representing the equilibrium present in a saturated solution.	$Fe(OH)_2(s) \rightleftharpoons Fe^{2+}(aq) + 2\,OH^-(aq)$
2. Let *s* be the molar solubility of $Fe(OH)_2$. The concentrations of Fe^{2+} and OH^- are then *s* and 2*s* respectively.	$s \qquad s \qquad 2s$
3. Write the corresponding K_{sp} expression.	$K_{sp} = [Fe^{2+}][OH^-]^2$
4. Look up the K_{sp} value for $Fe(OH)_2$ and substitute in the concentrations of ions.	$4.9 \times 10^{-17} = (s)\,(2s)^2$ $4.9 \times 10^{-17} = 4s^3$
5. Simplify and solve.	$s = \sqrt[3]{4.9 \times 10^{-17}/4}$ $= 2.3 \times 10^{-6}$ M

Sample Problem 4.3.2(b) — Calculating Solubility from K_{sp}

What mass is dissolved in 275 mL of saturated silver bromate?

What to Think About	How to Do It
1. The formula is $AgBrO_3$. Write an equation representing the equilibrium present in a saturated solution.	$AgBrO_3(s) \rightleftharpoons Ag^+(aq) + BrO_3^-(aq)$
2. Let *s* be the molar solubility of $AgBrO_3$. The concentrations of Ag^+ and BrO_3^- are then both *s*.	$s \qquad s \qquad s$
3. Write the corresponding K_{sp} expression.	$K_{sp} = [Ag^+][BrO_3^-]$
4. Look up the K_{sp} value for $AgBrO_3$ and substitute in the concentrations of ions.	$5.3 \times 10^{-5} = (s)\,(s)$ $= s^2$
5. Solve for the molar solubility.	$s = 7.3 \times 10^{-3}$ M
6. To calculate the mass, use the molar mass of $AgBrO_3$ and the given volume of solution.	$\text{mass} = 0.275\ \cancel{L} \times \frac{7.3 \times 10^{-3}\ \cancel{mol}}{1\ \cancel{L}} \times \frac{235.8\ g}{1\ \cancel{mol}}$ $= 0.47$ g

© Edvantage Interactive 2019

Practice Problems 4.3.2 — Calculating Solubility from K_{sp}

1. Calculate the solubility of the following:
   (a) silver chloride in mol/L

   (b) iron (II) sulfide in g/mL

   (c) lead(II) iodate in M

   (d) strontium fluoride in g/L

2. What is the concentration of hydroxide in a saturated solution of iron(III) hydroxide? Hint: Write out the dissociation equation and K_{sp} expression first. This example is different than the ones shown.

3. What mass of calcium oxalate is dissolved in 650. mL of saturated solution?

Types of Salts

To summarize, we have introduced two types of salts: AB (such as AgCl) and AB_2 (such as $PbCl_2$) salts.

For AB salts, $K_{sp} = (\text{solubility})^2$

For AB_2 or A_2B salts, $K_{sp} = 4(\text{solubility})^3$

4.3 Activity: Experimentally Determining the K_{sp} of $CaCO_3$

Question

What is the K_{sp} of $CaCO_3$?

Background

The K_{sp} of a substance is temperature dependent. Your task is to design an experiment to determine the K_{sp} of calcium carbonate at a predetermined temperature.

Procedure

1. Choose a temperature between 10°C and 30°C. Design an experiment to determine the K_{sp} of calcium carbonate at that temperature. Your experiment should include:
   - a list of reagents
   - a list of apparatus
   - a detailed step-by-step procedure
   - appropriate data tables

Results and Discussion

1. Describe how you would analyze the data and perform calculations to determine the K_{sp}.

2. What would be some sources of error?

3. Compare your procedure to that of another group. Was their procedure the same?

© Edvantage Interactive 2019

4.3 Review Questions

1. Write equilibrium equations and the corresponding K_{sp} expressions for each of the following solutes in saturated aqueous solution.

   (a) $Al(OH)_3$

   (b) $Cd_3(AsO_4)_2$

   (c) $BaMoO_4$

   (d) calcium sulfate

   (e) lead(II) iodate

   (f) silver carbonate

2. Consider a saturated solution of $BaSO_3$.
   (a) Write the equation that represents the equilibrium in the solution.

   (b) Explain the difference between the solubility and the solubility product constant of $BaSO_3$.

3. A saturated solution of $ZnCO_3$ was prepared by adding excess solid $ZnCO_3$ to water. The solution was analyzed and found to contain $[Zn^{2+}] = 1.1 \times 10^{-5}$ M. What is the K_{sp} for $ZnCO_3$?

4. When a student evaporated 250. mL of a saturated solution of silver phosphate, 0.0045 g of solute remained. Calculate the K_{sp} for silver phosphate.

© Edvantage Interactive 2019

5. Gypsum is used in drywall and plaster, and occurs naturally in alabaster. It has the formula $CaSO_4 \cdot 2\ H_2O$ and its K_{sp} is 9.1×10^{-6}. What mass of gypsum is present in 500. mL of saturated solution?

6. Naturally occurring limestone contains two forms of $CaCO_3$ called calcite and aragonite. They differ in their crystal structure. High-grade calcite crystals were used in World War II for gun sights, especially in anti-aircraft weaponry. Aragonite is used in jewelry and glassmaking. Using the following K_{sp} values, calculate the solubility of each in g/L.
(a) K_{sp} calcite = 3.4×10^{-9}

(b) K_{sp} aragonite = 6.0×10^{-9}

7. Lead(II) arsenate, $Pb_3(AsO_4)_2$, was commonly used as an insecticide, especially against codling moths. Because of the toxic nature of lead compounds, it was banned in the 1980s. It has a solubility of 3.0×10^{-5} g/L. Calculate the K_{sp} for lead(II) arsenate.

8. A student compares the K_{sp} values of cadmium carbonate ($K_{sp} = 1.0 \times 10^{-12}$) and cadmium hydroxide ($K_{sp} = 7.2 \times 10^{-15}$) and concludes that the solubility of cadmium carbonate is greater than the solubility of cadmium hydroxide. Do you agree or disagree? Support your answer with appropriate calculations.

9. A titration was carried out to determine the unknown concentration of Cl^- ion in solution. The standard solution was $AgNO_3$ and an indicator of K_2CrO_4 was used. The equivalence point was reached when the solution turned the red color of Ag_2CrO_4, signaling that virtually all of the Cl^- ions had been used up. Explain why a precipitate of AgCl formed before a precipitate of Ag_2CrO_4. Use data from the K_{sp} table provided in this section.

10. Silver carbonate is used as an antibacterial agent in the production of concrete. What mass of silver carbonate must be dissolved to produce 2.5 L of saturated solution?

© Edvantage Interactive 2019

4.4 Precipitation Formation and the Solubility Product K_{sp}

Warm Up

1. Describe how to make a saturated solution of silver chloride, given solid silver chloride and pure water. How does the concentration of Ag^+ compare to the concentration of Cl^-?

____

____

2. A student mixed 25 mL of 0.10 M silver nitrate with 15 mL of 0.085 M sodium chloride.
   (a) Calculate the $[Ag^+]$ and $[Cl^-]$ before a reaction occurred in the mixed solution.

   (b) How does the $[Ag^+]$ compare with the $[Cl^-]$ before the reaction? Explain why they are not equal.

   ____

   (c) Write a net ionic equation for this reaction.

Precipitates That Form When Solutions Are Mixed Together

In the previous section, we investigated saturated solutions formed by attempting to dissolve an excess of solute in water. In such a case, the concentrations of the ions are directly related to one another. For example, if we attempt to dissolve excess AgCl in water, the $[Ag^+]$ equals the $[Cl^-]$. Similarly, if we use an excess of $PbCl_2$, the $[Cl^-]$ is double the $[Pb^{2+}]$.

In this section, we will be examining situations in which the ions forming the precipitate do not come from the same solute. Because of this, the concentrations of the ions in solution are not related to one another, but instead depend on the concentrations and the volumes of the solutions being combined. When determining ion concentrations, it is always important to *consider the source* of each ion.

Predicting Whether a Precipitate Will Form

When two solutions are mixed, we can predict whether a precipitate will form. The K_{sp} value represents the maximum product of the ion concentrations in a saturated solution. If the product of the ion concentrations present exceeds this value, the ions will not remain dissolved in solution and a precipitate will form. On the other hand, if the product of the ion concentrations is less than the value of K_{sp}, the ions remain dissolved in solution, and no precipitate forms.

The concentrations in a K_{sp} expression are the *equilibrium* concentrations of ions in a saturated solution. If an equilibrium is not present in solution, then we calculate a **trial ion product (TIP)**, also called a trial K_{sp} value or reaction quotient (Q).

If the TIP > K_{sp}, a precipitate forms.
If the TIP < K_{sp}, no precipitate forms.
If the TIP = K_{sp}, the solution is saturated.

Sample Problem 4.4.1 — Predicting Whether a Precipitate Will Form

Will a precipitate form when 23 mL of 0.020 M Na_2CO_3 is added to 12 mL of 0.010 M $MgCl_2$?

What to Think About	How to Do It
1. Determine the precipitate that will potentially form using the solubility table. Then write an equation representing the equilibrium present in a saturated solution.	$Na_2CO_3 + MgCl_2 \rightarrow MgCO_3(s) + 2\ NaCl$ $MgCO_3(s) \rightleftharpoons Mg^{2+}(aq) + CO_3^{2-}(aq)$
2. Write the corresponding K_{sp} expression and its value.	$K_{sp} = [Mg^{2+}][CO_3^{2-}] = 6.8 \times 10^{-6}$
3. When one solution is added to another, *both* are diluted. Calculate the concentration of each solution before the reaction occurs.	$[Na_2CO_3] = \frac{0.020\ mol}{1\ \cancel{L}} \times \frac{0.023\ \cancel{L}}{0.035 L} = 0.013\ M$ $[MgCl_2] = \frac{0.010\ mol}{1\ \cancel{L}} \times \frac{0.012\ \cancel{L}}{0.035\ L} = 0.0034\ M$
4. Determine the $[Mg^{2+}]$ and $[CO_3^{2-}]$ in the diluted solutions. Be sure to consider the source of the ions to determine whether these concentrations should be multiplied by a whole number.	$[CO_3^{2-}] = 0.013\ M$ $[Mg^{2+}] = 0.0034\ M$
5. Calculate the value of TIP.	$TIP = [Mg^{2+}]\ [CO_3^{2-}] = (0.013)(0.0034) = 4.4 \times 10^{-5}$
6. Compare the TIP with the real K_{sp}.	TIP > K_{sp} so a precipitate forms.

Practice Problems 4.4.1 — Predicting Whether a Precipitate Will Form

1. Will a precipitate form when 8.5 mL of 6.3×10^{-2} M lead(II) nitrate is added to 1.0 L of 1.2×10^{-3} M sodium iodate?

2. Will a precipitate form when 1.5 mL of 4.5×10^{-3} M ammonium bromate is added to 120.5 mL of 2.5×10^{-3} M silver nitrate?

3. No precipitate forms when 24 mL of 0.17 M sodium fluoride is added to 55 mL of 0.22 M cadmium nitrate. From this information, what can you conclude about the numerical value for the K_{sp} of CdF_2? (State the K_{sp} value as a range.)

© Edvantage Interactive 2019

Using K_{sp} to Calculate the Concentration of Ions in Solution

These problems are very similar to the ones you analyzed in the previous section, except that the ions that form the precipitate are from different stock reagent sources. First, determine the concentrations of any ions present in the solution. Once another solution is added, consider the potential precipitate that might form. Then, as always, you should write an equation for the equilibrium present in a saturated solution (the dissociation of the precipitate) and then the K_{sp} expression.

Consider a solution of 0.025 M $Pb(NO_3)_2$. By writing a dissociation equation for lead(II) nitrate, we can calculate the concentration of each ion in solution:

$$Pb(NO_3)_2(aq) \rightarrow Pb^{2+}(aq) + 2\,NO_3^-(aq)$$
$$0.025\text{ M} \qquad 0.025\text{ M} \qquad 0.050\text{ M}$$

If a solution of NaCl is added, the precipitate that may form is $PbCl_2(s)$. If a precipitate forms, then a saturated solution of $PbCl_2$ is present and is governed by its K_{sp}.

$$PbCl_2(s) \rightleftharpoons Pb^{2+}(aq) + 2\,Cl^-(aq)$$

$$K_{sp} = [Pb^{2+}][Cl^-]^2$$

Note that the original $[Pb^{2+}]$ and $[Cl^-]$ are unrelated to each other because they came from *different* sources. The maximum concentration of Cl^- that can exist in this solution can be calculated from the K_{sp} and the concentration of Pb^{2+} provided by the $Pb(NO_3)_2$ source. From the concentration of chloride, the mass of solute required can be calculated using its molar mass.

$$1.2 \times 10^{-5} = (0.025)\,[Cl^-]^2$$
$$[Cl^-] = 0.022\text{ M} = [NaCl]$$

Sample Problem 4.4.2(a) — Forming a Precipitate in a Solution

What mass of sodium sulfate is required to start precipitation in 500. mL of 0.030 M calcium chloride? (Assume the volume remains constant.)

What to Think About	How to Do It
1. Determine the precipitate that will form using the solubility table. Then write an equation representing the equilibrium present in a saturated solution.	$Na_2SO_4(aq) + CaCl_2(aq) \rightarrow CaSO_4(s) + 2\,NaCl(aq)$ $CaSO_4(s) \rightleftharpoons Ca^{2+}(aq) + SO_4^{2-}(aq)$
2. Write the corresponding K_{sp} expression.	$K_{sp} = [Ca^{2+}][SO_4^{2-}]$
3. The calcium ions came from the 0.030 M $CaCl_2$ solution, and the sulfate ions came from $Na_2SO_4(s)$. The chloride ions and sodium ions are spectators. Calculate the concentration of Ca^{2+} in the $CaCl_2$ solution.	$CaCl_2(aq) \rightarrow Ca^{2+}(aq) + 2\,Cl^-(aq)$ $0.030\text{ M} \qquad 0.030\text{ M}$
4. Substitute the value of K_{sp} (from the K_{sp} table, Table 4.3.1) and the known ion concentration to solve for the unknown $[SO_4^{2-}] = [Na_2SO_4]$.	$7.1 \times 10^{-5} = (0.030)\,[SO_4^{2-}]$ $[SO_4^{2-}] = 2.4 \times 10^{-3}\text{ M}$
5. Calculate the mass of solid sodium sulfate required to be dissolved in 500. mL of solution from $[SO_4^{2-}]$ and the molar mass of sodium sulfate.	$\text{mass } Na_2SO_4 = 0.500\text{ L} \times \frac{2.4 \times 10^{-3}\text{ mol}}{1\text{ L}} \times \frac{142.1\text{ g}}{1\text{ mol}}$ $= 0.17\text{ g}$

Sample Problem 4.4.2(b) — Forming a Precipitate in Solution

What is the maximum $[SO_4^{2-}]$ that can exist in a saturated solution of $CaCO_3$?

What to Think About	How to Do It
1. Calculate the $[Ca^{2+}]$ in a saturated solution of $CaCO_3$.	$CaCO_3(s) \rightleftharpoons \underset{s}{Ca^{2+}(aq)} + \underset{s}{CO_3^{2-}(aq)}$ $K_{sp} = [Ca^{2+}][CO_3^{2-}]$ $5.0 \times 10^{-9} = s^2$ $s = 7.1 \times 10^{-5}\ M = [Ca^{2+}]$
2. The calcium ions form a precipitate with the sulfate ions. Write the equation for the equilibrium present in the saturated solution of $CaSO_4$.	$CaSO_4(s) \rightleftharpoons Ca^{2+}(aq) + SO_4^{2-}(aq)$
3. Substitute the value of K_{sp} for $CaSO_4$ (from the K_{sp} table, Table 4.3.1) and the known $[Ca^{2+}]$ and solve for the $[SO_4^{2-}]$.	$K_{sp} = [Ca^{2+}][SO_4^{2-}]$ $7.1 \times 10^{-5} = (7.1 \times 10^{-5})[SO_4^{2-}]$ $[SO_4^{2-}] = 1.0\ M$

Practice Problems 4.4.2 — Forming a Precipitate In Solution

1. Calculate the maximum $[Sr^{2+}]$ that can exist in solutions of the following:
   (a) 0.045 M sodium fluoride (Remember to consider the source of the fluoride ion.)

   (b) 2.3×10^{-4} M lithium carbonate

   (c) 0.011 M sulfuric acid

2. Sodium carbonate may be added to hard water to remove the Mg^{2+} ions. What mass of sodium carbonate is required to soften 10.0 L of hard water containing 3.2×10^{-3} M Mg^{2+}? (Assume no volume change occurs.)

3. What is the maximum $[Ag^+]$ that can exist in a saturated solution of PbI_2?

© Edvantage Interactive 2019

The Common Ion Effect

We defined the solubility of a substance as the maximum amount of solute that will dissolve in a given volume of solvent at a specific temperature. You know that solubility depends on temperature, but it also depends on the solvent's identity. Up to now, we have only considered pure water as the solvent. The presence of other ions in the solvent also has an effect on the solubility of a solute.

The solubility of a substance depends on the presence of other ions in solution and the temperature. The K_{sp} of a substance depends on temperature only.

Consider a saturated solution of Ag_2CO_3:

$$Ag_2CO_3(s) \rightleftharpoons 2\,Ag^+(aq) + CO_3^{2-}(aq)$$

At a given temperature, the amount of Ag^+ and CO_3^{2-} in solution is governed by the K_{sp}. If the solvent already contained Ag^+ ions, the $[Ag^+]$ is increased. To maintain the value of K_{sp}, the $[CO_3^{2-}]$ must decrease. According to Le Châtelier's principle, an increase in $[Ag^+]$ causes the equilibrium to shift left. This shift causes the $[CO_3^{2-}]$ to decrease and the amount of solid Ag_2CO_3 to increase. The presence of silver ions in the solvent effectively decreases the solubility of Ag_2CO_3. This is called the *common ion effect* because the solubility of Ag_2CO_3 is decreased due to the common ion Ag^+ in the solvent. The presence of CO_3^{2-} in the solvent would cause a similar effect and resulting decrease in the solubility.

$$Ag_2CO_3(s) \rightleftharpoons 2\,Ag^+(aq) + CO_3^{2-}(aq)$$

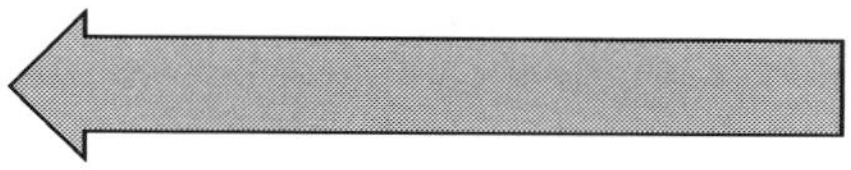

Adding Ag^+ or CO_3^{2-} causes the equilibrium to shift left, so the solubility of Ag_2CO_3 decreases.

The solubility of a solute is decreased by the presence of a second solute in a solvent containing a common ion.

According to Le Châtelier's principle, the solubility of Ag_2CO_3 may be increased by removing the Ag^+ or CO_3^{2-} ions. This would cause the equilibrium to shift right. An example of this would be the presence of HCl in the solvent. You have learned that carbonates dissolve in acid solutions. The presence of H_3O^+ from the acid causes the $[CO_3^{2-}]$ to decrease, which in turn causes more $Ag_2CO_3(s)$ to dissolve. Additionally, the chloride ion from the acid precipitates the silver ion from the solution. The removal of the silver ion causes a further right shift, increasing the solubility of silver carbonate even further.

Quick Check

1. Consider a saturated solution of AgCl.
   (a) How can you change the K_{sp} for AgCl?

   (b) How can you change the solubility of AgCl?

2. List two substances that would decrease the solubility of $Mg(OH)_2$. Use Le Châtelier's principle to explain each.

3. List two substances that would increase the solubility of $Mg(OH)_2$. Use Le Châtelier's principle and a K_{sp} expression to explain each.

Calculating Solubility With a Common Ion Present

The presence of a common ion in the solvent decreases the solubility of a solute. Let's compare the solubility of $Mg(OH)_2$ in water to its solubility in 0.10 M $MgCl_2$.

 © Edvantage Interactive 2019

Sample Problem 4.4.3 — Calculating Solubility With a Common Ion Present

What is the solubility of $Mg(OH)_2$ in (a) water? (b) 0.10 M $MgCl_2$?

What to Think About	How to Do It
(a) in water	
1. Write the equilibrium for a saturated solution of $Mg(OH)_2$.	$Mg(OH)_2(s) \rightleftharpoons Mg^{2+}(aq) + 2\,OH^-(aq)$ s $\quad$ $2s$
2. Write the corresponding K_{sp} expression.	$K_{sp} = [Mg^{2+}][OH^-]^2$
3. Look up the value for K_{sp} on the K_{sp} table (Table 4.3.1) and solve for the solubility.	$5.6 \times 10^{-12} = (s)(2s)^2 = 4s^3$ $s = 1.1 \times 10^{-4}$ M = solubility of $Mg(OH)_2$
(b) in 0.10 M $MgCl_2$	
1. Write the equilibrium for a saturated solution of $Mg(OH)_2$.	$Mg(OH)_2(s) \rightleftharpoons Mg^{2+}(aq) + 2\,OH^-(aq)$
2. The equilibrium for the saturated solution is shifted on the addition of the common ion Mg^{2+} from the $MgCl_2$. Use an ICE table. In the $MgCl_2$, there is initially 0.10 M Mg^{2+}. The amount of $Mg(OH)_2$ that dissolves will increase the $[Mg^{2+}]$ and $[OH^-]$ by x and $2x$ respectively.	$Mg(OH)_2(s) \rightleftharpoons Mg^{2+}(aq) + 2\,OH^-(aq)$ I: – $\quad$ 0.10 $\quad$ 0 C: – $\quad$ $+x$ $\quad$ $+2x$ E: – $\quad$ $0.10 + x$ $\quad$ $2x$
3. The amount of Mg^{2+} that dissolves from the $Mg(OH)_2$ (represented by x) is very small compared to the amount of Mg^{2+} in solution from the $MgCl_2$ (0.10 M). Assume that $[Mg^{2+}] = 0.10 + x = 0.10$.	
4. Substitute $[Mg^{2+}]$ and $[OH^-]$ at equilibrium into a K_{sp} expression.	$K_{sp} = [Mg^{2+}][OH^-]^2$ $5.6 \times 10^{-12} = (0.10)(2x)^2$
5. Solve for the solubility, x.	$5.6 \times 10^{-11} = (2x)^2 = 4x^2$ $x = 3.7 \times 10^{-6}$ M

Practice Problems 4.4.3 — Calculating Solubility With a Common Ion Present

1. Calculate the molar solubility of silver iodate in 0.12 M sodium iodate.

2. Calculate the molar solubility of lead(II) iodide in 0.10 M KI.

3. Calculate the solubility (in g/L) of barium sulfate in 0.050 M barium nitrate.

4.4 Activity: Experimentally Determining the K_{sp} Of Copper(II) Iodate

Question

What is the approximate value of K_{sp} for copper(II) iodate?

Background

A TIP calculation can be used to determine if a precipitate will form. If TIP > K_{sp}, a precipitate forms. If TIP < K_{sp}, no precipitate forms. Five different dilutions of copper(II) nitrate and sodium iodate were prepared and mixed together. By observing which mixed solutions contained a precipitate, information about the K_{sp} can be deduced.

Procedure:

1. Five different dilutions of copper(II) nitrate and sodium iodate were prepared as shown in the data table below. The given volume of each solution was mixed together with water and the formation of a precipitate was noted. Answer the questions below.

	Mixture 1	Mixture 2	Mixture 3	Mixture 4	Mixture 5
Volume 0.010 M $Cu(NO_3)_2$ (mL)	10.0	8.0	6.0	4.0	2.0
Volume 0.020 M $NaIO_3$ (mL)	10.0	8.0	6.0	4.0	2.0
Volume water added (mL)	0.0	4.0	8.0	12.0	16.0
Observation	precipitate	precipitate	precipitate	no precipitate	no precipitate

Results and Discussion

1. Write balanced formula, complete ionic, and net ionic equations for this reaction.

2. Calculate the $[Cu^{2+}]$ in each of the mixtures.

3. Calculate the $[IO_3^-]$ in each of the mixtures.

4. Write the equation for the equilibrium involving the precipitate, and the K_{sp} expression.

 © Edvantage Interactive 2019

5. Calculate a TIP value for each mixture.

6. State the K_{sp} as a range of values from this data.

7. Compare your range to the stated K_{sp} value on the K_{sp} table (Table 4.3.1).

4.4 Review Questions

1. The following solutions were mixed together. Write the equilibrium equation for the precipitate that forms and its K_{sp} expression.
   (a) $FeCl_2$ and Na_2S

   (b) $Sr(OH)_2$ and $MgBr_2$

   (c) silver nitrate and ammonium chromate

2. A student mixed equal volumes of 0.2 M solutions of sulfuric acid and calcium chloride together.
   (a) What precipitate forms?

   (b) Write an equation for the equilibrium present and the K_{sp} expression.

   (c) In the resulting solution, does $[SO_4^{2-}] = [Ca^{2+}]$? Explain.

3. What is the maximum $[Pb^{2+}]$ that can exist in 0.015 M $CuSO_4$?

4. Kidney stones are crystals of calcium oxalate that form in the kidney, ureter, or bladder. Small kidney stones are passed out of the body easily, but larger kidney stones may block the ureter causing severe pain. If the $[Ca^{2+}]$ in blood plasma is 5×10^{-3} M, what $[C_2O_4^{2-}]$ must be present to form a kidney stone?

5. What is the maximum $[CO_3^{2-}]$ that can exist in a saturated solution of AgBr?

6. A 100.0 mL sample of seawater was tested by adding one drop (0.2 mL) of 0.20 M silver nitrate. What mass of NaCl is present in the seawater to form a precipitate?

© Edvantage Interactive 2019

7. Does a precipitate form when 2.5 mL of 0.055 M $Sr(NO_3)_2$ is added to 1.5 L of 0.011 M $ZnSO_4$? Justify your answer with calculations.

8. Does a precipitate form when 0.068 g of lead(II) nitrate is added to 2.0 L of 0.080 M NaCl? Justify your answer with calculations. (Assume no volume change.)

9. The addition of Ag^+ to a solution containing Cl^- and I^- will cause precipitates of both AgCl and AgI to form. Because AgCl and AgI have quite different K_{sp} values, you can use this information to separate Cl^- from I^- in solution by carefully manipulating the $[Ag^+]$ so that only one of Cl^- or I^- precipitates at a time. Consider a solution containing 0.020 M Cl^- and 0.020 M I^-. Solid silver nitrate is slowly added without changing the overall volume of solution.

   (a) Write the equilibrium equation for each precipitate that forms.

   (b) Beside each equilibrium equation, write the corresponding K_{sp} expression and value from your K_{sp} table.

   (c) Based on the K_{sp} values, which precipitate will form first?

   (d) Calculate the $[Ag^+]$ required just to start precipitation of the first precipitate.

   (e) Calculate the $[Ag^+]$ required just to start precipitation of the second precipitate.

   (f) State the range of $[Ag^+]$ required to precipitate I^- but not Cl^-.

   (g) What $[I^-]$ remains in solution just before the formation of AgCl?

   (h) What percentage of I^- is precipitated out before the AgCl starts to precipitate?

10. Washing soda, $Na_2CO_3 \cdot 10\ H_2O$ is used to treat hard water containing Ca^{2+} and Mg^{2+}. A 1.0 L sample contained 12 mg of Mg^{2+}. What mass of washing soda is required to precipitate out the Mg^{2+}?

11. List two substances that, when added to water, that would decrease the solubility of lead(II) iodate. Explain each.

12. Explain why $BaSO_4$ is less soluble in a solution of Na_2SO_4 than in water.

13. Is iron(III) hydroxide more or less soluble in water than in 0.1 M HCl? Explain.

14. An aqueous suspension of $BaSO_4$ is used as a contrast agent to improve the quality of intestinal X-rays. The patient drinks a suspension of $BaSO_4$. However, Ba^{2+} is toxic, so the $BaSO_4$ is dissolved in a solution of 0.10 M Na_2SO_4.
(a) Calculate the maximum mass of $BaSO_4$ that can be dissolved in 200. mL of water. (Assume no volume change.)

(b) Calculate the maximum mass of $BaSO_4$ that can be dissolved in 200. mL of 0.10 M Na_2SO_4 without forming a precipitate.

© Edvantage Interactive 2019

5 Acid-Base Equilibrium

This chapter focuses on the following AP Units from the College Board:

Unit 4: Chemical Reactions
Unit 7: Equilibrium.
Unit 8: Acids and Bases

By the end of this chapter, you should be able to do the following:

- Identify acids and bases through experimentation
- Identify various models for representing acids and bases
- Analyze balanced equations representing the reaction of acids or bases with water
- Classify an acid or base in solution as either weak or strong, with reference to its electrical conductivity
- Analyze the equilibria that exist in weak acid or weak base systems
- Identify chemical species that are amphiprotic
- Analyze the equilibrium that exists in water
- Perform calculations relating pH, pOH, $[H_3O^+]$, and $[OH^-]$
- Explain the significance of the K_a and K_b equilibrium expressions
- Perform calculations involving K_a and K_b

By the end of this chapter, you should know the meaning of these **key terms**:

- acid
- acid ionization constant (K_a)
- amphiprotic
- Arrhenius
- base
- base ionization constant (K_b)
- Brønsted-Lowry
- conjugate acid-base pair
- electrical conductivity
- ion product constant
- mass action expression
- pH
- pK_w
- pOH
- polarized
- strong acid
- strong base
- water ionization constant (K_w)
- weak acid
- weak base

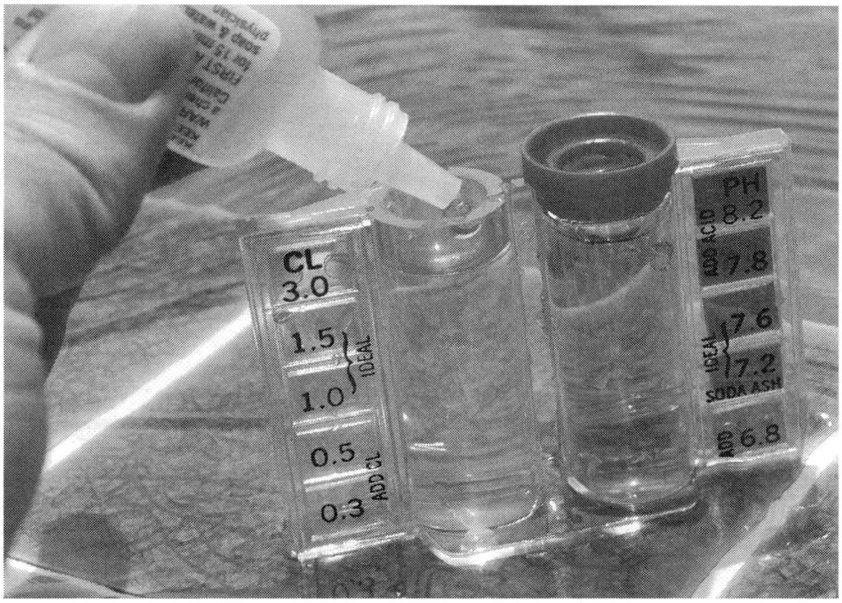

Testing swimming pool water involves acid-base interactions.

5.1 Identifying Acids and Bases

Warm Up

A student tested a number of unknown solutions and recorded the following observations. Based on each observation, place a check mark in the corresponding column that identifies the unknown solution as containing an acid, a base, or either one.

Observation	Acid	Base
Turns phenolphthalein pink		
Feels slippery		
Has pH = 5.0		
Tastes sour		
Conducts electricity		
Reacts with metal to produce a gas		

The Arrhenius Theory of Acids and Bases

In previous years, you learned how to identify an acid or base using a concept developed by a chemist named Svante Arrhenius. According to the Arrhenius theory, acids release H^+ ions in solution, and bases release OH^- ions.

Typically, when an Arrhenius acid and base react together, a salt and water form. A salt is an ionic compound that does not contain H^+ or OH^- ions. The cation from the base and the anion from the acid make up the salt.

Example: $HCl(aq) + NaOH(aq) \rightarrow NaCl(aq) + H_2O(l)$
acid base salt water

Sample Problem 5.1.1 — Identifying Arrhenius Acids and Bases

Classify each of the following substances as an Arrhenius acid, an Arrhenius base, a salt or a molecular compound.

(a) HNO_3
(b) $Al(OH)_3$
(c) $Al(NO_3)_3$
(d) NO_2

What to Think About	How to Do It
(a) An acid releases H^+ ions.	HNO_3 is an acid.
(b) A base releases OH^- ions.	$Al(OH)_3$ is a base.
(c) A salt is an ionic compound not containing H^+ or OH^- ions.	$Al(NO_3)_3$ is a salt.
(d) A molecule is not made up of ions.	NO_2 is a molecular compound.

 © Edvantage Interactive 2019

Practice Problems 5.1.1 — Identifying Arrhenius Acids and Bases

1. Classify each of the following as an Arrhenius acid, an Arrhenius base, a salt, or a molecular compound.

   (a) H_2SO_4 ____________________

   (b) XeF_6 ____________________

   (c) CH_3COOH ____________________

   (d) $NaCH_3COO$ ____________________

   (e) KOH ____________________

   (f) NH_3 ____________________

2. Complete the following neutralization equations. Make sure each equation is balanced, and circle the salt produced.

   (a) $CH_3COOH + LiOH \rightarrow$

   (b) $HI + Ca(OH)_2 \rightarrow$

   (c) $Mg(OH)_2 + H_3PO_4 \rightarrow$

3. Write the formula of the parent acid and the parent base that react to form each salt listed.

	Parent Acid	Parent Base
(a) KNO_2		
(b) NH_4Cl		
(c) CuC_2O_4		
(d) $NaCH_3COO$		

Brønsted-Lowry Acids and Bases

Arrhenius' definition worked well to classify a number of substances that displayed acidic or basic characteristics. However, some substances that acted like acids or bases could not be classified using this definition. A broader definition of acids and bases was required.

In the practice problem above, you may have classified NH_3 as molecular. While it is molecular, a solution of NH_3 also feels slippery, has a pH greater than 7, and turns phenolphthalein pink. It clearly has basic characteristics, but it is not an Arrhenius base.

Chemists Johannes Brønsted and Thomas Lowry suggested a broader definition of acids and bases:

> **Brønsted-Lowry acid** — a substance or species that donates a hydrogen ion, H^+ (a proton)
> **Brønsted-Lowry base** — a substance or species that accepts a hydrogen ion, H^+

Consider the reaction that occurs in aqueous HCl:

$$\underset{\text{acid}}{HCl(aq)} + \underset{\text{base}}{H_2O(l)} \rightarrow \underset{\text{hydronium}}{H_3O^+(aq)} + Cl^-(aq)$$

In this example, the HCl donates a hydrogen ion (H^+) to the water molecule. The HCl is therefore acting as a Brønsted-Lowry acid. The water accepts the H^+ ion so it is acting as a Brønsted-Lowry base.

The H_3O^+ ion is called a **hydronium ion**. It is simply a water molecule with an extra H^+ ion (Figure 5.1.1). It is also called a protonated water molecule.

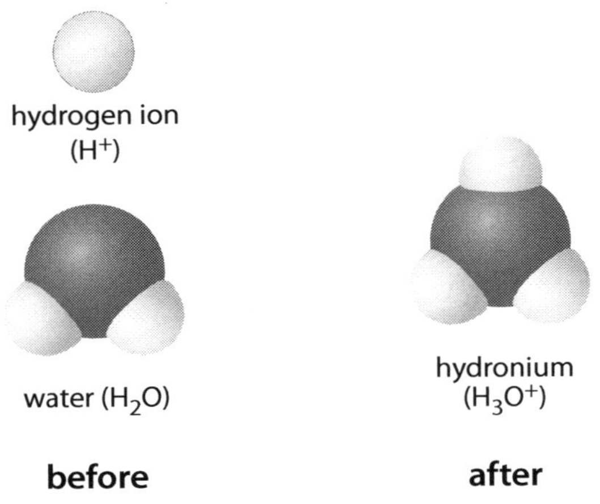

Figure 5.1.1 *A hydronium ion is a water molecule with an extra H+ ion.*

Let's look at NH_3 now. In a solution of ammonia (NH_3) the following reaction occurs:

$$\underset{\text{base}}{NH_3(aq)} + \underset{\text{acid}}{H_2O(l)} \rightleftharpoons NH_4^+(aq) + OH^-(aq)$$

The ammonia molecule accepted a H^+ ion from the water, so NH_3 is acting as a Brønsted-Lowry base, and water is acting as a Brønsted-Lowry acid.

You may notice that in the equation for HCl, a one-way arrow was used, but in the equation for NH_3, an equilibrium arrow was used. The reasons for this will be explained in the next section. Just remember that if you see an equilibrium arrow, then equilibrium is established. More importantly, in an equilibrium, you have both reactants and products present in the system. Both forward and reverse reactions occur. If we look at the reverse reaction for the ammonia system, we can identify Brønsted-Lowry acids and bases:

$$\underset{\text{base}}{NH_3(aq)} + \underset{\text{acid}}{H_2O(l)} \rightleftharpoons \underset{\text{acid}}{NH_4^+(aq)} + \underset{\text{base}}{OH^-(aq)}$$

In the reverse reaction, the NH_4^+ ion donates a proton to the OH^- ion. According to Brønsted-Lowry definitions, the NH_4^+ ion is acting as an acid, and the OH^- ion is acting as a base.

In a Brønsted-Lowry equilibrium, there are two acids and two bases: one for the forward reaction, and one for the reverse reaction. An acid and a base react to form a different acid and base.

Two substances that differ by one H^+ ion are called a **conjugate acid-base pair.**

In the example above, the NH_3 and NH_4^+ together form one conjugate acid-base pair, and the H_2O and OH^- form the other conjugate acid-base pair.

 © Edvantage Interactive 2019

Sample Problems 5.1.2 — Identifying Conjugate Acid-Base Pairs

1. In the following equilibrium, identify the acids and bases, and the two conjugate acid-base pairs:

$$HF(aq) + CN^-(aq) \rightleftharpoons HCN(aq) + F^-(aq)$$

2. Complete the following table:

Conjugate Acid	Conjugate Base
$H_2C_2O_4$	
	SO_3^{2-}
HCO_3^-	
	H_2O

3. Complete the following equilibrium, which represents the reaction of a Brønsted-Lowry acid and base. Circle the substances that make up one of the conjugate acid-base pairs.

$$NO_2^-(aq) + H_2CO_3(aq) \rightleftharpoons$$

What to Think About

1. An acid donates a proton and a base accepts a proton.

In the forward reaction, the HF is the acid and the CN– is the base. In the reverse reaction, the HCN is the acid and the F– is the base.

The substances in a conjugate acid-base pair differ by one H^+ ion.

2. An acid donates a proton. Find the conjugate base of an acid by removing one H^+. Be careful of your charges on the ions! A base accepts a proton. Find the conjugate acid of a given base by adding one H^+.

3. An acid must be able to donate a H^+ ion. Only the H_2CO_3 has a H^+ to donate. When it donates a H^+ ion, HCO_3^- forms. The NO_2^- ion is forced to accept the H^+, making the NO_2^- a base. When the NO_2^- accepts a proton, it forms HNO_2. The total charge on the reactant side should equal the total charge on the product side. Balance reactions for both.

Note: H_2CO_3 only donates ONE H^+ ion. Substances in a conjugate acid-base pair differ by only ONE H^+ ion. Balance both sides of the equation for number of atoms and charge.

How to Do It

1. The two conjugate acid-base pairs are: HF/F^- and CN^-/HCN.

$$\underset{\text{acid}}{HF(aq)} + \underset{\text{base}}{CN^-(aq)} \rightleftharpoons \underset{\text{acid}}{HCN(aq)} + \underset{\text{base}}{F^-(aq)}$$

2.

Conjugate acid			Conjugate base
$H_2C_2O_4$	→	remove H^+	$HC_2O_4^-$
HSO_3^-	←	add H^+	SO_3^{2-}
HCO_3^-	→	remove H^+	CO_3^{2-}
H_3O^+	←	add H^+	H_2O

3.

$$NO_2^-(aq) + H_2CO_3(aq) \rightleftharpoons HNO_2(aq) + HCO_3^-(aq)$$

Circle around either of the following: NO_2^-/HNO_2 or H_2CO_3/HCO_3^-

Practice Problems 5.1.2 — Identifying Conjugate Acid-Base Pairs

1. For the following equilibria, label the acids and bases for the forward and reverse reactions.

   (a) $HIO_3 + NO_2^- \rightleftharpoons HNO_2 + IO_3^-$

   (b) $HF + HC_2O_4^- \rightleftharpoons H_2C_2O_4 + F^-$

   (c) $Al(H_2O)_6^{3+} + SO_3^{2-} \rightleftharpoons HSO_3^- + Al(H_2O)_5OH^{2+}$

2. Complete the following table:

Conjugate Acid	Conjugate Base
H_2O_2	
	$H_2BO_3^-$
HCOOH	
	$C_6H_5O_7^{3-}$

3. Complete the following equilibria. Label the acids and bases for the forward and reverse reactions. Circle one conjugate acid-base pair in each equilibria.

   (a) $HNO_2 + NH_3 \rightleftharpoons$

   (b) $H_3C_6H_5O_7 + CN^- \rightleftharpoons$

   (c) $PO_4^{3-} + H_2S \rightleftharpoons$

Amphiprotic Species

Consider the two equilibria below:

$$NH_3(aq) + \underset{\text{acid}}{H_2O(l)} \rightleftharpoons NH_4^+(aq) + OH^-(aq) \qquad HF(aq) + \underset{\text{base}}{H_2O(l)} \rightleftharpoons H_3O^+(aq) + F^-(aq)$$

In the first reaction, water acts as a Brønsted-Lowry acid. In the second reaction, water acts as a Brønsted-Lowry base. An **amphiprotic** substance has the ability to act as an acid or a base, depending on what it is reacting with. Water is a common amphiprotic substance. Many anions also display amphiprotic tendencies. For a substance to be amphiprotic, it must have a proton to donate and be able to accept a proton. Examples of amphiprotic anions include HCO_3^-, $HC_2O_4^-$, and $H_2PO_4^-$. Uncharged species, with the exception of water, are generally not amphiprotic. For example, HCl will donate one H^+ ion (proton) to form Cl^-, but will not accept a proton to form H_2Cl^+. You should recognize many of the species that form.

Quick Check

1. Write an equation for a reaction between HCO_3^- and CN^- where HCO_3^- acts as an acid.

2. Write an equation for a reaction between HCO_3^- and H_2O where HCO_3^- acts as a base.

3. Circle amphiprotic substances in the following list:

   (a) CH_3COOH (b) $H_2PO_4^-$ (c) PO_4^{3-} (d) $H_2C_2O_4$ (e) $HC_2O_4^-$

© Edvantage Interactive 2019

5.1 Activity: Conjugate Pairs Memory Game

Question

How many conjugate acid-base pairs can you identify?

Materials

- grid of conjugate pairs, cut into cards
- scissors

Procedure

1. Go to edvantagescience.com for a page of symbols and formulas.
2. Cut along the grid lines to make a set of cards. Each card will have one symbol or formula on it.
3. Place the cards face down on the table in a 6 × 6 grid.
4. Play in groups of two or three. The first player turns over two cards. If the two substances are a conjugate acid-base pair, the player keeps the two cards and gets one more turn. If they are not a conjugate acid-base pair, the player turns the cards face down again after everyone has seen them.
5. The next player turns over two cards, again looking for a conjugate pair.
6. The play continues until all conjugate acid-base pair cards are collected. The winner is the player with the most cards.

Results and Discussion

1. Define an acid-base conjugate pair.

2. Explain why H_2SO_3 and SO_3^{2-} are not a conjugate pair.

5.1 Review Questions

1. How are the Arrhenius and Brønsted-Lowry definitions of an acid and base similar? How are they different? Use examples.

2. Explain why the H^+ ion is the same as a proton.

3. A hydronium ion is formed when water accepts a proton. Draw a Lewis structure for water, and explain why water will accept a proton. Draw the Lewis structure for a hydronium ion.

4. In the following equations, identify the acids and bases in the forward and reverse reactions. Identify the conjugate acid-base pairs.
   (a) $NH_3 + H_3PO_4 \rightleftharpoons NH_4^+ + H_2PO_4^-$

   (b) $H_2PO_4^- + SO_3^{2-} \rightleftharpoons HSO_3^- + HPO_4^{2-}$

   (c) $CH_3NH_2 + CH_3COOH \rightleftharpoons CH_3COO^- + CH_3NH_3^+$

5. Formic acid, HCOOH, is the substance responsible for the sting in ant bites. Write an equation showing it acting as an acid when reacted with water. Label the acids and bases in the forward and reverse reactions. Identify the two conjugate acid-base pairs.

6. Pyridine, C_5H_5N, is a Brønsted-Lowry base. It is used in the production of many pharmaceuticals. Write an equation showing it acting as a base when reacted with water. Label the acids and bases in the forward and reverse reactions. Identify the two conjugate acid-base pairs.

© Edvantage Interactive 2019

7. Sodium hypochlorite solution is also known as bleach. It contains the hypochlorite ion ClO^-.
   (a) Write an equation for the reaction between hypochlorite ion and ammonium ion. Label the acids and bases in the forward and reverse reactions. Identify the two conjugate acid-base pairs.

   (b) This equilibrium favors the reactants. Which of the acids is stronger and donates protons more readily?

8. (a) Explain how to write the formula for the conjugate acid of a given base. Use an example.

   (b) Explain how to write the formula for the conjugate base of a given acid. Use an example.

9. (a) Hydrogen peroxide, H_2O_2, is a Brønsted Lowry acid. It is used as an antiseptic and bleaching agent. Write the formula for the conjugate base of hydrogen peroxide.

   (b) Hydrazine, N_2H_4, is a Brønsted-Lowry base used as a rocket fuel. Write the formula for the conjugate acid of hydrazine.

   (c) Phenol, HOC_6H_5, is a Brønsted-Lowry acid used to make plastics, nylon, and slimicides. Write the formula for its conjugate base.

   (d) Aniline, $C_6H_5NH_2$, is a Brønsted-Lowry base used to make polyurethane. Write the formula for its conjugate acid.

10. Define the term *amphiprotic*. List four amphiprotic substances.

11. Baking soda contains sodium bicarbonate.
    (a) Write two equations demonstrating the amphiprotic nature of the bicarbonate ion with water. Describe a test you could perform to identify which equilibrium is more likely to occur.

    (b) Bicarbonate produces CO_2 gas in the batter of cookies or cakes, which makes the batter rise as it bakes. Which of the two equations in (a) represents the action of bicarbonate ion in baking?

12. Water is amphiprotic. Write a reaction showing a water molecule acting as an acid reacting with a water molecule acting as a base. Label the acids and bases for the forward and reverse reactions. Identify the conjugate acid-base pairs.

© Edvantage Interactive 2019

5.2 The Strengths of Acids and Bases

Warm Up

1. How can you tell from a formula whether a substance is ionic or molecular?

____

____

2. What must be present in a solution if it conducts electricity?

____

3. Define the term *conjugate acid-base pair* and give an example.

____

____

The Meaning of Strong and Weak

Consider Figure 5.2.1, which shows electricity being conducted through two solutions of different acids.

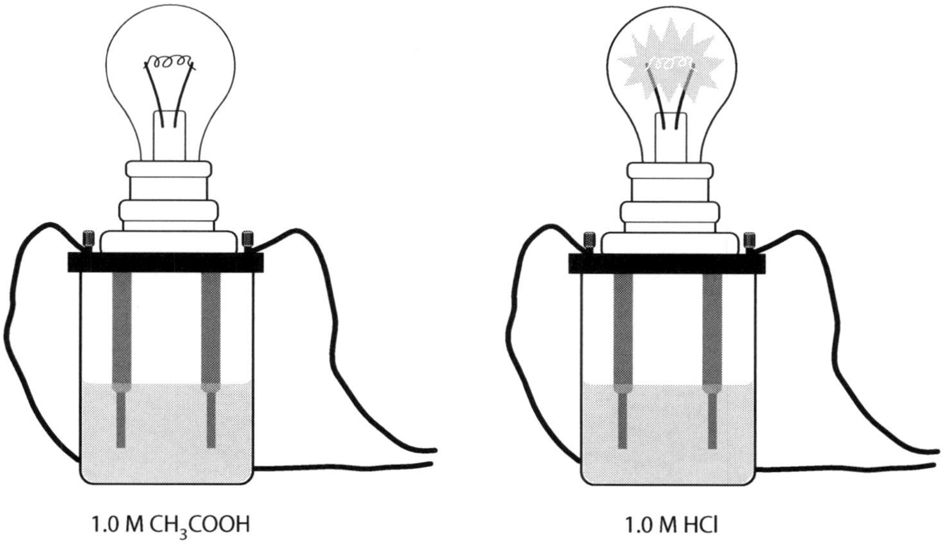

Figure 5.2.1 *Although these acids are the same concentration, they don't both conduct electricity.*

In order for a solution to conduct electricity, ions must be present. In Figure 5.2.1, you can see that the solution on the right conducts electricity much better than the solution on the left, even though both acids are the same concentration.

You may also notice that when looking at the formulas of the acids, they appear to be molecular. Obviously, there must be more ions present in 1.0 M HCl than in 1.0 M CH_3COOH. Acid molecules enter solution as molecules, but then water splits some or all of the acid molecules into ions in a process called ionization.

Chemists use the words "strong and "weak" to describe the ability of an acid or base to produce ions in solution.

A **strong acid** is a substance that completely ionizes in aqueous solution.
A **weak acid** is a substance that only partially ionizes in aqueous solution.

In Figure 5.2.1, HCl must be a strong acid. We can show how HCl acts in an aqueous solution in two ways:

$$HCl(aq) \rightarrow H^+(aq) + Cl^-(aq)$$

or

$$HCl(aq) + H_2O(l) \rightarrow H_3O^+(aq) + Cl^-(aq)$$

The second equation shows HCl acting as a Brønsted-Lowry acid. We will use this version of the equation more commonly in this unit. The hydronium ion is formed when water accepts a H^+ ion. H_3O^+ and H^+ may be used interchangeably to represent the acid ion present in solution. Notice also that the arrow in both equations is a one-way arrow. This shows that the reaction goes to completion, and that the HCl completely ionizes. In an aqueous solution, there are almost no molecules of HCl, only the ions H^+ and Cl^-. Other strong acids include $HClO_4$, HI, HBr, HNO_3, and H_2SO_4.

In Figure 5.2.1, the CH_3COOH solution conducts electricity poorly. You can infer from this that there are few ions present in solution. Most of the CH_3COOH molecules remain intact. Because of this, CH_3COOH is called a *weak* acid. In a solution of CH_3COOH, there are very few ions:

$$CH_3COOH(aq) \rightleftharpoons H^+(aq) + CH_3COO^-(aq)$$

or

$$CH_3COOH(aq) + H_2O(l) \rightleftharpoons H_3O^+(aq) + CH_3COO^-(aq)$$

Notice the use of an equilibrium arrow in the equations, signifying that the acid only partly ionizes. At equilibrium, the forward and reverse reaction rates are equal, thus all of the species shown are present in the solution.

There are many weak acids. You will learn later in this section how to classify an acid as weak or strong based on its formula.

Similarly to acids, bases can be classified as strong or weak.

A **strong base** is a substance that completely dissociates in aqueous solution.
A **weak base** is a substance that produces few ions in solution.

Strong bases are typically oxides or hydroxides of group I and II metal ions. Examples include NaOH, KOH, $Ca(OH)_2$, and $Mg(OH)_2$. Even though $Mg(OH)_2$ is slightly soluble in water, the amount that does dissolve completely ionizes. A very common weak base in water is ammonia, NH_3. Other weak bases include amines such as methylamine, CH_3NH_2. There are many anions that are weak Brønsted-Lowry bases. They will accept a H^+ ion from another substance to produce OH^- ions and their conjugate acid. The nitrite ion is one such example:

$$NO_2^-(aq) + H_2O(l) \rightleftharpoons HNO_2(aq) + OH^-(aq)$$

© Edvantage Interactive 2019

Quick Check

1. Explain the difference between a concentrated acid and a strong acid. Is it possible to have a concentrated weak acid? Give an example.

____

____

____

2. What is the concentration of ions in 1.0 M HNO_3? How would the concentration of ions in 1.0 M CH_3COOH compare?

____

____

3. A student tests the electrical conductivity of 0.1 M NaOH and 0.1 M NH_3. Draw a diagram showing what you would expect to see. Under each diagram, write the chemical equation representing what is happening in each solution.

4. Will the Cl^- ion act as a Brønsted-Lowry base in water? Explain.

____

____

The Acid and Base Ionization Constant

Let's go back to our discussion of CH_3COOH. The equilibrium present is:

$$CH_3COOH(aq) + H_2O(l) \rightleftharpoons H_3O^+(aq) + CH_3COO^-(aq)$$

As with all equilibria, we can write a K_{eq} expression for acetic acid, which is customized for acids by calling it a K_a expression. The K_a is called the **acid ionization constant**.

$$K_a = \frac{[H_3O^+][CH_3COO^-]}{[CH_3COOH]}$$

Notice that we do not include the $[H_2O]$ in the K_a expression. As you have learned, the concentration of water does not change appreciably, so it is treated as part of the constant. For any weak acid in solution, we can write a general equation and K_a expression:

$$HA(aq) + H_2O(l) \rightleftharpoons H_3O^+(aq) + A^-(aq) \qquad K_a = \frac{[H_3O^+][A^-]}{[HA]}$$

In a weak acid solution of appreciable concentration, most of the acid molecules remain intact or un-ionized. Only a few ions are formed. Equal concentrations of different acids produce different H_3O^+ concentrations. The K_a values for weak acids are less than 1.0. The K_a corresponds to the percentage ionization. A greater K_a signifies a greater $[H_3O^+]$ in solution.

Likewise, a weak Brønsted-Lowry base such as ammonia establishes an equilibrium in solution:

$$NH_3(aq) + H_2O(l) \rightleftharpoons NH_4^+(aq) + OH^-(aq)$$

$$K_b = \frac{[NH_4^+][OH^-]}{[NH_3]}$$

where K_b is called the **base ionization constant**. Generally, for a molecule acting as a weak Brønsted-Lowry base in aqueous solution:

$$B(aq) + H_2O(l) \rightleftharpoons HB^+(aq) + OH^-(aq) \qquad K_b = \frac{[HB^+][OH^-]}{[B]}$$

Quick Check

1. HF is a weak acid. Write an equation showing how HF acts in solution; then write the K_a expression for HF.

2. Explain why we would not typically write a K_b expression for NaOH.

   ____

   ____

3. Ethylamine is a weak base with the formula $CH_3CH_2NH_2$. Write an equation showing how ethylamine acts in water, then write the K_b expression.

4. The hydrogen oxalate ion is amphiprotic. Write two equations, one showing how this ion acts as an acid and the other showing this ion acting as a base. Beside each equation, write its corresponding K_a or K_b expression.

Comparing Acid and Base Strengths

Recall that the larger the K_a or K_b, the greater the $[H_3O^+]$ or $[OH^-]$ respectively. To compare the relative strengths of weak acids and bases, we can use in Table 5.2.1 on the next page.

As you look at the table, note the following points:

- Acids are listed on the left of the table, and their conjugate bases are listed on the right.
- The strong acids are the top six acids on the table. Their ionization equations include a one-way arrow signifying that they ionize 100%. Their K_a values are too large to be useful.

© Edvantage Interactive 2019

Table 5.2.1 *Relative Strengths of Brønsted-Lowry Acids and Bases (In aqueoous solution at room temperature)*

STRENGTH OF ACID (STRONG at top → WEAK at bottom); STRENGTH OF BASE (WEAK at top → STRONG at bottom)

Name of Acid	Acid		Base	K_a
Perchloric	$HClO_4$	→	$H^+ + ClO_4^-$	very large
Hydriodic	HI	→	$H^+ + I^-$	very large
Hydrobromic	HBr	→	$H^+ + Br^-$	very large
Hydrochloric	HCl	→	$H^+ + Cl^-$	very large
Nitric	HNO_3	→	$H^+ + NO_3^-$	very large
Sulfuric	H_2SO_4	→	$H^+ + HSO_4^-$	very large
Hydronium Ion	H_3O^+	⇄	$H^+ + H_2O$	1.0
Iodic	HIO_3	⇄	$H^+ + IO_3^-$	1.7×10^{-1}
Oxalic	$H_2C_2O_4$	⇄	$H^+ + HC_2O_4^-$	5.9×10^{-2}
Sulfurous ($SO_2 + H_2O$)	H_2SO_3	⇄	$H^+ + HSO_3^-$	1.5×10^{-2}
Hydrogen sulfate ion	HSO_4^-	⇄	$H^+ + SO_4^{2-}$	1.2×10^{-2}
Phosphoric	H_3PO_4	⇄	$H^+ + H_2PO_4^-$	7.5×10^{-3}
Hexaaquoiron ion, iron(III) ion	$Fe(H_2O)_6^{3+}$	⇄	$H^+ + Fe(H_2O)_5(OH)^{2+}$	6.0×10^{-3}
Citric	$H_3C_6H_5O_7$	⇄	$H^+ + H_2C_6H_5O_7^-$	7.1×10^{-4}
Nitrous	HNO_2	⇄	$H^+ + NO_2^-$	4.6×10^{-4}
Hydrofluoric	HF	⇄	$H^+ + F^-$	3.5×10^{-4}
Methanoic, formic	$HCOOH$	⇄	$H^+ + HCOO^-$	1.8×10^{-4}
Hexaaquochromium ion, chromium(III) ion	$Cr(H_2O)_6^{3+}$	⇄	$H^+ + Cr(H_2O)_5(OH)^{2+}$	1.5×10^{-4}
Benzoic	C_6H_5COOH	⇄	$H^+ + C_6H_5COO^-$	6.5×10^{-5}
Hydrogen oxalate ion	$HC_2O_4^-$	⇄	$H^+ + C_2O_4^{2-}$	6.4×10^{-5}
Ethanoic, acetic	CH_3COOH	⇄	$H^+ + CH_3COO^-$	1.8×10^{-5}
Dihydrogen citrate ion	$H_2C_6H_5O_7^-$	⇄	$H^+ + HC_6H_5O_7^{2-}$	1.7×10^{-5}
Hexaaquoaluminum ion, aluminum ion	$Al(H_2O)_6^{3+}$	⇄	$H^+ + Al(H_2O)_5(OH)^{2+}$	1.4×10^{-5}
Carbonic ($CO_2 + H_2O$)	H_2CO_3	⇄	$H^+ + HCO_3^-$	4.3×10^{-7}
Monohydrogen citrate ion	$HC_6H_5O_7^{2-}$	⇄	$H^+ + C_6H_5O_7^{3-}$	4.1×10^{-7}
Hydrogen sulfite ion	HSO_3^-	⇄	$H^+ + SO_3^{2-}$	1.0×10^{-7}
Hydrogen sulfide	H_2S	⇄	$H^+ + HS^-$	9.1×10^{-8}
Dihydrogen phosphate ion	$H_2PO_4^-$	⇄	$H^+ + HPO_4^{2-}$	6.2×10^{-8}
Boric	H_3BO_3	⇄	$H^+ + H_2BO_3^-$	7.3×10^{-10}
Ammonium ion	NH_4^+	⇄	$H^+ + NH_3$	5.6×10^{-10}
Hydrocyanic	HCN	⇄	$H^+ + CN^-$	4.9×10^{-10}
Phenol	C_6H_5OH	⇄	$H^+ + C_6H_5O^-$	1.3×10^{-10}
Hydrogen carbonate ion	HCO_3^-	⇄	$H^+ + CO_3^{2-}$	5.6×10^{-11}
Hydrogen peroxide	H_2O_2	⇄	$H^+ + HO_2^-$	2.4×10^{-12}
Monohydrogen phosphate ion	HPO_4^{2-}	⇄	$H^+ + PO_4^{3-}$	2.2×10^{-13}
Water	H_2O	⇄	$H^+ + OH^-$	1.0×10^{-14}
Hydroxide ion	OH^-	←	$H^+ + O^{2-}$	very small
Ammonia	NH_3	←	$H^+ + NH_2^-$	very small

- The other acids between, and including, hydronium and water are weak. Their ionization equations include an equilibrium arrow and an associated K_a value.
- Even though OH^- and NH_3 are listed on the left of the table, they do NOT act as acids in water. The reaction arrow does not go in the forward direction. They do NOT give up H^+ ions in water.
- There are two bold arrows along the sides of the table. On the left, acid strength increases going up the table. Notice that this arrow stops for OH^- and NH_3 because they are not weak acids; they will not donate a hydrogen ion in water. On the right, base strength increases going down the table. This arrow stops for the conjugate bases of the strong monoprotic acids because these ions (Cl^-, Br^-, and so on) do not act as weak bases. They will not accept a hydrogen ion from water.
- The K_a values listed are for aqueous solutions at room temperature. Like any equilibrium constant, K_a and K_b values are temperature dependent.
- The table lists the K_a values for weak acids. You will learn how to calculate the K_b of a weak base in an upcoming section. For now, you can rank the relative strength of a base from its position on this table. The lower a base is on the right side, the stronger it is. This means that the stronger an acid is, the weaker its conjugate base will be and vice versa. The more willing an acid is to donate a hydrogen ion, the more reluctant its conjugate base will be to take it back.
- Some ions appear on both sides of the table. They are amphiprotic and able to act as an acid or a base. One example of this is the bicarbonate ion, HCO_3^-.

Quick Check

1. Classify the following as a strong acid, strong base, weak acid, or weak base.

   (a) sulfuric acid ______________________

   (b) calcium hydroxide ______________________

   (c) ammonia ______________________

   (d) benzoic acid ______________________

   (e) cyanide ion ______________________

   (f) nitrous acid ______________________

2. For the weak acids or bases above, write an equation demonstrating their behavior in water and their corresponding K_a or K_b expression.

3. A student tests the electrical conductivity of 0.5 M solutions of the following: carbonic acid, methanoic acid, phenol, and boric acid. Rank these solutions in order from most conductive to least conductive.

   ____

   ____

© **Edvantage Interactive 2019**

Effects of Structure on Acid Strength

Strong acids ionize to produce more hydronium ions than weak acids when placed in water. That is, strong acids donate their hydrogen ions more readily. Why do some acids ionize more than others? To answer this question, we must examine an acid's structure. The structure of an acid influences how readily a hydrogen ion may leave the molecule (Figure 5.2.2).

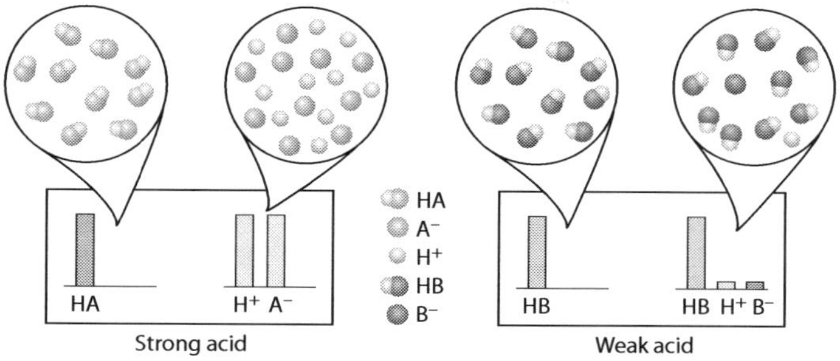

Figure 5.2.2 *Strong acids ionize completely in water. Weak acids ionize only partially. The weaker the acid, the lower the degree of ionization. In this representation, hydronium ion, H_3O^+ is simplified to H^+.*

Binary Acid Strength

The strength of a binary acid, HX depends primarily on the attraction between the nucleus of the hydrogen atom and the electrons that surround the atom X. There is also an attractive force between the electron of the hydrogen atom and the nucleus of X. As the size of X increases, the distance between the nucleus of one atom and the electrons of its neighbor increases. An increased distance results in a longer bond length, less bond strength, and a stronger acid. Binary acids of the halogen family provide a good illustration (Figure 5.2.3).

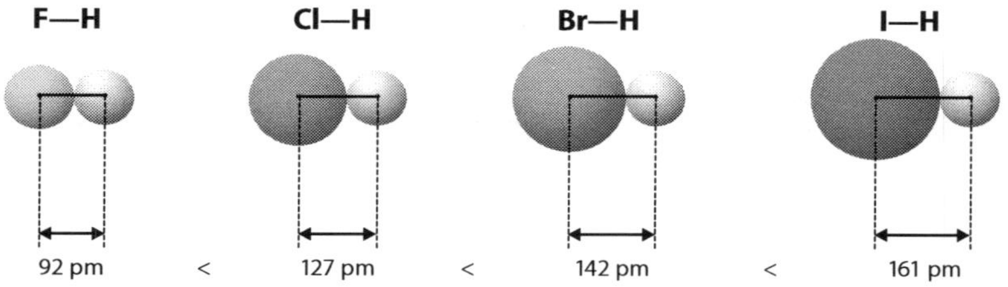

Figure 5.2.3 *Hydrofluoric acid is the weakest member of the hydrohalic acids due to the strong bond between hydrogen and fluorine. Binary acids of the halogen family increase in strength as the bond length increases — the longer the bond length, the more easily they can ionize.*

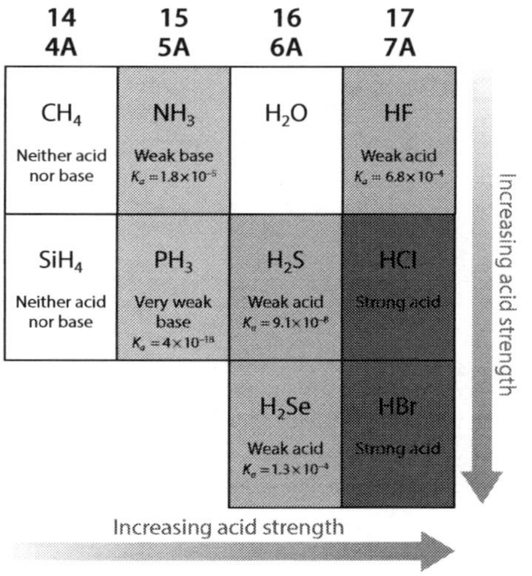

Figure 5.2.4 *In general, the acidity of binary acids increases as the non-metal attached to the hydrogen is further to the right in a period or closer to the bottom in a family of the periodic table.*

Binary acids containing more than one hydrogen atom are weaker than the hydrohalic acid in the same period (Figure 5.2.4). The presence of more hydrogen atoms bound to the central non-metal strengthens the H–X bonds in an H_nX molecule.

Acids weaker than water do not behave as acids in aqueous solution. Thus ammonia and methane are not commonly considered to be acids. Water is only treated as an acid in the context of aqueous solution chemistry.

Ternary Acid Strength

The strength of ternary or oxo-acids depends on two things:
1. the number of oxygen atoms, and
2. the electronegativity of the central non-metal atom

Ternary acids ionize more easily when the O–H bond is readily **polarized** (Figure 5.2.5). The bond is polarized when the pair of electrons shared between the oxygen and hydrogen atoms is drawn away from the hydrogen toward the center of the molecule. This occurs most readily when there are more oxygen atoms and the central non-metal atom is highly electronegative.

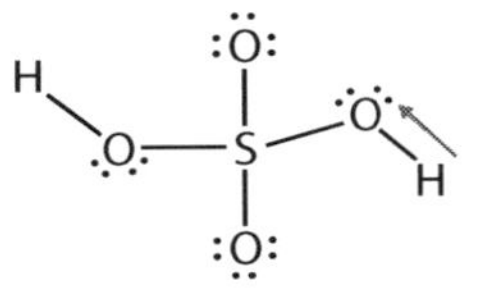

Figure 5.2.5 *Polarization of the O–H bond in an oxo-acid such as sulfuric acid (H_2SO_4) leads to increased strength*

Carboxylic Acids

The strength of carboxylic acids also depends on polarization of the O–H bond. The bond is more easily polarized if the carbon skeleton is shorter and if there are electronegative atoms attached to the carbon skeleton of the molecule (Figure 5.2.6).

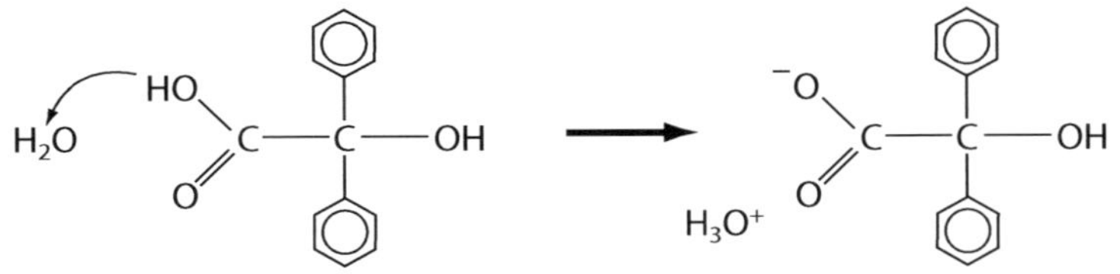

Figure 5.2.6 *The H atom from the carboxylic acid group (–COOH) on the left side of benzillic acid is the most ionizable H atom due to electron withdrawal by the extra oxygen double bonded to the carbon in the group. The electron withdrawal polarizes the H–O bond, causing the acid to ionize.*

 © **Edvantage Interactive 2019**

Quick Check

1. Study the acids shown here. Which acid is stronger? Clearly explain your answer.

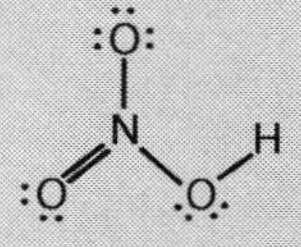

Acid 1

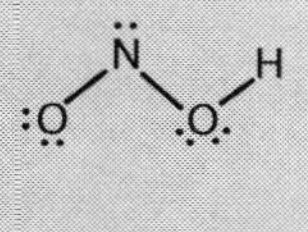

Acid 1

____

____

____

____

2. Study this table of binary acids. Rank the compounds below from strongest to weakest in terms of acid strength. Give a complete explanation of your reasoning.

Binary compound	Hydrobromic acid (HBr)	Hydrochloric acid (HCl)	Hydroiodic acid (HI)	Hydroselenic acid(H_2Se)	Hydrosulfuric acid (H_2S)	Methane (CH_4)	Water (H_2O)
Lewis structure	H–Br	H–Cl	H–I	H–Se–H	H–S–H	CH_4 (C bonded to four H)	H–O–H

____

____

3. Study the ternary acids shown here. Rank the compounds below from weakest to strongest in terms of acid strength. Give a complete explanation of your reasoning.

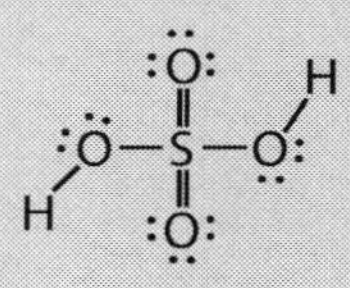

(H_2SO_4)

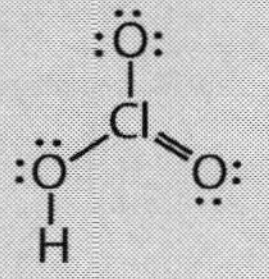

($HClO_3$)

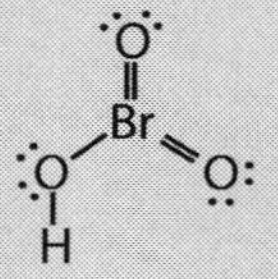

($HBrO_3$)

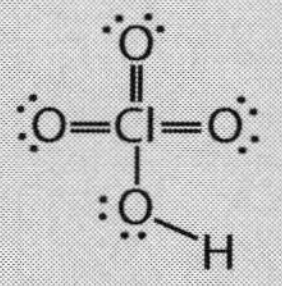

($HClO_4$)

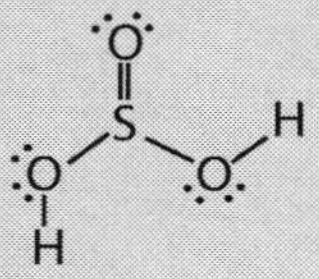

(H_2SO_3)

____

____

____

____

4. Use Table 5.2.1 to rank benzoic, ethanoic, and methanoic acids in terms of strength. Arrange the acids from greatest to least polarizable O–H bond.

The Position of Equilibrium and Relative Strengths

When a Brønsted-Lowry acid and base react, the position of the equilibrium results from the relative strengths of the acids and bases involved. If K_{eq} is greater than 1, products are favored. If K_{eq} is less than 1, reactants are favored. Acids that are stronger are more able to donate H^+ ions, so the position of the equilibrium is determined by the stronger acid and base reacting. Consider the reaction between ammonia and methanoic acid:

$$\underset{\text{base}}{NH_3(aq)} + \underset{\text{acid}}{HCOOH(aq)} \rightleftharpoons \underset{\text{acid}}{NH_4^+(aq)} + \underset{\text{base}}{HCOO^-(aq)}$$

We can label the acids and bases for the forward and reverse reactions as above. The two acids are methanoic acid and the ammonium ion. According to the K_a table, methanoic acid is a stronger acid than the ammonium ion, so it donates H^+ ions more readily. Therefore, the forward reaction happens to a greater extent than the reverse reaction. Additionally, NH_3 is a stronger base than $HCOO^-$, so it accepts H^+ ions more readily. Therefore, the forward reaction proceeds to a greater extent than the reverse reaction, and products are favored at equilibrium.

Equilibrium favors the reaction in the direction of the stronger acid and base forming the weaker acid and base.

Sample Problem 5.2.1(a) — Predicting Whether Reactants or Products Will Be Favored in a Brønsted-Lowry Acid-Base Equilibrium

Predict whether reactants or products will be favored when HCN reacts with HCO_3^-.

What to Think About	How to Do It
1. Recognize that both HCN and HCO_3^- can act as weak acids, but only HCO_3^- can act as a weak base. This means that HCN will be the acid, and HCO_3^- will be the base. The acid donates a H^+ ion and the base accepts the H^+ ion. We can complete the equilibrium.	$HCN + HCO_3^- \rightleftharpoons CN^- + H_2CO_3$
2. The acid in the forward reaction is HCN, and the acid in the reverse reaction is H_2CO_3.	acid + base ⇌ base + acid
3. According to the K_a table, H_2CO_3 is a stronger acid than HCN. H_2CO_3 will donate H^+ ions more readily than HCN. It is evident from the table that CN^- is a stronger base than HCO_3^-. The stronger acid and base will always appear on the same side of an equilibrium.	weaker acid + weaker base ⇌ stronger acid + stronger base
4. The equilibrium favors the direction in which the stronger acid and base react to form the weaker conjugate acid and base.	The reverse reaction is favored, so reactants are favored at equilibrium.

Consider the reaction between HSO_4^- and $HC_2O_4^-$. Both of these species are amphiprotic. If two amphiprotic species react, then the stronger acid of the two will donate the H^+ ion, unless one of the species is water. When an amphiprotic species reacts with water, the reaction that occurs to a greater extent is determined by comparing the K_a to the K_b of the amphiprotic species. You will learn how to do this in an upcoming section.

© Edvantage Interactive 2019

Sample Problem 5.2.1(b) — Predicting Whether Reactants or Products Will Be Favored in a Brønsted-Lowry Acid-Base Equilibrium

Predict whether reactants or products will be favored when HSO_4^- reacts with $HC_2O_4^-$.

What to Think About	How to Do It
1. Both substances are amphiprotic. Since HSO_4^- is a stronger acid than $HC_2O_4^-$, the HSO_4^- acts as the acid and donates a H^+ ion to $HC_2O_4^-$.	$HSO_4^- + HC_2O_4^- \rightleftharpoons SO_4^{2-} + H_2C_2O_4$
2. The acid in the forward reaction is HSO_4^-, and the acid in the reverse reaction is $H_2C_2O_4$.	acid + base $\rightleftharpoons$ base + acid
3. According to the K_a table, $H_2C_2O_4$ is a stronger acid than HSO_4^-. $H_2C_2O_4$ will donate H^+ ions more readily than HSO_4^-. It is evident from the table that SO_4^{2-} is a stronger base than $HC_2O_4^-$. The stronger acid and base will always appear on the same side of an equilibrium.	weaker acid + weaker base $\rightleftharpoons$ stronger acid + stonger base
4. The equilibrium favors the direction in which the stronger acid and base react to form the weaker conjugate acid and base.	Reverse reaction favored, so reactants are favored at equilibrium.

Practice Problems 5.2.1 — Predicting Whether Reactants or Products Will Be Favored in a Brønsted-Lowry Acid-Base Equilibrium

1. For the following, complete the equilibrium and predict whether reactants or products are favored at equilibrium.
   (a) hydrogen peroxide + hydrogen sulfite ion $\rightleftharpoons$
   (b) citric acid + ammonia $\rightleftharpoons$
   (c) hydrogen carbonate ion + dihydrogen phosphate ion $\rightleftharpoons$

2. Arsenic acid (H_3AsO_4) reacts with an equal concentration of sulfate ion. At equilibrium, $[H_3AsO_4] > [HSO_4^-]$. Write the equation for this reaction and state which acid is the stronger one.

3. Consider the reaction between the sulfite ion and the hexaaquochromium ion. Write the equation for this reaction, and predict whether K_{eq} *is greater or less than 1.*

The Levelling Effect

According to the K_a table, all strong acids in water are equally strong. Remember that "strong" means that it ionizes 100%. When each of the strong acids ionizes in water, hydronium ions form:

$$HCl(aq) + H_2O(l) \rightarrow H_3O^+(aq) + Cl^-(aq)$$

$$HBr(aq) + H_2O(l) \rightarrow H_3O^+(aq) + Br^-(aq)$$

Therefore, in a solution of a strong acid, no molecules of the strong acid remain — only the anion and hydronium ion are left. In the same manner, all strong bases dissociate completely to form OH^- ions.

In aqueous solution, the strongest acid actually present is H_3O^+ and the strongest base actually present is OH^-. Water levels the strength of strong acids and bases.

All strong acids in aqueous solution have equal ability to donate a H^+ ion to form H_3O^+. This is analogous to your chemistry teacher and a football player being able to lift a 5 kg weight. Both are able to lift the weight easily, so there is no observed difference in their strengths. Increasing the difficulty of the task (by increasing the amount of weight) would allow us to observe a difference in strength. Likewise, HCl and HI have no observable difference in strength when reacting with water, but when reacting with pure CH_3COOH, their different strengths become apparent.

© Edvantage Interactive 2019

5.2 Activity: Determining the Relative Strengths of Six Acids

Question

You are given six unknown weak acid solutions of the same concentration. The three weak acid indicators (HIn) are first mixed with HCl and NaOH. Can you build a table of relative acid strengths for six unknown solutions?

Procedure

1. Consider the following data collected when the indicated solutions are mixed:

	HIn_1/In_1^-	HIn_2/In_2^-	HIn_3/In_3^-
HCl	red	yellow	colorless
NaOH	yellow	red	purple
HA_1/A_1^-	red	yellow	purple
HA_2/A_2^-	red	yellow	colorless
HA_3/A_3^-	yellow	yellow	purple

2. There are six unknown weak acid solutions containing a conjugate acid-base pair. Three of the acids are HA_1, HA_2, and HA_3. The other three acids are chemical indicators HIn_1, HIn_2, and HIn_3. A chemical indicator is a weak acid in which its conjugate acid has a different color than its conjugate base. In the indicator solution, both the acid form (HIn) and the base form (In^-) exist in equilibrium.
3. When indicator 1 (HIn_1) is mixed with HCl, the HCl will donate a H^+ ion because it is a strong acid. If HCl acts as an acid, then it will donate a H^+ ion to the base form of the indicator:
   $HCl + In_1^- \rightarrow HIn_1 + Cl^-$
   According to the data in step 1, indicator 1 turns red in HCl. Therefore, HIn must be red. Likewise, In^- must be yellow because the OH^- in NaOH accepts a H^+ ion from HIn to form In^-. We know then that HIn = red and In^- = yellow.
4. When we mix unknown acid 1 (HA_1) with indicator 1 (HIn_1) we see red. The equilibrium established may be written as:
   $HA_1 + In_1^- \rightleftharpoons HIn_1 + A_1^-$
   yellow red
   Knowing that HIn_1 is red, we conclude that products are favored in this equilibrium. Therefore, HA_1 is a stronger acid than HIn_1.
5. Fill in the table below by comparing the strength of each pair of acids HA to HIn. The first one has been filled in for you from the discussion above.

	HIn_1/In_1^-	HIn_2/In_2^-	HIn_3/In_3^-
HA_1/A_1^-	$HA_1 > HIn_1$		
HA_2/A_2^-			
HA_3/A_3^-			

Results and Discussion

1. Rank the six unknown acids in order from strongest to weakest:
   ________ > ________ > ________ > ________ > ________ > ________
2. Construct a table similar to Table 5.2.1 Relative Strengths of Brønsted-Lowry Acids and Bases using the six unknown acids. Be sure to include ionization equations and arrows on each side of the table labelled: "Increasing strength of acid" and "Increasing strength of base."

5.2 Review Questions

1. Classify the following as strong or weak acids or bases.
   (a) sodium oxide — used in glass making

   (b) boric acid — used to manufacture fiberglass, antiseptics, and insecticides

   (c) perchloric acid — used to make ammonium perchlorate for rocket fuel

   (d) phosphate ion — present in the cleaner TSP (trisodium phosphate)

2. For any of the substances above that are weak, write an equation showing how they react in water, then write its corresponding K_a or K_b expression.

3. A student tests the electrical conductivity of a 2.0 M oxalic acid solution and compares it to the conductivity of 2.0 M hydroiodic acid. Explain how the hydroiodic acid could have a greater conductivity than the oxalic acid.

4. Calculate the total ion concentration in a solution of 2.0 M nitric acid. Explain why you cannot use this method to calculate the concentration of ions in 2.0 M nitrous acid.

5. Give an example of a
   (a) concentrated weak base

   (b) dilute strong acid

© **Edvantage Interactive 2019**

6. (a) Rank the following 0.1 M solutions in order from least electrical conductivity to greatest electrical conductivity: carbonic acid, citric acid, sulfuric acid, sulfurous acid, and water.

(b) Rank the following bases in order from strongest to weakest: monohydrogen phosphate ion, carbonate ion, fluoride ion, ammonia, nitrite ion, and water.

7. Write the equation for the reaction of each of the following acids in water and its corresponding K_a expression:
(a) monohydrogen citrate ion

(b) dihydrogen citrate ion

(c) aluminum ion

(d) hydrogen peroxide

8. Write the equation for the reaction of each of the following bases in water and its corresponding K_b expression:
(a) ammonia

(b) benzoate ion

(c) acetate ion

(d) monohydrogen citrate ion

(e) pyradine (C_5H_5N).

9. For the following, complete the equilibria, then state whether reactants or products are favored.

(a)

$Fe(H_2O)_6^{3+}(aq) + HO_2^-(aq) \rightleftharpoons$

(b)

$H_2SO_3(aq) + IO_3^-(aq) \rightleftharpoons$

(c)

$CN^-(aq) + H_2PO_4^-(aq) \rightleftharpoons$

10. Using the substances H_2CO_3, HCO_3^-, $H_2C_2O_4$ and $HC_2O_4^-$, write an equilibrium equation with a $K_{eq} > 1$.

11. Consider the following equilibria:

$H_2SiO_3 + BrO^- \rightleftharpoons HBrO + HSiO_3^- \quad K_{eq} = 0.095$

$HClO + BrO^- \rightleftharpoons HBrO + ClO^- \quad K_{eq} = 14$

Rank the acids H_2SiO_3, HClO, and HBrO from strongest to weakest.

12. Explain why HCl, HBr, and HI are equally strong in water. Use balanced chemical equations in your answer.

© **Edvantage Interactive 2019**

5.3 The Ionization of Water

Warm Up

1. Describe the difference between a weak acid and a strong acid.

2. Compare the relative electrical conductivities of 1.0 M HCl, 1.0 M CH_3COOH, and distilled water. Explain your reasoning.

3. On your K_a table, find the equation for water acting as an acid and reproduce it here. Write the K_a expression for water.

The Ion-Product Constant of Water

In the previous Section, you saw that water can act as either a Brønsted-Lowry weak acid or weak base. Water is amphiprotic and so can form both hydronium and hydroxide ions. In a Brønsted-Lowry equilibrium, we can see how one water molecule donates a proton to another water molecule (Figure 5.3.1). This is called **autoionization**.

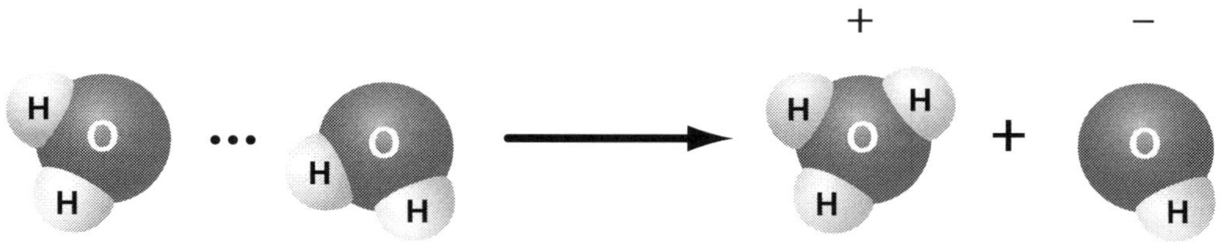

$$H_2O(l) + H_2O(l) \rightleftharpoons H_3O^+(aq) + OH^-(aq)$$

Figure 5.3.1 *Autoionization of water*

As with any equilibrium equation, we can write a corresponding equilibrium constant expression:

$$K_w = [H_3O^+][OH^-]$$

where K_w is the **water ionization constant** or **ion product constant**.

Remember that the value of an equilibrium constant depends on the temperature.

At 25°C, $K_w = 1.00 \times 10^{-14} = [H_3O^+][OH^-]$

From this information, we can calculate the $[H_3O^+]$ and $[OH^-]$ in water at 25°C. It is obvious from the equilibrium that the $[H_3O^+] = [OH^-]$ at any temperature. Because of this, water is neutral.

$$H_2O(l) + H_2O(l) \rightleftharpoons \underset{x}{H_3O^+(aq)} + \underset{x}{OH^-(aq)}$$

$$K_w = 1.00 \times 10^{-14} = [H_3O^+][OH^-]$$
$$= (x)(x) = x^2$$
$$x = 1.00 \times 10^{-7}\text{ M}$$
$$[H_3O^+] = [OH^-] = 1.0 \times 10^{-7}\text{ M}$$

Quick Check

1. The autoionization of water is endothermic. If the temperature of water is increased, what happens to the concentration of hydronium ion, hydroxide ion, and K_w?

____

____

2. At higher temperatures, how will the concentration of hydronium ion and hydroxide ion compare to each other?

____

____

3. At 10°C, $K_w = 2.9 \times 10^{-15}$. Calculate $[H_3O^+]$ and $[OH^-]$ in water at this temperature.

Adding Acid or Base to Water

When we add an acid or base to water, we cause the equilibrium present in water to shift in response. In 1.0 M HCl, HCl, which is a strong acid, thus ionizes 100% to produce 1.0 M H_3O^+ and 1.0 M Cl^- ions:

$$HCl(aq) + H_2O(l) \rightarrow \underset{1.0\text{ M}}{H_3O^+(aq)} + \underset{1.0\text{ M}}{Cl^-(aq)}$$

The added hydronium ions cause the water equilibrium to shift left and the concentration of hydroxide to decrease.

Likewise, when a strong base dissolves in water, the added hydroxide ions cause a shift left, and a corresponding hydronium ion concentration to decrease.

An increase in $[H_3O^+]$ causes a decrease in $[OH^-]$, and vise versa. The $[H_3O^+]$ is inversely proportional to $[OH^-]$.

Both H_3O^+ and OH^- ions exist in all aqueous solutions:

- If $[H_3O^+] > [OH^-]$, the solution is acidic.
- If $[H_3O^+] = [OH^-]$, the solution is neutral.
- If $[H_3O^+] < [OH^-]$, the solution is basic.

© Edvantage Interactive 2019

Sample Problem 5.3.1 — Calculating $[H_3O^+]$ and $[OH^-]$ in Solutions of a Strong Acid or Strong Base

What is the $[H_3O^+]$ and $[OH^-]$ in 0.50 M HCl? Justify that the solution is acidic.

What to Think About	How to Do It
1. HCl is a strong acid and so will ionize 100%. Thus $[HCl] = [H_3O^+]$.	$[H_3O^+] = 0.50$ M
2. The temperature is not specified. Assume 25°C.	$K_w = 1.00 \times 10^{-14} = [H_3O^+][OH^-]$
3. Substitute into K_w and solve for $[OH^-]$.	$1.00 \times 10^{-14} = (0.50\text{ M})[OH^-]$ $[OH^-] = 2.0 \times 10^{-14}$ M Because the $[H_3O^+] > [OH^-]$, the solution is acidic.

Practice Problems 5.3.1 — Calculating $[H_3O^+]$ and $[OH^-]$ in Solutions of a Strong Acid or Strong Base

(Assume the temperature in each case is 25°C.)

1. Calculate the $[H_3O^+]$ and $[OH^-]$ in 0.15 M $HClO_4$. Justify that this solution is acidic.

2. Calculate the $[H_3O^+]$ and $[OH^-]$ in a saturated solution of magnesium hydroxide. (Hint: this salt has low solubility, but is a strong base.)

3. A student dissolved 1.42 g of NaOH in 250. mL of solution. Calculate the resulting $[H_3O^+]$ and $[OH^-]$. Justify that this solution is basic.

Mixing Solutions of Strong Acids and Bases

When we react strong acids with strong bases, we need to consider two factors: solutions will dilute each other when mixed, and then acids will neutralize bases. The resulting solution will be acidic, basic, or neutral depending on whether more acid or base is present after neutralization.

Sample Problem 5.3.2 — What Happens When a Strong Acid Is Added to a Strong Base?

What is the final $[H_3O^+]$ in a solution formed when 25 mL of 0.30 M HCl is added to 35 mL of 0.50 M NaOH?

What to Think About	How to Do It
1. When two solutions are combined, both are diluted. Calculate the new concentrations of HCl and NaOH in the mixed solution.	HCl is a strong acid, so $[HCl] = [H_3O^+]$ NaOH is a strong base, so $[NaOH] = [OH^-]$ $[HCl] = \frac{0.30 \text{ mol}}{\cancel{L}} \times \frac{0.025 \cancel{L}}{0.060 \text{ L}} = 0.125 \text{ M}$ $[NaOH] = \frac{0.50 \text{ mol}}{\cancel{L}} \times \frac{0.035 \cancel{L}}{0.060 \text{ L}} = 0.292 \text{ M}$
2. The hydronium ions and hydroxide ions will neutralize each other. Since there is more hydroxide, there will be hydroxide left over. Calculate how much will be left over.	$[H_3O^+]_{initial} = 0.125 \text{ M}$ $[OH^-]_{initial} = 0.292 \text{ M}$ $[OH^-]_{excess} = [OH^-]_{initial} - [H_3O^+]_{initial}$ $= 0.292 \text{ M} - 0.125 \text{ M}$ $= 0.167 \text{ M} = 0.17 \text{ M}$
3. Use K_w to calculate the hydronium ion concentration from the hydroxide ion concentration.	$K_w = [H_3O^+][OH^-]$ $1.00 \times 10^{-14} = [H_3O^+](0.17 \text{ M})$ $[H_3O^+] = 6.0 \times 10^{-14} \text{ M}$

Practice Problems 5.3.2 — What Happens When a Strong Acid Is Added to a Strong Base?

1. Calculate the final $[H_3O^+]$ and $[OH^-]$ in a solution formed when 150. mL of 1.5 M HNO_3 is added to 250. mL of 0.80 M KOH.

2. Calculate the mass of solid NaOH that must be added to 500. mL of 0.20 M HI to result in a solution with $[H_3O^+] = 0.12$ M. Assume no volume change on the addition of solid NaOH.

3. Calculate the resulting $[H_3O^+]$ and $[OH^-]$ when 18.4 mL of 0.105 M HBr is added to 22.3 mL of 0.256 M HCl.

© Edvantage Interactive 2019

5.3 Activity: Counting Water Molecules and Hydronium Ions

Question

How many water molecules does it take to produce one hydronium ion?

Procedure

1. Calculate the number of water molecules present in 1.0 L of water using the density of water (1.00 g/mL) and its molar mass.
2. Calculate the number of hydronium ions in 1.0 L of water. (Hint: You need the [H_3O^+] in pure water from step 1.)
3. Using the above answers, calculate the ratio of ions/molecules. This is the percentage ionization of water.
4. Using the ratio above, calculate the number of water molecules required to produce one hydronium ion.

Results and Discussion

1. From the ratio of ions to molecules, it is evident that an extremely small percentage of water molecules actually ionize. Because there are an enormously large number of molecules present in the solutions we use, a reasonable number of hydronium and hydroxide ions are present. What volume of water contains only one hydronium ion?

5.3 Review Questions

1. In its pure liquid form, ammonia (NH_3) undergoes autoionization. Write an equation to show how ammonia autoionizes.

2. Complete the following table:

$[H_3O^+]$	$[OH^-]$	Acidic, Basic, or Neutral?
	6.0 M	
3.2×10^{-4} M		
	9.2×10^{-12} M	
2.5 M		
	4.7×10^{-5} M	

3. The autoionization of water has $\Delta H = 57.1$ kJ/mol. Write the equation for the autoionization of water including the energy term. Explain how the value of K_w changes with temperature.

4. The K_w for water at 1°C is 1.0×10^{-15}. Calculate the $[H_3O^+]$ and $[OH^-]$ in 0.20 M HI at this temperature.

5. Human urine has a $[H_3O^+] = 6.3 \times 10^{-7}$ M. What is the $[OH^-]$, and is urine acidic, basic, or neutral?

6. Complete the table:

Temperature	K_w	$[H_3O^+]$	$[OH^-]$	Acidic, Basic, or Neutral?
50° C	5.5×10^{-14}			
100° C	5.1×10^{-13}			

 © **Edvantage Interactive 2019**

7. Heavy water (D_2O) is used in CANDU reactors as a moderator. In heavy water, the hydrogen atoms are H-2 called *deuterium* and symbolized as D. In a sample of heavy water at 50°C, $[OD^-] = 8.9 \times 10^{-8}$ M. Calculate K_w for heavy water.

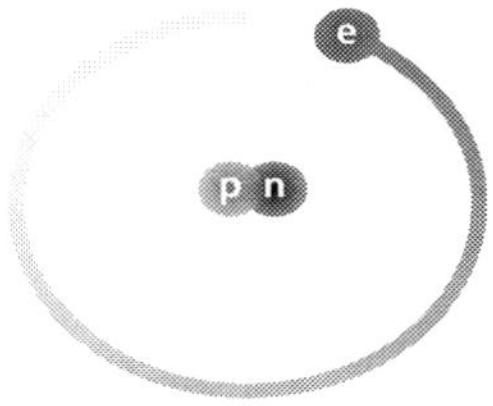

8. Calculate the $[H_3O^+]$ and $[OH^-]$ in a saturated solution of calcium hydroxide. ($K_{sp} = 4.7 \times 10^{-6}$)

9. A student combines the following solutions:
Calculate the $[H_3O^+]$ and $[OH^-]$ in the resulting solution.

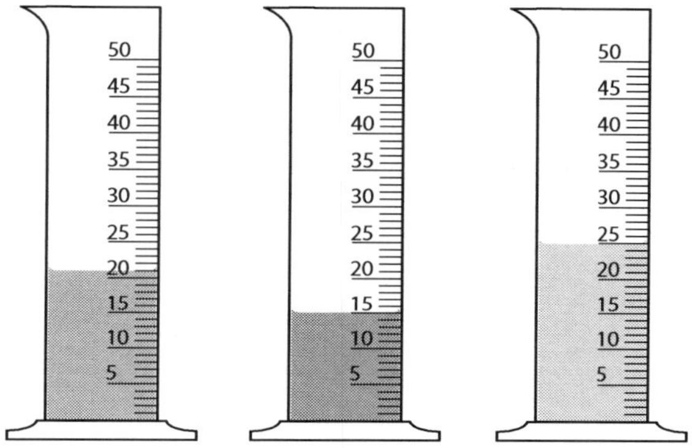

0.80 M HCl   1.2 M NaOH   0.60 M HI

10. What mass of strontium hydroxide must be added to 150. mL of 0.250 M nitric acid to produce a solution with $[OH^-] = 0.010$ M?

5.4 pH and pOH

Warm Up

1. Complete the following table.

Solution	$[H_3O^+]$	$[OH^-]$
A. 1.0 M NaOH		
B. 1.0 M HCl		

2. Determine the $[H_3O^+]$ and $[OH^-]$ in the solution formed when equal volumes of solution A and solution B are combined.

3. Calculate the volume of solution A required to obtain 1.0 mol of H_3O^+ ions.

The pH Scale

Look at your answers to question 1 in the Warm Up and consider the magnitude of the difference between the $[H_3O^+]$ and $[OH^-]$ in solution A and solution B — it is 100 trillion times! Consider also that during the neutralization described in question 2, each ion concentration changes instantly by 10 million times to equal the other. Now think about the volume your answer to question 3 actually represents: 10^{14} L of 1.0 M NaOH solution would be required to obtain 1.0 mol of hydronium ions!

Let's try to appreciate how large a volume this is. The average flow rate of large river is approximately 3.5×10^6 L/s (Figure 5.4.1). At this rate, to observe 10^{14} L of water flow by, you would have to watch this mighty river for more than 330 days!

Figure 5.4.1 *A powerful river flows through a narrow valley.*

The point behind the above discussion is that a linear arithmetic scale is not only inconvenient, it is cumbersome. It is also often inadequate to use when representing the typically very small hydronium and hydroxide concentrations in most aqueous solutions and the extent to which they can change in a neutralization reaction.

A much more convenient and compact approach was introduced in 1909 by the great Danish chemist S.P. Sorensen. Sorensen's scale is called the **pH** ("potency" or "power" of hydrogen) scale. It is a logarithmic or "power of 10" way to specify the concentration of hydronium ions in a solution.

We define pH as the negative logarithm of the molar concentration of hydronium ions:

$$\mathbf{pH = -log\,[H_3O^+]}$$

© Edvantage Interactive 2019

The logarithm of a number is the power to which 10 must be raised to obtain that number. For example:

$$\log 100 = \log (1 \times 10^2) = 2.0$$
$$\log 0.01 = \log (1 \times 10^{-2}) = -2.0$$

Logarithms and Significant Figures

When we take the logarithm of a number, we must be careful to record the answer to the proper number of significant figures. To understand how to do this, consider the following example:

Determine the pH of a 0.0035 M H_3O^+ solution and record the answer to the proper number of significant figures.

Solution: Note that in the molar concentration, there are two significant figures because the leading zeros are not considered significant. It should make sense to you that any operation done on those zeros yields a value that is also not considered significant. In the solution below, the significant figures are underlined:

$$\begin{aligned} pH &= -\log [H_3O^+] \\ &= -\log (0.00\underline{35}) \text{ (two significant figures)} \\ &= -\log (\underline{3.5} \times 10^{-3}) \end{aligned}$$

(*Note that the log of the product of two numbers equals the sum of the logs of those numbers so that:* log (A × B) = log A + log B)

$$= -\log \underline{3.5} \text{ (significant)} + -\log 10^{-3}$$

(The exponent 3 is not a measured value. Rather, it is an exact number and consequently does not limit the number of significant figures in the answer.)

$$\begin{aligned} &= -0.\underline{54}41 \text{ (significant)} + 3 \\ &= 2.\underline{45}59 \\ &= 2.\underline{46} \text{ (two significant figures)} \end{aligned}$$

We can generalize this into a rule governing logarithms and significant figures:

> When taking the logarithm of a number, the result must have the same number of *decimal places* as there are *significant figures* in the original number.

Measuring pH

The pH of a solution is usually determined with an acid-base indicator or, more precisely, by using an instrument called a pH meter (Figure 5.4.2). (Acid-base indicators will be discussed in more detail in Chapter 6.)

A pH meter consists of specially designed electrodes that are sensitive to the concentration of H_3O^+ ions. When the electrodes are dipped into a solution, a voltage between the measuring electrode and a reference electrode is generated that depends on the solution's pH. That voltage is read on a meter which is calibrated in pH units.

Figure 5.4.2 *A pH meter*

Quick Check

1. Convert each of the following hydronium concentrations to pH values. Make sure to record your answers to the proper number of significant figures.

Solution	$[H_3O^+]$	pH
orange juice	3.2×10^{-4} M	
milk of magnesia	2.52×10^{-11} M	
stomach acid	0.031 M	

2. During a titration, if the pH of a solution decreased quickly by 5 units from 8 to 3 at the equivalence point, did the $[H_3O^+]$ increase or decrease and by how much?

____

3. A 100.0 mL sample of an aqueous solution labeled as 0.10 M H_3O^+ is diluted to 1.0 L. Has the pH of the solution increased or decreased and by how much?

____

Antilogarithms

You will be expected to determine the pH of a solution given its hydronium concentration. You must also be able to convert pH values into hydronium concentrations in the reverse process. This is accomplished using the following relationship:

$$[H_3O^+] = 10^{-pH}$$

This is sometimes called taking the antilogarithm, and in this case, we are taking the antilogarithm of the *negative pH value*. It is simply expressing the negative logarithm in its original exponential form. Depending on the type of calculator you use, you should become familiar with the calculation steps to perform this operation. Usually, this requires employing the "10^x," "Y^x," or "inverse" "log" keys.

Sample Problem 5.4.1 — Converting pH to $[H_3O^+]$

The pH of a beaker of lemon juice is measured and found to be 2.31. Calculate the concentration of hydronium ions in this solution.

What to Think About	How to Do It
1. Because the pH is well below 7.00, expect the hydronium concentration to be much greater than 1.0×10^{-7} M. The solution is therefore acidic.	$[H_3O^+] = 10^{-pH}$ $[H_3O^+] = 10^{-2.31}$
2. Two decimal places in the pH value will correspond to a molar concentration recorded to two significant figures.	$[H_3O^+] = 4.9 \times 10^{-3}$ M

© Edvantage Interactive 2019

Practice Problems 5.4.1 — Converting pH to $[H_3O^+]$

1. Complete the following table and record your answers to the proper number of significant figures:

$[H_3O^+]$	No. of sig. figures	pH
5.00×10^{-5} M		
		3.34
6.4×10^{-11} M		
		6.055
0.00345 M		

2. During a titration, the pH at the equivalence point changed quickly from 4.35 to 9.65. Calculate the $[H_3O^+]$ just before and just after the equivalence point was reached.

3. A student calculates the pH of a sample of concentrated nitric acid to be –1.20. She thinks she has made a mistake because the value is negative. Calculate the hydronium concentration in this acid solution and decide if an error was made. Why do you think expressing pH values for concentrated strong acid solutions are not really necessary?

Expanding the "p" Concept

The success of the pH concept for representing small hydronium concentrations allowed it to be extended to cover other typically small values. In general:

$$\mathbf{pX = -log\ X}$$

Accordingly, we can also represent the hydroxide concentrations in aqueous solutions in a logarithmic way and call that value **pOH**.

$$\mathbf{pOH = -log\ [OH^-]}$$

For example, in a 0.10 M solution of NaOH, we know that the $[OH^-] = 0.10$ M. This allows us to determine the pOH as follows:

$$\begin{aligned} pOH &= -\log 0.10 \\ &= -\log (1.0 \times 10^{-1}) = 1.00 \end{aligned}$$

Recall that the concentrations of hydronium and hydroxide ions in aqueous solutions are inversely related through the equilibrium constant we call K_w. This always equals 1.00×10^{-14} at 25°C as given by: $[H_3O^+][OH^-] = K_w = 1.00 \times 10^{-14}$

We can use this to derive another very useful relationship for any aqueous solution. Begin with:

$$[H_3O^+][OH^-] = K_w$$

Take the negative log of both sides:

$$-\log\left[[H_3O^+][OH^-]\right] = -\log K_w$$

$$= -\log [H_3O^+] + -\log [OH^-] = -\log K_w$$

This is simply:

$pH + pOH = pK_w$

The above relationship is always true for any aqueous solution at any temperature. If we assume a temperature of 25°C, then:

$pH + pOH = 14.00$

In Figure 5.4.3(a), note the graphical relationship showing the inverse relationship between hydronium and hydroxide concentration in aqueous solutions as given by $[H_3O^+][OH^-] = 10^{-14}$.

Note how the negative logarithm of both sides of the relationship translates to the graphical relationship in (b) as given by pH + pOH = 14.00.

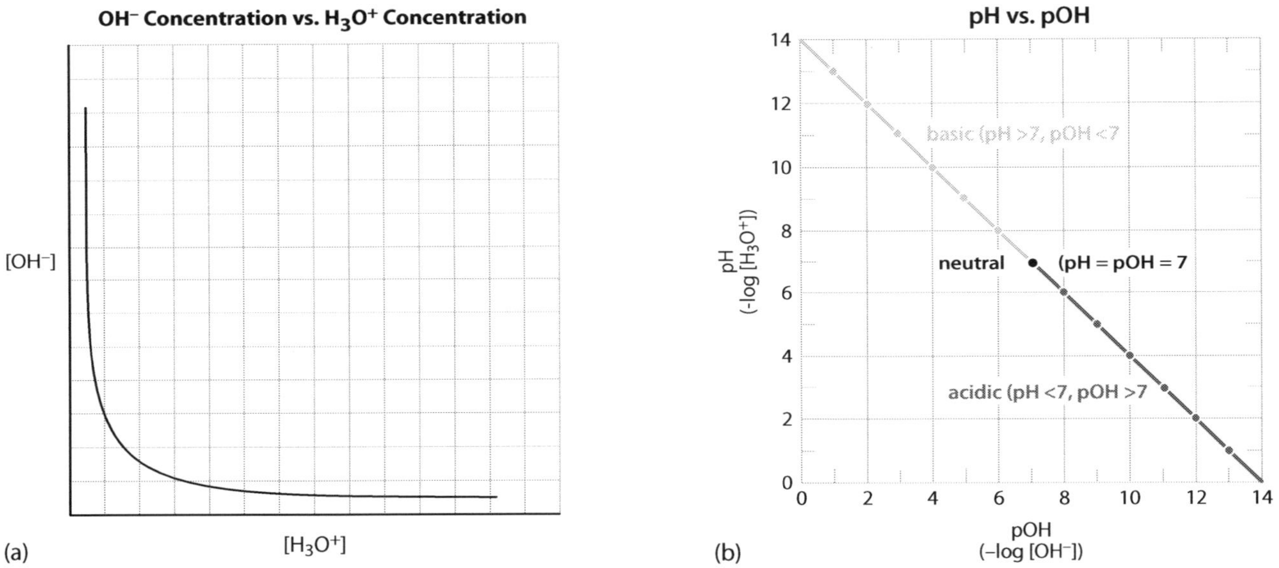

Figure 5.4.3 *(a) The inverse relationship between hydronium and hydroxide concentration in aqueous solutions; (b) This graph uses the negative logs of both sides of the relationship shown in (a).*

This relationship allows us to add to our criteria for designating aqueous solutions as acidic, basic, or neutral by incorporating both pH and pOH (Table 5.4.1).

Table 5.4.1 *pH and pOH Criteria for Designating Aqueous Solutions as Acidic, Basic, or Neutral*

Aqueous Solution at Any Temperature	Aqueous Solution at 25°C	Result
pH = pOH	pH = pOH = 7	Solution is *neutral.*
pH < pOH	pH < 7 and pOH > 7	Solution is *acidic.*
pH > pOH	pH > 7 and pOH < 7	Solution is *basic.*

© Edvantage Interactive 2019

This relationship also means that for any aqueous solution, if we are given any one of pH, pOH, $[H_3O^+]$, or $[OH^-]$, we can always calculate the remaining three. Consider Figure 5.4.4.

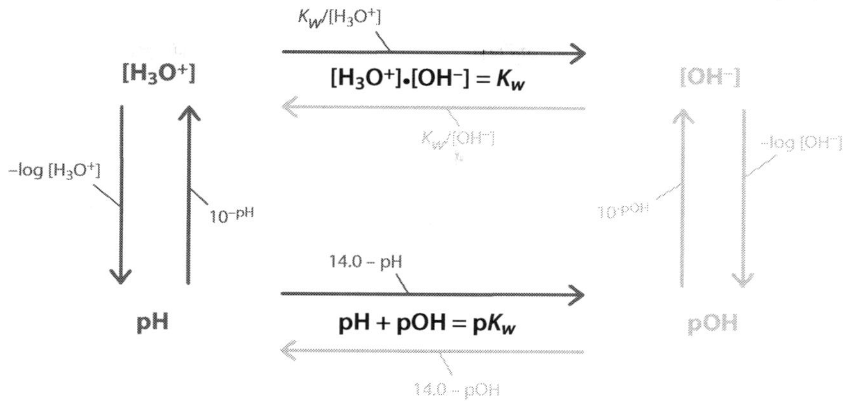

Figure 5.4.4 *This diagram shows how, by knowing one of pH, pOH, $[H_3O^+]$, or $[OH^-]$, we can calculate the other three.*

We can therefore summarize the relationship between pH, pOH, $[H_3O^+]$, and $[OH^-]$ for any aqueous solution at 25°C as shown in Figure 5.4.5. On the chart, consider the "cursor" that sits over the middle of the scale, highlighting a neutral solution. Imagine that this cursor is transparent and movable. It could be moved to the left or the right to identify the conditions associated with increasingly acidic or basic solutions respectively.

← Solution becomes more ***acidic.*** | Solution becomes more ***basic.*** →

$[H_3O^+]$	1	10^{-1}	10^{-2}	10^{-3}	10^{-4}	10^{-5}	10^{-6}	**10^{-7}**	10^{-8}	10^{-9}	10^{-10}	10^{-11}	10^{-12}	10^{-13}	10^{-14}
pH	0	1	2	3	4	5	6	**7**	8	9	10	11	12	13	14
pOH	14	13	12	11	10	9	8	**7**	6	5	4	3	2	1	0
$[OH^-]$	10^{-14}	10^{-13}	10^{-12}	10^{-11}	10^{-10}	10^{-9}	10^{-8}	**10^{-7}**	10^{-6}	10^{-5}	10^{-4}	10^{-3}	10^{-2}	10^{-1}	1

← **CURSOR** →

↑

Solution is
neutral.

Figure 5.4.5 *The "cursor" on the chart highlights the pH, pOH, $[H_3O^+]$, and $[OH^-]$ for any aqueous solution at 25°C.*

Sample Problem 5.4.2 — Calculating pH, pOH, $[H_3O^+]$, and $[OH^-]$

A 0.10 M aqueous solution of Aspirin (acetylsalicylic acid) at 25°C is found to have a pH of 2.27. Determine the $[H_3O^+]$, $[OH^-]$, and pOH for this solution.

What to Think About

1. This solution is acidic so expect the $[H_3O^+]$ to be greater than $[OH^-]$. It is very important to recognize which is the *predominant ion* in a solution such as this. For acids, the $[H_3O^+]$ always predominates. This means it is more prevalent.
2. Two decimal places in the pH correspond to two significant figures in the concentration. Be sure to keep all figures through the entire calculation. Only round to the appropriate number of significant figures at the very end.
3. Consider Figure 5.4.4 and note that there is more than one order in which the calculations can be performed. For example, we could answer the questions in the order they are asked, or we could begin by calculating pOH and then determine $[OH^-]$ and $[H_3O^+]$.

How to Do It

Perform the calculations in the order they are asked. In terms of Figure 5.4.3, begin in the lower left corner and move around clockwise to answer the questions:

$$[H_3O^+] = 10^{-pH} = 10^{-2.27}$$
$$= 5.4 \times 10^{-3}\ M$$

$$[OH^-] = K_w/[H_3O^+]$$

$$[OH^-] = \frac{1.0 \times 10^{-14}}{5.4 \times 10^{-3}} = 1.9 \times 10^{-12}\ M$$

$$pOH = -\log\ (1.86 \times 10^{-12}\ M) = 11.73$$

OR

$$pOH = 14.00 - 2.27 = 11.73$$

$$[OH^-] = 10^{-11.73} = 1.9 \times 10^{-12}\ M$$

$$[H_3O^+] = \frac{1.0 \times 10^{-14}}{1.9 \times 10^{-12}} = 5.4 \times 10^{-3}\ M$$

Practice Problems 5.4.2 — pH and pOH

(Unless otherwise indicated, assume all aqueous solutions are at 25°C.)

1. Complete the following table.

Solution	$[H_3O^+]$	$[OH^-]$	pH	pOH	Acidic/Basic/Neutral?
Orange Juice				10.5	
Tears	3.98×10^{-8} M				
Blood			7.40		
Milk		3.16×10^{-8} M			

2. Consider the equations above relating pH, pOH, $[H_3O^+]$, and $[OH^-]$ for an aqueous solution, and complete the following statements:
   (a) As a solution becomes more acidic, both $[H_3O^+]$ and pOH ____________ (increase or decrease) and both $[OH^-]$ and pH ____________ (increase or decrease).
   (b) A basic solution has a pOH value that is ____________ (greater or less) than 7, and $[H_3O^+]$ that is ____________ (greater or less) than 10^{-7} M.
   (c) If the pH of a solution equals 14.0, the $[OH^-]$ equals _________ M.
   (d) If the pOH of a solution decreases by 5, then the $[H_3O^+]$ has ____________ (increased or decreased) by a factor of ____________.
3. For pure water at 10°C, $K_w = 2.55 \times 10^{-15}$. Calculate the pH of water at 10°C and state whether the water is acidic, basic, or neutral.

© Edvantage Interactive 2019

When Strong Acids and Strong Bases Are Mixed

Look again at your answer to the Warm Up question 2 at the beginning of this section. In this example, hydronium ions from a strong acid reacted with an equal number of moles of hydroxide ions from a strong base. The resulting aqueous solution was neutral because neither ion was in excess following the neutralization reaction. Therefore, the $[H_3O^+]$ and $[OH^-]$ were both 1.0×10^{-7} M, so both the pH and pOH were equal to 7.00.

However, if an excess of either hydronium or hydroxide ions remains in a solution following the reaction of a strong acid with a strong base, the solution will not be neutral. Recall that the net ionic equation for the reaction of a strong acid with a strong base is given by:

$$H_3O^+(aq) + OH^-(aq) \rightarrow 2\,H_2O(l)$$

This allows us to easily determine which ion will be in excess and by how much after a strong acid and a strong base are mixed together. We can then determine pH and/or pOH values.

A convenient approach is to calculate the starting or diluted $[H_3O^+]$ and $[OH^-]$ when the solutions are poured together but *before they react* and then to simply subtract the lesser concentration from the greater concentration to determine the final concentration of the ion in excess. Let us designate those starting concentrations as: $[H_3O^+]_{ST}$ and $[OH^-]_{ST}$. Depending on which of these two concentrations is greater, we use one of the two equations below to calculate the pH or pOH:

If $[H_3O^+]_{ST} > [OH^-]_{ST}$, then we use: $[H_3O^+]_{XS} = [H_3O^+]_{ST} - [OH^-]_{ST}$ to calculate pH or pOH.

If $[OH^-]_{ST} > [H_3O^+]_{ST}$, then we use: $[OH^-]_{XS} = [OH^-]_{ST} - [H_3O^+]_{ST}$ to calculate pH or pOH.

Sample Problem 5.4.3(a) — Mixing Strong Acids and Bases

Calculate the pH of the solution resulting from mixing 30.0 mL of 0.40 M HNO_3 with 70.0 mL of 0.20 M NaOH.

What to Think About

1. Nitric acid is a strong acid and so the concentration of the acid is also the $[H_3O^+]$ in that solution due to 100% ionization.
2. The final volume will be 100.0 mL so each ion concentration will be reduced accordingly upon mixing.

How to Do It

$[H_3O^+]_{ST} = 0.40\text{ M} \times \frac{30.0\text{ mL}}{100.0\text{ mL}} = 0.12\text{ M}$

$[OH^-]_{ST} = 0.20\text{ M} \times \frac{70.0\text{ mL}}{100.0\text{ mL}} = 0.14\text{ M}$

$[OH^-]_{XS} = 0.14\text{ M} - 0.12\text{ M} = 0.02\text{ M}$

$pOH = -\log(0.02) = 1.7$

And so $pH = 14.0 - 1.7 = 12.3$

An alternative approach would be to calculate the total number of moles of each ion and then subtract the lesser from the greater. Then divide the difference by the final volume to obtain the concentration of the ion is excess.

$\text{mol } H_3O^+ = 0.0300\text{ L} \times 0.40 \frac{\text{mol } H_3O^+}{\text{L}} = 0.012\text{ mol } H_3O^+$

$\text{mol } OH^- = 0.0700\text{ L} \times 0.20 \frac{\text{mol } OH^-}{\text{L}} = 0.014\text{ mol } OH^-$

$\text{mol } OH^- \text{ in excess} = 0.014\text{ mol} - 0.012\text{ mol} = 0.002\text{ mol } OH^- \text{ in excess}$

$\text{The final } [OH^-] = \frac{0.002\text{ mol } OH^-}{0.1000\text{ L}} = 0.02\text{ M}$

$pOH = -\log 0.02 = 1.7$ so $pH = 14.0 - 1.7 = 12.3$

Sample Problem 5.4.3(b) — Mixing Strong Acids and Bases

Determine the pH of the solution that results when 50.0 mL of 0.200 M H_2SO_4 is mixed with 100.0 mL of 0.400 M NaOH.

What to Think About

1. The final volume will be 150.0 mL and so each ion concentration should be diluted accordingly.
2. H_2SO_4 is a diprotic acid and so the $[H_3O^+]_{ST}$ should be calculated accordingly.
3. The final pH must be recorded to three decimal places.

How to Do It

$$[H_3O^+]_{ST} = 0.200\ \frac{\text{mol } H_2SO_4}{L} \times \frac{2\text{ mol } H_3O^+}{\text{mol } H_2SO_4} \times \frac{50.0\text{ mL}}{150.0\text{ mL}}$$

$$= 0.1333\text{ M}$$

$$[OH^-]_{ST} = 0.400\text{ M} \times \frac{100.0\text{ mL}}{150.0\text{ mL}} = 0.2667\text{ M}$$

$$[OH^-]_{XS} = 0.2667\text{ M} - 0.1333\text{ M} = 0.1333\text{ M}$$

$$pOH = -\log(0.1333) = 0.875$$

$$pH = 14.000 - 0.875 = 13.125$$

Sample Problem 5.4.3(c) — Mixing Strong Acids and Bases

A student adds 35.0 mL of an HCl solution with a pH of 2.00 to 15.0 mL of NaOH solution with a pH of 12.00. Calculate the pH of the final solution.

What to Think A bout

1. The predominant ion in the first solution (with a pH of 2.00) is clearly the hydronium ion, and the predominant ion in the second (pH = 12.00) is hydroxide.
2. Accordingly, determine each ion concentration as shown previously.
3. Record two decimal places in the final pH.

How to Do It

In the acidic solution: $[H_3O^+] = 10^{-2.00} = 0.010\text{ M}$

In the basic solution: $pOH = 14.00 - 12.00 = 2.00$

$$[OH^-] = 10^{-2.00} = 0.010\text{ M}$$

$$[H_3O^+]_{ST} = 0.010\text{ M} \times \frac{35.0\text{ mL}}{50.0\text{ mL}} = 0.0070\text{ M}$$

$$[OH^-]_{ST} = 0.010\text{ M} \times \frac{15.0\text{ mL}}{50.0\text{ mL}} = 0.0030\text{ M}$$

$$[H_3O^+]_{XS} = 0.0070\text{ M} - 0030\text{ M} = 0.0040\text{ M}$$

$$pH = -\log(0.0040) = 2.40$$

© Edvantage Interactive 2019

Sample Problem 5.4.3(d) —Mixing Strong Acids and Bases

What mass of NaOH must be added to 500.0 mL of a solution of 0.020 M HI to obtain a solution with a pH of 2.50?

What to think about

1. The final solution still has an excess of H_3O^+ ions so the equation that applies is:

$$[H_3O^+]_{XS} = [H_3O^+]_{ST} - [OH^-]_{ST}$$

2. Solve for $[OH^-]_{ST}$ because both the $[H_3O^+]_{XS}$ and $[H_3O^+]_{ST}$ are provided either directly or indirectly in the question. Therefore manipulate the above equation to give:

$$[OH^-]_{ST} = [H_3O^+]_{ST} - [H_3O^+]_{XS}$$

Then convert your answer from moles per liter to grams required for 0.500 L.

How to Do It

$[H_3O^+]_{ST} = 0.020\ M$

$[H_3O^+]_{XS} = 10^{-2.50} = 0.00316\ M$

$[OH^-]_{ST} = [H_3O^+]_{ST} - [H_3O^+]_{XS}$

$= 0.020\ M - 0.00316\ M$

$= 0.0168\ M\ NaOH$

$0.0168\ \frac{mol}{L} \times 40.0\ \frac{g\ NaOH}{mol} \times 0.500\ L$

$= 0.34\ g\ NaOH$ (2 significant figures)

Practice Problems 5.4.3 — Mixing Strong Acids and Bases

1. Calculate the pH of the solution that results from mixing 25.0 mL of 0.40 M HCl with 15.0 mL of 0.30 M KOH.

2. A solution of HCl has a pH of 0.60. A 1.0 g sample of NaOH is dissolved in 250.0 mL of this HCl solution. Calculate the pOH of the resulting solution, assuming no volume change.

3. Calculate the pH of the solution that results when 25.0 mL of a solution with a pOH of 12.00 is mixed with 45.0 mL of a solution with a pH of 11.00.

4. What mass of HCl(*g*) must be dissolved in 1.50 L of a NaOH solution having a pH of 11.176 to produce a solution with a pH of 10.750? (Assume no volume change.)

5.4 Activity: Finding Acidic and Basic Common Solutions

Question

Can you identify a series of common solutions as being acidic, basic, or neutral?

Background

Many common aqueous solutions used around your house are either acidic or basic. Some have pH values that are high or low enough to qualify them as being as hazardous as many chemicals used in the laboratory.

Procedure

1. For each of the common solutions listed below, only one of the four values has been provided. Determine the other three for each solution. (Assume all solutions are at 25°C.)
2. Classify each solution as either acidic, basic, or neutral.

Solution	pH	pOH	$[H_3O^+]$ M	$[OH^-]$ M	Acidic/Basic/Neutral
Unpolluted rainwater	5.5				
Saliva		7.3			
Stomach acid			0.031		
Tears				2.5×10^{-7}	
Vinegar	2.9				
Milk		7.6			
Milk of magnesia			3.2×10^{-11}		
Lemon juice				2.0×10^{-12}	
Tomato juice	4.2				
Orange juice		10.5			
Grapefruit juice			0.0010		
Liquid drain cleaner				1.0	
Black coffee	5.1				
Urine		8.0			
Blood			4.0×10^{-8}		
Laundry bleach				0.010	
Windex	10.7				
Pepto-Bismol		8.2			
Household ammonia			1.3×10^{-12}		
Red wine				3.2×10^{-12}	

 © Edvantage Interactive 2019

Results and Discussion

1. Once you have completed the table, consider the last column. Are many of the solutions listed (or others that you found) actually neutral? Explain.

2. Do the majority of the solutions used for cleaning purposes have a low or a high pH? Try to find them in your home and see how many have a hazardous warning on their label.

3. Are the solutions that you consume generally acidic or basic?

5.4 Review Questions

(Assume all solutions are at 25°C unless otherwise indicated.)

1. Define pH and pOH using a statement and an equation for each.

2. Why do we use Sorensen's pH and pOH scales to express hydronium and hydroxide concentrations in aqueous solutions?

3. Complete the following table, expressing each value to the proper number of significant figures.

$[H_3O^+]$	pH	Acidic/Basic/Neutral
3.50×10^{-6} M		
	11.51	
0.00550 M		
	0.00	
6.8×10^{-9} M		

4. Complete the following table, expressing each value to the proper number of significant figures.

$[OH^-]$	pOH	Acidic/Basic/Neutral
7.2×10^{-9} M		
	9.55	
4.88×10^{-4} M		
	14.00	
0.000625 M		

5. Complete the following statements:
   (a) As a solution's pOH value and $[H_3O^+]$ both decrease, the solution becomes more _______________ (acidic or basic).

   (b) As a solution's pH value and $[OH^-]$ both decrease, the solution becomes more _______________ (acidic or basic)

   (c) The ____________________ (sum or product) of the $[H_3O^+]$ and $[OH^-]$ equals K_w.

   (d) The ____________________ (sum or product) of pH and pOH equals pK_w.

© Edvantage Interactive 2019

6. Complete the following table, expressing each value to the proper number of significant figures.

$[H_3O^+]$	pOH	Acidic/Basic/Neutral
0.0342 M		
	8.400	
7.2×10^{-12} M		
	3.215	

7. For pure water at 60.0°C, the value of $pK_w = 13.02$. Calculate the pH at this temperature and decide if the water is acidic, basic, or neutral.

8. Calculate the pH of a 0.30 M solution of $Sr(OH)_2$.

9. A 2.00 g sample of pure NaOH is dissolved in water to produce 500.0 mL of solution. Calculate the pH of this solution.

10. A sample of HI is dissolved in water to make 2.0 L of solution. The pH of this solution is found to be 2.50. Calculate the mass of HI dissolved in this solution.

11. Complete the following table, expressing each value to the proper number of significant figures.

$[H_3O^+]$	$[OH^-]$	pOH	pH	Acidic/Basic/Neutral
5.620×10^{-5} M				
	0.000450 M			
		12.50		
			10.5	

12. Calculate the pH resulting from mixing 75.0 mL of 0.50 M HNO_3 with 125.0 mL of a solution containing 0.20 g NaOH.

13. Calculate the pH of the solution that results from mixing 200.0 mL of a solution with a pH of 1.50 with 300.0 mL of a solution having a pOH of 1.50.

14. Calculate the pH of a solution that is produced when 3.2 g of HI is added to 500.0 mL of a solution having a pH of 13.00. Assume no volume change.

15. The following three solutions are mixed together:
25.0 mL of 0.20 M HCl + 35.0 mL of 0.15 M HNO_3 + 40.0 mL of 0.30 M NaOH
Calculate the pH of the final solution.

16. What mass of HCl should be added to 450.0 mL of 0.0350 M KOH to produce a solution with a pH of 11.750? (Assume no volume change.)

17. What mass of LiOH must be added to 500.0 mL of 0.0125 M HCl to produce a solution with a pH of 2.75? (Assume no volume change.)

 © **Edvantage Interactive 2019**

5.5 Calculations Involving K_a and K_b

Warm Up

Three of the binary acids containing halogens (hydrohalic acids) are strong acids, while one of them is a weak acid.

1. (a) Write a chemical equation representing the reaction of hydrochloric acid with water and identify the two conjugate acid-base pairs.

   (b) If the concentration of this *strong* acid solution is 0.50 M, what would you expect the $[H_3O^+]$ and the pH of the solution to be?

2. (a) Write a chemical equation representing the reaction of hydrofluoric acid with water and identify the two conjugate acid-base pairs. Which side of this equilibrium is favored?

   (b) If the concentration of this *weak* acid solution is also 0.50 M, would you expect the pH of this solution to be the same as for 0.50 M HCl? Why or why not?

3. Write K_a or K_b expressions for the following species in aqueous solutions:

   (a) K_a for HNO_2 =

   (b) K_b for $C_2O_4^{2-}$ =

   (c) K_a for $HC_2O_4^-$ =

   (d) K_b for NH_3 =

Part A: Calculations for Weak Acids

Most of the substances that we identify as acids ionize only to a slight extent in water and are therefore considered to be weak acids. As you have learned the following equilibrium exists in an aqueous solution of a weak acid HA:

$$HA(aq) + H_2O(l) \rightleftharpoons A^-(aq) + H_3O^+(aq)$$

In this chemical equilibrium system, the weaker an acid HA is, the less ionization occurs, the more the reactants are favored, and the smaller the value of the acid ionization constant K_a. In strong acids, the ionization is effectively 100%. In weak acids, because most of the original HA remains intact, the concentration of hydronium ions at equilibrium is *much less* than the original concentration of the acid.

Consider the data presented in one of the sample questions in the previous section:

"A 0.10 M solution of Aspirin (acetylsalicylic acid) at 25°C is found to have a pH of 2.27."

This pH corresponds to a hydronium ion concentration of only 5.4×10^{-3} M. It tells us that acetylsalicylic acid must be a weak acid because only a small percentage of the original 0.10 mol/L of the acid has ionized. If the ionization were complete, we would expect the hydronium ion concentration to also be 0.10 M, corresponding to a pH of 1.00.

For a strong acid, because almost all of the original acid has been converted to hydronium ions, the $[H_3O^+]$ in the solution is the same as the original acid concentration.

Is there also a way that we could calculate the equilibrium concentration of hydronium ions (and therefore the pH) of a *weak acid* solution if we knew the initial acid concentration? The answer is yes because using an ICE table you learned how to calculate equilibrium concentrations of chemical species given initial concentrations and a value for the equilibrium constant K_{eq}. Let's begin the discussion of calculating this value and others for weak acid equilibria.

The acid ionization constant K_a is given by:

$$K_a = \frac{[A^-][H_3O^+]}{[HA]}$$

This equation will be used to solve the majority of calculations that you will perform, and the three values that we normally care most about are K_a, [HA], and $[H_3O^+]$. Because we are concerned with three variables, there are really three types of problems that you will be expected to solve for weak acids. Let's consider examples of each.

Problem Type 1: Calculating $[H_3O^+]$ (and so usually pH) given K_a and $[HA]_{initial}$

Let's return to our Warm Up example:
Calculate the pH of 0.50 M solution of hydrofluoric acid (HF). K_a for HF = 3.5×10^{-4}

Note the following:

1. The concentration given refers to how the solution *was prepared* — namely, $[HA]_{initial}$.
2. The question is asking us to determine the *equilibrium* concentration of hydronium ions (from which we calculate pH), given the *initial* concentration of the acid and the value of K_a. This suggests the use of an ICE table.
3. We are given the value for K_a. If the value is not given, you will be expected to find that value by referring to the Table of Relative Strengths of Brønsted-Lowry Acids and Bases (Table 5.2.1 and inside back cover).
4. For most weak acid problems, it will be necessary to construct an ICE table underneath the balanced equation for the equilibrium existing in the aqueous solution.
5. Any problem that requires us to calculate a value *on the ICE table itself* will also require us to define a value for that unknown (as *x*, for example). These problems usually involve $[H_3O^+]$ or the $[HA]_{initial}$
6. HF is a monoprotic acid, but even if we are given a polyprotic weak acid, *the first ionization* (donation of the first proton) is *the predominant reaction determining pH*. Subsequent ionizations with much smaller K_a values are of no relative consequence in determining pH and can therefore be considered insignificant.
7. As only the first proton is donated, there is always a 1:1:1 mole ratio in the change line of such problems.
8. You should always read the question carefully — more than once if necessary — so that you are certain of the type of problem you are given, and what you are being asked to calculate. Let's begin solving this problem: Let *x* equal the equilibrium concentration of hydronium ions: $[H_3O^+]_{eq}$

   Now let's construct the ICE table, fill it in, and discuss the entries in Table 5.5.1.

Table 5.5.1 *ICE Table for Example Problem*

		HF +	H_2O ⇌	F^- +	H_3O^+
Initial Concentration	**(I)**	0.50		0	0
Change in Concentration	**(C)**	$-x$		$+x$	$+x$
Equilibrium Concentration	**(E)**	$0.50 - x$		x	x

 © Edvantage Interactive 2019

When filling in the table, we start by making two assumptions:

1. We don't include the concentration of water for the same reason we don't include it in a K_a expression. We can assume the $[H_2O]$ remains constant because the extent to which the large concentration of water (55.6 M) actually *changes* is insignificant, given the relatively tiny amount of ionization that actually occurs.
2. We know that the initial $[H_3O^+]$ in pure water (prior to the ionization of the weak acid) is really 10^{-7} M. However, the fact that the K_a of this acid is so much greater than K_w means that we can assume that this initial $[H_3O^+]$ (resulting from the autoionization of water) is insignificant compared to the equilibrium $[H_3O^+]$ resulting from the ionization of this weak acid. Consequently, the initial $[H_3O^+]$ is given as zero.

At this point we could attempt to solve for x:

$$K_a = \frac{[F^-][H_3O^+]}{HF} = \frac{x^2}{0.50 - x} = 3.5 \times 10^{-4}$$

However, that process would require the use of the quadratic formula. We can avoid this if we make another simplifying assumption based on the relative magnitudes of $[HF]_{initial}$ and K_a. The value of K_a is so small compared to the initial concentration of the acid that the percent of the acid that actually ionizes will not significantly change the original concentration. As a result, we can make the following assumption:

$[HF]_{eq} = 0.50 - x \approx 0.50$

It is important to note that the assumption *is not always* justified. This assumption is valid if the percent ionization of the weak acid is ≤ 5%. The percent ionization is given by the following equation:

$$\%\text{ ionization} = \frac{[H_3O^+]_{eq}}{[HA]_{initial}} \times 100\%$$

A good rule-of-thumb is:

If the $[HA]_{initial}$ is at least 10^3 times larger than the K_a value, the assumption is valid.

It may surprise you to know that, as the initial concentration of the acid decreases, the percent ionization *increases*. This means that the assumption is normally only valid for relatively high weak-acid concentrations. Table 5.5.2 demonstrates this, using data for three different concentrations of acetic acid.

Table 5.5.2 *Data for Three Concentrations of Acetic Acid*

$[CH_3COOH]$	Percent Ionization	Assumption
0.15 M	1.1%	valid
0.015 M	3.5%	valid
0.0015 M	11%	invalid

In most, if not all of the problems you will encounter in this course, the assumption will be justified and the use of the quadratic formula can therefore be avoided. However, it is still necessary to *explicitly state the assumption each time you solve such a problem*. If you simply ignore x, it constitutes a chemical error. Having made the assumption, let's return to our example. We now have:

$$\frac{x^2}{0.50} = 3.5 \times 10^{-4} \qquad x = \sqrt{(3.5 \times 10^{-4})(0.50)} = 0.0\underline{13}2\ M\ H_3O^+$$

$$\text{pH} = -\log(0.0\underline{13}2) = 1.\underline{88} \text{ (two significant figures)}$$

Let's calculate the % ionization as a check to see if our most recent assumption was valid:

$$\% \text{ ionization} = \frac{[H_3O^+]_{eq}}{[HF]_{initial}} \times 100\% = \frac{0.0132 \text{ M}}{0.50 \text{ M}} \times 100\% = 2.6\% \text{ (the assumption was valid)}$$

Quick Check

1. Why don't we include water's concentration when we complete an ICE table?

____

____

2. Why are we justified in assuming that the initial concentration of hydronium ions prior to the ionization of a weak acid is effectively zero?

____

____

3. What allows us to assume that $[HA]_{eq} \approx [HA]_{initial}$ in weak acid equilibria?

____

____

Sample Problem 5.5.1 — Calculating pH given K_a and $[HA]_{initial}$

Hydrogen sulfide is a poisonous flammable gas whose "rotten egg" smell is perceptible at concentrations as low as 0.00047 ppm. It is also a weak acid when dissolved in water. Calculate the pH of 0.0500 M H_2S.

What to Think About

1. The K_a value isn't given. Refer to the table.: $K_a = 9.1 \times 10^{-8}$
   This value has two significant figures so our final pH should reflect that.
2. H_2S is a diprotic acid, but the first ionization is all that significantly determines pH.
3. Define *x* and solve for it using an ICE table.
4. Remember to state the assumption mentioned above.

How to Do It

Let $x = [H_3O^+]_{eq}$

$$H_2S + H_2O \rightleftharpoons HS^- + H_3O^+$$

	H_2S	H_2O	HS^-	H_3O^+
I	0.0500	X	0	0
C	$-x$	X	$+x$	$+x$
E	$0.0500 - x$	X	x	x

Assume $0.0500 - x \approx 0.0500$

$$K_a = \frac{[HS^-][H_3O^+]}{[H_2S]} = \frac{x^2}{0.0500} = 9.1 \times 10^{-8}$$

$$x = \sqrt{(9.1 \times 10^{-8})(0.0500)} = \underline{6.7}4 \times 10^{-5} \text{ M}$$

$$pH = -\log(\underline{6.7}4 \times 10^{-5}) = 4.\underline{17} \text{ (two sig figs)}$$

© Edvantage Interactive 2019

Practice Problems 5.5.1 — Calculating pH given K_a and $[HA]_{initial}$

1. Methanoic acid is the simplest carboxylic acid and is found naturally in the venom of bee and ant stings. (It is also called formic acid, from the Latin word for ant, *formica*). Calculate the pH of a 0.50 M solution of methanoic acid.

2. Household vinegar is an aqueous solution of acetic acid. A sample of vinegar is analyzed by titration and found to be 0.850 M CH_3COOH. Calculate the pH of this solution.

3. Calculate the percent ionization in a 0.10 M solution of aspirin with a pH of 2.27. Would our simplifying assumption stated above be valid in this case?

Problem Type 2: Calculating $[HA]_{initial}$ given K_a and pH

In this type of problem, we are given the pH of the solution from which we calculate the equilibrium concentration of hydronium ions. We then use that value and the K_a to calculate the initial concentration of the weak acid.

As we are once again solving for an unknown on the ICE table, we still must define *x* as that unknown. However, there are a couple of differences between this unknown and the one in the previous problem type:

1. We place this "*x*" in the "**I**nitial" row, rather than the "**E**quilibrium" row of the table.
2. This unknown will be the largest of any quantity appearing in the ICE table because it's the initial concentration of the acid. Therefore, no assumption regarding its insignificance applies.

Consider the sample problem below. Note that the use of the quadratic isn't necessary to solve this problem. Therefore, there is no need to assume that the amount of ionization of the benzoic acid that occurs relative to the initial concentration is insignificant. However, if the $[H_3O^+]_{eq}$ is sufficiently large relative to the K_a value, the assumption may be valid. Even so, until you have acquired ample experience solving these types of problems, if you don't *have to* make such an assumption to solve the problem, then don't. (Calculate the percentage ionization in the sample problem to see if such an assumption would have been valid in this case.)

Sample Problem 5.5.2 — Calculating $[HA]_{initial}$, given K_a and pH

Benzoic acid is used as a food preservative and a precursor in many organic synthesis reactions. It is the most commonly used chemical standard in calorimetry. What concentration of benzoic acid is required to produce a solution with a pH of 3.30?

What to Think About

1. Once again an ICE table and a "Let x = " statement are required.
2. The unknown now represents the initial acid concentration.
3. Use the given pH to calculate the $[H_3O^+]_{eq}$.
4. Look up the value of K_a for benzoic acid: $K_a = 6.5 \times 10^{-5}$

How to Do It

Let $x = [C_6H_5COOH]_{initial}$

$$[H_3O^+]_{eq} = 10^{-3.30} = 0.000501 \text{ M}$$

$$C_6H_5COOH + H_2O \rightleftharpoons C_6H_5COO^- + H_3O^+$$

	C_6H_5COOH	H_2O	$C_6H_5COO^-$	H_3O^+
I	x		0	0
C	−0.000501		+0.000501	+0.000501
E	$x - 0.000501$		0.000501	0.000501

$$K_a = \frac{[C_6H_5COO^-][H_3O^+]}{[C_6H_5COOH]} = \frac{(0.000501)^2}{(x - 0.000501)}$$

$$= 6.5 \times 10^{-5}$$

$$x - 0.000\underline{501} = \frac{(0.000\underline{501})^2}{6.5 \times 10^{-5}}$$

$x = 0.00\underline{44}$ M (2 significant figures)

Practice Problems 5.5.2 — Calculating $[HA]_{initial}$, given K_a and pH

1. Citric acid is one of the acids responsible for the sour taste of lemons. What concentration of citric acid would be required to produce a solution with a pH of 2.50?

2. Rhubarb's sour taste is due in part to the presence of oxalic acid. A solution of oxalic acid has had the label removed. What concentration should appear on the label if the pH of the solution is found to be 0.55?

3. Nitrous acid is one of the components of acid rain. An aqueous solution of nitrous acid is found to have a pH of 1.85. Calculate the concentration of the acid.

© Edvantage Interactive 2019

Problem Type 3: Calculating K_a given $[HA]_{initial}$ and pH

This type of problem does not require us to solve for an unknown *x* on the ICE table because all of the entries in the table are available directly or indirectly from the information provided in the question. The pH allows us to determine $[H_3O^+]_{eq}$. Although there is *no need* for a simplifying assumption, we are given enough information to calculate percentage ionization to determine if the assumption is justified.

Let's return to acetylsalicylic acid in the following sample problem.

Sample Problem 5.5.3 — Calculating K_a, given $[HA]_{initial}$ and pH

A 0.100 M solution of acetylsalicylic acid (Aspirin) is found to have a pH of 2.27. Calculate the K_a for this acid. The formula for acetylsalicylic acid is $C_8H_7O_2COOH$.

What to Think About

1. Use pH to calculate $[H_3O^+]_{eq}$ and then use that value to complete the entries in the ICE table.

   Note that we cannot ignore 0.00537 M compared to 0.10 M.

2. Record the K_a value to two significant figures.

How to Do It

$[H_3O^+]_{eq} = 10^{-2.27} = 0.00537\ M$

$C_8H_7O_2COOH + H_2O \rightleftharpoons C_8H_7O_2COO^- + H_3O^+$

	$C_8H_7O_2COOH$	H_2O	$C_8H_7O_2COO^-$	H_3O^+
I	0.100		0	0
C	−0.00537		+0.00537	+0.00537
E	0.0946		0.00537	0.00537

$$K_a = \frac{[C_8H_7O_2COO^-][H_3O^+]}{[C_8H_7O_2COOH]} = \frac{(0.00537)^2}{0.0946}$$

$= \underline{3.0} \times 10^{-4}$ (2 significant figures)

Practice Problems 5.5.3 — Calculating K_a, given $[HA]_{initial}$ and pH

1. One form of vitamin C is ascorbic acid, $H_2C_6H_6O_6$. The name originates from the fact that ascorbic acid prevents scurvy — a fact first discovered in 1747 by British surgeon John Lind. This subsequently resulted in citrus juice (from limes and lemons) being supplied to sailors in the Royal Navy. A 0.100 M solution of ascorbic acid is found to have a pH of 3.00. Calculate the K_a for ascorbic acid.

2. Lactic acid ($C_3H_6O_3$) is a weak acid produced in muscle tissue during anaerobic respiration and is the acid present in sour milk. It's also responsible for the sour taste of sauerkraut. A 0.025 M solution of lactic acid is found to have a pH of 2.75. Calculate the K_a for lactic acid.

Part B: Calculations for Weak Bases

As with acids, most bases are weak. Water can both accept and donate a proton (hydrogen ion), so weak bases also participate in equilibria with water. Using the symbol "B" for a weak base, we can represent this as:

$$B(aq) + H_2O(l) \rightleftharpoons HB^+(aq) + OH^-(aq)$$

We can therefore write the following expression for the base ionization constant. K_b:

$$K_b = \frac{[HB^+][OH^-]}{[B]}$$

Although the three main types of problems associated with weak bases that you will be expected to solve are similar to those identified above for weak acids, additional calculations are often required.

For example, if you are given a problem that includes a weak base from the Table of Relative Strengths of Brønsted-Lowry Acids and Bases, you cannot simply look up the K_b value as you are able to with K_a values. Rather, you must *calculate the* K_b *for that base by using the* K_a *value of its conjugate acid*. Let's derive the equation that you will need to perform that calculation below.

Consider the conjugate acid/base pair of NH_4^+ and NH_3 and their respective K_a and K_b expressions:

$$K_a \text{ for } NH_4^+ = \frac{[NH_3][H_3O^+]}{[NH_4^+]} \quad \text{and} \quad K_b \text{ for } NH_3 = \frac{[NH_4^+][OH^-]}{[NH_3]}$$

Note that two common terms appear in each equation. Let's take advantage of that by multiplying the two expressions together and cancelling those common terms:

$$K_a \times K_b = \frac{\cancel{[NH_3]}[H_3O^+]}{\cancel{[NH_4^+]}} \times \frac{\cancel{[NH_4^+]}[OH^-]}{\cancel{[NH_3]}} = [H_3O^+][OH^-] = K_w$$

This allows us to formulate the following relationship for *conjugate acid-base pairs*:

$$K_a \text{ (conjugate acid)} \times K_b \text{ (conjugate base)} = K_w = 1.00 \times 10^{-14} \text{ (at 25°C)}$$

Taking the negative logarithm of both sides of the above equation, we obtain:

$$pK_a \text{ (conjugate acid)} + pK_b \text{ (conjugate base)} = pK_w = 14.00 \text{ (at 25°C)}$$

This allows us to calculate the K_b value for any weak base in the table. For example:

$$K_b \text{ for } NH_3 = \frac{K_w}{K_a \text{ for } NH_4^+} = \frac{1.00 \times 10^{-14}}{5.6 \times 10^{-10}} = 1.8 \times 10^{-5}$$

You must be careful to use the *correct* K_a value when performing this calculation, especially when dealing with amphiprotic ions. Before you begin the calculation, first locate the weak base on the *right side* of the table. Then look over to the left side of that equation to find the appropriate conjugate acid. The K_a value for *that acid* is the correct value to use in the calculation.

© Edvantage Interactive 2019

Quick Check

1. Complete the following table by choosing the correct conjugate acid and corresponding K_a value and then calculating the K_b value for each weak base. Consider carefully the first three that are done for you.

	Weak Base	Conjugate Acid	Appropriate K_a Value	Calculated K_b
(a)	$HC_2O_4^-$	$H_2C_2O_4$	5.9×10^{-2}	1.7×10^{-13}
(b)	$H_2PO_4^-$	H_3PO_4	7.5×10^{-3}	1.3×10^{-12}
(c)	HPO_4^{2-}	$H_2PO_4^-$	6.2×10^{-8}	1.6×10^{-7}
(d)	NO_2^-			
(e)	$HC_6H_5O_7^{2-}$			
(f)	HCO_3^-			
(g)	CN^-			

2. Calculate the pK_a and pK_b values for all of the chemical species above. How do the sizes of pK_a values for acids and pK_b values for bases relate to their strength?

Problem Type 1: Calculating $[OH^-]$ (and usually pH) given K_b and $[B]_{initial}$

In the same way we discussed each of the three main problem types associated with weak acids, let's now begin that discussion for solutions of weak bases.

Remember that if the question involves a weak base from the table, we have to calculate the K_b rather than simply looking it up and also that solving for "x" gives us $[OH^-]$ rather than $[H_3O^+]$. This means that an extra calculation will be necessary if we are asked to determine pH. Remember this point. Consider the sample problems below.

Notice that, in the second sample problem, the cyanide *ion* is reacting with water and functioning as a weak base. Such an event is known as **hydrolysis**. For now, simply treat ions as you would any other weak base in water.

Note that the only *uncharged* weak base (except for water) in the table of acids and bases is NH_3. Most of the remaining weak bases on the table are anions. Many neutral weak bases are organic compounds called amines containing nitrogen whose lone electron pair is available to accept a proton from water.

Sample Problem 5.5.4(a) — Calculating [OH⁻] and pH using K_b and $[B]_{initial}$

One of the compounds responsible for the odor of herring brine is methylamine, CH_3NH_2. ($K_b = 4.4 \times 10^{-4}$) Calculate the pH of a 0.50 M solution of methylamine.

What to Think About

1. Once again, construct an ICE table. Add the proton from water to the nitrogen in methylamine. Be careful with charges.
2. A value on the ICE table is being solved so, once again, define x.
3. The K_b value is provided so you don't have to calculate it.
4. The relative magnitudes of K_b and $[OH^-]_{initial}$ allow the assumption to be valid.

How to Do It

Let $x = [OH^-]_{eq}$

$$CH_3NH_2 + H_2O \rightleftharpoons CH_3NH_3^+ + OH^-$$

	CH_3NH_2	H_2O	$CH_3NH_3^+$	OH^-
I	0.50		0	0
C	$-x$		$+x$	$+x$
E	$0.50 - x$		x	x

Assume $0.50 - x \approx 0.50$

$$K_b = \frac{[CH_3NH_3^+][OH^-]}{[CH_3NH_2]} = \frac{x^2}{0.50} = 4.4 \times 10^{-4}$$

$x = 0.0148$ M OH^- so $pOH = -\log 0.0148 = 1.829$

$pH = 14.00 - 1.829 = 12.17$

Sample Problem 5.5.4(b) — Calculating [OH⁻] and pH using K_b and $[B]_{initial}$

Calculate the pH of a solution containing 0.20 M CN^-.

What to Think About

1. Calculate the K_b value using the K_a for HCN.
2. As CN^- is a relatively strong weak base, expect this solution to have a relatively high pH.
3. Remember to convert the $[OH^-]$ to pH.

How to Do It

$$K_b \text{ for } CN^- = \frac{K_w}{K_a \text{ for HCN}} = \frac{1.00 \times 10^{-14}}{4.9 \times 10^{-10}}$$

$$= 2.04 \times 10^{-5}$$

Let $x = [OH^-]_{eq}$

$$CN^- + H_2O \rightleftharpoons HCN + OH^-$$

	CN^-	H_2O	HCN	OH^-
I	0.20		0	0
C	$-x$		$+x$	$+x$
E	$0.20 - x$		x	x

Assume $0.20 - x \approx 0.20$

$$K_b = \frac{[HCN][OH^-]}{[CN^-]} = \frac{x^2}{0.20} = 2.04 \times 10^{-5}$$

$x = 0.00202$ M OH^- so $pOH = -\log(0.00202)$
$= 2.695$

$pH = 14.00 - 2.695 = 11.31$

© Edvantage Interactive 2019

Practice Problems 5.5.4 — Calculating $[OH^-]$ and pH using K_b and $[B]_{initial}$

1. Hydrazine, N_2H_4 is used in rocket fuel, in producing polymer foams, and in the production of air bags. The K_b for hydrazine is 1.7×10^{-6}. Calculate the pH of the solution prepared by dissolving 12.0 g of hydrazine in 500.0 mL of solution.

2. Calculate the $[OH^-]$, $[H^+]$, pOH, and pH of a 0.60 M solution of $HCOO^-$.

3. Calculate the K_a and pK_a values for the following:
   (a) methylammonium, $CH_3NH_3^+$
   (b) hydrazinium, $N_2H_5^+$

Problem Type 2: Calculating $[B]_{initial}$, given K_b and pH (or pOH)

This type of problem may require us to calculate both $[OH^-]_{eq}$ (from pH) and K_b (from a K_a) at the beginning of the solution process. We then continue in much the same way as we would for this type of problem when dealing with weak acids. Consider the sample problem below.

Sample Problem 5.5.5 — Calculating $[B]_{initial}$, given K_b and pH (or pOH)

What concentration of NH_3 would be required to produce a solution with a pH = 10.50?

What to Think About

1. Calculate both the K_b for NH_3 (using the K_a for NH_4^+) and the $[OH^-]_{eq}$ (from the given pH).
2. The unknown x will represent the $[NH_3]_{initial}$.
3. No assumption regarding x is part of solving this problem.

How to Do It

$$K_b \text{ for } NH_3 = \frac{K_w}{K_a \text{ for } NH_4^+} = \frac{1.00 \times 10^{-14}}{5.6 \times 10^{-10}} = 1.78 \times 10^{-5}$$

$$pOH = 14.00 - 10.50 = 3.50$$

$$[OH^-]_{eq} = 10^{-3.50} = 3.16 \times 10^{-4}\ M$$

Let $x = [NH_3]_{initial}$

$$NH_3 + H_2O \rightleftharpoons NH_4^+ + OH^-$$

	NH_3	H_2O	NH_4^+	OH^-
I	x	X	0	0
C	-3.16×10^{-4}	X	$+3.16 \times 10^{-4}$	$+3.16 \times 10^{-4}$
E	$x - 3.16 \times 10^{-4}$	X	3.16×10^{-4}	3.16×10^{-4}

$$K_b = \frac{[NH_4^+][OH^-]}{[NH_3]} = \frac{(3.16 \times 10^{-4})^2}{x - 3.16 \times 10^{-4}}$$

$$= 1.78 \times 10^{-5}$$

$$x - 3.16 \times 10^{-4} = \frac{(3.16 \times 10^{-4})^2}{1.78 \times 10^{-5}}$$

$$x = 0.0059\ M$$

Practice Problems 5.5.5 — Calculating $[B]_{initial}$ given K_b and pH (or pOH)

1. Ethylamine ($C_2H_5NH_2$) is a pungent colorless gas used extensively in organic synthesis reactions. It is also a weak base with $K_b = 5.6 \times 10^{-4}$. What mass of ethylamine is dissolved in 250.0 mL of a solution having a pH of 11.80?

Continued on the next page

 © Edvantage Interactive 2019

Practice Problems 5.5.5 (*Continued*)

2. What concentration of CN^- would produce a solution with a pH of 11.50?

3. Using the K_b provided above for hydrazine, calculate the $[N_2H_4]$ required to produce a solution with a $[H_3O^+] = 1.0 \times 10^{-10}$ M.

Problem Type 3: Calculating K_b given $[B]_{initial}$ and pH (or pOH)

As was the case with an acidic system, this final type of problem requires no simplifying assumption (although it may prove to be justified), and no unknown to be solved in the ICE table. All of the entries in the table are available, either directly or indirectly, from the information provided in the question. Consider the sample problem below.

Sample Problem 5.5.6 — Calculating K_b, given $[B]_{initial}$ and pH (or pOH)

A solution is prepared by dissolving 9.90 g of the weak base hydroxylamine, NH_2OH, in enough water to produce 500.0 mL of solution. The pH of the solution is found to be 9.904. Calculate the K_b for hydroxylamine.

What to Think About

1. Convert grams of the compound dissolved in 500.0 mL to moles per liter to determine $[NH_2OH]_{initial}$.
2. Use the pH to determine $[OH^-]_{eq}$. That value shows that the % ionization is small enough to assume $0.600 - x \approx 0.600$.
3. Record the final answer to three significant figures.

How to Do It

$$[NH_2OH]_{initial} = 9.90\text{ g } \frac{NH_2OH}{0.5000\text{ L}} \times \frac{1\text{ mol}}{33.0\text{ g}} = 0.600\text{ M}$$

$$pOH = 14.000 - 9.904 = 4.096$$

$$[OH^-]_{eq} = 10^{-4.096} = 8.0168 \times 10^{-5}\text{ M}$$

$$NH_2OH + H_2O \rightleftharpoons NH_2OH_2^+ + OH^-$$

	NH_2OH	H_2O	$NH_2OH_2^+$	OH^-
I	0.600		0	0
C	-8.0168×10^{-5}		$+8.0168 \times 10^{-5}$	$+8.0168 \times 10^{-5}$
E	≈ 0.600		8.0168×10^{-5}	8.0168×10^{-5}

$$K_b = \frac{[NH_2OH_2^+]}{[NH_2OH]} = \frac{(8.0168\ 10^{-5})^2}{0.600} = 1.07 \times 10^{-8}$$

Practice Problems 5.5.6 — Calculating K_b, given $[B]_{initial}$ and pH (or pOH)

1. A 0.400 M solution of the weak base methylamine, CH_3NH_2, is found to have a pH of 12.90. Calculate the K_b of methylamine and the percentage ionization. Compare your calculation of this K_b value with the sample problem above involving methylamine. What might this indicate about the temperature of this solution?

2. One of the most effective substances at relieving intense pain is morphine. First developed in about 1810, the compound is also a weak base. In a 0.010 M solution of morphine, the pOH is determined to be 3.90. Calculate the K_b and pK_b for morphine. (Let "Mor" and "$HMor^+$" represent the conjugate pair in your equilibrium reaction.)

3. Quinine, $C_{20}H_{24}N_2O_2$, is a naturally occurring white crystalline base used in the treatment of malaria. It is also present in tonic water. Calculate the K_b for this weak base if a 0.0015 M solution has a pH of 9.84. (Let "Qui" and "$HQui^+$" represent the conjugate pair in your equilibrium reaction.)

© Edvantage Interactive 2019

5.5 Activity: An Organically Grown Table of Relative Acid Strengths

Question

Can you construct your own table of relative acid strengths using the relationships you have learned in this section to calculate the K_a values for a series of organic compounds?

Background

The vast majority of chemical compounds are organic (carbon-based) compounds and some of those are weak acids and bases. Given sufficient data, you can use various calculations to organize a collection of these compounds into a table from strongest to weakest acids similar to the Table of Relative Strengths of Brønsted-Lowry Acids and Bases (Table 5.2.1 and Table A5), which you have already seen.

Procedure

1. You will be given data relating to 15 organic compounds, 9 of which are weak acids, and 6 of which are weak bases. The data could include K_b, pK_b, pK_a, pH, and pOH information. None of the compounds appear on Table of Relative Strengths of Brønsted-Lowry Acids and Bases (Table 5.2.1 and Table A5). The data will not be presented in any particular order.
2. If given the acid, write the formula for the conjugate base and vice versa.
3. Use the data given to calculate the K_a value for each weak acid or for the conjugate acid of each weak base using any of the relationships discussed in this section. Before beginning, you may want to review the relationships below.
4. Place the equilibrium equation for each weak acid (or conjugate acid) reacting with water in order from strongest down to weakest acid as in an example provided.
5. Include in the right-hand section of the table you construct the K_a value you have calculated.
6. All of the acids are monoprotic carboxylic acids (containing –COOH) and so all of their conjugate bases will appear as $-COO^-$ following donation of the proton to water.
7. All of the weak bases are neutral amines containing nitrogen and so all of their conjugate acids will have an extra "H" on the nitrogen and a "+" charge following acceptance of a proton from the hydronium ion.
8. Consider the following when calculating the K_a values (Assume 25°C):
    - For conjugate acid-base pairs: $K_a \times K_b = K_w = 1.00 \times 10^{-14}$
    - For conjugate acid-base pairs: $pK_a + pK_b = pK_w = 14.00$
    - Review how to calculate K_a and K_b, given pH (or pOH) and $[HA]_{initial}$ (or $[B]_{initial}$).
9. Fill in the missing items in the table below and use the data provided to calculate the K_a values for all the acids and conjugate acids of the bases given in the table.
10. Then arrange all of the acids and conjugate acids in the correct order in the table, including the appropriate equilibrium equation for the examples given. Note that "soln" stands for "solution."

Compound Name	Formula for Conjugate Acid	Formula for Conjugate Base	Calculate K_a for Acid or Conjugate Acid Given
Acids			
chloroacetic acid	$ClCH_2COOH$		$pK_a = 2.85$
phenylacetic acid	C_7H_7COOH		pH of 1.0 M soln = 2.155
propanoic acid	C_2H_5COOH		K_b for conjugate base = 7.7×10^{-10}
pyruvic acid	C_2H_3OCOOH		pK_b for conjugate base = 11.45
lactic acid	C_2H_5OCOOH		pOH of 0.10 M soln = 11.57
acetylsalicylic acid	$C_8H_7O_2COOH$		K_b for conjugate base = 2.8×10^{-11}
glycolic acid	CH_3OCOOH		$pK_a = 3.82$
glyoxylic acid	CHOCOOH		pK_b for conjugate base = 10.54
glyceric acid	$C_2H_5O_2COOH$		pH of 1.0 M soln = 1.77
Bases			
pyridine		C_5H_5N	$K_b = 1.7 \times 10^{-9}$
trimethylamine		$(CH_3)_3N$	pOH of 0.10 M soln = 2.60
piperidine		$C_5H_{10}NH$	$pK_b = 2.89$
tert-butylamine		$(CH_3)_3CNH_2$	pH of a 1.0 M soln = 12.34
ethanolamine		$C_2H_5ONH_2$	pK_a of conjugate acid = 9.50
n-propylamine		$C_3H_7NH_2$	$pK_b = 3.46$

© Edvantage Interactive 2019

Relative Strengths of Some Organic Acids and Bases

Strength of Acid	Equilibrium Reaction With Water: Acid + H_2O $\rightleftharpoons$ H_3O^+ + Base	K_a Value	Strength of Base
Stronger ↑	$\rightleftharpoons$		Weaker ↓
	$\rightleftharpoons$		
	$\rightleftharpoons$		
	$\rightleftharpoons$		
	$\rightleftharpoons$		
	$\rightleftharpoons$		
	$\rightleftharpoons$		
	$\rightleftharpoons$		
	$\rightleftharpoons$		
	$\rightleftharpoons$		
	$\rightleftharpoons$		
	$\rightleftharpoons$		
	$\rightleftharpoons$		
	$\rightleftharpoons$		
Weaker	$\rightleftharpoons$		Stronger

Sample:

	HCOOH (given an acid) + H_2O $\rightleftharpoons$ H_3O^+ + $HCOO^-$	1.8×10^{-4}	
	NH_4^+ + H_2O $\rightleftharpoons$ H_3O^+ + **NH_3** (given a base)	5.6×10^{-10}	

Results and Discussion

1. Are the K_a values for these monoprotic carboxylic acids significantly different from each other in their orders of magnitude? ________________
2. Which acid is the strongest and which base is the strongest? ____
3. Use the K_a vlaues you have calculated to expand the Table of Relative Strengths of Acids and Bases, if you want to include these organic compounds.

5.5 Review Questions

1. Calculate the $[H_3O^+]$, $[OH^-]$, pH, and pOH that results when 23.0 g of HCOOH is dissolved in enough water to produce 500.0 mL of solution.

2. At standard temperature and pressure, 5.6 L of H_2S is dissolved in enough water to produce 2.50 L of solution. Calculate the pH of this solution and percent ionization of H_2S.

3. The percent ionization of 0.100 M solution of an unknown acid is 1.34%. Calculate the pH of this solution and identify the acid.

4. Because of its high reactivity with glass, hydrofluoric acid is used to etch glass. What mass of HF would be required be required to produce 1.5 L of an aqueous solution with a pH of 2.00?

5. Phosphoric acid is used in rust removal and also to add a tangy sour taste to cola soft drinks. A solution of phosphoric acid is found to have a pOH of 12.50. Calculate the concentration of this acid.

© **Edvantage Interactive 2019**

6. Oxalic acid is a white crystalline solid. Some of its uses include rust removal, bleaching pulpwood, and even as an ingredient in baking powder. A 250.0 mL sample of an oxalic solution is found to have a pH of 2.35. What mass of oxalic acid would remain if this aqueous solution were evaporated to dryness?

7. Hypochlorous acid (HClO) is used mainly as an active sanitizer in water treatment. A 0.020 M solution of hypochlorous acid is found to have a pH of 4.62. Calculate the K_a for hypochlorous acid.

8. Phenylacetic acid ($C_6H_5CH_2COOH$) is used in some perfumes and in the production of some forms of penicillin. A 0.100 M solution of phenylacetic acid has a pOH of 11.34. Calculate the K_a of phenylacetic acid.

9. Complete the following table:

Conjugate Acid	Conjugate Base	K_a for Acid	pK_a	K_b for Base	pK_b
	NO_2^-				
H_2O_2					
	$C_6H_5O^-$				
HSO_4^-					

10. Complete the following table of amphiprotic ions:

Conjugate Acid	Conjugate Base	K_a for Acid	pK_a	K_b for Base	pK_b
	HPO_4^-				
$H_2C_6H_5O_7^-$					
	$H_2BO_3^-$				
HCO_3^-					

11. An aqueous solution is prepared by dissolving 5.6 L of NH_3 gas, measured at STP, in enough water to produce 750.0 mL of solution. Calculate the pH of this solution.

12. Isopropylamine, $(CH_3)_2CHNH_2$, is a weak base ($K_b = 4.7 \times 10^{-4}$) used in herbicides such as Roundup and some chemical weapons. Calculate the pOH and pH of a 0.60 M solution of isopropylamine.

13. What concentration of sulfite ions will produce a solution with a pH of 10.00?

14. Trimethylamine, $(CH_3)_3N$ is a weak base ($K_b = 6.3 \times 10^{-5}$). It is one of the compounds responsible for the smell of rotting fish and is used in a number of dyes. What volume of this gas, measured at STP, must be dissolved in 2.5 L of solution to give that solution a pOH of 2.50?

15. A 0.10 M solution of ethylamine, $C_2H_5NH_2$, is found to have a pOH of 2.14. Calculate the K_b for ethylamine.

 © Edvantage Interactive 2019

6 Applications of Acid-Base Reactions

This chapter focuses on the following AP Units from the College Board:

Unit 4: Chemical Reactions
Unit 7: Equilibrium.
Unit 8: Acids and Bases

By the end of this chapter, you should be able to do the following:

- Demonstrate an ability to design, perform, and analyze a titration experiment involving the following:
  - primary standards
  - standardized solutions
  - titration curves
  - appropriate indicators
- Describe an indicator as an equilibrium system
- Perform and interpret calculations involving the pH in a solution and K_a for an indicator
- Describe the hydrolysis of ions in salt solutions
- Analyse the extent of hydrolysis in salt solutions
- Describe buffers as equilibrium systems
- Describe the preparation of buffer systems
- Predict what will happen when oxides dissolve in rain water

---

By the end of this chapter, you should know the meaning of these **key terms**:

- acid rain
- buffers
- dissociation
- equation
- equivalence point (stoichiometric point)
- hydrolysis
- hydrolysis reaction
- indicator
- primary standards
- salt
- titration
- titration curve
- transition point

The freshwater African chichlid requires water having a pH between 8.0 and 9.2 to survive. The South American chichlid requires water with a pH between 6.4 and 7.0.

6.1 Hydrolysis of Salts — The Reactions of Ions with Water

Warm Up

Consider the neutralization reactions described below.

1. (a) When equal volumes of 0.10 M HNO_3 and 0.10 M KOH solutions react together, what salt solution exists in the reaction vessel following the reaction?

   ____

   (b) Consider the dissociated ions of this salt. Is either of the ions located on the table of relative strengths of Brønsted-Lowry acids and bases (Table A5, at the back of the book)? If so, where? Does this help you predict if the pH of this solution will be equal to, above, or below 7?

   ____

   ____

2. (a) When equal volumes of 0.10 M CH_3COOH and 0.10 M NaOH solutions react together, what salt solution exists in the reaction vessel following the reaction?

   ____

   (b) Consider the dissociated ions of the salt. Is either of the ions located on the table of relative strengths of acids and bases (Table A5)? If so, where? Does this help you predict if the pH of this solution will be equal to, above, or below 7?

   ____

   ____

Neutralization Reactions

In previous Chemistry classes you have been introduced to several reaction types. One of those reaction types is *neutralization* in which an acid and a base react to produce a salt and water. The name suggests that when an equal number of moles of hydronium ions from an acid and hydroxide ions from a base react together, the resulting solution will be neutral and thus have a pH of 7.

It might surprise you to know that many such neutralizations produce salt solutions that are actually acidic or basic. This phenomenon occurs because one or both of the dissociated *ions of the product salt* behave as weak acids or bases and thus react with water to generate hydronium or hydroxide ions. This is known as hydrolysis.

Hydrolysis is the reaction of an ion with water to produce either the conjugate base of the ion and *hydronium ions* or the conjugate acid of the ion and *hydroxide ions*.

Whether or not the ions of a salt will hydrolyze can often be determined by considering the acids and bases from which the salt was produced. In each case, we look at the dissociated ions of each type of salt individually and assess their ability to either donate protons to or accept protons from water. This allows us to predict if aqueous solutions of those salts will be acidic, basic, or neutral. Let's begin that discussion below.

© Edvantage Interactive 2019

A. Neutral Salts: Salts Containing the Anion of a Strong Acid and the Cation of a Strong Base

Consider the first Warm Up question above. When equal amounts of nitric acid and potassium hydroxide solutions are combined, an aqueous solution of potassium nitrate is produced. The dissociated ions present in this solution are the K^+ cations from the strong base and the NO_3^- anions from the strong acid.

Like all aqueous ions, the alkali ions in the solution become surrounded by water molecules in the hydration process, but no reaction between those ions and water occurs. The same is true for all alkali (Group 1) ions and most alkaline earth (Group 2) ions (except beryllium). *These are the cations of strong bases and they do not hydrolyze.* We therefore consider them *spectator ions.*

Like all ions that are the conjugate bases of strong acids, NO_3^- ions have no measurable ability to accept protons from water. Notice on the table of relative strengths of Brønsted-Lowry acids and bases (Table A5) that all such anions of strong acids are located at the top right corner of the table and on the receiving end of a *one-way arrow* — they are thus incapable of accepting protons and so cannot function as bases. Like the cations mentioned above, all anions of strong monoprotic acids are hydrated in water, but no further reaction occurs. *The anions of strong monoprotic acids do not hydrolyze.* They are considered *spectator ions in water.* (Note that the bisulfate anion, HSO_4^-, although unable to *accept* protons from water, is a relatively strong weak acid and therefore *donates* protons to water.) We can generalize these results into the conclusion stated below.

A salt containing the anion of a strong monoprotic acid and the cation of a strong base will produce a neutral solution in water because neither of the ions undergoes hydrolysis.

Quick Check

1. Circle the ions in the following list that represent cations of strong bases.

   Al^{3+} Rb^+ Fe^{3+} Cr^{3+} Ca^{2+} Sn^{4+} Cs^+ Ba^{2+}

2. Circle the ions in the following list that represent the conjugate bases of strong acids.

   F^- ClO_2^- ClO_4^- SO_4^{2-} Cl^- NO_2^- CH_3COO^- CN^- NO_3^-

3. Circle the following salts whose ions will not hydrolyze when dissociated in water.

   NH_4Cl Na_2CO_3 $RbClO_4$ Li_2SO_3 BaI_2 NH_4HCOO KIO_3 CsF $CaBr_2$

B. Basic Salts: Salts Containing the Anion of a Weak Acid and the Cation of a Strong Base

Look at the second Warm Up question at the beginning of this section. When equal amounts of acetic acid and sodium hydroxide solutions are combined, an aqueous solution of sodium acetate is produced. The dissociated ions present in this solution are the Na^+ ions from the strong base and the CH_3COO^- ions from the weak acid. We have already stated that alkali ions are incapable of undergoing hydrolysis and thus cannot affect the solution's pH.

However, the acetate anion is the conjugate base of a weak acid and therefore has a measurable ability to accept protons from water. Being a weak base, the acetate anion will react with water by accepting protons in the following hydrolysis reaction:

$$CH_3COO^-(aq) + H_2O(l) \rightleftharpoons CH_3COOH(aq) + OH^-(aq)$$

As a result of the hydrolysis, this solution will be basic with a pH above 7.

A salt containing the anion of a weak monoprotic acid and the cation of a strong base will produce a basic solution in water because the anion acts as a weak base, producing hydroxide ions, and the cation does not react.

Quick Check

1. Which of the following salts contain the anion of a weak acid?

   NH_4Cl $NaClO_4$ $Fe(CH_3COO)_3$ KF LiCl

   $Al(NO_3)_3$ NH_4HSO_4 $Pb(NO_2)_2$ NH_4I $Ba(CN)_2$

2. Which of the following salts will produce a basic aqueous solution due to anionic hydrolysis?

   $AlBr_3$ $Ca(HCOO)_2$ $RbClO_4$ $SrCO_3$ $Mg(CN)_2$

   $NaCH_3COO$ $Cr(NO_3)_3$ LiC_6H_5COO FeI_3 K_3PO_4

Qualitatively, we can predict that such solutions will be basic due to anionic hydrolysis, but we can also perform all of the same types of calculations for these dissolved anions that we introduced in the previous section for any weak base in water. Consider the Sample Problem below.

Sample Problem 6.1.1 — Calculating the pH of a Basic Salt Solution

A 9.54 g sample of $Mg(CN)_2$ is dissolved in enough water to make 500.0 mL of solution. Calculate the pH of this solution.

What to Think About

1. First calculate the concentration of the compound and then write the dissociation equation to determine the initial concentration of each ion.
2. Then consider each of the dissociated ions separately and decide if either is capable of hydrolyzing.
3. Mg^{2+} will not hydrolyze, but CN^- is the conjugate base of a very weak acid and is therefore a relatively strong weak base. Consequently, expect the pH of this solution to be well above 7.
4. Write an equilibrium equation under which you can construct an ICE table.
5. To calculate the $[OH^-]_{eq}$, first calculate the K_b of the cyanide anion.
6. Remember that you are solving for $[OH^-]_{eq}$ on the ICE table and so an extra step is required to determine pH.

How to Do It

$$\frac{9.54\ \text{g}}{0.5000\ \text{L}} \times \frac{1\ \text{mol } Mg(CN)_2}{76.3\ \text{g}} = 0.250\ \text{M}$$

$$\underset{0.250\ \text{M}}{Mg(CN)_2(s)} \rightarrow \underset{0.250\ \text{M}}{Mg^{2+}(aq)} + \underset{0.500\ \text{M}}{2\ CN^-(aq)}$$

$$K_b \text{ for } CN^- = \frac{K_w}{K_a \text{ for } HCN} = \frac{1.00 \times 10^{-14}}{4.9 \times 10^{-10}}$$

$$= 2.04 \times 10^{-5}$$

Let $x = [OH^-]_{eq}$

$$CN^- + H_2O \rightleftharpoons HCN + OH^-$$

	CN^-	H_2O	HCN	OH^-
I	0.500		0	0
C	$-x$		$+x$	$+x$
E	$0.500 - x$		x	x

Assume $0.500 - x \approx 0.500$

$$K_b = \frac{[HCN][OH^-]}{[CN^-]} = \frac{x^2}{0.500} = 2.04 \times 10^{-5}$$

$$x = 3.19 \times 10^{-3}\ \text{M} = [OH^-]_{eq}$$

$$pOH = -\log(0.00319) = 2.496$$

$$pH = 14.00 - 2.496 = 11.50 \text{ (2 sig. figures)}$$

 © Edvantage Interactive 2019

Practice Problems 6.1.1 — Basic Salt Solutions

1. Without performing any calculations, rank the following salts in order of decreasing pH of their 0.10 M aqueous solutions:
   Na_2SO_3 LiF KNO_2 RbCN $Na_2C_2O_4$ K_2CO_3

   ________ > ________ > ________ > ________ > ________ > ________

2. Sodium carbonate is used in the manufacture of glass and also as a laundry additive to soften water. A 200.0 mL aqueous solution of 0.50 M Na_2CO_3 is diluted to 500.0 mL. Calculate the pH of the resulting solution.

3. What concentration of NaHCOO would be required to produce an aqueous solution with a pH of 9.20? Begin by writing the equation for the predominant equilibrium present in the solution.

C. Acidic Salts I: Salts Containing the Conjugate Base of a Strong Acid and the Conjugate Acid of a Weak Base

When equal amounts of NH_3 (a weak base) and HCl (a strong acid) are combined, the neutralization reaction that occurs is:

$$NH_3(aq) + HCl(aq) \rightarrow NH_4Cl(aq)$$

Following the reaction, the two ions present in the solution are NH_4^+ and Cl^-. We have already noted that chloride ions, like all conjugate bases of the strong acids, are incapable of accepting protons by reacting with water. However, the ammonium cation is the conjugate acid of a weak base and is therefore a weak acid capable of donating protons to water in the cationic hydrolysis reaction shown below:

$$NH_4^+(aq) + H_2O(l) \rightleftharpoons NH_3(aq) + H_3O^+(aq)$$

As a result of the hydrolysis, this solution will be acidic with a pH below 7.

A salt containing the cation of a weak base and the anion of a strong monoprotic acid will produce an acidic solution in water because the cation acts as a weak acid producing hydronium ions and the anion does not react.

Quick Check

1. Write the hydrolysis equation for the conjugate acids of the following weak bases reacting with water and the appropriate K_a expressions:
   (a) methylamine, CH_3NH_2

   (b) *n*-propylamine, $C_3H_7NH_2$

   (c) trimethylamine $(CH_3)_3N$

2. Calculate the K_a for the conjugate acids of the above weak bases given the following data:
   (a) K_b for methylamine = 4.4×10^{-4}

   (b) K_b for n–propylamine = 3.5×10^{-4}

   (c) K_b for trimethylamine = 6.3×10^{-5}

Sample Problem 6.1.2 — Calculating the pH of an Acidic Salt

The K_b for pyridine, C_5H_5N, is 4.7×10^{-9}. Calculate the pH of a 0.10 M solution of $C_5H_5NHNO_3$.

What to Think About

1. The dissociation equation yields $C_5H_5NH^+$ and NO_3^- ions, each at 0.10 M concentrations.
   The NO_3^- ion will not hydrolyze as it is the conjugate base of a strong acid.
   The $C_5H_5NH^+$ cation, however will donate protons to water as it is the conjugate acid of a weak base. That hydrolysis will make the solution acidic.
2. Calculate the K_a for the cation using K_w and the given K_b for pyridine.
5. Construct an ICE table under the equilibrium equation for hydrolysis of the cation.
6. Calculate the pH.

How to Do It

$$C_5H_5NHNO_3(s) \rightarrow C_5H_5NH^+(aq) + NO_3^-(aq)$$
$$\quad 0.10\ M \qquad\qquad 0.10\ M$$

$$K_a \text{ for } C_5H_5NH^+ = \frac{K_w}{K_b \text{ for } C_5H_5N} = \frac{1.00 \times 10^{-14}}{4.7 \times 10^{-9}}$$
$$= 2.13 \times 10^{-6}$$

Let $x = [H_3O^+]_{eq}$

$$C_5H_5NH^+ + H_2O \rightleftharpoons C_5H_5N + H_3O^+$$

	$C_5H_5NH^+$	H_2O	C_5H_5N	H_3O^+
I	0.10		0	0
C	$-x$		$+x$	$+x$
E	$0.10 - x$		x	x

Assume $0.10 - x \approx 0.10$

$$K_a \text{ for } C_5H_5NH^+ = \frac{[C_5H_5N]\,[H_3O^+]}{[C_5H_5NH^+]} = \frac{x^2}{0.10}$$
$$= 2.13 \times 10^{-6}$$

$x = \sqrt{2.13 \times 10^{-7}} = 4.61 \times 10^{-4}$

$pH = -\log(4.61 \times 10^{-4}) = 3.34$ (2 sig. figures)

 © Edvantage Interactive 2019

Practice Problems 6.1.2 — Acidic Salt Solutions

1. Ammonium nitrate is used in fertilizers, the production of explosives, and instant cold packs. Calculate the pH of the solution produced when 16.0 g of NH_4NO_3 is dissolved in enough water to produce 500.0 mL of solution.

2. The pH of a 0.50 M solution of N_2H_5Cl is found to be 4.266. Calculate the K_a for $N_2H_5^+$. Check your answer, given that the K_b for $N_2H_4 = 1.7 \times 10^{-6}$.

3. What mass of C_5H_5NHCl would be required to produce 250.0 mL of an aqueous solution with a pH = 3.00? (See the Sample Problem above for K_a value.)

D. Acidic Salts II: Salts Containing the Anion of a Strong Acid and a Small Highly Charged Metal Cation

Look closely at the table of relative strengths of acids and bases (Table A5). Notice that several of the weak acids are actually hydrated metal cations that are capable of donating protons to water. For example, consider the Al^{3+} cation. The ion itself is not a Brønsted-Lowry acid. However, when it is surrounded by six water molecules in its hydrated form, the combination of its small size and relatively high charge (called a high "charge density" by chemists) draws the oxygens of the attached water molecules very close. This further polarizes their O–H bonds. This increases the tendency of those molecules to donate protons, making the hydrated cation complex a weak acid. Consider the diagram of the hydrated cation in Figure 6.1.1.

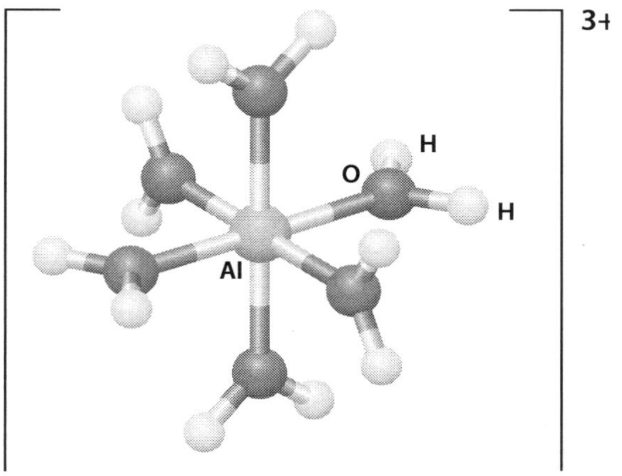

Figure 6.1.1 *The hydrated cation formed from the Al^{3+} cation surrounded by six water molecules*

We would not expect this to occur when larger cations with a smaller charge are hydrated. This explains why the alkali metals and all but one of the alkaline earth cations do not hydrolyze. Can you suggest a reason why Be^{2+} *does* react with water to some extent?

The hydrolysis reaction for the hexaaquoaluminum cation is shown below:

$$Al(H_2O)_6^{3+}(aq) + H_2O(l) \rightleftharpoons Al(H_2O)_5OH^{2+}(aq) + H_3O^+(aq)$$

Note that in the hydrolysis reaction, the number of bound water molecules decreases by one (from six to five) when the proton is donated to water and generates an OH^-. This reduces the overall charge of the cation from 3+ to 2+.

Other hydrated cations such as Fe^{3+}, Cr^{3+}, Sn^{2+}, and Cu^{2+} show similar behavior. Generally, each ion will form an acidic hydrate with the number of water molecules equal to twice the magnitude of the charge on the cation. As a result, a salt containing one of these cations and an anion from a strong monoprotic acid would produce an acidic aqueous solution.

A salt containing the anion of a strong monoprotic acid and a small highly charged metal cation will produce an acidic solution in water because the hydrated cation acts as a weak acid producing hydronium ions and the anion does not react.

Quick Check

1. Circle the salts below that will produce acidic aqueous solutions.

   $NaNO_2$ NH_4I $CaBr_2$ $CrCl_3$ $Sr(CN)_2$ $RbCH_3COO$ $Fe(NO_3)_3$ Li_2SO_3

2. Write the hydrolysis reactions for the following hydrated cations:

   (a) $Sn(H_2O)_4^{2+}$

   (b) $Cu(H_2O)_4^{2+}$

   (c) $Fe(H_2O)_6^{3+}$

Sample Problem 6.1.3 — Acidic Salts II

What mass of $CrCl_3$ would be required to produce 250.0 mL of an aqueous solution with a pH of 2.75?

What to Think About

1. The aqueous solution contains Cl^- ions which will not hydrolyze and hydrated Cr^{3+} ions which will react with water to produce H_3O^+ ions.
2. Use the pH to determine the $[H_3O^+]_{eq}$. Use the $[H_3O^+]_{eq}$, together with the K_a value for $Cr(H_2O)_6^{3+}$ from the table, to calculate the $[Cr^{3+}]_{initial}$.

How to Do It

$[H_3O^+]_{eq} = 10^{-pH} = 10^{-2.75} = 0.00178\ M$

Let $x = [Cr^{3+}]_{initial} = [Cr(H_2O)_6^{3+}]_{initial}$

$Cr(H_2O)_6^{3+} + H_2O \rightleftharpoons Cr(H_2O)_5OH^{2+} + H_3O^+$

	$Cr(H_2O)_6^{3+}$	H_2O	$Cr(H_2O)_5OH^{2+}$	H_3O^+
I	x		0	0
C	−0.00178		+0.00178	+0.00178
E	$x - 0.00178$		0.00178	0.00178

Continued opposite

© Edvantage Interactive 2019

Sample Problem 6.1.3 (*Continued*)

What to Think About	How to Do It
3. $[CrCl_3]_{initial} = [Cr^{3+}]_{initial} = [Cr(H_2O)_6^{3+}]_{initial}$	$K_a = \frac{[Cr(H_2O)_5OH^{2+}][H_3O^+]}{[Cr(H_2O)_6^{3+}]} = \frac{(0.00178)^2}{x - 0.00178} = 1.5 \times 10^{-4}$ $1.5 \times 10^{-4}x - 2.67 \times 10^{-7} = 3.17 \times 10^{-6}$ $x = 2.29 \times 10^{-2}$ mol/L $2.29 \times 10^{-2} \frac{\text{mol } CrCl_3}{L} \times \frac{158.5 \text{ g}}{\text{mol}} \times 0.2500 \text{ L}$ $= 0.91$ g (2 sig. figures)

Practice Problems 6.1.3 — Acidic Salts II

1. Iron(III) nitrate solutions are used by jewellers to etch silver and silver alloys. Calculate the pH of a 6.0 M $Fe(NO_3)_3$ solution.

2. What concentration of $AlBr_3$ would be required to produce an aqueous solution with a pH of 3.25?

3. Unlike the other alkaline earth cations, the hydrated beryllium ion will hydrolyze by donating protons to water. The K_a for $Be(H_2O)_4^{2+}$ is 3.2×10^{-7}. Calculate the pH of a 0.400 M aqueous solution of BeI_2.

Magnitudes of K_a and K_b Values

Whether the two remaining classes of salts produce acidic, basic, or neutral solutions depends on the relative magnitudes of the K_a and K_b values for their ions. For the most part, you will not be expected to calculate the pH of such solutions, but calculations will be necessary to determine if those pH values will be above, below, or equal to 7.

E. Salts Containing Weakly Acidic Cations and Weakly Basic Anions

Consider the ions present in a 0.10 M solution of NH_4CN. The ammonium ion is the conjugate acid of a weak base (NH_3), and the cyanide ion is the conjugate base of a weak acid (HCN). As a result, both dissociated ions will react with water and influence the pH of the salt solution. Those two hydrolysis reactions and the corresponding equilibrium constant values are shown below:

$NH_4^+(aq) + H_2O(l) \rightleftharpoons NH_3(aq) + H_3O^+(aq) \qquad K_a = 5.6 \times 10^{-10}$

$CN^-(aq) + H_2O(l) \rightleftharpoons HCN(aq) + OH^-(aq) \qquad K_b = 2.0 \times 10^{-5}$

Note that the K_b of the cyanide ion is greater than the K_a of the ammonium ion. This tells us that the anionic hydrolysis reaction that generates hydroxide ions occurs to a much greater extent than the cationic hydrolysis reaction that produces hydronium ions. Consequently the $[OH^-]$ will exceed the $[H_3O^+]$ and the solution will be basic with a pH greater than 7.

Thus by comparing the K_a and the K_b values of the ions which hydrolyze, we can determine if the solution will be acidic, basic, or neutral. Below are guides for using this comparison to determine the acidity of a solution.

A salt containing a weakly acidic cation and a weakly basic anion will produce a solution that is:
- acidic if K_a for the cation > K_b for the anion
- basic if K_a for the cation < K_b for the anion
- neutral if K_a for the cation = K_b for the anion

Quick Check

1. Which of the following salts will dissociate into ions that will *both* react with water?

   KI $\quad NH_4NO_2 \quad Fe(CN)_3 \quad Sn(NO_3)_2 \quad Rb_2C_2O_4 \quad CrBr_3 \quad NaCH_3COO \quad AlF_3$

2. Write out the two hydrolysis reactions that occur when a sample of NH_4F dissolves in water.

3. Which of the two hydrolysis reactions in question 2 above will occur to a greater extent? How do you know?

   ____

   ____

Sample Problem 6.1.4 — Determining if a Salt Solution is Acidic, Basic, or Neutral

Determine if an aqueous solution of $Cr(CH_3COO)_3$ will be acidic, basic, or neutral and include the hydrolysis reactions that occur.

What to Think About	How to Do It
1. Both of the dissociated ions will hydrolyze.	$Cr(H_2O)_6^{3+}(aq) + H_2O(l) \rightleftharpoons Cr(H_2O)_5OH^{2+}(aq) + H_3O^+(aq)$
2. Use the K_a for the hydrated Cr^{3+} ion from Table A5.	$K_a = 1.5 \times 10^{-4}$
3. Calculate the K_b for the acetate ion using K_w and the K_a for acetic acid.	$CH_3COO^-(aq) + H_2O(l) \rightleftharpoons CH_3COOH(aq) + OH^-(aq)$ $K_b = \dfrac{K_w}{K_a \text{ for } CH_3COOH} = \dfrac{1.00 \times 10^{-14}}{1.8 \times 10^{-5}} = 5.6 \times 10^{-10}$ As the value of K_a for $Cr(H_2O)_6^{3+}$ is greater than the value of K_b for CH_3COO^-, the hydrolysis of the cation-producing hydronium ions predominates. We would expect this solution to be acidic.

© Edvantage Interactive 2019

Practice Problems 6.1.4 — Determining if a Salt Solution is Acidic, Basic, or Neutral

1. Determine if a solution of NH_4CH_3COO will be acidic, basic, or neutral, and include the hydrolysis reactions that occur. Can you predict the approximate pH of this solution?

2. Ammonium phosphate is used in fire extinguishers and also in bread making to promote the growth of the yeast. Determine if an aqueous solution of $(NH_4)_3PO_4$ will be acidic, basic, or neutral and include the hydrolysis reactions that occur.

3. Arrange the following 0.10 M salt solutions in order of decreasing pH:

   $FeCl_3$ $(NH_4)_2CO_3$ $Al(CH_3COO)_3$ $NaNO_3$

   ____________ > ____________ > ____________ > ____________

F. Salts Containing the Cation of a Strong Base and an Amphiprotic Anion

When aqueous solutions containing an equal number of moles of NaOH and H_3PO_4 are combined, only a *partial neutralization* of the triprotic acid occurs, producing an aqueous solution of NaH_2PO_4. This solution contains sodium ions, which we know will not hydrolyze, and the amphiprotic dihydrogen phosphate ion, which is capable of both donating protons to and accepting protons from water. To determine which hydrolysis reaction predominates, we must once again compare a K_a to a K_b value, except in this case those values are for the *same ion*.

> A salt containing a cation of a strong base and an amphiprotic anion will produce a solution that is: acidic if K_a for the anion > K_b for the anion
> basic if K_a for the anion < K_b for the anion

Table 6.1.1 *Summary Table of Hydrolysis*

Type of Salt: Cation	Type of Salt: Anion	Examples	Ion That Hydrolyzes	Result for Solution
A. Of a strong base	Of a strong acid	KNO_3, NaCl	neither	neutral
B. Of a strong base	Of a weak acid	KCN, $NaCH_3COO$	anion	basic
C. Of a weak base†	Of a strong acid	NH_4I, NH_4Br	cation	acidic
D. Small highly charged	Of a strong acid	$FeCl_3$, $Al(NO_3)_3$	cation	acidic
E. Weakly acidic	Weakly basic	NH_4CN, $Fe(NO_2)_2$	both	acidic or basic*
F. Of a strong base	Amphiprotic	$NaHCO_3$, $KHSO_3$	anion	acidic or basic*

† *Conjugate acid of* weak base
*Acidic if $K_a > K_b$, basic if $K_a < K_b$

Sample Problem 6.1.5 — Determining if a Salt Solution Containing the Cation of a Strong Base and an Amphiprotic Anion Will be Acidic or Basic

Determine if a 0.10 M solution of NaH_2PO_4 will be acidic or basic and include the hydrolysis reactions that occur.

What to Think About	How to Do It
1. The sodium ions will not hydrolyze, but the dihydrogen phosphate anion can. It is amphiprotic.	$H_2PO_4^-(aq) + H_2O(l) \rightleftharpoons HPO_4^{2-}(aq) + H_3O^+(aq)$ $K_a = 6.2 \times 10^{-8}$
2. Use the K_a for the anion from Table A5. Calculate the K_b using K_w and the K_a for phosphoric acid.	$H_2PO_4^-(aq) + H_2O(l) \rightleftharpoons H_3PO_4(aq) + OH^-(aq)$ $K_b = \frac{K_w}{K_a \text{ for } H_3PO_4} = \frac{1.00 \times 10^{-14}}{7.5 \times 10^{-3}} = 1.3 \times 10^{-12}$ As the value of K_a is greater than the value of K_b for the anion, the hydrolysis reaction producing hydronium ions is the predominant one and the solution will therefore be slightly acidic.

Practice Problems 6.1.5 — Determining if a Salt Solution Containing the Cation of a Strong Base and an Amphiprotic Anion Will be Acidic or Basic

1. Determine if a 0.10 M solution of K_2HPO_4 will be acidic or basic and include the hydrolysis reactions that occur.

2. Arrange the following 0.10 M aqueous solutions in order of increasing pH:

   $NaHSO_3$ $LiHCO_3$ $KHSO_4$

   ______ < ______ < ______

3. Are any calculations required to determine if an aqueous solution of $KHSO_4$ will be acidic or basic? Why or why not?

© Edvantage Interactive 2019

6.1 Activity: Hydrolysis — A Rainbow of Possibilities

Question

Can you predict the color that a universal indicator solution will display when added to a series of 10 different 0.1 M aqueous salt solutions?

Background

A universal indicator solution is a mixture of several chemical indicators, each of which undergoes a different color change over a different pH range. When the indicators are mixed, their colors and color changes combine over the entire range of the pH scale to display a series of rainbow-like hues depending on the hydronium concentration of the particular solution as shown in the table below.

pH	1	2	3	4	5	6	7	8	9	10	11	12	13	14
Colour	RED		ORANGE		YELLOW		GREEN			BLUE		PURPLE-VIOLET		

Procedure

1. Calculate the pH of the following 0.1 M aqueous solutions to determine the color displayed by the universal indicator when added to that solution. (The pH values for the first two salts are provided for you.)
   (a) $NaHSO_4$ (pH $\leq$ 3)

   (b) K_3PO_4 (pH $\geq$ 11)

   (c) NH_4NO_3

   (d) $Na_2C_2O_4$

2. Write the formula for each salt underneath the appropriate pH value and color in the diagram below.

3. Determine if the following 0.1 M aqueous solutions are acidic, basic, or neutral by comparing the K_a value for the cation to the K_b value for the anion in each salt.
   (a) $(NH_4)_2CO_3$

(b) $Fe_2(SO_4)_3$

(c) $(NH_4)_2C_2O_4$

4. The three solutions above have the following three pH values: 3.8, 6.5, and 8.5. Match each solution above to one of the pH values and write the formula for that salt underneath the appropriate pH value and color in the diagram below.

5. Determine if the following 0.1 M aqueous solutions should be acidic, basic, or neutral by comparing the K_a value to the K_b value for the anion in each salt.
(a) KH_2PO_4

(b) $NaHSO_3$

(c) $KHCO_3$

6. The three solutions above have the following three pH values: 5.5, 4.0, and 9.0. Match each solution above to one of the pH values and write the formula for that salt underneath the appropriate pH value and color in the diagram below.

pH	1	2	3	4	5	6	7	8	9	10	11	12	13	14
Colour	RED		ORANGE		YELLOW		GREEN			BLUE		PURPLE-VIOLET		

Formulas

Results and Discussion

1. If possible, ask your teacher if you can test the results of your calculations by preparing as many of the above solutions as possible. Add a few drops of universal indicator to each and/or measure the pH values with a pH meter.

© Edvantage Interactive 2019

6.1 Review Questions

1. Three separate unmarked beakers on a lab bench each contain 200 mL samples of 1.0 M clear, colorless aqueous solutions. You are told that one beaker contains $Ca(NO_3)_2$, one beaker contains K_3PO_4, and one beaker contains $Al(NO_3)_3$. Using the principles learned in this section, describe a simple test to identify the solutes in each solution.

2. Complete the following table for the six aqueous solutions by filling in the missing entries.

Salt Formula	**Ion(s) that Hydrolyze(s)**	**Result for Aqueous Solution (Acidic, Basic, or Neutral)**	**Equation(s) for Hydrolysis Reaction(s) (if any)**
$(NH_4)_2SO_3$			
$Al(IO_3)_3$			
RbF			
SrI_2			
KHC_2O_4			
$Fe_2(SO_4)_3$			

3. A 50.0 mL solution of 0.50 M KOH is combined with an equal volume of 0.50 M CH_3COOH.
   (a) Write the chemical equation for this neutralization reaction.

   (b) What salt concentration exists in the reaction vessel following the reaction?

(c) Calculate the pH of this solution. Begin by writing the equation for the predominant equilibrium that exists in the solution.

4. A 25.2 g sample of Na_2SO_3 is dissolved in enough water to make 500.0 mL of solution. Calculate the pH of this solution.

5. Copper(II) chloride dihydrate is a beautiful blue-green crystalline solid. The K_a for the tetraaquocopper(II) ion is 1.0×10^{-8}. What mass of $CuCl_2 \cdot 2\,H_2O$ would be required to produce 250.0 mL of an aqueous solution with a pH of 5.00?

6. Sodium cyanide is mainly used to extract gold and other precious metals in mining. Cyanide salts are also among the most rapidly acting of all poisons. A 300.0 mL aqueous solution of sodium cyanide is found to have a pH of 9.50. What mass of NaCN exists in this solution?

© Edvantage Interactive 2019

7. One of the main uses for ammonium perchlorate is in the production of solid rocket propellants. Calculate the pH of the solution produced by dissolving 470 g of the salt in enough water to make 5.0 L of solution.

8. Without performing any calculations, arrange the following 0.1 M aqueous solutions in order of increasing pH.

RbI NH_4Br KCN Li_2CO_3 $NaHSO_4$ $Cr(NO_3)_3$ Na_3PO_4 $FeCl_3$

________ < ________ < ________ < ________ < ________ < ________ < ________ < ________

9. (a) What mass of KNO_2 will remain when 350.0 mL of an aqueous solution with a pH of 8.50 is evaporated to dryness?

(b) How will you observe the pH change as the volume of the solution decreases? Why?

10. Calculate the pH of a 0.500 M aqueous solution of N_2H_5Cl. The K_b for $N_2H_4 = 1.7 \times 10^{-6}$.

6.2 The Chemistry of Buffers

Warm Up

1. Consider a 1.0 L aqueous solution of 0.10 M CH_3COOH. Calculate the pH of this solution and begin by writing the equation for the predominant chemical equilibrium in the solution.

2. From the $[H_3O^+]$ calculated above, determine the percent ionization of the acetic acid.

3. A student adds 0.10 mol of $NaCH_3COO$ to the solution described in question 1.

   (a) In which direction will the equilibrium shift after the addition of the salt?

   ____

   (b) What is the name of this type of effect?

   ____

   (c) How will the percent ionization of the acetic acid and the pH of the solution be affected?

   ____

   (d) What two chemical species participating in the equilibrium will predominate in the solution following the addition of the salt? Can these species react *with each other*?

   ____

Definition of a Buffer

Most biological fluids are solutions whose pH must be maintained within a very narrow range. In your body for example, the ability of your blood to transport oxygen depends on its pH remaining at or very near 7.35. If the pH of your blood were to deviate much more than one-tenth of a unit beyond that, it would lose the capacity to perform its vital function. Yet many products of the multiple metabolic processes occurring right now in your body are acidic compounds, each potentially able to lower your blood pH to fatal levels. In addition, many of the foods you enjoy are full of acidic compounds. If your blood were a solution incapable of effectively and continually resisting changes to its pH level, these foods would kill you. A solution capable of maintaining a relatively constant pH is known as a buffer.

An acid-base **buffer** is a solution that resists changes in pH following the addition of relatively small amounts of a strong acid or strong base.

 © Edvantage Interactive 2019

The Components of a Buffer

To understand how (and how well) a buffer solution resists pH changes, we must first discuss the *components* of a buffer. Let's start with the same 1.0 L solution of 0.10 M CH_3COOH from the Warm Up above. Only a very small percent of the weak acid is ionized, symbolized using enlarged and reduced fonts in the reaction shown below.

$$\mathbf{CH_3COOH}(aq) + H_2O(l) \rightleftharpoons CH_3COO^-(aq) + H_3O^+(aq)$$

If a relatively small amount of a strong base such as NaOH is added to this solution, a "reservoir" of *almost all* of the original 0.10 mol of acetic acid is available to neutralize the added hydroxide ions. However, this same minimal ionization means that the solution has *almost no ability* to counter the effects of added hydronium ions from an acid because the concentration of the conjugate base in this solution is so low. This solution therefore cannot be considered to be a buffer.

To give this solution the ability to also absorb *added acid*, we must increase the concentration of the conjugate base. We can do this by adding a soluble salt of that anion in the form of, for example, sodium acetate. The weak base added is normally *the conjugate base of the weak acid already in solution*. This prevents the two species from neutralizing each other.

Let's now add 0.10 mol of $NaCH_3COO$ to this acidic solution with no volume change and consider the effects. The Na^+ is a spectator ion in the solution, but according to Le Châtelier's principle, the added acetate ions will shift the weak acid equilibrium to the left in favor of the molecular acid and further suppress its already minimal ionization. This qualifies as the common ion effect that you learned about in Chapter 4. As the shift occurs, the percent ionization of the acetic acid drops from the original 1.3% to only 0.018%. The corresponding decrease in hydronium concentration results in a pH increase in the solution from 2.87 to 4.74.

Recall the pH calculations for weak acids. There, we assumed that the equilibrium concentrations of those acids were effectively equal to the initial concentrations if the percent ionization was less than 5%. In this solution, the assumption is even more justified. Also, the equilibrium concentration of the acetate ion in this solution is slightly more than 0.10 M because of that very small percent ionization. However, because the ionization is so minimal, the equilibrium concentration of the acetate ion is effectively equal to the concentration of that anion resulting from the added salt. Also any hydrolysis of the acetate ion can be ignored because of the presence of the acetic acid.

Our solution is therefore effectively a 0.10 M solution of both acetic acid and its conjugate base, the acetate anion. Appreciable quantities of each component give the solution the capacity to resist large pH changes equally well following the addition of relatively small amounts of either a strong base or a strong acid.

This is because significant (and approximately equal) reservoirs of *both* a weak acid *and* a weak base are available in the solution to neutralize those stresses. Thus, the buffer has the ability to shift to the left or the right in response to either acidic or basic stress.

$$\underset{\approx 0.10\text{ M}}{\mathbf{CH_3COOH}}(aq) + H_2O(l) \rightleftharpoons \underset{\approx 0.10\text{ M}}{\mathbf{CH_3COO^-}}(aq) + H_3O^+(aq)$$

> A buffer solution normally consists of a weak acid and its conjugate weak base in appreciable and approximately equal concentrations.

We refer to this solution as an **acidic buffer** because it will buffer a solution in the acidic region of the pH scale. Note that it's not necessary for the concentrations of the weak acid and its conjugate base to be equal — only that they are each relatively large. Normally, however, we attempt to keep those concentrations as close to equal as possible so as to give the buffer the ability to resist both acid and base stresses equally well. We'll discuss this in more detail below.

To understand how these components allow the buffer to resist significant pH changes, we begin by manipulating the K_a expression for this weak acid. Our goal is to derive an equation that tells us what determines the hydronium concentration of this buffer solution.

Because: $K_a = \dfrac{[CH_3COO^-][H_3O^+]}{[CH_3COOH]}$ then: $[H_3O^+] = K_a \dfrac{[CH_3COOH]}{[CH_3COO^-]}$

Or in general: $\mathbf{[H_3O^+] = K_a \dfrac{[HA]}{[A^-]}}$

This simple but important equation means that the hydronium ion concentration (and therefore the pH) of a buffer solution depends on two factors:

- the K_a value for the weak acid and
- the *ratio* of the concentration of that weak acid to its conjugate base in the solution

Examining the above equation more closely reveals some additional details:

1. If the concentrations of the acid and its conjugate base are equal, a ratio of 1 means that the hydronium concentration in the buffer solution is simply equal to the K_a value for the weak acid. Thus, in our example, the $[H_3O^+] = K_a$ for acetic acid $= 1.8 \times 10^{-5}$ M.

2. At a constant temperature, only one of the two factors determining $[H_3O^+]$ (and therefore its maintenance) is variable. As the value of K_a is a constant, only the weak acid/conjugate base concentration ratio can be changed. Specifically: if the $[HA]/[A^-]$ ratio *increases*, the $[H_3O^+]$ *increases*, and if the $[HA]/[A^-]$ ratio *decreases*, the $[H_3O^+]$ *decreases*.

3. When we dilute a buffer solution, the concentrations of both the weak acid and its conjugate base are reduced equally. Therefore, their ratio remains constant. This means that the hydronium ion concentration (and so the pH) *does not change* when a buffer solution is diluted.

Quick Check

1. Why do we normally attempt to make the concentrations of the weak acid and its conjugate base in a buffer solution approximately equal?

 ____

2. In a buffer containing HA and A^-, the conjugate base A^- will react to neutralize added acid. As a result, following the addition of a small amount of strong acid to a buffer solution, the $[HA]/[A^-]$ ratio will ______________ (increase or decrease), the $[H_3O^+]$ will ______________ (increase or decrease) slightly, and the pH will ______________ (increase or decrease) slightly.

3. Circle the pairs of chemical species below that could be used to prepare a buffer solution.

 HNO_3 and $NaNO_3$ KF and HF HNO_2 and HNO_3 HCOOH and LiHCOO

 $NaHSO_4$ and Na_2SO_4 K_2CO_3 and $K_2C_2O_4$ HCl and NaCl KH_2PO_4 and K_2HPO_4

pH Change Resistance after the Addition of a Strong Acid to an Acidic Buffer

Let's use some of the above points as we discuss the chemistry of buffers in more detail.

We'll begin by using our acetic acid/acetate ion buffer as an example. First, we'll consider how the components of a buffer allow it to resist pH changes after the addition of a relatively small amount of either a strong acid or a strong base.

When a small amount of strong acid is added to a buffer, the reservoir of conjugate base (resulting from the added salt) reacts with the hydronium ions from the acid. In our example, this yields the following net ionic equation:

$$CH_3COO^-(aq) + H_3O^+(aq) \rightarrow CH_3COOH(aq) + H_2O(l)$$

 © Edvantage Interactive 2019

All of the hydronium ions from the strong acid are converted to the weak acid and water in the reaction. This increases the $[CH_3COOH]$ and decreases the $[CH_3COO^-]$ by a stoichiometric amount equal to the number of moles of hydronium ions added from the strong acid. The result is that the buffer component *ratio* increases, which increases the overall $[H_3O^+]$ but *only by a very small amount.*

Although a quantitative treatment of buffer chemistry will likely not be expected in this course, discussing some numbers will demonstrate how effective a buffer is at maintaining a relatively constant pH.

In our original buffer solution, the component ratio was equal to 1. Therefore, the $[H_3O^+]$ was equal to the K_a for acetic acid, namely 1.8×10^{-5} M. We now add 0.010 mol HCl to 1.0 L of our buffer solution containing 0.10 M CH_3COOH and 0.10 M CH_3COO^- with no volume change. The 0.010 mol H_3O^+ will be consumed according to the above reaction and therefore decrease the $[CH_3COO^-]$ by 0.010 mol/L and increase the $[CH_3COOH]$ by 0.010 mol/L. The result for our 1.0 L buffer solution will be as shown in Table 6.2.1.

Table 6.2.1 *Results of Adding 0.010 mol H_3O^+ to the Buffer Solution*

	$[CH_3COOH]$	$[CH_3COO^-]$	$[CH_3COOH]/[CH_3COO^-]$ Ratio
Before 0.010 M H_3O^+ added	0.10 M	0.10 M	0.10 M/0.10 M = 1.0
After 0.010 M H_3O^+ added	0.11 M	0.09 M	0.11 M/0.09 M = 1.222

The initial and final $[H_3O^+]$ are calculated below according to the equation:

$$[H_3O^+] = (K_a \text{ for acetic acid}) \times \frac{[CH_3COOH]}{[CH_3COO^-]}$$

Initial $[H_3O^+] = (1.8 \times 10^{-5}\text{ M}) \times (1.0) = \mathbf{1.8 \times 10^{-5}\ M}$ so $\text{pH} = -\log(1.8 \times 10^{-5}) = \mathbf{4.74}$

Final $[H_3O^+] = (1.8 \times 10^{-5}\text{ M}) \times (1.22) = \mathbf{2.20 \times 10^{-5}\ M}$ so $\text{pH} = -\log(2.196 \times 10^{-5}) = \mathbf{4.66}$

The pH has indeed decreased, but *only* by 0.08 units. To appreciate how effective this buffer is at maintaining the pH, consider the result of adding 0.010 mol HCl to 1.0 L of pure water. The $[H_3O^+]$ would increase from 1.0×10^{-7} M to 1.0×10^{-2} M. This represents a *100 000 times increase* in hydronium ion concentration and a *5 unit decrease* in pH from 7.00 to 2.00!

pH Change Resistance after the Addition of a Strong Base to a Buffer Solution

When a small amount of strong base is added to a buffer, the reservoir of weak acid reacts with the hydroxide ions from the base. For our example, this results in the following net ionic equation:

$$CH_3COOH(aq) + OH^-(aq) \rightarrow CH_3COO^-(aq) + H_2O(l)$$

All of the hydroxide ions from the strong base are converted to the conjugate base of the weak acid and water in the reaction. This decreases the $[CH_3COOH]$ and increases the $[CH_3COO^-]$ by a stoichiometric amount equal to the number of moles of hydroxide ions added from the strong base. The result is that the buffer component *ratio* decreases, which decreases the overall $[H_3O^+]$ but once again, *only by a very small amount.*

Using the same 1.0 L buffer solution containing 0.10 M CH_3COOH and 0.10 M CH_3COO^-, we add 0.010 mol NaOH with no volume change. The 0.010 mol OH^- will be consumed according to the above reaction and therefore decrease the $[CH_3COOH]$ by 0.010 mol/L and increase the $[CH_3COO^-]$ by 0.010 mol/L. The result for our 1.0 L buffer solution is shown in Table 6.2.2.

Table 6.2.2 *Results of Adding 0.010 mol OH^- to the Buffer Solution*

	$[CH_3COOH]$	$[CH_3COO^-]$	$[CH_3COOH]/[CH_3COO^-]$ Ratio
Before 0.010 M OH^- added	0.10 M	0.10 M	0.10 M/0.10 M = 1.0
After 0.010 M OH^- added	0.09 M	0.11 M	0.09 M/0.11 M = 0.82

We can once again calculate the final $[H_3O^+]$ by multiplying the K_a for acetic acid by the new reduced ratio:

Final $[H_3O^+] = (1.8 \times 10^{-5}\text{ M}) \times (0.82) = \mathbf{1.48 \times 10^{-5}\text{ M}}$ so final pH = $-\log(1.48 \times 10^{-5}) = \mathbf{4.83}$

The pH value has increased, but once again only slightly — by just 0.09 units. The effectiveness of this buffer at maintaining a relatively constant pH is again evident if we consider that adding 0.010 mol NaOH to 1.0 L of pure water would reduce the $[H_3O^+]$ from 1.0×10^{-7} M to 1.0×10^{-12} M. This represents a *100 000 times decrease* in hydronium ion concentration and a *5 unit increase* in pH from 7.00 to 12.00!

Figure 6.2.1 summarizes our examples above. Note the appropriate net ionic equation below each section of the diagram.

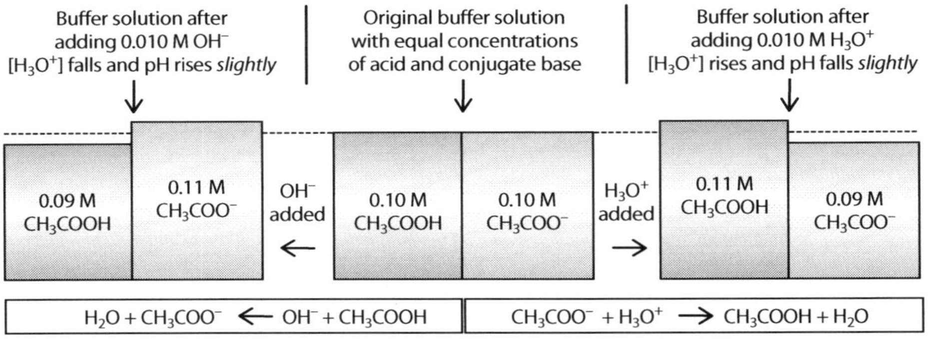

Figure 6.2.1 *The effects on pH of adding a strong base or a strong acid to an acidic buffer*

Sample Problem 6.2.1 — Acidic Buffers

Consider a 1.0 L buffer solution composed of 1.0 M HNO_2 and 1.0 M $NaNO_2$.

(a) Write the equation for the weak acid equilibrium in this solution and highlight the predominant species in that equilibrium.

(b) Write the net ionic equation for the reaction that occurs when a small amount of HCl is added to this solution.

(c) How will the $[HNO_2]/[NO_2^-]$ ratio, the $[H_3O^+]$, and the pH change following the addition of this acid? What equation do you use to make these decisions?

What to Think About

1. The concentrations of both HNO_2 and NO_2^- can be safely assumed to be ≈ 1.0 M, making these the major species.
2. The addition of a small amount of the strong acid HCl introduces H_3O^+ ions into the solution, which react with the nitrite anions to form HNO_2 and water.
3. This reduces the $[NO_2^-]$ and increases the $[HNO_2]$ increasing the concentration ratio of weak acid to conjugate base.

   This increases the $[H_3O^+]$ and lowers the pH slightly according to the equation given earlier.

How to Do It

(a) $HNO_2(aq) + H_2O(l) \rightleftharpoons NO_2^-(aq) + H_3O^+(aq)$

(b) $NO_2^-(aq) + H_3O^+(aq) \rightarrow HNO_2(aq) + H_2O(l)$

(c) The above equation means that the $[HNO_2]/[NO_2^-]$ ratio will increase. This causes the $[H_3O^+]$ to increase slightly and the pH to decrease slightly as per the following equation:

$$[H_3O^+] = (K_a \text{ for } HNO_2) \times \frac{[HNO_2]}{[NO_2^-]}$$

 © Edvantage Interactive 2019

Practice Problems 6.2.1 — Acidic Buffers

1. (a) Fill in the blanks in the statement below.
   Following the addition of a small amount of strong base to a buffer solution, the [HA]/[A^-] ratio _______________ (increases or decreases), the [H_3O^+] _______________ (increases or decreases) slightly, and the pH _______________ (increases or decreases) slightly.

   (b) Write the net ionic equation for the reaction occurring when a small amount of NaOH is added to the buffer solution discussed in the Sample Problem above.

   (c) How will the [HNO_2]/[NO_2^-] ratio, the [H_3O^+], and the pH of this solution change following the addition of this strong base?

2. (a) If 100.0 mL of the buffer solution discussed in the sample problem is diluted to 1.0 L, the pH will be the same as the original buffer solution. How many moles of HNO_2 and NO_2^- are available to neutralize added H_3O^+ and OH^- ions in 1.0 L of this diluted solution compared with 1.0 L of the undiluted buffer solution?

   (b) If 0.11 mol HCl is now added to each of these 1.0 L buffer solutions, would they be equally able to resist a significant change in their pH levels? Why or why not?

3. Determine if each of the following solutions qualifies as a buffer. Briefly explain your answer in each case.
   (a) 0.10 M HI/0.10 M NaI

   (b) 0.50 M NaF/0.50 M NaCN

   (c) 1.0 M $K_2C_2O_4$/1.0 M KHC_2O_4

   (d) 0.20 M HF/0.20 M HCN

Buffering a Solution in the Basic pH Region

We can also prepare a solution that buffers in the basic region of the pH scale. This is called a **basic buffer**. Although some minor differences exist, the chemistry associated with the maintenance of solution pH is very similar to the chemistry for an acidic buffer.

Consider 1.0 L of an aqueous solution of 0.10 M $NH_3(aq)$ and 0.10 M $NH_4Cl\ (aq)$. The equilibrium and predominant participating species can be represented as shown below:

$$\underset{\approx 0.10\ M}{\mathbf{NH_3}}(aq) + H_2O(l) \rightleftharpoons \underset{\approx 0.10\ M}{\mathbf{NH_4^+}}(aq) + OH^-(aq)$$

This solution has appreciable quantities of both a weak base and its conjugate acid in approximately equal amounts. (Note that the chloride ion from the salt is simply a spectator ion in this aqueous solution.) The buffer solution has the capacity to resist large pH changes equally well following the addition of relatively small amounts of both a strong acid and a strong base because significant (and approximately equal) reservoirs of *both* a weak base and a weak acid are available in the solution to neutralize those stresses.

In terms of the hydroxide concentration in a solution of this basic buffer, we can derive an equation similar to the one when we began with an acid ionization earlier. In our example:

Because: $K_b = \dfrac{[NH_4^+][OH^-]}{[NH_3]}$ then: $[OH^-] = K_b\dfrac{[NH_3]}{[NH_4^+]}$

Or in general for any buffer containing a weak base B: $\mathbf{[OH^-] = K_b\dfrac{[B]}{[HB^+]}}$

> The hydroxide ion concentration (and therefore the pH) of this buffer solution depends on two factors:
> - the K_b value for the weak base and
> - the *ratio* of the concentration of that weak base to its conjugate acid in the solution

Similar to an acidic buffer, the equation tells us that the hydroxide ion concentration and ultimately the pH of the solution depend on a constant and the ratio of the concentrations of a conjugate acid-base pair. The equation tells us that *if* the $[B]/[HB^+]$ ratio *increases*, the $[OH^-]$ *increases*, and *if* the $[B]/[HB^+]$ ratio *decreases*, the $[OH^-]$ *decreases*.

We can appreciate the effectiveness of this basic buffer by quantitatively investigating the results of adding a relatively small amount of both a strong acid and strong base to 1.0 L of the solution. We will add the same amount of each to the basic buffer as we did to the acidic buffer discussed earlier.

pH Change Resistance after the Addition of a Strong Acid

When a small amount of strong acid is added, the reservoir of weak base reacts with the hydronium ions from the acid. In our example, this yields the following net ionic equation:

$$NH_3(aq) + H_3O^+(aq) \rightarrow NH_4^+(aq) + H_2O(l)$$

All of the hydronium ions from the strong acid are converted to the conjugate acid of the weak base and water in the reaction. This increases the $[NH_4^+]$ and decreases the $[NH_3]$ by a stoichiometric amount equal to the number of moles of hydronium ions added from the strong acid. The result is that the buffer component *ratio* decreases, which decreases the overall $[OH^-]$ but *only by a very small amount*.

Assume that we add 0.010 mol HCl to this solution with no volume change. The 0.010 mol H_3O^+ will be consumed according to the above reaction. It will therefore decrease the $[NH_3]$ by 0.010 mol/L and increase the $[NH_4^+]$ by 0.010 mol/L. The result for our 1.0 L buffer solution is shown in Table 6.2.3

 © Edvantage Interactive 2019

Table 6.2.3 *Results of Adding 0.010 mol H_3O^+ to the Buffer Solution*

	$[NH_3]$	$[NH_4^+]$	$[NH_3]/[NH_4^+]$ Ratio
Before 0.010 M H_3O^+ added	0.10 M	0.10 M	0.10 M/0.10 M = 1.0
After 0.010 M H_3O^+ added	0.09 M	0.11 M	0.09 M/0.11 M = 0.82

The initial and final [OH⁻] along with the initial and final pH values are calculated below:

$$[OH^-] = (K_b \text{ for } NH_3) \times \frac{[NH_3]}{[NH_4^+]} \quad (\text{Remember: } K_b \text{ for } NH_3 = K_w / K_a \text{ for } NH_4^+)$$

Initial $[OH^-] = (1.8 \times 10^{-5}\text{ M}) \times (1.0) = \mathbf{1.8 \times 10^{-5}\ M}$

So initial $[H_3O^+] = \dfrac{1.00 \times 10^{-14}}{1.8 \times 10^{-5}} = \mathbf{5.6 \times 10^{-10}\ M}$ so initial pH = $-\log(5.6 \times 10^{-10}) = \mathbf{9.25}$

Final $[OH^-] = (1.8 \times 10^{-5}\text{ M}) \times (0.82) = \mathbf{1.48 \times 10^{-5}\ M}$

So final $[H_3O^+] = \dfrac{1.00 \times 10^{-14}}{1.48 \times 10^{-5}} = \mathbf{6.76 \times 10^{-10}\ M}$ so final pH = $-\log(6.76 \times 10^{-10}) = \mathbf{9.17}$

Contrast this minimal increase in hydronium concentration and corresponding minimal decrease in pH with the huge changes to both after the addition of 0.010 mol HCl to 1.0 L of pure water, discussed earlier in the section.

pH Change Resistance after the Addition of a Strong Base

When a small amount of strong base is added, the reservoir of the weak conjugate acid (from the added salt) reacts with the hydroxide ions from the base. For our example, this results in the following net ionic equation:

$NH_4^+(aq) + OH^-(aq) \rightarrow NH_3(aq) + H_2O(l)$

All of the hydroxide ions from the strong base are converted to the weak base and water in the reaction. This increases the $[NH_3]$ and decreases the $[NH_4^+]$ by a stoichiometric amount equal to the number of moles of hydroxide ions added from the strong base. The result is that the buffer component *ratio* increases, which increases the overall [OH⁻] once again by a very small amount.

Using the same 1.0 L basic buffer solution above, we add 0.010 mol NaOH with no volume change. The 0.010 mol OH^- will be consumed according to the above reaction. It will therefore increase the $[NH_3]$ by 0.010 mol/L and decrease the $[NH_4^+]$ by 0.010 mol/L. The result for our 1.0 L buffer solution is shown in Table 6.2.4.

Table 6.2.4 *Results of Adding 0.010 mol OH^- to the Buffer Solution*

	$[NH_3]$	$[NH_4^+]$	$[NH_3]/[NH_4^+]$ Ratio
Before 0.010 M OH^- added	0.10 M	0.10 M	0.10 M/0.10 M = 1.0
After 0.010 M OH^- added	0.11 M	0.09 M	0.11 M/0.09 M = 1.22

We can once again calculate the final [OH⁻] according to the following:

Final $[OH^-] = (1.8 \times 10^{-5}\text{ M}) \times (1.222) = \mathbf{2.20 \times 10^{-5}\ M}$

So final $[H_3O^+] = \dfrac{1.00 \times 10^{-14}}{2.20 \times 10^{-5}} = \mathbf{4.55 \times 10^{-10}\ M}$ and final pH = $-\log(4.55 \times 10^{-10}) = \mathbf{9.34}$

Obviously, if *less* than a 0.10 pH unit change occurs in our basic buffer solution after adding either 0.010 mol of strong acid or 0.010 mol of strong base, the buffer is extremely efficient at maintaining a reasonably constant pH compared to pure water.

Consider once again that the same maintenance of relatively constant pH occurs whether we discuss an acid ionization or a base ionization. Table 6.2.2 summarizes the changes we have just discussed for this basic buffer. Note again the appropriate net ionic equations beneath each section of the diagram.

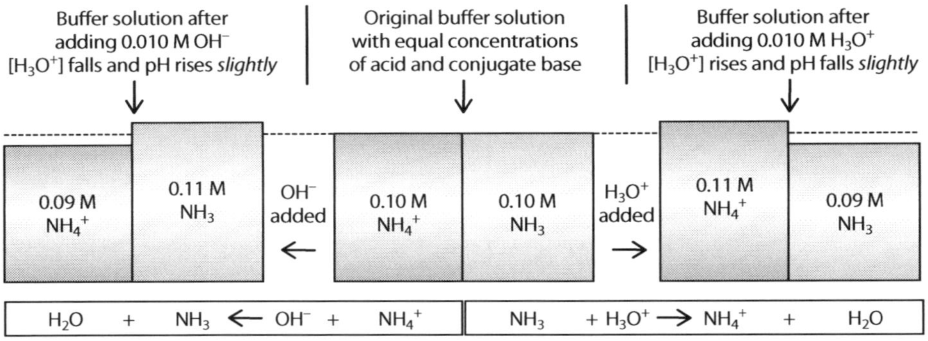

Figure 6.2.2 *The effects on pH of adding a strong base or a strong acid to a basic buffer*

Sample Problem 6.2.2 — Basic Buffers

1. Hydrazine, N_2H_4, is a weak base with a $K_b = 1.7 \times 10^{-6}$. What compound could you add to a 0.50 M solution of hydrazine to make a basic buffer solution?
2. Extension: If the concentration of that compound in the final solution were also 0.50 M, what $[H_3O^+]$ would exist in the buffer solution?

What to Think About

1. To make this solution a buffer, add a soluble salt of the conjugate acid of hydrazine.
2. If the concentration of that conjugate acid is also 0.50 M, then according to the equation discussed above, the hydroxide ion concentration in the solution is equal to the K_b for hydrazine. Calculate the hydronium concentration based on that.

How to Do It

The conjugate acid of N_2H_4 is $N_2H_5^+$. Therefore an appropriate compound to add to this solution would be N_2H_5Cl.

If the solution contained 0.50 M N_2H_4 and also 0.50 M N_2H_5Cl, then in the buffer solution:

$[OH^-] = K_b$ for $N_2H_4 = 1.7 \times 10^{-6}$ M

Thus: $[H_3O^+] = \dfrac{K_w}{[OH^-]} = \dfrac{100 \times 10^{-14}}{1.7 \times 10^{-6}} = 5.9 \times 10^{-9}$ M

Practice Problems 6.2.2 — Basic Buffers

1. Each of the following solutions contains a weak base. What compounds (in what concentrations ideally) would make each a buffer solution?

Weak Base	Added Compound
(a) 1.0 M CH_3NH_2	
(b) 0.80 M N_2H_4	
(c) 0.20 M $(CH_3)_2NH$	

2. Write the six net ionic equations representing the reactions occurring when a small amount of strong acid and also a small amount of strong base are added to each of the above basic buffer solutions.

Net Ionic Equation When Acid Added	Net Ionic Equation When Base Added
(a)	
(b)	
(c)	

© Edvantage Interactive 2019

The Henderson-Hasselbalch Equation

A very useful relationship for buffers can be derived from the equation we have discussed in this section, namely:

$$[H_3O^+] = K_a \times \frac{[HA]}{[A^-]}$$

Taking the negative logarithm of both sides of this equation yields:

$$-\log [H_3O^+] = -\log K_a + -\log\left[\frac{[HA]}{[A^-]}\right]$$

(Note the inversion of the ratio when the sign of the log is changed.)

From which we can obtain: $pH = pK_a + \log\left[\frac{[A^-]}{[HA]}\right]$

If we generalize the ratio for any conjugate acid-base pair, we write what is known as the **Henderson-Hasselbalch equation:**

$$\mathbf{pH = pK_a + \log\left[\frac{[base]}{[acid]}\right]}$$

Again, buffer calculations will not likely be required in this course, but any discussion of buffers should include some reference to this equation because, as we will see below, it represents a convenient tool for both analyzing and preparing buffer solutions.

The Capacity of a Buffer

The above equation reinforces that the pH of a given buffer is dependent only on the component ratio in the solution resulting from the relative concentrations of the conjugate base and weak acid. For example, a 0.010 M CH_3COO^-/0.010 M CH_3COOH buffer solution will have the same pH as a buffer solution containing 1.0 M CH_3COO^- and 1.0 M CH_3COOH. However, their ability to *resist changes* to those pH values will be different because that ability depends on the absolute concentrations of their buffer components. The former solution can neutralize only a small amount of acid or base before its pH changes significantly. The latter can withstand the addition of much more acid or base before a significant change in its pH occurs.

Buffer capacity is defined as the amount of acid or base a buffer can neutralize before its pH changes significantly.

A more concentrated or *high-capacity* buffer will experience less of a pH change following the addition of a given amount of strong acid or strong base than a less concentrated or *low-capacity* buffer will. Stated another way, to cause the same pH change, more strong acid or strong base must be added to a high-capacity buffer than to a low-capacity buffer.

Following the addition of an equal amount of H_3O^+ or OH^- ions, the $[A^-]/[HA]$ ratio (and hence the pH) changes more for a solution of a low-capacity buffer than for a high-capacity buffer.

Preparation of a Buffer

The buffer solutions we have discussed in this section contain equal concentrations of conjugate acid-base pairs. There is a reason for that. The Henderson-Hasselbalch equation clearly shows that the more the component ratio changes, the more the solution pH changes. In addition, simple calculations with the same equation show that the more similar the component concentrations are to each other (the closer the $[A^-]/[HA]$ ratio is to 1) in a buffer solution, the less that ratio changes after the addition of a given amount of strong acid or strong base. Conversely, a buffer solution whose component concentrations are very different will experience a greater change in pH following the addition of the same amount of H_3O^+ or OH^- ions. Practically speaking, if the $[A^-]/[HA]$ ratio is less than 0.1 or greater than 10, the buffer can no longer maintain its pH level when a small amount of strong acid or base is added. This means that a buffer is effective only if the following condition is met:

$$10 \geq \frac{[\mathbf{A^-}]}{[\mathbf{HA}]} \geq 0.1$$

As a result, when we prepare a buffer, we attempt to find a weak acid whose pK_a is as close as possible to the desired pH so that the component ratio is within the desired range and ideally as close as possible to 1.

More on Buffer Preparation

Preparations of buffer solutions for biological and environmental purposes are a common task for researchers and laboratory technicians. The Henderson-Hasselbalch equation and the above rules are routinely employed in the process. The desired pH of the solution usually dictates the choice of the conjugate acid-base pair. Because a buffer is *most effective* when the component concentration ratio is *closest to 1*, the *best weak acid* will be the one whose pK_a is *closest* to that target pH value. Once that acid is chosen, the Henderson-Hasselbalch equation is used to choose the appropriate ratio of $[A^-]/[HA]$ that achieves the desired pH. As mentioned at the beginning of this section, the equilibrium and initial concentrations of the buffer components are almost the same. This allows the equation to yield the following:

$$\text{Desired pH} = pK_a + \log\left[\frac{[A^-]_{\text{initial}}}{[HA]_{\text{initial}}}\right]$$

When the actual concentrations are chosen, the fact that higher concentrations make better buffers means that low concentrations are normally avoided. For most applications, concentrations between 0.05 M and 0.5 M are sufficient. The Sample Problem below is offered for demonstration purposes only.

Sample Problem 6.2.3 — Preparing a Buffer

An environmental chemist requires a solution buffered to pH 5.00 to study the effects of acid rain on aquatic microorganisms. Decide on the most appropriate buffer components and suggest their appropriate relative concentrations.

What to Think About	How to Do It
1. Choose an acid whose pK_a value is close to 5.00. The sodium salt of its conjugate base will then be the second buffer component.	The K_a for acetic acid $= 1.8 \times 10^{-5}$. This corresponds to a $pK_a = 4.74$. Therefore this buffer solution can be prepared from acetic acid and sodium acetate. According to the Henderson-Hasselbalch equation, $pH = 5.00 = 4.74 + \log\left[\frac{[CH_3COO^-]_{initial}}{[CH_3COOH]_{initial}}\right]$
2. Determine the proper $[A^-]/[HA]$ ratio according to the Henderson-Hasselbalch equation to obtain the desired buffer pH.	so $\log\left[\frac{[CH_3COO^-]_{initial}}{[CH_3COOH]_{initial}}\right] = 0.26$ and thus $\left[\frac{[CH_3COO^-]_{initial}}{[CH_3COOH]_{initial}}\right] = 10^{0.26} = 1.8$ A ratio of 1.8 to 1.0 could be accomplished with many combinations. For example: 1.8 M and 1.0 M, 0.18 M and 0.10 M, and 0.90 M and 0.50 M are all correct concentrations for CH_3COO^- and CH_3COOH respectively in this buffer. The choice depends on the required capacity of the buffer.

© Edvantage Interactive 2019

Practice Problems 6.2.3 — Buffer Capacity and Preparation

1. Rank the following four buffer solutions (by letter) in order from lowest to highest capacity.
   (a) 0.48 M HF and 0.50 M NaF
   (b) 0.040 M HCOOH and 0.060 M KHCOO
   (c) 1.0 M CH_3COOH and 1.0 M $LiCH_3COO$
   (d) 0.10 M H_2S and 0.095 M NaHS

   ______ < ______ < ______ < ______

2. *Buffer range* is the pH range over which a buffer acts effectively. Given that the $[A^-]/[HA]$ ratio should be no less than 0.1 and no more than 10 for a buffer to be effective, use the Henderson-Hasselbalch equation to determine how far away the pH of a buffer solution can be (+ or –) from the pK_a of the weak acid component before that buffer becomes ineffective. Your answer represents the normally accepted range of a buffer.

3. Prior to being used to measure the pH of a solution, pH meters are often calibrated with solutions buffered to pH = 7.00 and also pH = 4.00 or pH = 10.00. Use the table of relative strengths of acids and bases (Table A5) and the Henderson-Hasselbalch equation to select three appropriate conjugate acid-base pairs that could be used to prepare these buffer solutions and complete the table below.

Desired pH	Weak Acid	Weak Acid pK_a	Salt of Conjugate Base
4.00			
7.00			
10.00			

The Maintenance of Blood pH

Two of the most important functions of your blood are to transport oxygen and nutrients to all of the cells in your body and also to remove carbon dioxide and other waste materials from them.

This essential and complex system could not operate without several buffer systems.

The two main components of blood are blood plasma, the straw-colored liquid component of blood, and red blood cells, or *erythrocytes*. Erythrocytes contain a complex protein molecule called hemoglobin, which is the molecule that transports oxygen in your blood. Hemoglobin (which we will represent as HHb) functions effectively as a weak monoprotic acid according to the following equilibrium:

$$\underset{\text{hemoglobin}}{HHb(aq)} + O_2(aq) + H_2O(l) \rightleftharpoons \underset{\text{oxyhemoglobin}}{HbO_2^-(aq)} + H_3O^+(aq)$$

The system functions properly when oxygen binds to hemoglobin producing oxyhemoglobin. That oxygen is eventually released to diffuse out of the red blood cells to be absorbed by other cells to carry out metabolism. For this to occur properly, several buffer systems maintain the pH of the blood at about 7.35.

If the $[H_3O^+]$ is too low (pH greater than about 7.50), then the equilibrium shown above shifts so far to the right that the $[HbO_2^-]$ is too high to allow for adequate release of O_2. This is called *alkalosis*.

If the $[H_3O^+]$ is too high (pH lower than about 7.20), then the equilibrium shifts far enough to the left that the $[HbO_2^-]$ is too low. The result is that the hemoglobin's affinity for oxygen is so reduced that the molecules won't bind together. This is called *acidosis*.

The most important buffer system managing blood pH involves H_2CO_3 and HCO_3^-. $CO_2(aq)$

produced during metabolic processes such as respiration is converted in the blood to H_2CO_3 by an enzyme called carbonic anhydraze. The carbonic acid then rapidly decomposes to bicarbonate and hydrogen ions. We can represent the process in the equation shown below:

$$CO_2(aq) + H_2O(l) \rightleftharpoons H_2CO_3(aq) \rightleftharpoons HCO_3^-(aq) + H^+(aq)$$

We can clearly see the buffer components in the above equilibrium system. For example, any addition of hydrogen ions will reduce the $[HCO_3^-]/[H_2CO_3]$ ratio and lower the pH only slightly. Coupled with the above system is the body's remarkable ability to alter its breathing to modify the concentration of dissolved CO_2. In the above example, rapid breathing would increase the loss of CO_2 to the atmosphere in the form of gaseous CO_2. This would then lower the concentration of $CO_2(aq)$ and further help to remove any added H^+ by driving the above equilibrium to the left.

Quick Check

1. Another buffer system present in blood and in other cells is the $H_2PO_4^-/HPO_4^{2-}$ buffer system.
   (a) Write the net ionic equation representing the result of adding hydronium ions to a solution containing this buffer system.

   (b) Write the net ionic equation representing the result of adding hydroxide ions to a solution containing this buffer system.

2. People under severe stress will sometimes hyperventilate, which involves rapid inhaling and exhaling. This can lower the $[CO_2]$ in the blood so much that a person may lose consciousness.
   (a) Consider the above equilibrium and suggest the effect of hyperventilating on blood pH if the concentration of carbon dioxide is too low.

   (b) Why might breathing into a paper bag reduce the effects of hyperventilation?

© Edvantage Interactive 2019

6.2 Activity: Over-The-Counter Buffer Chemistry

Question

What kinds of buffers are used in over-the-counter medicines?

Background

Many common over-the-counter medicines employ chemical principles that you are learning about. One of the most common and effective pain relievers or "analgesics" is the weak acid acetylsalicylic acid (ASA), $C_8H_7O_2COOH$. This product is marketed under various brands but the best-known one is Aspirin by the Bayer Corporation. (*Note that anyone under the age of 18 should not use ASA as children may develop Reye's syndrome, a potentially fatal disease that may occur with ASA use in treating flu or chickenpox.*)

One form of the product contains a "buffering agent" because some people are sensitive to the acidity level of this medication. That same "buffering agent" is used in several antacid remedies to neutralize excess stomach acid (HCl).

Procedure

1. Consider the advertisement shown here and answer the questions below.
   (a) Identify the ion in the compound listed on the box that acts as the "acid neutralizer" and buffers the ASA.

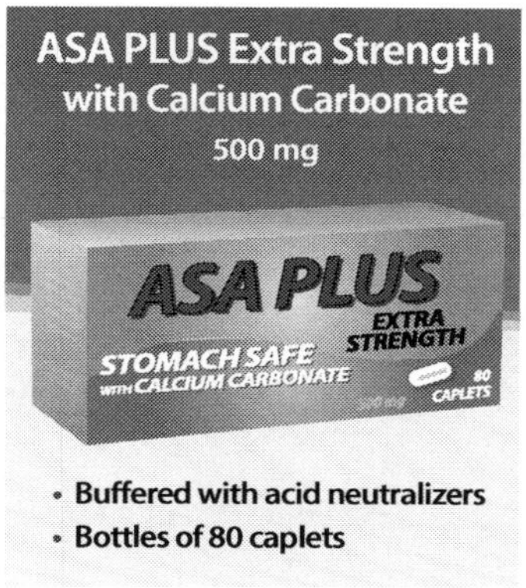

   (b) Write the net ionic equation corresponding to the reaction involving the "acid neutralizer" reacting with a small amount of strong acid.

   (c) Write the net ionic equation corresponding to the reaction occurring when a small amount of strong base is added to a relatively concentrated solution of ASA.

   (d) Consider the above net ionic equations and decide if a solution containing significant quantities of ASA and the ion identified as the acid neutralizer in question 1 would function well as a buffer solution? Why or why not?

2. Consider the antacid label shown here and note that the active ingredient is the same compound used to buffer the ASA above.

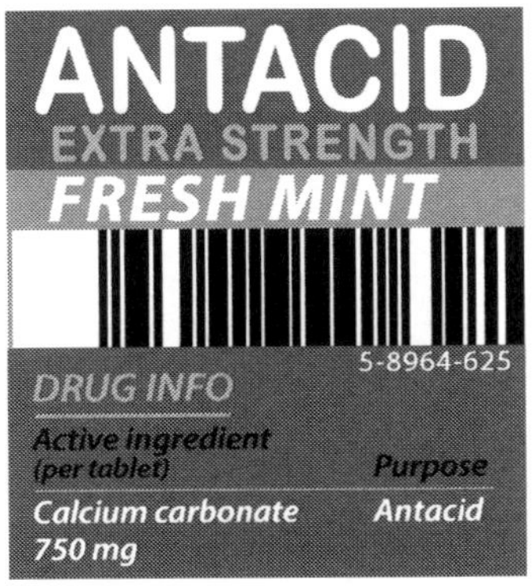

(a) Determine the pH of a buffer solution containing a 0.10 M solution of both the anion in the compound listed on the label and its conjugate acid.

(b) Would this solution be considered an acidic or a basic buffer?

3. Next time you're in a pharmacy, locate other antacid or "buffered" products on the shelves. Read the labels to determine if the active ingredient is the same or different than in the products listed here. If different, think about the chemistry associated with that ingredient and try to figure out how it works. (Thinking about the chemistry you encounter every day is *always* a good idea!)

 © **Edvantage Interactive 2019**

6.2 Review Questions

1. What is the purpose of an acid-base buffer?

2. Why do you think that the components of a buffer solution are normally a conjugate acid-base pair rather than any combination of a weak acid and a weak base?

3. Explain why a solution of 0.10 M HNO_3 and 0.10 M $NaNO_3$ cannot function as a buffer solution.

4. Each of the following compound pairs exists at a concentration 0.50 M in their respective solutions. Circle the solutions that represent buffers:

   Na_2CO_3/KOH $NaCl/HCl$ C_6H_5COOH/KC_6H_5COO HNO_3/KNO_2

   N_2H_4/NH_3 $CH_3NH_3NO_3/CH_3NH_2$ $K_2SO_3/KHSO_3$ CH_3COOH/HI

   $HBr/NaOH$ KIO_3/HIO_3 $NaHS/H_2S$ HF/LiF $H_2O_2/RbHO_2$

5. Consider a buffer solution containing 0.30 M HCN and 0.30 M NaCN.
   (a) Without performing any calculations, state the $[H_3O^+]$ in the solution.

   (b) Is this solution considered to be an acidic or a basic buffer? Why?

   (c) Write the net ionic equation for the reaction occurring when a small amount of HCl is added to the solution. What happens to the pH of the solution after the HCl is added?

   (d) Write the net ionic equation for the reaction occurring when a small amount of NaOH is added to the solution. What happens to the pH of the solution after the NaOH is added?

6. Complete the following table for a buffer solution containing equal concentrations of HA and A^- when a small amount of strong acid is added and when a small amount of strong base is added.

Stress Applied	Net Ionic Equation	How $[HA]/[A^-]$ Changes	How pH Changes
H_3O^+ added			
OH^- added			

7. Without performing any calculations, consult the table of K_a values (Table A5) and arrange the following buffer solutions (by letter) in order from lowest $[H_3O^+]$ to highest $[H_3O^+]$:
(a) 1.0 M H_2S/1.0 M NaHS
(b) 0.50 M HCN/0.50 M KCN
(c) 0.25 M $NaHC_2O_4$/0.25 M $Na_2C_2O_4$
(d) 2.0 M HCOOH/2.0 M LiHCOO

_________ < _________ < _________ < _________

8. What is meant by the term *buffer capacity* and what does it depend upon? Which of the buffer solutions listed in question 7 above would have the highest capacity?

9. List the following four buffer solutions (by letter) in order from highest to lowest capacity.
(a) 0.010 M KNO_2/0.010 M HNO_2
(b) 0.10 M CH_3COOH/0.10 M $NaCH_3COO$
(c) 0.0010 M NH_3/0.0010 M NH_4Cl
(d) 1.0 M HF/1.0 M NaF

_________ > _________ > _________ > _________

10. What is meant by the term *buffer range*? How is it related to the pK_a value for the weak acid component of a buffer solution?

11. Describe the effect of lowering the $[CO_2]$ in blood on the pH of the blood.

© Edvantage Interactive 2019

12. Describe the effect of *alkalosis* on the ability of hemoglobin to transport oxygen.

13. Describe the effect of *acidosis* on the ability of hemoglobin to transport oxygen.

14. **Challenge:** Consider carefully the components of a buffer solution and decide if a buffer solution could be *prepared* from 1.0 L of 1.0 M HNO_2 and sufficient NaOH? If so, how?

15. Use the Henderson-Hasselbalch equation to calculate the pH of each of the buffers mentioned in question 9 above.

16. Use the Henderson-Hasselbalch equation to answer the following:
    (a) A student requires a solution buffered to pH = 10.00 to study the effects of detergent runoff into aquatic ecosystems. She has just prepared a 1.0 L solution of 0.20 M $NaHCO_3$. What mass of Na_2CO_3 must be added to this solution to complete the buffer preparation? Assume no volume change.

    (b) Calculate the pH of this buffer solution following the addition of 0.0010 mol HCl.

17. Calculate the pH of the following buffer solutions:
   (a) 75.0 mL of 0.200 mol/L CH_3COOH mixed with 75.0 mL of 0.300 mol/L $NaCH_3COO$

   (b) 300. mL of 0.100 mol/L NH_3 combined with 200. mL of 0.200 mol/L NH_4Cl

18. A buffer solution contains 0.400 mol/L of CH_3COOH and 0.400 mol/L of $NaCH_3COO$. What is the pH of the buffer under the following conditions?
   (a) Before any acid or base is added

   (b) After adding 0.050 mol of HCl to 1.00 L of the buffer. Assume the total volume remains constant.

   (c) After adding 0.050 mol of NaOH to 1.00 L of the buffer. Assume the total volume remains constant.

© Edvantage Interactive 2019

19. A solution contains 0.0375 mol of HCOOH and 0.0325 mol of NaHCOO in a total volume of 1.00 L. Determine the pH following the addition of 0.0100 mol of HCl with no significant change in volume.

20. What ratio of [NaF]/[HF] is required to produce a buffer with a pH of 4.25?

21. How many grams of NH_4Br must be added to 0.500 mol of NH_3 to produce 1.00 L of buffer with a pH of 9.05?

22. (a) What is the pH of 1.00 L of buffer containing 0.180 mol of CH_3COOH and 0.200 mol of $NaCH_3C$

(b) How many moles of HCl must be added to this buffer to change the pH to:

(i) 4.600

(ii) 0.900

(c) The purpose of a buffer is to maintain a relatively constant pH when strong acids or bases are added. What caused the large drop in pH in (b)(ii)?

6.3 Acid-Base Titrations — Analyzing with Volume

Warm Up

1. What is the typical purpose of a titration?

____

2. Determine the pH of the following solutions:

0.10 M HCl	0.10 M HCN

3. Assume that 25.0 mL of each of the above solutions is reacted with a 0.10 M NaOH solution. How will the volume of the NaOH solution required to neutralize the HCl compare with that required to neutralize the HCN?

____

Criteria for Titration

Titrations are among the most important of all the analytical procedures that chemists use. A titration is a form of volumetric analysis. During a titration, the number of moles of solute in a solution is determined by adding a sufficient volume of another solution of known concentration to *just produce a complete reaction*. Once determined, that number of moles can then be used to calculate other values such as concentration, molar mass, or percent purity.

Any reaction being considered for a titration must satisfy three criteria:

1. Only one reaction can occur between the solutes contained in the two solutions.
2. The reaction between those solutes must go rapidly to completion.
3. There must be a way of signaling the point at which the complete reaction has been achieved in the reaction vessel. This is called the **equivalence point** or **stoichiometric point** of the titration.

The equivalence point in an acid-base titration occurs in the reaction vessel when the total number of moles of H_3O^+ from the acid equals the total number of moles of OH^- from the base.

To ensure that the reaction between the acid and the base goes to completion, at least one of the two reacting species must be strong. A complete reaction means that *the volume of added solution required to reach the equivalence point depends only on the moles of the acid and base present and the stoichiometry of the reaction*. Prior to the titration, a small amount of an appropriate chemical indicator is added to the reaction vessel containing the solution being analyzed. The correct indicator is one that will undergo a color change *at or very near* the pH associated with the equivalence point. This color change signals when the titration should stop. A pH meter used to monitor the pH of the reaction mixture during the course of a titration will also indicate when the equivalence point has been reached.

 © Edvantage Interactive 2019

Titration Accuracy

Recall that quantitative analytical procedures such as titrations require precise instruments and careful measurements to ensure the accuracy of the results. Let's review the equipment and procedures associated with a titration. Figure 6.3.1 shows the apparatus used for a typical titration.

A precise volume of the solution to be analyzed is drawn into a volumetric pipette and transferred into an Erlenmeyer (conical) flask. The shape of the flask allows for swirling of the reaction mixture during the course of the titration without loss of contents. A small amount of an appropriate indicator is then added to this solution. The flask is placed under a burette containing the solution of known concentration called a **standard** or **standardized solution**. The solution in the burette is referred to as the *titrant* and the solution in the flask is called the *analyte*. Normally, the approximate concentration of the analyte is known, which allows a titrant of similar concentration to be prepared. If the titrant is too concentrated, then only a few drops might be required to reach the equivalence point. If the titrant is too dilute, then the volume present in the burette may not be enough to reach the equivalence point.

The standard solution is carefully added to the solution in the flask until the first permanent color change just appears in the indicator. This is called the **transition point** or **endpoint** of the indicator. It should signal when the equivalence point in the titration has been reached.

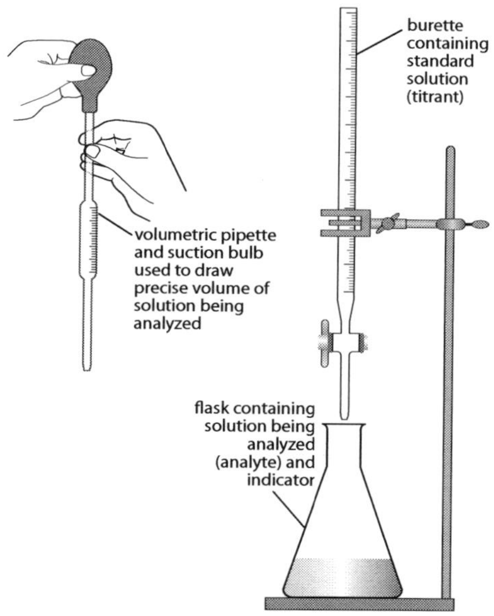

Figure 6.3.1 *Titration apparatus*

> The transition point is the point in a titration at which the indicator changes color.

At the transition point, the valve on the burette is closed to stop the titration and the volume of standard solution added from the burette is determined.

It is important to remember that *the pH at the transition point is dependent only on the chemical nature of the indicator* and is independent of the equivalence point. The *pH at the equivalence point is dependent only on the chemical nature of the reacting species*. As mentioned above, the pH at which the endpoint occurs should be as close as possible to the pH of the solution at the equivalence point.

A titration should always be repeated as an accuracy check. Incomplete mixing of solutions, incorrect pipetting techniques, or errors made when reading burettes can contribute to inaccuracies in the data collected, particularly for beginning students.

Those experienced at performing titrations normally expect that the volumes added from the burette in each trial should agree with each other within 0.02 mL (less than a drop). Students performing titrations for the first time should expect agreement within 0.1 mL.

If the volumes delivered from the burette in the first two trials do not agree within the desired uncertainty, then the titration must be repeated until they do. Once agreement between two trials occurs, the volumes added in those trials are averaged, and the other data is discarded. For example, consider Table 6.3.1, which lists the volumes of standard solution required to reach the equivalence point in three separate titration trials.

Table 6.3.1 *Volumes of Standard Solution Required for Equivalence Points*

Titration Trial	Volume of Std. Solution
1	21.36 mL
2	21.19 mL
3	21.21 mL

Note that a third trial was required because the first two volumes differed by 0.17 mL, which is beyond the range of acceptable agreement. The volume recorded for trial 3 agrees well with that of trial 2 and so those two volumes are averaged to obtain the correct volume of standard solution, while the data from trial 1 is discarded. (It is common to overshoot a titration on the first trial.)

$$\text{Average volume of standard solution} = \frac{21.19\text{ mL} + 21.21\text{ mL}}{2} = 21.20\text{ mL}$$

Quick Check

1. What ensures that an acid-base titration goes to completion?

____

2. Distinguish between an endpoint and an equivalence point in an acid-base titration.

____

____

3. A student performing a titration for the first time lists the volumes of standard solution required to reach the equivalence point in three separate titration trials.

Titration Trial	Volume of Std. Solution
1	23.88 mL
2	23.67 mL
3	23.59 mL

What is the correct volume of standard solution that should be recorded by the student?

____

Standard Solutions

A successful titration requires that the concentration of the standard solution be very accurately known. There are two ways to obtain a standard solution.

1. A standard solution can be prepared if the solute is a stable, non-deliquescent, soluble compound available in a highly pure form. Such a compound is known as a **primary standard.**
   - Two examples of **acidic primary standards** are:
   (a) potassium hydrogen phthalate, $KHC_8H_4O_4$, a monoprotic acid often abbreviated as simply KHP.
   (b) oxalic acid dihydrate, $H_2C_2O_4 \cdot 2\,H_2O$, a diprotic acid.
   - A common example of a **basic primary standard** is anhydrous sodium carbonate, Na_2CO_3, which will accept two protons in a reaction with an acid.
   - Each of the above stable, pure compounds can be used to prepare a standard solution whose concentration can be accurately known directly.

2. If the solute is not available in a highly pure form and/or readily undergoes reaction with, for example, atmospheric water vapor or carbon dioxide, then the solution must be *standardized* to accurately determine its concentration before it can be used in a titration. This is accomplished by titrating the solution in question against a primary standard. For example, a solution of the strong base sodium hydroxide is often used as a standard solution in a titration. However, solid NaOH rapidly absorbs water vapor from the air. Both solid and aqueous NaOH readily react with

© Edvantage Interactive 2019

atmospheric CO_2 as shown in the equation below:

$$2\ NaOH + CO_2 \rightarrow Na_2CO_3 + H_2O$$

This means that before a solution of NaOH can be used as a standard solution in a titration, its concentration must first be accurately determined by titrating it against an acidic primary standard such as KHP or $H_2C_2O_4 \cdot 2\ H_2O$. For each titration, phenolphthalein is a suitable indicator. KHP reacts with NaOH as shown in this equation:

$$KHC_8H_4O_4(aq) + NaOH(aq) \rightarrow NaKC_8H_4O_4(aq) + H_2O(l)$$

Oxalic acid dihydrate reacts with sodium hydroxide in a 2:1 mole ratio:

$$H_2C_2O_4(aq) + 2\ NaOH(aq) \rightarrow Na_2C_2O_4(aq) + 2\ H_2O(l)$$

For example, if KHP is used to standardize the NaOH solution, a precise mass of KHP (usually sufficient to prepare a 0.1000 M solution), is dissolved in water, transferred into a volumetric flask, and diluted to the required volume. A volumetric pipette is then used to transfer a precise volume to an Erlenmeyer flask into which a few drops of phenolphthalein indicator are added. The NaOH solution to be standardized is then gradually added from a burette into the acid solution. At the equivalence point, all of the KHP in the flask has been neutralized and so the next drop of NaOH solution added makes the reaction mixture basic enough to cause the indicator to turn pink. The volume of the NaOH solution required in the titration allows for the accurate determination of its concentration. Once that concentration is known, the standardized NaOH solution can then be added to an acid solution in a titration procedure.

To standardize an acidic solution, a titration against a basic primary standard such as Na_2CO_3 is performed. Appropriate indicators for this reaction would be either bromcresol green or methyl red. In a reaction with a monoprotic acid such as HCl, the carbonate anion will react in a 2:1 mole ratio:

$$Na_2CO_3(aq) + 2\ HCl(aq) \rightarrow 2\ NaCl(aq) + CO_2(g) + H_2O(l)$$

When standardizing a solution, its *approximate* concentration is often known. Because the concentration of the other solution is known, the approximate volume required of the solution being standardized in the titration can be estimated before the procedure.

Quick Check

1. Is a 4.00 g sample of NaOH likely to contain 0.100 mol of this compound? Why or why not?

   ____

2. Which piece of equipment and/or procedure employed during a titration ensures the following:
   (a) Accurate and precise measurement of the volume of the solution being analyzed in the reaction flask

   ____

   (b) Accurate and precise determination of the concentration of the titrant

   ____

   (c) Accurate and precise measurement of the volume of titrant required in the titration

   ____

   (d) Correct determination of the equivalence point during the titration

   ____

Sample Problem 6.3.1 — Standardizing a Solution

A student standardizing a solution of NaOH finds that 28.15 mL of that solution is required to neutralize 25.00 mL of a 0.1072 M standard solution of KHP. Calculate the [NaOH].

What to Think About	How to Do It
1. To solve titration problems, begin with writing the balanced equation for the reaction. The mole ratio in the balanced equation is 1 mol NaOH : 1 mol KHP	$KHC_8H_4O_4 + NaOH \rightarrow NaKC_8H_4O_4 + H_2O$ mol KHP = 0.02500 ~~L~~ × 0.1072 $\frac{\text{mol KHP}}{\text{~~L~~}}$ = 0.002680 mol mol NaOH = mol KHP = 0.002680 mol
2. The [NaOH] should be slightly less than 0.107**2** M because the volume of NaOH solution required in the titration is greater than 25.00 mL.	$[NaOH] = \frac{0.002680 \text{ mol NaOH}}{0.02815 \text{ L}} = 0.09520 \text{ M}$ (4 sig. figures)
	Look at the above solution. Can you identify *three steps* in the solution process?

Practice Problems 6.3.1 — Standardizing a Solution

1. If 21.56 mL of a NaOH solution is required to neutralize 25.00 mL of a 0.0521 M standard oxalic acid solution, calculate the [NaOH].

2. A 1.546 g sample of pure anhydrous sodium carbonate is diluted to 250.0 mL in a volumetric flask. A 25.00 mL aliquot of this standard solution required 23.17 mL of a nitric acid solution to be neutralized. Calculate the $[HNO_3]$.

Common Titration Calculations

The majority of titration calculations you will be expected to perform in this course involve determining a solution concentration, solution volume, molar mass, or percent purity.

Regardless of which acid or base is involved, *the total number of moles of H^+ from the acid equals the total number of moles of OH^- from the base at the equivalence point*. Therefore, for any type of titration problem you are solving, it is *strongly suggested* that you begin by writing the balanced chemical equation for the titration reaction if it isn't provided.

- The first step in the calculation process normally involves using the data provided to determine the number of moles of one of the reactant species used.
- The second step uses the moles determined in the first step and the mole ratio in the balanced equation to determine the moles of the second reactant consumed.
- The third step uses the moles calculated in step 2 to determine a solution concentration, solution volume, molar mass, or percent purity.

© Edvantage Interactive 2019

Because a titration represents a quantitative analytical procedure, accuracy and precision are paramount. This means that you must pay particular attention to significant figures when performing titration calculations.

Calculating Solution Concentration

This represents the most common type of titration calculation you will encounter in this course. If you look again at Sample Problem 6.3.1 above for standardizing a solution, you will recognize this problem type and the application of the above steps to solve it.

Sample Problem 6.3.2 — Calculating Solution Concentration

A 25.0 mL sample of H_2SO_4 requires 46.23 mL of a standard 0.203 M NaOH solution to reach the equivalence point. Calculate the $[H_2SO_4]$.

What to Think About	How to Do It
1. The balanced equation shows a 2:1 mole ratio between the reacting species.	$2\ NaOH(aq) + H_2SO_4(aq) \rightarrow Na_2SO_4(aq) + 2\ H_2O(l)$ $\text{mol NaOH} = 0.04623\ \cancel{L} \times \frac{0.203\ \text{mol}}{\cancel{L}} = 0.009385\ \text{mol}$
2. Ensure that your final answer has three significant figures.	$\text{mol } H_2SO_4 = 0.009385\ \cancel{\text{mol NaOH}} \times \frac{1\ \text{mol } H_2SO_4}{2\ \cancel{\text{mol NaOH}}}$ $= 0.004692\ \text{mol } H_2SO_4$
3. As molarity × mL = millimoles, solve the question using mol and L, *or* mmol and mL.	$[H_2SO_4] = \frac{0.004692\ \text{mol } H_2SO_4}{0.0250\ \text{L}} = 0.188\ \text{M}$ (3 sig. figures)
4. A solution using each set of units is shown on the right.	*Alternatively:* $\text{mmol NaOH} = 46.23\ \cancel{\text{mL}} \times \frac{0.203\ \text{mmol}}{\cancel{\text{mL}}} = 9.385\ \text{mmol}$ $\text{mmol } H_2SO_4 = 9.385\ \cancel{\text{mmol NaOH}} \times \frac{1\ \text{mmol } H_2SO_4}{2\ \cancel{\text{mmol NaOH}}}$ $= 4.692\ \text{mmol } H_2SO_4$ $[H_2SO_4] = \frac{4.692\ \text{mmol } H_2SO_4}{25.0\ \text{mL}} = 0.188\ \text{M}$

Practice Problems 6.3.2 — Calculating Solution Concentration

1. The equivalence point in a titration is reached when 25.64 mL of a 0.1175 M KOH solution is added to a 50.0 mL solution of acetic acid. Calculate the concentration of the acetic acid.

Continued on next page

Practice Problems 6.3.2 *(Continued)*

2. Lactic acid, C_2H_5OCOOH, is found in sour milk, yogurt, and cottage cheese. It is also responsible for the flavor of sourdough breads. Three separate trials, each using 25.0 mL samples of lactic acid, are performed using a standardized 0.153 M NaOH solution. Consider the following table listing the volume of basic solution required to reach the equivalence point for each trial.

Titration Trial	Volume of NaOH Solution
1	33.42 mL
2	33.61 mL
3	33.59 mL

Calculate the concentration of the lactic acid.

3. Methylamine, CH_3NH_2, is found in herring brine solutions, used in the manufacture of some pesticides, and serves as a solvent for many organic compounds. A titration is performed to determine the concentration of methylamine present in a solution being prepared for a commercial pesticide. A 0.185 M HCl solution is added to 50.0 mL samples of aqueous methylamine in three separate titration trials. The data table below shows the results.

Titration Trial	Burette Readings	
	Initial Volume	Final Volume
1	20.14 mL	47.65 mL
2	9.55 mL	36.88 mL
3	15.84 mL	43.11 mL

Calculate the concentration of the methylamine solution.

Calculating Solution Volume

If you are asked to calculate a solution volume from titration data, you will probably be given the concentrations of both the acid and the base solutions. If you aren't given the concentrations directly, you will be given enough information to calculate them. The final step in the solution process involves converting the moles of reactant determined in the second step into a volume using the appropriate concentration value.

It is important to remember that because *the reaction goes to completion*, the volume of standard solution required in a titration is only dependent on the stoichiometry of the reaction and the moles of the species (acid or base) that it must neutralize. *It does not depend on the strength of those species.*

Review your answer to Warm Up question 3. The volume of standard NaOH solution required to neutralize 25.0 mL of 0.10 M HCl will be *the same* as that required to neutralize 25.0 mL of 0.10 M HCN.

© Edvantage Interactive 2019

Sample Problem 6.3.3 — Calculating Solution Volume

What volume of a standard $Sr(OH)_2$ solution with a pH of 13.500 is needed to neutralize a 25.0 mL solution of 0.423 M HCl?

What to Think About	How to Do It
1. The pH allows the concentration of the basic solution to be calculated. 2. The balanced equation shows a 2:1 mole ratio between the reacting species. 3. Express the final answer to three significant figures.	$2\ HCl(aq) + Sr(OH)_2(aq) \rightarrow SrCl_2(aq) + 2\ H_2O(l)$ $\text{mmol HCl reacting} = 25.0\ \cancel{mL} \times \frac{0.423\ \text{mmol HCl}}{\cancel{mL}}$ $= 10.58\ \text{mmol HCl}$ $\text{mmol } Sr(OH)_2 = 10.58\ \cancel{\text{mmol HCl}} \times \frac{1\ \text{mmol } Sr(OH)_2}{2\ \cancel{\text{mmol HCl}}}$ $= 5.290\ \text{mmol } Sr(OH)_2$ $pOH = 14.000 - 13.500 = 0.500$ $[OH^-] = 10^{-0.500} = 0.3162\ M$ $[Sr(OH)_2] = \frac{[OH^-]}{2} = 0.1581\ M = 0.1581\ \frac{\text{mmol}}{\text{mL}}$ Volume $Sr(OH)_2$ solution $=$ $5.290\ \cancel{\text{mmol } Sr(OH)_2} \times \frac{1\ \text{mL}}{0.1581\ \cancel{\text{mmol}}} = 33.4\ \text{mL}$ (3 sig. figures)

Practice Problems 6.3.3 — Calculating Solution Volume

1. How many milliliters of a 0.215 M KOH solution are required to neutralize 15.0 mL of a 0.173 M H_2SO_4 solution?

2. A solution of HCl is standardized and found to have a pH of 0.432. What volume of this solution must be added to 25.0 mL of a 0.285 M $Sr(OH)_2$ solution to reach the equivalence point?

3. A 5.60 L sample of NH_3 gas, measured at STP, is dissolved in enough water to produce 500.0 mL of solution. A 20.0 mL sample of this solution is titrated with a 0.368 M HNO_3 solution. What volume of standard solution is required to reach the equivalence point?

Calculating Molar Mass

The molar mass of an unknown acid (or base) can be determined from a titration as long as we know if that acid (or base) is monoprotic or diprotic, etc. This tells us the molar ratio in the neutralization reaction that occurs. This in turn allows us to calculate the moles of the unknown compound that react during the titration. Depending on how the information is provided, we can then choose to calculate the molar mass in one of two ways, as shown in the following sample problems.

Sample Problem 6.3.4(a) — Calculating Molar Mass 1

A 0.328 g sample of an unknown monoprotic acid, HA, is dissolved in water and titrated with a standardized 0.1261 M NaOH solution. If 28.10 mL of the basic solution is required to reach the equivalence point, calculate the molar mass of the acid.

What to Think About	How to Do It
1. The mole ratio in the balanced equation is 1:1 so the mol of NaOH reacted = the mol of HA present in 0.328 g.	$NaOH(aq) + HA(aq) \rightarrow NaA(aq) + H_2O(l)$ $\text{mmol NaOH} = 28.10\ \cancel{\text{mL}} \times \frac{0.1261\ \text{mmol}}{\cancel{\text{mL}}} = 3.543\ \text{mmol}$
2. The mass of the unknown acid divided by the moles present equals the molar mass.	$\text{mmol HA} = 3.543\ \cancel{\text{mmol NaOH}} \times \frac{1\ \text{mmol HA}}{\cancel{\text{mmol NaOH}}}$ $= 3.543\ \text{mmol HA} = 0.003543\ \text{mol HA}$ $\text{molar mass of HA} = \frac{0.328\ \text{g HA}}{0.003543\ \text{mol HA}} = 92.6\ \text{g/mol}$ (3 sig. figures)

Sample Problem 6.3.4(b) — Calculating Molar Mass 2

A 2.73 g sample of an unknown diprotic acid is placed in a volumetric flask and then diluted to 500.0 mL. A 25.0 mL sample of this solution requires 30.5 mL of a 0.1112 M KOH solution to completely neutralize the acid in a titration. Calculate the molar mass of the acid.

What to Think About	How to Do It
1. Two moles of KOH are required to neutralize each mole of diprotic acid, H_2A.	$2\ KOH(aq) + H_2A(aq) \rightarrow K_2A(aq) + 2\ H_2O(l)$ $\text{mol KOH} = 0.0305\ \cancel{\text{L}} \times \frac{0.1112\ \text{mol}}{\cancel{\text{L}}} = 0.003392\ \text{mol}$
2. Calculate the concentration of the acid solution and use the volume of the original solution to determine the moles of H_2A present. This will allow you to determine the molar mass using the mass of the original acid sample.	$\text{mol } H_2A = 0.003392\ \cancel{\text{mol KOH}} \times \frac{1\ \text{mol } H_2A}{2\ \cancel{\text{mol KOH}}} = 0.001696\ \text{mol}$ $[H_2A] = \frac{0.001708\ \text{mol } H_2A}{0.0250\ \text{L}} = 0.06783\ \text{M}$ $\text{mol } H_2A \text{ in original 500.0 mL} = \frac{0.06832\ \text{mol}}{\cancel{\text{L}}} \times 0.5000\ \cancel{\text{L}}$ $= 0.03392\ \text{mol } H_2A$ $\text{molar mass } H_2A = \frac{2.73\ \text{g } H_2A}{0.03392\ \text{mol}} = 80.5\ \text{g/mol}$ (3 sig. figures)

 © Edvantage Interactive 2019

Practice Problems 6.3.4 — Calculating Molar Mass

1. A 3.648 g sample of an unknown monoprotic acid is dissolved in enough water to produce 750.0 mL of solution. When a 25.0 mL sample of this solution is titrated to the equivalence point, 12.50 mL of a 0.1104 M NaOH solution is required. Calculate the molar mass of the acid.

2. A 0.375 g sample of an unknown diprotic acid is dissolved in water and titrated using 0.2115 M NaOH. The volumes of standard solution required to neutralize the acid in three separate trials are given below.

Titration Trial	Volume of NaOH Solution
1	37.48 mL
2	37.36 mL
3	37.34 mL

Calculate the molar mass of the acid.

3. A 2.552 g sample of a monoprotic base is diluted to 250.0 mL in a volumetric flask. A 25.0 mL sample of this solution is titrated with a standardized solution of 0.05115 M HCl. If 17.49 mL of the acid solution is required to reach the equivalence point, calculate the molar mass of the base.

Calculating Percent Purity

If a solid sample of an impure acid or base is dissolved in solution and titrated against a standard solution, the actual number of moles of the pure solute can be determined. Depending on how the information is presented, this allows percent purity to be calculated. For example, we may be told that a small mass of an impure solid is dissolved in enough water to form the solution that is titrated directly. In this case, the percent purity can be calculated by dividing the *actual mass of pure solute* present in the sample, as determined by the titration, by the *given mass of the impure sample.*

$$\text{percent purity} = \frac{\text{actual mass of pure solute (from titration)}}{\text{given mass of impure solute}} \times 100\%$$

We may also be told that a mass of impure solid is dissolved in a given volume of solution, and then a portion of that solution is withdrawn and analyzed in the titration. In this case, we can choose to calculate the percent purity by dividing the *actual solution concentration*, as determined by the titration, by the *expected concentration* in the original solution if the sample had been pure.

$$\text{percent purity} = \frac{\text{actual concentration (from titration)}}{\text{expected concentration (from original mass)}} \times 100\%$$

There are other possible approaches, but each uses a true value provided by the titration and compares it to a given value to determine percent purity.

Sample Problem 6.3.5(a) — Calculating Percent Purity 1

A 0.3470 g sample of impure $NaHSO_3$ is dissolved in water and titrated with a 0.1481 M NaOH solution. If 20.26 mL of the standard solution is required, calculate the percent purity of the $NaHSO_3$ sample.

What to Think About

1. The mole ratio in the balanced equation is 1:1.
2. The titration will allow you to calculate the actual number of moles of $NaHSO_3$ in the sample from which you can obtain percent purity.

How to Do It

$NaOH(aq) + NaHSO_3(aq) \rightarrow Na_2SO_3(aq) + H_2O(l)$

$\text{mol NaOH} = 0.02026\ \cancel{L} \times \frac{0.1481\ \text{mol}}{\cancel{L}} = 0.003000\ \text{mol}$

$\text{mol pure } NaHSO_3 = \text{mol NaOH} = 0.003000\ \text{mol}$

$\text{actual mass pure } NaHSO_3 = 0.003000\ \cancel{\text{mol}} \times \frac{104.1\ \text{g } NaHSO_3}{\cancel{\text{mol}}}$

$= 0.3123\ \text{g } NaHSO_3$

$\%\ \text{purity} = \frac{\text{actual mass pure } NaHSO_3}{\text{given mass impure } NaHSO_3} \times 100\%$

$= \frac{0.3123\ \cancel{g}}{0.3470\ \cancel{g}} \times 100\% = 90.00\%$ (4 sig. figures)

Sample Problem 6.3.5(b) — Calculating Percent Purity 2

A 2.70 g sample of impure $Sr(OH)_2$ is diluted to 250.0 mL in a volumetric flask. A 25.0 mL portion of this solution is then neutralized in a titration using 31.39 mL of 0.131 M HCl. Calculate the percent purity of the $Sr(OH)_2$.

What to Think About

1. The balanced equation shows a 2:1 mole ratio for the reactants.
2. Compare the actual concentration of the solution to the expected concentration to determine percent purity.
3. Round the answer to three significant figures.

How to Do It

$2\ HCl(aq) + Sr(OH)_2(aq) \rightarrow SrCl_2(aq) + 2\ H_2O(l)$

$\text{mmol HCl} = 31.39\ \cancel{\text{mL}} \times \frac{0.131\ \text{mmol}}{\cancel{\text{mL}}} = 4.112\ \text{mmol}$

$\text{mmol } Sr(OH)_2 = 4.112\ \cancel{\text{mmol HCl}} \times \frac{1\ \text{mmol } Sr(OH)_2}{2\ \cancel{\text{mmol HCl}}}$

$= 2.056\ \text{mmol } Sr(OH)_2$

$\text{actual } [Sr(OH)_2] = \frac{2.056\ \text{mmol } Sr(OH)_2}{25.0\ \text{mL}} = 0.08224\ \text{M}$

$\text{expected } [Sr(OH)_2] = \frac{2.70\ \text{g } \cancel{Sr(OH)_2}}{0.2500\ \text{L}} \times \frac{1\ \text{mol } Sr(OH)_2}{121.6\ \cancel{g}}$

$= 0.08882\ \text{M}$

$\%\ \text{purity} = \frac{\text{actual } [Sr(OH)_2]}{\text{expected } [Sr(OH)_2]} \times 100\%$

$= \frac{0.08224\ \cancel{M}}{0.08882\ \cancel{M}} \times 100\% = 92.6\%$ (3 sig. figures)

© Edvantage Interactive 2019

Practice Problems 6.3.5 — Calculating Percent Purity

1. Benzoic acid, C_6H_5COOH, is a white crystalline solid. It is among the most common food preservatives and is also used as an antifungal skin treatment. A 0.3265 g sample of impure benzoic acid is dissolved in enough water to form 25.0 mL of solution. In a titration, 23.76 mL of a 0.1052 M NaOH solution is required to reach the equivalence point. Calculate the percent purity of the acid.

2. A 1.309 g sample of impure $Ca(OH)_2$ is dissolved in water to produce 750.0 mL of solution. A 25.0 mL sample of this solution is titrated against a standard solution of 0.0615 M HCl. If 17.72 mL of the acid solution is required in the titration, calculate the percent purity of the $Ca(OH)_2$.

3. Nicotinic acid, C_5H_4NCOOH, (also known as niacin or vitamin B_3) is considered an essential human nutrient and is available in a variety of food sources such as chicken, salmon, eggs, carrots, and avocados. A 1.361 g sample of impure nicotinic acid is dissolved in water to form 30.00 mL of solution. The acid solution requires 20.96 mL of 0.501 M NaOH to reach the equivalence point. Calculate the percent purity of the acid.

6.3 Activity: Titration Experimental Design

Question

Can you identify the equipment and procedures associated with a typical titration and then employ them in designing a titration?

Background

As you have learned in this section, a titration is one of the most valuable analytical procedures employed by chemists. This activity is intended to review the equipment and reagents involved in a titration and then present you with the task of designing such an investigation.

Procedure

1. What is the function of each the following in a titration?
   (a) burette

   (b) volumetric pipette

   (c) Erlenmeyer flask

   (d) indicator

   (e) standard solution

   (f) acidic or basic primary standard

2. Why must every titration be repeated?

3. The concentration of a solution of acetylsalicylic acid, $C_8H_7O_2COOH$, must be determined very accurately for a clinical trial. The equipment and chemical reagents available to you to accomplish this are listed below. Using all of them, describe in point form and in order the laboratory procedures you would use.

Equipment	Reagents
• analytical balance • 100 mL beaker • 2 funnels • wash bottle • 250 mL volumetric flask • two 125 mL Erlenmeyer flasks • 50 mL burette • two 25 mL pipettes with suction bulbs • ring stand • burette clamp • safety goggles • lab apron	• pure oxalic acid dihydrate crystals • NaOH solution (approximately 0.1 M) • ASA solution (approximately 0.1 M) • phenolphthalein indicator solution

 © Edvantage Interactive 2019

Titration Procedure

Results and Discussion

1. Write the balanced equation for the reaction that occurs during standardization of the basic solution and for the titration of the ASA solution.

2. (a) What salt solution exists at the equivalence point of the ASA titration?

   (b) Would you expect the pH of the solution at the equivalence point to be 7? Why or why not?

3. What concentration might be appropriate for the oxalic acid solution that you prepare?

4. Identify at least three possible sources of error and their impact on the experimental results.

6.3 Review Questions

1. A student intends to titrate two 25.0 mL acidic solutions, each with a known concentration of approximately 0.1 M. One solution is hydrochloric acid and the other solution is acetic acid. He expects to require more of a standard NaOH solution to reach the equivalence point when titrating the HCl solution because it is a strong acid with a higher $[H_3O^+]$. Do you agree or disagree with the prediction? Explain your answer.

2. During a titration, a student adds water from a wash bottle to wash down some reactant solution that has splashed up in the Erlenmeyer flask. Although this changes the volume of the solution in the flask, she is confident that the accuracy of the titration will not be affected. Do you agree or disagree? Explain your answer.

3. A student must titrate a 25.0 mL sample of acetic acid solution whose concentration is known to be approximately 0.2 M. After adding a small amount of phenolphthalein indicator to the reaction flask, the student fills a 50 mL burette with a standardized 0.0650 M solution of NaOH and prepares to begin the titration. His lab partner insists that the titration cannot succeed. Do you agree or disagree with the lab partner? Explain your answer.

4. A student requires a standard solution of NaOH for a titration with a concentration as close as possible to 0.500 M. Using a digital balance, she carefully measures 20.00 g of NaOH. She quantitatively transfers it to a 1 L volumetric flask and adds the precise amount of water. She then calculates the concentration of the resulting solution to be 0.500 M and prepares to fill a burette and begin the titration. Her lab partner insists that the concentration is inaccurate. Do you agree or disagree with the lab partner? Would you expect the calculated concentration to be too high or too low? Explain your answer.

5. A student standardizing a solution of NaOH finds that 25.24 mL of that solution is required to neutralize a solution containing 0.835 g of KHP. Calculate the [NaOH].

 © Edvantage Interactive 2019

6. A 21.56 mL solution of NaOH is standardized and found to have a concentration of 0.125 M. What mass of oxalic acid dihydrate would be required to standardize this solution?

7. A solution of NaOH is standardized and found to have a pH of 13.440. What volume of this solution must be added to 25.0 mL of a 0.156 M $H_2C_2O_4$ solution in a titration to neutralize the acid?

8. A 4.48 L sample of HCl gas, measured at STP, is dissolved in enough water to produce 400.0 mL of solution. A 25.0 mL sample of this solution is titrated with a 0.227 M $Sr(OH)_2$ solution. What volume of standard solution is required to reach the equivalence point?

9. A 0.665 g sample of an unknown monoprotic acid, HA, is dissolved in water and titrated with a standardized 0.2055 M KOH solution. If 26.51 mL of the basic solution is required to reach the equivalence point, calculate the molar mass of the acid.

10. A 5.47 g sample of an unknown diprotic acid is placed in a volumetric flask and then diluted to 250.0 mL. A 25.0 mL sample of this solution requires 23.6 mL of a 0.2231 M $Sr(OH)_2$ solution to completely neutralize the acid in a titration. Calculate the molar mass of the acid.

11. Tartaric acid, $C_4H_6O_6$, is a white crystalline diprotic organic acid. It occurs naturally in many plants, such as grapes and bananas, is often added to foods to give them a sour taste, and is one of the main acids found in wine. A 7.36 g sample of impure tartaric acid is diluted to 250.0 mL in a volumetric flask. A 25.0 mL portion of this solution is transferred to an Erlenmeyer flask and titrated against a 0.223 M standardized NaOH solution. If 40.31 mL of the basic solution is required to neutralize the acid, calculate the percent purity of the tartaric acid.

12. Sorbic acid, C_5H_7COOH, is a monoprotic organic acid that was first isolated from the berries of the mountain ash tree in 1859. It is a white crystalline solid used primarily as a food preservative. A 0.570 g sample of impure sorbic acid is dissolved in water to form 25.00 mL of solution. The acid solution requires 27.34 mL of 0.178 M KOH to reach the equivalence point. Calculate the percent purity of the sorbic acid.

13. Phenylacetic acid, C_7H_7COOH, is used in some perfumes and possesses a honey-like odor in low concentrations. A 0.992 g sample of impure phenylacetic acid dissolved in solution is titrated against a 0.105 M standard $Sr(OH)_2$ solution. If 31.07 mL of the standard solution is required to reach the equivalence point, calculate the percent purity of the acid.

14. Why is a titration considered to be a "volumetric" analysis?

© **Edvantage Interactive 2019**

6.4 A Closer Look at Titrations

Warm Up

Consider each pair of reactants in the three titrations below.

	Titration 1	Titration 2	Titration 3
Solution in burette	0.100 M NaOH	0.100 M NaOH	0.100 M HCl
Solution in flask	0.100 M HCl	0.100 M CH_3COOH	0.100 M NH_3

1. Write the formula equation for each titration.

   Titration 1:

   Titration 2:

   Titration 3:

2. What salt solution exists in each reaction flask at each of the equivalence points?

   Titration 1: ______________________

   Titration 2: ______________________

   Titration 3: ______________________

3. Indicate whether you would expect the pH of each solution at the equivalence point to be below, equal to, or above 7, and explain your decision.

   Titration 1:

   ____

   Titration 2:

   ____

   Titration 3:

   ____

Measuring pH with Acid-Base Indicators

Titrations are described as a form of volumetric chemical analysis. We will now take a closer look at the procedure by monitoring the pH changes in the reaction mixture during several types of titrations. In doing so, we'll also see how the principles of hydrolysis and buffer chemistry apply to and give us a better understanding of the titration process.

Usually we measure pH using either an acid-base indicator or a pH meter. Let's begin by describing the behavior and role of an acid-base indicator in a titration. Acid-base indicators are weak (usually monoprotic) organic acids whose conjugate pairs display different and normally intense colors. Those intense colors mean that only a small amount of an indicator is needed for a titration. If the appropriate indicator has been chosen, the change from one color to another will signal when the equivalence point has been reached.

Acid-base indicators are complex organic molecules and so we normally represent their formulas as simply "HIn." A typical indicator is a weak acid as shown in the aqueous equilibrium below.

$$\mathbf{HIn}(aq) \quad + \quad H_2O(l) \quad \rightleftharpoons \quad \mathbf{In^-}(aq) \quad + \quad H_3O^+(aq)$$

↑	↑
Acidic form and color predominate when $[H_3O^+]$ is relatively high and the equilibrium favors the reactant side.	**Basic form** and color predominate when $[H_3O^+]$ is relatively low and the equilibrium favors the product side.

If a small amount of the indicator is placed in a solution where the hydronium concentration is relatively high, this equilibrium will favor the reactant side. Thus, the acidic form of the indicator, **HIn**, and its color will predominate. In a basic solution, where the hydronium concentration is low, the equilibrium will favor the product side and so the basic form, **In⁻**, and its color will be prominent. For example, Figure 6.4.1 shows the acidic and basic forms of bromthymol blue.

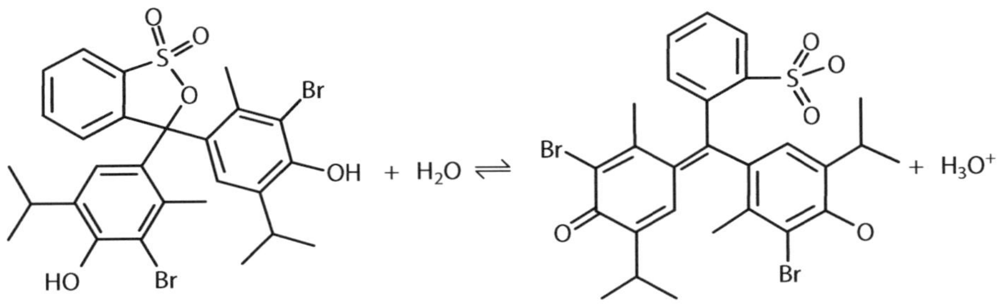

Acidic (yellow) form of bromthymol blue predominates in an acidic solution with a pH below **6.0**.

Basic (blue) form of bromthymol blue predominates in an alkaline solution with a pH above **7.6**.

Figure 6.4.1 *The acidic and basic forms of bromthymol blue*

Table A6 Acid-Base Indicators (at the back of the book) tells us that changes in indicator colors occur over a *range* of pH values rather than instantly at one pH. This is because our eyes are limited in their ability to perceive slight changes in shades of color. Normally during a titration, about *one tenth* of the initial form of an indicator must be converted to the other form (its conjugate) for us to notice a color change.

It is useful to follow the progress of a typical titration in terms of the position of the indicator equilibrium and the relative amount of each member of the conjugate pair present in the reaction flask as the titrant is added.

For example, in a flask containing an indicator in an acidic solution, the acid form of the indicator, HIn, predominates. If we now begin adding a basic solution from a burette, the OH^- ions reduce the $[H_3O^+]$ in the flask and the position of the $[In^-]/[HIn]$ equilibrium begins to shift towards In^- according to Le Châtelier's principle. As the [HIn] decreases and the $[In^-]$ increases, we eventually reach a point where the $[In^-]/[HIn]$ ratio = 0.10. Here, we notice *the first color change.*

As the addition of OH^- ions continues to reduce the $[H_3O^+]$, the ratio continues to increase until the $[HIn] = [In^-]$. An equal concentration of each form of the indicator will now combine to produce an *intermediate color* in the solution. The point at which we see this intermediate color, where the indicator is *half-way through its color change*, is called the **transition point** or **end point** of the indicator. At the transition point, as $[HIn] = [In^-]$, then

$$K_a = \frac{[H_3O^+]\cancel{[In^-]}}{\cancel{[HIn]}} \text{ reduces to: } \boldsymbol{K_a = [H_3O^+]}$$

 © Edvantage Interactive 2019

This tells us that the $[H_3O^+]$ at the transition point equals the value of the K_a for the indicator (sometimes called K_{In}).

> If we take the negative logarithm of both sides of the above equation, we see that:
> the pK_a of an indicator = the pH at its transition point

When you refer to the table of acid-base indicators (Table A6), you will notice that different indicators change colors at different pH values. Those pH values reflect the pK_a values for each indicator.

As we continue adding base, we would see the indicator's color change complete when only about *one-tenth* of the initial acid form HIn remains in the flask, that is, when $[In^-]/[HIn] = 10$. We can summarize this progression in Table 6.4.1 beginning with the first detectable color change as the basic solution is added and ending when the color change is seen to be complete.

Table 6.4.1 *Indicator Color Change During the Titration of an Acid with a Base*

Indicator Color Change First Seen	Indicator Transition Point Occurs	Indicator Color Change Complete
$\frac{[In^-]}{[HIn]} = \frac{1}{10}$ so $K_a = [H_3O^+](0.1)$ and $pK_a = pH + -\log(0.1)$ or $pK_a = pH + 1$ so $\mathbf{pH = pK_a - 1}$	$\frac{[In^-]}{[HIn]} = 1$ so $K_a = [H_3O^+]$ and $pK_a = pH$ or $\mathbf{pH = pK_a}$	$\frac{[In^-]}{[HIn]} = \frac{10}{1}$ so $K_a = [H_3O^+](10)$ and $pK_a = pH + -\log(10)$ or $pK_a = pH - 1$ so $\mathbf{pH = pK_a + 1}$
The first color change is seen when the pH of the solution is about one pH unit below the pK_a of the indicator.	The transition point and intermediate color occur when the pH of the solution equals the pK_a of the indicator.	The color change is complete when the pH of the solution is about one pH unit above the pK_a of the indicator.

We see from the above table that the range over which an indicator's color changes is normally about two pH units extending from approximately one pH unit below to one pH unit above the indicator's pK_a. This corresponds to a 100-fold change in the $[In^-]/[HIn]$ ratio and tells us that the useful pH range for an indicator in a titration is usually given by $\mathbf{pK_a \pm 1}$.

As we will discuss later in this section, depending on the reagents used in a titration, the pH at the equivalence point can be quite different. We normally attempt to choose an indicator whose pK_a is within one unit of the pH at the equivalence point.

Had we applied the above discussion to bromthymol blue, we would have noticed the indicator's yellow color begin to change at pH = 6 and continue changing until it appears completely blue at about pH = 7.6. Halfway through that change, at an *average of the two pH values*, the transition point pH of 6.8 is reached, which equals the indicator pK_a. At the transition point, bromthymol blue displays an intermediate green color.

> An indicator's transition point pH and pK_a value can be estimated by averaging the two pH values associated with the range over which the indicator changes color.

Look again at the table of acid-base indicators (Table A6) and consider the order that those indicators appear top-to-bottom. Notice that the pH values over which the color changes occur increase as we move down the table from the acidic end of the pH scale to the basic end. This means that the pK_a values of those indicators must also increase.

As an increase in pK_a corresponds to a *decrease in* K_a, this tells us that the indicator acid strength decreases as we move down the table in the same way as it does in Table A5 showing the relative strengths of Brønsted-Lowry acids and bases (see Table A5 at the back of the book).

Combining Acid-Base Indicators — A Universal Indicator

Several different indicators that each go through a different color change over a different pH range can be combined into a single indicator solution. This solution will display different colors over a wide range of pH values. A universal indicator solution can also be added to absorbent strips of paper so that when the solvents evaporate, the individual test strips can be dipped into solutions to estimate pH values.

In a universal indicator, the colors of the component indicators at each pH combine to display virtually all the colors of the visible spectrum. Commercially available universal indicators are often composed of the indicator combination shown in Table 6.4.2 The indicator colors combine over the entire range of the pH scale to produce the results shown in Table 6.4.3. (The original universal indicator recipe was patented by the Japanese chemist Yamada in 1923.)

Table 6.4.2 *Indicators That Make up a Typical Universal Indicator*

Indicator	pK_a Value	Color of Acid Form	Color of Base Form
Thymol blue*	2.0 (pK_{a1})	red	yellow
Methyl red	5.6	red	yellow
Bromthymol blue	6.8	yellow	blue
Thymol blue*	8.8 (pK_{a2})	yellow	blue
Phenolphthalein	9.1	colorless	pink

Table 6.4.3 *Indicator Colors When Combined in a Universal Indicator*

Indicator	pH < 2	pH 3–4	pH 5-6	pH 7-8	pH 9-11	pH >12
Thymol Blue*	red/orange	yellow	yellow	yellow	green/blue	blue
Methyl Red	red	red	orange/yellow	yellow	yellow	yellow
Bromthymol Blue	yellow	yellow	yellow	green/blue	blue	blue
Phenolphthalein	colorless	colorless	colorless	colorless	pink	pink
Combined color	***red/orange***	***orange/yellow***	***yellow***	***yellow/green***	***green/blue***	***purple***

* Note. Thymol blue undergoes a *color change over two different pH ranges*. What does this tell us about the chemical nature of this acid?

 © Edvantage Interactive 2019

Sample Problem 6.4.1(a) — Estimating Indicator K_a and pK_a values

Eight acid-base indicators listed on the acid-base indicators table (Table A6) display an orange color at their transition points. Identify which of those has a $K_a = 5 \times 10^{-8}$.

What to Think About

1. Calculate the pK_a value from the given K_a.
2. That pK_a represents the average of one of the pair of pH values listed for indicators on the table. Focus on the middle of the indicator table.
3. Once you calculate it, immediately focus on a particular region of the table to find the appropriate indicator.

How to Do It

$pK_a = -\log(5 \times 10^{-8}) = 7.3$

Phenol red undergoes its color change from yellow to red between pH 6.6 and 8.0. The intermediate color is orange.

Averaging the two pH values, we obtain:

$$\frac{6.6 + 8.0}{2} = 7.3$$

The indicator is phenol red.

Sample Problem 6.4.1(b) — Estimating Solution pH

Samples of a solution were tested with three different indicators. Determine the pH range of the solution given the results shown below.

Indicator	Color
thymolphthalein	colorless
bromthymol blue	blue
thymol blue	Yellow

What to Think About

1. Use each data entry to identify a range of possible pH values for the solution.
2. Give the final answer as a narrow pH range rather than an exact value.

How to Do It

First data entry: pH ≤ 9.4
Second data entry: pH ≥ 7.6
Third data entry: pH ≤ 8

The pH range of the solution is given by:

$$7.6 \leq \text{pH} \leq 8.0$$

Practice Problems 6.4.1 — Acid-Base Indicators

1. The indicator bromphenol blue appears yellow below pH = 3.0 and blue above pH = 4.5. Estimate the pK_a and K_a of the indicator and determine the color it will display in a 1.8×10^{-4} M HCl solution.

2. Estimate the $[H_3O^+]$ in a solution given the following data:

Indicator	Color
Phenol red	red
Phenolphthalein	colorless

Continued on next page

Practice Problems 6.4.1 *(Continued)*

3. A few drops of alizarin yellow are added to 25.0 mL of a 0.0010 M NaOH solution. What color should the indicator display? Explain your answer by showing the work.

4. Like thymol blue, the indicator alizarin also undergoes a color change over two different pH ranges. Use the table below to estimate the K_{a1} and K_{a2} values for alizarin.

	Below pH 5.6	**Above pH 7.3**	**Below pH 11.0**	**Above pH 12.4**
Alizarin color	yellow	red	red	purple

5. The following 0.10 M salt solutions have had their labels removed: $NaHSO_4$, Na_2CO_3, NaH_2PO_4, and NH_4CH_3COO. The solutions are tested with three indicators and the following results were observed.

	Bromthymol Blue	**Methyl Orange**	**Phenolphthalein**
Solution A	blue	yellow	pink
Solution B	green	yellow	colorless
Solution C	yellow	yellow	colorless
Solution D	yellow	red	colorless

Identify each solution: A ____________ B ____________

C ____________ D ____________

Acid-Base Titration Curves

We now begin a more detailed discussion of acid-base titrations by focusing on the pH changes that occur in the reaction flask as the titrant is added from the burette. We will look at three different types of titrations and apply our knowledge of indicators in each case.

An efficient way to monitor the progress of an acid-base titration is to plot the pH of the solution being analyzed as a function of the volume of titrant added. Such a diagram is called a titration curve.

> A **titration curve** is a plot of the pH of the solution being analyzed versus the volume of titrant added.

Each of the three types of titrations we will consider has a different net ionic equation, a different titration curve with a characteristic shape and features, and a different equivalence point pH requiring selection of a suitable indicator.

© Edvantage Interactive 2019

I. Strong Acid — Strong Base Titration Curves

We will begin by considering the titration of the strong acid HCl(*aq*) with the strong base NaOH(*aq*). The formula and net ionic equations for the titration are given below:

$$HCl(aq) + NaOH(aq) \rightarrow NaCl(aq) + H_2O(l)$$

$$H_3O^+(aq) + OH^-(aq) \rightarrow 2\ H_2O(l)$$

The titration curve for the titration of a 25.00 mL solution of 0.100 M HCl with a 0.100 M NaOH solution is shown in Figure 6.4.2. An analysis of the curve reveals several important features.

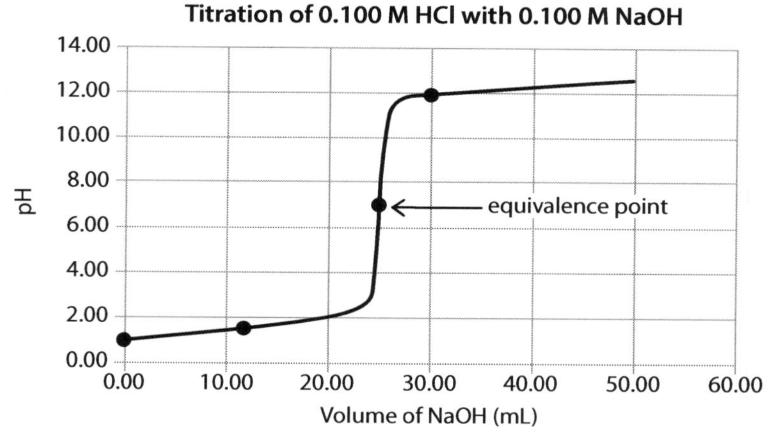

Figure 6.4.2 *Titration curve for a 25.00 mL solution of 0.100 M HCl titrated with a 0.100 M NaOH solution*

Important Features of a Strong Acid–Strong Base Titration Curve

1. Because the acid is strong and therefore the initial $[H_3O^+]$ is high, *the pH starts out low.* As the titration proceeds, as long as there is *excess strong acid* in the flask, the pH will remain low and increase only very slowly as the NaOH is added.
2. The slow increase in pH continues until the moles of NaOH added almost equal the moles of H_3O^+ initially present in the acid. Then, when the titration is within one or two drops of the equivalence point, the slope of the curve increases dramatically. The next drop of titrant neutralizes the last of the acid at the equivalence point and then introduces a tiny excess of OH^- ions into the flask. When this occurs, *the line becomes almost vertical and the pH rises by six to eight units almost immediately.*
3. Following the steep rise in pH at the equivalence point, the pH then increases slowly as excess OH^- is added.

Look at the titration curve above in Figure 6.4.2. Four points have been placed on the curve, representing key stages during the titration. Let us consider the chemical species present in the reaction flask and *calculate the pH at these four key stages.*

Stage 1: *The pH prior to the addition of any titrant*
Before any NaOH has been added, the reaction flask contains 25.00 mL of 0.100 M HCl(*aq*). As HCl is a strong acid, the $[HCl] = [H_3O^+] = 0.100$ M. Therefore the $pH = -\log(0.100) = 1.000$.
(Note the location of the *first* point on the above titration curve.)

Stage 2: *The pH approximately halfway to the equivalence point*
Once we begin adding NaOH, two changes occur in the solution in the flask that influence its pH: some of the acid has been neutralized by the added base, and the volume has increased.

Calculating the pH at this stage is similar to the process of a strong acid being mixed with a strong base. Recall that the calculation involves determining the diluted concentrations of H_3O^+ and OH^- (designated as $[H_3O^+]_{ST}$ and $[OH^-]_{ST}$) before the reaction and then subtracting the lesser concentration from the greater concentration to determine the concentration of the ion in excess.

Although this method will work again in this situation, as we move forward through this and the other types of titration calculations, you will learn another approach.

This method allows us to organize and manage information efficiently when solutions are mixed and involve limiting and excess reactants. The process involves the use of an **ICF** table, which is a variation on the ICE table you are already familiar with. The "**I**" and the "**C**" still represent the "**I**nitial" and "**C**hange" in reagent concentrations, but because titration reactions go to completion, the "E" has been replaced with an "**F**" representing the "**F**inal" concentrations present when the reaction is complete. Let's use this method to calculate the pH of the solution present in the flask at stage 2, following the addition of 12.50 mL of the 0.100 M NaOH to the 25.00 mL of 0.100 M HCl in the flask — that is *halfway* to the equivalence point. Consider the Sample Problem below.

Sample Problem 6.4.2(a) — Calculating pH Halfway to the Equivalence Point

Calculate the pH of the solution produced in the reaction flask during a titration following the addition of 12.50 mL of 0.100 M NaOH to 25.00 mL of 0.100 M HCl.

What to Think About

1. Determine the diluted [HCl] and [NaOH] before the neutralization reaction. Enter these into the "Initial" row on the table as "$[HCl]_{IN}$" and "$[NaOH]_{IN}$".
2. In step 2, construct and complete an ICF table underneath the balanced equation using the $[HCl]_{IN}$ and $[NaOH]_{IN}$ determined in step 1. Notice that the *NaOH is the limiting reactant.* Omit the states (*aq*) and (*l*) in the table.
3. Use the species present in the reaction flask when the reaction is complete to determine the pH.
4. As the reactant acid and base are both strong, *neither of the ions in the product salt* can react with water to affect the pH of the solution. The product salt is therefore *neutral.*

How to Do It

$$[HCl]_{IN} = 0.100\ M \times \frac{25.00\ \cancel{mL}}{37.50\ \cancel{mL}} = 0.06667\ M$$

$$[NaOH]_{IN} = 0.100\ M \times \frac{12.50\ \cancel{mL}}{37.50\ \cancel{mL}} = 0.03333\ M$$

$$HCl + NaOH \rightarrow NaCl + H_2O$$

	HCl	NaOH	NaCl	H_2O
I	0.06667	0.03333	0	
C	− 0.03333	− 0.03333	+ 0.03333	
F	0.03334	≈ 0	0.03333	

Although the $[OH^-]$ cannot actually be zero (recall that $[H_3O^+][OH^-]$ must $= 10^{-14}$), as the excess HCl is the major species present, the $[OH^-]$ is insignificant.

final [HCl] = final $[H_3O^+]$

$pH = -\log(0.03334) = 1.477$ (3 sig. figures)

(Note the location of the *second* point on the curve.)

Stage 3: *The pH at the equivalence point*

After 25.00 mL of 0.100 M NaOH has been added to the original 25.00 mL of 0.100 M HCl, the equivalence point is reached. At this point, the total number of moles of H_3O^+ from the acid now equals the total number of moles of OH^- from the base. Consider the Sample Problem on the next page.

© Edvantage Interactive 2019

Sample Problem 6.4.2(b) — Calculating pH at the Equivalence Point

Determine the pH of the solution produced in the reaction flask when 25.00 mL of 0.100 M NaOH has been added to 25.00 mL of 0.100 M HCl.

What to Think About

1. Approach this problem in the same way as the problem above.
2. The $[HCl]_{IN}$ and $[NaOH]_{IN}$ are equal to each other and so neither will be in excess following the reaction.
3. At the equivalence point, the reaction flask will contain only water and NaCl(*aq*). As *neither ion is capable of hydrolysis, the solution in the flask will be neutral.*

How to Do It

$$[HCl]_{IN} = 0.100\ M \times \frac{25.00\ mL}{50.00\ mL} = 0.05000\ M$$

$$[NaOH]_{IN} = 0.100\ M \times \frac{25.00\ mL}{50.00\ mL} = 0.05000\ M$$

	HCl	+ NaOH	→ NaCl	+ H_2O
I	0.05000	0.05000	0	
C	− 0.05000	− 0.05000	+ 0.05000	
F	≈ 0	≈ 0	0.05000	

Neither the $[H_3O^+]$ nor the $[OH^-]$ can be zero because their product must equal 10^{-14}. However, neither is in excess so final $[H_3O^+]$ = final $[OH^-] = 1.00 \times 10^{-7}$ M and $pH = -\log(1.00 \times 10^{-7}\ M) = 7.000$.

(Note the location of the *third point* on the curve.)

As mentioned above, as neither ion in the product salt is capable of reacting with water, the pH of the solution at the equivalence point is 7.

The titration of a strong monoprotic acid by a strong base will produce a solution with a pH of 7 at the equivalence point because neither of the ions present in the product salt can undergo hydrolysis to affect the pH.

As discussed, the appropriate indicator for a titration should ideally have a pK_a value that is as close as possible to the equivalence point (normally within about one pH unit). For a strong acid–strong base titration, however, the *large jump in pH* that occurs with the addition of a single drop of titrant at the equivalence point means that we have more flexibility in our choice of indicators. The table of acid-base indicators (Table A6) shows us that several indicators undergo their color change over the steep portion of the curve. Therefore, the indicators with transition points as low as pH 5 and as high as pH 9 (from methyl red to phenolphthalein) on the table are suitable for such a titration.

Stage 4: *The pH beyond the equivalence point*

After all of the acid has been neutralized, the solution now becomes increasingly basic as excess OH^- ions are added from the burette. We will use the ICF table below to calculate the pH of the solution in the reaction flask after 30.00 mL of the NaOH solution has been added.

Quick Check

1. Write the net ionic equation for a strong acid–strong base titration.

2. Although we have a choice of several indicators for such a titration, phenolphthalein is often chosen for practical reasons. Why?

   ____

3. Why is the pH at the equivalence point of a strong acid–strong base titration equal to 7?

   ____

A Reverse Scenario

Now let's consider the reverse scenario in which a 0.100 M NaOH solution is titrated with a 0.100 M HCl solution. The titration curve is effectively inverted compared to a strong acid titrated with a strong base, but the net ionic equation, general shape, and important features are the same. Note the inclusion of the same points at the four key stages of this titration on the curve in Figure 6.4.3.

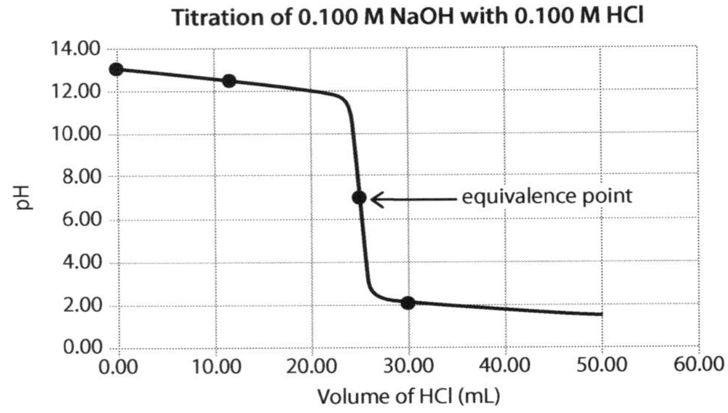

Figure 6.4.3 *Titration curve for a 0.100 M NaOH solution is titrated with a 0.100 M HCl solution*

Sample Problem 6.4.2(c) — Calculating pH beyond the Equivalence Point

Calculate the pH of the solution produced in the reaction flask when 30.00 mL of 0.100 M NaOH has been added to 25.00 mL of 0.100 M HCl.

What to Think About

1. The $[NaOH]_{IN}$ will exceed the $[HCl]_{IN}$ because the equivalence point has been passed by 5.00 mL. We therefore expect the pH to be well above 7.
2. As [NaOH] will be in excess, the final [HCl] will appear as zero on the table. Although the $[H_3O^+]$ cannot actually be zero, its final concentration is insignificant.
3. The subtraction yielding the final $[OH^-]$ gives an answer to two significant figures.

How to Do It

$$[HCl]_{IN} = 0.100\ M \times \frac{25.00\ \text{mL}}{55.00\ \text{mL}} = 0.04545\ M$$

$$[NaOH]_{IN} = 0.100\ M \times \frac{30.00\ \text{mL}}{55.00\ \text{mL}} = 0.05454\ M$$

	HCl +	NaOH →	NaCl +	H_2O
I	0.04545	0.05454	0	
C	− 0.04545	− 0.04545	+ 0.04545	
F	≈ 0	0.00909	0.04545	

final $[OH^-]$ = final [NaOH] = 0.00909 M

pOH = − log (0.00909) = 2.041

pH = 14.000 − 2.041 = 11.96 (2 sig. figures)

(Note the location of the *fourth point* on the curve.)

© Edvantage Interactive 2019

Practice Problems 6.4.2 — Strong Acid–Strong Base Titration Curves

1. Consider the titration described above in the sample problems. Use an ICF table to calculate the pH of the solution in the reaction flask after 24.95 mL of 0.100 M NaOH has been added to the 25.00 mL of 0.100 M HCl. (This corresponds to about *1 drop before the equivalence point.*)

2. Use an ICF table to calculate the pH of the solution in the same flask after 25.05 mL of 0.100 M NaOH has been added to the 25.00 mL of 0.100 M HCl. (This corresponds to about *1 drop beyond the equivalence point.*)

3. Would you expect the complete neutralization of sulfuric acid by a sodium hydroxide solution in a titration to produce a neutral solution at the equivalence point? Why or why not? (Begin your answer by writing the balanced formula equation for the reaction.)

II. Weak Acid–Strong Base Titration Curves

Let's now consider the titration of the *weak acid* $CH_3COOH(aq)$ with the strong base $NaOH(aq)$. The formula and net ionic equations for the reaction are shown below:

$$CH_3COOH(aq) + NaOH(aq) \rightarrow NaCH_3COO(aq) + H_2O(l)$$

$$CH_3COOH(aq) + OH^-(aq) \rightarrow CH_3COO^-(aq) + H_2O(l)$$

Note that the acid is weak so it ionizes only to a small extent. Therefore, the predominant species reacting with the hydroxide ion from the strong base is the intact molecular acid.

The diagram in Figure 6.4.4 shows the curve obtained when we titrate 25.0 mL of a 0.100 M CH_3COOH solution with a 0.100 M NaOH solution. Once again, we can identify a number of important features.

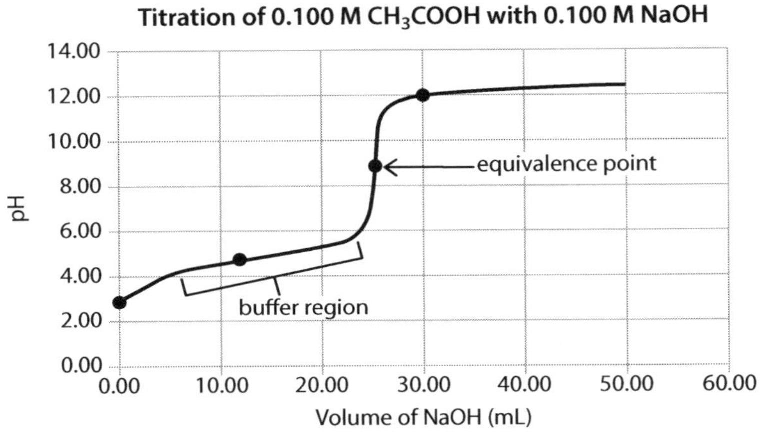

Figure 6.4.4 *Titration curve for 25.0 mL of a 0.100 M CH_3COOH solution titrated with 25.0 mL of a 0.100 M NaOH solution*

Important Features of a Weak Acid–Strong Base Titration Curve

1. Because the acid is weak and thus ionizes only to a slight extent, the initial $[H_3O^+]$ is lower and so *the initial pH is higher* than for a strong acid.
2. There is an initial small jump in pH, but then the pH increases more slowly over a portion of the curve called the *buffer region* (labeled above) just before the steep rise to the equivalence point. However, *the pH in this region still changes more quickly than it does during a strong acid–strong base titration.* The buffer region occurs because large enough quantities of both the weak acid and its conjugate base exist in the reaction flask. This will be discussed in detail below.
3. The steep rise to the equivalence point occurs *over a smaller pH range* than when a strong acid is titrated with a strong base and *the pH at the equivalence point is greater than 7.* The solution at the equivalence point contains the anion from a weak acid (CH_3COO^-) and the cation from a strong base (Na^+). Although the cation can't react with water, the anion is a weak base and will therefore *accept protons from water, producing OH^- ions.* Hence the pH is greater than 7.
4. Beyond the equivalence point, the pH once again increases slowly as excess OH^- is added.

Note that we have again placed points on the curve at the same four key stages as we discussed in the strong acid–strong base titration. Let's once again consider the chemical species present in the reaction flask and calculate the pH at those four key stages. The calculations are different because of the minimal ionization of the weak acid and the hydrolysis reaction of its conjugate base with water.

Stage 1: *The pH prior to the addition of any titrant*
You may recognize this calculation as the first type of weak acid calculation, namely calculating the pH of a weak acid solution given the initial concentration and the K_a value. Recall that the minimal ionization (less than 5%) of the acid allowed us to assume that its initial and equilibrium concentrations were approximately equal. Using the same approach here, the initial concentration of 0.100 M and the K_a for acetic acid of 1.8×10^{-5} allows us to perform the calculation below.

Let $x = [H_3O^+]_{eq}$
Assume $0.100 - x \approx 0.100$

$$CH_3COOH + H_2O \rightleftharpoons CH_3COO^- + H_3O^+$$

	CH_3COOH	H_2O	CH_3COO^-	H_3O^+
I	0.100		0	0
C	$-x$		$+x$	$+x$
E	$0.100 - x$		x	x

© Edvantage Interactive 2019

$$K_a = \frac{[CH_3COO^-][H_3O^+]}{[CH_3COOH]} = \frac{x^2}{0.100} = 1.8 \times 10^{-5}$$

$$x = \sqrt{(1.8 \times 10^{-5})(0.100)} = 1.342 \times 10^{-3}\ M$$

So pH = – log (1.342 × 10^{-3} M) = 2.87 (2 sig. figures)

(Note the location of the *first point* on the titration curve in Figure 6.4.4.)

Stage 2: *The pH approximately halfway to the equivalence point*
As we begin adding NaOH from the burette, the OH^- ions react with the CH_3COOH in the flask to produce CH_3COO^- and H_2O. Therefore, from the beginning of the titration until the equivalence point is reached, the flask will contain *a mixture of a weak acid and its conjugate base*. This means that, for most of that time, the reaction mixture will qualify as a buffer solution. When you look at the titration curve, you can see that the *buffer region* represents the interval over which there are sufficient quantities of both CH_3COOH and CH_3COO^- for the solution to be a buffer.

To calculate the pH of the reaction mixture at about halfway to the equivalence point, we can use the same sequence of calculations with the ICF table as for a strong acid–strong base titration. Consider the Sample Problem below.

Sample Problem 6.4.3(a) — Calculating pH Just before Halfway to the Equivalence Point

Calculate the pH of the solution produced in the reaction flask *just prior to halfway to the equivalence point* when 12.00 mL of 0.100 M NaOH has been added to 25.00 mL of 0.100 M CH_3COOH.

What to Think About

1. Once again calculate the diluted concentrations of reactant acid and base before the reaction.
2. The final concentrations of CH_3COOH and CH_3COO^- in the solution are significant and thus constitute a buffer.
3. Therefore calculate the pH either by manipulating the K_a expression for acetic acid or, by way of extension, using the Henderson-Hasselbalch equation (see below).

How to Do It

$$[CH_3COOH]_{IN} = 0.100\ M \times \frac{25.00\ mL}{37.00\ mL} = 0.06757\ M$$

$$[NaOH]_{IN} = 0.100\ M \times \frac{12.00\ mL}{37.00\ mL} = 0.03243\ M$$

$$CH_3COOH + NaOH \rightarrow NaCH_3COO + H_2O$$

	CH_3COOH	NaOH	$NaCH_3COO$	H_2O
I	0.06757	0.03243	0	
C	– 0.03243	– 0.03243	+ 0.03243	
F	0.03514	≈ 0	0.03243	

$$K_a = \frac{[H_3O^+][CH_3COO^-]}{[CH_3COOH]},\ \text{so}\ [H_3O^+] = \frac{K_a\,[CH_3COOH]}{[CH_3COO^-]}$$

$$[H_3O^+] = \frac{(1.8 \times 10^{-5})(0.03514)}{(0.03243)} = 1.95 \times 10^{-5}\ M$$

so pH = – log (1.95 × 10^{-5}) = 4.71 (2 sig. figures)

(Note the location of the *second point* on the curve.)

Using the Henderson-Hasselbalch Equation

Because a buffer solution exists in the reaction flask, we could have also chosen to solve the above problem using the Henderson-Hasselbalch equation as follows:

$$pH = pK_a + \log\left[\frac{[CH_3COO^-]}{[CH_3COOH]}\right] = 4.745 + \log\left[\frac{(0.03243)}{(0.03514)}\right] = 4.745 + (-0.0348) = 4.71$$

pH of Solution = pK_a at Halfway Point

The above methods show us that just before halfway to the equivalence point in the titration, *the log of the ratio is negative* because the [base]/[acid] ratio is less than one. This means that *just before halfway to the equivalence point, the solution pH is always less than the pK_a.*

Note that *exactly halfway to the equivalence point*, half of the acid has been converted to its conjugate base, so $[CH_3COOH] = [CH_3COO^-]$. We therefore see that:

$$[H_3O^+] = \frac{K_a\cancel{[CH_3COOH]}}{\cancel{[CH_3COO^-]}} \quad \text{and} \quad pH = pK_a + \log\frac{\cancel{[CH_3COO^-]}}{\cancel{[CH_3COOH]}}$$

so $\mathbf{[H_3O^+] = K_a} = 1.8 \times 10^{-5}$ so $pH = pK_a + \log 1$

$$\mathbf{pH = pK_a} = 4.74$$

The fact that the pH of the solution halfway to the equivalence point equals the pK_a of the weak acid being titrated is a useful relationship. This allows us to determine the K_a of a weak acid by titrating it with a strong base and noting the pH of the solution exactly halfway to the equivalence point on the titration curve.

Sample Problem 6.4.3(b) — Calculating pH Just beyond Halfway to the Equivalence Point

Calculate the pH of the solution produced in the reaction flask *just beyond halfway to the equivalence point* when 13.00 mL of 0.100 M NaOH has been added to 25.00 mL of 0.100 M CH_3COOH.

What to Think About

1. Calculate the diluted concentrations and enter them into the ICF table.
2. The solution in the reaction flask once again qualifies as a buffer.
3. Use the final concentrations of CH_3COOH and CH_3COO^- to calculate the pH of the solution in two ways as in the previous example.

How to Do It

$$[CH_3COOH]_{IN} = 0.100\ M \times \frac{25.00\ \cancel{mL}}{38.00\ \cancel{mL}} = 0.06579\ M$$

$$[NaOH]_{IN} = 0.100\ M \times \frac{13.00\ \cancel{mL}}{38.00\ \cancel{mL}} = 0.03421\ M$$

$$CH_3COOH + NaOH \rightarrow NaCH_3COO + H_2O$$

	CH_3COOH	$NaOH$	$NaCH_3COO$	H_2O
I	0.06579	0.03421	0	
C	− 0.03421	− 0.03421	+ 0.03421	
F	0.03158	0	0.03421	

$$K_a = \frac{[H_3O^+][CH_3COO^-]}{[CH_3COOH]} \quad \text{so} \quad [H_3O^+] = \frac{K_a\,[CH_3COOH]}{[CH_3COO^-]}$$

$$[H_3O^+] = \frac{(1.8 \times 10^{-5})\,(0.03158)}{(0.03421)} = 1.66 \times 10^{-5}\ M$$

so $pH = -\log(1.66 \times 10^{-5}) = 4.78$ (2 sig. figures)

Using the Henderson-Hasselbalch Equation

Once again, we could have chosen to solve the above problem using the Henderson-Hasselbalch equation as follows:

$$pH = pK_a + \log\left[\frac{[CH_3COO^-]}{[CH_3COOH]}\right] = 4.745 + \log\left[\frac{(0.03421)}{(0.03158)}\right] = 4.74 + (0.0347) = 4.78$$

pH of Solution > pK_a beyond Halfway and Prior to the Equivalence Point

We can therefore see that beyond halfway to the equivalence point in the titration, *the log of the ratio is positive* because the [base]/[acid] is greater than one. This means that *beyond halfway to the equivalence point, the solution pH is always greater than the pK_a.*

© Edvantage Interactive 2019

During the titration of a weak acid with strong base:

- prior to halfway to the equivalence point: $[H_3O^+] > K_a$ and so $pH < pK_a$
- halfway to the equivalence point: $[H_3O^+] = K_a$ and so $pH = pK_a$
- beyond halfway and prior to the equivalence point: $[H_3O^+] < K_a$ and so $pH > pK_a$

Stage 3: *The pH at the equivalence point*

If you look again at the weak acid–strong base titration curve (Figure 6.4.4), you'll notice that the volume of 0.100 M NaOH required to neutralize 25.00 mL of 0.100 M CH_3COOH at the equivalence point is *exactly the same* as that required to neutralize the same volume of 0.100 M HCl. This reminds us that the strength of an acid has *no bearing* on the volume of base required to neutralize it in a titration.

At the equivalence point, all of the acid originally present has reacted with the added NaOH. The reaction flask therefore contains an aqueous solution of the salt produced from a weak acid and a strong base, namely $NaCH_3COO$. As noted above, although the Na^+ ion cannot react with water, the CH_3COO^- ion from a weak acid is itself a weak base and will therefore accept protons from water, producing OH^- ions. This means that the pH at the equivalence point will be above 7 due to the presence of a basic salt.

The titration of a weak acid by a strong base will produce a basic solution with a pH greater than 7 at the equivalence point because the anion present in the product salt will undergo hydrolysis to produce OH^- ions and the cation will not hydrolyze.

To correctly calculate the pH at the equivalence point, we must first consider the initial reaction that *goes to completion*. This requires the use of the IC**F** table. We must then use the IC**E** table to manage the hydrolysis reaction of the acetate anion with water, which involves an *equilibrium*. This is illustrated in the Sample Problem below.

Sample Problem 6.4.3(c) — Calculating pH at the Equivalence Point

Calculate the pH of the solution produced in the reaction flask when 25.00 mL of 0.100 M NaOH has been added to 25.00 mL of 0.100 M CH_3COOH

What to Think About

1. Once again dilute the acid and base and then enter those values into the ICF table for the reaction that goes to completion.
2. Examine the bottom line of the ICF table. It reveals that a 0.0500 M solution of $NaCH_3COO$ exists in the reaction flask at the equivalence point.

How to Do It

Part 1

$$[CH_3COOH]_{IN} = 0.100\text{ M} \times \frac{25.00\text{ mL}}{50.00\text{ mL}} = 0.0500\text{ M}$$

$$[NaOH]_{IN} = 0.100\text{ M} \times \frac{25.00\text{ mL}}{50.00\text{ mL}} = 0.0500\text{ M}$$

$$CH_3COOH + NaOH \rightarrow NaCH_3COO + H_2O$$

	CH_3COOH	$NaOH$	$NaCH_3COO$	H_2O
I	0.0500	0.0500	0	
C	− 0.0500	− 0.0500	+ 0.0500	
F	≈ 0	≈ 0	0.0500	

Continued on next page

Sample Problem 6.4.3(c) *(Continued)*

What to Think About

3. The anion of the dissociated salt is the conjugate base of a weak acid and is thus capable of accepting protons from water in a hydrolysis reaction.

4. For the second part of the calculation, enter the 0.0500 M CH_3COO^- in the **I**nitial row of the ICE table for the hydrolysis equilibrium.

5. Calculate the pH of the solution resulting from the anionic hydrolysis of the acetate ion.

How to Do It

Part 2

Let $x = [OH^-]_{eq}$

$$CH_3COO^- + H_2O \rightleftharpoons CH_3COOH + OH^-$$

	CH_3COO^-	H_2O	CH_3COOH	OH^-
I	0.0500		0	0
C	$-x$		$+x$	$+x$
E	$0.0500 - x$		x	x

Assume $0.0500 - x \approx 0.0500$

$$K_b = \frac{[CH_3COOH][OH^-]}{[CH_3COO^-]} = \frac{K_w}{K_a} = \frac{1.0 \times 10^{-14}}{1.8 \times 10^{-5}} = 5.6 \times 10^{-10}$$

$$\frac{x^2}{0.0500} = 5.6 \times 10^{-10} \quad \text{so} \quad x = \sqrt{(0.0500)(5.6 \times 10^{-10})}$$

$x = [OH^-] = 5.29 \times 10^{-6}$ M so pOH $= -\log(5.292 \times 10^{-6})$

pOH $= 5.27$ and so pH $= 14.000 - 5.27 = 8.72$

(2 sig. figures)

(Note the location of the *third point* on the curve.)

Choosing the Right Indicator

Because the vertical region on the titration curve around the equivalence point is shorter than for a strong acid–strong base titration, we are more limited when choosing the proper indicator. The table of acid-base indicators (Table A6) shows us that either phenolphthalein or thymol blue (based on its second transition point) would be an appropriate indicator in this case. Methyl red would not.

Stage 4: *The pH beyond the equivalence point*

After all of the acid has been neutralized, the solution again becomes increasingly basic with the addition of excess OH^- ions. Although a relatively high concentration of the weakly basic acetate ion remains in the reaction flask beyond the equivalence point, the presence of excess hydroxide ions in the flask is far more significant in determining the pH. The excess NaOH is a *strong base* and the increasing $[OH^-]$ from that base forces the weak base hydrolysis equilibrium even further to the left.

$$CH_3COO^-(aq) + H_2O(l) \rightleftharpoons CH_3COOH(aq) + \mathbf{OH^-}(aq)$$

The result is that we can safely ignore any contribution to the $[OH^-]$ in the flask by the acetate ion and thus use only the ICF table to calculate the pH. Consider that Sample Problem below.

 © Edvantage Interactive 2019

Sample Problem 6.4.3(d) — Calculating pH beyond the Equivalence Point

Calculate the pH of the solution produced in the reaction flask when 30.00 mL of 0.100 M NaOH has been added to 25.00 mL of 0.100 M CH_3COOH.

What to Think About	How to Do It
1. Because the equivalence point has been passed by 5.00 mL, once again expect the pH to be well above 7.	$[CH_3COOH]_{IN} = 0.100\ M \times \frac{25.00\ mL}{55.00\ mL} = 0.04545\ M$ $[NaOH]_{IN} = 0.100\ M \times \frac{30.00\ mL}{55.00\ mL} = 0.05454\ M$
2. As [NaOH] will be in excess, ignore the final $[CH_3COO^-]$ when calculating pH.	$CH_3COOH + NaOH \rightarrow NaCH_3COO + H_2O$
3. The subtraction yielding the final $[OH^-]$ gives an answer to three significant figures. This specifies the decimal places in the final pH.	See table and calculation below

	CH_3COOH	$NaOH$	$NaCH_3COO$	H_2O
I	0.04545	0.05454	0	
C	− 0.04545	− 0.04545	+ 0.04545	
F	≈ 0	0.00909	0.04545	

final $[OH^-]$ = final $[NaOH] = 0.00909\ M$

$pOH = -\log(0.00909) = 2.041$

$pH = 14.000 - 2.041 = 11.959$ (3 sig. figures)

(Note the location of the *fourth point* on the curve.)

Comparing Titration Curves

Note that the pH at this *final stage* is the same as for the titration of 0.100 M HCl by 0.100 M NaOH, although the pH values at *the first three stages are different.*

Figure 6.4.5 compares the two titration curves. Note the position of the weak acid–strong base titration curve relative to the strong acid–strong base curve *before the equivalence point.* As the strength of the acid being titrated decreases, the portion of the titration curve before the equivalence point will shift farther and farther up so that each of the first three stages we have discussed will be associated with higher and higher pH values during the titration. Yet despite the acid's strengths being different, the volume of base required to reach equivalence remains the same!

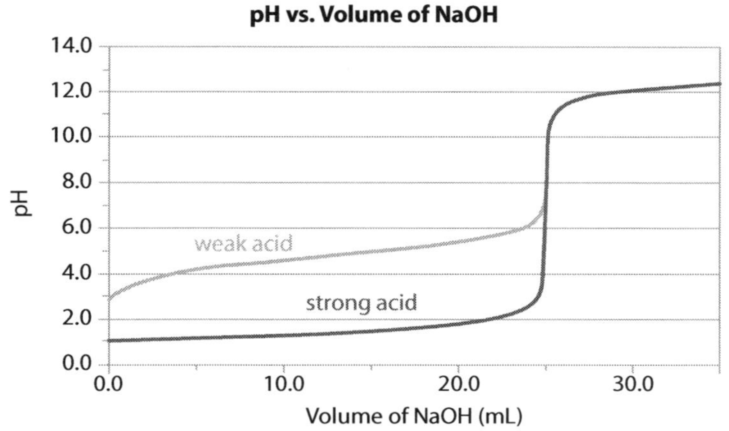

Figure 6.4.5 *Comparison of titration curves*

Quick Check

1. Why do we label a region of a weak acid–strong base titration curve before the equivalence point as a "buffer region"?

2. Why is the pH at the equivalence point of a weak acid–strong base titration higher than 7?

3. When titrating acetic acid with sodium hydroxide, why can we ignore any contribution to the $[OH^-]$ by the acetate anion beyond the equivalence point when calculating pH?

4. *On Figure 6.4.5 above,* sketch the titration curve for the titration of 25.0 mL 0.100 M hypochlorous acid, HClO, with a solution of 0.100 M NaOH, given the following information:

Initial pH of HClO Solution	pH Halfway to Equivalence Point	pH at Equivalence Point
4.27	7.54	10.12

Practice Problems 6.4.3 — Weak Acid–Strong Base Titration Curves

1. (a) Calculate the pH of the solution produced when 9.00 mL of 0.200 M NaOH has been added to 20.0 mL of 0.200 M HCOOH. Is this value less than or greater than the pK_a of HCOOH?

   (b) Calculate the pH at the equivalence point of this titration.

2. A student titrates an unknown weak monoprotic acid with a standard solution of KOH and draws a titration curve. Halfway to the equivalence point, the pH of the solution is identified to be 4.187. Identify the acid.

3. (a) A 20.0 mL sample of 0.450 M HNO_2 is titrated with a 0.500 M NaOH solution. What $[H_3O^+]$ will exist in the reaction flask exactly halfway to the equivalence point?

   (b) The equivalence point is reached when 18.00 mL of the basic solution has been added to the original nitrous acid solution. Calculate the pH at the equivalence point.

 © Edvantage Interactive 2019

III. Weak Base–Strong Acid Titration Curves

The third type of titration we will discuss can be considered the opposite of the previous type — namely, the titration of a *weak base* by a *strong* acid. Recall that the curve for a strong base titrated with a strong acid is the *same shape* as a strong acid titrated with a strong base, but is *inverted.* The same is true of the titration curve for a weak base titrated with a strong acid compared with the curve for a weak acid titrated with a strong base: *the shape is the same but inverted.*

Let's investigate the titration of a 0.100 M NH_3 solution with a 0.100 M HCl. The formula and net ionic equations for the reaction are shown below:

$$NH_3(aq) + HCl(aq) \rightarrow NH_4^+(aq) + Cl^-(aq)$$

$$NH_3(aq) + H_3O^+(aq) \rightarrow NH_4^+(aq) + H_2O(l)$$

If we compare the titration curve for the above reaction to that for a *strong base* titrated with a strong acid, we can once again identify a number of important features. Consider those two curves in Figure 6.4.6 below.

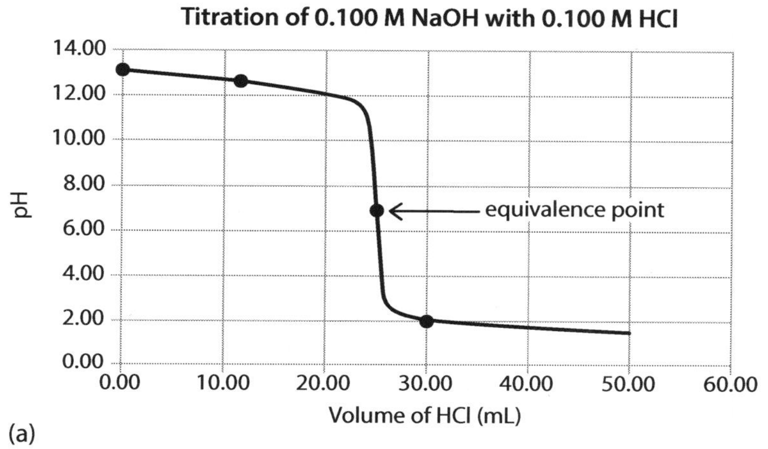

(a)

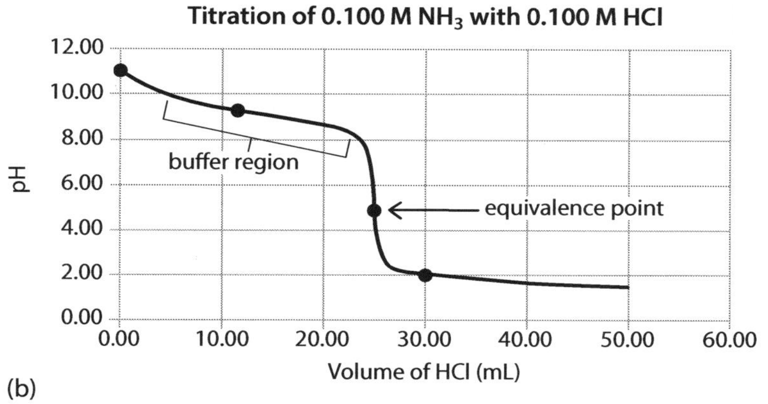

(b)

Figure 6.4.6 *Titration curves for solutions of (a) 0.100 M NaOH and (b) 0.100 M* NH_3 *titrated with 0.100 M HCl*

Important Features of a Weak Base–Strong Acid Titration Curve

1. Because the solution we begin with is a *weak* base, we expect the initial pH to be above 7, but *lower* than if we were starting with a *strong base*.
2. There is an initial small drop in pH as the titration begins, but then the pH decreases more slowly over a *buffer region* during which significant amounts of the weak base (NH_3) and its conjugate acid (NH_4^+) are present in the flask. However, the pH in this region still changes *more quickly* than it does during a strong base–strong acid titration. The buffer region ends just before the steep drop in pH associated with the equivalence point.

3. The steep drop at the equivalence point occurs *over a smaller pH range* than when a *strong base* is titrated with a strong acid and *the pH at the equivalence point is below 7*. The solution at the equivalence point contains the anion from a strong acid (Cl^-) and the cation from a weak base (NH_4^+). Although the anion can't accept protons from water, *the cation is a weak acid and will therefore donate protons to water, producing* H_3O^+ *ions*. Hence the pH is below 7.

4. Beyond the equivalence point, the pH decreases slowly as excess H_3O^+ is added.

The four points have once again been placed at the same key stages of the titration. And once again, by considering the species present in the reaction flask at these stages, we can calculate the pH of the solution. The calculations are similar to the previous titration type in that they reflect, in this case, the minimal ionization of the weak base and the hydrolysis reaction of its conjugate with water.

Stage 1: *The pH before the addition of any titrant*

This calculation is the first type we discussed for weak bases: the pH of a weak base solution is determined given the initial concentration and the K_b value. The slight ionization of the NH_3 allows us to assume that its initial and equilibrium concentrations are approximately equal. Consider the following pH calculation:

$$K_b \text{ for } NH_3 = \frac{K_w}{K_a \text{ for } NH_4^+} = \frac{1.00 \times 10^{-14}}{5.6 \times 10^{-10}} = 1.8 \times 10^{-5}$$

Let $x = [OH^-]_{eq}$

Assume $0.100 - x \approx 0.100$

	NH_3	+ H_2O $\rightleftharpoons$	NH_4^+	+ OH^-
I	0.100		0	0
C	$-x$		$+x$	$+x$
E	$0.100 - x$		x	x

$$K_b = \frac{[NH_4^+][OH^-]}{[NH_3]} = \frac{x^2}{0.100} = 1.8 \times 10^{-5}$$

$x = \sqrt{(1.8 \times 10^{-5})(0.100)} = 1.34 \times 10^{-3}\text{ M} = [OH^-]$

so $pOH = -\log(1.34 \times 10^{-3}) = 2.872$ and

$pH = 14.000 - 2.872 = 11.13$

(Note the location of the *first point* on the curve.)

Stage 2: *The pH approximately halfway to the equivalence point*

As the titration begins and HCl is added to the flask, the H_3O^+ ions react with the NH_3 to produce NH_4^+ and H_2O. Thus, from the beginning of the titration until the equivalence point is reached, the flask will contain *a mixture of a weak base and its conjugate acid*. This means once again that, for most of that time, the reaction mixture will qualify as a buffer solution. If you look at the titration curve, you can see that the *buffer region* represents the interval over which there are significant quantities of both NH_3 and NH_4^+ in the solution.

The use of the ICF table will again allow us to efficiently organize and manage the information provided in the question.

© Edvantage Interactive 2019

Sample Problem 6.4.4(a) — Calculating pH before Halfway to the Equivalence Point

Calculate the pH of the solution produced during a titration following the addition of 12.00 mL of 0.100 M HCl to 25.00 mL of 0.100 M NH_3. This is almost *halfway* to the equivalence point.

What to Think About

1. Once again determine the diluted concentrations and enter those values into the ICF table.
2. Use the final concentrations at the completion of the reaction to determine the pH.
3. As we are almost halfway to the equivalence point, the $[NH_3]$ and $[NH_4^+]$ are sufficient to constitute a buffer.
4. The $[Cl^-]$ cannot react with water and so will not affect the pH of the solution.

How to Do It

$$[NH_3]_{IN} = 0.100\ M \times \frac{25.00\ mL}{37.00\ mL} = 0.06757\ M$$

$$[HCl]_{IN} = 0.100\ M \times \frac{12.00\ mL}{37.00\ mL} = 0.03243\ M$$

	NH_3 +	HCl →	NH_4^+ +	Cl^-
I	0.06757	0.03243	0	0
C	− 0.03243	− 0.03243	+ 0.03243	+ 0.03243
F	0.03514	≈ 0	0.03243	0.03243

$$K_b = \frac{[NH_4^+][OH^-]}{[NH_3]}, \quad \text{so} \quad [OH^-] = \frac{K_b\,[NH_3]}{[NH_4^+]}$$

$$[OH^-] = \frac{(1.8 \times 10^{-5})(0.03514)}{(0.03243)} = 1.95 \times 10^{-5}\ M$$

$$pOH = -\log(1.95 \times 10^{-5}) = 4.710$$

so pH = 14.000 − 4.710 = 9.29 (2 sig. figures)

(Note the location of the *second point* on the curve.)

Using the Henderson-Hasselbalch Equation

Because a buffer solution exists in the reaction flask, we could have again chosen to solve the above problem using the Henderson-Hasselbalch equation. In the equation, we use the pK_a for the conjugate acid of NH_3.
The pK_a for $NH_4^+ = -\log(5.6 \times 10^{-10}) = 9.252$.

$$pH = pK_a + \log\left[\frac{[NH_3]}{[NH_4^+]}\right] = 9.252 + \log\left[\frac{[0.03514]}{[0.03243]}\right] = 9.252 + (0.0349) = 9.29$$

Note that, because the [base]/[acid] ratio is greater than 1, *the log of the ratio is positive*. This means that just prior to halfway to the equivalence point, *the pH is greater than the* pK_a

$pOH = pK_b$ of Weak Base at Halfway Point

Note that *exactly halfway to the equivalence point* half of the base has been converted to its conjugate acid. Therefore $[NH_3] = [NH_4^+]$. This means that:

$$[OH^-] = \frac{K_b\cancel{[NH_3]}}{\cancel{[NH_4^+]}} \qquad pOH = pK_b + \log\frac{\cancel{[NH_3]}}{\cancel{[NH_4^+]}}$$

so $\mathbf{[OH^-] = K_b} = 1.8 \times 10^{-5}$ so $pOH = pK_b + \log 1$

and $[H_3O^+] = \dfrac{1.00 \times 10^{-14}}{1.8 \times 10^{-5}} = 5.6 \times 10^{-10}$ $\mathbf{pOH = pK_b} = 4.745$

$\mathbf{[H_3O^+] = K_a}$ (for NH_4^+) $\mathbf{pH = pK_a}$ (for NH_4^+) = 9.25

The fact that the pOH of the solution halfway to the equivalence point equals the pK_b of the weak base is a similar scenario to that of a *weak acid–strong base* titration. In this case, we can determine the K_b of a weak base by titrating it with a strong acid and noting the pOH of the solution exactly halfway to the equivalence point on the titration curve. (Had we chosen to use the Henderson-Hasselbalch equation, we would have calculated the same pH value.)

Stage 3: *The pH at the equivalence point*

At the equivalence point, all of the base initially present in the flask has reacted with the added HCl. The flask therefore contains an aqueous solution of the salt produced from a strong acid and a weak base — in this case, NH_4Cl. We noted above that the Cl^- ion cannot react with water, but the NH_4^+ is weakly acidic and will therefore react with water to produce H_3O^+ ions. This means that the pH at the equivalence point will be below 7 due to the presence of an acidic salt.

> The titration of a weak base by a strong acid will produce an acidic solution with a pH below 7 at the equivalence point because the cation present in the product salt will undergo hydrolysis to produce H_3O^+ ions and the anion will not hydrolyze.

To calculate the pH at the equivalence point, we must once again consider the initial reaction that *goes to completion*, and then the hydrolysis reaction of the ammonium anion with water that involves an *equilibrium*. Consider next Sample Problem.

Sample Problem 6.4.4(b) — Calculating pH at the Equivalence Point

Calculate the pH of the solution produced in the reaction flask when 25.00 mL of 0.100 M HCl has been added to 25.00 mL of 0.100 M NH_3.

What to Think About

1. Dilute the acid and base and enter those values into the ICF table for the reaction that goes to completion.
2. Examine the bottom line of the ICF table. It shows that a 0.0500 M NH_4Cl solution exists in the reaction flask at the equivalence point.
3. The cation of the dissociated salt is weakly acidic and is thus capable of donating protons to water in a hydrolysis reaction.
4. For the second part of the calculation, enter the 0.05000 M NH_4^+ into the **I**nitial row of the ICE table for the hydrolysis equilibrium.
5. Calculate the pH of the solution resulting from the cationic hydrolysis of the ammonium ion.

How to Do It

Part 1

$$[NH_3]_{IN} = 0.100\ M \times \frac{25.00\ mL}{50.00\ mL} = 0.0500\ M$$

$$[HCl]_{IN} = 0.100\ M \times \frac{25.00\ mL}{50.00\ mL} = 0.0500\ M$$

	NH_3 +	HCl →	NH_4^+ +	Cl^-
I	0.0500	0.0500	0	0
C	− 0.0500	− 0.0500	+ 0.0500	+ 0.0500
F	≈ 0	≈ 0	0.0500	0.0500

Part 2

Let $x = [H_3O^+]_{eq}$

	NH_4^+	+ H_2O ⇌	NH_3	+ H_3O^+
I	0.0500		0	0
C	− x		+ x	+ x
E	0.0500 − x		x	x

Assume $0.0500 - x \approx 0.0500$

$$K_a = \frac{[NH_3][H_3O^+]}{[NH_4^+]} = 5.6 \times 10^{-10}$$

$$\frac{x^2}{0.0500} = 5.6 \times 10^{-10} \quad \text{so} \quad x = \sqrt{(0.0500)(5.6 \times 10^{-10})}$$

$$x = 5.292 \times 10^{-6}\ M \quad \text{so pH} = -\log(5.292 \times 10^{-6}) = 5.28$$

(Note the location of the *third point* on the curve.)

© Edvantage Interactive 2019

Selecting the Indicator

The relatively short vertical section of the curve near the pH at the equivalence point of 5.28 suggests that an appropriate indicator for this titration would be methyl red. The pK_a for methyl red is 5.4.

Stage 4: *The pH beyond the equivalence point*

After all of the base has been neutralized, the solution again becomes increasingly acidic with the addition of excess H_3O^+ ions. Although a relatively high concentration of the weakly acidic ammonium ion remains in the reaction flask beyond the equivalence point, its presence is insignificant in determining pH in the same way that excess acetate ions were insignificant beyond the equivalence point in the weak acid–strong base titration. In this case, the presence of excess H_3O^+ in the flask is the only significant factor in determining the pH. The excess HCl is a *strong acid* and the increasing $[H_3O^+]$ from that acid forces the weak acid hydrolysis equilibrium even further to the left.

$$NH_4^+(aq) + H_2O(l) \rightleftharpoons NH_3(aq) + \mathbf{H_3O^+}(aq)$$

The result is that we can safely ignore any contribution to the $[H_3O^+]$ in the flask by the ammonium ion and so need only use the ICF table to calculate the pH. Consider Sample Problem 6.4.4(c) below.

Sample Problem 6.4.4(c) — Calculating pH beyond the Equivalence Point

Calculate the pH of the solution produced in the reaction flask when 30.00 mL of 0.100 M HCl has been added to 25.00 mL of 0.100 M NH_3

What to Think About

1. Because the equivalence point has been passed by 5.00 mL, expect the pH to be well below 7.
2. As [HCl] will be in excess, ignore the final $[NH_4^+]$ when calculating pH. Also ignore the $[Cl^-]$.
3. The subtraction yielding the final $[H_3O^+]$ gives an answer to three significant figures. This determines the decimal places in the final pH.

How to Do It

$$[NH_3]_{IN} = 0.100\text{ M} \times \frac{25.00\text{ mL}}{55.00\text{ mL}} = 0.04545\text{ M}$$

$$[HCl]_{IN} = 0.100\text{ M} \times \frac{30.00\text{ mL}}{55.00\text{ mL}} = 0.05454\text{ M}$$

	NH_3	+ HCl	→ NH_4^+	+ Cl^-
I	0.04545	0.05454	0	0
C	− 0.04545	− 0.04545	+ 0.04545	+ 0.04545
F	≈ 0	0.00909	0.04545	0.04545

final $[HCl]$ = final $[H_3O^+]$ = 0.00909 M

pH = − log (0.00909) = 2.04 (2 sig. figures)

(Note the location of the *fourth point* on the curve.)

Practice Problems 6.4.4 — Weak Base–Strong Acid Titration Curves

1. Calculate the pH of the solution produced during the titration described above after 13.0 mL of 0.100 M HCl has been added to 25.0 mL of 0.100 M NH_3. (This is just beyond halfway to the equivalence point). Should your answer be greater than or less than the pK_a of NH_4^+?

2. Explain how the titration curve for a weak base titrated by a strong acid can be used to determine the K_b of the weak base.

3. Calculate the pH of the solution produced in the titration described above after 40.0 mL of 0.100 M HCl has been added to 25.0 mL of 0.100 M NH_3. Does the pH value you calculate agree with the titration curve?

Quick Check

1. Why is the pH at the equivalence point of a weak base–strong acid titration lower than 7?

___

2. Phenolphthalein is an appropriate indicator for the first two types of titrations we discussed in this section. Why is phenolphthalein a poor indicator choice for the titration of a weak base with a strong acid?

___

3. When titrating aqueous ammonia with hydrochloric acid, why can we ignore any contribution to the [H_3O^+] by the ammonium cation beyond the equivalence point when calculating pH?

___

© Edvantage Interactive 2019

6.4 Activity: A Titration Curve Summary

Question

How can you summarize the important aspects of each of the three types of titrations discussed in this section?

Background

As you have learned in this section, each type of titration we have considered has a different net ionic equation, a different titration curve with a characteristic shape and features, and a different equivalence point pH.

Procedure

1. Consider each of the titration types listed at the top of each column in the table on the next page. Complete each box in the table for each titration type using "HA" as the general formula for a typical weak acid and "B" as the general formula for a typical weak base.
2. Assume that the reacting solutions in each titration are at 0.100 M concentrations and that we begin with 25.0 mL aliquots in each reaction flask.
3. Although only a sketch of each curve is required, on each curve, clearly label the:
   - *x*- and *y*-axes
   - approximate pH at each equivalence point
   - volume of titrant required to reach the equivalence point
   - buffer region (if applicable)
4. In the boxes beneath each curve, state the reason that the equivalence pH is below, equal to, or above 7. Include any relevant chemical equation if applicable.
5. Use the completed table for review before your quizzes or tests.

A Titration Curve Summary Table

Strong Acid + Strong Base	Weak Acid + Strong Base	Weak Base + Strong Acid
Net Ionic Equation	**Net Ionic Equation**	**Net Ionic Equation**
Sketch of Titration Curve	**Sketch of Titration Curve**	**Sketch of Titration Curve**
Reason for Equivalence Point pH Value	**Reason for Equivalence Point pH Value**	**Reason for Equivalence Point pH Value**
Hydrolysis Reaction (if any)	**Hydrolysis Reaction (if any)**	**Hydrolysis Reaction (if any)**

Results and Discussion

1. The volume of titrant required to reach the equivalence point in each titration should be exactly the same. Explain why.

2. Explain how each of the two "weak–strong" titration curves can be used to determine one of either a K_a or a K_b value.

 © Edvantage Interactive 2019

6.4 Review Questions

1. Consider the following for a hypothetical indicator: $K_a = \dfrac{[H_3O^+][In^-]}{[HIn]} = 1.0 \times 10^{-7}$

   So, given that $\dfrac{K_a}{[H_3O^+]} = \dfrac{[In^-]}{[HIn]}$

   Complete the following table for three different solutions given that HIn is *yellow* and In^- is *blue*.

Solution	**$[In^-]/[HIn]$ Ratio in Solution**	**Solution Color**
0.0010 M HCl		
Pure water		
0.0010 M NaOH		

2. Equal concentrations of an indicator, HIn, and one of three different acids are placed in three separate flasks and the following data was obtained for each pair of compounds:

Solution →	**0.1 M HNO_3**	**0.1 M HA1**	**0.1 M HA2**
0.1 M HIn color	red	yellow	red

   Use the above data to list the three acids, HA1, HA2, and HIn, in order of increasing strength and explain your reasoning.

   ________ < ________ < ________

3. You are given four 0.10 M solutions without labels and told they are HCl, NaOH, $FeCl_3$, and NaCN. You are also told to choose only three indicators that will positively identify each solution. Complete the table below showing your choice of indicators and their colors in each solution.

Solution →	**0.10 M HCl**	**0.10 M NaOH**	**0.10 M $FeCl_3$**	**0.10 M NaCN**
Indicator 1:				
Indicator 2:				
Indicator 3:				

4. Complete the table below showing the reactants in three different titrations.
   (a) State if the pH at the equivalence point of each titration will be below, equal to, or above 7.
   (b) Select an appropriate indicator from the table of acid-base indicators (Table A6) for each titration. (There may be more than one correct choice for each titration.)

	HNO_3 + KOH	**NaOH + HCOOH**	**HBr + NH_3**
pH at equivalence pt.			
Indicator			

5. Bromcresol purple undergoes its color change from yellow to purple as pH increases from 5.2 through to 6.8.
   (a) Is bromcresol purple a stronger or a weaker acid than acetic acid? Explain your answer.

   (b) Would bromcresol purple be a good indicator to indicate that acetic acid is acidic? Why or why not?

6. The following 0.10 M solutions have had their labels removed: NaCl, K_3PO_4, LiHCOO, CH_3COOH, and HIO_3. The solutions are tested with three indicators and the results in the table below were observed.

	Bromthymol Blue	Methyl Orange	Thymolphthalein
Solution A	yellow	red	colorless
Solution B	green	yellow	colorless
Solution C	blue	yellow	blue
Solution D	yellow	yellow	colorless
Solution E	blue	yellow	colorless

Identify each solution:

A ___________ B___________ C___________ D___________ E___________

7. Complete the following table:

Indicator	pK_a	K_a	Color in Pure Water	Color Displayed in 0.010 M NaOH	Color Displayed in 0.010 M HCl
Phenol red					
Methyl orange					
Alizarin yellow					

8. Complete each of the following statements relating to weak–strong titrations by placing the words "lower" or "higher" in each of the blank spaces in each statement.
   (a) In a weak acid–strong base titration, the weaker the acid being titrated, the ___________ (lower or higher) the initial pH of the solution will be, and the ___________ (lower or higher) the pH at the equivalence point will be.
   (b) In a weak base–strong acid titration, the weaker the base being titrated, the ___________ (lower or higher) the initial pH of the solution will be, and the ___________ (lower or higher) the pH at the equivalence point will be.

9. The chemistry of buffers and the hydrolysis of salts must both be considered when calculating the pH at different stages during the final two types of titrations we have discussed in this section. For each type of titration below, explain why in the appropriate space in the table:

	Calculating pH Halfway to the Equivalence Point (Chemistry of Buffers)	Calculating pH at the Equivalence Point (Hydrolysis of Salts)
Titration of a weak acid by a strong base		
Titration of a weak base by a strong acid		

 © Edvantage Interactive 2019

10. Explain why the calculation of pH at the equivalence point for each of the titration types in question 8 above requires a *two-step* process.

11. A titration is performed in which a standard 0.200 M solution of NaOH is added to a 20.0 mL sample of a 0.250 M HCOOH solution.
(a) Determine the pH halfway to the equivalence point.

(b) Calculate the volume of standard solution required to reach the equivalence point.

(c) Calculate the pH at the equivalence point.

12. A student titrates a solution of a weak monoprotic acid with a standardized NaOH solution. She monitors the pH with a pH meter and draws the titration curve. The curve reveals that, halfway to the equivalence point, the pH of the reaction mixture was 3.456. Identify the weak acid.

13. A solution of the weak base ethanolamine, $HOCH_2CH_2NH_2$, is titrated with a standard HCl solution. The pH is monitored with a pH meter and the titration curve is drawn. The curve reveals that, halfway to the equivalence point, the pH of the reaction mixture was 9.50. Calculate the K_b for ethanolamine.

14. The curve below shows the titration of a 0.10 M NaOH solution with a 0.10 M HCl solution. On the *same set of axes below*:

(a) Sketch the titration curve for a 0.20 M NaOH solution being titrated with the same acid. Choose an appropriate indicator.

(b) Sketch the titration curve for a 0.10 M NH_3 solution being titrated with the same acid. Choose an appropriate indicator.

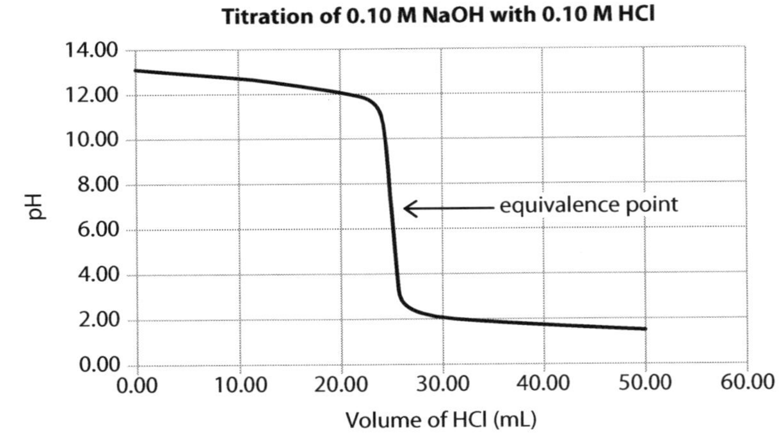

15. The curves we have discussed for the titration of both strong and weak acids have been limited to monoprotic acids. What do you think the titration curve might look like if the titration involved the titration of a weak *diprotic* acid with a strong base?

(a) Sketch your suggested curve below:

(b) What would you need to consider when selecting an indicator for such a titration?

 © Edvantage Interactive 2019

6.5 Non-metal and Metal Oxides in Water

Warm Up

1. Recall some of the information about chemical bonding that you have studied. Consider the electronegativity values of the main-group elements in groups 1 and 2 and 13 through 17, as shown in the chart below.

Electronegativities of the Elements

H 2.1																	He
Li 1.0	Be 1.5											B 2.0	C 2.5	N 3.0	O 3.5	F 4.0	Ne
Na 0.9	Mg 1.2											Al 1.5	Si 1.8	P 2.1	S 2.5	Cl 3.0	Ar
K 0.8	Ca 1.0	Sc 1.3	Ti 1.5	V 1.6	Cr 1.6	Mn 1.5	Fe 1.8	Co 1.8	Ni 1.8	Cu 1.9	Zn 1.6	Ga 1.6	Ge 1.8	As 2.0	Se 2.4	Br 2.8	Kr
Rb 0.8	Sr 1.0	Y 1.3	Zr 1.4	Nb 1.6	Mo 1.8	Tc	Ru 2.2	Rh 2.2	Pd 2.2	Ag 1.9	Cd 1.7	In 1.7	Sn 1.8	Sb 1.9	Te 2.1	I 2.5	Xe
Cs 0.7	Ba 0.9	La 1.1	Hf 1.3	Ta 1.5	W 1.7	Re 1.9	Os 2.2	Ir 2.2	Pt 2.2	Au 2.4	Hg 1.9	Tl 1.8	Pb 1.8	Bi 1.9	Po 2.0	At 2.2	Rn
Fr 0.7	Ra 0.9	Ac 1.1															

Ce 1.1	Pr 1.1	Nd 1.2	Pm	Sm 1.2	Eu 1.2	Gd 1.1	Tb 1.2	Dy 1.2	Ho 1.2	Er 1.2	Tm 1.2	Yb 1.1	Lu 1.2
Th 1.3	Pa 1.5	U 1.7											

(a) Elements from which two of these seven groups will form the *most ionic* oxides?

____

(b) In which region of the periodic table are elements located that will form the *most covalent* oxides?

____

2. Consider the chemical equations below, representing the typical reaction of two different oxide compounds with water:

$Na_2O(s) + H_2O(l) \rightarrow 2\,NaOH(aq)$

$SO_3(g) + H_2O(l) \rightarrow H_2SO_4(aq)$

Determine the type of chemical bonds in each of the reactant oxide compounds and complete the following *general* statements:

(a) *In general*, the reaction of ____________ (ionic or covalent) oxides with water will produce *basic* solutions.

(b) *In general*, the reaction of ____________ (ionic or covalent) oxides with water will produce *acidic* solutions.

Basic Anhydrides

The periodic table summarizes an enormous amount of empirical data about the elements by classifying them according to their chemical and physical properties. One of the most important of these classifications is the designation of an element as either a metal or a non-metal. Within each of these categories, the elements and the compounds they form often behave in characteristic and predictable ways in several important types of chemical reactions.

One example of such a chemical change is the reaction between two of the most common compounds on our planet — the oxides of the elements and water. *In general,* metal oxides react with water to form bases, and non-metal oxides react with water to form acids.

As with most general statements in chemistry, there are exceptions. For a metal oxide to react with water and produce a *basic* solution, it must be both *highly ionic and soluble*. These criteria are only met by the oxides formed from the group 1 *alkali* metals and all but one of the group 2 *alkaline* earth metals. These families are so-named because their oxides (except for Be) react with water to produce alkaline or basic solutions. Metal oxides that react with water in this way are called *basic anhydrides* ("anhydride" means "without water"). Although the group 2 metal oxides are less soluble than the alkali metal oxides, their aqueous solutions are basic.

Metal oxides formed from the group 1 alkali metals and the group 2 alkaline earth metals (except Be) react with water to produce basic solutions. These oxides are referred to as *basic anhydrides.*

When basic anhydrides react with water, the metal ions are actually spectators. It is really the *dissociated oxide ions that react with water.*

If you locate the oxide ion on the Table of Relative Strengths of Brønsted-Lowry Acids and Bases (Table A5), you will notice that it is found on the bottom right corner of the table where it is identified as a *strong base*. Because of its *enormous affinity for protons*, each oxide ion in water will remove a proton from a water molecule. This converts both itself and the water into hydroxide ions.

We can demonstrate the initial dissociation of a metal oxide and the subsequent reaction of its oxide ion with water (written as "HOH") by using sodium oxide as an example:

Dissociation: $Na_2O(s) \rightarrow 2\ Na^+(aq) + O^{2-}(aq)$

Net ionic equation: $O^{2-}(aq) + HOH(l) \rightarrow OH^-(aq) + OH^-(aq)$

Overall reaction: $Na_2O(s) + H_2O(l) \rightarrow 2\ Na^+(aq) + 2\ OH^-(aq)$

Not all metal oxides are considered to be basic anhydrides. Metal oxides are solid at room temperature, but many are not soluble in water. The oxide ions are locked so tightly in the crystal lattice structure of these compounds that they cannot react with water to generate hydroxide ions.

There are also several metal oxides that are referred to as *amphoteric*. This means that, depending on the reaction conditions, they can behave as either acidic oxides or basic oxides. Some of these compounds include the group 2 metal oxide, BeO, and also Cr_2O_3, Al_2O_3, Ga_2O_3, SnO_2, and PbO_2.

Finally, some transition metal oxides in which the metal has a high oxidation number actually act as *acidic* oxides. (You will learn about oxidation numbers in the next chapter.) For example, manganese(VII) oxide and chromium(VI) oxide both react with water to produce acids:

$$Mn_2O_7(s) + H_2O(l) \rightarrow \underset{\text{permanganic acid}}{2\ HMnO_4(aq)}$$

$$CrO_3(s) + H_2O(l) \rightarrow \underset{\text{chromic acid}}{H_2CrO_4(aq)}$$

 © Edvantage Interactive 2019

Quick Check

1. What two criteria must be met for a metal oxide to be considered a basic anhydride?

___

2. Which two families in the periodic table contain elements that satisfy these criteria?

___

3. Calcium oxide, or quicklime, is a component of dry Portland cement, which, when mixed with water, will eventually harden into concrete. Explain why continual contact of your hands with fresh Portland cement can lead to irritation.

___

Acidic Anhydrides

Non-metal oxides that react with water are known as *acidic anhydrides*. In their reactions with water, these molecular or *covalent* oxides produce acids that are also molecular compounds.

In such a reaction, because *no oxide ions are released into water, no hydroxide ions are produced* in the aqueous solution. Instead, the water molecule binds to the molecular oxide, forming a molecular acid. Figure 6.5.1 and Figure 6.5.2 show the Lewis structures of two gaseous non-metal oxides as they react with water to form acids.

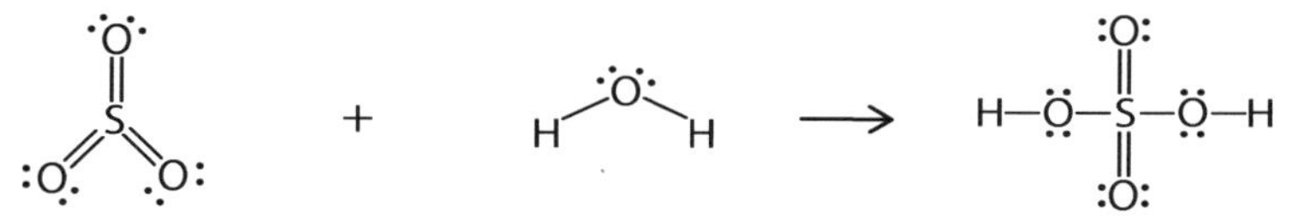

$$SO_3(g) + H_2O(l) \longrightarrow H_2SO_4(aq)$$

Figure 6.5.1 *The formation of sulfuric acid from sulfur trioxide and water.*

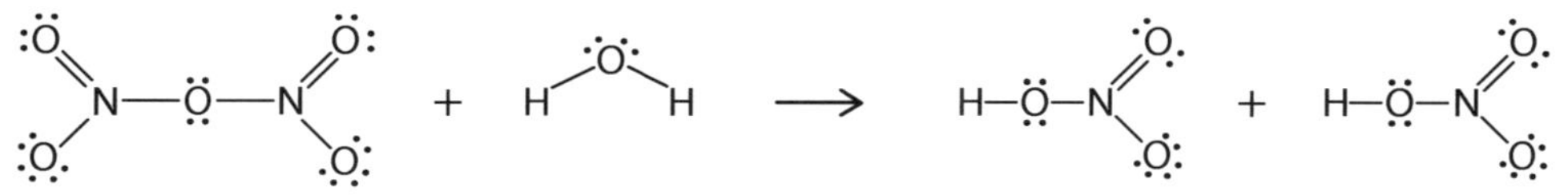

$$N_2O_5(g) + H_2O(l) \longrightarrow HNO_3(aq) + HNO_3(aq)$$

Figure 6.5.2 *The formation of two nitric acid molecules from dinitrogen pentaoxide and water*

Acidic anhydrides are normally those containing non-metals with relatively high oxidation states such as SO_3, N_2O_5, and Cl_2O_7. For now, we can interpret that to simply mean molecules containing at least two oxygen atoms per non-metal atom. The "lower" non-metal oxides, such as NO and CO, do *not* react with water to form acids and so are not considered to be acidic anhydrides.

Non-metal oxides that react with water to produce acids are called *acidic anhydrides.*

As we discussed earlier, several metal oxides react with water to produce *acidic* solutions, but *no non-metal oxides that react with water are known to produce basic solutions.*

Although carbon monoxide does not combine with water to form an acid, carbon dioxide does. The reaction of CO_2 and water produces the weak acid carbonic acid, which is too unstable to be isolated in its pure form. Therefore, aqueous solutions of CO_2 contain varying amounts of the bicarbonate and hydronium ions and can be represented as shown below. This reaction explains why pure water will gradually become acidic when exposed to air containing CO_2 and why unpolluted rainwater is slightly acidic with a pH of about 5.6.

$$CO_2(g) + 2\ H_2O(l) \rightleftharpoons H_3O^+(aq) + HCO_3^-(aq)$$

In addition to making general statements about the reactions of metal oxides and non-metal oxides with water, we can also detect a *periodic trend* in the acid-base properties of the element oxides of the main group elements.

In general, as elements become less metallic, their oxides that react with water produce more acidic solutions. This occurs as we move both left to right across a chemical period and bottom to top up a chemical family.

Quick Check

1. A student adds a few drops of universal indicator to a small beaker of pure water and sees the expected pale green color indicating a pH of slightly less than 7. She then repeatedly blows exhaled air through a straw into the solution and notices the green color slowly change to yellow and then to pale orange. Explain these results.

   ____

2. Why are no hydroxide ions formed when covalent oxides react with water?

   ____

Sample Problem 6.5.1 — Metal and Non-metal Oxides

Two 500. mL aqueous solutions on a lab bench have had their labels removed. One solution contains 0.50 mol of Li_2O and one solution contains 0.50 mol of SO_3. How could phenolphthalein be used to identify each solution? Include the chemical equations as part of your answer.

What to Think About	How to Do It
1. One of the solutes is an alkali metal oxide. This solution must be basic.	The Li_2O reacts with water to produce a basic solution of LiOH according to the following:
2. One of the solutes is a covalent oxide that reacts with water. This solution must be acidic.	$Li_2O(s) + H_2O(l) \rightarrow 2\ LiOH(aq)$
3. Phenolphthalein is pink in a basic solution.	Phenolphthalein will be *pink* in this solution.
	The SO_3 reacts with water to form a strong acid according to the following:
	$SO_3(g) + H_2O(l) \rightarrow H_2SO_4(aq)$
	Phenolphthalein will be *colorless* in this solution.

 © Edvantage Interactive 2019

Practice Problems 6.5.1 — Metal and Non-metal Oxides

1. Complete and balance the following formula equations:

   (a) $K_2O(s) + H_2O(l) \rightarrow$

   (b) $MgO(s) + H_2O(l) \rightarrow$

2. (a) Each of the following third period oxides reacts with water to produce acids. Arrange these oxides in order from least acidic to most acidic.

   SO_3 Cl_2O_7 SiO_2 P_4O_{10} Al_2O_3

   ________ < ________ < ________ < ________ < ________

   (b) Two of the above oxides react with water to produce strong acids. Write the balanced equations for those reactions below.

3. Complete the following statements using either "ionic" or "molecular" in the blank spaces.

   (a) In general, *ionic oxides* react with water to produce ______________ (ionic or molecular) bases.

   (b) In general, *molecular oxides* that react with water produce acids. Acids are ______________ (ionic or molecular) compounds.

The Problem of Acid Rain

Many of the advantages we enjoy and often take for granted in our industrialized and mobile society also come with environmental costs. One of the most serious and widespread is the problem of acid precipitation in the form of rain, snow, fog, and even dry deposits on particles.

As noted earlier, normal rainwater has a pH of about 5.6 because of dissolved CO_2. If the pH of rainwater is below 5.3, it is referred to as *acid rain*.

Although natural causes also exist, virtually all of the acid precipitation that humankind is responsible for can ultimately be traced back to the burning of fossil fuels in our homes, vehicles, and power plants, and the processing of mineral ores in industry. The products of such activities and the reactions they undergo are further examples of the important impact chemistry has on our lives.

The Human Causes of Acid Rain

Precipitation in any form is an atmospheric event that involves water. Because our atmosphere is a gaseous solution, it should come as no surprise that the major substances responsible for acid precipitation are themselves gases that react with water. *Each is a non-metal oxide that reacts with water to produce an acid.*

Let's discuss how our modern society produces each of the gaseous substances that cause acids to fall from the sky.

Sources of Sulfur Oxides

Many coal and oil deposits contain sulfur impurities. When electrical power plants burn these fossil fuels to drive steam turbines, the sulfur is oxidized to SO_2. For example, the main sulfur impurity in coal is iron disulfide or *pyrite*, FeS_2. The combustion of the coal also burns the pyrite and produces SO_2 according to the following reaction:

$$4\ FeS_2(s) + 11\ O_2(g) \rightarrow 2\ Fe_2O_3(s) + 8\ SO_2(g)$$

Although the levels of sulfur impurities are often less than 3%, the huge quantities of fossil fuels burned worldwide result in the production of hundreds of millions of tonnes of SO_2.

Another source of SO_2 is the process of *smelting*, which extracts metals from their ores by heating. Several important metals such as copper, lead, and zinc are present in Earth's crust, mainly as sulfides. The first step in the smelting of these minerals usually involves *roasting*, in which the sulfides are heated at high temperatures in air. For example, when ZnS is heated to about 700°C, the following reaction occurs in the roaster:

$$2\ ZnS(s) + 3\ O_2(g) \rightarrow 2\ ZnO(s) + 2\ SO_2(g)$$

Much like carbonic acid, the weak acid produced from the reaction of SO_2 and water, called sulfurous acid, H_2SO_3, is unstable and doesn't exist in its molecular form in water. As a result, we can represent aqueous solutions of sulfur dioxide as follows:

$$SO_2(g) + 2\ H_2O(l) \rightleftharpoons H_3O^+(aq) + HSO_3^-(aq)$$

This means that rainwater falling through gaseous SO_2 will be more acidic than normal when it reaches the ground.

The problem becomes worse in polluted air containing ozone, O_3, and fine dust particles where, especially in the presence of sunlight, oxygen and ozone will oxidize some of the SO_2 to SO_3:

$$2\ SO_2(g) + O_2(g) \rightarrow 2\ SO_3(g)$$

$$SO_2(g) + O_3(g) \rightarrow SO_3(g) + O_2(g)$$

Sulfur trioxide now reacts with water to form the *strong acid* sulfuric acid:

$$SO_3(g) + H_2O(l) \rightarrow H_2SO_4(aq)$$

Because 100% ionization occurs when sulfuric acid reacts with water, rainwater in the presence of this acid is much more acidic. A gaseous mixture of SO_2 and SO_3 is sometimes referred to as SO_x.

Natural processes such as volcanic eruptions also introduce enormous amounts of sulfur oxides into the atmosphere, but they represent only about 5% to 10% of the total released by human activities.

Sources of Nitrogen Oxides

The air we breathe is composed of about 79% nitrogen and 21% oxygen. These two gases will not react with each other under normal conditions of temperature and pressure because the activation energy for the reaction is far too high. However, when air is mixed with fossil fuels and burned in the internal combustion engine of vehicles or in electric power plants, the high temperatures and pressures generated cause the two atmospheric gases to react according to the following reaction:

$$N_2(g) + O_2(g) \rightarrow 2\ NO(g)$$

When the NO gas in a hot exhaust stream encounters cooler outside air, it reacts with oxygen gas to produce NO_2 gas. This gaseous mixture of NO and NO_2 is often referred to as NO_x.

Nitrogen dioxide gas reacts with water in the atmosphere to produce the strong acid HNO_3 and the weak acid HNO_2 as shown below:

$$2\ NO_2(g) + H_2O(l) \rightarrow HNO_3(aq) + HNO_2(aq)$$

As with sulfur oxides, nature also generates a significant amount of nitrogen oxides. Lightning and decaying vegetation are both sources of NO, but we can do nothing to affect those processes.

Figure 6.5.3 summarizes the causes and effects of acid rain.

 © Edvantage Interactive 2019

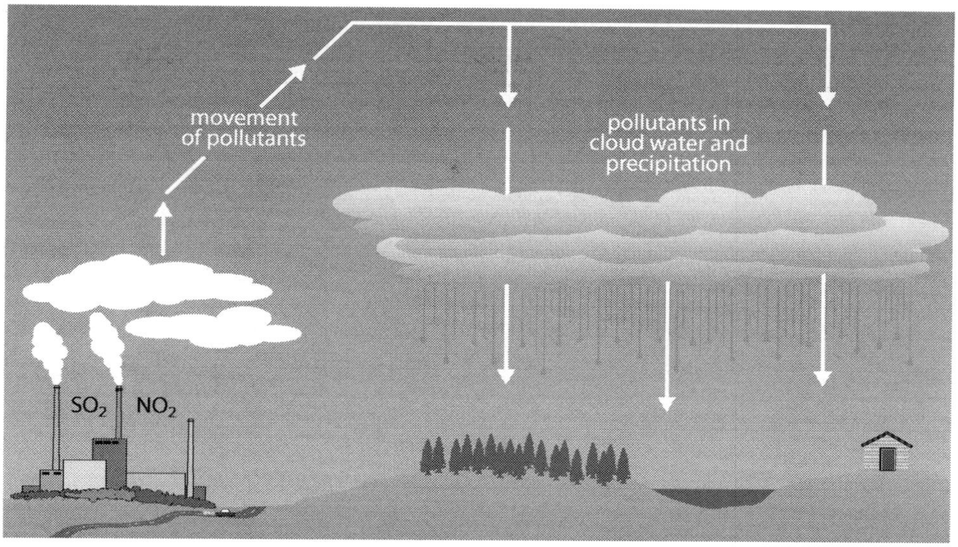

Figure 6.5.3 *Acid rain kills plants, pollutes rivers, lakes, and streams and erodes stone.*

Quick Check

1. Identify the three non-metal oxides that react with water in the atmosphere to produce acid precipitation.

____

2. How do coal-burning electrical power plants produce the sulfur oxide responsible for acid rain?

____

3. Why can the problem of sulfur oxide acid precipitation become worse in polluted air?

____

Consequences of Acid Rain

Acid precipitation in the form of rain, snow, fog, or dry deposits on particles has been recorded on every continent on Earth — even at the north and south poles! Because the oxides of sulfur and nitrogen that cause acid precipitation are gases that are carried into the atmosphere, prevailing winds can potentially push clouds containing these oxides more than 1500 km from their sources. For example, Scandinavia receives acid precipitation from Germany, England, and countries in eastern Europe. Southern Ontario and Quebec can receive the acid precipitation that originated anywhere in the U.S. industrial belt extending from Chicago to Boston.

Measurements taken in Europe and North America confirm how acidic some precipitation can be. Rainwater with a pH of 2.7 (approximately equal to vinegar) has been recorded in Sweden and a pH of 1.8 (almost equal to *stomach acid*) has been recorded for rain in West Virginia.

The effects of acid rain are both serious and widespread. Both aquatic and terrestrial ecosystems can be severely affected when exposed to acidic conditions. Most species of fish die at pH levels below 5, and entire forests have been devastated by acidic precipitation.

Obviously, contaminating the water supplies that our species depends on also has serious direct and indirect consequences. The soils in many areas contain aluminum salts that are nearly insoluble in normal groundwater, but begin to dissolve in more acidic solutions. This dissolving soil not only releases the Al^{3+} ions that are very toxic to fish, but also leaches out many valuable nutrients from the soil, which are lost in the runoff. Figure 6.5.4 shows some examples of acid rain damage.

Many buildings, monuments, and even cemetery headstones contain $CaCO_3$ in the form of either marble or limestone. Carbonate salts dissolve in acids and long-term exposure to acid rain significantly damages such structures. Although not an environmental consequence, the cost of such damage to our society is significant.

Figure 6.5.4 *Trees, soil, water, and fish can all be damaged or destroyed by acid rain*

Figure 6.5.5 *This statue shows the damage from years of exposure to acid rain.*

Some Reasons for Optimism

Some lakes in regions where acid precipitation occurs are naturally protected because they are bounded by soils rich in limestone. The same reaction that dissolves the calcium carbonate in statues and buildings allows these lakes to resist changes in their pH. As the limestone dissolves, the hydronium ions from acid rain cause more bicarbonate ions to form as shown below.

$$CO_3^{2-}(aq) + H_3O^+(aq) \rightleftharpoons HCO_3^-(aq) + H_2O(l)$$

Over time, as the $[HCO_3^-]$ increases, the lakes become effective bicarbonate/carbonate buffer systems and maintain a relatively constant pH.

If a lake's soil does not contain sufficient limestone, a *temporary* solution is to add $CaCO_3$ or CaO directly to the lake. Over time, however, such lakes will eventually once again suffer the effects of acid rain unless the sources of the SO_2 and NO_2 are controlled.

Growing environmental awareness on a global scale over the past several decades has focused the attention of the public, the politicians who represent them, and the scientific community on attempting to solve the problem of acid precipitation. There is still much work to be done, but there are few disciplines as powerful as chemistry when it comes to solving our problems and so there are reasons for optimism.

Strict government emission standards are forcing automobile manufacturers to produce much cleaner and more efficient vehicles. Modern vehicles are equipped with a catalytic converter, which significantly reduces the levels of carbon monoxide, unburned hydrocarbons, and nitrogen oxides released into the atmosphere. One of the reaction chambers in the converter uses catalytic materials such as transition metal oxides and palladium or platinum metals to convert gaseous nitrogen oxides in the exhaust stream to nitrogen and oxygen gas before it leaves the tailpipe. The catalyzed reaction can be represented as shown below.

$$2\ NO_x(g) \rightarrow x\ O_2(g) + N_2(g)$$

(The value of "*x*" is either 1 or 2.)

Over the past several years, most major car companies have produced "hybrid" vehicles, which normally use two distinct power sources to move the vehicle. The most common hybrid vehicles are hybrid electric vehicles (HEVs), which combine an internal combustion engine with one or more electric motors. In addition, several major car companies including General Motors and Nissan have

 © Edvantage Interactive 2019

invested heavily in the production of electric vehicles such as the Volt and the Leaf, which are available to the general public.

Industrial efforts to reduce sulfur and nitrogen oxide emissions have also intensified over the past several decades. One method of removing sulfur dioxide gas from the exhaust stream of a coal-fired power plant or a metal smelter is by a process called *scrubbing*. This involves first blowing powdered limestone ($CaCO_3$) into the combustion chamber where heat decomposes it to CaO and CO_2. The calcium oxide (lime) then combines with the sulfur dioxide gas to produce solid calcium sulfite:

$$CaO(s) + SO_2(g) \rightarrow CaSO_3(s)$$

As a second step, to remove the $CaSO_3$ and any unreacted SO_2, an aqueous suspension of CaO is then sprayed into the exhaust gases before they reach the smokestack to produce a thick suspension of $CaSO_3$ called a slurry. The process is not without its drawbacks, however. First, it is expensive and consumes a great deal of energy. Second, because no use has yet been found for the $CaSO_3$, the great quantities of this compound that are produced by the process are usually buried in landfills.

A recently developed process for removing SO_2 involves using H_2S gas to convert the SO_2 into elemental sulfur according to the following reaction:

$$16\ H_2S(g) + 8\ SO_2(g) \rightarrow 3\ S_8(s) + 16\ H_2O(l)$$

To reduce the nitrogen oxide emissions from power plants, gaseous ammonia is reacted with the hot stack gases to produce nitrogen and water vapor:

$$4\ NO(g) + 4\ NH_3(g) + O_2(g) \rightarrow 4\ N_2(g) + 6\ H_2O(l)$$

The problem of acid precipitation has not yet been solved. A number of major hurdles must still be overcome, particularly as they relate to international agreements and enforcement. Economics, employment, industrial development, political will, environmental protection, and scientific advancement do not always merge harmoniously on our planet.

As you read this, consider the problem a challenge to you and your generation. Although the stakes are very high and the problems are significant, human ingenuity and chemistry have combined to surmount many enormous challenges in our world in the past. Maybe it's your turn to begin such an endeavor now!

Sample Problem 6.5.2 — Acid Rain

Lead is most commonly found in Earth's crust as lead(II) sulfide, PbS, a mineral called *galena*. The first step in smelting lead converts the galena to lead(II) oxide by the process of *roasting*.

(a) Write the formula equation for the reaction.

(b) Identify the product of the reaction that contributes to acid precipitation.

What to Think About	How to Do It
1. Roasting reacts oxygen in air with the sulfide mineral.	$2\ PbS(s) + 3\ O_2(g) \rightarrow 2\ PbO(s) + 2\ SO_2(g)$
2. The non-metal oxide product is precursor to acid precipitation.	Both the SO_2 and the SO_3 that it can produce contribute to acid precipitation.

Practice Problems 6.5.2 — Acid Rain

1. Write the formula equations for the reactions between each of the three oxides and water that result in the production of the acids responsible for acid precipitation.

2. Explain why the release of Al^{3+} ions into aquatic ecosystems poses a serious threat to the organisms living there

3. How does the process of "scrubbing" remove sulfur dioxide gas from exhaust streams at coal-fired power plants and smelters? Include the relevant chemical equations in your answer.

 © Edvantage Interactive 2019

6.5 Activity: The Canada–United States Air Quality Agreement Then and Now — Some Reasons for Optimism

Question

What can you learn from about efforts to reduce acid rain from the major international agreement between Canada and the United States relating to the control of acid rain?

Background

The *Canada-United States Air Quality Agreement* was signed by Canada and the United States in Ottawa, Ontario, on March 13, 1991, to address trans-boundary air pollution leading to acid rain.

Procedure

Part 1: The Original Document

1. Perform an Internet search using the title: "Canada-U.S. Air Quality Agreement."
2. When you locate the document, scroll down to "Section 1." Review the document carefully as you answer the following questions about sulfur dioxide and nitrogen oxide emissions for each country.
   (Note that 1 tonne = 1.1 tons)

Sulfur Dioxide

A. For the United States
   What was the target permanent national emissions cap for SO_2 produced by electrical utilities by the year 2010?

B. For Canada
   What was the target total permanent national emissions cap for SO_2 by the year 2000?

Nitrogen Oxides

A. For the United States
   Before the Acid Rain Program (ARP) was implemented, the projected annual NO_x emission levels from stationary sources for the year 2000 were 8.1 million tons. How far below this did the ARP set as a target level for total annual NO_x emissions for the year 2000? (Note that *stationary sources* refers to power plants, major combustion sources, and metal smelting operations, and *mobile sources* refers to all vehicles.)

B. For Canada
   Before the ARP was implemented, the projected annual NO_x emission levels from stationary sources for the year 2000 were 970 000 tonnes. How far below this did the ARP set as a target level for total annual NO_x emissions for the year 2000?

Part 2: The 2010 Progress Report

1. From the original page that loaded for the Air Quality Agreement, select the icon: "Canada-U.S. Air Quality Agreement Progress Report 2010."
2. Load the PDF file and select the "Acid Rain Annex." Review the document carefully as you answer the following questions.

Sulfur Dioxide Emission Reductions

A. For Canada

(a) In 2008, what were Canada's total SO_2 emissions and what percentage of the national cap established by the ARP do these represent?

(b) What continues to be the largest source of SO_2 emissions in Canada?

B. For the United States

(a) Consider the graph labeled "Figure 2. U.S. Emissions from Acid Rain Program Electric Generating Units, 1990–2009." In 2009, what were the total SO_2 emissions from the electric power sector and what percentage of the 2010 cap established by the ARP does this represent?

(b) Note that the ARP for the United States did *not* cover SO_2 emissions from non-electric power generators such as metal smelting. What were the *total* SO_2 emissions from all sources in the U.S. in 1980 and also in 2008? What percentage of that total do the emissions from the electric power sector represent?

Nitrogen Oxide Emission Reductions

A. For Canada

(a) In 2008, what were Canada's total NO_x emissions from stationary sources and what percentage of the original forecast for the year 2000 do they represent?

(b) What percentage of the total NO_x emissions do transportation sources represent?

B. For the United States

(a) In 2009, what were the total NO_x emissions from stationary sources (those covered by the ARP)?

(b) Before the Acid Rain Program (ARP) was implemented, the projected annual NO_x emission levels from stationary sources for the year 2000 were 8.1 million tons. What percentage of this projected amount does your answer to (a) represent?

Results and Discussion

The *Canada–United States Air Quality Agreement* is a large document with many clauses and statistics and many more questions (and discussions) are possible than the few we have mentioned here. Consider these questions to be merely the beginning of a much broader conversation concerning the problem of and potential solutions to acid rain. Your answers to the questions should convince you that there are reasons for optimism, but you should also note the final sentence of the "Overview" at the beginning of the 2010 Progress Report:

"However, despite these achievements, studies in each country indicate that although some damaged ecosystems are showing signs of recovery, further efforts are necessary to restore these ecosystems to their pre-acidified conditions."

Consider that restoration to be one of the challenges to you and your generation.

 © Edvantage Interactive 2019

6.5 Review Questions

1. Complete the following formula equations:

(a) $Rb_2O(s) + H_2O(l) \rightarrow$

(b) $SrO(s) + H_2O(l) \rightarrow$

(c) $SeO_2(s) + H_2O(l) \rightarrow$

(d) $N_2O_5(g) + H_2O(l) \rightarrow$

2. Calcium oxide (lime) is often added to lawns to *sweeten* the soil and help reduce moss growth. Write the chemical equation for the reaction that occurs in moist soil and indicate what is meant by the term *sweeten*.

3. Tetraphosphorus decaoxide, P_4O_{10}, is a potent dehydrating agent. This acidic anhydride is a white solid that reacts vigorously with water to produce a molecular acid that is listed on the Table of Relative Strengths of Brønsted-Lowry Acids and Bases (Table A5). Write the balanced equation for this reaction below.

4. Even though nitrogen and oxygen account for more than 99% of the gases in our atmosphere, they don't react to produce NO gas as they do when fossil fuels are burned in internal combustion engines. Why not?

5. In point-form below, identify four serious problems associated with acid precipitation.

6. Complete the following equations associated with the formation of acid rain:

(a) $SO_3(g)$ + $H_2O(l)$ →

(b) $NO_2(g)$ + $H_2O(l)$ →

7. Why can acid precipitation occur great distances from where the non-metal oxides causing the problem are actually produced?

8. Why are some lakes naturally protected from acid precipitation and what temporary protection can be employed to help those lakes that aren't?

9. (a) What is the purpose of "scrubbers" in coal-burning electrical power plants and smelters?

(b) What problems are associated with the process of scrubbing?

10. How does the catalytic converter in a vehicle's exhaust system help to reduce the problem of acid rain?

11. What role does ammonia play in the reduction of NO_x emissions from power plants?

© Edvantage Interactive 2019

7 Oxidation-Reduction and Its Applications

This chapter focuses on the following AP Units from the College Board:

Unit 4: Chemical Reactions
Unit 6: Thermodynamics
Unit 9: Applications of Thermodynamics

By the end of this chapter, you should be able to do the following:

- Describe oxidation and reduction processes
- Analyze the relative strengths of reducing and oxidizing agents
- Balance equations for redox reactions
- Determine the concentration of a species by performing a redox titration
- Analyze an electrochemical cell in terms of its components and their functions
- Describe how electrochemical concepts can be used in various practical applications
- Analyze the process of metal corrosion in electrochemical terms
- Analyze an electrolytic cell in terms of its components and their functions
- Describe how electrolytic concepts can be used in various practical applications

---

By the end of this chapter, you should know the meaning of these **key terms**:

- cathodic protection
- corrosion
- electrochemical cell
- electrode
- electrolysis
- electrolytic cell
- electroplating
- electrorefining
- Faraday's law
- half-cell
- half-reaction
- oxidation
- oxidation number
- oxidizing agent
- redox reaction
- redox titration
- reducing agent
- reduction
- volt

An old ship undergoing a redox reaction — rusting

7.1 Oxidation-Reduction

Warm Up

1. Complete the following table of compounds of multivalent metals.

Name	Formula	Metal Ion Charge
	$FeCl_3$	
	$Fe(CH_3COO)_2$	
	$Mn(BrO_3)_2$	
	MnO_2	
	$KMnO_4$	

2. How did you determine the ion charge of the metal in each case?

____

____

Electrochemistry

Throughout this course you have learned about the importance of chemistry to our everyday lives. We use conversions of chemical energy to other energy forms to do work for us, such as heating our homes and moving our vehicles. The heat or enthalpy stored in chemical bonds is being used at this very moment to sustain every living cell in your body.

There is another form of chemical conversion that is critical to life. This is the conversion of chemical to electrical energy. This conversion and the reverse change of electrical to chemical energy make up the study of **electrochemistry.**

Electrochemistry is the study of the interchange of chemical and electrical energy.

All electrochemical reactions have one thing in common. They involve the transfer of electrons from one reacting species to another. Most of the major types of chemical reactions you learned about in previous years involve electron transfer.

Synthesis and decomposition reactions involving species in elemental form always involve electron transfer. Single replacement and combustion reactions also fall into this category.

Reactions that involve electron transfer are commonly called **oxidation-reduction reactions.** Such reactions are often referred to as **redox reactions** for short.

Double replacement reactions are the major group of reactions that do not involve electron transfer. Synthesis and decomposition reactions involving oxides are a smaller group. Reactions that *do not* involve electron transfer are referred to as **metathesis reactions.**

 © Edvantage Interactive 2019

Oxidation Numbers: A System for Tracking Electrons

The easiest way to determine whether electrons have been transferred between elements during a chemical reaction is to keep track of each atom's **oxidation number** (also referred to as the **oxidation state**).

> The **oxidation number** is the real or apparent charge of an atom or ion when all bonds in the species containing the atom or ion are considered to be ionic.

In previous science classes you may have referred to the oxidation number as the *combining capacity*. Multivalent metals such as iron, for example, may combine with chlorine to form $FeCl_2$ or $FeCl_3$, depending on the oxidation number of the iron ion involved. The compound containing iron with an oxidation number of +2 has the formula $FeCl_2$ and is called iron(II) chloride. This distinguishes it from $FeCl_3$ or iron(III) chloride, which contains iron with an oxidation number of +3. Notice that the charge is indicated before the number in an oxidation number.

Oxidation numbers (states) extend beyond combining capacities as they may be assigned to any atom in any aggregation, whether the atom exists in an element, a monatomic ion, or as part of a polyatomic ion or compound. The aggregation is simply the arrangement of atoms the element is in. As we're assuming all species are ionic in order to assign oxidation numbers, we should remember that the more electronegative elements gain electrons, so all electrons in an ionic bond should be assumed to belong to the more electronegative element. The easiest way to assign oxidation numbers to atoms is to follow the simple set of rules given in Table 7.1.1.

Table 7.1.1 *Rules for Assigning Oxidation numbers*

Rule	Statement about Oxidation Number	Examples
1.	Atoms in elemental form = 0	Na, O_2, P_4, As, Zn
2.	Monatomic ions = the ion's charge	K^{+1},Ca^{+2}, Fe^{+2}, Fe^{+3}, Cl^{-1}
3.	Oxygen = −2 except in peroxides (O_2^{2-}) = −1 and OF_2 = +2	Na_2O_2, OF_2
4.	Hydrogen = +1 except in **metal** hydrides = −1	CaH_2, LiH
5.	Oxidation numbers in compounds must sum to zero.	CuCl, $CuCl_2$ contain copper(I) and copper(II)
6.	Oxidation numbers in polyatomic ions must sum to the ion charge.	ClO_4^{1-}, ClO_3^{1-} contain chlorine = +7 and +5
7.	Always assign the more electronegative element a negative oxidation number.	PF_5 contains F = −1 and thus P = +5
8.	In a compound or ion containing more than two elements, the element written furthest to the right takes its most common oxidation number.	SCN^- contains N = −3 (most common), S = −2 (negative value), thus C = +4.

If the species contains oxygen and/or hydrogen, it is usually a good idea to assign their oxidation numbers first. For a species containing multiple types of atoms, assign the more electronegative element first. If the more electronegative element can have more than one oxidation number, use its most common oxidation number.

It is important to note that we always calculate the oxidation number of *one* atom of a particular element. While they are useful in the *calculation* of oxidation numbers, the subscripts that may be assigned to a particular atom have *no effect* on the oxidation number of that atom.

Sample Problem 7.1.1 — Assigning Oxidation Numbers

Assign the oxidation number of each atom in the following species:

(a) H_2SiO_3 (b) AsO_4^{3-} (c) $Pb(NO_3)_2$ (d) C_4H_{10}

What to Think About	How to Do It
(a) H_2SiO_3 1. Assign oxidation numbers to hydrogen and oxygen first, as this will help you discover the value for silicon most easily.	Neither hydrogen nor oxygen is in elemental form (H_2 or O_2). This is not an exception for oxygen (the compound is not a peroxide nor is it OF_2) or hydrogen (the compound is not a metal hydride).
2. Apply rule 3 for oxygen and rule 4 for hydrogen. Assign their usual oxidation numbers.	Hydrogen is **+1** and oxygen is **−2**. For hydrogen, $(2 \times +1)$ = a total of +2. For oxygen, (3×-2) = a total of −6.
3. Apply rule 5 to calculate the oxidation number for the middle atom in the formula, in this case, silicon.	Thus for silicon: $(+2) + (\ \ ) + (-6) = 0$; the oxidation number must be **+4**.
(b) AsO_4^{3-} 1. Assign the oxidation number of oxygen first, following rule 3.	Oxygen is not in elemental form, nor is it in a peroxide or OF_2. Consequently, oxygen is assigned its usual oxidation number of **−2**.
2. Apply rule 6 to calculate the oxidation number for the arsenic.	For oxygen, (4×-2) = a total of −8. Thus for arsenic: $(\ \ ) + (-8) = -3$; the oxidation number must be **+5**.
(c) $Pb(NO_3)_2$ 1. Begin by considering the nitrate ion, NO_3^- as a group and follow rule 5 to calculate the oxidation number of lead.	As there are two NO_3^- groups, each with an overall charge of 1−, the oxidation number of the Pb must be **+2**.
2. Remembering that subscripts have no effect on the oxidation number assigned to an individual element, despite the brackets. Treat NO_3^- as if there was only one nitrate group. Apply rules 3 and 6 to complete the problem.	Assign oxygen its usual oxidation number: **−2**. Hence, for oxygen, (3×-2) = a total of −6 Now for nitrogen: $(\ \ ) + (-6) = -1$; the oxidation number must be **+5**.
(d) C_4H_{10} 1. Begin by considering the hydrogen atom, H. Apply rule number 4.	In this case, though it appears second in the formula, assign H its usual oxidation number of **+1** because C_4H_{10} is not a metal hydride.
2. Apply rule 5 to calculate the oxidation number for carbon.	For hydrogen, $(10 \times +1)$ = a total of −10. Thus, for carbon, $(\ \ ) \times 4 = -10$ since the overall charge of the compound is zero. Finally, for each carbon, the oxidation number must = −10/4 = −2 and ½ or **−2.5** each.

Practice Problems 7.1.1 — Assigning Oxidation Numbers

Assign the oxidation number of each atom in the following species:

1. H_2O
2. Cs_2O_2
3. CO_3^{2-}
4. $Na_2Cr_2O_7$
5. BaH_2
6. NH_4^+
7. S_8
8. $Al_2(SO_4)_3$

Oxidation and Reduction

When an atom gains electrons during a reaction, its oxidation number becomes less positive or more negative. This is logical as the electrons being gained are negative particles. A substance whose oxidation number becomes smaller is being reduced.

A *decrease in oxidation number* is called **reduction**.

On the other hand, when an atom loses electrons during a reaction, its oxidation number becomes more positive. This is because the number of protons (positive charges) does not change, but there are fewer electrons. Consequently, the atom now has more positive protons than negative electrons and hence the net charge is greater. The substance whose oxidation number increases is being oxidized.

An *increase in oxidation number* is called **oxidation**.

In the equation shown below, the oxidation number of the iron increases by two, while the oxidation number of the Cu^{2+} ion decreases by two. Hence, iron metal is oxidized and copper(II) ion is reduced.

It is important to realize that reduction and oxidation always occur together in a reaction. If one atom has its oxidation number increase due to a loss of electrons, another substance must have its oxidation number decrease due to a gain of electrons. This is why reactions that involve electron transfer are called oxidation-reduction reactions or redox reactions for short. These reactions are always *coupled* and the oxidation number changes are entirely due to the transfer of electrons.

oxidation

$$Fe(s) + Cu^{2+}(aq) \rightarrow Fe^{2+}(aq) + Cu(s)$$

reduction

Remember that we always state the oxidation number for just *one* atom of a particular element, *no matter what subscript or coefficient* may be associated with the atom. Figure 7.1.1 shows a handy mnemonic device to help you remember what happens to electrons during the redox process.

A *gain of electrons* is **REDUCTION**, while a *loss of electrons* is **OXIDATION**.

LEO goes GER

lose electrons = oxidation gain electrons = reduction

Figure 7.1.1 *Leo can help you remember the redox process.*

Quick Check

Study the following reaction:

$$2\ Al + Fe_2O_3 \rightarrow Al_2O_3 + 2\ Fe$$

0 +3 +3 0

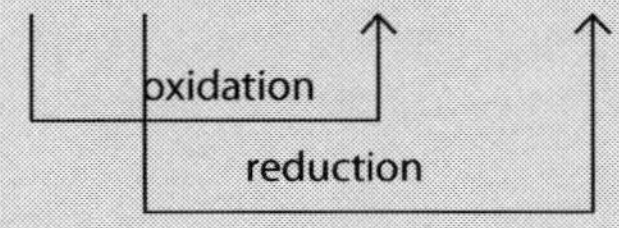

1. (a) Are electrons gained or lost by each iron(III) ion? ________________

   How many? ______________

   (b) Are electrons are gained or lost by each Al atom? ________________

   How many? ______________

2. How many electrons were transferred in total during the reaction? ______________

3. What happened to the oxide ion, O^{2-}, during the reaction?

   ____

Agents Cause Electron Transfer

Examination of the Quick Check above indicates that the number of electrons lost by the species being oxidized must always equal the number of electrons gained by the species being reduced.

So far we have examined electron transfer in terms of the species that lost or gained the electrons. Another approach is to view the event from the perspective of the species that cause the electron loss or gain. In this sense, the species that gets oxidized causes another species to gain electrons and be reduced. For this reason, the species that gets oxidized is called a reducing agent. A similar argument describes the chemical that takes electrons from another species and is consequently reduced, as an oxidizing agent (Figure 7.1.2).

A substance that is *reduced* acts as an **oxidizing agent**, while a substance that is *oxidized* acts as a **reducing agent**.

© Edvantage Interactive 2019

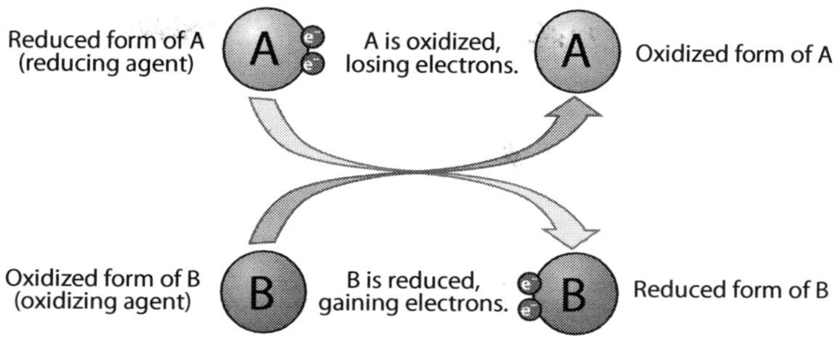

Figure 7.1.2 *Species being oxidized and reduced act as reducing and oxidizing agents.*

Quick Check

Get a pair of stoppers (or even a pair of test tubes) from your teacher. Pretend these are electrons. Give the "electrons" to your lab partner.

1. Were you just "oxidized" or "reduced"? ____________________

   What about your partner?____________________

2. Which partner acted as an oxidizing agent? ____________________

   A reducing agent? ____________________

3. What happened to your oxidation number? ____________________

   What about happened to your partner? ____________________

   Trade roles and repeat the Quick Check. Try it with other partners until you feel confident with the new vocabulary you've learned.

Solving Problems with Redox Reactions

In the sample problem below, the second example may not appear to fit any of the traditional five categories of classification from our past chemistry studies. (It is the combustion of ammonia.) Often redox reactions do not fit our classic categories. You will encounter many more of these in the rest of this chapter.

Sample Problem 7.1.2 — Recognizing Oxidizing and Reducing Agents

Indicate the oxidizing and reducing agent in each of the following reactions:

(a) $Mg(s) + 2\ HCl(aq) \rightarrow MgCl_2(aq) + H_2(g)$ (b) $4\ NH_3(g) + 7\ O_2(g) \rightarrow 4\ NO_2(g) + 6\ H_2O(l)$

What to Think About	How to Do It
(a) $Mg(s) + 2\ HCl(aq) \rightarrow MgCl_2(aq) + H_2(g$	
1. Assign oxidation numbers to all atoms in the equation. (You may wish to write these values above each atom to help keep track.)	Mg: $0 \rightarrow +2$ H: $+1 \rightarrow 0$ Cl: $-1 \rightarrow -1$
2. Indicate the increase in oxidation number as an oxidation and the decrease in oxidation number as a reduction.	Magnesium atom was oxidized. Hydrogen ion was reduced.
3. The species that was oxidized is the reducing agent. The one that was reduced is the oxidizing agent. This is a classic single replacement reaction.	Reducing agent: magnesium atom (Mg) Oxidizing agent: hydrogen ion (H^+) Notice that the Mg atom lost two electrons, while each H^+ ion gained one.
(b) $4\ NH_3(g) + 7\ O_2(g) \rightarrow 4\ NO_2(g) + 6\ H_2O(l)$	
1. Assign oxidation numbers to all elements in the equation. Notice that even though hydrogen is written second in the formula for ammonia, ammonia is not a *metal* hydride so hydrogen is assigned its usual oxidation number of +1.	H: $+1 \rightarrow +1$ O: $0 \rightarrow -2$ (in both products) N: $-3 \rightarrow +4$
2. Indicate the increase in oxidation number as an oxidation and the decrease in oxidation number as a reduction.	Oxygen gas was reduced. N in ammonia was oxidized.
3. The species that was oxidized is the reducing agent. The one that was reduced is the oxidizing agent.	Oxidizing agent: oxygen gas (O_2) Reducing agent: ammonia (NH_3) NOTE: When the atom that is oxidized or reduced belongs to a covalent compound, we indicate the *entire species* as the agent.

Practice Problems 7.1.2 — Recognizing Oxidizing and Reducing Agents

Determine the oxidizing and reducing agent in each of the following reactions. Write the appropriate formula for each agent. Begin by clearly indicating the oxidation numbers of all elements in each equation. Question 1 is done as an example. Hint: Always show the agent as it would appear in a *net ionic equation*. (See H^+ in Sample Problem 7.1.1 above, as HCl is a strong acid.)

0 0 −4+1

1. $C(s) + 2\ H_2(g) \rightarrow CH_4(g)$ O.A. = C(*s*) R.A. = $H_2(g)$

2. $3\ Sr(s) + 2\ FeBr_3(aq) \rightarrow 2\ Fe(s) + 3\ SrBr_2(aq)$

3. $5\ CO(g) + Cl_2O_5(s) \rightarrow 5\ CO_2(g) + Cl_2(g)$

4. $4\ PH_3(g) \rightarrow P_4(g) + 6\ H_2(g)$

5. $Ba(s) + 2\ H_2O(l) \rightarrow Ba(OH)_2(s) + H_2(g)$

7.1 Activity: Compare and Contrast Oxidizing and Reducing Agents

Question

How can you compare and contrast oxidizing and reducing agents?

Background

In previous activities you learned how useful it is to summarize the concepts you learn in "chunks" of material. You created a set of summary notes in the form of a table or chart of information. For this section, you will use the "compare and contrast" method to create a table as part of your summary notes for this section.

Procedure:

1. Use the outline provided below to organize what you've learned about oxidizing and reducing agents.
2. The first row has been completed as an example of what is expected. Note that there may be many other comparisons and contrasts (or similarities and differences) that you can add to your table. Don't feel limited to only those lines where clues have been provided.

Characteristic	Oxidizing Agent	Reducing Agent
Causes another species to be…	oxidized	reduced
Is itself _____ during reaction.		
Its oxidation number is__during reaction.		
Causes electrons to be...		
__________ electrons.		

Results and Discussion

You will find it very helpful to produce similar charts to help you summarize material for study. Add these to the dedicated section of your notebook for summary notes and refer to them from time to time to help you prepare for your unit and final examinations.

7.1 Review Questions

1. Elements that get oxidized (act as reducing agents) form (a)__________________ ions when they react. This means reducing agents are generally (b)__________________. Reducing agents may also be (c)__________________ charged ions. The most active reducing agents likely belong to the (d)__________________ family on the periodic table. The most active oxidizing agents must belong to the (e)__________________ family.

2. Give the oxidation number for the underlined element in each of the following species:

   (a) $\underline{CaI}_2$ (b) $\underline{O}F_2$ (c) $\underline{C}_6H_{12}O_6$ (d) $Rb_2\underline{O}_2$ (e) $\underline{S}_2O_3^{2-}$ (f) $Be\underline{H}_2$ (g) $\underline{Br}O^-$ (h) $\underline{Cl}_2$

3. (a) What is an oxidizing agent?

   (b) What is a reducing agent?

   (c) How would you expect electronegativity to be related to the strength of each?

4. For each of the following reactions, indicate the species being oxidized and reduced and show the oxidation numbers above their symbols.

   (a) $2\ KBrO_3(s) \rightarrow 2\ KBr(s) + 3\ O_2(g)$ Oxidized: Reduced:

   (b) $Sr(s) + 2\ CuNO_3(aq) \rightarrow Sr(NO_3)_2(aq) + 2\ Cu(s)$ Oxidized: Reduced:

   (c) $2\ F_2(g) + O_2(g) \rightarrow 2\ OF_2(g)$ Oxidized: Reduced:

   (d) $NH_4NO_3(s) \rightarrow N_2O(g) + 2\ H_2O(l)$ Oxidized: Reduced:

 © Edvantage Interactive 2019

5. Determine the oxidizing and reducing agent in each of the following reactions. Then indicate the number of electrons transferred by one atom of the reducing agent.

(a) $2\ Sn(s) + O_2(g) \rightarrow 2\ SnO(s)$ OA: RA: No. e^-:

(b) $2\ V(s) + 5\ I_2(g) \rightarrow 2\ VI_5(s)$ OA: RA: No. e^-:

(c) $Sr(s) + 2\ HCl(aq) \rightarrow SrCl_2(aq) + H_2(g)$ OA: RA: No. e^-:

(d) $C_3H_8(g) + 5\ O_2(g) \rightarrow 3\ CO_2(g) + 4\ H_2O(g)$ OA: RA: No. e^-:

6. The pictures indicate the same reacting system following a 12 h period.

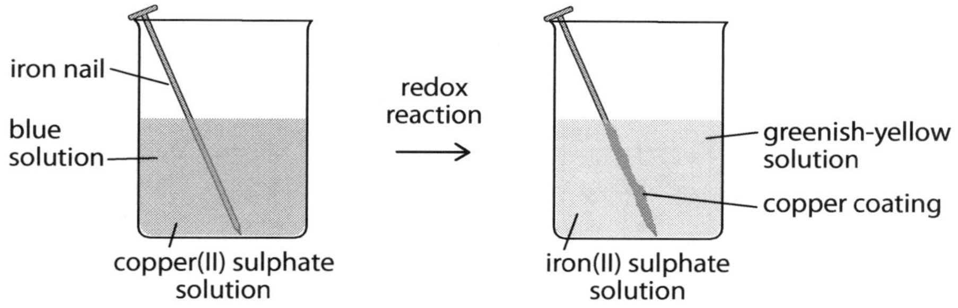

(a) Write a balanced redox equation (in net ionic form) to show what has occurred in the beaker over time.

(b) Which substance is the oxidizing agent? The reducing agent?

(c) How many electrons were transferred in the equation?

7. Give the oxidation number of the underlined element in each species:

(a) $\underline{P}^{3-}$ (b) $(NH_4)_2\underline{Zr}(SO_4)_3$ (c) $Na_2\underline{C}_2O_4$ (d) $\underline{N}_2H_5Cl$ (e) $\underline{Mn}O_4^{\ 2-}$

8.

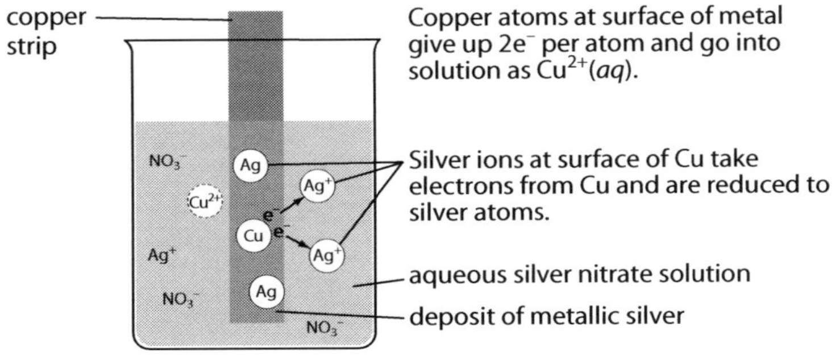

(a) Write a balanced net ionic equation to represent the redox reaction occurring in the beaker.

(b) Which substance is getting oxidized? Reduced?

(c) Which substance is the reducing agent? The oxidizing agent?

(d) How many electrons are transferred in each reaction?

9. What family on the periodic table would likely contain:

(a) The strongest reducing agents?

(b) The strongest oxidizing agents?

10. (a) Which of the following substances could be formed by the oxidation of ClO^-: ClO_4^-, Cl_2, ClO_2^-, Cl^-, ClO_3^-?

(b) The reduction of ClO^-?

© Edvantage Interactive 2019

7.2 Balancing Oxidation-Reduction Equations

Warm Up

Examine the following equation: $Zn(s) + \quad Cu^{+}(aq) \rightarrow \quad Zn^{2+}(aq) + \quad Cu(s)$

1. Which species acts as a reducing agent and consequently is oxidized? ____________________

2. Which species acts as an oxidizing agent and consequently is reduced? ____________________

3. How many electrons are lost by each atom of the reducing agent as it is oxidized? ____________

4. A Cu^{+} ion accepts only one electron to become a neutral Cu atom. How many Cu^{+} ions does it take to accept two electrons?
   ____

5. Add coefficients to the equation so that the number of electrons donated by the reducing agent equals the number of electrons received by the oxidizing agent.

6. Does the net charge of the reactants now equal the net charge of the products? _____________

The Conservation of Mass *and* Charge

For the past several years, you've been applying Antoine Lavoisier's law of conservation of mass to every chemical reaction you've encountered. This law states that the mass of the products equals the mass of the reactants in any chemical reaction. This is because no atoms are gained or lost during a chemical reaction. In junior science, you learned to place coefficients in front of various chemical species to make sure that the total number of atoms of each type on the reactant side would equal the total number of atoms of the same type on the product side of the equation.

In previous years, you learned to write net ionic equations for a variety of reaction types. In these equations, it was necessary to balance the charge as well as the number of each type of each atom. In oxidation-reduction reactions, charge is balanced by making certain that the number of electrons lost equals the number gained. This is sometimes done by simple inspection. An example is the reduction of copper(I) ion by zinc metal in the Warm Up question above. Examination reveals that two Cu^{+} ions are reduced for every Zn atom oxidized, so the balanced equation is:

$$Zn(s) + 2\ Cu^{+}(aq) \rightarrow Zn^{2+}(aq) + 2\ Cu(s)$$

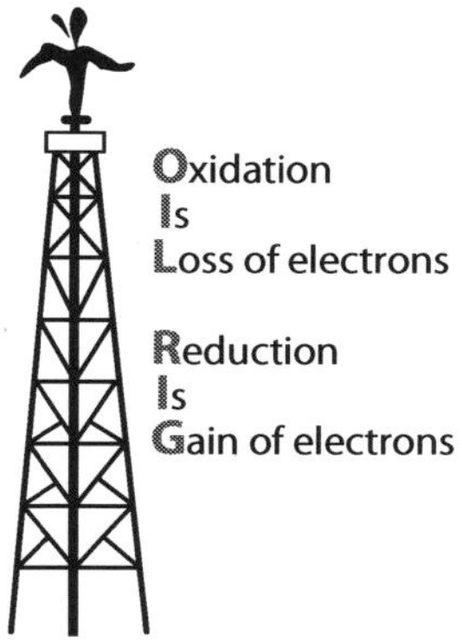

Figure 7.2.1 *Remember the OIL RIG.*

As luck would have it, there are many oxidation-reduction reactions that are considerably more complex than this simple example. For these more complicated cases, we require a system to help us determine the number of electrons lost and gained so we can balance not only the number of atoms of each type, but also the number of electrons transferred.

Half-Reactions

It is possible to separate out the reduction and oxidation portions of a redox reaction and to represent them as two separate **half-reactions**. For example, the sample reaction from the Warm Up may be broken into the following half-reactions:

$$Zn \rightarrow Zn^{2+} + 2e^{-} \text{ (oxidation) } \textit{and } Cu^{+} + e^{-} \rightarrow Cu \text{ (reduction)}$$

Notice that the half-reactions include the number of electrons lost, in the case of oxidation, or gained, in the case of reduction.

A **half-reaction** is an equation representing either an oxidation or a reduction, including the number of electrons lost or gained.

Balancing questions usually specify whether the reaction is occurring under acidic or basic conditions. Sometimes this will be readily apparent from the chemical reactants. If this isn't obvious or isn't stated, the conditions are likely acidic. It is possible, however, that it is occurring under neutral conditions. This means that when you balance it, you find that any H^+ or OH^- ions will cancel out and not appear in the final reaction statement.

Balancing Half-Reactions

Balancing a half-reaction requires the application of the following steps:

OTHER atoms — Balance atoms other than H and O.

All atoms *except* oxygen and hydrogen should be balanced first. This is not always necessary, so people tend to forget to balance the "other" atoms. Do *not* forget this step and watch the way coefficients affect charges.

OXYGEN atoms — Balance oxygen atoms by adding H_2O.

Redox reactions occur in aqueous solution. Consequently, you may add as many water molecules as required to balance the number of oxygen atoms.

HYDROGEN atoms — Balance hydrogen atoms by adding H^+ ions.

As most reactions occur in an acidic environment, you may add as many hydrogen ions, H^+, as are needed.

CHARGE — Balance the charge by adding electrons.

Always add the electrons to the *more positive* (or less negative) side. Add the number of electrons needed to ensure that the charge is the *same* on both sides of the equation. This is a good time to *check* that the total number of atoms of each type is in fact the same on both sides, so the equation is indeed balanced in terms of mass and charge.

© Edvantage Interactive 2019

Sample Problem 7.2.1(a) — Balancing Half-Reactions in Acidic Conditions

Balance the following half-reaction occurring under acidic conditions: $ClO_4^- \rightarrow Cl_2$

Does this represent an oxidation or a reduction?

What to Think About	How to Do It
1. Balance atoms *other than* O and H. This requires a coefficient 2 in front of the perchlorate ion, ClO_4^-. Because the "other" atoms are often already balanced, students frequently do not need to balance them and as a result they tend to forget to apply the first step. *Always* check the "other" atoms first.	$2\ ClO_4^- \rightarrow Cl_2$
2. Balance *oxygen atoms* by adding *H_2O molecules*. As there are now 8 oxygen atoms on the reactant side, add 8 water molecules to the products.	$2\ ClO_4^- \rightarrow Cl_2 + 8\ H_2O$
3. Balance *hydrogen atoms* by adding *H^+ ions*. As there are now 16 hydrogen atoms on the product side, add 16 H^+ ions on the reactant side.	$16\ H^+ + 2\ ClO_4^- \rightarrow Cl_2 + 8\ H_2O$
4. Balance the charge by adding the e^- to the *more positive side*. As the total charge on the reactant side is +14 and there is no charge on the product side, add 14 electrons on the reactant side.	$14\ e^- + 16\ H^+ + 2\ ClO_4^- \rightarrow Cl_2 + 8\ H_2O$ An **oxidation number check** is helpful to perform on half-reactions. Note that the number of electrons gained matches the oxidation number change. $\overset{+7}{2\ ClO_4^-} \rightarrow \overset{0}{Cl_2}$ [Gain of $7e^-$ (×2) = $14e^-$ gained.] ✓
Electrons are gained (they are "reactants").	This is a **reduction**.

While all redox reactions occur in aqueous solution, some occur in basic, rather than acidic conditions. When balancing a reaction that is occurring under basic conditions, chemists simply add a step to our sequence to convert from an acidic to a basic environment. When a redox reaction is to be balanced in base, *the hydrogen ions must be neutralized*. This is accomplished by adding hydroxide ions, OH^-, to cancel any H^+ ions. If hydroxide ions are added to one side of the equation, the same number must be added to the other side.

Thus, complete the first four steps and then…

BASE — Add OH^- ions to both sides to neutralize all H^+ Ions.

The number of OH^- ions added to neutralize the H^+ must be balanced by adding the same number of OH^- ions to the other side of the reaction. Free H^+ and OH^- ions on the same side of the equation should be combined to form the corresponding number of H_2O molecules. This step may result in water molecules showing up on both sides of the equation. Be sure to cancel so that H_2O appears on one side of the equation only.

It is critically important to pay close attention to all charges during the balancing process. Dropping the charge from an ion or inadvertently changing a charge will lead to a wrong answer every time!

Sample Problem 7.2.1(b) — Balancing Half-Reactions in Basic Conditions

Balance the following half-reaction: $I_2 \rightarrow IO_4^-$ in base.
Does this represent an oxidation or a reduction?

What to Think About	How to Do It
1. Balance atoms *other than* O and H. A coefficient 2 is needed in front of IO_4^-.	$I_2 \rightarrow 2\,IO_4^-$
2. Balance *oxygen atoms* by adding *H_2O molecules.* As there are 8 oxygen atoms on the product side, add 8 H_2O molecules as reactants.	$8\,H_2O + I_2 \rightarrow 2\,IO_4^-$
3. Balance *hydrogen atoms* by adding *H^+ions* to the product side. As there are now 16 hydrogen atoms on the reactant side, add 16 H^+ to the product side.	$8\,H_2O + I_2 \rightarrow 2\,IO_4^- + \mathbf{16}\,H^+$
4. Add the e^- to the *more positive side*. As the total charge on the product side is +14 and there is no charge on the reactant side, add 14 electrons on the product side.	$8\,H_2O + I_2 \rightarrow 2\,IO_4^- + 16\,H^+ + \mathbf{14e^-}$
5. The objective for balancing a reaction in base is to *neutralize the H^+ions*. As there are 16 H^+ ions on the product side, add 16 OH^- ions to both sides. Each combination of H^+ with OH^- forms an H_2O molecule. Water molecules present on both sides of the equation algebraically cancel. *NEVER leave H_2O molecules on both sides.*	~~$8\,H_2O$~~ $+ I_2 \rightarrow 2\,IO_4^- + 16$ ~~H^+~~ $+ 14e^-$ $\mathbf{16\,OH^-}$ $\qquad$ $\mathbf{16\,OH^-}$ $16\,OH^- + I_2 \rightarrow 2\,IO_4^- + 8\,H_2O + 14\,e^-$
Electrons are produced-hence they are lost.	**Oxidation number check:** 0 $\quad$ +7 $I_2 \rightarrow 2\,IO_4^-$ $\quad$ [Loss of $7e^-$ (x2) = $14e^-$ lost] ✓ This process is an **oxidation.**

Practice Problems 7.2.1 — Balancing Half-Reactions in Acidic and Basic Conditions

Balance the following half-reactions. Assume the reactions occur in acid unless specified otherwise. In each case, indicate whether the half-reaction is an oxidation or a reduction.

1. $Sm \rightarrow Sm^{3+}$
2. $NO_3^- \rightarrow NH_4^+$
3. $IO_4^- \rightarrow IO_3^-$ (basic)
4. $S_2O_3^{2-} \rightarrow SO_4^{2-}$
5. $BrO_3^- \rightarrow Br_2$ (basic)

© Edvantage Interactive 2019

Redox Reactions

The equation for an oxidation-reduction reaction is a combination of two of the half-reactions we have just finished balancing (an oxidation and a reduction). When a reducing agent is oxidized, the electrons are not actually *lost* in the usual sense of the word. In fact, chemists know exactly where those electrons go. They are, of course, gained by an oxidizing agent that will become reduced. The goal of balancing a redox reaction is to ensure the number of electrons lost by a reducing agent (as it becomes oxidized) exactly equals the number of electrons gained by the oxidizing agent (as it becomes reduced).

> Oxidation-reduction (redox) reactions are characterized by a balanced loss and gain of electrons.

There are two common methods for balancing redox reactions. We will begin by focusing on the method that involves balancing two half-reactions. This method is appropriately called the *half-reaction method*. It consists of the following steps:

SEPARATE the redox equation into its half-reactions.

In most cases, it is easy to identify the two half-reactions by noting species in the reactants that contain atoms in common with species in the products.

↓

BALANCE each half-reaction.

Give yourself plenty of room and don't forget to compare the change in oxidation numbers with the electron gain or loss.

↓

MULTIPLY each half-reaction by an integer to balance the transfer of electrons.

Take the time and space to rewrite each reaction and take care as you transcribe the formulas and coefficients to avoid errors.

↓

ADD the half-reactions together.

Algebraically cancel those species that appear on both sides of the equation. Again: be care*ful* — not care*less*! No common species should remain on both sides of the equation.

↓

***If the equation is basic*, ADD OH^- to *both sides* to neutralize the H^+ ions *only after* recombining the equations.**

Balancing redox equations can seem tedious at times, as there are many steps involved. Errors made early will lead to a series of mistakes but even one late error will result in the wrong answer. Taking care in transcribing steps and checking each process as you go will lead to consistent success.

Sample Problem 7.2.2 — Balancing Redox Reactions: Acidic

Balance the following redox reaction: $IO_3^- + HSO_3^- \rightarrow SO_4^{2-} + I_2$

What to Think About	How to Do It
1. Separate the redox equation Into its two half-reactions. Look for common atoms to assist you. IO_3^- and I_2 both contain iodine. HSO_3^- and SO_4^{2-} both contain sulfur.	$IO_3^- \rightarrow I_2$ $HSO_3^- \rightarrow SO_4^{2-}$
2. Balance each half-reaction. Note: There must be an electron *gain* on one side and *loss* on the other. If not, you have made an error!	$10e^- + 12\,H^+ + 2\,IO_3^- \rightarrow I_2 + 6\,H_2O$ $H_2O + HSO_3^- \rightarrow SO_4^{2-} + 3\,H^+ + 2e^-$ Don't forget to do a quick check of oxidation numbers at this point. $\overset{+5}{2\,IO_3^-} \rightarrow \overset{0}{I_2}$ $\quad \overset{+4}{HSO_3^-} \rightarrow \overset{+6}{SO_4^{2-}}$
3. Balance the electron loss and gain. Look for the *lowest common multiple*. Multiply the second half-reaction by 5 and rewrite both equations.	$(-5 \times 2 = 10e^-\text{ gain})$ $\quad (+2 = 2e^-\text{ lost})$ ✓ $1(10e^- + 12\,H^+ + 2\,IO_3^- \rightarrow I_2 + 6\,H_2O)$ $5(H_2O + HSO_3^- \rightarrow SO_4^{2-} + 3\,H^+ + 2e^-)$
4. Add the balanced half-reactions together, cancelling where appropriate.	$\cancel{10e^-} + 12\,H^+ + 2\,IO_3^- \rightarrow I_2 + 6\,H_2O$ $5\,H_2O + 5\,HSO_3^- \rightarrow 5\,SO_4^{2-} + 15\,H^+ + \cancel{10e^-}$ $5\,HSO_3^- + 2\,IO_3^- \rightarrow 5\,SO_4^{2-} + 3\,H^+ + I_2 + H_2O$

Once you have balanced a full redox reaction, it is worth taking the time to do a full balancing check. You may have performed similar checks when balancing standard equations at some point in your chemistry past. A table is a helpful tool:

Species	Reactants	Products
Hydrogen	5	5
Sulfur	5	5
Oxygen	21	21
Iodine	2	2
Charge	–7	–7

✓

The charge is perhaps the most important part of the check. Be sure to take care with your counting and as mentioned earlier, don't drop or change ion charges during the transcribing. More than one student has done a wonderful job of correctly balancing an equation that wasn't assigned to them because they changed one of the species.

© Edvantage Interactive 2019

Practice Problems 7.2.2 — Balancing Redox Reactions in Acid

Balance each of the following equations in acidic solution. Perform a check for each.

1. $H_3AsO_4 + Zn \rightarrow AsH_3 + Zn^{2+}$

2. $C_2H_5OH + NO_3^- \rightarrow CH_3COOH + N_2O_4$

Disproportionation Reactions

Some redox reactions can be rather difficult to break into half-reactions. One of the most troublesome almost appears, at first glance, to be a half-reaction. Take the reaction,

$$Sn^{2+} \rightarrow Sn^{4+} + Sn$$

The tin(II) ion is both oxidized (to form the tin(IV) ion) and reduced (to form tin metal). A reaction such as this is called a disproportionation reaction.

A **disproportionation** reaction is a redox reaction in which the same species is both oxidized and reduced.

Occasionally, multiple reactants form only one product. A chemical change of this sort is called a **comproportionation** reaction. This may be the reverse of a disproportionation in which one species is reduced to form a product and a different species is oxidized to give the same product.

Sample Problem 7.2.3 — Balancing Disproportionation Reactions: Basic

Balance the following in base: $IAsO_4 \rightarrow AsO_4^{3-} + I_2 + IO_3^-$

What to Think About

1. Separate the half-reactions. Both half-reactions must contain the same reactant, so this is a disproportionation reaction. Arsenic must be a product in both half-reactions. Hence the remaining two iodine-containing species must be split between the two half-reactions.
2. Balance each half-reaction and check the oxidation numbers with the electron loss and gain.
3. Multiply the second half-reaction by 3.
4. Sum the two halves with appropriate cancelling.
5. To balance in base, add 18 OH^- ions to each side; then cancel 9 H_2O's.

   A final check is always a good idea.

How to Do It

$IAsO_4 \rightarrow AsO_4^{3-} + I_2$

$IAsO_4 \rightarrow AsO_4^{3-} + IO_3^-$

$6e^- + 2\,IAsO_4 \rightarrow 2\,AsO_4^{3-} + I_2$

$3\,H_2O + IAsO_4 \rightarrow AsO_4^{3-} + IO_3^- + 6\,H^+ + 2e^-$

$\overset{+3}{2\,IAsO_4} \rightarrow AsO_4^{3-} + \overset{0}{I_2}$ $(-3 \times 2 = \text{gain } 6e^-)$

$\overset{+3}{IAsO_4} \rightarrow AsO_4^{3-} + \overset{+5}{IO_3^-}$ $(+2 = \text{loss of } 2e^-)$ ✓

$6e^- + 2\,IAsO_4 \rightarrow 2\,AsO_4^{3-} + I_2$

$9\,H_2O + 3\,IAsO_4 \rightarrow 3\,AsO_4^{3-} + 3\,IO_3^- + 18\,H^+ + 6e^-$

$9\,H_2O + 5\,IAsO_4 \rightarrow 5\,AsO_4^{3-} + 3\,IO_3^- + I_2 + 18\,H^+$

$(+\,18\,OH^-)$ $\qquad (+\,18\,OH^-)$

$18\,OH^- + 5\,IAsO_4 \rightarrow 5\,AsO_4^{3-} + 3\,IO_3^- + I_2 + 9\,H_2O$

Species	Products	Reactants
Hydrogen	18	18
Arsenic	5	5
Oxygen	38	38
Iodine	5	5
Charge	–18	–18

✔

© Edvantage Interactive 2019

Practice Problems 7.2.3 — Balancing Disproportionation Reactions

Balance the following reactions in a basic environment. Perform a check for each.

1. $HXeO_4^- \rightarrow XeO_6^{4-} + Xe + O_2$

2. $BrO_3^- + Br^- \rightarrow Br_2$ (a comproportionation)

3. $CH_3COO^- \rightarrow CH_4 + CO_2$

OOHe — <u>O</u>ther atoms, <u>O</u>xygen (with H_2O), <u>H</u>ydrogen (with H^+), <u>e</u>lectrons

7.2 Activity: A Balancing Short Cut (The Change in Oxidation Number Method)

Question

Is there a shorter way to balance redox reactions?

Background

The check we've been using for our half-reactions can be applied to full redox reactions to help determine the coefficients required to balance an equation without breaking it into halves. For many redox reactions, this can be fairly easy. In some cases, however, it can be extremely difficult.

Procedure

Study the examples shown below.

LEVEL I: $MnO_4^- + NO_2 \rightarrow NO_3^- + Mn^{2+}$

Level I problems do *not* require balancing of *"other" than O or H atoms*. There is only one species oxidized and one reduced.

Step 1: Assign oxidation numbers and identify the reduction and the oxidation number *changes*. We call these the ΔON values (change in oxidation number values).

+7------------------ ΔON = (–5)----------------2

+4 --- ΔON = (+1)-+5

$$MnO_4^- + NO_2 \rightarrow NO_3^- + Mn^{2+}$$

Step 2: Apply coefficients to make the increase in ΔON for the oxidation equal the decrease in ΔON for the reduction. This equalizes the electrons transferred.

$$MnO_4^- + 5\ NO_2 \rightarrow 5\ NO_3^- + Mn^{2+}$$

Step 3: Add the number of H_2O's needed to balance the oxygen atoms.

$$H_2O + MnO_4^- + 5\ NO_2 \rightarrow 5\ NO_3^- + Mn^{2+}$$

Step 4: Finish by adding H^+ ions to balance the hydrogen atoms.

$$H_2O + MnO_4^- + 5\ NO_2 \rightarrow 5\ NO_3^- + Mn^{2+} + 2\ H^+$$

Step 5: As always, perform a check at the end.

Species	Reactants	Products
Hydrogen	2	2
Manganese	1	1
Oxygen	15	15
Nitrogen	5	5
Charge	–1	–1

✔

LEVEL II: $P_4 \rightarrow HPO_4^{2-} + PH_3$ (basic)

This reaction is a disproportionation requiring the balance of an "other" atom to start.

Step 0: Begin by showing two P_4 molecules and placing coefficients to balance the P for each of the products as you would if you were using the half-reaction method.

$$P_4 + P_4 \rightarrow 4\ HPO_4^{2-} + 4\ PH_3$$

Step 1: Determine ΔON values. This becomes more difficult when there are "other" atoms to balance. As shown, each atom's oxidation number change must be accounted for.

0 -- ΔON = (+5 × 4 = <u>+20</u>) -- +5

0 ----------------ΔON = (–3 × 4 = <u>–12</u>) ---- –3

$$P_4 + P_4 \rightarrow 4\ HPO_4^{2-} + 4\ PH_3$$

 © Edvantage Interactive 2019

Step 2: Equalize the electrons transferred by applying coefficients. In this case, the lowest common multiple of 20 and 12 is 60, thus the multipliers are 3 and 5 respectively.

$$3\ P_4 + 5\ P_4 \longrightarrow 12\ HPO_4^{2-} + 20\ PH_3$$

Step 3: Add waters to balance oxygens.

$$48\ H_2O + 3\ P_4 + 5\ P_4 \longrightarrow 12\ HPO_4^{2-} + 20\ PH_3$$

Step 4: Add hydrogen ions to balance hydrogens.

$$48\ H_2O + 3\ P_4 + 5\ P_4 \longrightarrow 12\ HPO_4^{2-} + 20\ PH_3 + 24\ H^+$$

Basify: The addition of OH^- to both sides occurs at the very end only. In this case, you must reduce the coefficients to the lowest possible whole numbers.

$$48\ H_2O + 3\ P_4 + 5\ P_4 \longrightarrow 12\ HPO_4^{2-} + 20\ PH_3 + 24\ H^+$$
$$24\ OH^- \qquad\qquad 24\ OH^-$$

$$(24\ OH^- + 24\ H_2O + 8\ P_4 \longrightarrow 12\ HPO_4^{2-} + 20\ PH_3) \div 4$$

$$6\ OH^- + 6\ H_2O + 2\ P_4 \longrightarrow 3\ HPO_4^{2-} + 5\ PH_3$$

Step 5: Check:

Species	Reactants	Products
Hydrogen	18	18
Phosphorus	8	8
Oxygen	12	12
Charge	–6	–6

✔

It is always a good idea to add to your arsenal when it comes to problem-solving methods.
As practice makes perfect, try balancing these two reactions using the ΔON method. Check each.

1. $CN^- + ClO_3^- \longrightarrow CNO^- + Cl_2$ (acidic)

2. $Fe + As_2O_3 \longrightarrow AsH_3 + Fe^{3+}$ (basic)

Results and Discussion

1. Which method do you prefer when it comes to keeping your balance in the redox world? Explain why.

7.2 Review Questions

1. Electrons can be used to cancel positive charges or to increase negative charge. Complete the following table by indicating how many electrons must be added to the reactants or the products to balance the electrical charge.

	Reactants	Products	Add
e.g.	2+	3+	$1e^-$ to the products
(a)	3+	2–	
(b)	1–	3–	
(c)	2–	4+	
(d)	1+	5+	

Examine your answers. Are you following the suggestion to *always add electrons to the more positive side?*

2. Balance the electrical charge of each of the following half-reactions by adding the appropriate number of electrons to either the reactants or products. Indicate whether the half-reaction is an *oxidation* or a *reduction*.
(a) $2\,NO_3^- + 2\,H_2O \rightarrow N_2O_4 + 4\,OH^-$

(b) $2\,Cr^{3+} + 7\,H_2O \rightarrow Cr_2O_7^{2-} + 14\,H^+$

(c) $ClO_4^- + 4\,H_2O \rightarrow Cl^- + 8\,OH^-$

(d) $S_2O_5^{2-} + 3\,H_2O \rightarrow 2\,SO_4^{2-} + 6\,H^+$

© Edvantage Interactive 2019

3. Balance the following half-reactions under acidic conditions. Indicate whether each is an *oxidation* or a *reduction*.

(a) $ClO_4^- \rightarrow Cl_2$

(b) $FeO \rightarrow Fe_2O_3$

(c) $N_2O_4 \rightarrow NO_3^-$

4. Balance the following half-reactions under basic conditions. Indicate whether each is an *oxidation* or a *reduction*.

(a) $CrO_4^{2-} \rightarrow Cr(OH)_2$

(b) $S_2O_3^{2-} \rightarrow S_4O_6^{2-}$

(c) $IO_3^- + Cl^- \rightarrow ICl_2^-$

5. Balance the following reactions using the half-reaction method. Assume acidic conditions unless stated otherwise.

(a) $Sn^{2+} + MnO_4^- \rightarrow Sn^{4+} + MnO_2$ (basic)

(b) $V^{2+} + H_2SO_3 \rightarrow V^{3+} + S_2O_3^{2-}$

(c) $IO_3^- + I^- \rightarrow I_2$ (basic)

(d) $ClO_3^- + N_2H_4 \rightarrow NO + Cl^-$

(e) $NO_3^- + Zn \rightarrow Zn^{2+} + NO$ (basic)

© Edvantage Interactive 2019

(f) $ClO_3^- \rightarrow ClO_4^- + Cl^- + Cl_2$
Use the ΔON values to help you determine how to break this into two half-reactions.

(g) $SnS_3O_3 + MnO_4^- \rightarrow MnO_2 + SO_4^{2-} + Sn^{4+}$ (basic)

(h) $Mg_3(AsO_4)_2 + SiO_2 + C \rightarrow As_4 + MgSiO_3 + CO$

6. Balance the following using the ΔON method. Assume acidic conditions unless otherwise indicated.
(a) $SeO_3^{2-} + F^- \rightarrow Se + F_2$

(b) $ReO_4^- + Sb_2O_3 \rightarrow ReO_2 + Sb_2O_5$ (basic)

(c) $Pd + NO_3^- + I^- \rightarrow PdI_6^{2-} + NO$

(d) $Pb(OH)_4^{2-} + BrO^- \rightarrow PbO_2 + Br^-$ (basic)

7. Use the half-reaction method to balance the following reactions occurring in aqueous solution:

   (a) $K_2Cr_2O_7 + CH_3CH_2OH + HCl \rightarrow CH_3COOH + KCl + CrCl_3 + H_2O$

   You must first convert the equation into net ionic form, balance the net ionic equation, and then convert it back into the original formula equation. This is the reaction performed in the prototype BAT (Breath Alcohol Testing) mobiles.

   (b) C.W. Scheele prepared chlorine gas in 1774 using the following reaction:

   $NaCl + H_2SO_4 + MnO_2 \rightarrow Na_2SO_4 + MnCl_2 + H_2O + Cl_2$

© Edvantage Interactive 2019

7.3 Using the Standard Reduction Potential (SRP) Table to Predict Redox Reactions

Warm Up

1. Compare Table A7 Standard Reduction Potentials of Half-Cells with Table A5 Relative Strengths of Brønsted-Lowry Acids and Bases at the back of the book. List four similarities between the tables.

   (a) ______________________________ (c) ______________________________

   (b) ______________________________ (d) ______________________________

2. The half-reactions in the SRP table are written as ______________________.

   This means the reactant species are all ______________________ agents.

3. Find the strongest reducing agents on the SRP table. What family do these reducing agents belong to?

   ____

4. What element is the strongest oxidizing agent? __________ What family does this element belong to?

   ____

Using the Standard Reduction Potential (SRP) Table

Chemists use the standard reduction potential (SRP) table to predict whether a chemical species will spontaneously give electrons to or take electrons from another species. The oxidizing agents, which are the species that take electrons, are on the left side of the SRP table. The reducing agents, which are the species that give electrons, are on the right side of the SRP table.

> Chemical species in the left column of the SRP table will only take electrons spontaneously from species *below them* in the right column.

In chemical terms, oxidizing agents only spontaneously oxidize the reducing agents below them in the SRP table. For example, Br_2 spontaneously oxidizes Ag but not Cl^- (Figure 7.3.1).

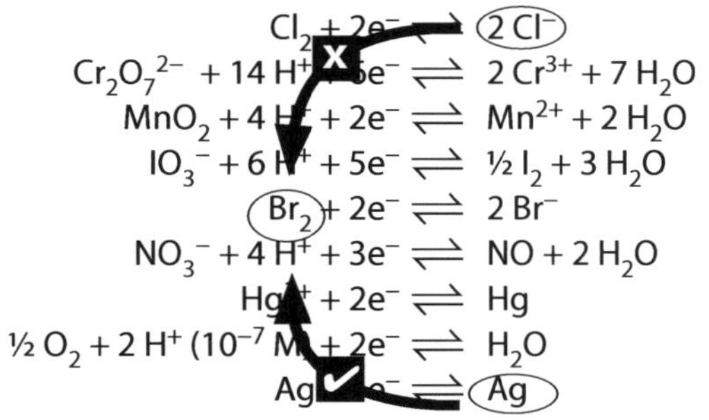

Figure 7.3.1 *You can tell that Br_2 spontaneously oxidizes Ag because Ag is below Br_2 in the SRP table.*

Of course, the event can also be described from the reducing agent's point of view.

> Chemical species in the right column only give electrons spontaneously to chemicals *above them* in the left column.

In chemical terms, reducing agents only spontaneously reduce the oxidizing agents above them in the SRP table. For example, Ag reduces Br_2 but Cl^- doesn't. Thus, spontaneous redox reactions occur with the oxidation half-reaction below the reduction half-reaction on the SRP table. Electrons are passed in a clockwise direction. Remember that the oxidizing agent (Br_2) gets reduced and the reducing agent (Ag) gets oxidized.

reduction ½ reaction →

$$Br_2 + 2e^- \rightleftharpoons 2\,Br^-$$
$$NO_3^- + 4\,H^+ + 3e^- \rightleftharpoons NO + 2\,H_2O$$
$$Hg^{2+} + 2e^- \rightleftharpoons Hg$$
$$\tfrac{1}{2}\,O_2 + 2\,H^+\,(10^{-7}\,M) + 2e^- \rightleftharpoons H_2O$$
$$Ag^+ + e^- \rightleftharpoons Ag$$

← oxidation ½ reaction

$$2\,Ag \rightarrow 2\,Ag^+ + \cancel{2e^-}$$
$$Br_2 + \cancel{2e^-} \rightarrow 2\,Br^-$$
$$2\,Ag + Br_2 \rightarrow 2\,Ag^+ + 2\,Br^-$$

Sample Problem 7.3.1 — Determining Whether a Spontaneous Redox Reaction Will Occur

For each of the following, state whether a reaction will spontaneously occur. If so, write the balanced equation for the reaction.

(a) $Fe^{3+} + Cl^-$ (b) $Ca + Zn^{2+}$ (c) $I^- + Al$

What to Think About	How to Do It
(a) $Fe^{3+} + Cl^-$ 1. Identify the oxidizing agent and the reducing agent.	Fe^{3+} is an oxidizing agent. Cl^- is a reducing agent.
2. Oxidizing agents only take electrons spontaneously from reducing agents below them in the SRP table.	Cl^- is not below Fe^{3+} in the SRP table so Fe^{3+} will not oxidize it. No reaction.
(b) $Ca + Zn^{2+}$ 1. Identify the oxidizing agent and the reducing agent.	Ca is a reducing agent. Zn^{2+} is an oxidizing agent.
2. Oxidizing agents can only take electrons spontaneously from reducing agents below them in the SRP table.	Ca is below Zn^{2+} in the SRP table so Zn^{2+} will oxidize it.
3. Write the two half-reactions, balance the transfer of electrons if necessary and then add the half-reactions together.	$Ca \rightarrow Ca^{2+} + \cancel{2e^-}$ $Zn^{2+} + \cancel{2e^-} \rightarrow Zn$ $Zn^{2+} + Ca \rightarrow Ca^{2+} + Zn$
(c) $I^- + Al$ 1. Identify the oxidizing agent and the reducing agent.	I^- and Al are both reducing agents so no reaction occurs.

© Edvantage Interactive 2019

Practice Problems 7.3.1 — Determining Whether a Spontaneous Redox Reaction Will Occur

For each of the following, state whether a spontaneous reaction will occur and if so, write the balanced equation for the reaction.

1. $I^- + Br_2$
2. $F_2 + Al^{3+}$
3. $Ag^+ + Sn$
4. $I_2 + Cl^-$

Single Replacement Reactions

Recall that both metals and non-metals are more stable as ions because as ions they have complete valence shells. Non-metals have high electron affinities, needing only one, two, or three electrons to complete their valence shells. Non-metals, as strong oxidizing agents, are found at the top left side of the SRP table, where they are shown being reduced to form anions (negatively charged ions). Non-metals can also be oxidized to form non-metallic oxides and oxyanions. For example, chlorine can be oxidized to chlorine dioxide (ClO_2), the hypochlorite ion (ClO^-), the chlorite ion (ClO_2^-), the chlorate ion (ClO_3^-), or the perchlorate ion (ClO_4^-). Metals, on the other hand, can only be oxidized. A metal empties its valence shell and the complete shell beneath it becomes its new valence shell. Most metals, as strong reducing agents, are found at the bottom, right side of the SRP table, where they are shown being oxidized to form cations (positively charged ions).

Recall that one chemical species passes or loses one or more electrons to another species in redox reactions. In the synthesis of ionic compounds, metals give electrons to non-metals and both form ions that are more stable than their neutral atoms. In the SRP table, this is reflected by most of the non-metals being above most of the metals. Single replacement reactions are also a type of redox reaction. In single replacement reactions, a non-metal oxidizes a different non-metal's anion, or a metal reduces a different metal's cation. Think of a non-metal replacement reaction as an electron tug-of-war between two non-metals for the "extra" electron(s) that one of them already possesses. A metal replacement reaction can be viewed as a metal atom trying to force its valence electron(s) onto a different metal's stable ion. In both cases, we use the SRP table to determine which chemical species wins.

Sample Problem 7.3.2 — Determining the Outcome of a Single Replacement Reaction

Will chlorine and sodium bromide spontaneously react to produce bromine and sodium chloride? If so, write the balanced net ionic equation for the reaction.

What to Think About	How to Do It
1. Write the balanced formula equation.	$Cl_2 + 2\ NaBr \rightarrow Br_2 + 2\ NaCl$
2. Write the complete ionic equation.	$Cl_2 + 2\ Na^+ + 2\ Br^- \rightarrow Br_2 + 2\ Na^+ + 2\ Cl^-$
3. Write the net ionic equation.	$Cl_2 + 2\ Br^- \rightarrow Br_2 + 2\ Cl^-$
4. Identify the oxidizing agent and the reducing agent.	Cl_2 is an oxidizing agent. Br^- is a reducing agent.
5. Oxidizing agents only spontaneously take electrons from reducing agents below them in the SRP table.	Br^- is below Cl_2 in the SRP table so Cl_2 can oxidize it as shown in part 3 above.

The chlorine atoms won the electron tug-of-war with the bromide ions in the sample problem above. The chlorine atoms that were sharing a pair of valence electrons to complete their valence shells now each have an electron of their own and the bromine atoms are forced to share valence electrons (Br_2). The sodium ions were spectator ions because they were unchanged by the reaction. We began with chlorine dissolved in a solution of sodium bromide and finished with bromine dissolved in a solution of sodium chloride.

Practice Problems 7.3.2 — Determining the Outcome of a Single Replacement Reaction

For each of the following, determine whether a reaction will occur and if so, write the balanced net ionic equation for the reaction.

1. $I_2 + CaF_2$

2. $Al + CuSO_4$

3. $Cl_2 + NaCl$

4. $Sn + Al(NO_2)_3$

The Strength of Oxidizing and Reducing Agents

Have you noticed that oxidizing and reducing agents closely parallel Brønsted-Lowry acids and bases? Brønsted-Lowry acids and bases pass protons back and forth. Oxidizing and reducing agents pass electrons back and forth. An acid and its conjugate base are the same chemical species with and without the proton. A reducing agent and its complementary oxidizing agent are the same chemical species with and without the electron. In the Warm Up exercise you identified similarities between the SRP table (Table A7) and the table of acid strengths (Table A6).

Recall that the weaker an acid, the stronger its conjugate base because the less an acid's tendency to give its proton away, the greater its conjugate base's tendency to take it back. Although the term *conjugate* is not used by chemists to describe the reduced and oxidized forms of a chemical species, the same inverse relationship exists between their strengths.

The stronger a reducing agent (A^-) is, the weaker its complementary oxidizing agent (A) is.

In other words, if a chemical species has a strong tendency to give an electron away then it will have a weak tendency to take it back.

Oxidizing Agents		**Reducing Agents**
STRONG	$F_2 + 2e^- \rightarrow 2\,F^-$	WEAK
↑	$2\,H^+ + 2e^- \rightarrow H_2$	↓
WEAK	$Li^+ + e^- \rightarrow Li$	STRONG

 © Edvantage Interactive 2019

Just as there are amphiprotic species that can act as both proton donors and acceptors, there are also some chemical species that can act as both reducing agents and oxidizing agents. Multivalent transition metals have ions such as Cu^+, Sn^{2+}, and Fe^{2+} that can be further oxidized or reduced back to the metal. H_2O_2 can also be an oxidizing agent or a reducing agent. Can you find it in both columns of the SRP table?

The halogens are a little difficult to spot in the SRP table. An element's oxidizing strength corresponds with its electronegativity. Its ability to oxidize various chemical species corresponds with how strongly it attracts the shared pair of electrons in a covalent bond. Electronegativity increases as you move up a group in the periodic table and thus the relative positions of the halogens in the SRP table are the same as they are in the periodic table (Table 7.3.1). Fluorine can therefore oxidize any of the other halide ions. Chlorine can oxidize any halide ion other than fluoride, etc.

Table 7.3.1 *The Position of the Halogens in the SRP Table*

$F_2 + 2e^-$	$\rightleftharpoons$	$2\,F^-$
$S_2O_8^{2-} + 2e^-$	$\rightleftharpoons$	$2\,SO_4^{2-}$
$H_2O_2 + 2\,H^+ + 2e^-$	$\rightleftharpoons$	$2\,H_2O$
$MnO_4^- + 8\,H^+ + 5e^-$	$\rightleftharpoons$	$Mn^{2+} + 4\,H_2O$
$Au^{3+} + 3e^-$	$\rightleftharpoons$	Au
$BrO_3^- + 6\,H^+ + 5e^-$	$\rightleftharpoons$	$\frac{1}{2}\,Br_2 + 3\,H_2O$
$ClO_4^- + 8\,H^+ + 8e^-$	$\rightleftharpoons$	$Cl^- + 4\,H_2O$
$Cl_2 + 2e^-$	$\rightleftharpoons$	$2\,Cl^-$
$Cr_2O_7^{2-} + 14\,H^+ + 6e^-$	$\rightleftharpoons$	$2\,Cr^{3+} + 7\,H_2O$
$\frac{1}{2}\,O_2 + 2\,H^+ + 2e^-$	$\rightleftharpoons$	H_2O
$MnO_2 + 4\,H^+ + 2e^-$	$\rightleftharpoons$	$Mn^{2+} + 2\,H_2O$
$IO_3^- + 6\,H^+ + 5e^-$	$\rightleftharpoons$	$\frac{1}{2}\,I_2 + 3\,H_2O$
$Br_2 + 2e^-$	$\rightleftharpoons$	$2Br^-$
$AuCl_4^- + 3e^-$	$\rightleftharpoons$	$Au + 4\,Cl^-$
$NO_3^- + 4\,H^+ + 3e^-$	$\rightleftharpoons$	$NO + 2\,H_2O$
$Hg^{2+} + 2e^-$	$\rightleftharpoons$	Hg
$\frac{1}{2}\,O_2 + 2\,H^+\,(10^{-7}\,M) + 2e^-$	$\rightleftharpoons$	H_2O
$2\,NO_3^- + 4\,H^+ + 2e^-$	$\rightleftharpoons$	$N_2O_4 + 2\,H_2O$
$Ag^+ + e^-$	$\rightleftharpoons$	Ag
$\frac{1}{2}\,Hg_2^{2+} + e^-$	$\rightleftharpoons$	Hg
$Fe^{3+} + e^-$	$\rightleftharpoons$	Fe^{2+}
$O_2 + 2\,H^+ + 2e^-$	$\rightleftharpoons$	H_2O_2
$I_2 + 2e^-$	$\rightleftharpoons$	$2\,I^-$

Some redox terminology is counter-intuitive. For instance, the strength of an oxidizing agent is called its **reduction potential** (E°). *Reduction potential* means *potential to be reduced*, not *potential to reduce*. Oxidizing agents get reduced and therefore have a reduction potential. Reduction and oxidation potentials are measured in volts. $F_2(g)$ is the strongest oxidizing agent shown in the SRP table, with a reduction potential of 2.87 V. Note that the *-ates* ions (e.g., bromate, permanganate, chlorate, dichromate) are strong oxidizing agents.

Likewise, **oxidation potentials** measure the strength of reducing agents since reducing agents become oxidized when they give up electrons. When the reduction half-reactions are read backwards, from right to left, they are oxidation half-reactions. Oxidation potentials of reducing agents are simply the opposite of the reduction potentials of their complementary oxidizing agents. For example, Al^{3+} has a reduction potential of −1.66 V while Al has an oxidation potential of +1.66 V. Li(*s*) is the strongest reducing agent shown in the SRP table we are using, with an oxidation potential of 3.04 V.

To change your standard reduction potential (SRP) table into a standard oxidation potential (SOP) table, you would turn it around 180° so it reads upside down and backwards, and you would reverse the E° signs (+ to – and – to +).

Quick Check

1. Which is the stronger reducing agent, Co or Sr? ____________
2. Which is the stronger oxidizing agent, Fe^{3+} or Al^{3+}? ____________
3. Which has the greater oxidation potential, Br^- or I^-? ____________
4. Which has the greater reduction potential, Cr^{3+} or Sn^{2+}? ____________
5. A and B are hypothetical elements. A^{2+} is a stronger oxidizing agent than B. Which has the greater oxidation potential, A or B^-? ____________
6. What is the reduction potential of Ag^+? ____________
7. What is the oxidation potential of Ca? ____________

Determining the Predominant Redox Reaction

In chemical mixtures, there are sometimes more than two chemical species available to react. We use the SRP table to predict which species will react.

The predominant redox reaction between the chemicals in a mixture will be between the strongest available oxidizing agent and the strongest available reducing agent.

© Edvantage Interactive 2019

Sample Problem 7.3.3 — Determining the Predominant Redox Reaction

Write the predominant redox reaction that will occur in a mixture of Cl_2, Ag^+, Sn^{2+}, and I^-.

What to Think About	How to Do It
1. Identify the oxidizing agent(s) and the reducing agent(s).	Cl_2, Ag^+, and Sn^{2+} are oxidizing agents. Sn^{2+} and I^- are reducing agents.
2. Use the SRP table to determine which species is the strongest oxidizing agent and which species is the strongest reducing agent.	(see table below) Cl_2 is a stronger oxidizing agent than Ag^+ or Sn^{2+}. Sn^{2+} is a stronger reducing agent than I^-.
3. The strongest oxidizing agent will oxidize the strongest reducing agent.	Cl_2 will oxidize Sn^{2+}.
4. Write the two half-reactions and balance the transfer of electrons if necessary. Then add the half-reactions together.	$Sn^{2+} \rightarrow Sn^{4+} + 2e^-$ $Cl_2 + 2e^- \rightarrow 2\ Cl^-$ $Cl_2 + Sn^{2+} \rightarrow Sn^{4+} + 2\ Cl^-$

Oxidizing Agents (Increasing Strength ↑) / Reducing Agents (Increasing Strength ↓)

Oxidizing Agents		Reducing Agents
$ClO_4^- + 8\ H^+ + 8e^-$	$\rightleftharpoons$	$Cl^- + 4\ H_2O$
$Cl_2 + 2e^-$	$\rightleftharpoons$	$2\ Cl^-$
$Cr_2O_7^{2-} + 14\ H^+ + 6e^-$	$\rightleftharpoons$	$2\ Cr^{3+} + 7\ H_2O$
$Br_2 + 2e^-$	$\rightleftharpoons$	$2\ Br^-$
$NO_3^- + 4\ H^+ + 3e^-$	$\rightleftharpoons$	$NO + 2\ H_2O$
$Hg^{2+} + 2e^-$	$\rightleftharpoons$	Hg
$\frac{1}{2}\ O_2(g) + 2\ H^+ (10^{-7}\ M) + 2e^-$	$\rightleftharpoons$	H_2O
$Ag^+ + e^-$	$\rightleftharpoons$	Ag
$I_2 + e^-$	$\rightleftharpoons$	$2\ I^-$
$H_2SO_3 + 4\ H^+ + 4e^-$	$\rightleftharpoons$	$S + 3\ H_2O$
$Cu^{2+} + 2e^-$	$\rightleftharpoons$	Cu
$SO_4^{2-} + 4\ H^+ + 2e^-$	$\rightleftharpoons$	$H_2SO_3 + H_2O$
$Sn^{4+} + 2e^-$	$\rightleftharpoons$	Sn^{2+}
$S + 2\ H^+ + 2e^-$	$\rightleftharpoons$	H_2S
$2\ H^+ + 2e^-$	$\rightleftharpoons$	H_2
$Pb^{2+} + 2e^-$	$\rightleftharpoons$	Pb
$Sn^{2+} + 2e^-$	$\rightleftharpoons$	Sn
$Ni^{2+} + 2e^-$	$\rightleftharpoons$	Ni

In the sample problem above, there are many other reactions that would occur but in every case the products can be oxidized by Cl_2 or reduced by Sn^{2+}. For example, Ag^+ can also oxidize I^- forming Ag and I_2 but this I_2 would then be reduced back to I^- by Sn^{2+} and the Ag would be oxidized back to Ag^+ by Cl_2. In every instance, the products would ultimately end up being those shown in the solution to the sample problem. Also keep in mind that if one species runs out, then the strongest remaining agent is "next up to bat."

Practice Problems 7.3.3 — Determining the Predominant Redox Reaction

Write the predominant redox reaction that will occur in each of the following mixtures:

1. Sn^{4+}, Br^-, Zn^{2+}, and Ni

2. $CuBr_2$(*aq*) and Al(*s*)

3. Na^+, Cu^+, and F^-

4. Copper and bromine in a solution of iron(III) chloride

Redox Titrations

All the general principles of titrations apply to redox titrations. A chemist titrates an acid with a base or vice versa. Similarly, a chemist titrates an oxidizing agent with a reducing agent or vice versa. The chemist must choose a titrant that is a strong enough oxidizing agent to react with the reducing agent or a strong enough reducing agent to react with the oxidizing agent.

The indicator of an acid-base titration is itself a weak acid with a different color in its base form. Similarly, the indicator of a redox titration is itself a reducing agent with a different color in its oxidized form. Otherwise, redox indicators operate in a much simpler way than acid-base indicators. A chemist chooses a redox indicator that is a weaker oxidizing or reducing agent than the analyte (the chemical being analyzed) so that the indicator's reaction indicates that the analyte has been completely consumed.

In redox titrations it is not uncommon for the titrant to act as its own indicator. The purple permanganate ion is sometimes used as an oxidizing agent to titrate a chemical species. The permanganate ion is reduced to the very faint pink Mn^{2+} under acidic conditions. When the permanganate solution is slowly added to a reducing agent of unknown molarity, the permanganate ion is reduced, and the purple color disappears. Eventually a drop is added and the purple color remains. At this point, the chemist knows that the chemical species that was reducing the permanganate ion has been totally consumed, and the equivalence point has been reached.

Sample Problem 7.3.4 — Determining a Chemical's Concentration via Redox Titration

To titrate a 25.0 mL solution of Fe^{2+} to the equivalence point, 16.7 mL of 0.0152 M MnO_4^- in acidic solution was needed. What was the $[Fe^{2+}]$?

What to Think About	How to Do It
1. Write the balanced net ionic equation for the titration reaction.	$5\ Fe^{2+} + MnO_4^- + 8\ H^+ \rightarrow 5\ Fe^{3+} + Mn^{2+} + 4\ H_2O$
2. Calculate the moles of MnO_4^- reacted.	$0.0167\ L \times 0.0152\ \frac{mol}{L} = 2.54 \times 10^{-4}\ mol\ MnO_4^-$
3. Calculate the moles of Fe^{2+} reacted.	$2.54 \times 10^{-4}\ mol\ MnO_4^- \times \frac{5\ mol\ Fe^{2+}}{1\ mol\ MnO_4^-} = 1.27 \times 10^{-3}\ mol\ Fe^{2+}$
4. Calculate the $[Fe^{2+}]$ in the original sample.	$[Fe^{2+}] = \frac{1.27 \times 10^{-3}\ mol}{0.0250\ L} = .0508\ M\ Fe^{2+}$
	Note: Under basic conditions the permanganate ion is reduced to MnO_2(*s*), as shown on the SRP table (+.60 V).

© Edvantage Interactive 2019

Practice Problems 7.3.4 — Determining a Chemical's Concentration via Redox Titration

1. Potassium dichromate is used to titrate a solution of iron(II) chloride. The dichromate ion acts as its own indicator. As the $Cr_2O_7^{2-}$ solution is added to the Fe^{2+} solution, the orange dichromate ion is reduced to green Cr^{3+} as it oxidizes the Fe^{2+} to Fe^{3+}. The equivalence point is evident when the orange color remains indicating that all the Fe^{2+} has reacted. An amount of 15.0 mL of 0.0200 M $Cr_2O_7^{2-}$ solution was required to titrate 20.0 mL of acidified $FeCl_2$.

   (a) Balance the redox equation for this titration: $Cr_2O_7^{2-} + Fe^{2+} \rightarrow Cr^{3+} + Fe^{3+}$

   (b) What was the $[FeCl_2]$?

2. A student uses 16.3 mL of an acidified $KMnO_4$ solution to titrate 1.00 g $Na_2C_2O_4$ to the equivalence point. The balanced equation is:

   $5\,C_2O_4^{2-} + 2\,MnO_4^- + 16\,H^+ \rightarrow 10\,CO_2 + 2\,Mn^{2+} + 8\,H_2O$

   Calculate the $[KMnO_4]$.

3. The following redox reaction occurs between the dichromate ion and ethanol:

   $3\,CH_3CH_2OH + 2\,Cr_2O_7^{2-} + 16\,H^+ \rightarrow 3\,CH_3COOH + 4\,Cr^{3+} + 11\,H_2O$

   ethanol (CH₃CH₂OH); orange ($Cr_2O_7^{2-}$); ethanoic acid (CH₃COOH); green (Cr^{3+})

   A chemist uses 26.25 mL of 0.500 M $Cr_2O_7^{2-}$ to titrate a 10.0 mL sample of wine to the equivalence point.

   (a) What is the $[CH_3CH_2OH]$ in the wine?

   (b) The concentration of ethanol in alcoholic beverages is expressed as percent by volume. If a wine is 10% alcohol, it means that there are 10 mL of ethanol for every 100 mL of the beverage. The density of ethanol is 0.789 g/mL. Convert your answer in part (a) into percent by volume.

7.3 Activity: Making an SRP Table

Question

How can you make a standard reduction potential table from a set of experimental data?

Background

Each redox reaction allows you to determine the relative position of its two half-reactions in the table. For example, from the following reaction in which L reduces M^{2+} you can infer that M^{2+} is a stronger oxidizing agent than L^+. M^+ is therefore above L^+ in the SRP table.

$L + M^{2+} \rightarrow 2\,L^+ + M$

reduction ½ reaction $\longrightarrow$

$M^{2+} + 2e^- \rightarrow M$

$L^+ + e^- \leftarrow L$

$\longleftarrow$ oxidation ½ reaction

Procedure

Use the following information to produce an SRP table with six half-reactions.

1. $L + M^{2+} \rightarrow 2\,L^+ + M$
2. P^- reduces D^{3+} to D^{2+}.
3. Element Q is the strongest oxidizing agent. ($Q + e^- \rightarrow Q^-$)
4. $M + 2\,P \rightarrow M^{2+} + 2\,P^-$
5. L^+ oxidizes C to C^{2+}.

Results and Discussion

1. Fill in the SRP table below:

Oxidizing Agents		Reducing Agents
______________	$\rightleftharpoons$	______________
______________	$\rightleftharpoons$	______________
______________	$\rightleftharpoons$	______________
______________	$\rightleftharpoons$	______________
______________	$\rightleftharpoons$	______________
______________	$\rightleftharpoons$	______________

2. Which chemical species is the weakest reducing agent? ______________

3. Which chemical species has the lowest reduction potential? ______________

© Edvantage Interactive 2019

7.3 Review Questions

1. Will iodine spontaneously oxidize: (a) Fe^{2+}? (b) Sn?

2. Identify a metal ion that will spontaneously oxidize I^- but not Cl^-.

3. For each of the following, state whether a spontaneous reaction will occur and if so, write the balanced equation for the reaction.
   (a) $Mg + Al^{3+} \rightarrow$

   (b) $Cl^- + I_2 \rightarrow$

   (c) $Hg^{2+} + Ag \rightarrow$

4. Complete the following table:

Metals	Non-metals
bottom right of SRP table	
	tend to take electrons
give e^- to chemicals above them on the left	

5. For each of the following, state whether a spontaneous reaction will occur and if so, write the balanced net ionic equation for the reaction.
   (a) $Fe + Sn(NO_3)_2 \rightarrow$

   (b) $F_2 + KBr \rightarrow$

   (c) $Cu + NaI \rightarrow$

6. (a) Write the net ionic equation for the reaction between KI and $FeCl_3$.

   (b) Write the net ionic equation for the reaction between Br_2 and $FeCl_2$.

7. When tin(II) nitrate dissolves in acid the two dissociated ions react with each other. Write the net ionic equation for this reaction.

8. Would it be practical to store a 0.5 M $FeCl_3$ solution in an aluminum container? Explain.

9. State whether the forward or the reverse reaction is spontaneous.
(a) $Sn^{4+} + 2\ Fe^{2+} \leftarrow\ ?\ \rightarrow 2\ Fe^{3+} + Sn^{2+}$

(b) $Cr_2O_7^{2-} + 14\ H^+ + 3\ Cu \leftarrow\ ?\ \rightarrow 2\ Cr^{3+} + 7\ H_2O + 3\ Cu^{2+}$

10. One characteristic of acids is that they react with magnesium, liberating hydrogen gas. Write the balanced redox equation for this reaction.

11. Explain why silver oxidizes and then dissolves in 1 M nitric acid but not in 1 M hydrochloric acid.

12. A few drops of phenolphthalein are added to a petri dish of water. A small piece of sodium reacts violently when placed in the water, leaving pink tracks as it skips across the water's surface. The air ignites above the sodium producing a small flame. Write the redox reaction that occurs and briefly explain the pink tracks and the flame.

13. (a) Which has the greatest reduction potential, I_2, Ag^+, or Mg^{2+}?

(b) Which has the greatest oxidation potential, I^-, Ag, or Mg?

14. The surface of a sheet of aluminum is observed to darken after being placed in a solution of gallium nitrate. From this observation, determine which has the greater reduction potential, Al^{3+} or Ga^{3+}.

15. (a) What is the reduction potential of $Br_2(l)$?

(b) What is the oxidation potential of Zn(*s*)?

16. Write the predominant redox reaction that will occur in each of the following mixtures:
(a) Co^{2+}, Cu, Mn^{2+}, and Fe

(b) Cu, Hg, Cu^+, and Cr^{2+}

(c) $CuCl_2(aq) + SnI_2(aq)$

 © Edvantage Interactive 2019

17. If a zinc sheet were placed into a solution of $Cu^{2+}(aq)$ and $Fe^{3+}(aq)$ what would the predominant reaction be?

18. Each of the following redox reactions is spontaneous in the forward direction:

$A^{2+} + B \rightarrow B^{2+} + A$ $\quad$ $2\,C^{3+} + A \rightarrow 2\,C^{2+} + A^{2+}$ $\quad$ $B^{2+} + 2\,D \rightarrow 2\,D^{+} + B$

Which of the chemical species involved in these reactions is:

(a) the strongest oxidizing agent

(b) the strongest reducing agent

19. A chemist titrates 15.0 mL of KI(aq) to the equivalence point with 32.8 mL of 0.200 M $Na_2Cr_2O_7$. What is the [KI]?

$Cr_2O_7^{2-} + 14\,H^{+} + 6\,I^{-} \rightarrow 2\,Cr^{3+} + 3\,I_2 + 7\,H_2O$

20. A $KMnO_4$ solution is standardized with oxalic acid. The equation for the redox reaction is:

$5\,H_2C_2O_4 + 2\,MnO_4^{-} + 6\,H^{+} \rightarrow 10\,CO_2 + 2\,Mn^{2+} + 8\,H_2O$

What is the molar concentration of the $KMnO_4$ solution if 18.6 mL of the solution was required to titrate 0.105 g $H_2C_2O_4 \cdot 2H_2O$?

21. The legal limit for intoxication while driving has been a blood alcohol content (BAC) of 0.08% by mass for many years. Now the National Traffic Safety Board (NTSB) has called for reducing the limit to 0.05%. A 5.00 g sample of blood is titrated with 10.15 mL of 0.0150 M $K_2Cr_2O_7$. The dichromate ion acts as an oxidizing agent in the reaction of ethanol, C_2H_5OH, to form carbon dioxide and the Cr^{3+} ion.

(a) Balance the equation for the reaction that occurs during the titration.

(b) Calculate the percent alcohol by mass in the blood sample. Would this driver be considered legally impaired under the newly called for guidelines of a BAC of 0.05%?

7.4 The Electrochemical Cell

Warm Up

1. A charged atom or group of atoms is called a(n) ______________.
2. The charged subatomic particle that travels around the nucleus is called a(n) ______________.
3. Current electricity is a steady flow of electric charge. A current of 1 amp means that one coulomb of charge is flowing past the point of measurement each second. The charge of a single electron is only 1.60×10^{-19} C. How many electrons does it take to make up one coulomb of charge?

The Standard Electrochemical Cell

Electrons are transferred from one chemical species to another in all redox reactions. An **electrochemical cell** is a portable source of electricity, in which the electricity is produced by a spontaneous redox reaction within the cell. Electrochemical cells are also referred to as voltaic cells and galvanic cells. The electrochemical cell is the most common application of redox reactions and is also the best tool for measuring the tendency of redox reactions to occur.

The basic design of an electrochemical cell isolates an oxidation half-reaction from a reduction half-reaction within the device. Electrons can travel only from the reducing agent to the oxidizing agent when the two agents are connected through an external circuit. The basic components of an electrochemical cell are two different conductive materials (electrodes) immersed in the same or different electrolyte solutions. If each electrode is immersed in a separate solution then two half-cells are created. The two half-cells must be connected in some manner that allows ion migration between them. For example, a salt bridge is a U-tube filled with an electrolyte solution or gel that allows ion migration (Figure 7.4.1).

How does an electrochemical cell work? The chemical species in the two half-cells exert forces on each other's electrons through the wire that connects the two half-cells. Electrons spontaneously flow through the wire from the strongest available reducing agent to the strongest available oxidizing agent.

One type of half-cell consists of a metal electrode immersed in a solution containing ions of the same metal. Either the metal electrode gives electrons to the other half-cell or the metal ions receive electrons from the other half-cell. Let's consider a cell with two metal | metal ion half-cells. The cell in Figure 7.4.1 has one half-cell with a magnesium electrode immersed in a solution containing magnesium ions and another half-cell with a copper electrode immersed in a solution containing copper(II) ions. Although the metals are not in physical contact with the other half-cell's ions, they are electrically connected through the wire connecting the two half-cells.

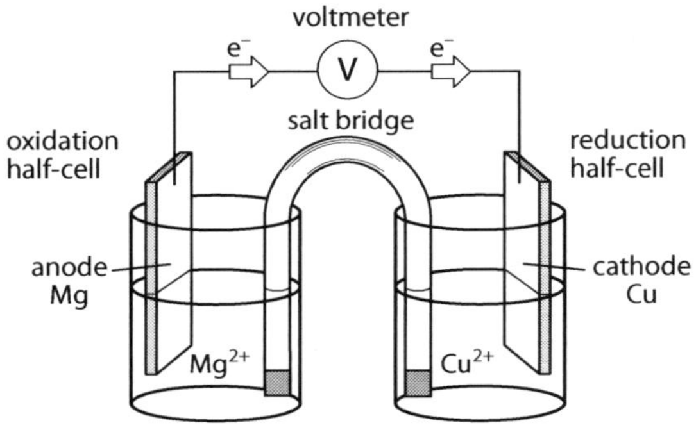

Figure 7.4.1 *A standard electrochemical cell*

The predominant redox reaction will be between the strongest available oxidizing agent and the strongest available reducing agent, just as though the chemicals were all in the same container. In fact, the SRP table (Table A7) specifically provides the tendency of redox reactions to occur between standard half-cells. A standard cell has ion concentrations of 1 M at 25°C as shown just below the heading of the SRP table. The SRP table thus allows us to predict the resulting direction of electron flow under standard conditions:

 © Edvantage Interactive 2019

reduction ½ reaction →

$$\begin{array}{lcl} Cu^{2+} + 2e^- & \rightarrow & Cu \\ Pb^{2+} + 2e^- & \rightleftharpoons & Pb \\ Co^{2+} + 2e^- & \rightleftharpoons & Co \\ Zn^{2+} + 2e^- & \rightleftharpoons & Zn \\ Mg^{2+} + 2e^- & \leftarrow & Mg \end{array}$$

← oxidation ½ reaction

$$\begin{array}{rcl} Mg & \rightarrow & Mg^{2+} + \cancel{2e^-} \\ Cu^{2+} + \cancel{2e^-} & \rightarrow & Cu \\ \hline Cu^{2+} + Mg & \rightarrow & Mg^{2+} + Cu \end{array}$$

The **anode** is defined as the electrode where oxidation occurs. The **cathode** is defined as the electrode where reduction occurs.

> Oxidation occurs at the anode.
> Reduction occurs at the cathode.

Thus in the cells in Figure 7.4.1, the magnesium electrode is the anode and the copper electrode is the cathode. Note that although reduction occurs at the cathode, it isn't the cathode itself that is being reduced. In our example, it is the copper(II) ions (Cu^{2+}) that are being reduced and plating out as copper metal (Cu) at the cathode. In any cell where plating occurs, it will be at the cathode. While the cathode thus increases in mass, the anode decreases in mass as metal atoms donate electrons and become ions, which dissolve into solution.

A conductor doesn't increase in mass or become charged when an electric current flows through it. When electrons move into a copper wire, they displace or push the wire's free moving valence electrons ahead. Magnesium's two electrons need only move one atom toward the copper half-cell to displace electrons all the way through the wire and pop two electrons out the other end to the waiting Cu^{2+} ions. This is similar to what happens when water flows from a tap into a hose that is already full of water, immediately pushing some water out the other end of the hose.

The Salt Bridge

A salt bridge or a porous barrier allows ion migration that completes the circuit. In effect, the ion migration electrically counterbalances the electron flow. Without this ion migration, a charge build-up would occur: the reduction half-cell would become negative and the oxidation half-cell would become positive. This would create a polarization that would stop the electron flow. The natural ion migration prevents such a charge build-up. Consider a cell and its external circuit as one continuous loop with the negatively charged particles (electrons and anions) flowing in a continuous clockwise or counter-clockwise direction. In Figure 7.4.2, the negatively charged particles flow in a clockwise direction.

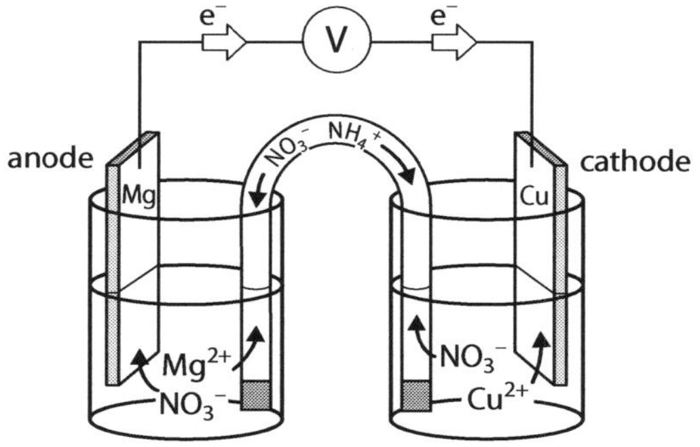

Figure 7.4.2 *Ion migration in an electrochemical cell*

> Anions migrate toward the anode.
> Cations migrate toward the cathode.

The oxidation half-cell above consists of a Mg electrode in $Mg(NO_3)_2(aq)$. The reduction half-cell consists of a Cu electrode in $Cu(NO_3)_2(aq)$. The salt bridge contains $NH_4NO_3(aq)$. The anion (NO_3^-) moves toward the anode while the cations (NH_4^+, Cu^{2+}, and Mg^{2+}) move toward the cathode.

Students sometimes ask whether the anode is the positive or the negative electrode. It is neither. The electrodes do not have any significant charge. Why then do commercial cells have a (–) label and a (+) label on them? The anode and the cathode each have a (–) and a (+) terminal or end, just as a magnet has a north and a south pole. Electrons flow externally from the (–) terminal of the anode to the (+) terminal of the cathode while internally anions migrate from the (–) terminal of the cathode to the (+) terminal of the anode (Figure 7.4.3).

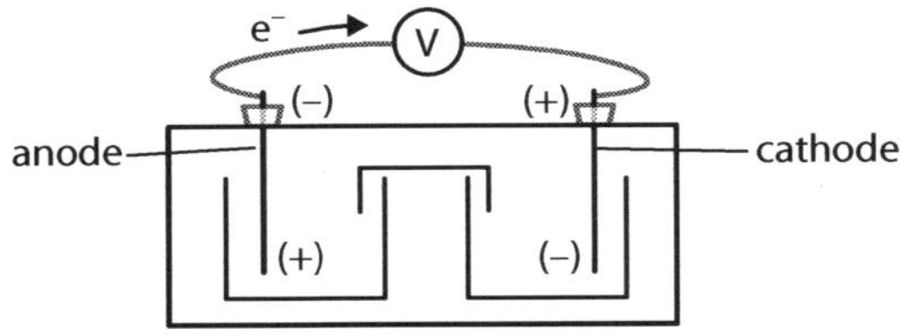

Figure 7.4.3 *Electrons move through the wire connecting the electrodes while ions move through the salt bridge.*

Non-metal | Non-metal Ion Half-Cells

Another type of half-cell consists of a non-metal electrode immersed in a solution containing ions of the same non-metal. What does a non-metal electrode such as a chlorine electrode look like? Obviously, a gas or a liquid electrode can't simply be a piece of the substance. They are essentially an inverted test tube filled with the liquid or gas (Figure 7.4.4). A platinum (inert metal) wire runs through the liquid or gas and connects at the bottom, open end of the tube to a piece of porous platinum foil where most of the electron transfer occurs. The gas is fed into the tube at 1 atm pressure through a side arm at the closed, top end of the tube. There are several variations on this design. Sometimes, an inert electrode is simply suspended above the open end of a tube that feeds gas bubbles into the solution. Many of the bubbles make contact with and even adhere to the electrode as they rise up through the solution.

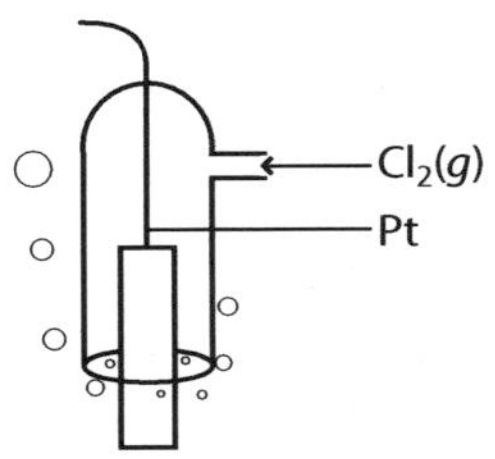

Figure 7.4.4 *A chlorine electrode*

A chlorine electrode immersed in a solution containing chloride ions is an example of a non-metal | non-metal ion half-cell. Either the non-metal electrode receives electrons from the other half-cell or the non-metal ions give electrons to the other half-cell when the electrochemical cell is operating. Hydrogen cells are an exception. Either the hydrogen electrode gives electrons to the other half-cell or the hydrogen ions receive electrons from the other half-cell. If a hydrogen | hydrogen ion half-cell were connected to a chlorine | chloride ion half-cell then electrons would flow from the hydrogen half-cell to the chlorine half-cell. The hydrogen gas would be oxidized and the chlorine gas would be reduced.

reduction ½ reaction →

$$\begin{array}{rcl} Cl_2 + 2e^- & \rightarrow & 2\,Cl^- \\ Br_2 + 2e^- & \rightleftharpoons & 2\,Br^- \\ I_2 + 2e^- & \rightleftharpoons & 2\,I^- \\ Cu^{2+} + 2e^- & \rightleftharpoons & Cu \\ 2\,H^+ + 2e^- & \leftarrow & H_2 \end{array}$$

← oxidation ½ reaction

$$\begin{array}{rcl} H_2 & \rightarrow & 2\,H^+ + \cancel{2e^-} \\ Cl_2 + \cancel{2e^-} & \rightarrow & 2\,Cl^- \\ \hline Cl_2 + H_2 & \rightarrow & 2\,H^+ + 2\,Cl^- \end{array}$$

Predicting Standard Cell Potentials (Voltages)

The simple design of the standard electrochemical cell makes it ideal for measuring redox potentials. The redox potential is the tendency of a redox reaction to occur. Standard cell potentials are measured in volts. Voltage can be thought of as the difference in electrical pressure that causes the flow of electrons in much the same way that a difference in air pressure causes a flow of air (wind). Cell voltages measure the net tendency for electron transfer between one redox tandem (oxidizing agent–reducing agent) and another. Cell voltages do not apply outside the context of standard

 © Edvantage Interactive 2019

Quick Check

For the cell shown on the right:

1. Which electrode is the anode? ____________

2. In which direction do the electrons flow through the wire?

   ____

3. In which direction do the cations flow through the salt bridge?

   ____

4. Which electrode gains in mass? ______________

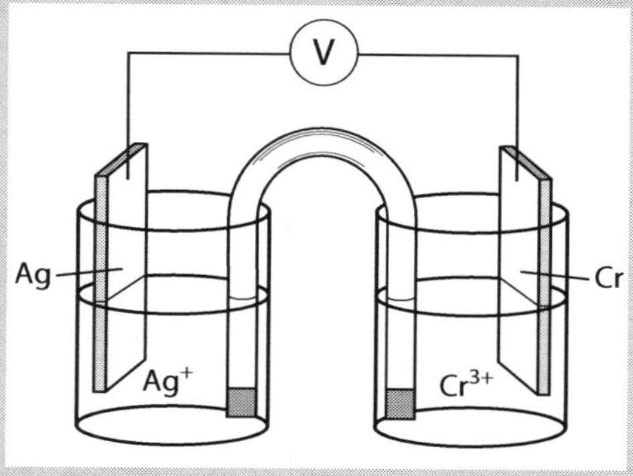

electrochemical cells. However, they can still be useful for predicting the spontaneity of a reaction between these species in other circumstances.

By now you are discovering that answering redox questions is all about knowing how to use the SRP table (Table A7). The SRP table not only allows us to predict the direction of electron flow in standard cells, it also allows us to predict the tendency of electron flow. All E° values in this table are reported relative to the $H_2(g)$ half-cell. The hydrogen electrode is thus referred to as a *reference* electrode. The result of any other "competition" can be determined by a third-party comparison against what might be considered their common enemy, H^+. This is like predicting the result of a football game by comparing how the two teams did against a common opponent. If Team A defeats Team B by 14 points and Team B defeats Team C by 10 points then we would predict that Team A would defeat Team C by 24 points. Third party comparisons are not always valid in sports, but they do work for predicting the voltages of half-cell combinations in electrochemical cells.

The half-reactions highlighted below show that, under standard conditions, a Ni | Ni^{2+} half-cell would lose to a hydrogen half-cell by 0.26 V. However an I_2 | I^- half-cell would win against a hydrogen half-cell by 0.54 V. It's predictable that, when a Ni | Ni^{2+} half-cell and a I_2 | I^- half-cell are connected, the result would be a 0.80 V victory for the I_2 | I^- half-cell.

reduction ½ reaction	$I_2 + 2e^-$	$\rightarrow$	$2\,I^-$	+0.54 V
	$Cu^+ + e^-$	$\rightleftharpoons$	Cu	+0.52 V
	$H_2SO_3 + 4\,H^+ + 2e^-$	$\rightleftharpoons$	$S + 3\,H_2O$	+0.45 V
	$Cu^{2+} + 2e^-$	$\rightleftharpoons$	Cu	+0.34 V
	$SO_4^{\,2-} + 4\,H^+ + 2e^-$	$\rightleftharpoons$	$H_2SO_3 + H_2O$	+0.17 V
	$Cu^{2+} + e^-$	$\rightleftharpoons$	Cu^+	+0.15 V
	$Sn^{4+} + 2e^-$	$\rightleftharpoons$	Sn^{2+}	+0.15 V
	$S + 2\,H^+ + 2e^-$	$\rightleftharpoons$	H_2S	+0.14 V
	$2\,H^+ + 2e^-$	$\rightleftharpoons$	H_2	0.00 V
	$Pb^{2+} + 2e^-$	$\rightleftharpoons$	Pb	−0.13 V
	$Sn^{2+} + 2e^-$	$\rightleftharpoons$	Sn	−0.14 V
oxidation ½ reaction	$Ni^{2+} + 2e^-$	$\leftarrow$	Ni	−0.26 V

Voltage is also called *potential difference* because it measures the difference in electrical potential energy between two points in a circuit. The difference between the reduction potentials of Ni^{2+} and I_2 is 0.54 V – (–0.26 V) = 0.80 V. Perhaps the easiest way to determine standard cell voltages is to write each half-reaction the way it occurs and then add the half-cell potentials together. When a half-reaction is written in the opposite direction as that shown in the SRP table then its half-cell potential is also changed from (+) to (–) or vice versa.

Sometimes it is necessary to multiply one or both of the half-reactions by an integer in order to balance the transfer of electrons. A half-cell potential (E°) doesn't change when its half-reaction is multiplied by an integer. One volt is one joule of energy per coulomb of charge. One coulomb of charge represents 6.2×10^{18} electrons. Tripling the half-reaction does not affect the half-cell potential since the energy *per electron* (voltage) is unchanged. Changing the size of metal electrodes does not affect the cell voltage.

Sample Problem 7.4.1 — Determining Standard Cell Potentials (Voltages)

Determine the voltage of a standard cell consisting of a Ni | Ni^{2+} half-cell and an I_2 | I^- half-cell.

What to Think About	How to Do It
1. Write each half-reaction and its standard potential. The oxidation potential of Ni is +0.26 V because it is the reverse of the reduction potential of Ni^{2+} provided in the SRP table (Table A7).	$Ni \rightarrow Ni^{2+} + 2e^-$ E° = 0.26 V $I_2 + 2e^- \rightarrow 2\,I^-$ E° = 0.54 V
2. Add the reduction potential to the oxidation potential.	$I_2 + Ni \rightarrow Ni^{2+} + 2\,I^-$ E° = 0.80 V

A positive E° indicates that the reaction is spontaneous. A negative E° indicates that the reverse reaction is spontaneous. In the context of an electrochemical cell, a negative E° means that you wrote the half-reactions backwards. The beauty of the SRP table is that it displays the strength of oxidizing and reducing agents, while also allowing you to quickly calculate the standard cell voltage of hundreds of half-cell combinations. A two-dimensional table could also be used to directly display the standard cell voltages of a limited number of half-cell combinations. Table 7.4.1 shows an example.

Table 7.4.1 *Example of Table to Display Half-cell Combinations*

		Reduction Half-cell		
		$2\,H^+ + 2e^- \rightarrow H_2$	$Ni^{2+} + 2e^- \rightarrow Ni$	$I_2 + 2e^- \rightarrow 2\,I^-$
Oxidation Half-cell	$H_2 \rightarrow 2\,H^+ + 2e^-$		–0.26 V	0.54 V
	$Ni \rightarrow Ni^{2+} + 2e^-$	0.26 V		0.80 V
	$2\,I^- \rightarrow I_2 + 2e^-$	–0.54 V	–0.80 V	

Practice Problems 7.4.1 — Determining Standard Cell Potentials (Voltages)

Determine the standard cell potential of each of the following combinations of half-cells. Show the oxidation and reduction half-reactions as well as the overall redox reaction occurring in each cell.

1. $Ni \mid Ni^{2+}$ and $Br_2 \mid Br^-$

2. $Al(s) \mid Al^{3+}(aq) \mid\mid Cu^{2+}(aq) \mid Cu(s)$

3. $Pt(s) \mid I^-(aq) \mid I^2(s) \mid\mid Au^{3+}(aq) \mid Au(s)$

Non-Standard Conditions

A cell's conditions usually change as it operates. The voltages predicted using the SRP table are cell voltages under standard conditions (1 M, 25°C). As a cell operates, its voltage drops. Recall the $Mg \mid Mg^{2+} \mid\mid Cu^{2+} \mid Cu$ cell from the original examples in this section.

$$Cu^{2+} + Mg \rightarrow Mg^{2+} + Cu$$

For the purposes of this discussion let's consider Cu^{2+} to be having an electron tug-of-war with Mg^{2+} in this cell. Both Cu^{2+} and Mg^{2+} are, after all, oxidizing agents. The Cu^{2+} pulls Mg's valence electrons toward the $Cu \mid Cu^{2+}$ half-cell while Mg^{2+} pulls Cu's valence electrons toward the $Mg \mid Mg^{2+}$ half-cell. These are opposing forces even though they are pulling on different electrons because electrons cannot simultaneously flow in two directions through a wire. Just as water can, at any given time, flow only in one direction through a hose, electrons can at any given time flow only in one direction through a wire. If you connected two taps with a hose, the water would flow from the tap with the greatest pressure to that with the least pressure. The tap with the greatest pressure would win the "push-of-war," but the water pressure in the opposite direction would act as a resistance to that flow. Similarly, electrons flow from the $Mg \mid Mg^{2+}$ half-cell to the $Cu \mid Cu^{2+}$ half-cell and the electrical pressure in the opposite direction acts as a resistance. In other words, Cu^{2+} wins the electron tug-of-war against Mg^{2+}.

Now let's consider how the cell's conditions change as it operates and how those changes affect the cell's voltage. As the cell operates, Mg transfers electrons to Cu^{2+}, thereby decreasing the $[Cu^{2+}]$ and increasing the $[Mg^{2+}]$. The increased $[Mg^{2+}]$ increases its pulling force while the decreasing $[Cu^{2+}]$ decreases its pulling force. Eventually the pulling forces of the Mg^{2+} and Cu^{2+} become equal and the cell now has 0 V so it is "dead." As an analogy, consider a tug-of-war between 20 grade 12s and 20 grade 8s. Naturally the grade 12s would win. But what would happen if every time the rope moved one foot, the grade 12s lost one of their pullers and the grade 8s gained another puller? Eventually the grade 8s' pulling force and the grade 12s' pulling force would be equal and the contest would come to a draw.

Cell Equilibrium

A "dead" cell is often said to be at equilibrium. The equilibrium referred to in the context of an electrochemical cell is a static equilibrium of forces. It is **not** a dynamic chemical equilibrium because electrons cannot travel simultaneously in two directions through the same wire. This same redox reaction could develop a chemical equilibrium if the reactants were both present in the same solution. Just as protons (H^+) are passed back and forth in Brønsted-Lowry acid-base equilibria, electrons are passed back and forth in redox equilibria. A reaction's E° indicates essentially the same thing as its K_{eq}. A formula called the *Nernst equation* converts E°s into K_{eqs}. Even small cell voltages generally correspond to large equilibrium constants. The reactions go almost to completion before establishing equilibrium. Small negative cell voltages therefore correspond to small equilibrium constants for reactions that establish equilibrium with little product. Chemists use cell voltages and the Nernst equation to determine equilibrium constants that would be virtually impossible to determine by direct chemical analysis.

We have seen that changes to a cell's conditions will affect its voltage. If the reactant concentrations are greater than 1 M or the product concentrations are less than 1 M then the cell's potential will be greater than the standard cell potential because the forward reaction has to proceed further to achieve the equilibrium of forces. Conversely if the reactant concentrations are less than 1 M or the product concentrations are greater than 1 M, the cell's potential will be less than the standard cell potential. This is because the forward reaction has less reactant to consume before achieving the equilibrium of forces. The concentration of an ion may be lowered in a half-cell by precipitating some ions out of solution. For example, if some sodium sulfide were added to a Cu | Cu^{2+} half-cell then some Cu^{2+} ions would precipitate out with S^{2-} ions. This would cause the voltage in our Cu | Cu^{2+} || Mg | Mg^{2+} cell to drop.

The Nernst Equation

The Nernst equation is useful for converting E°_{cell} into *K* and vice versa. It can also be used to determine how E°_{cell} will change when non-standard ion concentrations are introduced into an electrochemical cell. Two different equations, both of which describe free energy, may be used to derive the Nernst equation. The first is from thermodynamics:

$$\Delta G = \Delta G^\circ + RT \ln Q \qquad \text{Equation I}$$

The second will be worked with in detail in an upcoming section.

$$\Delta G^\circ = -nFE^\circ \qquad \text{Equation II}$$

The symbol *F* in the second equation is called the Faraday constant. It has a numerical value of 96 500 C/mol e⁻. Substitution of Equation II into Equation I gives this new equation:

$$-nFE = -nFE^\circ + RT \ln Q \qquad \text{Equation III}$$

Division of both sides of Equation III by $-nF$ results in the following equation.

$$\frac{-\cancel{nF}E}{-\cancel{nF}} = \frac{-nFE^\circ + RT \ln Q}{-nF} = \frac{-\cancel{nF}E^\circ}{-\cancel{nF}} + \frac{RT \ln Q}{-nF}$$

Canceling of $-nF$ wherever possible results in an initial version of the Nernst equation:

$$E = E^\circ - \frac{RT}{nF} \ln Q \qquad \text{Equation IV}$$

At 25°C, substitution of known values such as

$R = 8.31$ J/mol·K
$T = 298$ K
$\ln Q = 2.303 \log Q$
$F = 96\,500$ C/mol e⁻

results in: $E = E^\circ - \frac{(8.31\,\text{J}/\cancel{\text{mol}\cdot\text{K}})(298\,\cancel{\text{K}})\,2.303}{n(96\,500\,\text{C}/\cancel{\text{mol}}\,\text{e}^-)} \log Q$

 © Edvantage Interactive 2019

Combining numerical values, and remembering that a joule/coulomb is equivalent to a volt, gives the final form of the Nernst equation. Note that *n* is the number of moles of electrons transferred.

$$E = E^\circ - \frac{0.0592}{n} \log Q$$

This equation allows us to calculate the cell voltage for an electrochemical cell whose half-cells contain any concentration of reactants and products. When a cell is at equilibrium, E = 0 and $Q = K$. This means that $0 = E^\circ - \frac{0.0592}{n} \log K$ or

$$E^\circ = \frac{0.0592}{n} \log K$$

The Danielli Cell

The historically important Danielli cell is often anglicized as the "Daniels cell." It involves copper and zinc electrodes in solutions of copper(II) and zinc ions (Figure 7.4.5).

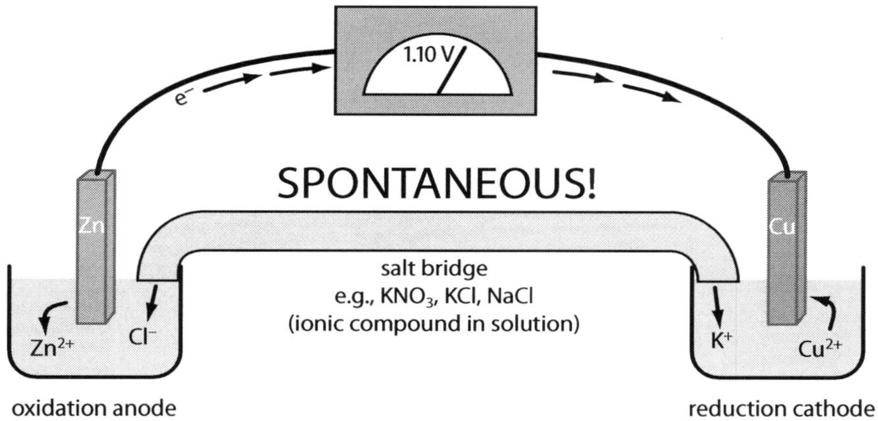

Figure 7.4.5 *The Danielli cell is made of zinc and copper half-cells.*

Zinc is the stronger reducing agent so it is oxidized and is the anode. Copper(II) ions are reduced at the cathode. The overall reaction is:

$$Zn(s) + Cu^{2+}(aq) \rightarrow Zn^{2+}(aq) + Cu(s)$$

Assuming the concentrations of both half-cells are standard, that is 1.0 *M*, the voltage for the cell is determined as explained earlier in this section.

Oxidation (at the anode):	$Zn(s) \rightarrow Zn^{2+}(aq) + 2e^-$	$E^\circ_{ox} = 0.76$ V
Reduction (at the cathode):	$Cu^{2+}(aq) + 2e^- \rightarrow Cu(s)$	$E^\circ_{red} = 0.34$ V
	$Zn(s) + Cu^{2+}(aq) \rightarrow Zn^{2+}(aq) + Cu(s)$	$E^\circ_{cell} = 1.10$ V

The E°_{cell} value and E_{cell} are the same as long as the concentrations of the ions in both half-cells are the same, since *Q* will equal 1 and the log of 1 equals zero:

$$E = E^\circ - \frac{0.0592}{n} \log Q = 1.10\,V - \frac{0.0592}{2} \log \frac{[Zn^{2+}]}{[Cu^{2+}]} = 1.10\,V - \frac{0.0592}{2} \log \frac{\cancel{1.0\,M}}{\cancel{1.0\,M}}$$

$$\text{Now, } 1.10\text{ V} - \frac{0.0592}{2}\log 1.0 = 1.10\text{ V} - \frac{0.0592}{2} \times 0 = 1.10\text{ V}$$

If, on the other hand, the concentration of one of the ions is made non-standard, the ratio of $[Zn^{2+}]/[Cu^{2+}]$ becomes greater or less than one. This leads to a $\log([Zn^{2+}]/[Cu^{2+}])$ with a positive or negative value. The consequence is an E_{cell} value larger or smaller than E°_{cell}.

Sample Problem 7.4.2(a) — The Nernst Equation

A Danielli cell is assembled with a standard half-cell for zinc, and one-tenth of the standard concentration of copper(II) in the copper half-cell. Determine the cell voltage.

What to Think About	How to Do It
1. Determine the balanced chemical equation.	$Zn(s) + Cu^{2+}(aq) \rightarrow Zn^{2+}(aq) + Cu(s)$
2. Determine the voltage for this reaction.	$E^\circ_{cell} = 0.76 + 0.34 = 1.10\text{ V}$
3. Use the Nernst equation.	$E = E^\circ - \frac{0.0592}{n}\log Q$, where $n = 2$ and $Q = \frac{[Zn^{2+}]}{[Cu^{2+}]} = \frac{(1.0\text{ M})}{(0.10\text{ M})}$
4. Proper substitution into the Nernst equation will lead to the correct cell voltage.	$E = 1.10\text{ V} - \frac{0.0592}{2}\log\frac{(1.0\text{ M})}{(0.10\text{ M})}$ $= 1.10\text{ V} - \frac{0.0592}{2}\log(10)$ $= 1.10\text{ V} - \frac{0.0592}{2} \times 1 = 1.07\text{ V}$
5. Always think about whether the answer makes sense. Although electrochemical cells are not at equilibrium, they are certainly driving toward equilibrium, which they will reach when the cell stops functioning and produces a voltage of zero. In this sense, the application of Le Chatêlier's principle may assist the prediction of how the voltage of a cell may be affected by changing molarities in half-cells.	Decreasing the concentration of a reactant ion (Cu^{2+}) would be expected to decrease the frequency of reactant particle collisions and hence to decrease the rate of the forward reaction. The result would be a left shift and a decrease in electron transfer. Hence the decrease in voltage makes sense.

Sample Problem 7.4.2(b) — The Nernst Equation

What is the equilibrium constant for the Danielli cell under standard conditions?

$Zn(s) + Cu^{2+}(aq) \rightarrow Zn^{2+}(aq) + Cu(s)$

What to Think About	How to Do It
1. Use the standard-conditions form of the Nernst equation.	$E = E^\circ - \frac{0.0592}{n}\log Q$
2. When *Q* becomes *K*, E becomes 0. This represents equilibrium conditions.	$0 = 1.10\text{ V} - \frac{0.0592}{2}\log K$

Continued

 © Edvantage Interactive 2019

Sample Problem 7.4.2(b) *(Continued)*

3. Solve for log *K*.

$1.10\text{ V} = \frac{0.0592}{2} \log K$

Thus $\log K = \frac{1.10\text{ J/C}}{\frac{0.0592}{2}} = 37.2$

4. Solve for *K*.

$K = 10^{37.2} = 1.45 \times 10^{37} = 1 \times 10^{37}$

(Recall the number of decimal places in the exponent determines the number of significant figures for logarithmic values.)

5. Does the answer make sense?

This is a large value for K. However, log K is positive and reasonably large, so considering that log K is really an exponent on the base 10, it makes sense that K should be large (in this case) and always positive.
In this case, the Danielli cell greatly favors the products.

Practice Problems 7.4.2 — The Nernst Equation

1. A standard-conditions iron-nickel cell is assembled to determine the voltage and equilibrium constant for the system. Determine E° and *K* for the cell. How does the voltage change when the concentration of Fe^{2+} ions is decreased to 0.05 M? Predict whether it will increase or decrease, and then calculate the new value.

2. A standard Zn^{2+}/Ni^{2+} cell is adjusted by the addition of nickel(II) ions to increase their concentration to 5.0 mol/L from 1.0 mol/L. Calculate the voltage for this cell.

3. Given a voltage of 0.45 V for an Fe^{2+}/Cu^{2+} cell, if the concentration of the iron(II) half-cell is standard, what is the reaction quotient for the cell? What is the concentration of the copper(II) half-cell?

Common Cells and Batteries

With the proliferation of handheld electronic devices, worldwide battery sales now top $70 billion annually. You obviously cannot put a standard electrochemical cell into a portable electronic device. The cells used in electronic devices are called *dry* cells because their electrolytes are in gels or pastes rather than ordinary aqueous solutions that would be more likely to leak. Most commercial cells have only one electrolyte and thus need no barrier at all between the locations of the two half-reactions.

Alkaline Dry Cell

A **battery** is a group or battery of cells. The common household 1.5 V battery that we use to power portable electronics is actually an individual alkaline dry cell. Two or more of them connected end to end are a battery. The modern alkaline cell was invented by Canadian engineer Lewis Urry in the 1950s. .

An alkaline cell's anode consists of zinc powder packed around a brass pin in the middle of the cell (Figure 7.4.6). Its cathode is a paste of solid manganese dioxide (MnO_2) and powdered carbon. The two electrodes are separated by a fibrous fabric. The alkaline cell is so named because its electrolyte is a moist paste of the base KOH.

The alkaline dry cell lasts longer and generates a steadier voltage than its predecessor, the Leclanché cell, which instead had a moist paste of the acidic salt, ammonium chloride (NH_4Cl) and zinc chloride ($ZnCl_2$). The alkaline cell's half-reactions are:

Anode	$Zn + 2\,OH^- \rightarrow ZnO(s) + H_2O + 2e^-$
Cathode	$2\,MnO_2 + H_2O + 2e^- \rightarrow Mn_2O_3(s) + 2\,OH^-$

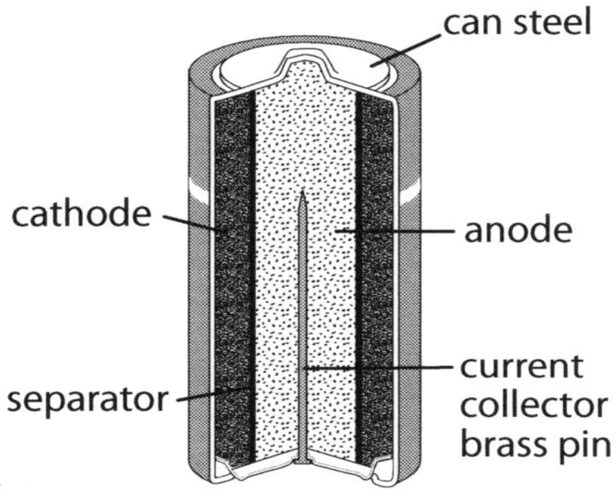

Figure 7.4.6 *An alkaline dry cell*

Other related cells include the button batteries used in calculators and watches, nickel-cadmium (Ni-Cad) batteries, and lithium ion batteries. Lithium ion batteries are a type of rechargeable battery used in everything from cellphones to electric vehicles.

Lead-Acid Storage Battery

A 12 V lead storage battery consists of six cells connected in series (Figure 7.4.7). This type of battery is most commonly used in cars. The anodes are lead alloy grids packed with spongy lead. The cathodes are lead alloy grids packed with lead oxide (PbO_2). The lead storage battery consists of true "wet" cells because its electrolyte is an aqueous solution of sulfuric acid. The cell doesn't have separate anode and cathode compartments because the oxidizing and reducing agents are both solids (PbO_2 and Pb) and both are immersed in the same electrolyte ($H_2SO_4(aq)$).

Anode	$Pb(s) + HSO_4^- \rightarrow PbSO_4(s) + H^+ + 2e^-$
Cathode	$PbO_2(s) + 3\,H^+ + HSO_4^- + 2e^- \rightarrow PbSO_4(s) + 2\,H_2O$

The product $PbSO_4(s)$ adheres to the electrodes' surfaces. When a car's engine is running, an alternator continuously recharges the battery. The alternator supplies an electric current to the battery, operating it "backwards" as an electrolytic cell to restore the original reactants.

 © Edvantage Interactive 2019

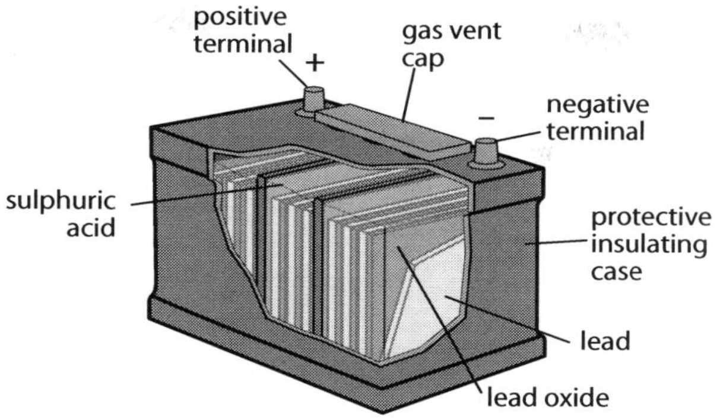

Figure 7.4.7 *A lead-acid storage battery*

For a cell to be classified as rechargeable, the redox reaction that occurs during the cell's operation must be "efficiently reversed" when the opposite electric potential is applied across the cell so that hundreds of recharging cycles are possible. Standard alkaline batteries are non-rechargeable cells because, in addition to the required reverse reactions, other reactions occur when the opposite electric potential is applied across the cell. Since not all of the original reactants are reformed during the reverse operation, the number of recharging cycles is very limited, with the cell lasting for a shorter period of time with each successive recharge. More importantly, recharging a standard alkaline battery is not safe because one of the side-products formed during the reverse operation is hydrogen gas, which can ignite and cause the battery to explode. (Non-rechargeable cells are also called primary cells.)

Fuel Cells

A **fuel cell** is a cell that has its reactants continuously resupplied from an external source as they are consumed. Fuel cells are used to power electric cars and buses as well as provide electricity for vehicles used in space travel. Fuel cells are also being used to provide backup, supplemental, and even mainstream power for industrial complexes and isolated communities. The most common fuel cell is the hydrogen-oxygen fuel cell (Figure 7.4.8). Hydrogen (the fuel) is oxidized at the anode while oxygen (the oxidizer) is reduced at the cathode. Both electrodes are composed of a porous carbon material.

Ballard Power Systems of Burnaby, Canada, is a world leader in fuel cell technology. In Ballard's current cell, the electrodes are bonded to a "cellophane-like" proton exchange membrane (PEM) that is coated with a very thin layer of platinum. The platinum catalyzes the half-reaction at the anode. The proton exchange membrane acts as an electrolyte medium conducting the hydrogen ions (protons) from the anode to the cathode.

Anode $2\,H_2(g) \rightarrow 4\,H^+ + 4e^-$

Cathode $O_2(g) + 4\,H^+ + 4e^- \rightarrow 2\,H_2O$

The overall reaction is: $2\,H_2 + O_2 \rightarrow 2\,H_2O$. The water produced at the cathode is vented out the bottom half of the cell as steam. The same reaction occurs when hydrogen burns or explodes in oxygen. The heat released from burning hydrogen could be converted into electricity in a variety of ways but the vast majority of that energy would be lost during the conversion from heat to electrical energy. By contrast, fuel cells' conversions of chemical energy directly into electrical energy are 40% to 60% efficient.

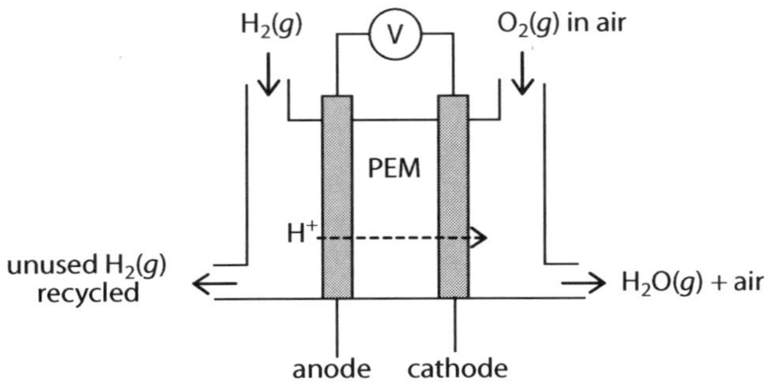

Figure 7.4.8 *A hydrogen fuel cell*

Quick Check

1. Complete the following table:

Type	Anode Material	Cathode Material	Electrolyte Medium	Use
Alkaline cell				
Lead-acid storage battery				
Fuel cell				

Corrosion

Corrosion is a term people use for *unwanted oxidation*, much like we use the term *weed* for an unwanted plant. **Rusting**, the corrosion of iron, is the most familiar and commercially important type of corrosion. Repairing rust damage to buildings, bridges, ships, cars, etc. costs billions of dollars each year.

Let's look at a simplified description of the rusting process. Droplets of water act as an electrolyte to create tiny voltaic cells on iron surfaces (Figure 7.4.9). Iron is more readily oxidized in some surface regions than others due to factors such as impurities and physical stresses such as being bent. When a water droplet forms over one of these "anode" regions, a pit forms as the iron is oxidized to Fe^{2+}:

Anode $\quad Fe(s) \rightarrow Fe^{2+} + 2e^-$

The lost electrons are passed through the iron itself to oxygen molecules at the edge of the droplet:

Cathode $\quad \frac{1}{2} O_2(g) + 2\,H^+ + 2e^- \rightarrow H_2O$ $\quad$ and/or

$\frac{1}{2} O_2(g) + H_2O + 2e^- \rightarrow 2\,OH^-$

Migrating Fe^{2+} ions are further oxidized to Fe^{3+} as they react with dissolved O_2 near the droplet's edge. The Fe^{3+} then readily reacts with water to form rust (hydrated iron (III) oxide), which, having low solubility, deposits on the iron's surface:

$$2\,Fe^{3+}(aq) + 4\,H_2O(l) \rightarrow \underset{\text{(rust)}}{Fe_2O_3 \cdot H_2O(s)} + 6\,H^+(aq)$$

© Edvantage Interactive 2019

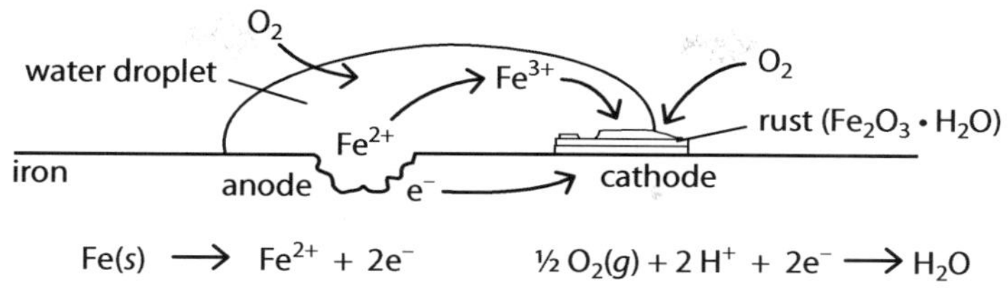

Figure 7.4.9 *Voltaic mechanism for rusting*

Dissolved salts in the water droplet increase its conductivity, thus increasing the corrosion rate. This is why cars generally rust faster in eastern United States where more road salt is used in the winter than on the west coast of the United States.

The tarnishing of silver is another example of corrosion. The black color typical of tarnishing results from silver reacting with sulfur compounds in the air or in materials that it touches.

Oxygen is capable of oxidizing most metals but most other metal oxides such as aluminum oxide, chromium oxide, and zinc oxide form hard, impenetrable coatings that protect their metals from further corrosion. By contrast, rust is porous and flaky and unable to shield the underlying metal from further oxidation.

The Prevention of Corrosion

Iron can be protected from rusting by coating it with paint or grease, by cathodic protection, or by galvanizing it.

One way to prevent a reaction from occurring is to prevent the reactants from coming into contact (collision theory). Rusting is commonly prevented by painting the iron's surface so that it is not directly exposed to water or air. To prevent a redox reaction from occurring, the paint must electrically insulate the iron as well as coat it. If the paint can conduct electrons to the oxidizing agent then its physical coating offers no protection from rusting.

Cathodic protection is another way to prevent rusting. In one form of cathodic protection, a metal is protected from corrosion by attaching a metal to it that is a stronger reducing agent. The attached metal gets oxidized instead of the metal you are protecting. The oxidizing agent draws electrons from the sacrificial metal through the metal being protected. As electrons from the oxidized metal move into the conductor, they displace or push the conductor's valence electrons through to the oxidizing agent. The exposed metal thus remains intact, acting only as a conductor for the electrons. Because the metal that is protected acts as a cathode, this process is called *cathodic protection*.

Cathodic protection is used to protect structures such as underground pipelines, steel reinforcing bars in concrete, deep-sea oil rigs, and ship hulls. Steel is an alloy consisting primarily of iron. Without protection, the steel hulls of ships would be quickly corroded by ocean water because of its salt content. Zinc bars are welded to ships' hulls. The cations in the ocean water preferentially oxidize the zinc through the steel hull and leave the steel alone. The zinc saves the iron from corrosion but the combination of the two metals causes the zinc to be oxidized much more quickly than if it had been exposed to the oxidizing agent alone. This is due to the increased surface area exposed to the oxidizing agent via conduction of its electrons through the iron. In a well-documented example of this phenomenon, the Statue of Liberty's internal support structure of iron ribs was corroded quickly by the moist sea air through the statue's copper skin.

Some iron materials are coated with zinc in a process known as **galvanizing**. Any chemical mixture that can oxidize iron can more easily oxidize zinc so how does the zinc coating offer the iron any protection? If the zinc is oxidized it forms zinc oxide. Zinc oxide forms a hard, impenetrable coating. Should the zinc or the zinc oxide coating be scratched off in some areas, the remaining zinc coating still provides cathodic protection.

Quick Check

1. What is the chemical name for rust? ______________________

2. Identify the reduction half-reaction responsible for rusting.

3. List three factors that influence the corrosion rate of iron.

   (a) ______________________

   (b) ______________________

   (c) ______________________

4. What are two methods that could be used to reduce the corrosion rate of iron?

   (a) ______________________

   (b) ______________________

© Edvantage Interactive 2019

7.4 Activity: Protecting the Environment for Future Generations

Question

How can you educate your family and school community about the potential environmental damage of burying dead batteries in your local landfill?

Background

You should never throw batteries in your household garbage. California residents have had a law prohibiting them from throwing batteries in their garbage since 2006. Batteries may contain toxic heavy metals such as mercury, cadmium, lithium, nickel, lead, and zinc, as well as corrosive electrolytes. When the casings of the batteries buried in our landfills corrode, these materials can leach into the groundwater. It is estimated that over 500 tonnes of dead batteries are being buried in North American landfills every day, yet recycling dead batteries would cost less than $4 per household per year.

Procedure

1. Set up a place in your house where your family members can dispose of their dead batteries (e.g., a plastic pail in the furnace room).
2. Find out the location of a disposal/recycling facility in your community where batteries are accepted.
3. Organize a one-week battery collection blitz in your school. Use your school announcements about the event to teach the staff and students at your school not to throw batteries into the garbage.

Results and Discussion

1. Household location for battery disposal: ______________________________

2. Community location for battery disposal: ______________________________

3. Number of batteries collected in school blitz: ____________

4. Mass of batteries collected in school blitz: ________ kg

5. Was this activity a success? ______

   Why or why not? ____

   ____

   ____

7.4 Review Questions

1. Complete the following table for an electrochemical (metal electrode/metallic ions) cell.

Anode	Cathode
	reduction occurs
mass decreases	
	attracts cations
electrons flow away	

2. The electrochemical cell below consists of a strip of iron in 1.0 M $Fe(NO_3)_2$ and a strip of nickel in 1.0 M $Ni(NO_3)_2$. A salt bridge containing 1.0 M NH_4NO_3 connects these half-cells. A voltmeter connects the two electrodes. (Make sure your answers to the following questions refer specifically to the cell below. Generic responses that are true for any cell, such as "oxidation occurs at the anode," will not be marked correct.)

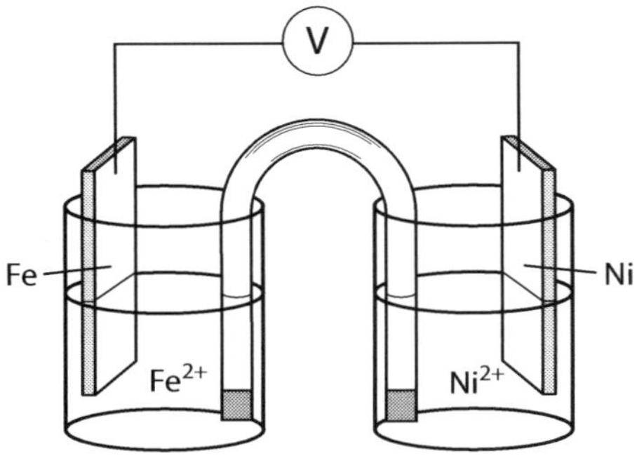

(a) Show the direction of electron flow on the diagram.
(b) In which half-cell does oxidation occur?

(c) Write the half-cell reactions involved.

(d) Label the anode and the cathode.
(e) What is the expected initial voltage?

(f) Describe the flow of the NH_4^+ and NO_3^- ions within the cell.

(g) Describe how the mass of each electrode changes as the cell operates.

 © Edvantage Interactive 2019

3. Elemental bromine does not exist in nature. Bromine is a corrosive, red-brown liquid at room temperature. Draw and label a bromine half-cell.

Use the following diagram for questions 4 and 5.

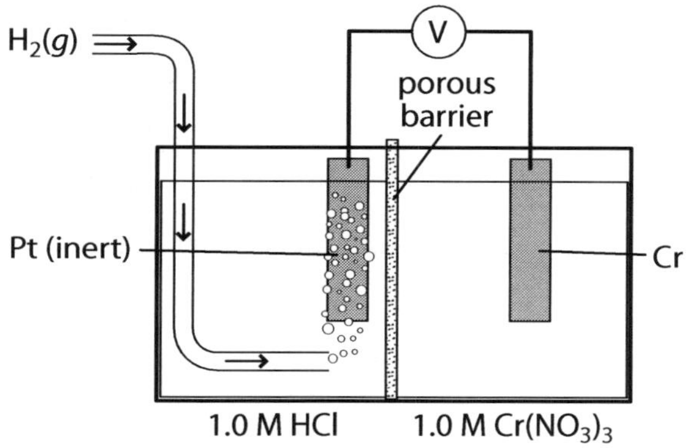

4. (a) Show the direction of electron flow on the above diagram.
   (b) In which half-cell does reduction occur?
   (c) Write the half-cell reactions involved.

5. (a) Label the anode and the cathode.
   (b) What is the expected initial voltage?
   (c) Describe the flow of ions within the cell.
   (d) Describe how the mass of each electrode changes as the cell operates.

6. (a) Draw a Zn | Zn^{2+} || F_2 | F^- electrochemical cell with the following labels:
   - electrodes (Zn, F_2)
   - solutions (1 M $ZnCl_2$, 1 M NaF)
   - anode and the cathode

   (b) Show the direction of electron flow on your diagram.
   (c) Show the direction of anion and cation flow on your diagram.
   (d) Write the cell's two half-reactions and overall redox reaction.
   (e) Calculate the cell's initial voltage.

7. What is the purpose of a salt bridge in an electrochemical cell?

8. Calculate the standard cell potential for the reaction: $Br_2 + 2\ Fe^{2+} \rightarrow 2\ Br^- + 2\ Fe^{3+}$

9. Suppose that the silver-silver ion electrode were used as the reference for E° values, instead of the hydrogen electrode. What would be the standard reduction potentials, E°, for these half-cell reactions?
   (a) $F_2(g) + 2e^- \rightleftharpoons 2\ F^-$

   (b) $Mg^{2+} + 2e^- \rightleftharpoons Mg(s)$

10. The standard cell potential for the following reaction is 2.33 V.

$$Sr + Cr^{2+} \rightarrow Sr^{2+} + Cr$$

Write the reduction half-reaction and determine its standard reduction potential (E°).

11. Given:

$$Pd^{2+} + Cu \rightarrow Pd + Cu^{2+} \qquad E° = 0.49\ V$$
$$2\ Np + 3\ Pd^{2+} \rightarrow 2\ Np^{3+} + 3\ Pd \qquad E° = 2.73\ V$$

   (a) What is the standard reduction potential (E°) of Pd^{2+}?

   (b) What is the standard reduction potential (E°) of Np^{3+}?

12. In the table below, fill in the missing cell voltages by using the voltages provided for other combinations of half-cells.

		Reduction Half-Cell	
		$Cd^{2+} + 2e^- \rightarrow Cd$	$Pt^{2+} + 2e^- \rightarrow Pt$
Oxidation Half-cell	$Pt \rightarrow Pt^{2+} + 2e^-$		0 V
	$Ni \rightarrow Ni^{2+} + 2e^-$	– 0.17 V	+ 1.43 V
	$Ce \rightarrow Ce^{3+} + 3e^-$	+ 1.93 V	

© Edvantage Interactive 2019

13. In an Fe(*s*) | Fe^{2+}(*aq*) || Pb^{2+}(*aq*) | Pb(*s*) standard cell, electrons are transferred from the Fe half-cell to the Pb half-cell.
   (a) What would be the effect on the voltage if $Pb(NO_3)_2$ were added to the lead half-cell?

   (b) What is the voltmeter reading when the cell reaches "equilibrium"?

   (c) What would be the effect on the voltage if sulfide ions (S^{2-}) were added to the Fe^{2+} ion compartment?

   (d) What would be the effect on the voltage if the size of the Fe electrode were doubled?

14. Sony demonstrated a paper cell at the Eco-Products 2011 Exhibition in Tokyo. Sony's bio-cell uses cellulase enzymes to hydrolyze paper into glucose, which is then oxidized. What features of this cell make it eco-friendly when compared to current commercial cells?

15. Describe how cathodic protection could be used to protect a steel stairway exposed to an ocean spray. Explain how this works.

16. Some steel nails are galvanized. Zinc is easier to oxidize than iron so how can coating a steel nail with zinc prevent it from corroding?

17. What adaptation to collision theory is necessary for redox reactions occurring in electrochemical cells?

18. Explain the graphic relationship shown here for the Danielli cell:

$Zn(s) + Cu^{2+}(aq) \rightarrow Zn^{2+}(aq) + Cu(s) \quad E^\circ_{cell} = 1.10\ V$

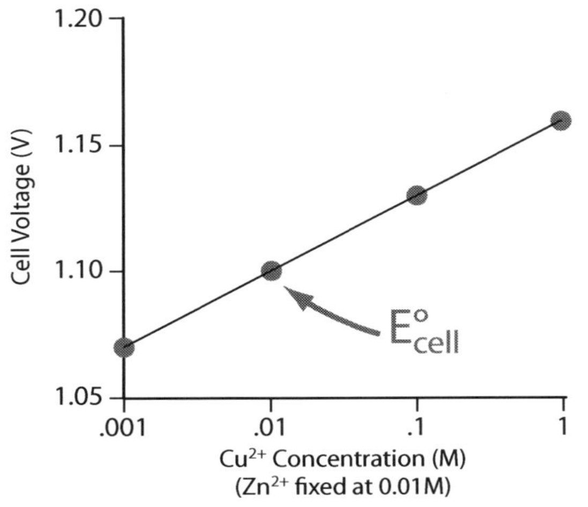

19. Use Table A7 Standard Reduction Potential of Half-Cells in the appendix to determine E° and *K* for the following reaction performed under standard conditions:

$I_2(s) + 5\ Cu^{2+}(aq) + 6\ H_2O(l) \rightarrow 2\ IO_3^-(aq) + 5\ Cu(s) + 12\ H^+(aq)$

20. (a) Calculate the voltage of the cell described by the following reaction. Then determine *K*. Assume standard temperature.

$2\ Al(s) + 3\ I_2(s) \rightarrow 2\ Al^{3+}(aq)\ (0.0040\ M) + 6\ I^-(aq)\ (0.010\ M)$

(b) How do these values compare to those for the cell operating under standard conditions? Explain.

21. Consider a cell in which the following reaction occurs at 25°C:

$Zn(s) + 2\ H^+(aq) \rightarrow Zn^{2+}(aq) + H_2(g)$

 © Edvantage Interactive 2019

(a) Calculate E°_{cell}.

(b) If the $[Zn^{2+}]$ is 0.10 M and $[H_2]$ is 1.0 M and the measured cell voltage is 0.542 V, what is the hydrogen ion concentration?

(c) What is the pH?

22. Examine the electrochemical cell shown here.

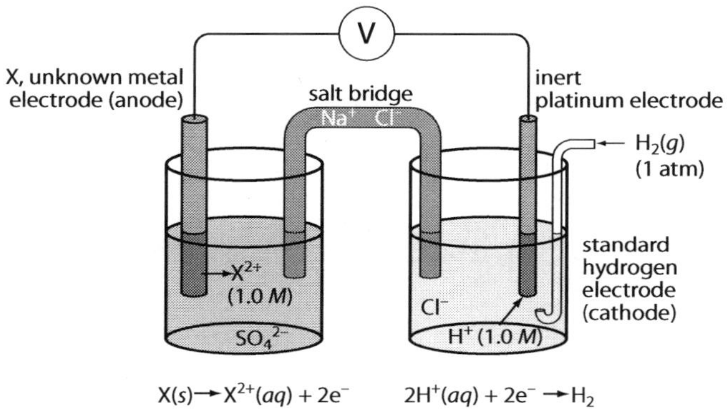

Under standard conditions, the equilibrium constant *K* for the cell's reaction is 6.1×10^8.

(a) What is E°_{cell}?

(b) What is the oxidation potential for the unknown metal?

(c) Identify the unknown metal.

7.5 The Electrolytic Cell

Warm Up

Complete the following table showing pairs of devices that perform opposite energy transformations. Each pair of devices transforms a different form of energy to and from electrical energy.

Device	Energy Conversion	
	From	To
light bulb	electrical energy	light energy
	light energy	electrical energy
speaker	electrical energy	
		electrical energy
heating element	electrical energy	
		electrical energy
motor	electrical energy	
		electrical energy
electrolytic cell	electrical energy	chemical energy
		electrical energy

The Structure and Function of the Electrolytic Cell

Current electricity is a flow of electrical charge. Although electrical charge is always carried by a particle, that particle is not always an electron. In solutions, ions are the particles responsible for carrying the charge. A chemical is an **electrolyte** if its aqueous solution conducts electricity. Whenever electricity is conducted through a molten electrolyte or an electrolyte solution, the process is called **electrolysis** and the apparatus is called an **electrolytic cell**.

For an electric current to exist, there must be a continuous path from the source's anode to its cathode. This continuous path is called a circuit. It would be simple if there were a chemical species in the electrolytic cell solution that picked up the electrons from one electrode and ferried them over to the other electrode but this is not the case. Instead, an oxidizing agent picks up the electrons from one electrode while an entirely different chemical species, a reducing agent, donates electrons at the other electrode. The circuit is complete. It doesn't matter that the electrons being removed from one electrode are not the same ones being released at the other electrode. "If you've seen one electron you've seen them all." It's like a con game where the electrons are being switched and the source never suspects.

© Edvantage Interactive 2019

In an electrolytic cell, oxidation occurs at the anode and reduction occurs at the cathode just like in an electrochemical cell. Figure 7.5.1 shows an electrolytic cell.

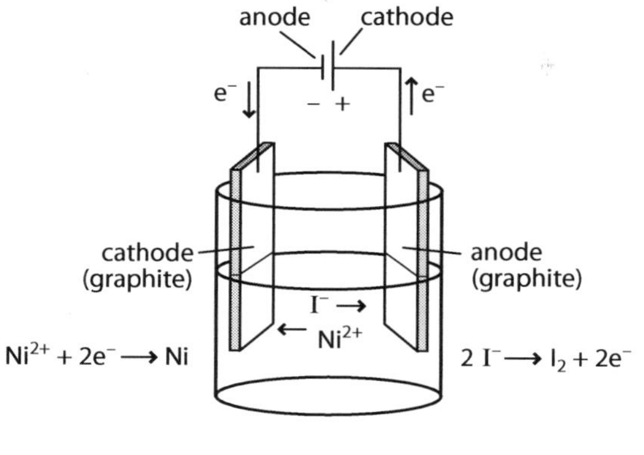

Figure 7.5.1 *An electrolytic cell*

The schematic symbol at the top of Figure 7.5.1 represents the electrochemical cell that serves as the source of direct current (DC) driving the electrolytic cell. Note that the electrochemical cell's anode is connected to the electrolytic cell's cathode. This makes sense if you think it through. Oxidation (electron loss) occurs at the anode; therefore, this is where the voltaic cell emits electrons. In the electrolytic cell, those electrons are accepted by a chemical species, which is thereby reduced. The site of reduction is the cathode. Likewise, the electrochemical cell's cathode is connected to the electrolytic cell's anode.

An electrolytic cell may superficially resemble an electrochemical cell but it performs the reverse energy transformation. In other words, an electrochemical cell generates electricity whereas an electrolytic cell uses electricity.

Electrolytic cells transform electrical energy into chemical energy.

The non-spontaneous reactions of electrolytic cells "read" in the reverse direction in the SRP table (Table A7) as the spontaneous reactions of electrochemical cells. In electrolytic cells, the oxidation half-reaction is above the reduction half-reaction. Try the following trick to remember which direction electrons are passed in the SRP table. Electrons are very "light" so they spontaneously float upward in the table but they must be pushed downward.

oxidation ½ reaction ⟵

$I_2 + 2e^-$	$\leftarrow$	$2\,I^-$	+0.54 V
$H_2SO_3 + 4\,H^+ + 2e^-$	$\rightleftharpoons$	$S + 3\,H_2O$	+0.45 V
$Cu^{2+} + 2e^-$	$\rightleftharpoons$	Cu	+0.34 V
$SO_4^{2-} + 4\,H^+ + 2e^-$	$\rightleftharpoons$	$H_2SO_3 + H_2O$	+0.17 V
$2\,H^+ + 2e^-$	$\rightleftharpoons$	H_2	0.00 V
$Sn^{2+} + 2e^-$	$\rightleftharpoons$	Sn	−0.14 V
$Ni^{2+} + 2e^-$	$\rightarrow$	Ni	−0.26 V

⟶ reduction ½ reaction

$$2\,I^- \rightarrow I_2 + 2e^-$$
$$Ni^{2+} + 2e^- \rightarrow Ni$$
$$Ni^{2+} + 2\,I^- \rightarrow I_2 + Ni$$

The net E° for the non-spontaneous reactions that occur in electrolytic cells is negative. The net E° gives us an estimation of how much voltage will be required to drive this electrolytic cell. In other words, the SRP table not only allows you to determine how much voltage an electrochemical cell will generate but also allows you to determine how much voltage an electrolytic cell will require to operate. This value will normally be less than the voltage actually required. The difference between the voltages the SRP table predicts will be necessary to drive electrolytic cells and the voltages actually required to drive those cells is referred to as **overpotential**.

The standard reduction potentials in the SRP table are derived solely from thermodynamic data. They represent the difference between the chemical potential energy of the reactants and the chemical potential energy of the products. However, the voltages required to drive electrolytic cells are also influenced by kinetic factors such as the reaction's activation energy and the reactants' localized concentrations at the electrodes. A cell's overpotential thus depends on the specific reactions involved and the cell's design.

Sample Problem 7.5.1 — Predicting the Voltage Required to Operate an Electrolytic Cell

Predict the voltage required to operate the electrolytic cell in Figure 7.5.1.

What to Think About	How to Do It
1. Write each half-reaction and its standard potential. The oxidation potential of I^- is – 0.54 V because it is the reverse of the reduction potential of I_2 provided in the SRP table.	$2I^- \rightarrow I_2 + 2e^-$ $E° = -0.54$ V $Ni^{2+} + 2e^- \rightarrow Ni$ $E° = -0.26$ V $Ni^{2+} + 2I^- \rightarrow I_2 + Ni$ $E° = -0.80$ V
2. Add the reduction potential to the oxidation potential.	A voltage of at least 0.80 V would be required to operate this cell.

Practice Problems 7.5.1 — Predicting the Voltage Required to Operate an Electrolytic Cell

Predict the voltage required to operate each of the following electrolytic cells given the pair of half-reactions occurring within each cell.

1. $Ag \rightarrow Ag^+ + e^-$ and $Ni^{2+} + 2e^- \rightarrow Ni$

2. $2F^- \rightarrow F_2 + 2e^-$ and $Cu^{2+} + 2e^- \rightarrow Cu$

3. $Sn \rightarrow Sn^{2+} + 2e^-$ and $Al^{3+} + 3e^- \rightarrow Al$

© Edvantage Interactive 2019

Comparing Electrochemical and Electrolytic Cells

In electrochemical cells, the strongest available reducing agent (lowest on the right in the SRP table) passes electrons *up* to the strongest available oxidizing agent (highest on the left in the SRP table). Thus, the half-reactions that occur in electrochemical cells are the ones that are farthest apart in the SRP table and generate the greatest possible voltage.

In electrolytic cells, the strongest available reducing agent (lowest on the right in the SRP table) passes electrons *down* to the strongest available oxidizing agent (highest on the left in the SRP table). Thus, the half-reactions that occur in electrolytic cells are the ones closest together in the SRP table and require the least voltage to drive them (Figure 7.5.2). Table 7.5.1 summarizes the differences between an electrochemical cell and an electrolytic cell.

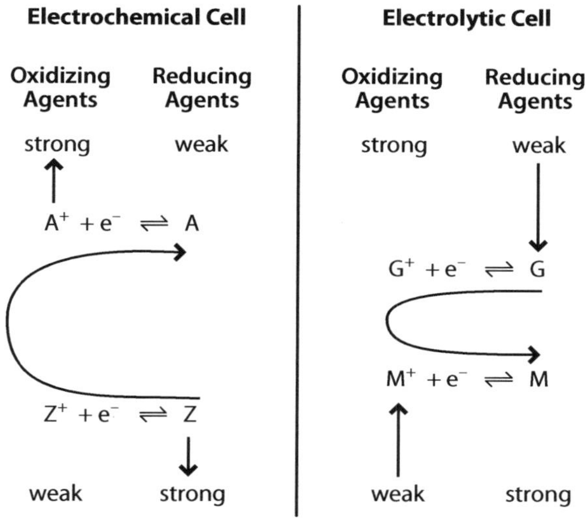

Figure 7.5.2 *Using the SRP table for electrochemical and electrolytic cells*

Table 7.5.1 *Contrasting the Electrochemical Cell and the Electrolytic Cell*

Electrochemical Cell	Electrolytic Cell
• exothermic • "makes" electricity • transforms chemical energy into electrical energy	• endothermic • "takes" electricity • transforms electrical energy into chemical energy
• is a DC voltage source	• requires a DC voltage source
• 2 half-cells	• 1 cell
• spontaneous redox reaction • E° is positive	• non-spontaneous redox reaction • E° is negative
• salt bridge or equivalent	• no salt bridge
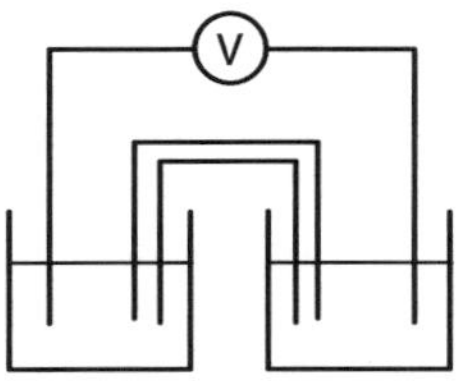	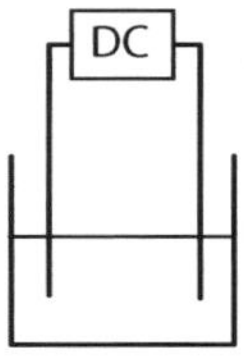
The oxidation half-reaction is below the reduction half-reaction in the SRP table. Think of the electrons floating upward.	The oxidation half-reaction is above the reduction half-reaction in the SRP table. Think of the electrons being pushed downward.
The half-reactions that are farthest apart in the SRP table will occur, generating the greatest possible voltage.	The half-reactions that are closest together in the SRP table will occur, requiring the least possible voltage to drive the cell.

Quick Check

What am I (an electrochemical cell, an electrolytic cell, or both)?

1. I have two half cells. ______________________
2. My oxidation half-reaction is $Ni \rightarrow Ni^{2+} + 2e^-$.
   My reduction half-reaction is $Fe^{2+} + 2e^- \rightarrow Fe$. ______________________
3. Oxidation occurs at my anode. ______________________
4. I transform chemical energy into electricity. ______________________
5. In order to flow, the electrical charge requires a complete path or circuit. ______________________
6. You can use the SRP table to calculate how much voltage it "takes" to operate me. ______________________
7. My E° is + 0.94 V. ______________________

Electrolytic Cell Types

There are three types of electrolytic cells:

- In type 1 cells, inert electrodes are immersed in a molten ionic compound. Only the molten ions (*1 type of thing*) can be oxidized and reduced.
- In type 2 cells, inert electrodes are immersed in an aqueous ionic solution. Only the ions or H_2O (*2 types of things*) can be oxidized and reduced.
- In type 3 cells, non-inert electrodes are immersed in an aqueous ionic solution. The ions, H_2O, or the anode itself (*3 types of things*) can be oxidized and the ions or H_2O can be reduced. Metals never form anions so the cathode itself is never reduced.

Type 1 Cells

Type 1 cells consist of inert electrodes (typically carbon or platinum) immersed in a molten ionic fluid. Electrolysis (electro-lysis) literally means *separation by electricity*. In a type 1 cell, the cations pick up the electrons and are reduced at the cathode, while the anions drop off electrons and are oxidized at the anode. In that way, the cations and anions are separated.

Consider an electrolytic cell having carbon electrodes immersed in molten magnesium chloride. The half-reactions occurring at the electrodes are:

Cathode $Mg^{2+}(l) + 2e^- \rightarrow Mg(l)$

Anode $2\ Cl^-(l) \rightarrow Cl_2(g) + 2e^-$

Magnesium chloride has a higher melting point than magnesium so the magnesium formed at the cathode is also liquid.

Type 2 Cells

Type 2 cells consist of inert electrodes immersed in an aqueous ionic solution. The first question generally asked about an electrolytic cell is, "What half-reactions occur within this cell?" A type 1 cell has only one type of chemical species that can react, the molten ions. In type 2 cells, either the dissolved ions or the water can react. A chemist uses the SRP table to determine whether a dissolved ion or water is reduced and whether a dissolved ion or water is oxidized.

The oxidation and the reduction of water have particularly high overpotentials. Under electrolytic conditions, these half-reactions must be moved relative to the others as shown on the SRP table. This is significant as type 2 and type 3 electrolytic cells conduct currents through aqueous solution. Because of the overpotential effect, water is a weaker reducing agent in electrolytic cells than Br^- and Cl^- ions, and a weaker oxidizing agent in electrolytic cells than Zn^{2+}, Cr^{3+}, and Fe^{2+} ions.

Water doesn't usually react in the spontaneous reactions of electrochemical cells but frequently reacts in the non-spontaneous reactions of electrolytic cells. Water can act as both a weak reducing agent (low oxidation potential) and as a weak oxidizing agent (low reduction potential). Since it is high on the right side of the SRP table, there are not many species above it on the left that it will reduce spontaneously. However, there are many below it that it will reduce non-spontaneously. Likewise, since it is low on the left side of the table, there are not many species below it on the right that it will oxidize spontaneously, but there are many species above it on the right that it will oxidize non-spontaneously.

 © Edvantage Interactive 2019

Sample Problem 7.5.2(a) — Predicting the Half-Reactions That Will Occur in a Type 2 Electrolytic Cell

Identify the half-reactions that occur in the electrolysis of an aqueous solution of manganese(II) bromide.

What to Think About

1. Identify the oxidizing agent(s) and the reducing agent(s).

How to Do It

Mn^{2+} and H_2O are oxidizing agents.
Br^- and H_2O are reducing agents.

What to Think About

2. Use the SRP table to determine which species is the strongest oxidizing agent and which species is the strongest reducing agent.

How to Do It

Oxidizing Agents		Reducing Agents
$ClO_4^- + 8\,H^+ + 8e^-$	⇌	$Cl^- + 4\,H_2O$
$Cl_2 + 2e^-$	⇌	$2\,Cl^-$
$Cr_2O_7^{2-} + 14\,H^+ + 6e^-$	⇌	$2\,Cr^{3+} + 7\,H_2O$
$\frac{1}{2}\,O_2 + 2\,H^+ + 2e^-$	⇌	H_2O
$MnO_2 + 4\,H^+ + 2e^-$	⇌	$Mn^{2+} + 2\,H_2O$
$IO_3^- + 6\,H^+ + 5e^-$	⇌	$\frac{1}{2}\,I_2 + 3\,H_2O$
$Br_2 + 2e^-$	⇌	$2\,Br^-$ (circled)
$AuCl_4 + 3e^-$	⇌	$Au + 4\,Cl^-$
$NO_3^- + 4\,H^+ + 3e^-$	⇌	$NO + 2\,H_2O$
$\frac{1}{2}\,O_2(g) + 2\,H^+ (10^{-7}\,M) + 2e^-$	⇌	H_2O (circled)
$Ag^+ + e^-$	⇌	Ag
$Cu^+ + e^-$	⇌	Cu
$Cu^{2+} + 2e^-$	⇌	Cu
$SO_4^{2-} + 4\,H^+ + 2e^-$	⇌	$H_2SO_3 + H_2O$
$2\,H^+ + 2e^-$	⇌	H_2
$Pb^{2+} + 2e^-$	⇌	Pb
$Ni^{2+} + 2e^-$	⇌	Ni
$2\,H_2O$ (circled) $+ 2e^-$	⇌	$H_2 + 2\,OH^- (10^{-7}\,M)$
$Fe^{2+} + 2e^-$	⇌	$Fe(s)$
$Ag_2S(s) + 2e^-$	⇌	$2\,Ag(s) + S^{2-}$
$Cr^{3+} + 3e^-$	⇌	$Cr(s)$
$Zn^{2+} + 2e^-$	⇌	$Zn(s)$
$Te(s) + 2\,H^+ + 2e^-$	⇌	H_2Te
$2\,H_2O + 2e^-$	⇌	$H_2(g) + 2\,OH^-$
Mn^{2+} (circled) $+ 2e^-$	⇌	$Mn(s)$

Increasing strength (oxidizing agents, upward) — Increasing strength (reducing agents, downward)

Overpotential Effect

What to Think About

3. The lowest available species on the right will pass electron(s) down to the highest available species on the left. Be mindful of the overpotential effect!
4. Write the two half-reactions balancing the transfer of electrons if necessary.

How to Do It

Br^- is a stronger reducing agent than H_2O (overpotential effect).
H_2O is a stronger oxidizing agent than Mn^{2+}.

$$2\,Br^- \rightarrow Br_2 + 2e^-$$
$$2\,H_2O + 2e^- \rightarrow H_2 + 2\,OH^-$$

$$2\,Br^- + 2\,H_2O \rightarrow Br_2 + 2\,OH^- + H_2$$

Type 3 Cells

Type 3 cells consist of non-inert electrodes immersed in an aqueous ionic solution. A type 3 cell adds the possibility that a metal anode itself could be oxidized.

Sample Problem 7.5.2(b) — Predicting the Half-Reactions That Will Occur in a Type 3 Electrolytic Cell

Identify the half-reactions that occur in an electrolytic cell consisting of copper electrodes in a solution of $CrBr_3$.

What to Think About

1. Identify the oxidizing agent(s) and the reducing agent(s).
2. Use the SRP table to determine which species is the strongest oxidizing agent and which species is the strongest reducing agent.
3. The lowest available species on the right will pass electron(s) down to the highest available species on the left.
4. Write the two half-reactions balancing the transfer of electrons if necessary.

How to Do It

Cr^{3+} and H_2O are oxidizing agents.
Br^-, H_2O and Cu are reducing agents.

Oxidizing Agents		Reducing Agents
$ClO_4^- + 8H^+ + 8e^-$	$\rightleftharpoons$	$Cl^- + 4H_2O$
$Cl_2 + 2e^-$	$\rightleftharpoons$	$2Cl^-$
$Cr_2O_7^{2-} + 14H^+ + 6e^-$	$\rightleftharpoons$	$2Cr^{3+} + 7H_2O$
$\frac{1}{2}O_2 + 2H^+ + 2e^-$	$\rightleftharpoons$	H_2O
$MnO_2 + 4H^+ + 2e^-$	$\rightleftharpoons$	$Mn^{2+} + 2H_2O$
$IO_3^- + 6H^+ + 5e^-$	$\rightleftharpoons$	$\frac{1}{2}I_2 + 3H_2O$
$Br_2 + 2e^-$	$\rightleftharpoons$	$2Br^-$
$AuCl_4 + 3e^-$	$\rightleftharpoons$	$Au + 4Cl^-$
$NO_3^- + 4H^+ + 3e^-$	$\rightleftharpoons$	$NO + 2H_2O$
$\frac{1}{2}O_2(g) + 2H^+ (10^{-7}\text{ M}) + 2e^-$	$\rightleftharpoons$	H_2O
$Ag^+ + e^-$	$\rightleftharpoons$	Ag
$Cu^+ + e^-$	$\rightleftharpoons$	Cu
$Cu^{2+} + 2e^-$	$\rightleftharpoons$	Cu
$SO_4^{2-} + 4H^+ + 2e^-$	$\rightleftharpoons$	$H_2SO_3 + H_2O$
$2H^+ + 2e^-$	$\rightleftharpoons$	H_2
$Pb^{2+} + 2e^-$	$\rightleftharpoons$	Pb
$Ni^{2+} + 2e^-$	$\rightleftharpoons$	Ni
$2H_2O + 2e^-$	$\rightleftharpoons$	$H_2 + 2OH^- (10^{-7}\text{ M})$
$Fe^{2+} + 2e^-$	$\rightleftharpoons$	$Fe(s)$
$Ag_2S(s) + 2e^-$	$\rightleftharpoons$	$2Ag(s) + S^{2-}$
$Cr^{3+} + 3e^-$	$\rightleftharpoons$	$Cr(s)$
$Zn^{2+} + 2e^-$	$\rightleftharpoons$	$Zn(s)$
$Te(s) + 2H^+ + 2e^-$	$\rightleftharpoons$	H_2Te
$2H_2O + 2e^-$	$\rightleftharpoons$	$H_2(g) + 2OH^-$
$Mn^{2+} + 2e^-$	$\rightleftharpoons$	$Mn(s)$

Increasing strength (oxidizing agents: upward); Increasing strength (reducing agents: downward); Overpotential Effect

Cu is a stronger reducing agent than Br^- or H_2O.
Cr^{3+} is a stronger oxidizing agent than H_2O (overpotential effect).

$$3Cu \rightarrow 3Cu^{2+} + 6e^-$$
$$2Cr^{3+} + 6e^- \rightarrow 2Cr$$
$$3Cu + 2Cr^{3+} \rightarrow 3Cu^{2+} + 2Cr$$

© Edvantage Interactive 2019

Practice Problems 7.5.2 — Predicting the Half-Reactions That Will Occur in an Electrolytic Cell

1. For each of the following, identify the type of electrolytic cell and the half-reactions occurring within it:
   (a) carbon electrodes in $MgI_2(l)$

   (b) platinum electrodes in $CaSO_4(aq)$

   (c) iron electrodes in $NaCl(aq)$

2. Draw an electrolytic cell having carbon electrodes in $NiBr_2(aq)$. Label the DC source, its terminals, and the anode and cathode of the electrolytic cell. Show each ion in the solution migrating toward the appropriate electrode. Write the half-reaction that occurs at each electrode and predict the voltage required to operate this cell.

Applications: Electrowinning, Electroplating, Electrorefining

Electrolytic cells are used extensively in mining and other metallurgy-related industries. **Electrowinning** is a metallurgical term for the electrolytic recovery of a metal from a solution containing its ions. The metal ions are reduced at the cathode where they deposit as metal. The world's largest zinc and lead smelter is the Cominco plant at Trail, B.C., Canada, Cominco electrowins zinc from zinc sulfate at this smelter.

Electroplating is a form of electrowinning in which a conductive material, usually a metal, is coated with a thin layer of a different metal. Electroplating is usually performed to provide a surface property such as wear resistance, corrosion protection, or lustre to a surface that lacks these properties. The technique is used widely in the manufacture of electronic and optic components and sensors, and to chrome plate bathroom fixtures and automobile parts.

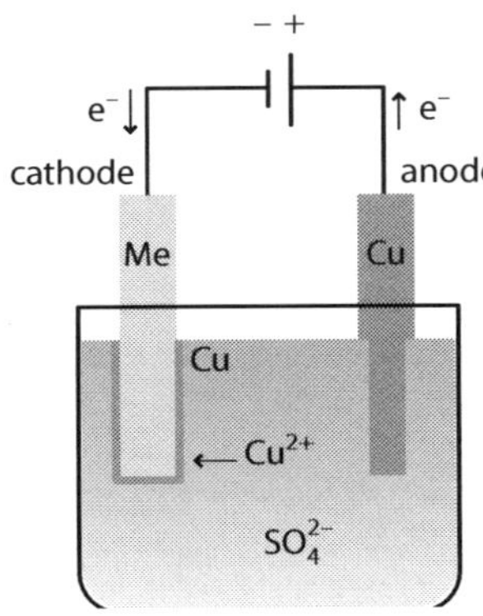

Figure 7.5.3 *Electroplating a metal (Me) with copper*

Consider an electrolytic cell having a metal object as its cathode, a copper anode, and a solution of $CuSO_4$ (Figure 7.5.3). Cu is a stronger reducing agent than SO_4^{2-} or H_2O. Cu^{2+} is a stronger oxidizing agent than H_2O (or SO_4^{2-} under acidic conditions). The half-reactions that occur in this cell are therefore:

$$Cu \rightarrow Cu^{2+} + 2e^-$$
$$Cu^{2+} + 2e^- \rightarrow Cu$$

Note that no net reaction occurs in this electrolytic cell. Copper ions from the solution are reduced at the cathode and plate out as metallic copper. Those copper ions are replaced by the oxidation of the copper anode. In effect, copper is simply being transferred from the anode to the cathode. This process can continue indefinitely as long as the anode is replaced after it has been consumed.

Electrorefining is another application of electrowinning. **Electrorefining** is the electrolytic purification of a metal. The metal of an impure anode is oxidized to ions that then migrate to the pure cathode where they are reduced back to the metal. The impurities remain behind. Sample Problem 7.5.2(b) would be an example of electrorefining if the anode were composed of impure copper and the cathode composed of pure copper. An impurity is anything that makes something impure. In chemistry, impurities are minority substances within a majority substance. Just because a substance is present in a material as an impurity doesn't mean that it isn't valuable. Many rare and valuable metals are recovered from the impurities left behind as *anode mud* during electrolysis. The electrorefining of lead by the Betts process, pioneered by Cominco's Trail Operations in 1902, is still the last step of lead production at the Trail complex. Significant quantities of silver and gold are recovered from the anode mud in this process. The cell voltage used is insufficient to oxidize silver or gold, which are much weaker reducing agents than lead.

Applications: The Héroult-Hall Process for Producing Aluminum

In 1885, aluminum was more valuable than gold. The most common mineral of aluminum is bauxite ($Al_2O_3 \cdot 3\,H_2O$). Aluminum cannot be produced from bauxite by electrowinning because water is a stronger oxidizing agent than Al^{3+}. Producing aluminum from the electrolysis of molten Al_2O_3 (type 1 cell) is very expensive because Al_2O_3's melting point is over 2050°C. In 1886, two 23-year-olds, Paul Héroult of France and Charles Hall of the USA independently discovered that aluminum oxide dissolves in molten cryolite ($Na_3AlF_6(l)$). This aluminum oxide-cryolite mixture melts at about 1000°C, making it much more economical to electrolyze than aluminum oxide alone. The Héroult-Hall process still consumes a tremendous amount of energy, both to melt the aluminum oxide-cryolite mixture and to electrolyze it. The aluminum produced in the electrolytic cell is also molten at 1000°C. Molten aluminum is denser than the aluminum oxide-cryolite mixture so it runs off through openings at the bottom of the cell where it collects.

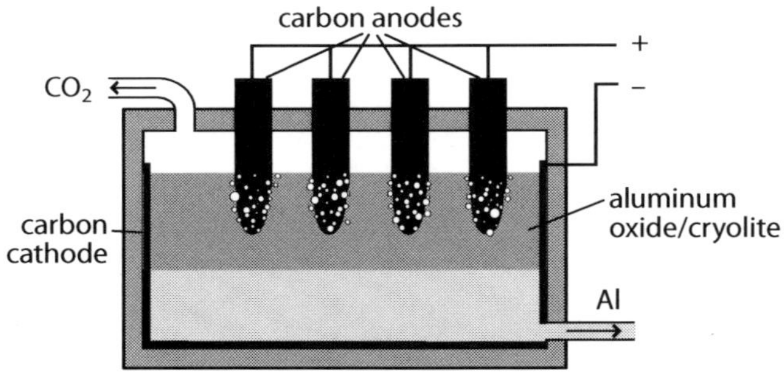

Figure 7.5.4 *The Héroult-Hall process*

© Edvantage Interactive 2019

Applications: The Chloralkali Industry

Sodium hydroxide and chlorine are both produced by the electrolysis of aqueous sodium chloride. The chemical industry based on this process is known as the chloralkali industry. Both sodium hydroxide and chlorine are among the world's top 10 chemicals (by mass) produced annually. Between 12 and 14 million tonnes of each are produced annually in the United States alone, for sales of approximately $4 billion. Sodium hydroxide and chlorine are used in the manufacture of a tremendous variety of everyday products from pharmaceuticals to plastics.

In the electrolysis of an aqueous sodium chloride solution, chloride ions are oxidized:

$$2\,Cl^- \rightarrow Cl_2 + 2e^-$$

and water molecules are reduced:

$$2\,H_2O + 2e^- \rightarrow H_2 + 2\,OH^-$$

The net reaction is:

$$2\,NaCl + 2\,H_2O \rightarrow Cl_2 + H_2 + 2\,NaOH$$

The sodium ions are uninvolved spectators in this process. They are dissolved with chloride ions in the reactants and with hydroxide ions in the products. Note that hydrogen gas is also produced in this process but it is generated more easily by other means.

Applications: Impressed Current Cathodic Protection

A form of cathodic protection is called "galvanic" cathodic protection because the reactions involved are spontaneous (positive E°) like those of a galvanic cell. Another form of cathodic protection called *impressed current* cathodic protection involves non-spontaneous (negative E°) reactions like those of an electrolytic cell. In this form of cathodic protection, the structure to be protected is connected to the negative terminal of a direct current source such as a rectifier or a battery. The positive terminal is usually connected to an inert electrode that must also be immersed in the solution or buried in the material containing the oxidizing agent(s). In this arrangement, the protected structure becomes the cathode in an electrolytic cell. Impressed current systems are generally less expensive and more effective than galvanic systems (particularly when used in combination with protective coatings). Despite the advantages of impressed current systems, galvanic systems continue to be more commonly used.

Quick Check

1. What is *electrowinning*?

   ____

2. What discovery was the key to designing an economical process for refining aluminum?

   ____

3. What two chemicals are produced in the chloralkali industry?

   ____

4. In what form of cathodic protection does the metal being protected act as the cathode in an electrolytic cell?

   ____

7.5 Activity: Location, Location, Location

Question

What criteria would a multinational corporation use when deciding where to locate an aluminum smelter?

Background

In 2015, North America produced 4.44 million tonnes of aluminum worth about \$6.6 billion. This makes us the world's third largest primary producer of aluminum, just behind the Gulf States 5.1 million tonnes and far behind China's 31.6 million tonnes.

Procedure

1. Reread the section on the Héroult-Hall process for producing aluminum.
2. There is a saying that the three most important criteria when purchasing real estate are location, location, and location. But what factors make one location more desirable than another? Imagine that you are the CEO of a multinational corporation planning to build an aluminum smelter. In the table provided below, list five important criteria that you would use when deciding where to build your smelter.

Results and Discussion

1.

Five Criteria for Choosing a Site

2. Look at the criteria of some of your classmates. Identify an important criterion that you didn't include in your table.

3. Kitimat, a coastal city in the Pacific Northwest, is a company town that was designed and built by the Aluminum Company of Canada (Alcan) in the 1950s. The Rio Tinto Alcan smelter is undergoing a \$6 billion modernization and expansion that was completed in 2014. The conversion of Kitimat's smelter will make it the "greenest" aluminum smelter in the world. Use the five criteria you listed in the above table to rate Kitimat as a location for an aluminum smelter.

© Edvantage Interactive 2019

7.5 Review Questions

1. Specialty sports drinks are called electrolyte drinks because they replenish the water and solutes, including electrolytes, that athletes lose in sweat during exercise. Which of the following ingredients of a typical sports drink are electrolytes: water, sucrose, dextrose, citric acid, sodium chloride, sodium citrate, and potassium dihydrogen phosphate?

2. Draw a type 1 electrolytic cell electrolyzing molten NaCl. Label the DC source, its terminals, and the anode and cathode of the electrolytic cell. Show each ion in the molten NaCl migrating toward the appropriate electrode. Write the half-reaction that occurs at each electrode and predict the voltage required to operate this cell.

3. Sodium is commercially produced by the electrolysis of molten NaCl in an apparatus called a Downs cell. A Downs cell directs the products into separate chambers to prevent them from coming into contact with each other. Why is it important to keep the two products physically separated as the cell operates?

4. Complete the following table:

	Cell Type (1,2,3)	Electrolyte	Anode/Cathode	Products	
				Anode	Cathode
(a)		$NaCl(l)$	Pt/Pt		
(b)		$NaCl(aq)$	Pt/C		
(c)		$CuBr_2(aq)$	C/C		
(d)		$AlF_3(aq)$	C/C		
(e)		$CuCl_2(aq)$	Cu/Cu		

5. An electrolytic cell contains inert electrodes in a solution of acidified copper(II) nitrate.
   (a) Write the half-reactions occurring at the anode and cathode.

   (b) Predict the voltage required to operate this cell.

6. Electrolysis is also used as a technique for the permanent removal of individual hairs. A very thin metal probe is inserted alongside the hair into the follicle beneath the skin's surface from which the hair emerges. This probe is the cathode of an electrolytic cell. Hydroxide ions formed at the cathode kill the cells that produce the hair. Write the half-reaction that produces the hydroxide ions.

7. How is electrorefining a special kind of electrowinning?

8. Why is it uneconomical to produce metallic aluminum by electrolyzing $Al_2O_3(l)$ and impossible to produce metallic aluminum by electrolyzing $Al_2O_3(aq)$?

9. Describe how impressed current cathodic protection is electrochemically different than galvanic cathodic protection.

10. Draw a type 3 electrolytic cell electroplating an aluminum spoon with silver. Label the DC source, its terminals, and the anode and cathode of the electrolytic cell. Predict the voltage required to operate this cell.

11. An electrolytic cell containing inert electrodes is used to electrolyze pure water.
    (a) What type of cell is this? Explain.

    (b) Identify a salt that could be added to water to increase its conductivity without the salt reacting.

12. What is the minimum voltage theoretically required to operate an electrolytic cell consisting of inert electrodes in an aqueous solution of $CuBr_2$?

© Edvantage Interactive 2019

7.6 The Stoichiometry of Electrochemistry – Faraday's Constant and Free Energy

Warm Up

Coulomb's law helps explain some of the trends in the periodic table. The coulomb is the SI unit of charge named after the great French physicist, Charles Augustin de Coulomb. One coulomb is the charge on 6.24×10^{18} electrons. For this Warm Up, write an equation using the number of electrons in 1 coulomb and Avogadro's number to determine the charge (in coulombs) on 1 mole of electrons.

Stoichiometry and Electrolysis

Michael Faraday was an English scientist who contributed a great deal to our understanding of electrochemistry. He was the first to describe a quantitative relationship, called **Faraday's law**, between the number of amperes used and the quantity of product formed or reactant consumed during an electrochemical process.

> The amount of substance produced (or consumed) at each electrode is directly proportional to the coulombs of charge flowing through an electrolytic cell.

In the warm-up exercise, you derived a conversion factor that represents the number of coulombs in each mole of electrons. The equation below outlines the process for this derivation. The number of coulombs in each mole of electrons is Faraday's constant and has the symbol *F*.

$$\frac{6.02 \times 10^{23}\ \cancel{\text{electrons}}}{\text{mole } e^-} \times \frac{1\ \text{coulomb}}{6.24 \times 10^{18}\ \cancel{e^-}} = 96\,500\ \text{C/mol } e^-$$

Using Faraday's law and the number of amperes, we can calculate the mass of product formed or reactant consumed in an electrochemical process. The ampere, named after the French physicist André-Marie Ampère, is the SI unit of electrical current. The symbol for amperes or amps is A. One ampere is equal to one coulomb of electrons flowing past a particular point in a conducting path each second.

> Faraday constant (F): $\dfrac{96\,500\ \text{C}}{\text{mole } e^-}$ = 1 faraday = the charge on 1 mol of electrons
>
> $$1\ \text{amp} = \frac{1\ \text{coulomb}}{\text{second}} \quad \text{or } 1\ \text{A} = 1\ \text{C/s}$$

Sample Problem 7.6.1(a) — Conversion of Reaction ⇔ Time Mass of Product

What mass of solid nickel can be deposited on a graphite cathode by passing 15.00 A of current through a solution of $NiCl_2$ for 2.25 h?

What to Think About	How to Do It
1. Determine the balanced chemical equation. This is the first step in any stoichiometry problem. In this case, it is a half-reaction.	Nickel will be produced by the reduction of the nickel (II) ion: $Ni^{2+}(aq) + 2e^- \rightarrow Ni(s)$
2. Perform the following conversions: hours → seconds (the unit in the denominator of amps) time → charge (use the current in amps expressed as C/s) charge → mol e^- (use the constant *F*) mole e^- → mol Ni (use the half reaction) mole Ni → mass Ni (use the molar mass)	$2.25\ \text{h} \times \frac{3600\ \text{s}}{1\ \text{h}} \times \frac{15.00\ \text{C}}{1\ \text{s}} \times \frac{1\ \text{mol } e^-}{96\,500\ \text{C}} \times \frac{1\ \text{mol Ni}}{2\ \text{mol } e^-} \times \frac{58.7\ \text{g Ni}}{1\ \text{mol Ni}} = 37.0\ \text{g Ni}$

Sample Problem 7.6.1(b) — Calculation of Current

What current is required to deposit 5.00 g of gold in 1.50 h from a solution containing gold(III) ions?

What to Think About	How to Do It
1. As always, determine the balanced chemical equation.	The reduction half reaction is: $Au^{3+}(aq) + 3e^- \rightarrow Au(s)$
2. Convert 5.00 g of gold into coulombs using the following series of conversions: mass → moles (use the molar mass) moles → mol e^- (use the half reaction) mole e^- → coulombs (use the constant *F*)	$5.00\ \text{g} \times \frac{1\ \text{mol Au}}{197.0\ \text{g}} \times \frac{3\ \text{mol } e^-}{1\ \text{mol Au}} \times \frac{96\,500\ \text{C}}{1\ \text{mol } e^-}$ $= 7347.7\ \text{C}$ (note there are three significant figures)
3. Divide the coulombs by the time (in seconds) to determine the current in amperes.	$\text{Current} = \frac{7347.7\ \text{C}}{1.50\ \text{h}} \times \frac{1\ \text{h}}{3600\ \text{s}} = 1.36\ \text{A}$

Practice Problems 7.6.1 — Stoichiometry and Electrolysis

1. Figure 7.5.4 depicts a Hall-Héroult cell used in the production of aluminum metal from bauxite ore, $Al_2O_3(s)$. What mass of aluminum is produced if 15.0 A of current passes through molten bauxite for 24.0 h?

Continued opposite

© Edvantage Interactive 2019

Practice Problems 7.6.1 (*Continued*)

2. Calculate the current required to deposit 15.0 g of silver metal in 2.5 h from a solution containing silver ions.

3. The peroxydisulfate ion forms during the electrolysis of a cold concentrated solution of potassium sulfate. The half reaction is:

   $2\ SO_4^{2-}(aq) \rightarrow S_2O_8^{2-}(aq) + 2e^-$

   (a) At which electrode does this reaction take place? Explain your answer.

   (b) Calculate the time required to produce 2.00 kg of $K_2S_2O_8$ with a current of 125 A.

Free Energy and Electrochemistry

Moving electrons through a wire requires work. What is the source of the energy to do this work? The work done when electrons move from one point to another on a conducting path depends on the electrical potential difference between the two points. The free energy of an oxidation-reduction reaction drives electrons through a circuit. As long as a reacting mixture is not at equilibrium, its free chemical energy ($\Delta G°$) provides electrical energy to do the work to move a given number of moles of electrons (n) across an electrical potential difference (E°).

As indicated earlier in this section, the unit of electrical potential difference (sometimes referred to as *electromotive force* or *emf*) is the **volt (V)**. One volt is equivalent to 1 joule of work per coulomb of charge transferred.

$$\textbf{potential difference (V)} = \frac{\textbf{work (J)}}{\textbf{charge (C)}}$$

When 1 coulomb of charge moves between two points in a circuit that differ by 1 volt of electrical potential, the chemical system produces or requires 1 joule of work. A simple algebraic manipulation of the equation above shows that work is the product of potential difference and charge. A review of the derivation of Faraday's constant shows that the charge transferred during a redox reaction, q, is equivalent to the product of the number of moles of electrons, n, and the constant, F. Substitution of $\Delta G°$ for maximum work provides the connection between thermodynamics and electrochemistry as $\Delta G° = -nFE°$. The equation is derived as follows:

$$\text{work (J)} = \text{potential difference}\left(\frac{J}{C}\right) \times \text{charge (C)} \quad \textit{or} \quad w_{max} = -E_{max}q$$

$$\text{Since } q = nF$$

$$w_{max} = -nFE° = \Delta G° \text{ thus:}$$

$$\boldsymbol{\Delta G° = -nFE°}$$

Spontaneous processes are never one hundred percent efficient. Some energy is always wasted in the form of heat. The values calculated for w_{max} and E_{max} assume 100% efficiency and are simplified to w and E° (assuming standard conditions) in this equation. The experimentally determined values of w and E° would likely be lower than the calculated values because the process is less than 100% efficient. The free energy is *produced by* the chemical system, therefore convention requires the insertion of a negative sign.

Spontaneous processes always result in a (+) E° value and a (–) ΔG° value.

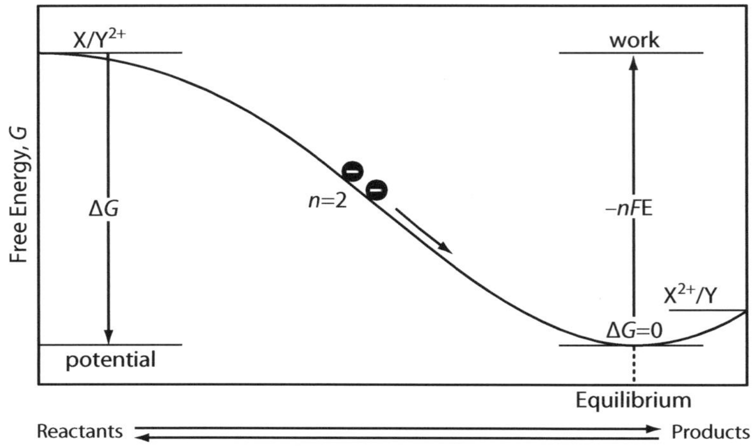

Figure 7.6.1 *This curve depicts the change in free energy when the reducing agent X transfers two electrons to the oxidizing agent Y^{2+} to form X^{2+} and Y. The change in free energy (ΔG°) is the amount of energy available to do electrical work. The maximum work available equals –nFE. This is a spontaneous process, and the negative sign indicates the work is done by the system.*

Sample Problem 7.6.2 — Free Energy and Electrochemistry: ΔG° ⇔ E°

Use Table A7 Standard Reduction Potentials of Half-Cells in the appendix to calculate E°_{cell} and ΔG° and to predict whether the following reaction is spontaneous:

$$Cl_2(g) + 2\,Br^-(aq) \rightarrow 2\,Cl^-(aq) + Br_2(l)$$

What to Think About	How to Do It
1. Calculate E° for the cell exactly as explained in sample problem 7.4.1.	Red: $Cl_2 + 2e^- \rightarrow 2\,Cl^-$ E° = 1.36 V Ox: $2\,Br^- \rightarrow Br_2 + 2\,e^-$ E° = –1.09 V Redox: $Cl_2 + 2\,Br^- \rightarrow 2\,Cl^- + Br_2$ E° = +0.27 V
2. Substitute E° into the equation ΔG° = –nFE° taking care with the signs. Remember that a volt is equivalent to a joule/coulomb.	$\Delta G^\circ = -\frac{2\ \text{mol } e^-}{\text{mol}_{rxn}} \times \frac{96\,500\ C}{\text{mol } e^-} \times \frac{0.27\ J}{1\ C} \times \frac{1\ kJ}{10^3\ J}$ $= -52\ kJ/mol_{rxn}$
3. Consider the sign of each value as it relates to spontaneity. Ensure the signs of E° and ΔG oppose one another.	Both (+) E° and (–) ΔG° indicate the reaction is spontaneous!

 © Edvantage Interactive 2019

Practice Problems 7.6.2 — Free Energy and Electrochemistry: $\Delta G° \Leftrightarrow E°$

1. Calculate E° and $\Delta G°$ when silver metal dissolves in nitric acid. Is this process thermodynamically favorable?

2. Cadmium metal spontaneously reduces copper(II) ions to copper metal, producing Cd^{2+} ions as well. $\Delta G°$ for this reaction is –143 kJ/mol_{rxn}. Determine the standard reduction potential for Cd^{2+}. Hint: Begin by finding E° for the redox reaction.

3. The reaction $6X^- + 2\ Al^{3+} \rightarrow 3\ X_2 + 2\ Al$ has a $\Delta G°$ value of 1270 kJ/mol_{rxn}.
   (a) Calculate E° for the reaction.

   (b) Use Table A7 Standard Reduction Potentials of Half-Cells in the appendix to determine the identity of the element X_2.

Pulling It All Together — Thermodynamics, Equilibrium, and Electrochemistry

As you continue your study of Chemistry for this course, remember the equations from the chapters on equilibrium, thermodynamics and oxidiation-reduction. These equations provide mathematical and conceptual connections between Big Ideas 3, 5, and 6 in the Curriculum Framework for AP Chemistry. These connections are depicted in the following diagram.

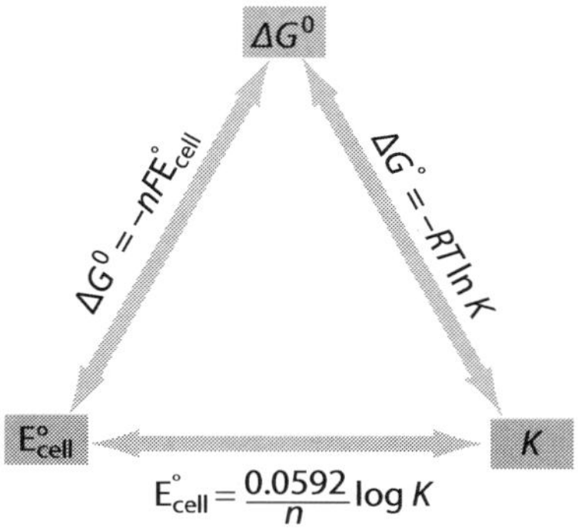

Figure 7.6.2 *$\Delta G°$, E°, and K form the apices of a triangle connected by three equations we have learned.*

Recall that *thermodynamically favorable* processes always have *positive* E° values, producing *negative* $\Delta G°$ values when substituted into the equation, $\Delta G° = -nFE°$.

Algebraic manipulation of either $\Delta G° = -RT \ln K$ or the Nernst equation shows that $K = e^{\Delta G°/-RT}$ or $K = 10^{E°n/0.0592}$. We see that *negative* $\Delta G°$ and/or *positive* E° values always result in *K* values that *exceed 1*. The greater the magnitude of $\Delta G°$ or E°, the larger the *K* value. If the signs of E° and $\Delta G°$ are reversed, *K* will be less than 1.

Table 7.6.1 *The Impact of $\Delta G°$, K, and E° on the Spontaneity of an Electrochemical Reaction*

$\Delta G°$	K	$E°_{cell}$	Reactions at standard-state conditions
<0	>1	>0	Spontaneous
0	1	0	At equilibrium
>0	<1	<0	Nonspontaneous

None of these factors, $\Delta G°$, K, or E°, *impact the kinetics* of a reaction. The magnitude of the activation energy and the rate constant influence the reaction rate. These things are *independent* of the thermodynamics, the electrochemistry, or the equilibrium position of a reaction. Only *temperature* influences the thermodynamics, electrochemistry, kinetics, *and* the equilibrium position of a chemical reaction.

© **Edvantage Interactive 2019**

7.6 Review Questions

1. Electroplating metals makes them more resistant to corrosion and may make them more attractive.
   (a) A motorcycle's exhaust pipe is plated with chromium by passing 55 A of current through a cell containing chromium(III) ions for 0.75 min. What mass of chromium is deposited on the pipe?

   (b) Steel screws for use in kitchen cabinetry are plated with nickel from a nickel(II) ion solution. If 125 mg of nickel are required for each screw and a current of 0.50 A is used, how long will it take to plate 32 screws for a set of kitchen cabinets?

   (c) An antique teapot requires a new silver surface with a mass of 12.0 g. If the plating process requires 1.50 h, what current should be used?

2. "Tin" cans are prepared by plating a steel can with tin.
   (a) What is the advantage of placing a layer of tin against the steel, which is mainly composed of iron?

   (b) The steel can is connected at the cathode in an electrolytic cell containing 1.00 L of 3.75 mol/L $SnCl_2(aq)$. A current of 2.50 A passes through the cell for 1.25 h.
   (i) What mass of tin is deposited on the steel can?

   (ii) What concentration of $SnCl_2(aq)$ remains in the cell once the plating is complete?

3. Pure bismuth is produced by the electrolysis of a solution containing BiO^+ ions. How long would it take to produce 15.0 g of bismuth using 10.0 A of current? Begin by writing a balanced reduction half reaction.

4. An aqueous solution of CoF_2 is electrolyzed with 3.50 A for 1.40 h. Both electrodes are made of graphite.
   (a) What mass of cobalt metal is collected?

   (b) What volume of oxygen gas evolves at the other electrode? Determine the volume at STP conditions.

   (c) Give two chemical tests to determine that the gas is, indeed, oxygen.

5. Calculate the standard cell potential E° *and* the change in free energy $\Delta G°$ for each of these reactions. Which reaction is spontaneous?
   (a) $2\ H_2O(l) \rightarrow 2\ H_2(g) + O_2(g)$ *decomposition of water*

   (b) $2\ Fe(s) + O_2(g) + 4\ H^+(aq) \rightarrow 2\ Fe^{2+}(aq) + 2\ H_2O(l)$ *rusting of Fe*

6. The reaction $Ag_2O(s) + Zn(s) + H_2O(l) \rightarrow 2\ Ag(s) + Zn^{2+}(aq) + 2\ OH^-(aq)$ occurs in some "button" batteries producing a cell potential of 1.104 V.
   (a) Calculate the standard reduction potential for the cathodic half reaction.

   (b) Calculate $\Delta G°$ for the spontaneous redox reaction.

© Edvantage Interactive 2019

7. The reaction $CH_4(g) + 2\ O_2(g) + 2\ OH^-(aq) \rightarrow CO_3^{2-}(aq) + 3\ H_2O(l)$ occurs in a methane-oxygen fuel cell producing energy at nearly 70% efficiency (compared to the 25% efficiency of a normal combustion reaction to produce steam in an electricity generating plant). E°_{cell} is 0.23 V for this reaction.

   (a) Calculate ΔG° for this reaction.

   (b) Given $E^\circ = 0.40$ V for $O_2(g) + 2\ H_2O(l) + 4\ e^- \rightarrow 4\ OH^-(aq)$, write the balanced oxidation half-reaction and determine E° for the anodic reaction.

8. If 0.40 g of a metal is deposited on a cathode by 5.0 A of current in 0.50 h, what mass of the *same* metal would be deposited by 1 faraday? Recall: 1 faraday is equivalent to 1 mole of electrons *or* 96 500 C.

9. Scientists and engineers have designed a wide variety of new rechargeable cells during the decade 2004 to 2014. A popular, though expensive, example is the silver-cadmium cell. The overall reaction is:
   $2\ AgO(s) + H_2O(l) + Cd(s) \rightarrow Ag_2O(s) + Cd(OH)_2(s)\ \Delta G^\circ = -257\ kJ/mol_{rxn}$
   What is the voltage for a silver-cadmium cell?

10. Scientists designed the first "transistor battery" shown here in the 1950s. It was commonly used to power the first portable transistor radios. Today, devices such as remote control cars, alarm systems, motion sensors, and smoke detectors use this same battery. The battery is actually a system of *six cells* each involving the standard dry cell reaction shown here:

$$2\ MnO_2(s) + H_2O(l) + Zn(s) \rightarrow Mn_2O_3(s) + 2\ OH^-(aq) + Zn^{2+}(aq)$$

$\Delta G°$ for this reaction is −299 kJ/mol_{rxn}. What is the overall voltage for a transistor battery?

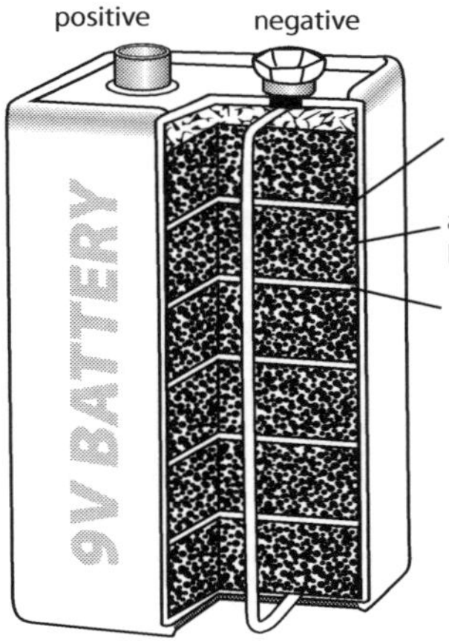

A transistor battery consists of six cells stacked vertically and connected in series.

11. The Hall-Héroult cell requires a low-voltage DC source (approximately 4.53 V) that applies current across inert graphite electrodes through molten bauxite (Al_2O_3) ore. The addition of cryolite (Na_3AlF_6) lowers the melting point of bauxite.

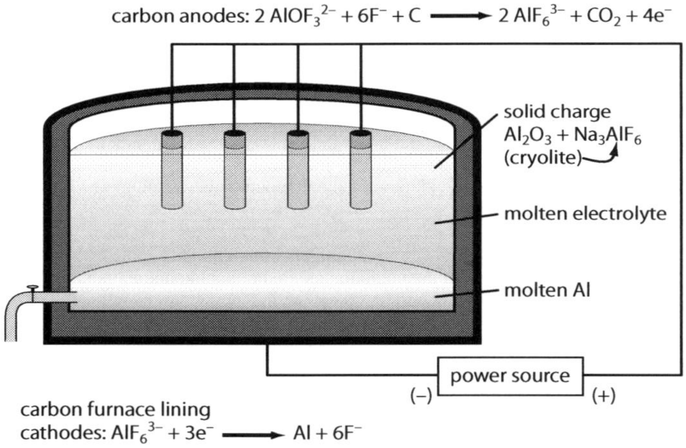

The Hall-Héroult process for the production of aluminum metal.

(a) Combine the anode and cathode half-reactions to give the overall equation for the Hall-Héroult process.

(b) Calculate the $\Delta G°$ value for the process.

 © Edvantage Interactive 2019

Appendix — Reference Tables

© Edvantage Interactive 2019

 © Edvantage Interactive 2019

Table A1 Atomic Masses of the Elements

Based on mass of carbon-12 at 12.00.

For elements that do not occur naturally, the atomic mass of the most stable or best known isotope is shown in parentheses.

Element	Symbol	Atomic Number	Atomic Mass
Actinium	Ac	89	(227)
Aluminum	Al	13	27.0
Americium	Am	95	(243)
Antimony	Sb	51	121.8
Argon	Ar	18	39.9
Arsenic	As	33	74.9
Astatine	At	85	(210)
Barium	Ba	56	137.3
Berkelium	Bk	97	(247)
Beryllium	Be	4	9.0
Bismuth	Bi	83	209.0
Boron	B	5	10.8
Bromine	Br	35	79.9
Cadmium	Cd	48	112.4
Calcium	Ca	20	40.1
Californium	Cf	98	(251)
Carbon	C	6	12.0
Cerium	Ce	58	140.1
Cesium	Cs	55	132.9
Chlorine	Cl	17	35.5
Chromium	Cr	24	52.0
Cobalt	Co	27	58.9
Copper	Cu	29	63.5
Curium	Cm	96	(247)
Dubnium	Db	105	(262)
Dysprosium	Dy	66	162.5
Einsteinium	Es	99	(252)
Erbium	Er	68	167.3
Europium	Eu	63	152.0
Fermium	Fm	100	(257)
Fluorine	F	9	19.0
Francium	Fr	87	(223)
Gadolinium	Gd	64	157.3
Gallium	Ga	31	69.7
Germanium	Ge	32	72.6
Gold	Au	79	197.0
Hafnium	Hf	72	178.5
Helium	He	2	4.0
Holmium	Ho	67	164.9
Hydrogen	H	1	1.0
Indium	In	49	114.8
Iodine	I	53	126.9
Iridium	Ir	77	192.2
Iron	Fe	26	55.8
Krypton	Kr	36	83.8
Lanthanum	La	57	138.9
Lawrencium	Lr	103	(262)
Lead	Pb	82	207.2
Lithium	Li	3	6.9
Lutetium	Lu	71	175.0
Magnesium	Mg	12	24.3
Manganese	Mn	25	54.9
Mendelevium	Md	101	(258)
Mercury	Hg	80	200.6
Molybdenum	Mo	42	95.9
Neodymium	Nd	60	144.2
Neon	Ne	10	20.2
Neptunium	Np	93	(237)
Nickel	Ni	28	58.7
Niobium	Nb	41	92.9
Nitrogen	N	7	14.0
Nobelium	No	102	(259)
Osmium	Os	76	190.2
Oxygen	O	8	16.0
Palladium	Pd	46	106.4
Phosphorus	P	15	31.0
Platinum	Pt	78	195.1
Plutonium	Pu	94	(244)
Polonium	Po	84	(209)
Potassium	K	19	39.1
Praseodymium	Pr	59	140.9
Promethium	Pm	61	(145)
Protactinium	Pa	91	231.0
Radium	Ra	88	(226)
Radon	Rn	86	(222)
Rhenium	Re	75	186.2
Rhodium	Rh	45	102.9
Rubidium	Rb	37	85.5
Ruthenium	Ru	44	101.1
Rutherfordium	Rf	104	(261)
Samarium	Sm	62	150.4
Scandium	Sc	21	45.0
Selenium	Se	34	79.0
Silicon	Si	14	28.1
Silver	Ag	47	107.9
Sodium	Na	11	23.0
Strontium	Sr	38	87.6
Sulfur	S	16	32.1
Tantalum	Ta	73	180.9
Technetium	Tc	43	(98)
Tellurium	Te	52	127.6
Terbium	Tb	65	158.9
Thallium	Tl	81	204.4
Thorium	Th	90	232.0
Thulium	Tm	69	168.9
Tin	Sn	50	118.7
Titanium	Ti	22	47.9
Tungsten	W	74	183.8
Uranium	U	92	238.0
Vanadium	V	23	50.9
Xenon	Xe	54	131.3
Ytterbium	Yb	70	173.0
Yttrium	Y	39	88.9
Zinc	Zn	30	65.4
Zirconium	Zr	40	91.2

Table A2 Names, Formulas, and Charges of Some Common Ions

** Aqueous solutions readily oxidized by air*

*** Not stable in aqueous solutions*

Positive Ions (Cations)

Al^{3+}	Aluminum	Pb^{4+}	Lead(IV), plumbic
NH_4^+	Ammonium	Li^+	Lithium
Ba^{2+}	Barium	Mg^{2+}	Magnesium
Ca^{2+}	Calcium	Mn^{2+}	Manganese(II), manganous
Cr^{2+}	Chromium(II), chromous	Mn^{4+}	Manganese(IV)
Cr^{3+}	Chromium(III), chromic	Hg_2^{2+}	Mercury(I)*, mercurous
Cu^+	Copper(I)*, cuprous	Hg^{2+}	Mercury(II), mercuric
Cu^{2+}	Copper(II), cupric	K^+	Potassium
H^+	Hydrogen	Ag^+	Silver
H_3O^+	Hydronium	Na^+	Sodium
Fe^{2+}	Iron(II)*, ferrous	Sn^{2+}	Tin(II)*, stannous
Fe^{3+}	Iron(III), ferric	Sn^{4+}	Tin(IV), stannic
Pb^{2+}	Lead(II), plumbous	Zn^{2+}	Zinc

Negative Ions (Anions)

Br^-	Bromide	OH^-	Hydroxide
CO_3^{2-}	Carbonate	ClO^-	Hypochlorite
ClO_3^-	Chlorate	I^-	Iodide
Cl^-	Chloride	HPO_4^{2-}	Monohydrogen phosphate
ClO_2^-	Chlorite	NO_3^-	Nitrate
CrO_4^{2-}	Chromate	NO_2^-	Nitrite
CN^-	Cyanide	$C_2O_4^{2-}$	Oxalate
$Cr_2O_7^{2-}$	Dichromate	O^{2-}	Oxide**
$H_2PO_4^-$	Dihydrogen phosphate	ClO_4^-	Perchlorate
CH_3COO^-	Ethanoate, acetate	MnO_4^-	Permanganate
F^-	Fluoride	$PO_4^{?-}$	Phosphate
HCO_3^-	Hydrogen carbonate, bicarbonate	SO_4^{2-}	Sulfate
$HC_2O_4^-$	Hydrogen oxalate, binoxalate	S^{2-}	Sulfide
HSO_4^-	Hydrogen sulfate, bisulfate	SO_3^{2-}	Sulfite
HS^-	Hydrogen sulfide, bisulfide	SCN^-	Thiocyanate
HSO_3^-	Hydrogen sulfite, bisulfite		

© Edvantage Interactive 2019

Table A3 Solubility of Common Compounds in Water

"Soluble" means > 0.1 mol/L at 25°C.

Negative Ions (Anions)	Positive Ions (Cations)	Solubility of Compounds
All	Alkali ions: Li^+, Na^+, K^+, Rb^+, Cs^+, Fr^+	Soluble
All	Hydrogen ion: H^+	Soluble
All	Ammonium ion: NH_4^+	Soluble
Nitrate, NO_3^-	All	Soluble
Chloride, Cl^- or Bromide, Br^- or Iodide, I^-	All others	Soluble
	Ag^+, Pb^{2+}, Cu^+	Low Solubility
Sulfate, SO_4^{2-}	All others	Soluble
	Ag^+, Ca^{2+}, Sr^{2+}, Ba^{2+}, Pb^{2+}	Low Solubility
Sulfide, S^{2-}	Alkali ions, H^+, NH_4^+, Be^{2+}, Mg^{2+}, Ca^{2+}, Sr^{2+}, Ba^{2+}	Soluble
	All others	Low Solubility
Hydroxide, OH^-	Alkali ions, H^+, NH_4^+, Sr^{2+}	Soluble
	All others	Low Solubility
Phosphate, PO_4^{3-} or Carbonate, CO_3^{2-} or Sulfite, SO_3^{2-}	Alkali ions, H^+, NH_4^+	Soluble
	All others	Low Solubility

Table A4 Solubility Product Constants at 25°C

Name	Formula	K_{sp}
Barium carbonate	$BaCO_3$	2.6×10^{-9}
Barium chromate	$BaCrO_4$	1.2×10^{-10}
Barium sulfate	$BaSO_4$	1.1×10^{-10}
Calcium carbonate	$CaCO_3$	5.0×10^{-9}
Calcium oxalate	CaC_2O_4	2.3×10^{-9}
Calcium sulfate	$CaSO_4$	7.1×10^{-5}
Copper(I) iodide	CuI	1.3×10^{-12}
Copper(II) iodate	$Cu(IO_3)_2$	6.9×10^{-8}
Copper(II) sulfide	CuS	6.0×10^{-37}
Iron(II) hydroxide	$Fe(OH)_2$	4.9×10^{-17}
Iron(II) sulfide	FeS	6.0×10^{-19}
Iron(III) hydroxide	$Fe(OH)_3$	2.6×10^{-39}
Lead(II) bromide	$PbBr_2$	6.6×10^{-6}
Lead(II) chloride	$PbCl_2$	1.2×10^{-5}
Lead(II) iodate	$Pb(IO_3)_2$	3.7×10^{-13}
Lead(II) iodide	PbI_2	8.5×10^{-9}
Lead(II) sulfate	$PbSO_4$	1.8×10^{-8}
Magnesium carbonate	$MgCO_3$	6.8×10^{-6}
Magnesium hydroxide	$Mg(OH)_2$	5.6×10^{-12}
Silver bromate	$AgBrO_3$	5.3×10^{-5}
Silver bromide	$AgBr$	5.4×10^{-13}
Silver carbonate	Ag_2CO_3	8.5×10^{-12}
Silver chloride	$AgCl$	1.8×10^{-10}
Silver chromate	Ag_2CrO_4	1.1×10^{-12}
Silver iodate	$AgIO_3$	3.2×10^{-8}
Silver iodide	AgI	8.5×10^{-17}
Strontium carbonate	$SrCO_3$	5.6×10^{-10}
Strontium fluoride	SrF_2	4.3×10^{-9}
Strontium sulfate	$SrSO_4$	3.4×10^{-7}
Zinc sulfide	ZnS	2.0×10^{-25}

© Edvantage Interactive 2019

Table A5 Relative Strengths of Brønsted-Lowry Acids and Bases

In aqueous solution at room temperature

STRONG ↑ STRENGTH OF ACID — WEAK

WEAK — STRENGTH OF BASE ↓ STRONG

Name of Acid	Acid		Base	K_a
Perchloric	$HClO_4$	→	$H^+ + ClO_4^-$	very large
Hydriodic	HI	→	$H^+ + I^-$	very large
Hydrobromic	HBr	→	$H^+ + Br^-$	very large
Hydrochloric	HCl	→	$H^+ + Cl^-$	very large
Nitric	HNO_3	→	$H^+ + NO_3^-$	very large
Sulfuric	H_2SO_4	→	$H^+ + HSO_4^-$	very large
Hydronium Ion	H_3O^+	⇄	$H^+ + H_2O$	1.0
Iodic	HIO_3	⇄	$H^+ + IO_3^-$	1.7×10^{-1}
Oxalic	$H_2C_2O_4$	⇄	$H^+ + HC_2O_4^-$	5.9×10^{-2}
Sulfurous (SO_2 +H_2O)	H_2SO_3	⇄	$H^+ + HSO_3^-$	1.5×10^{-2}
Hydrogen sulfate ion	HSO_4^-	⇄	$H^+ + SO_4^{2-}$	1.2×10^{-2}
Phosphoric	H_3PO_4	⇄	$H^+ + H_2PO_4^-$	7.5×10^{-3}
Hexaaquoiron ion, iron(III) ion	$Fe(H_2O)_6^{3+}$	⇄	$H^+ + Fe(H_2O)_5(OH)^{2+}$	6.0×10^{-3}
Citric	$H_3C_6H_5O_7$	⇄	$H^+ + H_2C_6H_5O_7^-$	7.1×10^{-4}
Nitrous	HNO_2	⇄	$H^+ + NO_2^-$	4.6×10^{-4}
Hydrofluoric	HF	⇄	$H^+ + F^-$	3.5×10^{-4}
Methanoic, formic	$HCOOH$	⇄	$H^+ + HCOO^-$	1.8×10^{-4}
Hexaaquochromium ion, chromium(III) ion	$Cr(H_2O)_6^{3+}$	⇄	$H^+ + Cr(H_2O)_5(OH)^{2+}$	1.5×10^{-4}
Benzoic	C_6H_5COOH	⇄	$H^+ + C_6H_5COO^-$	6.5×10^{-5}
Hydrogen oxalate ion	$HC_2O_4^-$	⇄	$H^+ + C_2O_4^{2-}$	6.4×10^{-5}
Ethanoic, acetic	CH_3COOH	⇄	$H^+ + CH_3COO^-$	1.8×10^{-5}
Dihydrogen citrate ion	$H_2C_6H_5O_7^-$	⇄	$H^+ + HC_6H_5O_7^{2-}$	1.7×10^{-5}
Hexaaquoaluminum ion, aluminum ion	$Al(H_2O)_6^{3+}$	⇄	$H^+ + Al(H_2O)_5(OH)^{2+}$	1.4×10^{-5}
Carbonic (CO_2 +H_2O)	H_2CO_3	⇄	$H^+ + HCO_3^-$	4.3×10^{-7}
Monohydrogen citrate ion	$HC_6H_5O_7^{2-}$	⇄	$H^+ + C_6H_5O_7^{3-}$	4.1×10^{-7}
Hydrogen sulfite ion	HSO_3^-	⇄	$H^+ + SO_3^{2-}$	1.0×10^{-7}
Hydrogen sulfide	H_2S	⇄	$H^+ + HS^-$	9.1×10^{-8}
Dihydrogen phosphate ion	$H_2PO_4^-$	⇄	$H^+ + HPO_4^{2-}$	6.2×10^{-8}
Boric	H_3BO_3	⇄	$H^+ + H_2BO_3^-$	7.3×10^{-10}
Ammonium ion	NH_4^+	⇄	$H^+ + NH_3$	5.6×10^{-10}
Hydrocyanic	HCN	⇄	$H^+ + CN^-$	4.9×10^{-10}
Phenol	C_6H_5OH	⇄	$H^+ + C_6H_5O^-$	1.3×10^{-10}
Hydrogen carbonate ion	HCO_3^-	⇄	$H^+ + CO_3^{2-}$	5.6×10^{-11}
Hydrogen peroxide	H_2O_2	⇄	$H^+ + HO_2^-$	2.4×10^{-12}
Monohydrogen phosphate ion	HPO_4^{2-}	⇄	$H^+ + PO_4^{3-}$	2.2×10^{-13}
Water	H_2O	⇄	$H^+ + OH^-$	1.0×10^{-14}
Hydroxide ion	OH^-	←	$H^+ + O^{2-}$	very small
Ammonia	NH_3	←	$H^+ + NH_2^-$	very small

Table A6 Acid-Base Indicators

Indicator	pH Range in Which Colour Change Occurs	Colour Change as pH Increases
Methyl violet	0.0 – 1.6	yellow to blue
Thymol blue	1.2 – 2.8	red to yellow
Orange IV	1.4 – 2.8	red to yellow
Methyl orange	3.2 – 4.4	red to yellow
Bromcresol green	3.8 – 5.4	yellow to blue
Methyl red	4.8 – 6.0	red to yellow
Chlorophenol red	5.2 – 6.8	yellow to red
Bromthymol blue	6.0 – 7.6	yellow to blue
Phenol red	6.6 – 8.0	yellow to red
Neutral red	6.8 – 8.0	red to amber
Thymol blue	8.0 – 9.6	yellow to blue
Phenolphthalein	8.2 – 10.0	colourless to pink
Thymolphthalein	9.4 – 10.6	colourless to blue
Alizarin yellow	10.1 – 12.0	yellow to red
Indigo carmine	11.4 – 13.0	blue to yellow

© Edvantage Interactive 2019

Table A7 Standard Reduction Potentials of Half-Cells

Ionic concentrations are at 1 M in water at 25°C.

Oxidizing Agents		Reducing Agents	E° (Volts)
$F_2(g) + 2e^-$	⇌	$2F^-$	+2.87
$S_2O_8^{2-} + 2e^-$	⇌	$2SO_4^{2-}$	+2.01
$H_2O_2 + 2H^+ + 2e^-$	⇌	$2H_2O$	+1.78
$MnO_4^- + 8H^+ + 5e^-$	⇌	$Mn^{2+} + 4H_2O$	+1.51
$Au^{3+} + 3e^-$	⇌	$Au(s)$	+1.50
$BrO_3^- + 6H^+ + 5e^-$	⇌	$\frac{1}{2}Br_2(\ell) + 3H_2O$	+1.48
$ClO_4^- + 8H^+ + 8e^-$	⇌	$Cl^- + 4H_2O$	+1.39
$Cl_2(g) + 2e^-$	⇌	$2Cl^-$	+1.36
$Cr_2O_7^{2-} + 14H^+ + 6e^-$	⇌	$2Cr^{3+} + 7H_2O$	+1.23
$\frac{1}{2}O_2(g) + 2H^+ + 2e^-$	⇌	H_2O	+1.23
$MnO_2(s) + 4H^+ + 2e^-$	⇌	$Mn^{2+} + 2H_2O$	+1.22
$IO_3^- + 6H^+ + 5e^-$	⇌	$\frac{1}{2}I_2(s) + 3H_2O$	+1.20
$Br_2(\ell) + 2e^-$	⇌	$2Br^-$	+1.09
$AuCl_4^- + 3e^-$	⇌	$Au(s) + 4Cl^-$	+1.00
$NO_3^- + 4H^+ + 3e^-$	⇌	$NO(g) + 2H_2O$	+0.96
$Hg^{2+} + 2e^-$	⇌	$Hg(\ell)$	+0.85
$\frac{1}{2}O_2(g) + 2H^+(10^{-7}\ M) + 2e^-$	⇌	H_2O	+0.82
$2NO_3^- + 4H^+ + 2e^-$	⇌	$N_2O_4 + 2H_2O$	+0.80
$Ag^+ + e^-$	⇌	$Ag(s)$	+0.80
$\frac{1}{2}Hg_2^{2+} + e^-$	⇌	$Hg(\ell)$	+0.80
$Fe^{3+} + e^-$	⇌	Fe^{2+}	+0.77
$O_2(g) + 2H^+ + 2e^-$	⇌	H_2O_2	+0.70
$MnO_4^- + 2H_2O + 3e^-$	⇌	$MnO_2(s) + 4OH^-$	+0.60
$I_2(s) + 2e^-$	⇌	$2I^-$	+0.54
$Cu^+ + e^-$	⇌	$Cu(s)$	+0.52
$H_2SO_3 + 4H^+ + 4e^-$	⇌	$S(s) + 3H_2O$	+0.45
$Cu^{2+} + 2e^-$	⇌	$Cu(s)$	+0.34
$SO_4^{2-} + 4H^+ + 2e^-$	⇌	$H_2SO_3 + H_2O$	+0.17
$Cu^{2+} + e^-$	⇌	Cu^+	+0.15
$Sn^{4+} + 2e^-$	⇌	Sn^{2+}	+0.15
$S(s) + 2H^+ + 2e^-$	⇌	$H_2S(g)$	+0.14
$2H^+ + 2e^-$	⇌	$H_2(g)$	+0.00
$Pb^{2+} + 2e^-$	⇌	$Pb(s)$	−0.13
$Sn^{2+} + 2e^-$	⇌	$Sn(s)$	−0.14
$Ni^{2+} + 2e^-$	⇌	$Ni(s)$	−0.26
$H_3PO_4 + 2H^+ + 2e^-$	⇌	$H_3PO_3 + H_2O$	−0.28
$Co^{2+} + 2e^-$	⇌	$Co(s)$	−0.28
$Se(s) + 2H^+ + 2e^-$	⇌	H_2Se	−0.40
$Cr^{3+} + e^-$	⇌	Cr^{2+}	−0.41
$2H_2O + 2e^-$	⇌	$H_2 + 2OH^-(10^{-7}\ M)$	−0.41
$Fe^{2+} + 2e^-$	⇌	$Fe(s)$	−0.45
$Ag_2S(s) + 2e^-$	⇌	$2Ag(s) + S^{2-}$	−0.69
$Cr^{3+} + 3e^-$	⇌	$Cr(s)$	−0.74
$Zn^{2+} + 2e^-$	⇌	$Zn(s)$	−0.76
$Te(s) + 2H^+ + 2e^-$	⇌	H_2Te	−0.79
$2H_2O + 2e^-$	⇌	$H_2(g) + 2OH^-$	−0.83
$Mn^{2+} + 2e^-$	⇌	$Mn(s)$	−1.19
$Al^{3+} + 3e^-$	⇌	$Al(s)$	−1.66
$Mg^{2+} + 2e^-$	⇌	$Mg(s)$	−2.37
$Na^+ + e^-$	⇌	$Na(s)$	−2.71
$Ca^{2+} + 2e^-$	⇌	$Ca(s)$	−2.87
$Sr^{2+} + 2e^-$	⇌	$Sr(s)$	−2.89
$Ba^{2+} + 2e^-$	⇌	$Ba(s)$	−2.91
$K^+ + e^-$	⇌	$K(s)$	−2.93
$Rb^+ + e^-$	⇌	$Rb(s)$	−2.98
$Cs^+ + e^-$	⇌	$Cs(s)$	−3.03
$Li^+ + e^-$	⇌	$Li(s)$	−3.04

STRONG — STRENGTH OF OXIDIZING AGENT — WEAK

WEAK — STRENGTH OF REDUCING AGENT — STRONG

Overpotential Effect (+0.82 → +1.39)

Overpotential Effect (−0.41 → −0.76)

Table A8 Thermodynamic Data at 25°C for Assorted Substances

Table A8-Inorganic *Thermodynamic data at 25°C for assorted inorganic substances.*

Substance	Enthalpy of formation ΔH_f^0, kJ/mol	Free energy of formation ΔG_f^0, kJ/mol	Entropy S^0, J/(K·mol)
Aluminum			
$Al(s)$	0	0	28.33
$Al^{3+}(aq)$	-524.7	-481.2	-321.7
$Al_2O_3(s)$	-1675.7	-1582.3	50.92
$Al(OH)_3(s)$	-1276	---	---
$AlCl_3(s)$	-704.2	-628.8	110.67
Antimony			
$SbH_3(g)$	145.11	147.75	232.78
$SbCl_3(g)$	-313.8	-301.2	337.80
$SbCl_5(g)$	-394.34	-334.29	401.94
Arsenic			
$As(s, gray)$	0	0	35.1
$As_2S_3(s)$	-169.0	-168.6	163.6
$AsO_4^{3-}(aq)$	-888.14	-648.41	-162.8
Barium			
$Ba(s)$	0	0	62.8
$Ba^{2+}(aq)$	-537.64	-560.77	9.6
$BaO(s)$	-553.5	-525.1	70.42
$BaCO_3(s)$	-1216.3	-1137.6	112.1
$BaCO_3(aq)$	-1214.78	-1088.59	-47.3
Boron			
$B(s)$	0	0	5.86
$B_2O_3(s)$	-1272.8	-1193.7	53.97
$BF_3(g)$	-1137.0	-1120.3	254.12
Bromine			
$Br_2(l)$	0	0	152.23
$Br_2(g)$	30.91	3.11	245.46
$Br(g)$	111.88	82.40	175.02
$Br^-(aq)$	-121.55	-103.96	82.4
$HBr(g)$	-36.40	-53.45	198.70
Calcium			
$Ca(s)$	0	0	41.42
$Ca(g)$	178.2	144.3	154.88
$Ca^{2+}(aq)$	-542.83	-553.58	-53.1
$CaO(s)$	-635.09	-604.03	39.79
$Ca(OH)_2(s)$	-986.09	-898.49	83.39
$Ca(OH)_2(aq)$	-1002.82	-868.07	-74.5

© Edvantage Interactive 2019

Table A8-Inorganic *Thermodynamic data at 25°C for assorted inorganic substances (continued).*

Substance	Enthalpy of formation ΔH_f^0, kJ/mol	Free energy of formation ΔG_f^0, kJ/mol	Entropy S^0, J/(K·mol)
$CaCO_3$(*s, calcite*)	-1206.9	-1128.8	92.9
$CaCO_3$(*s, aragonite*)	-1207.1	-1127.8	88.7
$CaCO_3$(*aq*)	-1219.97	-1081.39	-110.0
CaF_2(*s*)	-1219.6	-1167.3	68.87
CaF_2(*aq*)	-1208.09	-1111.15	-80.8
$CaCl_2$(*s*)	-795.8	-748.1	104.6
$CaCl_2$(*aq*)	-877.1	-816.0	59.8
$CaBr_2$(*s*)	-682.8	-663.6	130
CaC_2(*s*)	-59.8	-64.9	69.96
$CaSO_4$(*s*)	-1434.11	-1321.79	106.7
$CaSO_4$(*aq*)	-1452.10	-1298.10	-33.1
Carbon			
C(*s, graphite*)	0	0	5.740
C(*s, diamond*)	1.895	2.900	2.377
C(*g*)	716.68	671.26	158.10
CO(*g*)	-110.53	-137.17	197.67
CO_2(*g*)	-393.51	-394.36	213.74
CO_3^{2-}(*aq*)	-677.14	-527.81	-56.9
CCl_4(*l*)	-135.44	-65.21	216.40
CS_2(*l*)	89.70	65.27	153.34
HCN(*g*)	135.1	124.7	201.78
HCN(*l*)	108.87	124.97	112.84
Cerium			
Ce(*s*)	0	0	72.0
Ce^{3+}(*aq*)	-696.2	-672.0	-205
Ce^{4+}(*aq*)	-537.2	-503.8	-301
Chlorine			
Cl_2(*g*)	0	0	223.07
Cl(*g*)	121.68	105.68	165.20
Cl^-(*aq*)	-167.16	-131.23	56.5
HCl(*g*)	-92.31	-95.30	186.91
HCl(*aq*)	-167.16	-131.23	56.5
Copper			
Cu(*s*)	0	0	33.15
Cu^+(*aq*)	71.67	49.98	40.6
Cu^{2+}(*aq*)	64.77	65.49	-99.6
Cu_2O(*s*)	-168.6	-146.0	93.14
CuO(*s*)	-157.3	-129.7	42.63
$CuSO_4$(*s*)	-771.36	-661.8	109

Table A8-Inorganic ***Thermodynamic data at 25°C for assorted inorganic substances (continued).***

Substance	Enthalpy of formation ΔH_f^0, kJ/mol	Free energy of formation ΔG_f^0, kJ/mol	Entropy S^0, J/(K·mol)
Fluorine			
$F_2(g)$	0	0	202.78
$F^-(aq)$	-332.63	-278.79	-13.8
HF(g)	-271.1	-273.2	173.78
HF(aq)	-332.36	-278.79	-13.8
Hydrogen			
$H_2(g)$	0	0	130.68
H(g)	217.97	203.25	114.71
$H^+(aq)$	0	0	0
$H_2O(l)$	-285.83	-237.13	69.91
$H_2O(g)$	-241.82	-228.57	188.83
$H_2O_2(l)$	-187.78	-120.35	109.6
$H_2O_2(aq)$	-191.17	-134.03	143.9
$D_2(g)$	0	0	144.96
$D_2O(l)$	-294.60	-243.44	75.94
$D_2O(g)$	-249.20	-234.54	198.34
Iodine			
$I_2(s)$	0	0	116.14
$I_2(g)$	62.44	19.33	260.69
$I^-(aq)$	-55.19	-51.57	111.3
HI(g)	26.48	1.70	206.59
Iron			
Fe(s)	0	0	27.28
$Fe^{2+}(aq)$	-89.1	-78.90	-137.7
$Fe^{3+}(aq)$	-48.5	-4.7	-315.9
Fe_3O_4(s, magnetite)	-1118.4	-1015.4	146.4
Fe_2O_3(s, hematite)	-824.2	-742.2	87.40
FeS(s, *a*)	-100.0	-100.4	60.29
FeS(aq)	---	6.9	---
$FeS_2(s)$	-178.2	-166.9	52.93
Lead			
Pb(s)	0	0	64.81
$Pb^{2+}(aq)$	-1.7	-24.43	10.5
$PbO_2(s)$	-277.4	-217.33	68.6
$PbSO_4(s)$	-919.94	-813.14	148.57
$PbBr_2(s)$	-278.7	-261.92	161.5
$PbBr_2(aq)$	-244.8	-232.34	175.3
Magnesium			
Mg(s)	0	0	32.68

© Edvantage Interactive 2019

Table A8-Inorganic ***Thermodynamic data at 25°C for assorted inorganicsubstances (continued).***

Substance	Enthalpy of formation ΔH_f^0, kJ/mol	Free energy of formation ΔG_f^0, kJ/mol	Entropy S^0, J/(K·mol)
$Mg(g)$	147.70	113.10	148.65
$Mg^{2+}(aq)$	-466.85	-454.8	-138.1
$MgO(s)$	-601.70	-569.43	26.94
$MgCO_3(s)$	-1095.8	-1012.1	65.7
$MgBr_2(s)$	-524.3	-503.8	117.2
Mercury			
$Hg(l)$	0	0	76.02
$Hg(g)$	61.32	31.82	174.96
$HgO(s)$	-90.83	-58.54	70.29
$Hg_2Cl_2(s)$	-265.22	-210.75	192.5
Nitrogen			
$N_2(g)$	0	0	191.61
$NO(g)$	90.25	86.55	210.76
$N_2O(g)$	82.05	104.20	219.85
$NO_2(g)$	33.18	51.31	240.06
$N_2O_4(g)$	9.16	97.89	304.29
$HNO_3(l)$	-174.10	-80.71	155.60
$HNO_3(aq)$	-207.36	-111.22	146.4
$NO_3^-(aq)$	-205.0	-108.74	146.4
$NH_3(g)$	-46.11	-16.45	192.45
$NH_3(aq)$	-80.29	-26.50	111.3
$NH_4^+(aq)$	-132.51	-79.31	113.4
$NH_2OH(s)$	-114.2	---	---
$HN_3(g)$	294.1	328.1	238.97
$N_2H_4(l)$	50.63	149.34	121.21
$NH_4NO_3(s)$	-365.56	-183.87	151.08
$NH_4Cl(s)$	-314.43	-202.87	94.6
$NH_4ClO_4(s)$	-295.31	-88.75	186.2
Oxygen			
$O_2(g)$	0	0	205.14
$O_3(g)$	142.7	163.2	238.93
$OH^-(aq)$	-229.99	-157.24	-10.75
Phosphorus			
P(s, white)	0	0	41.09
$P_4(g)$	58.91	24.44	279.98
$PH_3(g)$	5.4	13.4	210.23
$P_4O_{10}(s)$	-2984.0	-2697.0	228.86
$H_3PO_3(aq)$	-964.0	---	---
$H_3PO_4(l)$	-1266.9	−1111.69	---

Table A8-Inorganic *Thermodynamic data at 25°C for assorted inorganic substances (continued).*

Substance	Enthalpy of formation ΔH_f^0, kJ/mol	Free energy of formation ΔG_f^0, kJ/mol	Entropy S^0, J/(K·mol)
H_3PO_4(*aq*)	-277.4	-1018.7	---
PCl_3(*l*)	-319.7	-272.3	217.18
PCl_3(*g*)	-287.0	-267.8	311.78
PCl_5(*g*)	-374.9	-305.0	364.6
PCl_5(*s*)	-443.5	---	---
Potassium			
K(*s*)	0	0	64.18
K(*g*)	89.24	60.59	160.34
K^+(*aq*)	-252.38	-283.27	102.5
KOH(*s*)	-424.76	-379.08	78.9
KOH(*aq*)	-482.37	-440.50	91.6
KF(*s*)	-567.27	-537.75	66.57
KCl(*s*)	-436.75	-409.14	82.59
KBr(*s*)	-393.80	-380.66	95.90
KI(*s*)	-327.90	-324.89	106.32
$KClO_3$(*s*)	-397.73	-296.25	143.1
$KClO_4$(*s*)	-432.75	-303.09	151.0
K_2S(*s*)	-380.7	-364.0	105
K_2S(*aq*)	-471.5	-480.7	190.4
Silicon			
Si(*s*)	0	0	18.83
SiO_2(*s*,α)	-910.94	-856.64	41.84
Silver			
Ag(*s*)	0	0	42.55
Ag^+(*aq*)	105.58	77.11	72.68
Ag_2O(*s*)	-31.05	-11.20	121.3
AgBr(*s*)	-100.37	-96.90	107.1
AgBr(*aq*)	-15.98	-26.86	155.2
AgCl(*s*)	-127.7	-109.79	96.2
AgCl(*aq*)	-61.58	-54.12	129.3
AgI(*s*)	-61.84	-66.19	115.5
AgI(*aq*)	50.38	25.52	184.1
$AgNO_3$(*s*)	-124.39	-33.41	140.92
Sodium			
Na(*s*)	0	0	51.21
Na(*g*)	107.32	76.76	153.71
Na^+(*aq*)	-240.12	-261.91	59.0
NaOH(*s*)	-425.61	-379.49	64.46
NaOH(*aq*)	-470.11	-419.15	48.1

© Edvantage Interactive 2019

Table A8-Inorganic *Thermodynamic data at 25°C for assorted inorganic substances (continued).*

Substance	Enthalpy of formation ΔH_f^0, kJ/mol	Free energy of formation ΔG_f^0, kJ/mol	Entropy S^0, J/(K·mol)
$NaCl(s)$	-411.15	-384.12	72.13
$NaBr(s)$	-361.06	-348.98	86.82
$NaI(s)$	-287.78	-286.06	98.53
Sulfur			
S(*s, rhombic*)	0	0	31.80
S(*s, monoclinic*)	0.33	0.1	32.6
$S^{2-}(aq)$	33.1	85.8	-14.6
$SO_2(g)$	-296.83	-300.19	248.22
$SO_3(g)$	-395.72	-371.06	256.76
$H_2SO_4(l)$	-813.99	-690.00	156.90
$H_2SO_4(aq)$	-909.27	-744.53	20.1
$SO_4^{2-}(aq)$	-909.27	-744.53	20.1
$H_2S(g)$	-20.63	-33.56	205.79
$H_2S(aq)$	-39.7	-27.83	121
$SF_6(g)$	-1209	-1105.3	291.82
Tin			
Sn(*s, white*)	0	0	51.55
Sn(*s, gray*)	-2.09	0.13	44.14
$SnO(s)$	-285.8	-256.9	56.5
$SnO_2(s)$	-580.7	-519.6	52.3
Zinc			
$Zn(s)$	0	0	41.63
$Zn^{2+}(aq)$	-153.89	-147.06	-112.1
$ZnO(s)$	-348.28	-318.30	43.64

Table A8-Organic *Thermodynamic data at 25°C for assorted organic substances.*

Substance	Enthalpy of combustion ΔH_c^0, kJ/mol	Enthalpy of formation ΔH_f^0, kJ/mol	Free energy of formation ΔG_f^0, kJ/mol	Entropy S^0, J/(K·mol)
Hydrocarbons				
CH_4(*g*), *methane*	-890	-74.81	-50.72	186.26
C_2H_2(*g*), *acethylene*	-1300	226.73	209.20	200.94
C_2H_4(*g*), *ethylene*	-1411	52.26	68.15	219.56
C_2H_6(*g*), *ethane*	-1560	-84.68	-32.82	229.60
C_3H_6(*g*), *propylene*	-2058	20.42	62.78	266.6
C_3H_6(*g*), *cyclopropane*	-2091	53.30	104.45	237.4
C_3H_8(*g*), *propane*	-2220	-103.85	-23.49	270.2
C_4H_{10}(*g*), *butane*	-2878	-126.15	-17.03	310.1
C_5H_{12}(*g*), *pentane*	-3537	-146.44	-8.20	349
C_6H_6(*l*), *benzene*	-3268	49.0	124.3	173.3
C_6H_6(*g*)	-3302	---	---	---
C_7H_8(*l*), *toluene*	-3910	12.0	113.8	221.0
C_7H_8(*g*)	-3953	---	---	---
C_6H_{12}(*l*), *cyclohexane*	-3920	-156.4	26.7	204.4
C_6H_{12}(*g*)	-3953	---	---	---
C_8H_{18}(*l*), *octane*	-5471	-249.9	6.4	358
Alcohols, phenols				
CH_3OH(*l*), *methanol*	-726	-238.86	-166.27	126.8
CH_3OH(*g*)	-764	-200.66	-161.96	239.81
C_2H_5OH(*l*), *ethanol*	-1368	-277.69	-174.78	160.7
C_2H_5OH(*g*)	-1409	-235.10	-168.49	282.70
C_6H_5OH(*s*), *phenol*	-3054	-164.6	-50.42	144.0

© Edvantage Interactive 2019

Table A8-Organic Thermodynamic data at 25 °C for assorted organic substances (continued).

Substance	Enthalpy of combustion ΔH_c^0, kJ/mol	Enthalpy of formation ΔH_f^0, kJ/mol	Free energy of formation ΔG_f^0, kJ/mol	Entropy S^0, J/(K·mol)
Aldehydes, ketones				
HCHO (g), formaldehyde	-571	-108.57	-102.53	218.77
CH_3CHO (l), acetaldehyde	-1166	-192.30	-128.12	160.2
CH_3CHO (g)	-1192	-166.19	-128.86	250.3
CH_3COCH_3 (l), acetone	-1790	-248.1	-155.4	200
Carboxylic acids				
HCOOH (l), formic acid	-255	-424.72	-361.35	128.95
CH_3COOH (l), acetic acid	-875	-484.5	-389.9	159.8
CH_3COOH (aq)	---	-485.76	-396.46	86.6
$(COOH)_2$ (s), oxalic acid	-254	-827.2	-697.9	120
C_6H_5COOH (s), benzoic acid	-3227	-385.1	-245.3	167.6
Sugars				
$C_6H_{12}O_6$ (s), glucose	-2808	-1268	-910	212
$C_6H_{12}O_6$ (aq)	---	---	-917	---
$C_6H_{12}O_6$ (s), fructose	-2810	-1266	---	---
$C_{12}H_{22}O_{11}$ (s), sucrose	-5645	-2222	-1545	360
Nitrogen compounds				
$CO(NH_2)_2$ (s), urea	-632	-333.51	-197.33	104.60
$C_6H_5NH_2$ (l), aniline	-3395	31.6	149.1	191.3
NH_2CH_2COOH (s), glycine	-969	-532.9	-373.4	103.51
[illegible]	[illegible]	[illegible]	[illegible]	[illegible]

A

absorbance (1.1) the amount of light that does not pass through a solution

acid ionization constant (4.2) a quantitative measure of the strength of an acid in solution

acidic buffer (5.2) solution that normally consists of a weak acid and its conjugate weak base in appreciable and approximately equal concentrations; it buffers a solution in the acidic region of the pH scale

acidic primary standard (5.3) a substance of known molar mass available in high purity, which is air-stable and non-hygroscopic, that can be used to prepare an acidic solution of known concentration

activated complex (1.4) an intermediate state that is formed during the conversion of reactants into products

activation energy (1.3) the minimum kinetic energy that the reacting species must have in order to react

amphiprotic (4.1) describes a substance that can act as an acid or a base; water is amphiprotic

anion (3.1) any atom or group of atoms with a negative charge

anode (7.4) the electrode where oxidation occurs

autoionization (4.3) in a Brønsted-Lowry equilibrium, process when one water molecule donates a proton to another water molecule

B

base ionization constant (4.2) a measure of the relative strength of a base

basic buffer (5.2) solution that has appreciable quantities of both a weak base and its conjugate acid in approximately equal amounts; it buffers a solution in the basic region of the pH scale

basic primary standard (5.3) a substance of known molar mass available in high purity, which is air-stable and non-hygroscopic, that can be used to prepare a basic solution of known concentration

battery (7.4) a group of electrochemical cells connected together

bimolecular (1.5) describes a reaction involving two molecules

bond energy (1.4) the chemical potential energy able to break a bond

Brønsted-Lowry acid (4.1) a substance or species that donates a hydrogen ion, H+, (a proton)

Brønsted-Lowry base (4.1) a substance or species that accepts a hydrogen ion, H+, (a proton)

buffer (5.2) a solution in which the pH remains relatively constant when small amounts of an acid or base are added

buffer capacity (5.2) the amount of acid or base a buffer can neutralize before its pH changes significantly

C

catalyst (1.2) a substance that increases the rates of chemical reactions without being used up

catalytic converter (1.5) a device that activates several oxidation and/or reduction reactions; usually found in a motor vehicle where a catalyst converts pollutant gases into less-harmful ones

cathode (7.4) the electrode where reduction occurs

cathodic protection (7.4) a way to prevent rusting. In one form of cathodic protection, a metal is protected from corrosion by sacrificing a metal that is a stronger reducing agent in place of the metal that must remain intact.

cation (3.1) an ion with fewer electrons than protons, giving it a positive charge

chemical equilibrium (2.1) condition in which the forward rate of a chemical reaction equals its reverse rate

chemical kinetics (1.1) the investigation of the rate at which the reactions occur and the factors that affect them

closed system (2.1) a system in which no chemicals are entering or leaving the defined boundaries of the system

collision theory (1.3) theory stating that reaction rates depend on the number of collisions per unit of time, and the fraction of these collisions that succeed in producing products

complete ionic equation (3.2) an equation for a reaction that represents soluble ionic compounds as separated ions

© Edvantage Interactive 2019

comproportionation (7.2) a chemical change in which multiple reactants form only one product

conjugate acid-base pair (4.1) two substances that differ by one H^+ ion

corrosion (7.4) a process in which a solid is eaten away and changed by chemical action; for example, the oxidation of iron in the presence of water by an electrolytic process

D

derived unit (1.1) a unit that consists of two or more other units

disproportionation (7.2) a redox reaction in which the same species is both oxidized and reduced

dissociation (3.1) the process of separating the positive and negative ions in solution

E

electrochemical cell (7.4) a portable source of electricity, in which the electricity is produced by a spontaneous redox reaction within the cell

electrochemistry 7.1) the study of the interchange of chemical and electrical energy

electrolysis (7.5) conduction of electricity through a molten electrolyte or an electrolyte solution

electrolyte (7.5) a solution that conducts electricity

electrolytic cell (7.5) an apparatus in which electrolysis occurs

electroplating (7.5) a form of electrowinning in which a conductive material, usually a metal, is coated with a thin layer of a different metal

electrorefining (7.5) the electrolytic purification of a metal

electrowinning (7.5) a metallurgical term for the electrolytic recovery of a metal from a solution containing its ions

elementary process (1.5) an individual step in a reaction

endothermic (1.4) a process or reaction in which the system absorbs energy from the surroundings in the form of heat

endpoint (5.3) the point in a titration at which neutralization is achieved

enthalpy (1.4) the heat content of a system at constant pressure

entropy (2.4) a substance's or system's state of disorganization or randomness

enzyme (1.5) catalyst in a biological system

equilibrium constant (2.5) the numerical value provided by the equilibrium expression; a ratio of concentrations of the products divided by the concentrations of the reactants, with all the coefficients in the chemical equation and the terms multiplied

equilibrium expression (2.5) the formula for the equilibrium constant in terms of the equilibrium concentrations of reactants and products

equilibrium position (2.2) the relative concentrations of reactants and products at equilibrium; usually expressed as percent yield

equilibrium system (2.2) a reacting system that is at or approaching equilibrium

equivalence point (5.3) the point in a titration at which the number of moles of the unknown solution is stoichiometrically equal to the number of moles of the standard solution; the reaction is complete

exothermic (1.4) a process or reaction that releases energy, usually in the form of heat

F

formula equation (3.2) a chemical equation consisting of the chemical formulas of the compounds and their states

fuel cell (7.4) a cell that has its reactants continuously resupplied from an external source as they are consumed

G

galvanizing (7.4) the process of applying a protective zinc coating to steel or iron to prevent rusting

H

half-reaction (7.2) an equation representing either oxidation or reduction, including the number of electrons lost or gained

Henderson-Hasselbalch equation (5.2) equation that describes the derivation of pH as a measure of acidity in biological and chemical systems

heterogeneous catalyst (1.5) the form of catalysis in which the phase of the catalyst differs from that of the reactants

heterogeneous reaction (1.2) when reactants are present in different states in a reacting system

homogeneous catalyst (1.5) catalyst that exists in the same phase as the rest of the reaction system

© Edvantage Interactive 2019

hydrolysis (5.1) the reaction of an ion with water to produce either the conjugate base of the ion and hydronium ions or the conjugate acid of the ion and hydroxide ions

hydronium ion (4.1) the positive ion H_3O^+ formed when a water molecule gains a hydrogen ion

I

ICE table (2.6) a simple table to help solve equilibrium problems. ICE is an acronym for **I**nitial concentration, **C**hange in concentration, and **E**quilibrium concentration.

ICF table (5.4) the "I" and the "C" represent the "initial" and "change" in reagent concentrations, but because titration reactions go to completion, the "E" from the ICE table has been replaced with an "F" representing the "**F**inal" concentrations present when the reaction is complete

inhibitor (1.2) substance that reduces the rate of a chemical reaction by combining with a reactant to stop it from reacting in its usual way

intermediate (1.5) a species that is formed in one step and consumed in a subsequent step and so does not appear in the overall reaction

ion product constant (K_w) (4.3) equilibrium constant in an autoionization equilibrium; water ionization constant

L

Le Châtelier's principle (2.2) principle stating that an equilibrium system subjected to a stress will shift to partially alleviate the stress and restore equilibrium

M

macroscopic (2.1) properties that are large enough to be measured or observed with the unaided eye

metalloenzyme (1.5) a protein that contains a metal ion cofactor

metathesis reaction (7.1) reaction that does not involve electron transfer

microstates (2.4) systems with lower entropy that have fewer variations or fewer degrees of freedom

mole ratio (1.1) the ratio between the amounts in moles of any two compounds involved in a chemical reaction. Mole ratios are used as conversion factors between products and reactants in many chemistry problems.

molecularity (1.5) in an elementary process, the number of reactant species that must collide to produce the reaction indicated by that step

N

net ionic equation (3.2) an equation in which only the ions that take part in the reaction appear

neutral (4.4) describes an aqueous solution with a pH of 7.0

O

overpotential (7.5) increase in potential difference beyond the calculated value for the cell potential

oxidation (7.1) the interaction between oxygen molecules and all the different substances they may contact; a process that involves complete or partial loss of electrons or a gain of oxygen

oxidation number (7.1) a positive or negative number assigned to a combined atom according to a set of arbitrary rules; does not represent the actual charges on atoms, but is a way to describe some properties of atoms in a compound

oxidation potential (7.3) a measure of the strength of a reducing agent because a reducing agent becomes oxidized when it gives up electrons

oxidation-reduction reaction (7.1) reaction that involves electron transfer

oxidation state (7.1) [see oxidation number]

oxidizing agent (7.1) a substance that accepts electrons in a reaction and therefore oxidizes the other reactant

P

partial pressure (1.2, 2.3) the portion of the total pressure contributed by one gas in a mixture of gases

percent yield (2.2) experimental (actual) yield of a reaction, expressed as a percentage of the predicted (theoretical) yield

pOH (4.4) hydroxide concentration in aqueous solution

potential energy diagram (1.4) a graphical representation of the energy changes that take place during a chemical or physical change

primary standard (5.3) a stable, non-deliquescent, soluble compound available in a highly pure form

R

rate constant (1.3) proportionality constant in the rate law of a chemical reaction

rate law (1.3) an expression that links the reaction rate with concentrations or pressures of reactants and constant parameters

© Edvantage Interactive 2019

rate-determining step (1.5) a step that limits the overall reaction rate
reactant orders (1.3) the values of *x* and *y* in a rate law
reaction mechanism (1.5) a series of steps that may be added together to give an overall chemical reaction
reaction quotient (Q) (2.5) the numerical value derived when any set of reactant and product concentrations are calculated in an equilibrium expression; trial K_{eq}
redox reaction (7.1) [see oxidation-reduction reaction]
reducing a7ent (7.1) a substance in a redox reaction that donates electrons; in the reaction, the reducing agent is oxidized
reduction (7.1) a decrease in the oxidation number
reduction potential (E°) (7.3) a measure of the tendency of a given half-reaction to occur as a reduction in an electrochemical cell
rusting (7.4) the corrosion of iron

S

saturated (3.1) the point at which a solution of a substance can dissolve no more of that substance and additional amounts of it will appear as a separate phase
shift left (2.2) when a system responds by changing some products into reactants, the response is referred to as a "shift left"
shift right (2.2) when a system responds by changing some reactants into products, the response is referred to as a "shift right"
solubility (3.1) the amount of a substance that dissolves in a given quantity of solvent at specified conditions of temperature and pressure to produce a saturated solution
solubility product constant (3.3) the equilibrium constant for the dissolving of an ionic solid
spectator ions (3.2) ions that are the same on both sides of the equation; ions that are not directly involved in the reaction
spontaneous process (2.4) a reaction or process that happens on its own with no outside intervention
standard or standardized solution (5.3) a solution of known concentration used when carrying out a titration
steady state (2.1) a state in which a system's properties are constant but the system is open
stoichiometric point (5.3) [see equivalence point]
stress (2.2) to an equilibrium system, any action that has a different effect on the forward reaction rate than it does on the reverse reaction rate, thus disrupting the equilibrium
strong acid (4.2) an acid that ionizes nearly 100% in aqueous solution
strong base (4.2) a based that dissociates nearly 100% in aqueous solution

T

termolecular (1.5) describes a reaction involving three molecules
titration curve (5.4) a plot of the pH of the solution being analyzed versus the volume of titrant added
transition point (5.3) [see endpoint]
transmittance (1.1) the amount of light detected by a photocell that passes through the solution as a percentage
trial ion product (TIP) (4.4) calculation of ion concentrations in a solution not in equilibrium; used to determine if the K_{sp} is exceeded; also called a trial K_{sp} or reaction quotient (Q)

U

unimolecular (1.5) describes a reaction involving one molecule

W

water ionization constant (K_w) (4.3) [see ion product constant]
weak acid (4.2) an acid that only partially ionizes in aqueous solution
weak base (4.2) a base that does not dissociate completely in aqueous solution

© Edvantage Interactive 2019

Throughout the test the following symbols have the definitions specified unless otherwise noted.

L, mL	=	liter(s), milliliter(s)	mm Hg	=	millimeters of mercury
g	=	gram(s)	J, k	=	joule(s), kilojoule(s)
nm	=	nanometer(s)	V	=	volt(s)
atm	=	atmosphere(s	mol	=	mole(s)

ATOMIC STRUCTURE

$E = h\nu$

$c = \lambda\nu$

E = energy

ν = frequency

λ = wavelength

Planck's constant, $h = 6.626 \times 10^{-34}$ J s

Speed of light, $c = 2.998 \times 10^{8}$ m s^{-1}

Avogadro's number $= 6.022 \times 10^{23}$ mol^{-1}

Electron charge, $e = -1.602 \times 10^{-19}$ coulomb

EQUILIBRIUM

$K_c = \dfrac{[C]^c[D]^d}{[A]^a[B]^b}$, where $a\,A + b\,B \rightleftarrows c\,C + d\,D$

$K_p = \dfrac{(P_C)^c(P_D)^d}{(P_A)^a(P_B)^b}$

$K_a = \dfrac{[H^+][A^-]}{[HA]}$

$K_b = \dfrac{[OH^-][HB^+]}{[B]}$

$K_w = [H^+][OH^-] = 1.0 \times 10^{-14}$ at 25°C

$= K_a \times K_b$

$pH = -\log[H^+],\ pOH = -\log[OH^-]$

$14 = pH + pOH$

$pH = pK_a + \log\dfrac{[A^-]}{[HA]}$

$pK_a = -\log K_a,\ pK_b = -\log K_b$

Equilibrium Constants

K_c (molar concentrations)

K_p (gas pressures

K_a (weak acid

K_b (weak base)

K_w (water)

KINETICS

$\ln[A]_t - \ln[A]_0 = -kt$

$\dfrac{1}{[A]_t} - \dfrac{1}{[A]_0} = kt$

$t_{1/2} = \dfrac{0.693}{k}$

k = rate constan

t = time

$t_{1/2}$ = half-lif

GASES, LIQUIDS, AND SOLUTIONS

$$PV = nRT$$

$$P_A = P_{\text{total}} \times X_A, \text{ where } X_A = \frac{\text{moles A}}{\text{total moles}}$$

$$P_{total} = P_A + P_B + P_C + \ldots$$

$$n = \frac{m}{\boldsymbol{M}}$$

$$K = {}^\circ C + 273$$

$$D = \frac{m}{V}$$

$$KE \text{ per molecule} = \frac{1}{2} mv^2$$

Molarity, M = moles of solute per liter of solution

$$A = abc$$

P = pressure
V = volume
T = temperature
n = number of moles
m = mass
$\boldsymbol{M}$ = molar mass
D = density
KE = kinetic energy
v = velocity
A = absorbance
a = molar absorptivity
b = path length
c = concentration

Gas constant, $R = 8.314 \text{ J mol}^{-1} \text{ K}^{-1}$
$= 0.08206 \text{ L atm mol}^{-1} \text{ K}^{-1}$
$= 62.36 \text{ L torr mol}^{-1} \text{ K}^{-1}$
1 atm = 760 mm Hg
= 760 torr
STP = 0.00 °C and 1.000 atm

THERMOCHEMISTRY/ ELECTROCHEMISTRY

$$q = mc\Delta T$$

$$\Delta S^\circ = \sum S^\circ \text{ products} - \sum S^\circ \text{ reactants}$$

$$\Delta H^\circ = \sum \Delta H_f^\circ \text{ products} - \sum \Delta H_f^\circ \text{ reactants}$$

$$\Delta G^\circ = \sum \Delta G_f^\circ \text{ products} - \sum \Delta G_f^\circ \text{ reactants}$$

$$\Delta G^\circ = \Delta H^\circ - T\Delta S^\circ$$
$$= -RT \ln K$$
$$= -nFE^\circ$$

$$I = \frac{q}{t}$$

q = heat
m = mass
c = specific heat capacity
T = temperature
S° = standard entropy
H° = standard enthalpy
G° = standard free energy
n = number of moles
E° = standard reduction potential
I = current (amperes)
q = charge (coulombs)
t = time (seconds)

Faraday's constant, F = 96,485 coulombs per mole of electrons

$$1 \text{ volt} = \frac{1 \text{ joule}}{1 \text{ coulomb}}$$

PERIODIC TABLE OF THE ELEMENTS

1 **H** 1.008																	2 **He** 4.00
3 **Li** 6.94	4 **Be** 9.01											5 **B** 10.81	6 **C** 12.01	7 **N** 14.01	8 **O** 16.00	9 **F** 19.00	10 **Ne** 20.18
11 **Na** 22.99	12 **Mg** 24.30											13 **Al** 26.98	14 **Si** 28.09	15 **P** 30.97	16 **S** 32.06	17 **Cl** 35.45	18 **Ar** 39.95
19 **K** 39.10	20 **Ca** 40.08	21 **Sc** 44.96	22 **Ti** 47.90	23 **V** 50.94	24 **Cr** 52.00	25 **Mn** 54.94	26 **Fe** 55.85	27 **Co** 58.93	28 **Ni** 58.69	29 **Cu** 63.55	30 **Zn** 65.39	31 **Ga** 69.72	32 **Ge** 72.59	33 **As** 74.92	34 **Se** 78.96	35 **Br** 79.90	36 **Kr** 83.80
37 **Rb** 85.47	38 **Sr** 87.62	39 **Y** 88.91	40 **Zr** 91.22	41 **Nb** 92.91	42 **Mo** 95.94	43 **Tc** (98)	44 **Ru** 101.1	45 **Rh** 102.91	46 **Pd** 106.42	47 **Ag** 107.87	48 **Cd** 112.41	49 **In** 114.82	50 **Sn** 118.71	51 **Sb** 121.75	52 **Te** 127.60	53 **I** 126.91	54 **Xe** 131.29
55 **Cs** 132.91	56 **Ba** 137.33	57 ***La** 138.91	72 **Hf** 178.49	73 **Ta** 180.95	74 **W** 183.85	75 **Re** 186.21	76 **Os** 190.2	77 **Ir** 192.2	78 **Pt** 195.08	79 **Au** 196.97	80 **Hg** 200.59	81 **Tl** 204.38	82 **Pb** 207.2	83 **Bi** 208.98	84 **Po** (209)	85 **At** (210)	86 **Rn** (222)
87 **Fr** (223)	88 **Ra** 226.02	89 **†Ac** 227.03	104 **Rf** (261)	105 **Db** (262)	106 **Sg** (266)	107 **Bh** (264)	108 **Hs** (277)	109 **Mt** (268)	110 **Ds** (271)	111 **Rg** (272)							

*Lanthanide Series	58 **Ce** 140.12	59 **Pr** 140.91	60 **Nd** 144.24	61 **Pm** (145)	62 **Sm** 150.4	63 **Eu** 151.97	64 **Gd** 157.25	65 **Tb** 158.93	66 **Dy** 162.50	67 **Ho** 164.93	68 **Er** 167.26	69 **Tm** 168.93	70 **Yb** 173.04	71 **Lu** 174.97
†Actinide Series	90 **Th** 232.04	91 **Pa** 231.04	92 **U** 238.03	93 **Np** (237)	94 **Pu** (244)	95 **Am** (243)	96 **Cm** (247)	97 **Bk** (247)	98 **Cf** (251)	99 **Es** (252)	100 **Fm** (257)	101 **Md** (258)	102 **No** (259)	103 **Lr** (262)

ATOMIC STRUCTURE

$\Delta E = h\nu$ $\quad c = \lambda\nu$

$\lambda = \dfrac{h}{m\upsilon}$ $\quad p = m\upsilon$

$$E = -\frac{2.178 \times 10^{-18}}{n^2} \text{ joule}$$

E = energy
ν = frequency
λ= wavelength
p = momentum
υ = velocity
n = principal quantum number
m = mass

Speed of light, $c = 3.00 \times 10^8 \text{ ms}^{-1}$

Planck's constant, $h = 6.63 \times 10^{-34}$ Js

Boltzmann's constant, $k = 1.38 \times 10^{-23} \text{ JK}^{-1}$

Avagadro's number = 6.022×10^{23} molecules mol^{-1}

Electron charge, $e = -1.602 \times 10^{-19}$ coulomb

1 electron volt/atom = 96.5 kJmol^{-1}

EQUILIBRIUM

$$K_a = \frac{[H^+][A^-]}{[HA]}$$

$$K_b = \frac{[OH^-][HB^+]}{[B]}$$

$K_w = [OH^-][H^+] = 10^{-14}$ @ 25°C
$= K_a \times K_b$

$pH = -\log[H^+]$, $pOH = -\log[OH^-]$
$14 = pH + pOH$

$$pH = pK_a + \log\frac{[A^-]}{[HA]}$$

$$pOH = pK_b + \log\frac{[HB^+]}{[B]}$$

$pK_a = -\log K_a$, $pK_b = -\log K_b$

$K_p = K_c(RT)^{\Delta n}$
where Δn = moles of product gas - moles reactant gas

<u>Equilibrium constants</u>

K_a (weak acid)
K_b (weak base)
K_w (water)
K_p (gas pressure)
K_c (molar concentration)
S^0 = standard entropy
H^0 = standard enthalpy
G^0 = standard free energy
E^0 = standard reduction potential
T = temperature
n = moles
m = mass
q = heat
c = specific heat capacity
C_p = molar heat capacity at constant pressure
E_a = activation energy
k = rate constant
A = frequency factor

Faraday's constant, $\Im$ = 96,500 coulombs per mole of electrons

Gas Constant, R = 8.31 $\text{Jmol}^{-1}\text{K}^{-1}$
= 0.0821 L atm $\text{mol}^{-1}\text{K}^{-1}$
= 8.31 volt coulomb $\text{mol}^{-1}\text{K}^{-1}$

THERMOCHEMISTRY/KINETICS

$\Delta S^0 = \sum S^0 \text{ products} - \sum S^0 \text{ reactants}$

$\Delta H^0 = \sum H^0_f \text{ products} - \sum H^0_f \text{ reactants}$

$\Delta G^0 = \sum G^0_f \text{ products} - \sum G^0_f \text{ reactants}$

$\Delta G^0 = \Delta H^0 - T\Delta S^0$
$= -RT \ln K = -2.303\, RT \log K$
$= -n\, \Im\, E^0$

$\Delta G = \Delta G^0 + RT \ln Q = \Delta G^0 + 2.303\, RT \log Q$

$q = mc\Delta T$

$$C_p = \frac{\Delta H}{\Delta T}$$

$\ln[A]_t - \ln[A]_0 = -kt$

$$\frac{1}{[A]_t} - \frac{1}{[A]_0} = kt$$

$$\ln k = \frac{-E_a}{R}\left(\frac{1}{T}\right) + \ln A$$

GASES, LIQUIDS, AND SOLUTIONS

$PV = nRT$

$$\left(P + \frac{n^2 a}{V^2}\right)(V - nb) = nRT$$

$P_A = P_{total} \times X_A$, where $X_A = \frac{\text{moles of A}}{\text{total moles}}$

$P_{total} = P_A + P_B + P_c + \ldots$

$n = \frac{m}{M}$

$K = °C + 273$

$$\frac{P_1 V_1}{T_1} = \frac{P_2 V_2}{T_2}$$

$D = \frac{m}{V}$

$$u_{rms} = \sqrt{\frac{3kT}{m}} = \sqrt{\frac{3RT}{M}}$$

KE per molecule $= \frac{1}{2} m\upsilon^2$

KE per mole $= \frac{3}{2}RT$

$$\frac{r_1}{r_2} = \sqrt{\frac{M_2}{M_1}}$$

molarity, M = moles solute per liter solution
molality = moles solute per kilogram solvent

$\Delta T_f = i\, K_f \times$ molality
$\Delta T_b = i\, K_b \times$ molality
$\Pi = MRT$
$A = abc$

P = pressure
V = volume
T = Temperature
n = number of moles
D = density
m = mass
υ= velocity

υ_{rms} = root mean square velocity
KE = kinetic energy
r = rate of effusion
M = molar mass
π= osmotic pressure
i= van't Hoff factor
K_f = molal freezing point depression constant
K_b = molal boiling point elevation constant
A = Absorbance
a = molar absorptivity
b = path length
c = concentration
Q = reaction quotient
I = current (amperes)
q = charge (coulombs)
t = time (seconds)
E^0 = standard reduction potential
K = equilibrium constant

Gas Constant, R $= 8.31\ \text{J mol}^{-1}\text{K}^{-1}$
$= 0.0821\ \text{L atm mol}^{-1}\text{K}^{-1}$
$= 8.31\ \text{volt coulomb mol}^{-1}\text{K}^{-1}$

Boltzmann's constant, $k = 1.38 \times 10^{-23}\ \text{JK}^{-1}$

K_f for $H_2O = 1.86\ \text{K kg mol}^{-1}$
K_b for $H_2O = 0.512\ \text{K kg mol}^{-1}$
1 atm = 760 mm Hg
= 760 torr
STP = 0.000°C and 1.000 atm
Faraday's constant, $\mathfrak{I}$ = 96500 coulombs per mol of electrons

OXIDATION REDUCTION; ELECTROCHEMISTRY

$$Q = \frac{[C]^c[D]^d}{[A]^a[B]^b}$$, where aA + bB → cC + dD

$I = \frac{q}{t}$

$$E_{cell} = E^0_{cell} - \frac{RT}{n\mathfrak{I}}\ln Q = E^0_{cell} - \frac{0.0592}{n}\log Q \quad @\ 25°C$$

$$\log K = \frac{nE^0}{0.0592}$$

Chapter 1 Answer Key

Page 3, Quick Check

1. Rate of decomposition of SO_2Cl_2.
2. The slope becomes less and less steep.
3. The rate decreases as the reaction proceeds.
4. -0.00023 mol/L/s (or +)
5. Rate is greater at 300 s than at 500 s.
6. Find the slope of a tangent drawn to the curve at that time.
7. 500 s: 09.2×10^{-5} M/s < 300 s: = 2.1×10^{-4} M/s

Page 6, Practice Problems

1. a) mass of Cu or mass of Ag, $[Cu(NO_3)_2]$ or $[AgNO_3]$, blue colour of $Cu(NO_3)_2$
b) pressure of entire closed system will increase or green colour of chlorine gas
c) volume or mass of carbon dioxide gas or increased partial pressure of CO_2 (in a closed system).
d) mass of $BaSO_4$ ppt formed, [either reactant], conductivity as ions are consumed
2. Volume change is generally associated with the formation of a gas.
3. Concentration change is associated with the formation or use of an aqueous species or a gas, not a solid or a liquid (except in the rare case of solid or liquid mixtures).

Page 8, Practice Problems

1. a) 0.0292 g/min
b) Rate is greatest at the beginning
c) Rate = 0 g/min in the last increment
d) This is because the HCl is all gone (limiting). Excess Zn left.
2. 2.55 x 10-4 mol/L/s

Page 9, Practice Problems

1. 5.1 x 1025 molecules/L
2. 4.02 min
3. 52.5 s

Page 11, 1.1 Review Questions

1. - The distance-time graph involves a vehicle changing position, while the rest of the data in this section involves a property of a chemical changing during a chemical reaction.
- The vehicle accelerates and then decelerates, while most reactions start at a maximum rate and decrease rate the entire time.
- The vehicle can stop moving entirely and then begin again. Once a reaction begins, it continues until it is finished.

2. a) i) 0.714 g/min ii) 0.172 g NO2/min iii) 0.0150 mol HNO3/min
b) i) 840. mL ii) 0.450 mol/L
c)
- Δ Conc HNO_3 by Titration using Buret, Flasks, Magnetic Mixer in *M* HNO_3/s to measure V_f and V_i
- Δ Mass Cu by Balance to measure m_f and m_i in units of g Cu/s
- Δ Pressure NO_2 by Manometer in closed system to measure P_f and P_i in units of kPa/s NO_2
- Δ Volume NO_2 by Eudiometer to measure V_f and V_i in units of mL/sNO_2
- Δ pH by pH meter to measure change in pH of HNO_3 per second
- Δ Mass of NO_2 gas by Balance to measure m_i and m_f in units of g/s
- Δ Conc $CuNO_3$ by Titration using buret, etc to find V_f and V_i in *M*/s

3.a)i) approx 32 mL/min
ii) approx 16 mL/min
iii) approx 3.3 mL/min
b) (a) > (b) > (c) As the reaction proceeds there are less reactant particles available to collide and react. Consequently, the rate decreases with time.
4. a) 1.29×10^{-4} mol/s
b) The [HCl] was decreasing. This led to less successful collisions.
c) One of the reactants (either the Sr disk or the HCl in solution) was completely consumed. Based on the reaction rate, the Sr disk was most likely the limiting reagent. The rate implies a reasonably large molarity of HCl.
5.

Time (seconds)	Absorbances (no unit)	Concentration of Copper(II) Ion (mol/L)
0 s	0	0 mol/L
20.	0.40	0.017
40.	0.70	0.030
60.	0.90	0.038
80.	1.00	0.042

a) 0.0014*M* HNO_3/s
b) 0.67 g
c) Cu(s) will decrease in size
Blue $Cu^{2+}(aq)$ will appear
Bubbles will be seen as gas forms
This is a very exothermic reaction so heat (and potentially some steam) will be given off
(Colourless NO(*g*) reacts immediately with oxygen in the air to form brownish orange $NO_2(g)$ or its dimer, $N_2O_4(g)$ which is also brownish orange.)

Page 22, 1.2 Review Questions

1. Factors affecting heterogeneous and homogeneous reactions:
Nature of reactants
Temperature
Concentration
Presence of a catalyst
2. Surface Area. You can only increase this area of contact for solids and rarely, liquids.
3. a) Platinum in the catalytic converter of a car.
b) Iron is used in the Haber Process to make ammonia.
c) Platinum is used in contact lens disinfectant disks to decompose hydrogen peroxide producing oxygen gas. The bubbling process helps clean the surface of the lenses.
d) A Magnesium Complex called Chlorophyll assists in photosynthesis.
4. $CaCO_3(s) + 2\ HNO_3(aq) \rightarrow Ca(NO_3)_2(aq) + H_2O(l) + CO_2(g)$
a) Increase – more frequent contact between reactants
b) Increase – more surface area leads to more contact between reactants
c) Decrease – less energetic collisions due to lower temperature
d) no effect – CO_2 is a product so increased contact has no effect on forward rate
5. 3.57×10^{-3} mol HCOOH/min
a) Less than half as much time (rxn most rapid a start) – under 30 seconds.
b) Considerably more time – much > 1 minute.
c) Approximately half as much time for each 10°C increase – about 30 seconds.
6. a) i) slow (due to solid C)
ii) fast (ionic species)
iii) slow (due to solid Mg)
Fastest: (ii) > (iii) > (i) Slowest
b) i) surface area of C(s), temperature of system, $[O_2]$ (volume of container) (partial pressure of O_2), an appropriate catalyst
ii) $[Pb^{2+}]$ and $[I^-]$, temperature of system, an appropriate catalyst
iii) $[CuCl_2]$, surface area of Mg(s), temperature of system, an appropriate catalyst
7. c > b > a
The greatest opportunity for contact between reactant particles is in system c. It appears to have the highest concentration/greatest partial pressure of each reactant gas. The next would be system b and the least opportunity would be system a.

Page 25, Quick Check

1. Rate = k[C][D]. This means that the rate of the reaction is directly related to the product of the concentrations of reactants C and D. Furthermore, it means the reaction is 1st order with respect to both reactants C and D.
(The overall reaction order = 1 + 1 = 2.)
2. a) The rate would double. b) The rate would half.
3. If the volume of the container were halved, the concentrations of both A and B would be doubled. Hence, the rate would be increased by a factor of 2 x 2 = 4 times.
4. Increased T → Increased Rate. Increased T must cause increased rate constant, k.

Page 27, Quick Check

1. Concentration (Volume of a Gas Sample), Surface Area, Temperature
2. Temperature, Presence of a Catalyst
3. Temperature

Page 29, Practice Problems

1. a) The added curve should have the same total area below it. The area below the curve and to the right of the vertical line representing E_a should be DOUBLED.
b) The added curve should have the same total area below it. The area below the curve and to the right of the vertical line representing E_a should be SIGNIFICANTLY INCREASED.
c) The added curve should have the same total area below it. The area below the curve and to the right of the vertical line representing E_a should be INCREASED BUT CLEARLY LESS THAN DOUBLE THAT IN CURVE (b).

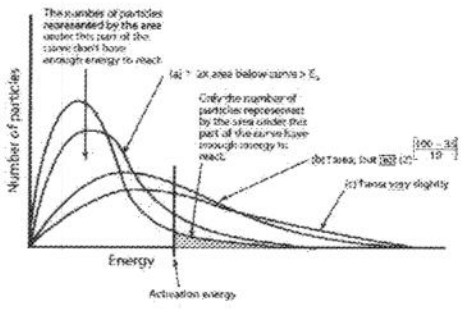

2.

Temperature	100°C	300°C
Frequency of Collisions	$2.00 \times 10^{15}\ s^{-1}$	$3.00 \times 10^{15}\ s^{-1}$
Force of Collisions (% Possessing E_a)	95.0%	97.0%
Frequency of Collisions Possessing Activation Energy	$1.90 \times 10^{15}\ s^{-1}$	$2.91 \times 10^{15}\ s^{-1}$

a) $\frac{97.0\%}{95.0\%}$ = 1.02X greater
b) $\frac{3.00 \times 10^{15}\ s^{-1}}{2.00 \times 10^{15}\ s^{-1}}$ = 1.50X greater
c) $\frac{2.91 \times 10^{15}\ s^{-1}}{1.90 \times 10^{15}\ s^{-1}}$ = 1.53X greater
d) Increased frequency of collisions.
e) Extremely forceful collisions may be too forceful to transfer KE of collisions into PE of new bonds. These forceful collisions may be unsuccessful resulting in reactants that simply bounce off one another.

Page 33, 1.3 Review Questions

1. The frequency of collisions and the fraction of these collisions that succeed.
2. Sufficient energy (E_a) and proper collision geometry.
3. a) Original surface area + 6/6(original surface area) since six new faces have been exposed. Thus 6.00 cm^2 + 6/6(6.00 cm^2) = 12.0 cm^2.
b) 6/6 + 6/6 = 12/6 or 2X as many collisions as before.
c) 2 (0.00120 mol Zn/min) = 0.00240 mol Zn/min
d) 242 mL H_2
4. a) 3 x 0.5 x (3.10×10^{-3} mol/L s) = 4.65×10^{-3} mol/L s
b) 1 x 4 x (3.10×10^{-3} mol/L s) = 1.24×10^{-2} mol/L s
c) The temperature was increased, perhaps by approximately 10°C. Or a catalyst was added.
d) 0.5 x 0.5 (3.10×10^{-3} mol/L s) = 7.75×10^{-4} mol/L s (note that both concentrations were halved)
5. a) The greatest concentration of HCl and the greatest surface area of $CaCO_3$ exists at the beginning of the reaction. Consequently, the reaction rate is greatest at the beginning as these circumstances allow for more successful collisions. As the reaction proceeds, there are less particles and surface available to collide and so the reaction rate decreases.
b)

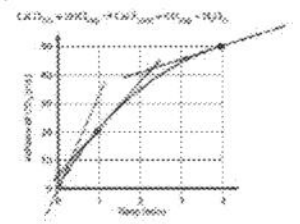

6. III > I > II The powdered zinc allows for the greatest contact at the surface and the 1.0*M* acid has the greatest number of particles available for collisions.
7. The Cl atoms must be able to contact one another to produce Cl_2 and NO_2. The particles must be drawn to allow this contact to directly occur.
8. a) Low temperatures decrease the frequency of collisions and decrease the fraction of collisions reaching Ea. This keeps the food from spoiling.
b) Fine bits of magnesium in the shavings (more surface area) allow more frequent collisions with the oxygen molecules. This allows a fire to start more readily. Its "nature" allows magnesium to react readily with oxygen with a low Ea.
c) Pt acts as a catalyst in the conversion of NO_x's into N_2. This means the collisions required for a successful reaction can occur with less energy or at lower temperatures.

Page 40, Practice Problems 1.4.1

1. Rate = k[NO][O_2] Trial 1 = X x 10^6 l/mol · sec
2. Rate = k[Y]
$k = 0.0070\ s^{-1}$
3. System 1: System 2: System 3:

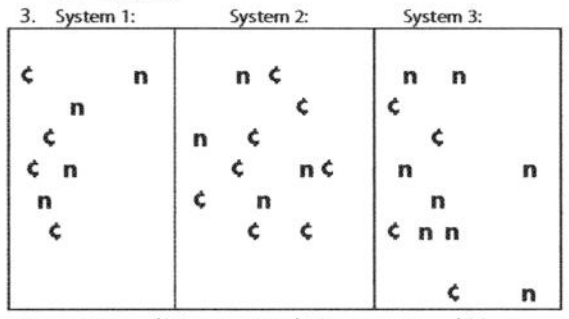

Rate = 0.010 mol/L/s 0.020 mol/L/s 0.080 mol/L/s

Page 42, 1.4 Review Questions

1. a) Rate = $k[X]^2[Y]$
b) k = 80 $L^2/mol^2/s$
c) Rate = 0.4 mol/L/s
2. a) Rate = $k[NO_2][F_2]$
b) k = 40.0 L/mol/s
3. a) Rate = $k[MnO_4^-]^2[H_2C_2O_4]$
k = $2.0 \times 10^5\ L^2/mol^2/$
b) If all the concentrations of all three reactants were doubled, the initial reaction rate would be: $(2)^2(2)^1(2)^0$ = 8x.
c) If the volume of the reaction system were doubled by adding distilled water, the reaction rate would be: $(½)^2(½)^1(½)^0$ = 1/8x.
4. a) Rate = $k[A]^2$
b) k = 4.00×10^{-3} L/mol/s
c) Trial 4: Rate = 3.60×10^{-4} mol/L/s

5. a) Rate = $k[MnO_4^-]^2$
b) k = 1.0×10^2 L/mol/min
c) Rate = 1.0×10^{-5} mol/L/min
d) $[MnO_4^-]$ = 4.8×10^{-4} mol/L
e) 5.2×10^{-6} mol/L/min MnO_4^-
6. Rate = $k[CH_3COCH_3][H^+]$
k = 0.0038 L/mol/s

Page 48, Practice Problems

1. $k = 2.57 \times 10^{-3} s^{-1}$
2. C = 0.982 mol/L (0.98 mol/L)
3. C = 2.16×10^{-2} mol/L (2.2×10^{-2} mol/L)

Page 49, Practice Problems

1. t = 2900 s (48 min)
2. Mass = 140 mg
3. t = 24 h

Page 53, Practice Problems 1.
Pseudo integrated rate analysis

Time (s)	Concentration (mol/L)	ln Concentration	1/Concentration (L/mol)
0	0.100	- 2.30 (-2.303)	10.0
30	0.074	- 2.6 (-2.60)	14
60	0.055	- 2.9 (-2.90)	18
90	0.041	- 3.2 (-3.19)	24

The substitution reaction is 1st order with respect to $[(CH_3)_3CBr]$.
$k = 0.0100\ s^{-1}$
2. $2\ NO_2(g) \rightarrow 2\ NO(g) + O_2(g)$

Time (s)	Concentration (mol/L)	ln Concentration	1/Concentration (L/mol)
0	0.0100	- 4.61 (-4.605)	100.
50.	0.0079	- 4.8 (-4.84)	130
100.	0.0065	- 5.6 (-5.04)	150
200.	0.0048	- 5.3 (-5.34)	210
300.	0.0038	- 5.6 (-5.57)	260
400.	0.0032	- 5.7 (-5.75)	310

a) Rate = $k[NO_2]_2$
k = 0.54 L/mol/s
b) i) If the initial concentration of NO2 increased, the reciprocal concentration would decrease, shifting the straight line graph down.
ii) If the temperature of the decomposition were elevated further, the slope (k) of the straight line graph would become steeper (k increases as temperature raises).

Page 56, Practice Problems 1. a)
$t_{1/2} = 4.6 \times 10^4$ s 770 min) (13 h)
b) C = 0.094 mol/L (0.09 mol/L)
2. a) k = $5.8 \times 10^{-3}\ s^{-1}$
b) C = 0.038 mol/L (0.04 mol/L)
c) t = 1.0×10^2 s

Page 58, Practice Problems

1. a) $t_{1/2}$ = 126 s
b) $\frac{1}{C}$ = 39.9 L/mol
C = 2.51×10^{-2} mol/L
2. If the half-life of a reaction is independent of the initial concentration of the reactants, then the reaction is first order.

Page 60, 1.5 Review Questions

1.

	a) first order	b) zero order	c) second order
i) rate of reaction	Decreases	Stays constant	Decreases
ii) rate constant	Stays constant	Stays constant	Stays constant
iii) half life	Stays constant	Decreases (half the previous)	Increases (double the previous)

2. C = 0.222 mol/L (0.22 mol/L)
3. C = 0.14 mol/L
4. C = 0.41 mol/L
5. a) k = 0.050 h^{-1}
b) t = 56 h
6. k = 0.00212 s^{-1}
7. $t_{1/2}$ = 7.30 s
8. Graphs for a 1st order equation are shown.
a) decrease in the initial concentration by a factor of ½ as evident by examination of the y-axis
b) decrease in the initial rate: a tangent drawn to the curves in the first graph at time zero now has about HALF the SLOPE
c) rate constant, k (determined by finding the slope of the lnC vs t graph) remains the SAME
d) temperature has increased. Only a change in temperature can change k.
e) the slope of the initial tangent line (= the rate) has increased and the temperature could increase the rate constant

9. Graphs for a 2nd order equation are shown.
   a) decrease in the initial concentration by a factor of ½ as evident by examination of the y-axis
   b) decrease in the initial rate: a tangent drawn to the curves in the first graph at time zero now has about HALF the SLOPE
   c) rate constant, k (determined by finding the slope of the 1/C vs t graph) remains the SAME
   d) temperature has decreased. Only a change in temperature can change k.
   e) the slope of the initial tangent line (= the rate) has decreased and the temperature could decrease the rate constant
10. Decomposition of aqueous sucrose to form the isomers glucose and fructose:

Time (min)	$[C_{12}H_{22}O_{11}]$ (mol/L)	$\ln[C_{12}H_{22}O_{11}]$	$1/[C_{12}H_{22}O_{11}]$ (L/mol)
0	0.316	- 1.15 (- 1.152)	3.17
39	0.274	- 1.30 (- 1.295)	3.65
80	0.238	- 1.44 (- 1.435)	4.20
140	0.190	- 1.66 (- 1.661)	5.26
210	0.146	- 1.92 (- 1.924)	6.85

   a) Rate = $k[C_{12}H_{22}O_{11}]$
   b) $k = 0.004\ s^{-1}$. Approximate value from graph slope.
   c) $t_{1/2}$ 1.13×10^4 s (189 min) (3.14 h). Approximate value from graph slope
   d) C = 0.166 mol/L (0.17 mol/L). Approximate value from graph slope.

11.

Time (s)	$[CH_3NC]$ (mol/L)	$\ln[CH_3NC]$	$1/[CH_3NC]$ (L/mol)
2000	0.0110	- 4.51 (- 4.510)	90.0
5000	0.0059	- 5.1 (- 5.13)	170
8000	0.0031	- 5.8 (- 5.78)	320
12000	0.0014	- 6.6 (- 6.57)	710
15000	0.0007	- 7 (- 7.3)	1000

   a) Rate = $k[CH_3NC]$
   b) $k == 0.0002\ s^{-1}$. Approximate value from graph slope.
   c) $t_{1/2} = 3000\ s$ $(50\ min)$ $(0.9\ h)$. Approximate value from graph slope.
   d) $C = 2 \times 10^{-4}\ mol/L$ $(10^{-4}\ mol/L)$. Approximate value from graph slope.
12. a) $k = 0.0105\ L/mol/s$
    b) $t_{1/2} = 316\ s$ this is the 1st half life
13. Assume 1.00 mol/L initial sample:
    t = 34.2 years
14. a) $t_{1/2} = 20\ (C_o)s$
    b) C = 0.13 mol/L
15. t = 75.4 s

Page 66, Quick Check

2. $2\ C_2H_6(g) + 7\ O_2(g) \rightarrow 4\ CO_2(g) + 6\ H_2O(l) + 2857.0\ kJ/mol_{rxn}$
   $2\ C_2H_6(g) + 7\ O_2(g) \rightarrow 4\ CO_2(g) + 6\ H_2O(l)$
   $\Delta H = -2857.0\ kJ/mol_{rxn}$
3. $72.2\ kJ/mol_{rxn} + 2\ HBr(g) \rightarrow H_2(g) + Br_2(l)$
   $2\ HBr(g) \rightarrow H_2(g) + Br_2(l)$ $\Delta H = +72.2\ kJ/mol_{rxn}$

Page 70, Practice Problems

1. a) endothermic
   b) i) 30 kJ/mol
      ii) +20 kJ/mol
      iii) 130 kJ/mol
      iv) 140 kJ/mol
2. I) Activation energy for the forward reaction.
   II) Potential energy for the reactants.
   III) Activation energy for the reverse reaction.
   IV) Enthalpy change.

Page 72, Quick Check

A) Reverse uncatalyzed activation energy. $E_{a(Reverse\ Uncatalyzed)}$ is #2 in Diagram 2.
B) Forward catalyzed activation energy. #3
C) Decrease in E_a due to catalysis. #4
D) ΔH. #7
E) Forward uncatalyzed activation energy. #6
F) Reverse catalyzed activation energy. #1
(Note that #5 is the PE of the activated complex – forward and reverse - uncatalyzed.)

Page 74, 1.6 Review Questions

1. a) $Fe_2O_3(s) + 2\ Al(s) \rightarrow Al_2O_3(s) + 2\ Fe(s)$ $\Delta H = -852\ kJ/mol_{rxn}$
   $Fe_2O_3(s) + 2\ Al(s) \rightarrow Al_2O_3(s) + 2\ Fe(s) + 852\ kJ/mol_{rxn}$
   b) $Ca(s) + O_2(g) + H_2(g) \rightarrow Ca(OH)_2(s)$ $\Delta H = -986\ kJ/mol_{rxn}$
   $Ca(s) + O_2(g) + H_2(g) \rightarrow Ca(OH)_2(s) + 986\ kJ/mol_{rxn}$
   c) $2\ H_2O(l) \rightarrow 2\ H_2(g) + O_2(g)$ $\Delta H = +572\ kJ/mol_{rxn}$
   $572\ kJ/mol_{rxn} + 2\ H_2O(l) \rightarrow 2\ H_2(g) + O_2(g)$
2. a&b)

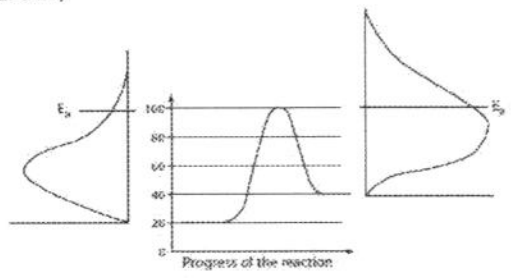

c) The particles above the E_a line in the first graph represent the particles whose collisions are successful (have energy > E_a and have good geometry).
e) An endothermic reaction has a greater number of successful collisions than the corresponding exothermic reaction. This indicates that the endothermic reaction is much more sensitive to an increase OR decrease in temperature's effect on its reaction rate. (Will find in Chapter 2 that an increase in T will always cause a shift in the ENDO direction.)

3. a) Endothermic sketch.
   b) 60 kJ/mol
   c) -35 kJ/mol
4. a) A = Activation energy for forward catalyzed reaction.
   B = ΔH
   C = Reverse uncatalyzed activation energy.
   D = Forward uncatalyzed activation energy.
   E = Reverse catalyzed activation energy.
   b) Exothermic
   c) No effect.
5. a) -50 kJ/mol
   b) Q + S → T + 50 kJ/mol
   Q + S → T $\Delta H = -50$ kJ/mol
   c) exothermic
   d) 150 kJ/mol
6. The energy released as more $CO_2(g)$ and $H_2O(g)$ is formed provides the activation energy needed to continue decomposing the hydrocarbon fuel.
7. The energy released during bond forming is greater than the energy required for bond breaking. As a result, there is a net release of energy. The bonds formed have less potential energy than the reactant bonds did.
8. The diagrams would be the same. The potential bond energy would be the same. The "reaction coordinate" is *NOT* a time axis!!
9. As particles approach one another their KE DECREASES (bond breaking requires energy – KE →→PE). Meanwhile, their PE INCREASES (see above). Once an activated complex has formed, the KE INCREASES (bond forming releases energy) and their PE decreases). The sum of KE and PE remains constant the entire time.

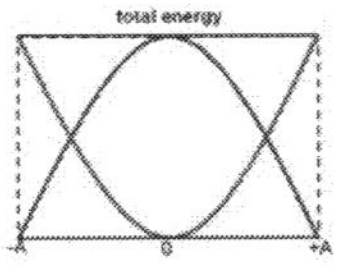

blue is PE, red (u-shape) is KE

10. a) exothermic
    b) 10 kJ/mol
    c) 25 kJ/mol
    d) -15 kJ/mol - no change at all when catalyzed.
    e) 15 kJ/mol - lower with a catalyst.
    f) increases the reaction rate.

Page 80, Quick Check

2. a)Bimolecular – Elementary Process
   b) Unimolecular – Elementary Process
   c) Termolecular – Overall Reaction

Page 83, Practice Problems

1. $O_3(g) \rightarrow O_2(g) +$ ~~$O(g)$~~ (slow)
   ~~$O(g)$~~ $+ O_3(g) \rightarrow 2\ O_2(g)$
   (ΔH value for entire reaction = - 284.6 kJ/mol)
   $2\ O_3(g) \rightarrow 3\ O_2(g)$
   There are no catalysts and O is the intermediate.

   Overall E_a is shown on the y-axis.

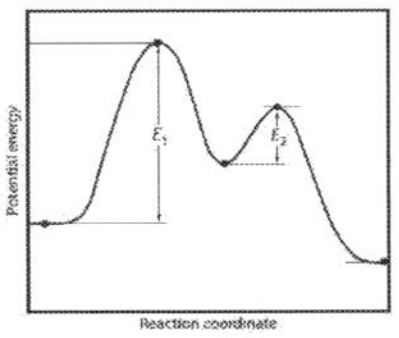

2. $H_2(g) +$ ~~$2\ Pd(s)$~~ → ~~$2\ Pd\text{-}H(s)$~~
   $C_2H_4(g) +$ ~~$Pd\text{-}H(s)$~~ → ~~$C_2H_5\text{-}Pd(s)$~~ (slowest step)
   ~~$C_2H_5\text{-}Pd(s)$~~ + ~~$Pd\text{-}H(s)$~~ → $C_2H_6(g) +$ ~~$2\ Pd(s)$~~
   $C_2H_4(g) + H_2(g) \rightarrow C_2H_6(g) + 136.9\ kJ/mol$

Catalyst is: Pd Intermediates are: Pd-H and C_2H_5Pd

Activation energy is between the dotted lines.

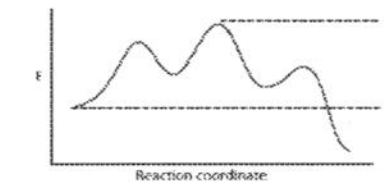

3.
$Cl_2(g) \rightarrow$ ~~$Cl(g)$~~ + ~~$Cl(g)$~~ initiation
$CH_4(g) +$ ~~$Cl(g)$~~ $\rightarrow CH_3Cl(g) +$ ~~$H(g)$~~) x 2 propagation
~~$H(g)$~~ + ~~$H(g)$~~ $\rightarrow H_2(g)$ termination

$2\ CH_4(g) + Cl_2(g) \rightarrow 2\ CH_3Cl(g) + H_2(g)$ chain mechanism

There are no catalysts. LIGHT provides E_a for the reaction. Intermediates include H's and Cl's (free radicals).

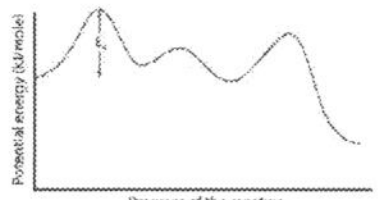

(The relative heights of the second and third step are not actually known from the information provided. The reaction is only slightly exothermic. Though the propagation step occurs twice, the reactant and product energies are the same, so it is shown only once.)

Page 87, Practice Problems

1. a) intermediates: HOCl, OH^-, HIO; catalyst: H_2O
   b) Rate = $k[I^-][OCl^-]/[OH^-]$
2. a) $Cl_2 \leftrightarrow$ ~~$2\ Cl$~~
   ~~Cl~~ $+ CHCl_3 \rightarrow HCl +$ ~~CCl_3~~
   ~~$Cl + CCl_3$~~ $\rightarrow CCl_4$
   $Cl_2 + CHCl_3 \rightarrow CCl_4 + HCl$
   b) intermediates: Cl, CCl_3
   c) Rate = $k[Cl_2]^{1/2}[CHCl_3]$

Page 91, 1.7 Review Questions

1. A series of steps that may be added together to give an overall chemical reaction.
2. The slowest elementary process in a reaction mechanism determines the overall reaction rate and is called the RATE-DETERMINING STEP.
3. Chemists determine these models by altering the concentration of species involved in the mechanism and examining the effects these alterations produce. Computer models are also very useful in the pursuit of mechanisms.
4. a) Hetero b) Homo c) Hetero
5.
   1st: $H_2O_2(aq) +$ ~~$I^-(aq)$~~ $\rightarrow H_2O(l) +$ ~~$IO^-(l)$~~ slow
   2nd $H_2O_2(aq) +$ ~~$IO^-(aq)$~~ $\rightarrow H_2O(l) + O_2(g) +$ ~~$I^-(aq)$~~ fast
   a) Overall Rxn: $2\ H_2O_2(aq) \rightarrow 2\ H_2O(l) + O_2(g)$
   b) Intermediates: IO^-
   c) catalyst is I^-
6. $NO_2 + F_2 \rightarrow NO_2F +$ ~~F~~ (RDS)
   $NO_2 +$ ~~F~~ $\rightarrow NO_2F$
   $2\ NO_2 + F_2 \rightarrow 2\ NO_2F$
7. a) 3
   b) 2nd step (middle step or step C)
   c) C
   d) B
   e) F
   f) endothermic
8.
   a) Mechanism One:
   Step 1:
   $2\ NO_2(g) \rightarrow NO_3(g) + NO(g)$ slow
   Step 2:
   $CO + NO_3 \rightarrow CO_2 + NO_2$ fast
   Overall Rxn:
   $CO(g) + NO_2(g) \rightarrow CO_2(g) + NO(g)$
   (Note that this is an example of ***authocatalysis.*** The reactant, NO_2, also acts as a catalyst for the reaction. Some autocatalyzed reactions involve the formation of the catalyst from the reactants in an early step.)

   Mechanism Two:
   Step 1:
   $2\ NO_2(g) \rightarrow N_2O_4(g)$ fast
   Step 2:
   $CO + N_2O_4 \rightarrow NO_2 + CO_2 + NO$ slow
   Overall Rxn:
   $CO(g) + NO_2(g) \rightarrow CO_2(g) + NO(g)$

   b) Mechanism 1 is correct as the CO is NOT in the RDS!
9. a) No – too many reactant particles (five) for a single step.
   b) $HBr + O_2 \rightarrow$ ~~$HOOBr$~~
   $HBr +$ ~~$HOOBr$~~ $\rightarrow$ ~~$2\ HOBr$~~
   $HBr +$ ~~$HOBr$~~ $\rightarrow H_2O + Br_2$
   $HBr +$ ~~$HOBr$~~ $\rightarrow H_2O + Br_2$
   $4\ HBr + O_2 \rightarrow 2\ H_2O + 2\ Br_2$
   c) Step One (both HBr and O_2 influence reaction rate).
   d)

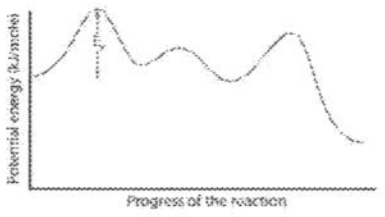

10.

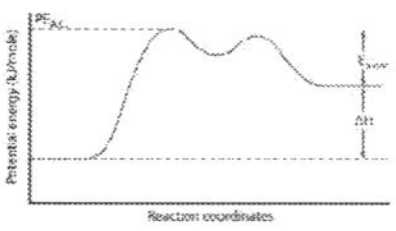

(Note the relative heights of steps one and two don't matter, but there must be AT LEAST two steps.)

11. a) intermediate: N_2O_2
    b) Rate = $k[NO]^2[O_2]$
12. Starting with each mechanism's temporary rate law based upon the slow step:
    Mechanism One: inconsistent with the provided rate law, rate = k[A][B]
    Rate = k'[M][A]
    $K_{eq} = \frac{[C][M]}{[A][B]}$
    $[M] = K_{eq}[A][B]/[C]$
    Rate = $k'K_{eq}[A]^2[B]/[C]$
    Rate = $k[A]^2[B]/[C]$
    N/A: if [M] in the rate law was substituted with the statement above, non-reactant species are also included
    Mechanism Two: consistent with the provided rate law, rate = k[A][B]
    Rate = k'[M][A]
    $K_{eq} = \frac{[M]}{[B]}$
    $[M] = K_{eq}[B]$
    Rate = $k'K_{eq}[A][B]$
    Rate = k[A][B]
    Mechanism Three: inconsistent with the provided rate law, rate = k[A][B]
    Rate = k'[M][A]
    $K_{eq} = \frac{[M]}{[A][B]}$
    $[M] = K_{eq}[A][B]$
    Rate = $k'K_{eq}[A]^2[B]$
    Rate = $k[A]^2[B]$
13. a) Step 1: NO + O2 ↔ ~~NO_3~~
    Step 2: ~~NO_3~~ $+ NO \rightarrow 2\ NO_2$
    $2\ NO + O_2 \rightarrow 2\ NO_2$
    b) Rate = $k[NO]^2[O_2]$
14. a) $NH_3 + OBr^- \leftrightarrow$ ~~$NH_2Br + OH^-$~~
    ~~NH_2Br~~ $+ NH_3 \rightarrow$ ~~$N_2H_5^+$~~ $+ Br^-$
    ~~$N_2H_5^+ + OH^-$~~ $\rightarrow N_2H_4 + H_2O$
    $2\ NH_3 + OBr^- \rightarrow N_2H_4 + Br^- + H_2O$ (basic)
    b) intermediates: NH_2Br, OH^-, $N_2H_5^+$
    c) Rate = $k[NH_3]^2[OBr^-]/[OH^-]$

Chapter 2

Page 99, Practice Problems,

1. 0.0082 mol/s (rate of its consumption = rate of its production at equilibrium)
2. $\frac{0.0041 \text{ mol } O_2}{s}$
3. $\frac{0.13 \text{ g } O_2}{s}$

Page 100, Quick Check

1. because the forward and reverse reactions continue to occur
2. i. constant macroscopic properties
   ii. closed system
   iii. a change in conditions causes an equilibrium shift
3. no chemicals are entering or leaving the defined system
4. a property that is large enough to be measured or observed with the unaided eye

Page 101, Quick Check

1. False
2. True
3. True
4. False

Page 104, 2.1 Review Questions

1. a. equilibrium
   b. steady state
   c. equilibrium
   d. steady state
   e. equilibrium
2. a. yes
   b. yes
   c. no
   d. yes
   e. no
3. a. $\frac{0.0040 \text{ mol } N_2O_4}{s}$
   b. $\frac{0.14 \text{ g } NH_3}{s}$
4. a. The rate of melting would become greater than the rate of freezing so net melting would occur and the ice cube would begin to decrease in size.
   b. Water is still evaporating but the water level is not dropping because the rate of condensation has become equal to the rate of evaporation.
5. No. Not until you reinstate the original temperature and the system shifts back to restore its original concentrations. Increasing the temperature may just have provided the activation energy to initiate a reaction.
6. a. The concentrations of the reactants and products remain relatively constant within the flame.
   b. The system isn't closed. The rate of the forward reaction does not equal the rate of the reverse reaction; in fact, there is no reverse reaction. (The concentrations of the reactants hold steady within the flame because reactants are continuously drawn into the flame to replace those being consumed; not because products are being converted back into reactants. The concentrations of the products hold steady within the flame because the products are leaving the flame at the same rate as new product particles are being formed; not because products are being converted back into reactants.)
7. Equilibria are closed whereas cyclic mechanisms such as this are open. The two steps in the cyclic mechanism are not the exact same reaction proceeding in opposite directions as is the case with an equilibrium. Each step in a two-step cyclic reaction consumes and produces chemicals not involved in the other step. As a result, equilibria are self-perpetuating since the forward and reverse reactions continuously supply each other with all their reactants whereas cyclic reactions stop as soon as one of their reactants runs out.
8. a. For example: otherwise the [NO] would not be constant.
   b. For example: otherwise the [H_2O] would not be constant.
9.

The Plot of Rate (forward and reverse) as a function of Time for a Reaction Achieving Equilibrium
0 5 10 15 20 25 30
time (s)

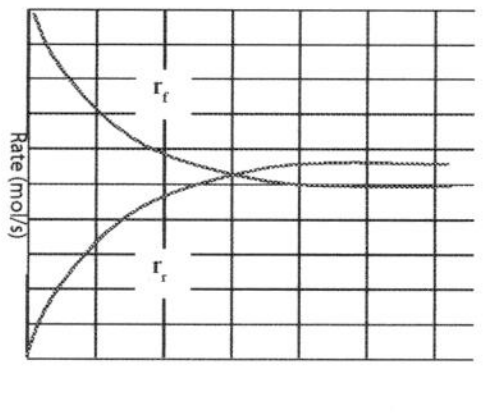

10. a. the orange gas would become paler
    b. the concentration of reactants (NO_2) decreases while the concentration of products (N_2O_4) increases
    c. the forward rate decreases while the reverse rate increases
11. It would establish equilibrium in the same way as usual but from the opposite direction. The concentration of the products and the reverse rate decrease while the concentration of reactants and the forward rate increase until the forward rate equals the reverse rate and equilibrium is re-established.

Page 110, Practice Problems

1. a. The system will restore equilibrium by removing some of the added Fe^{3+}.
   b. right
   c. [Fe^{3+}] and [$FeSCN^{2+}$] will be increased. [SCN^-] will be decreased.
2. a. The system will restore equilibrium by replacing some of the removed Fe^{3+}.
   b. left
   c. [Fe^{3+}] and [$FeSCN^{2+}$] will be decreased. [SCN^-] will be increased.
3.

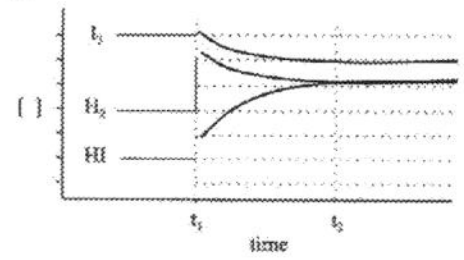

Page 112, Practice Problems

1. a. increases the reverse rate resulting in a net reverse reaction (shift left)
   b. decreases the reverse rate resulting in a net forward reaction (shift right)
   c. decreases the forward rate resulting in a net reverse reaction (shift left)
2. For example

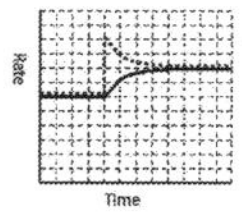

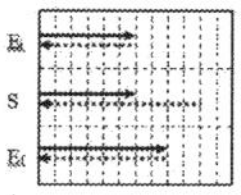

Page 114, Quick Check

1. For example: An equilibrium system subjected to a stress will restore equilibrium by partially alleviating the stress.
2. it will shift to replace some of the removed product
3. any action that has a different effect on the forward reaction rate than it does on the reverse reaction rate
4. it increases them both equally
5. True. This is a bit of a trick question. [HNO_2] will be greater than [H_2SO_3] regardless whether HNO_2 is the limiting reactant or it is the reactant in excess.

Page 116, 2.2 Review Questions

1. a. Equilibrium will be restored by removing some of the added NO
   b. right
   c. decreased
2. a. the forward rate decreases resulting in a net reverse rate (shift left)
   b. decreased
3. [Ag^+] and [$Ag(S_2O_3)_2^{3-}$] will be increased. [$S_2O_3^{2-}$] will be decreased.
   For example: Only some of the added Ag^+ is removed so its concentration increases. The system shifts left which decreases [$S_2O_3^{2-}$] and increases [$Ag(S_2O_3)_2^{3-}$].
4. a. The equilibrium would shift left thereby replacing some of the removed LDL and consuming some HDL in the process.
   b. Either add some X or remove some Y
5. Decrease the wine's pH (by adding H^+).
6.

		add NH_3	remove some H_2	add N_2
Equil. Conc.	N_2	Increase	Increase	Increase
	H_2	Increase	Decrease	Decrease
	NH_3	Increase	Decrease	Increase

7. a. Add H^+ (the system would shift left if you add P^- or remove HP but you don't know whether the shift would undershoot the equilibrium's original position and leave the solution yellow, overshoot the equilibrium's original position and turn the solution red, or regain the equilibrium's original position and turn the solution orange.)
   b. Add OH^- to remove (neutralize) some H^+.
8. a. left
   b. right
   c. right
   d. left
9. It increases the reverse rate by the same amount.
10. a. right b. gradually turn green
11. For example:

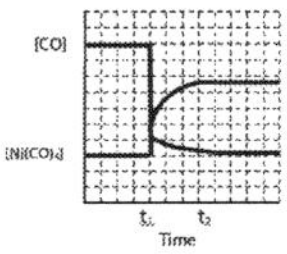

12. For example:

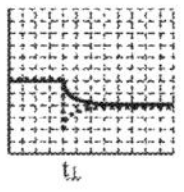

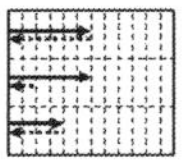

13. Increase. Equilibrium 2 shifts towards products to remove some of the added H^+. This decreases [NH_3] which in turn shifts equilibrium 1 left to replace some of the lost NH_3. This increases [Cu^{2+}].
14. The $AgCH_3COO(s)$ would slowly disappear. Equilibrium 2 shifts towards products to remove some of the added H^+. This decreases [CH_3COO^-] which in turn shifts equilibrium 1 right to replace some of the lost CH_3COO^-. This decreases the amount of $AgCH_3COO(s)$.
15. if NO is in excess (O_2 is limiting)
16. For example: Continuously remove product as it is formed or continuously replace reactant as it is consumed.

Page 121, Quick Check

1. by shifting to relieve some of the added pressure
2. the gas's or solutes part of the total pressure or the pressure exerted by this gas or solute alone in a mixture of gases or solutes.
3. by shifting to replace some of the lost osmotic pressure

Page 122, Practice Problems

1. Left. Increased number of NOCl; decreased numbers of NO and Cl_2. All concentrations increased due to compression.
2. Right. Increased numbers of Ag^+ and $S_2O_3^{2-}$; decreased number of $Ag(S_2O_3)_2^{3-}$. All concentrations decreased.
3. No. The system cannot relieve any of the added pressure by shifting in either direction.

Page 125, Practice Problems

1. The reverse rate would increase more than the forward rate resulting in a net reverse reaction (shift left).
2. The reverse rate would decrease more than the forward rate resulting in a net forward reaction (shift right).
3. For example:

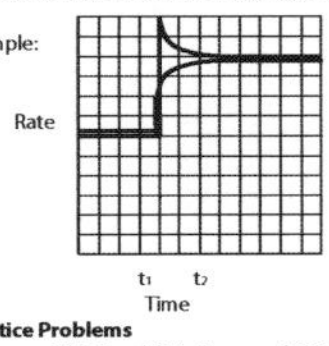

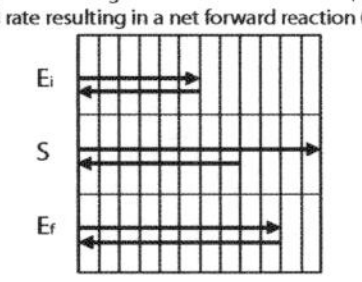

Page 126, Practice Problems

1. Left. Increased [SO_2] and [O_2]; decreased [SO_3].
2. Right. Increased [HI]; decreased [H_2] and [I_2].

Page 129, Practice Problems

1. The reverse rate would increase more than the forward rate resulting in a net reverse reaction (shift left).
2. The forward rate would decrease more than the reverse rate resulting in a net reverse reaction (shift left).
3. For example:

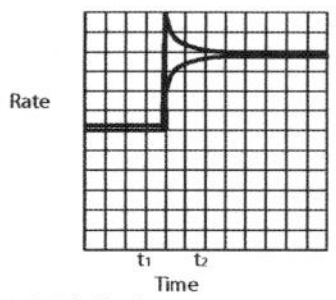

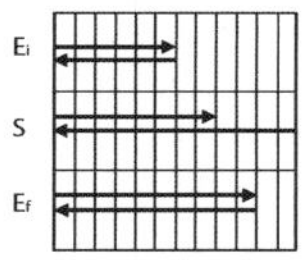

Page 130, Quick Check

1. Ammonia
2. adding a catalyst

Page 132, 2.3 Review Questions

1. a. The equilibrium will shift left to replace some of the lost osmotic pressure.
   b. increased number of SCN^- ions; decreased [SCN^-]
2. The reverse reaction rate decreases more than the forward reaction rate (greater sum of reaction coefficients) resulting in a net forward reaction (shift right).
3. The equilibrium will shift left to relieve some of the added pressure. (Note that the carbon atoms are in the solid phase.) The reverse reaction rate increases more than the forward reaction rate resulting in a net reverse reaction (shift left).
4. When the system's volume changes but the sum of the gaseous or aqueous reactant coefficients equals the sum of the gaseous or aqueous product coefficients in the balanced equation.
5. For example:

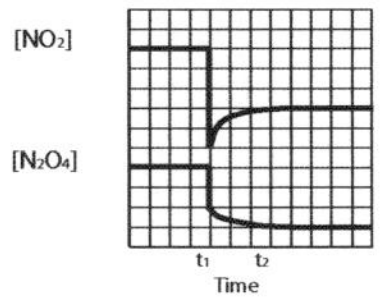

6. For example:

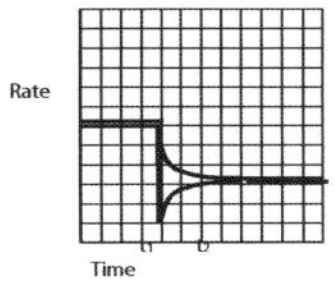

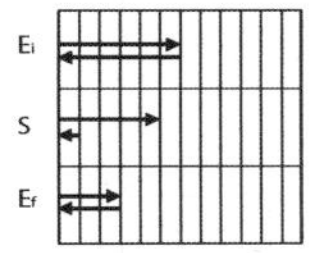

7. Less soluble. Increasing the temperature shifts the equilibrium to the left to remove some of the added kinetic energy and cool itself.

8. Right. Le Chatelier's Principle: Increasing the temperature shifts the equilibrium to the right to remove some of the added kinetic energy and cool itself. Chemical Kinetics: Increasing the temperature increases the forward reaction rate more than the reverse reaction rate resulting in a net forward reaction (shift right).
9. For example:

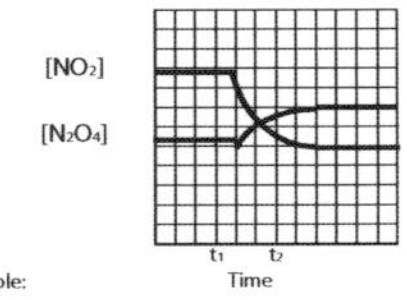

10. For example:

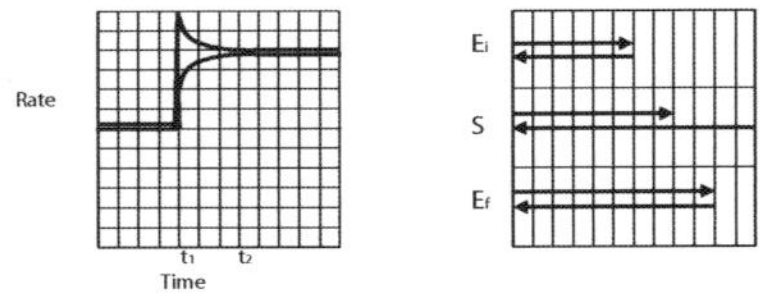

11. Endothermic. A decrease in temperature shifts an equilibrium in the exothermic direction to replace some of the lost kinetic energy and warm itself up. Cooling shifted this equilibrium to the left therefore the reverse reaction is exothermic and the forward reaction is endothermic.
12. a. left b. it was heated
13. Decreasing the temperature decreases the reverse reaction rate more than the forward reaction rate resulting in a net forward reaction (shift right).
14. An equilibrium's endothermic direction has a higher activation energy than its exothermic direction.
15. high temperature; low pressure
16. Lower temperatures slowly generate a high percent yield whereas higher temperatures quickly generate a low percent yield.
17.

		Decrease Volume	Decrease Temperature
Equil. Conc.	N_2	Increase	Decrease
	H_2	Increase	Decrease
	NH_3	Increase	Increase
Equil. No.	N_2	Decrease	Decrease
	H_2	Decrease	Decrease
	NH_3	Increase	Increase

18. Note: the forward rate is greater at the start of the reaction and equilibrium is achieved sooner with greater forward and reverse rates.

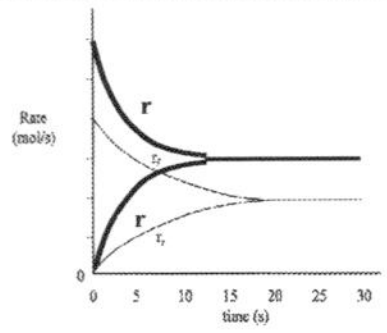

19. a. left
    b. right
    c. right
    d. left
20. a. left
    b. The shift would cause the piston to fall further. (In this situation, the shift would result in the volume decreasing at a constant pressure rather than decreasing the pressure in a constant volume.)

21.

$N_2(g) + 3H_2(g) \rightleftharpoons 2NH_3(g)$ ΔH = -92.4 kJ/mol				
Stress	**Le Chatelier Predicts**		**Chemical Kinetics Explains**	
	Response	**Shift**	**Effect**	**Net Rx**
add H_2	remove some of the added H_2	right	increase r_f	net forward rx
add NH_3	remove some of the added NH_3	left	increase r_r	net reverse rx
remove N_2	replace some of the removed N_2	left	decrease r_f	net reverse rx
decrease volume (compress)	relieve some of the added pressure	right	increase r_f more than r_r	net forward rx
decrease temperature	replace some of the lost K.E.	right	decrease r_r more than r_f	net forward rx

22. a. left
    b. right
    c. left
    d. right

Page 139, Quick Check

1. a substance's or system's state of disorganization or randomness
2. A perfect crystal at zero degrees Kelvin has 0 entropy.
3. Ag because more electrons provide more positional variability
4. H_2O_2 because larger and more complex molecules have more possible configurations (ways of positioning their parts relative to each other).

Page 141, Practice Problems

1. increases because the number of gas molecules increases ($0 \rightarrow 1$)
2. increases because the sulphur atoms go from being in a solid to being in a gas as well as splitting up to become part of 8 separate molecules.
3. increases because this is simply a solid melting ($s \rightarrow l$)

Page, 144 Practice Problems

1. not occur (both drives towards reactants)
2. exothermic (the drive towards increasing entropy is towards reactants therefore the drive towards decreasing enthalpy must be towards products)
3. entropy decreases (the drive towards decreasing enthalpy is towards products therefore the drive towards increasing entropy must be towards reactants)

Page 147, 2.4 Review Questions

1. a. $Br_2(g)$ because gases have more entropy than liquids
   b. $SO_3(g)$ because larger and more complex molecules have more possible configuratio
   c. Pb(s) because more electrons provide more positional variability
2. a. increasing because the number of gas molecules increases ($2 \rightarrow 4$)
   b. increasing because common items split up (Cl atoms go from being together in 1 molecule to being in 2 separate molecules. Unable to verify with standard entropies because $NOCl_2$ is an unstable reaction intermediate with no standard entropy value available.)
   c. decreasing because the number of gas molecules decreases ($3 \rightarrow 0$)
   d. increasing because common items split up
   e. increasing because the oxygen atoms go from being in a solid to being in a gas.
3. a. completion (both drives towards products)
   b. not occur (both drives towards reactants)
   c. equilibrium (enthalpy decreases towards products & entropy increases towards reactants)
   d. completion (both drives towards products)
4. endothermic; entropy increases towards products therefore enthalpy must decrease towards reactants
5. an endothermic reaction in which entropy decreases (entropy increases and enthalpy decreases towards reactants)
6. increasing; enthalpy decreases towards reactants therefore entropy must increase towards products
7. right; entropy increases towards reactants therefore enthalpy must decrease towards products. The equilibrium will shift in the exothermic direction to replace some of the lost kinetic energy and warm itself.
8. Maximum entropy is achieved just short of the completed reaction because even if the entropy of the products is much greater than the entropy of the reactants, a mixture containing a very small proportion of reactants will have a greater entropy than products alone.

Page 151, Practice Problems

1. $Keq = 0.019$
2. a. $Keq = 11.5$
   b. exothermic; When cooled, equilibria shift in the exothermic direction to replace some of the lost kinetic energy and warm themselves. The higher *Keq* indicates this reaction shifted to the right at the lower temperature therefore the forward reaction is exothermic.
3. $Keq = 1.7 \times 10^2$
   $[H_2] = 0.18$ M

Page 153, Quick Check

1. a. right
   b. no change
2. left; decrease; decrease
3. false

Page 154, Quick Check

1. $Keq = \dfrac{[H_2O]^3}{[B_2H_6]\,[O_2]^3}$.
2. $Keq = \dfrac{[Cl_2]^2\,[H_2O]^2}{[HCl]^4\,[O_2]}$
3. $Keq = \dfrac{[HBr]^2}{[H_2]}$
4. $Keq = [Ca^{2+}]\,[CO_3^{2-}]$

Page 154, Quick Check

1. 56
2. 0.13
3. 7.5

Page 156, Practice Problems

1. Trial $Keq = \dfrac{[CO]\,[H_2]^3}{[CH_4]\,[H_2O]} = \dfrac{(0.10)\,(0.30)^3}{(0.025)\,(0.045)} = 2.4$
   2.4 < 4.7 therefore the reaction will proceed to the right to achieve equilibrium
2. Trial $Keq = \dfrac{[N_2O_4]}{[NO_2]^2} = \dfrac{(4.0\ mol / 0.50\ L)}{(1.5\ mol / 0.50\ L)^2} = 0.89$
   0.89 < 0.940 therefore the reaction will proceed to the right to achieve equilibrium
3. $Keq = \dfrac{[H^+]\,[SO_4^{2-}]}{[HSO_4^-]} = \dfrac{(0.10)\,(0.10)}{(0.83)} = 0.012$
   Trial $Keq = \dfrac{(0.10)\,(0.20)}{(0.93)} = 0.022$
   0.022 > 0.012 therefore the system will shift left to restore equilibrium, increasing the $[HSO_4^-]$.

Page 157, Quick Check

1. completely
2. partially
3. completely

Page 159, 2.5 Review Questions

1. At equilibrium $r_f = r_r$ therefore: $2.7 \times 10^{-3}\,[N_2O_5] = 4.3 \times 10^{-2}\,[NO_2]\,[NO_3]$
   $Keq = \dfrac{[NO_2]\,[NO_3]}{[N_2O_5]} = \dfrac{2.7 \times 10^{-3}}{4.3 \times 10^{-2}} = 0.063$
2. No. The coefficients in a balanced chemical equation provide the ratio in which the reactants are consumed and the products are formed. The chemical equation in this question tells us that for each Cl_2 that reacts, 2 NO are consumed and 2 NOCl are produced but it provides no information about the ratio of the reactants and products present at equilibrium.
3. a. $Keq = \dfrac{[H^+]\,[NO_2^-]}{[HNO_2]}$
   b. $Keq = \dfrac{[SO_2]^2\,[O_2]}{[SO_3]^2}$
   c. $Keq = \dfrac{[NO]^4\,[H_2O]^6}{[NH_3]^4\,[O_2]^5}$
4. $Keq = 2.8$
5. a. $[COBr_2] = 0.060$ M; $[CO] = 0.030$ M; $[Br_2] = 0.040$ M
   b. to replace some of the lost pressure
   c. $Keq = 0.040$ at equilibrium initially
   $= 0.040$ when equilibrium is restored
6. 0.082 M
7. Trial $Keq = 0.59$
   0.59 < 1.0 therefore the reaction must proceed to the right to achieve equilibrium
8. a. $Keq = \dfrac{[H_2]\,[Fe^{2+}]}{[H^+]^2}$
   b. $Keq = \dfrac{[Cl^-]^2}{[I^-]^2\,[Cl_2]}$
   c. $Keq = \dfrac{1}{[CO_2]}$
   d. $Keq = \dfrac{[CO_2(aq)]}{[CO_2(g)]}$
   e. $Keq = [O_2]$
9. a. $Cl_2(g) \rightleftharpoons Cl_2(aq)$
   $Keq = \dfrac{[Cl_2(aq)]}{[Cl_2(g)]}$
   b. $CCl_4(g) \rightleftharpoons C(s) + 2Cl_2(g)$
   $Keq = \dfrac{[Cl_2]^2}{[CCl_4]}$
   c. $2MgO(s) + 2SO_2(g) + O_2(g) \rightleftharpoons 2MgSO_4(s)$
   $Keq = \dfrac{1}{[SO_2]^2\,[O_2]}$
10. a. 0.28
    b. 12.5
    c. 3.5
11. a. no effect
    b. no effect
    c. decrease
    d. no effect
12. No. An equilibrium's position depends upon the initial reactant concentrations as well as the equilibrium constant. The lower the initial $[H_2O(g)]$, the greater the percent yield at equilibrium. Calculations reveal that if the initial $[H_2O(g)]$ is 1.0 M then there will be a 33% yield at equilibrium so the reactants are favoured but if the initial $[H_2O(g)]$ is only 0.10 M then there will be a 70% yield at equilibrium so the products are favoured. From Le Chatelier's perspective, lowering the concentrations causes a shift to the right to replace some of the lost pressure.
13. No. It is difficult to make meaningful comparisons between the equilibrium constants of different equilibria unless their expressions have identical forms. Calculations reveal that if each reaction's initial reactant concentration is 1.0 M then both of these equilibria will have a 50% yield at equilbrium.
14. a. same (It increases forward and reverse rates equally.)
    b. same (There is only one chemical in the equilibrium expression so all of the lost O_2 is replaced.)
    c. decreased (The equilibrium shifts to the left to replace some of the lost K.E.)

Page 164, Practice Problems

1. $Keq = 3.0$
2. $Keq = 2.2$
3. $Keq = 0.13$

Page 168, Practice Problems

1. 1.2 mol Cl_2
2. $[C_2N_2]_{eq} = 1.89$ M

3. $[HCl]_{eq} = 8.5$ M

Page 169, Practice Problems

1. 0.75 M
2. 1.2 M
3. 0.26 M

Page 172, Practice Problems

1. a) $K_p = 0.133$
   b) $K_p = 1.04$
2. a) $x = \sqrt{0.3042} = 0.55$ atm
   b) x = 349 atm
3. 0.060
4. In (a), $\Delta n = 0$, so $K_p = K_c$. In (b), $\Delta n = -1$, so K_p does not equal K_c.

Page 174, 2.6 Review Questions

(a)	$H_2(g) + C_2N_2(g) \Leftrightarrow 2HCN(g)$		
I	6	0	0
C	-3.0	1.5	4.5
E	3.0	1.5	4.5

(a)	$2N_2(g) + 3H_2(g) \Leftrightarrow 3NH_3(g)$		
I	2.5	5.0	0
C	-0.5	-1.5	1.0
E	2.0	3.5	1.0

2. a. $[NO_2]_{eq} = 0.6$ M
   b. $Keq = 3$
3. a. $[A^{2+}]_{eq} = 0.80$ M
   b. $Keq = 20.$
4. a. $Keq = 1.20$
   [HCN] = 3.0
   b. $Keq = 1.20$
   $[C_2N_2] = 3.0$
5. [G3P] = 0.002 M
   [DHAP] = 0.038 M
6. $[H_2] = 0.522$ M
   [CO] = 0.678 M
7. [HCN] = 1.02 M
8. $[H_2] = 0.62$ mol H_2
9. a. $[BCl_3] = 2(0.1126) = 0.23$ M (rounded off to the appropriate number of sig.figs.)
   b. No, the reaction would run out of BN(*s*) and thus go to completion before reaching equilibrium. The flask only contains 1.0 g BN(*s*) but 1.40 g are required to achieve equilibrium
10. $Keq = 2.8$
11. a. $[H_2] = [Cl_2] = 3.00 - 0.778 = 2.22$ M
    [HCl] = 4.00 + 2(0.778) = 5.56 M
    b. The system shifted to the right and replaced some of the removed HCl.
12. $Keq = \frac{[FeSCN^{2+}]}{[Fe^{3+}][SCN^-]} = \frac{1.8}{(0.10)^2} = 180$

    $^*Keq = \frac{0.72 - x}{(0.040 + x)^2} = 180$ (*This equation is sufficient for the answer)

    $0.72 - x = 180(0.040 + x)^2 = 180(0.0016 + 0.08x + x^2) = 0.288 + 14.4x + 180x^2$

    $180x^2 + 15.4x - 0.432 = 0$

    Solve for x to give -0.108, 0.022 and ignore the negative value as it makes no sense from a chemistry perspective (and we'll blame the mathematicians for the negative ;)

13.

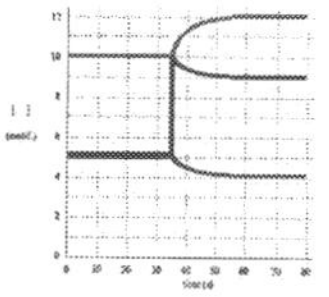

[H_2] = 4.0 M
[Br_2] = 9.0 M
[HBr] = 12 M

14.

b.	$N_2(g) + 3H_2(g) \rightleftharpoons 2NH_3(g)$		
I	2.5	5.0	0
C	− 0.5	− 1.5	+ 1.0
E	2.0	3.5	1.0

a. $[SO_3]_{eq} = 28.3 - 3.60 = 24.7$ M

b. 28.3 $\frac{mol}{L}$ x 0.500 L = 14.2 mol

15. $[H_2]_i = 1.0$ M
16. $[PCl_5]_i = 2.55$ M
17. 0.29 $\frac{mol}{L}$ O_2
18. a) $K_p = \frac{(P\,PCl_3)(P\,Cl_2)}{P\,PCl_5}$
    b) $K_p = \frac{P^2\,P_2O_5}{P^5\,O_2}$
    c) $K_p = \frac{1}{P\,CO_2}$
19. $K_p = K_c(RT)^{\Delta n}$
    Review Question 4: $K_p = 1.7 \times 10^{3}$
    Review Question 6: $K_p = 2.8 \times 10^{5}$
    Review Question 7: $K_p = 1.7 \times 10^{3}$
20. $Q = \frac{P^2\,SO_3}{(P^2\,SO_2)(P\,O_2)} = \frac{(0.10\text{ atm})^2}{(0.20\text{ atm})^2(0.20\text{ atm})}$
    $= 1.25 > 0.14 = K_p$
    As $Q > K_p$, the equilibrium shifts left to reach equilibrium.
21. a) $\Delta P_A = -1.5$ atm, $\Delta P_B = -1.5$ atm and $\Delta P_C = +1.5$ atm so $A + B \rightleftharpoons C$
    b) $K_p = \frac{P_C}{(P_A)(P_B)}$
    c) $K_p = 0.60$
    d) 15
22. $P\,N_2 = 3.0$ atm
    $P\,H_2 = 8.9$ atm
    $P\,NH_3 = 5.9$ atm
    $K_p = 0.017$
23. $K_p = 1.78$
24. a) $PCl_5(g) \rightleftharpoons PCl_3(g) + Cl_2(g)$. For every mole of PCl_5 decomposed, a total of 2 moles of PCl_3 and Cl_2 combined are produced. Therefore, as the reaction reaches equilibrium (shifts right), the total number of moles of gas increase and the pressure increases.
    b) When the system reaches equilibrium, P PCl_5 = 1.00 - 0.40 = 0.60 atm, P PCl_3 = 0.40 atm, P Cl_2 = 0.40 atm
    c) $K_p = 0.27$
    d) If the decomposition were to go to completion, P PCl_5 = 0.00 atm, P PCl_3 = 1.00 atm, P Cl_2 = 1.00 atm.
    Therefore, P_{total} 2.00 atm

Chapter 3

Page 183, Quick Check

1. a) a mole of liquid water has more disorder, or, entropy, and will occur spontaneously.
   b) the solution has more entropy and will occur spontaneously.
   c) the collection of pieces will occur spontaneously.
   d) the raw rubber has more entropy and will occur spontaneously.
   e) The randomly shuffled deck therefore has higher entropy and will occur spontaneously.

Page 185, Quick Check

1. $\Delta S = 109$ J/(K*mol)
2. a) Cl_2 has more layers of electrons (ie. more "shells") in which the electrons can position themselves than F_2. Therefore, there are more microstates and thus more entropy in Cl_2.
   b) CO_2 has more places where electrons can exist due to the bigger electron cloud and more total electron shells in CO_2 than CO. Therefore, there are more microstates and more entropy in CO_2.
   c) The right picture (pile of bricks) has more entropy since there is more disorder while the left brick wall is organized, thus low on entropy.

Page 186, Practice Problems

1. a) the gas particles have far more microstates than the liquid particles (the entropy change will be positive), and thus the entropy change is going to be positive and evaporation will be spontaneous.
   b) ΔS is going to be negative. The reaction will be non-spontaneous.
   c) ΔS is positive and the change is likely spontaneous.
   d) the entropy change is going to be positive and the dilution will be spontaneous.
2. a) $\Delta S = 174.51 - 413.61 = \frac{-239.1J}{mol\,rxn{*}K}$
   The reaction is non-spontaneous (not thermodynamically favourable) as ΔS<0. [This makes sense as the moles of gas have decreased.]
   b) The reaction is non-spontaneous as ΔS<0.

Page 187, Review Questions

1. a), ΔS is positive
   b) ΔS is negative
   c) ΔS is positive
   d) ΔS is negative
   e) ΔS is negative
   f) ΔS is negative
2. a) ΔS is negative
   b) ΔS is negative
   c) ΔS is positive
   d) ΔS is negative
   e). ΔS is positive
   f) ΔS is negative
3. S = 93.8 J/mol*K
4. $T = \frac{\Delta H^\circ}{\Delta S^\circ} == 373.8K = 100.6$°C. At room temperature is 25°C, formic acid is in liquid state at room temperature.
5. ΔS = -238 J/K
6. T = 150 °C
7. a) 229.6 J/mol_{rxn} K
   b) -311.4 kJ/mol_{rxn}
   c) 1065 °C
8. a) Sign of ΔS° will be negative as the reaction goes from 3 moles of gas to 2 moles of gas, and gases have much higher entropy than solids that the 3 moles of solid's entropy is negligible.
   b) -186.74 J/mol_{rxn} K
9. 205 J/mol O_2*K
10. a) -44.42 J/mol_{rxn} K
    b) -137.56 J/mol_{rxn} K
    c) -5.14 J/mol_{rxn} K
    d) -206.16 J/mol_{rxn} K
    e) 974 J/mol_{rxn} K

Page 193, Quick Check

1. a) Vapourizing any substance requires heat energy. Therefore, it is logical that this is an endothermic process (thus ΔH is positive).
   b) Gases have more microstates (occupy far more positions in space) than liquids, so a transition from liquid to gas results in an increase in entropy.
   c) 60.°C
   d) This temperature represents the boiling point for bromine.

Page 197, Practice Problems

1. -1325.33 kJ/mol rxn
2. −5296.9 kJ of work is available from oxidation of 1 mol of octane.
3. Method 1:
   ΔG° = ΔH° - T*ΔS° = 180.50 kJ/mol - 298 K*(24.77 J/K*mol) = 173.12 kJ/mol_{rxn}
   Method 2:
   ΔG° = 2*ΔG°$_f$ NO = 2* (86.55 kJ/mol) = 173.10 kJ/mol_{rxn}
   The values are very close.

Page 199, Practice Problems

1. a) ΔG° = 14.0 kJ/mol rxn
   b) ΔG° = -18.1 kJ/mol rxn
   c) The reaction becomes more favorable as temperature increases as ΔG° decreases as temperature increases.

Page 200, Review Questions

1. a) Change in enthalpy (ΔH) and change in entropy (ΔS) affect the spontaneity of a process
   b) ΔH is the change in potential energy available to be converted to heat and ΔS is the change in the number of microstates the matter can occupy.
   c) negative ΔH and positive ΔS are associated with spontaneity

2.

Sign of ΔH°	Sign of ΔS°	Temp	Sign of ΔG°	Spontaneous/ Non-spontaneous
-	+	Low	-	Spontaneous
-	+	High	-	Spontaneous
+	-	Low	+	Non-spontaneous
+	-	High	+	Non-spontaneous
-	-	Low	-	Spontaneous
+	+	High	-	Spontaneous
-	-	High	+	Non-spontaneous
+	+	Low	+	Non-spontaneous

3. Circle A:
   i) ΔH is positive, ΔS is also positive
   ii) spontaneous only at high temperatures as ΔG is negative only when T*ΔS is bigger than ΔH.

   Circle B:
   i) ΔH is negative, ΔS is also negative
   ii) spontaneous only at low temperatures as ΔG is negative only when T*ΔS is smaller than ΔH.
4. a) ΔS° is positive as there are more gas molecules (and thus more microstates) on the product side. ΔG° is negative as ΔG° = ΔH° - T*ΔS° and ΔH° is negative while ΔS° is positive, hence ΔG° = (-) - T(+) gives a negative value.
   b) This process is spontaneous at all temperatures - ΔG° = (-) - T(+) gives a negative answer no matter what the T value.
5. a) 3 H_2 (g) + N_2 (g) → 2 NH_3 (g)
   b) -92.22 kJ/mol_{rxn}
   c) ΔS°$_{rxn}$ is negative.
   d) As ΔH°$_{rxn}$ is negative and ΔS°$_{rxn}$ is also negative, and ΔG° = ΔH° - T*ΔS°, this process will be spontaneous only if temperature is low. Otherwise, -T*ΔS° will make ΔG° positive.
   e) The spontaneity of this reaction changes when ΔG°=0, so ΔG° = 0 = ΔH° - T*ΔS°, or, when T = ΔH°/ΔS°.
   ΔS° = -198.75 J/K*mol_{rxn}
   T = 191.0 °C
6. a) I_2 (g) → I_2 (s)
   b) T = 159.0°C
7. a) ΔS°$_{rxn}$ will be positive
   b) ΔS°$_{rxn}$ = 137.56 J/K*mol
   ΔG°$_{rxn}$ = -326.4 kJ/mol
   The predicted signs match the calculated signs, hence the predictions were accurate.
8. a) = -91.12 kJ/mol_{rxn}
   b) -91.73 kJ/mol_{rxn}
   c) 13374.0 kJ/mol_{rxn}
9. a) -74 kJ/mol_{rxn}
   b) 537 J/mol_{rxn}
   c) -228 kJ/mol_{rxn}
   d) Since the enthalpy change is negative and the entropy change is positive, the free energy change will be negative (and hence the reaction will be thermodynamically favourable - that is spontaneous) under all temperature conditions.
   e) The ability to produce fuel over a wide range of temperature conditions improves the economic feasibility. It is particularly expensive to maintain high temperatures during a chemical process, so being able to produce fuels without this necessity makes the process very attractive to a company trying to make money.
10. a) -47 J/K*mol_{rxn}
    b) As ΔS° is negative and ΔH° is also negative, ΔG° will be negative only when the temperature is low enough.
    c) -187 kJ/mol_{rxn}. The reaction is *still* spontaneous at this high temperature (though as expected, it is less spontaneous).

Page 207, Practice Problems

1. -36.31 kJ/mol_{rxn}
2. 1.26 kJ/mol_{rxn}

3. -33.38/ kJ/mol_{rxn}

Page 209, Practice Problems

1. 110 kJ/mol_{rxn}
2. a) 1×10^{6}
   b) 7×10^{-7}
   c) The K value for a) is much bigger than K value for b). This means the reaction in a) is very spontaneous in the forward direction while the reaction in b) is very spontaneous in the reverse direction. This is well suported by the values of $\Delta G°$, as negative value of $\Delta G°$ in a) indicates that the reaction is spontaneous while the positive value of $\Delta G°$ in b) indicates that the reaction is non-spontaneous or spontaneous in the reverse reaction.

Page 211, Review Questions

1. 163 kJ/mol
2. a) 48.3 $kJ/mol_{rxn} > 0$
   Therefore, the forward reaction is not spontaneous at room temperature.
   b) $\Delta S° = 175.0\ J/K{*}mol_{rxn} > 0$
   Entropy drives the reaction forward.
   $\Delta H° = 100.6\ kJ/mol_{rxn} > 0$
   Enthalpy drives the reaction in the reverse direction. Therefore, only entropy drives the reaction forward.
   c) 3×10^{-9}
   d) 301.9°C
   e) $\Delta G = \Delta H° - T{*}\Delta S°$ thus (+) - T(+) only becomes negative when T exceeds 299.9. As T increases further, ΔG becomes more negative and the reaction becomes more spontaneous.
3. a) When the barrel is wide open, $CH_4\ (g) + 2\ O_2\ (g) \rightarrow CO_2\ (g) + 2\ H_2O\ (g)$.
   $\Delta G° = -800.78\ kJ/mol_{rxn}$
   When the barrel is nearly closed, $CH_4\ (g) + 2\ O_2\ (g) \rightarrow CO_2\ (g) + 2\ H_2O\ (l)$.
   $\Delta G° = -817.90\ kJ/mol_{rxn}$
   b) When the barrel is wide open,
   $K = 2\times10^{140}$
   When the barrel is nearly closed,
   $K = 2\times10^{143}$
   c) As evidenced by larger K value and more negative $\Delta G°$, the combustion of methane is more spontaneous when the barrel is nearly closed.
   d) Opening barrel allows more O_2 gas to react to force reaction right.
4. a) $\Delta H° = -41.16\ kJ/mol_{rxn}$
   b) $\Delta S° = -42.08\ J/K{*}mol_{rxn}$
   c) $\Delta G° = -28.62\ kJ/mol_{rxn}$
   d) $K = 1{*}10^{5}$
   e) $K = 1.0{*}10^{3}$
   f) As temperature increased, the K value decreased. This means the reaction was exothermic - as temperature increases, the reaction shifts left to offset the additional heat energy, decreasing the K value.
   This agrees with the answer to part (a) as $\Delta H° = -41.16\ kJ/mol_{rxn} < 0$
5. a) The graphs are similar in that they show potential energy changes as reactants convert to products. Also both graphs represent reactions in which the products have less available energy than the reactants ("exo").
   b) The graphs are different in that the first graph shows changes in free energy as the reaction proceeds while the second graph shows changes in enthalpy. The second graph shows the activated complex while the first graph shows equilibrium point.
6. A: a) The sign of $\Delta H°$ is positive, as ice melts into water by absorbing heat from its surroundings.
   b) The sign of $\Delta S°$ is positive, as the state of water changes from solid to liquid (which has more microstates).
   c) Both $\Delta H°$ and $\Delta S°$ are positive, so at high temperatures, $\Delta G°$ is negative while at low temperatures it is positive.
   B: a) The sign of $\Delta H°$ is positive as the reverse reaction, the combustion of hydrogen, is exothermic.
   b) The sign of $\Delta S°$ is positive, as the reaction goes from 2 moles of gas to 3 moles of gas.
   c) $\Delta H°$ and $\Delta S°$ are both positive, so $\Delta G°$ will be negative at high temperatures and positive at low temperatures.
7. a) $\Delta G° = 4.73\ kJ/mol_{rxn}$
   b) $\Delta G = -1.53\ kJ/mol_{rxn}$
   c) As $\Delta G < 0$, the equilibrium will shift right, producing more NO_2 from N_2O_4. Therefore, the representation will have more NO_2 molecules and less N_2O_4 molecules.
8. a) = -60.3 kJ/mol_{rxn}
   b) The reaction is less spontaneous under these pressure conditions as $\Delta G° = -71.2\ kJ/molrxn < -60.3\ kJ/molrxn = \Delta G$
9. a) -4.0 kJ/mol_{rxn}
   b) The reaction is more spontaneous under these conditions than under standard conditions as $\Delta G = -14.02\ kJ/mol_{rxn} < 20.21\ kJ/mol_{rxn} = \Delta G°$
10. a) 27 kJ/mol_{rxn}
    b) -13. kJ/mol_{rxn}
    c) The reaction becomes thermodynamically favorable as ΔG is now negative.

Chapter 4

Page 219, Quick Check

1. No. Some salts are weak electrolytes. They do not dissolve to a significant extent.
2. a) molecular
   b) ionic
   c) ionic
   d)molecular
   e) ionic
3. Sample A is tap water. It has a low electrical conductivity due to low concentrations of dissolved salts in tap water. Sample B is carbon tetrachloride. It is molecular and does not conduct electricity. Sample C is seawater. It has a significant amount of dissolved ions present so will conduct electricity well.

Page 220, Quick Check

1. $CaCl_2(aq) \rightarrow Ca^{2+}(aq) + 2Cl^-(aq)$
2. $(NH_4)_2C_2O_4(aq) \rightarrow 2NH_4^+(aq) + C_2O_4^{2-}(aq)$
3. $Na_3PO_4(aq) \rightarrow 3Na^+(aq) + PO_4^{3-}(aq)$

Page 221, Quick Check

1. a) $Na_2C_2O_4(aq) \rightarrow 2Na^+(aq) + C_2O_4^{2-}(aq)$
   0.45 M   0.90 M   0.45 M
   total [ions] = 0.90 M + 0.45 M = 1.35 M
   b) $AlCl_3(aq) \rightarrow Al^{3+}(aq) + 3Cl^-(aq)$
   2.5 M   2.5 M   7.5 M
   total [ions] = 2.5 M + 7.5 M = 10.0 M
2. $LiOH(aq) \rightarrow Li^+(aq) + OH^-(aq)$
   1.0 M   1.0 M   1.0 M
   total ion concentration = 2.0 M
   $CaCl_2(aq) \rightarrow Ca^{2+}(aq) + 2Cl^-(aq)$
   0.8 M   0.8 M   1.6 M
   total ion concentration = 2.4 M
   The $CaCl_2$ will have the greater conductivity because it has a greater ion concentration.
3. $AlBr_3(aq) \rightarrow Al^{3+}(aq) + 3Br^-(aq)$
   According to the dissociation equation, 1 mole Al^{3+}: 3 mole Br^-. If $[Br^-] = 0.15$ M, then $[Al^{3+}] = 0.050$ M.

Page 222, Practice Problems 1. a)
$[NH_4^+] = 3(3.6 \times 10^{-3}) = 1.1 \times 10^{-2}$ M
$[PO_4^{3-}] = 3.6 \times 10^{-3}$ M
b) $[H^+] = 2.6$ M $[Cl^-] = 2.6$ M
2. mass of $Al_2(SO_4)_3 = 13$ g
3. total $[NH_4^+] = 0.58$ M, $[SO_4^{2-}] = 0.15$ M $[S^{2-}] = 0.14$ M

Page 223, Practice Problems

1. 5.4×10^{-2} M
2. Mass $Pb(IO_3)_2 = 7.5 \times 10^{-3}$ g
3. mol $CaCO_3$ 7.1×10^{-5} M

Page 224, Quick Check

1. $ZnCO_3(s) \rightleftharpoons Zn^{2+}(aq) + CO_3^{2-}(aq)$
2. $Al(OH)_3(s) \rightleftharpoons Al^{3+}(aq) + 3OH^-(aq)$
3. $Fe_2S_3(s) \rightleftharpoons 2Fe^{3+}(aq) + 3S^{2-}(aq)$

Page 226, 4.1 Review

1. a) any soluble salt or strong acid or base: NaCl, HCl, NaOH. Many answers possible.
   b) any molecular substance not including weak acids: CCl_4, SO_2, XeF_6
2. Both are acids with the same concentration, but $HClO_4$ is a strong acid that ionizes completely. H_3PO_4 is a weak acid, and remains largely in molecular form. Since there are more ions in the $HClO_4$, it will have a greater electrical conductivity.
3. a) $Mg(ClO_4)_2(aq) \rightarrow 2Mg^{2+}(aq) + 2ClO_4^-(aq)$
   b) $CaCr_2O_7(aq) \rightarrow Ca^{2+}(aq) + Cr_2O_7^{2-}(aq)$
   c) $Cu(CH_3COO)_2(aq) \rightarrow Cu^{2+}(aq) + 2CH_3COO^-(aq)$
   d) $Mn(SCN)_2(aq) \rightarrow Mn^{2+}(aq) + 2SCN^-(aq)$
   e) $Al(HC_2O_4)_3(aq) \rightarrow Al^{3+}(aq) + 3HC_2O_4^-(aq)$
   f) $Ba(OH)_2 \cdot 8H_2O(aq) \rightarrow Ba^{2+}(aq) + 2OH^-(aq) + 8\ H_2O(l)$
4. mol $BaSO_4 = 1.0 \times 10^{-5}$ M
5. mass $CaCO_3 = 1.8 \times 10^{-3}$ g
6. $[Na^+] = 0.025$ M $[Cr_2O_7^{2-}] = 0.013$ M
7. $[Mg^{2+}] = 0.80$ M, total $[Cl^-] = 4.9$ M, $[Na^+] = 3.3$ M
8. Measure out 1.0 L of water and add solid NaCl until there is undissolved solid remaining. Pour off until 1.0 L solution remains.
9. a$AgBrO_3(s) \rightleftharpoons Ag^+(aq) + BrO_3^-(aq)$
   b) $Al_2(CrO_4)_3(s) \rightleftharpoons 2Al^{3+}(aq) + 2CrO_4^{2-}(aq)$
   c) $Mg(OH)_2(s) \rightleftharpoons Mg^{2+}(aq) + 2OH^-(aq)$
   d) $PbSO_4(s) \rightleftharpoons Pb^{2+}(aq) + SO_4^{2-}(aq)$
   e) $Cu_3(PO_4)_2(s) \rightleftharpoons 3Cu^{2+}(aq) + 2PO_4^{3-}(aq)$

Page 230, Practice Problems

1. a) low solubility
   b) low solubility
   c) soluble
   d) soluble
   e) soluble
   d) soluble
2. (many answers possible)
   a) Na_2CO_3
   b) $SrSO_4$
   c) Ag^+
   d) NO_3^-
3. The sodium hydroxide contains sodium ions and hydroxide ions. Sodium ions form soluble compounds, so any precipitate must contain the hydroxide anion. The two compounds possible for the precipitate are $Mg(OH)_2$ and $Sr(OH)_2$. According to the Solubility Table, $Mg(OH)_2$ has low solubility and $Sr(OH)_2$ is soluble. The sample must contain strontium nitrate since no precipitate was observed.

Page 231, Quick Check

1. a) $BaSO_4$
   b) $Fe(OH)_2$
   c) $Zn_3(PO_4)_2$
   d) $CrCO_3$
   e) $Mn(OH)_2$
2. a)
   $Sr(OH)_2(aq) + 2AgNO_3(aq) \rightarrow 2AgOH(s) + Sr(NO_3)_2(aq)$
   $Sr^{2+}(aq) + 2OH^-(aq) + 2Ag^+(aq) + 2NO_3^-(aq) \rightarrow 2AgOH(s) + Sr^{2+}(aq) + 2NO_3^-(aq)$
   $Ag^+(aq) + OH^-(aq) \rightarrow AgOH(s)$
   b)
   $MgS(aq) + ZnCl_2(aq) \rightarrow ZnS(s) + MgCl_2(aq)$
   $Mg^{2+}(aq) + S^{2-}(aq) + Zn^{2+}(aq) + 2Cl^-(aq) \rightarrow ZnS(s) + Mg^{2+}(aq) + 2Cl^-(aq)$
   $Zn^{2+}(aq) + S^{2-}(aq) \rightarrow ZnS(s)$
   c)
   $Na_2CO_3(aq) + BaS(aq) \rightarrow BaCO_3(s) + Na_2S(aq)$
   $2Na^+(aq) + CO_3^{2-}(aq) + Ba^{2+}(aq) + S^{2-}(aq) \rightarrow BaCO_3(s) + 2Na^+(aq) + S^{2-}(aq)$
   $Ba^{2+}(aq) + CO_3^{2-}(aq) \rightarrow BaCO_3(s)$

Page 233, Practice Problems

(other answers possible)

1. First add NaCl. Filter out the AgCl(s)
   Then add Na_2S. Filter out the BeS(s)
   Finally add Na_2SO_4. Filter out the $BaSO_4(s)$
2. First add $Ca(NO_3)_2$. Filter out the $CaSO_4(s)$
   Then add $Cu(NO_3)_2$. Filter out the CuS(s)
   Finally add $AgNO_3$. Filter out the AgBr(s)
3. First add $Sr(NO_3)_2$. Filter out the $Sr_3(PO_4)_2(s)$
   Then add $Mg(NO_3)_2$. Filter out the $Mg(OH)_2(s)$
   Finally add $AgNO_3$. Filter out the $Ag_2S(s)$

Page 234, Quick Check

1. The color of the solution (for example, solutions containing Cu^{2+} are blue). Flame test color. Solubility – amount of precipitate formed, the speed at which a precipitate forms, or the ability of a precipitate to re-dissolve on the addition of NH_3 or HNO_3.
2. First add NaCl. A precipitate of both $PbCl_2$ and AgCl may form. Filter out the precipitate, dry it and measure its mass. Put the precipitate into a second beaker. To the original solution, add NaOH. If a precipitate forms, filter out the $Cu(OH)_2(s)$. To the second beaker, add 6 M NH_3. Any AgCl re-dissolves. Filter out the $PbCl_2(s)$. Dry the PbCl2(s) and measure its mass. If the mass had decreased, the presence of AgCl is confirmed.
3. First add HNO_3. The formation of bubbles confirms the presence of CO_3^{2-} ions. Next, add $CaCl_2$. If a precipitate forms, it is $Ca_3(PO_4)_2(s)$. Filter out the precipitate.

Page 238, 4.2 Review Questions

1. a) soluble
   b) low solubility
   c) low solubility
   d) soluble
   e) soluble
   f) soluble
2. Yes – there are silver and sulphate ions in solution. A low solubility simply means that very little will dissolve; **not** that it is insoluble.
3. mol $AgCH_3COO = 0.0665$ M
   0.0665 M < 0.1 M so $AgCH_3COO$ would have a low solubility.
4. A formula equation is written with substances as compounds and states shown.
   A complete ionic equation is written with soluble ionic compounds and strong acids in dissociated form, and compounds with low solubility undissociated. States are also shown.
   A net ionic equation only shows the substances that take part in the reaction. Spectator ions are not shown. States are also shown.
5. A spectator ion is one that does not take part in the reaction. Na^+ ions and NO_3^- ions are often spectators.
6.
   a) $(NH_4)_2S(aq) + FeSO_4(aq) \rightarrow (NH_4)_2SO_4(aq) + FeS(s)$
   $2NH_4^+(aq) + S^{2-}(aq) + Fe^{2+}(aq) + SO_4^{2-}(aq) \rightarrow 2NH_4^+(aq) + SO_4^{2-}(aq) + FeS(s)$
   $Fe^{2+}(aq) + S^{2-}(aq) \rightarrow FeS(s)$
   b) $H_2SO_3(aq) + CaCl_2(aq) \rightarrow 2HCl(aq) + CaSO_3(s)$
   $H_2SO_3(aq) + Ca^{2+}(aq) + 2Cl^-(aq) \rightarrow 2H^+(aq) + 2Cl^-(aq) + CaSO_3(s)$
   $H_2SO_3(aq) + Ca^{2+}(aq) + SO_3^{2-}(aq) \rightarrow 2H^+(aq) + CaSO_3(s)$
   c) $CuSO_4(aq) + CaS(aq) \rightarrow CuS(s) + CaSO_4(s)$
   $Cu^{2+}(aq) + SO_4^{2-}(aq) + Ca^{2+}(aq) + S^{2-}(aq) \rightarrow CuS(s) + CaSO_4(s)$
   $Cu^{2+}(aq) + SO_4^{2-}(aq) + Ca^{2+}(aq) + S^{2-}(aq) \rightarrow CuS(s) + CaSO_4(s)$
7. Na^+ and K^+ are alkali ions. Compounds containing alkali ions are soluble in water.
8. First add Na_2SO_4 to precipitate $CaSO_4$: $Ca^{2+}(aq) + SO_4^{2-}(aq) \rightarrow CaSO_4(s)$
   Filter out the precipitate
   Secondly, add Na_2S to precipitate Cr_2S_3: $2Cr^{3+}(aq) + 3S^{2-}(aq) \rightarrow Cr_2S_3\ (s)$
   Filter out the precipitate
   Finally add NaOH to precipitate $Mg(OH)_2$: $Mg^{2+}(aq) + 2OH^-(aq) \rightarrow Mg(OH)_2(s)$
   Filter out the precipitate
9. First add $Mg(NO_3)_2$ to precipitate $Mg_3(PO_4)_2$: $3Mg^{2+}(aq) + 2PO_4^{3-}(aq) \rightarrow Mg_3(PO_4)_2\ (s)$
   Filter out the precipitate
   Secondly, add $Fe(NO_3)_2$ to precipitate FeS: $Fe^{2+}(aq) + S^{2-}(aq) \rightarrow FeS(s)$
   Filter out the precipitate
   Finally add $AgNO_3$ to precipitate AgCl: $Ag^+(aq) + Cl^-(aq) \rightarrow AgCl(s)$
   Filter out the precipitate
10. Nitrates are soluble in water. If a precipitate forms when a nitrate is added, the precipitate must contain the cation of the nitrate.
11. AgCl can be dissolved in 6M NH_3, while AgI cannot. This can be used to separate AgCl from AgI or AgBr. Carbonates will dissolve on the addition of a strong acid such as HNO_3.
12. a) $2Ag^+(aq) + CO_3^{2-}(aq) \rightarrow Ag_2CO_3(s)$
    b) $Ag_2CO_3(s) + 2H^+(aq) \rightarrow CO_2(g) + H_2O(l) + 2Ag^+(aq)$
    $Ag_2CO_3(s) + 4NH_3(aq) \rightarrow 2Ag(NH_3)_2^+(aq) + CO_3^{2-}(aq)$
13. a) Hard water contains Ca^{2+} ions, Fe^{2+} ions and/or Mg^{2+} ions.
    Scale is $CaCO_3$ that collects inside water heaters, pipes, kettles and boilers.
    b) $CaCO_3(s) + 2HCl(aq) \rightarrow H_2O(l) + CO_2(g) + CaCl_2(aq)$
    $CaCO_3(s) + 2H^+(aq) + 2Cl^-(aq) \rightarrow H_2O(l) + CO_2(g) + Ca^{2+}(aq) + 2Cl^-(aq)$
    $CaCO_3(s) + 2H^+(aq) \rightarrow H_2O(l) + CO_2(g) + Ca^{2+}(aq)$
    c) Many answers are possible: Na_2CO_3
    d) Water softeners remove Ca^{2+} ions and Mg^{2+} ions from hard water. Soap scum can't form without these ions.

Page 242, Quick Check

1. a) $SrCO_3(s) \rightleftharpoons Sr^{2+}(aq) + CO_3^{2-}(aq)$
   b) $Mg(OH)_2(s) \rightleftharpoons Mg^{2+}(aq) + 2OH^-(aq)$
   c) $Ca_3(PO_4)_2(s) \rightleftharpoons 3Ca^{2+}(aq) + 2PO_4^{3-}(aq)$
2. a) $K_{sp} = [Sr^{2+}][CO_3^{2-}]$
   b) $K_{sp} = [Mg^{2+}][OH^-]^2$
   c) $K_{sp} = [Ca^{2+}]^3[PO_4^{3-}]^2$
3. The solubility is the maximum *amount* of solute that can be dissolved in a particular volume of solvent. The solubility product constant is the *product* of the ion concentrations raised to the power of the coefficients from the equilibrium.

Page 244, Practice Problems

1. a) $K_{sp} = 3.7 \times 10^{-9}$
   b) $K_{sp} = 1.9 \times 10^{-13}$
   c) $K_{sp} = 1.2 \times 10^{-10}$
   d) $K_{sp} = 5.2 \times 10^{-12}$
2. $K_{sp} = 5.2 \times 10^{-12}$
3. $K_{sp} = 9.0 \times 10^{-5}$

Page 247, Practice Problems

1. a) 1.3×10^{-5} M
   b) 6.8×10^{-11} g / mL
   c) 4.5×10^{-5} M
   d) 6.8×10^{-11} g
2. 3.0×10^{-10} M
3. 4.0×10^{-3} g

Page 249, 4.3 Review Questions

1. a) $Al(OH)_3(s) \rightleftharpoons Al^{3+}(aq) + 3OH^-(aq)$ $K_{sp} = [Al^{3+}][OH^-]^3$
   b) $Cd_3(AsO_4)_2\ (s) \rightleftharpoons 3Cd^{2+}(aq) + 2\ AsO_4^{3-}(aq)$
   $K_{sp} = [Cd^{2+}]^3[AsO_4^{3-}]^2$
   c) $BaMoO_4\ (s) \rightleftharpoons Ba^{2+}(aq) + MoO_4^{2-}(aq)$
   $K_{sp} = [Ba^{2+}][MoO_4^{2-}]$
   d) $CaSO_4(s) \rightleftharpoons Ca^{2+}(aq) + SO_4^{2-}(aq)$
   $K_{sp} = [Ca^{2+}][SO_4^{2-}]$
   e) $Pb(IO_3)_2(s) \rightleftharpoons Pb^{2+}(aq) + 2IO_3^-(aq)$
   $K_{sp} = [Pb^{2+}][IO^{3-}]^2$
   f)$Ag_2CO_3(s) \rightleftharpoons 2Ag^+(aq) + CO_3^{2-}(aq)$
   $K_{sp} = [Ag^+]^2[CO_3^{2-}]$
2.
   a) $BaSO_3(s) \rightleftharpoons Ba^{2+}(aq) + SO_3^{2-}(aq)$
   b) The solubility is the maximum amount of solute dissolved in a given volume of solvent. The solubility product constant is the solubility squared (s^2)
3. $K_{sp} = 1.2 \times 10^{-10}$
4. $K_{sp} = 9.5 \times 10^{-17}$
5. mass gypsum (g) =0.26 g
6. 7.7×10^{-6} g
7. $K_{sp} = 4.4 \times 10^{-36}$
8. Disagree. Even though the K_{sp} value for $CdCO_3$ (1.0×10^{-6} M) is greater than the K_{sp} for $Cd(OH)_2$ (1.2×10^{-5} M) its solubility is less.
9. The solubility of AgCl (1.3×10^{-5} M) is less than the solubility of Ag_2CrO_4 (6.5×10^{-5} M). All things being equal, the precipitate of AgCl will form first.
10. 9.0×10^{-2} g

Page 252, Practice Problems

1. TIP = 7.6×10^{-10}
   TIP > K_{sp} so a precipitate forms
2. TIP = 1.4×10^{-7}
   TIP < K_{sp} so no precipitate forms
3. TIP = 4.1×10^{-4}
   If no precipitate forms, then TIP < K_{sp} . K_{sp} must be greater than 4.1×10^{-4}.

Page 254, Practice Problems

1. a) $[Sr^{2+}] = 2.1 \times 10^{-6}$ M
   b) $[Sr^{2+}] = 2.4 \times 10^{-6}$ M
   c) $[Sr^{2+}] = 3.1 \times 10^{-5}$ M
2. 2.2 g
3. $[Ag^+] = 3.3 \times 10^{-14}$ M

Page 256, Quick Check

1. a) Only changing temperature changes the value of K_{sp}.
   b) Changing the temperature or the presence of certain ions in the solution can change the solubility of AgCl. For example, if there are Pb^{2+} ions in the solution, the solubility of AgCl would be increased.

2. To decrease the solubility, we need *more* $Mg(OH)_2\ (s)$, so we need to cause the equilibirum system to shift left. The $[Mg^{2+}]$ or $[OH^-]$ could be increased by adding $Mg(NO_3)_2$ or NaOH to the solution.
3. To increase the solubility, we need more $Mg(OH)_2\ (s)$ to *dissolve*, so we need to cause the equilibirum system to shift right. The $[Mg^{2+}]$ or $[OH^-]$ could be decreased by adding a substance to precipitate one of them out such as $Ca(NO_3)_2$ (to precipitate out the OH^-). Additionally, we could add an acid (such as HCl) to neutralize the OH^- ions.
   Since the value of K_{sp} does not change, a decrease in the $[Mg^{2+}]$ (or $[OH^-]$) causes the equilibrium above to shift right and the concentration of the other ion to increase.

Page 257 Practice Problems

1. $x = 2.7 \times 10^{-7}\ M = [Ag^+] = [AgIO_3]$ dissolved
2. $x = 8.5 \times 10^{-7}\ M = [Pb^{2+}] = [PbI_2]$ dissolved
3. 5.1×10^{-7} g/L

Page 260, 4.4 Review Questions

1. a) $FeS(s) \rightleftharpoons Fe^{2+}(aq) + S^{2-}(aq)$
   $K_{sp} = [Fe^{2+}][S^{2-}]$
   b) $Mg(OH)_2(s) \rightleftharpoons Mg^{2+}(aq) + 2OH^-(aq)$
   $K_{sp} = [Mg^{2+}][OH^-]^2$
   c) $Ag_2CrO_4(s) \rightleftharpoons 2Ag^+(aq) + CrO_4^{2-}(aq)$
   $K_{sp} = [Ag^+]^2[CrO_4^{2-}]$
2. a) $CaSO_4$
   b) $CaSO_4(s) \rightleftharpoons Ca^{2+}(aq) + SO_4^{2-}(aq)$
   $K_{sp} = [Ca^{2+}][SO_4^{2-}]$
   c) Not necessarily. The Ca^{2+} came from the $CaCl_2$ and the SO_4^{2-} came from the H_2SO_4. The concentrations of ions depend on the original concentrations of the $CaCl_2$ and the H_2SO_4.
3. $[Pb^{2+}] = 1.2 \times 10^{-6}$ M
4. $[C_2O_4^{2-}] = 5 \times 10^{-7}$ M
5. $[CO_3^{2-}] = 16$ M
6. 3×10^{-6} g
7. $TIP = [Sr^{2+}][SO_4^{2-}] = (9.2 \times 10^{-5})(1.1 \times 10^{-2}) = 1.0 \times 10^{-6}$
   $TIP > K_{sp}$ so precipitate forms
8. $TIP = [Pb^{2+}][Cl^-]^2 = (1.0 \times 10^{-4})(0.080)^2 = 6.6 \times 10^{-7}$ $TIP < K_{sp}$ so no precipitate forms
9. a) $K_{sp} = [Ag^+][Cl^-] = 1.8 \times 10^{-10}$
   $K_{sp} = [Ag^+][I^-] = 8.5 \times 10^{-17}$
   b) See above
   c) AgI
   d) $[Ag^+] = 4.3 \times 10^{-15}$ M
   e) $[Ag^+] = 9.0 \times 10^{-9}$ M
   f) $4.3 \times 10^{-15}\ M < [Ag^+] < 9.0 \times 10^{-9}\ M$
   g) $[I^-] = 9.4 \times 10^{-9}$ M
   h) $\% I^-$ remaining $= \dfrac{9.4 \times 10^{-9}\ M}{0.020\ M} \times 100\% = 0.00047\ \%$
   so $100.00000 - 0.00047 = 99.999953\ \%$ precipitated out.
10. 4.0 g
11. To decrease the solubility, the equilibrium must be shifted left. By adding $Pb(NO_3)_2$ or KI, the common ions (Pb^{2+} or I^-) cause an increase in their respective concentrations.
12. In Na_2SO_4, the common ion SO_4^{2-} exists, so equilibrium shifts left and solubility is decreased. In water, there are no Ba^{2+} or SO_4^{2-} ions.
13. In HCl, the H^+ ions will neutralize the OH^- ions, causing the $[OH^-]$ to decrease. The equilibrium will shift right and the solubility of $Fe(OH)_3$ will increase. It is more soluble in HCl than in water.
14. a) 4.7×10^{-4} g
    b) 5.1×10^{-8} g

Chapter 5

Page 265, Practice Problems

1. a) H_2SO_4 acid
   b) XeF_6 molecular
   c) CH_3COOH acid
   d) $NaCH_3COO$ salt
   e) KOH base
   f) NH_3 molecular (but also a base)
2. a) $CH_3COOH + LiOH \rightarrow LiCH_3COO + H_2O$ ($LiCH_3COO$: salt)
   b) $2HI + Ca(OH)_2 \rightarrow 2H_2O + CaI_2$ (CaI_2: salt)
   c) $3Mg(OH)_2 + 2H_3PO_4 \rightarrow 6H_2O + Mg_3(PO_4)_2$ ($Mg_3(PO_4)_2$: salt)

3.

	Parent Acid	Parent Base
a) KNO_2	HNO_2	KOH
b) NH_4Cl	HCl	NH_4OH (or NH_3)
c) CuC_2O_4	$H_2C_2O_4$	$Cu(OH)_2$
d) $NaCH_3COO$	CH_3COOH	NaOH

Page 268, Practice Problems

1. a) $HIO_3 + NO_2^- \leftrightarrow HNO_2 + IO_3^-$
   acid base acid base
   b) $HF + HC_2O_4^- \leftrightarrow H_2C_2O_4 + F^-$
   acid base acid base
   c) $Al(H_2O)_6^{3+} + SO_3^{2-} \leftrightarrow HSO_3^- + Al(H_2O)_5OH^{2+}$
   acid base acid base
2.

Conjugate acid	Conjugate base
H_2O_2	HO_2^-
H_3BO_3	$H_2BO_3^-$
HCOOH	$HCOO^-$
$HC_6H_5O_7^{2-}$	$C_6H_5O_7^{3-}$

3. a) $HNO_2 + NH_3 \leftrightarrow NO_2^- + NH_4^+$
   acid base base acid
   conjugate pairs: HNO_2/NO_2^- and NH_3/NH_4^+
   b) $H_3C_6H_5O_7 + CN^- \leftrightarrow H_2C_6H_5O_7^- + HCN$
   acid base base acid
   conjugate pairs: $H_3C_6H_5O_7/H_2C_6H_5O_7^-$ and CN^-/HCN
   c) $PO_4^{3-} + H_2S \leftrightarrow HPO_4^{2-} + HS^-$
   base acid acid base
   conjugate pairs: HPO_4^{2-}/PO_4^{3-} and H_2S/HS^-

Page 268, Quick Check

1. $HCO_3^- + CN^- \leftrightarrow CO_3^{2-} + HCN$
2. $HCO_3^- + H_2O \leftrightarrow H_2CO_3 + OH^-$
3. b) and e) are amphiprotic

Page 270, 5.1 Review Questions

1. Both Arrhenius and Bronsted Lowry acids contain H^+ ions. Definitions of a base differ. Arrhenius base contains OH^- ions. Bronsted Lowry base accepts H^+ ion.
2. A Hydrogen atom contains 1 proton and 1 electron. When a H^+ ion is formed, the electron is given away, leaving a single proton.
3.

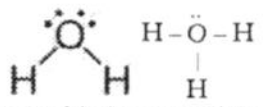

One of the lone pairs of electrons on the oxygen atom of water will attract the H^+ ion from an acid.

4.
a) $NH_3 + H_3PO_4 \leftrightarrow NH_4^+ + H_2PO_4^-$
base acid acid base

b) $H_2PO_4^- + SO_3^{2-} \leftrightarrow HSO_3^- + HPO_4^{2-}$
acid base acid base

c) $CH_3NH_2 + CH_3COOH \leftrightarrow CH_3COO^- + CH_3NH_3^+$
base acid base acid

5.
$HCOOH + H_2O \leftrightarrow HCOO^- + H_3O^+$
Acid base base acid

6.
$C_5H_5N + H_2O \leftrightarrow C_5H_5NH^+ + OH^-$
Base acid acid base

7.
$ClO^- + NH_4^+ \leftrightarrow HClO + NH_3$
Base acid acid base

b) HClO

8. a) Add a H^+ ion. Example: CN^- becomes HCN
   b) Remove a H^+ ion. Example: HNO_2 becomes NO_2^-
9. a) HO_2^-
   b) $N_2H_5^+$
   c) $OC_6H_5^-$
   d) $C_6H_5NH_3^+$
10. A substance that is able act as both an acid or a base depending on the other substance present. Examples: HSO_3^-, $H_2PO_4^-$, HPO_4^{2-}, H_2O
11. a) As an acid: $HCO_3^- + H_2O \leftrightarrow CO_3^{2-} + H_3O^+$; As a base: $HCO_3^- + H_2O \leftrightarrow H_2CO_3 + OH^-$
    Use litmus paper to test the solution. If it is acidic, the litmus will turn red. If it is basic, the litmus will turn blue.
    b) As a base. H_2O and CO_2 can be written as H_2CO_3.
12.
$H_2O + H_2O \leftrightarrow H_3O^+ + OH^-$
Acid base acid base

Page 275, Quick Check

1. Concentrated acids have a high molarity (ex. 6M acid) whereas a strong acid is one that ionizes completely (ex. HCl). You can have a concentrated weak acid - such as 6 M HF.
2. HNO_3 is a strong acid so ionizes completely:
   $HNO_3(aq) + H_2O(l) \rightarrow H_3O^+(aq) + NO_3^-(aq)$
   1.0 M 1.0 M

   $CH_3COOH(aq) + H_2O(l) \leftrightarrow H_3O^+(aq) + CH_3COO^-(aq)$
   1.0 M very few very few

   Because both acids are the same concentration, but HNO_3 is strong and CH_3COOH is weak, the HNO_3 will have more ions in solution.
3. In 0.1 M NaOH: a bright light In 0.1 M NH_3: very dim light or no light visible
   $NaOH(aq) \rightarrow Na^+(aq) + OH^-(aq)$ $NH_3(aq) + H_2O(l) \leftrightarrow NH_4^+(aq) + OH^-(aq)$
4. No, Cl^- will not accept an H^+ ion. HCl is a strong acid and completely ionizes.

Page 276, Quick Check

1. $HF(aq) + H_2O(l) \leftrightarrow H_3O^+(aq) + F^-(aq)$ $K_a = [H_3O^+][F^-]/[HF]$
2. NaOH is a strong base, which means that it ionizes completely. There is no equilibrium present, so no K_b.
3. $CH_3CH_2NH_2(aq) + H_2O(l) \leftrightarrow OH^-(aq) + CH_3CH_2NH_3^+(aq)$
   $K_b = [OH^-][CH_3CH_2NH_3^+]/[CH_3CH_2NH_2]$
4. Acid: $HC_2O_4^-(aq) + H_2O(l) \leftrightarrow H_3O^+(aq) + C_2O_4^{2-}(aq)$
   $K_a = [H_3O^+][C_2O_4^{2-}]/[HC_2O_4^-]$
   Base: $HC_2O_4^-(aq) + H_2O(l) \leftrightarrow OH^-(aq) + H_2C_2O_4(aq)$
   $K_b = [OH^-][H_2C_2O_4]/[HC_2O_4^-]$

Page 278, Quick Check

1. a) strong acid
   b) strong base
   c) weak base
   d) weak acid
   e) weak base
   f) weak acid
2. c) weak base: $NH_3(aq) + H_2O(l) \leftrightarrow NH_4^+(aq) + OH^-(aq)$
   $K_b = [NH_4^+][OH^-]/[NH_3]$
   d) weak acid: $C_6H_5COOH(aq) + H_2O(l) \leftrightarrow H_3O^+(aq) + C_6H_5COO^-(aq)$
   $K_a = [H_3O^+][C_6H_5COO^-]/[C_6H_5COOH]$
   e) weak base: $CN^-(aq) + H_2O(l) \leftrightarrow HCN(aq) + OH^-(aq)$
   $K_b = [HCN][OH^-]/[CN^-]$
   f) weak acid: $HNO_2(aq) + H_2O(l) \leftrightarrow H_3O^+(aq) + NO_2^-(aq)$
   $K_a = [H_3O^+][NO_2^-]/[HNO_2]$
3. Methanoic acid > carbonic acid > boric acid > phenol
   $HCOOH > H_2CO_3 > H_3BO_3 > C_6H_5OH$

Page 281, Quick Check

1. There are more oxygen atoms (which are highly electronegative) attached to the central nitrogen atom - therefore, the O-H bond in Acid 1 is more polarized than in Acid 2 (as 3 oxygen atoms pull electrons away from hydrogen to a greater extent than 2 oxygen atoms do) and hydrogen will be donated more easily in Acid 1. As a result, Acid 1 is stronger than Acid 2.
2. Since the presence of more hydrogen atoms bound to the central atom strengthens the bond between hydrogen and that atom, HBr, HCl, HI > H_2Se, H_2S, H_2O > CH_4 in terms of acid strength.
   I > Br > Cl in terms of size. And as the halogen atoms' size increases, the bond length between the halogen atom and hydrogen increases, so the bond strength decreases, allowing H to be donated more easily and making the acid stronger. Therefore, HI > HBr > HCl in terms of acid strength.
   For the same reason, Se > S > O in terms of size and $H_2Se > H_2S > H_2O$ in terms of acidity. Therefore, $HI > HBr > HCl > H_2Se > H_2S > H_2O > CH_4$ in terms of acid strength.
3. The more oxygen atoms are attached to the central atom, the more polarized the O-H bond is. Therefore, H_2SO_4, $HClO_4$ > $HClO_3$, $HBrO_3$, H_2SO_3 in terms of acid strength.
   Between H_2SO_4 and $HClO_4$, since Cl is more electronegative than H_2SO_4 and pulls electrons away from H more than S does, hydrogen in $HClO_4$ is donated more easily than in H_2SO_4. Therefore, $HClO_4 > H_2SO_4$ in terms of acid strength.
   For similar reasons, H_2SO_3 is weaker than $HClO_3$ and $HBrO_3$ (since Cl and Br are both electronegative halogens while S is not).
   Finally, since Br is less electronegative than Cl, the O-H bond is more polarized in chloric acid than in bromic. This allows hydrogen to be donated more easily. Therefore, $HBrO_3 > HClO_3 > H_2SO_3$.
   Therefore overall, $HClO_4 > H_2SO_4 > HBrO_3 > HClO_3 > H_2SO_3$.
4. Methanoic acid and benzoic acid have main carbon chain lengths of 1 while ethanoic acid has a carbon chain of length 2. Therefore, ethanoic acid's O-H bond is the least polarizable. Furthermore, benzoic acid has a huge group of carbon atoms - a benzene ring (phenyl group) - attached to the 1 carbon chain that allows any charge to disperse between the many carbon & hydrogen atoms in the benzene group, so its O-H bond is the less polarizable than that of methanoic acid.
   Therefore, methanoic acid > benzoic acid > ethanoic acid in terms of polarity of O-H bond and consequently strength.

Page 283, Practice Problems

1a) $H_2O_2 + HSO_3^- \leftrightarrow H_2SO_3 + HO_2^-$; reactants favored

b) $H_3C_6H_5O_7 + NH_3 \leftrightarrow H_2C_6H_5O_7^- + NH_4^+$; products favored

c) $HCO_3^- + H_2PO_4^- \leftrightarrow H_2CO_3 + HPO_4^{2-}$; reactants favored

2. $H_3AsO_4 + SO_4^{2-} \leftrightarrow H_2AsO_4^- + HSO_4^-$; HSO_4^- is stronger
3. $SO_3^{2-} + Cr(H_2O)_6^{3+} \leftrightarrow HSO_3^- + Cr(H_2O)_5OH^{2+}$ products favored so $K_{eq} > 1$

Page 283, 5.2 Review Questions

1. a) strong base
   b) weak acid
   c) Strong acid
   d) weak base
2. $H_3BO_3 + H_2O \leftrightarrow H_2BO_3^- + H_3O^+$ $K_a = [H_2BO_3^-][H_3O^+]/[H_3BO_3]$
   $PO_4^{3-} + H_2O \leftrightarrow HPO_4^{2-} + OH^-$ $K_b = [HPO_4^{2-}][OH^-]/[PO_4^{3-}]$

3. Both acids have the same concentration. Oxalic acid is a weak acid and hydriodic acid is strong. Conductivity depends on ions in solution. Since hydriodic acid is a strong aci, it will ionize completely. Oxalic acid is weak, so it ionizes to a lesser extent, forming fewer ions in solution.
4. HNO_3 is a strong acid so ionizes completely:
$HNO_3(aq) + H_2O(l) \rightarrow H_3O^+(aq) + NO_3^-(aq)$
2.0 M 2.0 M total [ion] = 4.0 M
HNO_2 is a weak acid, so does ionize completely.
5. a) 6 M NH_3
b) 0.001 M HCl
6. a) water < carbonic acid < citric acid < sulphurous acid < sulphuric acid
b) carbonate > ammonia > monohydrogen phosphate > fluoride > nitrite > water
7. $HC_6H_5O_7^{2-} + H_2O \leftrightarrow C_6H_5O_7^{3-} + H_3O^+$
$K_a = [C_6H_5O_7^{3-}][H_3O^+] / [HC_6H_5O_7^{2-}]$

$H_2C_6H_5O_7^- + H_2O \leftrightarrow HC_6H_5O_7^{2-} + H_3O^+$
$K_a = [HC_6H_5O_7^{2-}][H_3O^+] / [H_2C_6H_5O_7^-]$

$Al(H_2O)_6^{3+} + H_2O \leftrightarrow Al(H_2O)_5OH^{2+} + H_3O^+$
$K_a = [Al(H_2O)_5OH^{2+}][H_3O^+] / [Al(H_2O)_6^{3+}]$

$H_2O_2 + H_2O \leftrightarrow HO_2^- + H_3O^+$
$K_a = [HO_2^-][H_3O^+] / [H_2O_2]$

8. $NH_3 + H_2O \leftrightarrow NH_4^+ + OH^-$
$K_b = [NH_4^+][OH^-] / [NH_3]$

$C_6H_5COO^- + H_2O \leftrightarrow C_6H_5COOH + OH^-$
$K_b = [C_6H_5COOH][OH^-] / [C_6H_5COO^-]$

$CH_3COO^- + H_2O \leftrightarrow CH_3COOH + OH^-$
$K_b = [CH_3COOH][OH^-] / [CH_3COO^-]$

$HC_6H_5O_7^{2} + H_2O \leftrightarrow C_6H_5O_7^- + OH^-$
$K_b = [C_6H_5O_7^-][OH^-] / [HC_6H_5O_7^{2-}]$

$C_5H_5N + H_2O \leftrightarrow C_5H_5NH^+ + OH^-$
$K_b = [C_5H_5NH^+][OH^-] / [C_5H_5N]$

9.
a) $Fe(H_2O)_6^{3+}(aq) + HO_2^-(aq) \rightleftharpoons H_2O_2 + Fe(H_2O)_5OH^{2+}$ products
b) $H_2SO_3(aq) + IO_3^-(aq) \rightleftharpoons HSO_3^- + HIO_3$ reactants
c) $CN^-(aq) + H_2PO_4^-(aq) \rightleftharpoons HCN + HPO_4^{2-}$ products
10. $H_2C_2O_4 + HCO_3^- \leftrightarrow H_2CO_3 + HC_2O_4^-$
11. HClO > HBrO > H_2SiO_3
12. All are strong acids so completely ionize in solution to form H_3O^+:
$HCl + H_2O \rightarrow H_3O^+ + Cl^-$
$HBr + H_2O \rightarrow H_3O^+ + Br^-$
$HI + H_2O \rightarrow H_3O^+ + I^-$

Page 290, Quick Check

1. energy + $2H_2O \leftrightarrow H_3O^+ + OH^-$
If temperature increases, equilibrium shifts right and the concentrations of H_3O^+ and OH^- both increase.
$K_w = [H_3O^+][OH^-]$
Therefore, K_w will increase as well.
2. $[H_3O^+] = [OH^-]$
3. 5.4×10^{-8} M = $[H_3O^+] = [OH^-]$

Page 291, Practice Problems

1. $[H_3O^+] = 0.15$ M because $HClO_4$ is a strong acid; $[OH^-] = 6.67 \times 10^{-14}$ M
acidic because $[H_3O^+] > [OH^-]$
2. $[OH^-] = 2s = 2.2 \times 10^{-4}$ M; $[H_3O^+] = 4.5 \times 10^{-11}$ M
basic because $[H_3O^+] < [OH^-]$
3. $[OH^-] = 0.142$ M; $[H_3O^+] = 7.04 \times 10^{-14}$ M
basic because $[H_3O^+] < [OH^-]$

Page 292, Practice Problems

1. $[OH^-] = 2 \times 10^{-13}$ M
2. 2 g
3. $[OH^-] = 5.32 \times 10^{-14}$ M

Page 294, 5.3 Review Questions

1. $NH_3 + NH_3 \leftrightarrow NH_4^+ + NH_2^-$
2.

$[H_3O^+]$	$[OH^-]$	Acidic, basic or neutral ?
1.7×10^{-15}	6.0*M*	basic
3.2×10^{-4}*M*	3.1×10^{-11}	acidic
1.1×10^{-3}	9.2×10^{-12}*M*	acidic
2.5*M*	4.0×10^{-15}	acidic
2.1×10^{-10}	4.7×10^{-5} *M*	basic

3. 57.1 kJ + $2H_2O \leftrightarrow H_3O^+ + OH^-$
As temperature increases, equilibrium shifts right and $[H_3O^+]$ and $[OH^-]$ increase, so K_w increases.
4. $[OH^-] = 5.0 \times 10^{-15}$ M
5. $[OH^-] = 1.6 \times 10^{-8}$ M
acidic because $[H_3O^+] > [OH^-]$

6. Complete the table:

Temp	K_w	$[H_3O^+]$	$[OH^-]$
50° C	5.5×10^{-14}	2.3×10^{-7} M	2.3×10^{-7} M
100° C	5.1×10^{-13}	7.1×10^{-7} M	7.1×10^{-7} M

Both are neutral at given temperatures

7.

$K_w = 7.9 \times 10^{-15}$
8. $[OH^-] = 2s = 0.0211$ M
$[H_3O^+] = 4.7 \times 10^{-13}$ M
9. $[OH^-] = 4.3 \times 10^{-14}$ M
10. 3.2 g

Page 298, Quick Check

1.

Solution	$[H_3O^+]$	pH
orange juice	3.2×10^{-4}*M*	3.49
milk of magnesia	2.52×10^{-11} *M*	10.598
stomach acid	0.031 *M*	1.51

2. The $[H_3O^+]$ increased because the pH decreased. A 5 unit pH decrease corresponds to a
10^5 times increase in hydronium concentration.
3. Initial pH (prior to dilution) = 1.00
After the dilution, the $[H_3O^+]$= 2.00

Page 299, Practice Problems

1.

$[H_3O^+]$	No. of sig. digits	pH
5.00×10^{-5} *M*	3	4.301
4.6×10^{-4} *M*	2	3.34
6.4×10^{-11} *M*	2	10.19
8.81×10^{-7} *M*	3	6.055
0.00345 *M*	3	2.462

2. Just before the equivalence point was reached: $[H_3O^+] = 4.5 \times 10^{-5}$ *M*
Just after the equivalence point was reached: $[H_3O^+] = 2.2 \times 10^{-10}$ *M*
3. Because pH is defined as a negative logarithm, converting a negative pH value to a concentration involves the following:
$[H_3O^+]$ = 16 *M*
The pH scale is not necessary to conveniently express concentrations this large.

Page 302, Practice Problems

1.

Solution	$[H_3O^+]$	$[OH^-]$	pH	pOH	Acidic/Basic/Neutral?
Orange Juice	3×10^{-4} *M*	3×10^{-11} *M*	3.5	10.5	Acidic
Tears	3.98×10^{-8} *M*	2.51×10^{-7} *M*	7.40	6.60	Basic
Blood	4.0×10^{-8}*M*	2.5×10^{-7} *M*	7.40	6.60	Basic
Milk	3.16×10^{-7} *M*	3.16×10^{-8} *M*	6.500	7.500	Acidic

2.
a) As a solution becomes more acidic, both $[H_3O^+]$ and pOH increase and both $[OH^-]$ and pH decrease.
b) A basic solution has a pOH value which is less than 7, and $[H_3O^+]$ which is greater than 10^{-7} *M*.
c) If the pH of a solution equals 14.0, the $[OH^-]$ equals 1 *M*. (1 sig. digit)
d) If the pOH of a solution decreases by 5, then the $[H_3O^+]$ has decreased by a factor of 10^5.
3. We would expect the K_w for water at 10°C to be less than 10^{-14} because the autoionization of water is endothermic. Regardless of the temperature, pure water is always neutral and so:
For pure water at any temperature: $[H_3O^+] = [OH^-]$ and pH = pOH
Therefore, because pH + pOH = pK_w, when we calculate the value of pK_w, the pH (and also the pOH) must be *half the value of* pK_w.
$pK_w = -\log(2.55 \times 10^{-15}) = 14.593$ Therefore, pH (and pOH) = $\underline{14.5934}$ = 7.297

Page 304, Practice Problems

1. 0.86
2. 0.82
3. 2.53
4. 0.0513 g HCl

Page 308, 5.4 Review Questions

1. The pH of a solution is defined as the negative logarithm of the concentration of hydronium ions.
Equation: pH = $-\log[H_3O^+]$
The pOH of a solution is defined as the negative logarithm of the concentration of hydroxide ions.
Equation: pOH = $-\log[OH^-]$
2. Sorenson's logarithmic pH and pOH scales are a convenient and compact way of expressing the typically very small concentrations of hydronium and hydroxide ions respectively and the extent by which they can change in aqueous solutions
3.

$[H_3O^+]$	pH	Acidic/Basic/Neutral
3.50×10^{-6} *M*	5.456	Acidic
3.1×10^{-12} *M*	11.51	Basic
0.00550 *M*	2.260	Acidic
1.0 *M*	0.00	Acidic
6.8×10^{-9} *M*	8.17	Basic

4.

$[OH^-]$	pOH	Acidic/Basic/Neutral
7.2×10^{-9} *M*	8.14	Acidic
2.8×10^{-10} *M*	9.55	Acidic
4.88×10^{-4} *M*	3.312	Basic
1.0×10^{-14} *M*	14.00	Acidic
0.000625 *M*	3.204	Basic

5.
a) As a solution's pOH value and $[H_3O^+]$ both decrease, the solution becomes more basic.
b) As a solution's pH value and $[OH^-]$ both decrease, the solution becomes more acidic.
c) The product of the $[H_3O^+]$ and $[OH^-]$ equals K_w.
d) The sum of pH and pOH equals pK_w.
6.

$[H_3O^+]$	pOH	Acidic/Basic/Neutral
0.0342 *M*	12.534	Acidic
2.51×10^{-6} *M*	8.400	Acidic
7.2×10^{-12} *M*	2.86	Basic
1.64×10^{-11} *M*	3.215	Basic

7. Pure water is always neutral at any temperature and so pH = pOH.
Therefore pH 6.51 (2 sig. digits)
8. pH = 13.78
9. 13.000
10. 0.81 g
11.

$[H_3O^+]$	$[OH^-]$	pOH	pH	Acidic/Basic/Neutral
5.620×10^{-5} *M*	1.779×10^{-10} *M*	9.7497	4.2503	Acidic
2.22×10^{-11} *M*	0.000450 *M*	3.347	10.653	Basic
3.2×10^{-2} *M*	3.2×10^{-13} *M*	12.50	1.50	Acidic
3×10^{-11} *M*	3×10^{-4} *M*	3.5	10.5	Basic

12. 0.79
13. 11.8
14. 12.7
15. 12.24
An alternative approach would be to calculate the total number of moles of hydronium ions from the acid solutions and then subtract that total from the moles of hydroxide ions from the basic solution. The excess moles of hydroxide ions present in the final 100.0 mL are then used to calculate final pH.
16. 0.483 g HCl
17. 0.128 g LiOH

Page 314, Quick Check

1. The amount of water that a weak acid will convert to hydronium ions is insignificant compared to the magnitude of water's concentration (55.6 *M*). The concentration of water is thus assumed to be constant and so is not included in an ICE table.
2. Because the K_a of a weak acid is normally so much greater than K_w, we can assume that the initial $[H_3O^+]$ resulting from the autoionization of water is insignificant compared to the equilibrium $[H_3O^+]$ resulting from the ionization of this weak acid.
3. The value of K_a is small enough compared to the initial concentration of the acid that the percent of the acid which actually ionizes will not significantly change that original concentration. Remember that this assumption is only valid if the percent ionization of the weak acid is ≤ 5 %.

Page 315, Practice Problems

1. 2.02
2. 2.41 (2 sig. digits)
3. 5.4 %
The simplifying assumption would not be valid in this case because the percent ionization is greater than 5 %

Page 316, Practice Problems

1. 0.017 *M*
2. 1.6 *M*
3. 0.45 *M*

Page 317, Practice Problems

1. 1.0×10^{-5}
2. 1.4×10^{-4}
3. 6.56×10^{-5} (The acid is most likely benzoic acid)

Page 319, Quick Check

1.

Weak Base	Conjugate Acid	Appropriate K_a Value	pK_a Value	Calculated K_b	pK_b Value
$HC_2O_4^-$	$H_2C_2O_4$	5.9×10^{-2}	1.23	1.7×10^{-13}	12.77
$H_2PO_4^-$	H_3PO_4	7.5×10^{-3}	2.12	1.3×10^{-12}	11.88
HPO_4^{2-}	$H_2PO_4^-$	6.2×10^{-8}	7.21	1.6×10^{-7}	6.79
NO_2^-	HNO_2	4.6×10^{-4}	3.34	2.2×10^{-11}	10.66
$HC_6H_5O_7^{2-}$	$H_2C_6H_5O_7^-$	1.7×10^{-5}	4.77	5.9×10^{-10}	9.23
HCO_3^-	H_2CO_3	4.3×10^{-7}	6.37	2.3×10^{-8}	7.63
CN^-	HCN	4.9×10^{-10}	9.31	2.0×10^{-5}	4.69

Page 321, Practice Problems

1. 11.05
2. $x = [OH^-] = 5.8 \times 10^{-6}$ *M* so pOH = $-\log(5.8 \times 10^{-6}) = 5.24$
pH = 14.00 - 5.24 = 8.76 and $[H_3O^+] = 10^{-8.76} = 1.7 \times 10^{-9}$ *M*

3. (a) Methylammonium, $CH_3NH_3^+$
$K_a = 2.3 \times 10^{-11}$
$pK_a = 10.64$
(b) Hydrazinium, $N_2H_5^+$
$K_a = 5.9 \times 10^{-9}$
$pK_a = 8.23$

Page 322, Practice Problems
1. 0.87 g $C_2H_5NH_2$
2. 0.49 *M*
3. 6.0×10^{-3} *M*

Page 324, Practice Problems
1. $K_b = 0.020$; Percent ionization = 20. %
This calculated K_b value is greater than the K_b given in the sample problem (4.4×10^{-4}). This indicates that the temperature of the solution is higher than 25° C.
2. $K_b = 2 \times 10^{-6}$ (1 sig. digits)
$pK_b = -\log(1.6 \times 10^{-6}) = 5.79$
3. 3.3×10^{-6}

Page 328, 5.5 Review Questions
1. pH = - log (0.01342) = 1.87 (2 sig. digits) $[H_3O^+] = 10^{-1.87} = 0.013$ M
pOH = 14.00 - 1.87 = 12.13 $[OH^-] = 10^{-12.13} = 7.4 \times 10^{-13}$ M
2. pH = 4.02; Percent ionization = 0.095 %
3. pH = 2.873; $K_a = 1.80 \times 10^{-5}$ (The unknown acid is acetic acid.)
4. 8.9 g HF
5. 0.16 *M* H_3PO_4
6. 0.11 g $H_2C_2O_4$
7. 2.9×10^{-8}
8. 4.9×10^{-5}
9.

Conjugate Acid	Conjugate Base	K_a for acid	pK_a	K_b for base	pK_b
HNO_2	NO_2^-	4.6×10^{-4}	3.34	2.2×10^{-11}	10.66
H_2O_2	HO_2^-	2.4×10^{-12}	11.62	4.2×10^{-3}	2.38
C_6H_5OH	$C_6H_5O^-$	1.3×10^{-10}	9.89	7.7×10^{-5}	4.11
HSO_4^-	SO_4^{2-}	1.2×10^{-2}	1.92	8.3×10^{-13}	12.08

10.

Conjugate Acid	Conjugate Base	K_a for acid	pK_a	K_b for base	pK_b
$H_2PO_4^-$	HPO_4^{2-}	6.2×10^{-8}	7.21	1.6×10^{-7}	6.79
$H_2C_6H_5O_7^-$	$HC_6H_5O_7^{2-}$	1.7×10^{-5}	4.77	5.9×10^{-10}	9.23
H_3BO_3	$H_2BO_3^-$	7.3×10^{-10}	9.14	1.4×10^{-5}	4.86
HCO_3^-	CO_3^{2-}	5.6×10^{-11}	10.25	1.8×10^{-4}	3.75

11. 11.39
12. 12.23
13. 0.10 *M*
14. 9.1 L
15. 4.2×10^{-4}

Chapter 6

Page 333, Quick Check
1. Rb^+, Ca^{2+}, Cs^+, Ba^{2+}
2. ClO_2^-, Cl^-, NO_3^-
3. $RbClO_4$, BaI_2, $CaBr_2$

Page 334, Quick Check
1. $Fe(CH_3COO)_3$, KF, $Pb(NO_2)_2$, $Ba(CN)_2$
2. $Ca(HCOO)_2$, $SrCO_3$, $Mg(CN)_2$, $NaCH_3COO$, LiC_6H_5COO, K_3PO_4

Page 335, Practice Problems
1. K_2CO_3 > RbCN > Na_2SO_3 > $Na_2C_2O_4$ > LiF > KNO_2
2. 11.78
3. 4.5 M

Page 336, Quick Check
1.
a) $CH_3NH_3^+(aq) + H_2O(l) \rightleftharpoons CH_3NH_2(aq) + H_3O^+(aq)$
$K_a = \frac{[CH_3NH_2][H_3O^+]}{[CH_3NH_3^+]}$
b) $C_3H_7NH_3^+(aq) + H_2O(l) \rightleftharpoons C_3H_7NH_2(aq) + H_3O^+(aq)$
$K_a = \frac{[C_3H_7NH_2][H_3O^+]}{[C_3H_7NH_3^+]}$
c) $(CH_3)_3NH^+(aq) + H_2O(l) \rightleftharpoons (CH_3)_3N(aq) + H_3O^+(aq)$
$K_a = \frac{[(CH_3)_3N][H_3O^+]}{[(CH_3)_3NH^+]}$
2.
a) 2.3×10^{-11}
b) 2.9×10^{-11}
c) 1.6×10^{-10}

Page 337, Practice Problems
1. 4.82
2. 5.9×10^{-9}
3. 14 g

Page 338, Quick Check
1. NH_4I, $CrCl_3$, $Fe(NO_3)_3$
2.
(a). $Sn(H_2O)_4^{2+}(aq) + H_2O(l) \rightleftharpoons Sn(H_2O)_3(OH)^+(aq) + H_3O^+(aq)$
(b) $Cu(H_2O)_4^{2+}(aq) + H_2O(l) \rightleftharpoons Cu(H_2O)_3(OH)^+(aq) + H_3O^+(aq)$
(c) $Fe(H_2O)_6^{3+}(aq) + H_2O(l) \rightleftharpoons Fe(H_2O)_5(OH)^{2+}(aq) + H_3O^+(aq)$

Page 339, Practice Problems
1. 0.72
2. 0.023 M
3. 3.45

Page 340, Quick Check
1. NH_4NO_2, $NaCH_3COO$, AlF_3
2. $NH_4^+(aq) + H_2O(l) \rightleftharpoons NH_3(aq) + H_3O^+(aq)$
$F^-(aq) + H_2O(l) \rightleftharpoons HF(aq) + OH^-(aq)$
3. K_a for $NH_4^+ = 5.6 \times 10^{-10}$
K_b for $F^- = 2.9 \times 10^{-11}$
As the K_a for NH_4^+ is greater than the K_b for F^-, the hydrolysis of the ammonium ion will occur to a greater extent than the hydrolysis of the fluoride ion.

Page 341, Practice Problems
1. K_a for $NH_4^+ = 5.6 \times 10^{-10}$
K_b for $CH_3COO^- = 5.6 \times 10^{-10}$
As the K_a for NH_4^+ is equal to the K_b for CH_3COO^-, each hydrolysis reaction will occur to the same extent and so the approximate pH of the solution will be 7.
2.
$NH_4^+(aq) + H_2O(l) \rightleftharpoons NH_3(aq) + H_3O^+(aq)$
$PO_4^{3-}(aq) + H_2O(l) \rightleftharpoons HPO_4^-(aq) + OH^-(aq)$
K_a for $NH_4^+ = 5.6 \times 10^{-10}$
K_b for $PO_4^{3-} = \frac{K_w}{K_a \text{ for } HPO_4^-} = \frac{1.0 \times 10^{-14}}{2.2 \times 10^{-13}} = 0.045$
As the K_b for PO_4^{3-} is much greater than the K_a for NH_4^+, the anionic hydrolysis reaction will occur to a far greater extent and so the solution will be basic.
3. $(NH_4)_2CO_3$ > $NaNO_3$ > $Al(CH_3COO)_3$ > $FeCl_3$

Page 342, Practice Problems
1. K_a for $HPO_4^{2-} = 2.2 \times 10^{-13}$ K_b for HPO_4^{2-} 1.6×10^{-7}
As the K_b for HPO_4^{2-} is greater than its K_a, the hydrolysis reaction involving the production of hydroxide ions will occur to a greater extent and so the solution will be basic.
2. $KHSO_4$ < $NaHSO_3$ < $LiHCO_3$
3. No calculations are required to determine if an aqueous solution of $KHSO_4$ will be acidic or basic because the bisulphate anion is *the conjugate base of a strong acid*. This means that the ion cannot accept protons from water and thus can only act as a weak acid. Therefore, an aqueous solution of $KHSO_4$ will be acidic.

Page 345, 6.1 Review Questions
1. Placing a few drops of universal indicator solution into each of the three beakers will identify the solutes.
The $Al(NO_3)_3$ solution will be acidic because the hydrated Al^{3+} ion is a weak acid and the NO_3^- ion will not hydrolyze. Therefore, universal indicator will appear ***dark orange*** or ***red*** in this solution.
The $Ca(NO_3)_2$ solution will be neutral because neither ion will hydrolyze. Therefore, universal indicator solution will appear ***light green*** in this solution.
The K_3PO_4 solution will be basic because the PO_4^{3-} ion is a relatively strong weak base and the K^+ will not hydrolyze. Therefore, universal indicator will appear ***purple*** in this solution.
2.

Salt Formula	Ion(s) Which Hydrolyze(s)	Result for Aqueous Solution (Acidic, Basic, or Neutral)	Equation(s) for Hydrolysis Reaction(s) (if any)
$(NH_4)_2SO_3$	both	basic as $K_b > K_a$	$NH_4^+ + H_2O \rightleftharpoons NH_3 + H_3O^+$ $SO_3^{2-} + H_2O \rightleftharpoons HSO_3^- + OH^-$
$Al(IO_3)_3$	both	acidic as $K_a > K_b$	$Al(H_2O)_6^{3+} + H_2O \rightleftharpoons Al(H_2O)_5(OH)^{2+} + H_3O^+$ $IO_3^- + H_2O \rightleftharpoons HIO_3 + OH^-$
RbF	F^-	basic	$F^- + H_2O \rightleftharpoons HF + OH^-$
SrI_2	neither	neutral	N/A
KHC_2O_4	$HC_2O_4^-$	acidic as $K_a > K_b$	$HC_2O_4^- + H_2O \rightleftharpoons C_2O_4^{2-} + H_3O^{3+}$ $HC_2O_4^- + H_2O \rightleftharpoons H_2C_2O_4 + OH^-$
$Fe_2(SO_4)_3$	both	acidic as $K_a > K_b$	$Fe(H_2O)_6^{3+} + H_2O \rightleftharpoons Fe(H_2O)_5(OH)^{2+} + H_3O^+$ $SO_4^{2-} + H_2O \rightleftharpoons HSO_4^- + OH^-$

3. a) $CH_3COOH(aq) + KOH(aq) \rightarrow KCH_3COO(aq) + H_2O(l)$
b) The salt solution that exists in the reaction vessel is 0.25 M KCH_3COO
c) 9.07
4. 10.30
5. 0.43 g
6. 0.0012 g
7. 4.67
8. $NaHSO_4$ < $FeCl_3$ < $Cr(NO_3)_3$ < NH_4Br < RbI < KCN < Li_2CO_3 < Na_3PO_4
9. a) 14 g
b) The pH of the solution will increase as evaporation proceeds because the concentration of the basic anion is increasing.
10. 4.27

Page 350, Quick Check
1. Equal concentrations of a weak acid and its conjugate base allow the buffer to resist changes to its pH *equally well* following the addition of relatively small amounts of *both* strong acid and strong base.
2. In a buffer containing HA and A^-, the conjugate base, A^-, will react to neutralize added acid. As a result, following the addition of a small amount of strong acid to a buffer solution, the $[HA]/[A^-]$ ratio will increase, the $[H_3O^+]$ will increase slightly, and the pH will decrease slightly.
3. KF and HF + HCOOH and LiHCOO
$NaHSO_4$ and Na_2SO_4 + KH_2PO_4 and K_2HPO_4

Page 353, Practice Problems
1. a) Following the addition of a small amount of strong base to a buffer solution, the $[HA]/[A^-]$ decreases, the $[H_3O^+]$ decreases slightly, and the pH increases slightly.
b) $HNO_2(aq) + OH^-(aq) \rightarrow NO_2^-(aq) + OH^-(aq)$
c) Following the addition of this strong base, the $[HNO_2]/[NO_2^-]$ ratio will decrease, the $[H_3O^+]$ will decrease slightly, and the pH of this solution will increase slightly.
2.(a) In 1.0 L of the diluted buffer solution, only 0.10 moles of HNO_2 and NO_2^- are available to neutralize added H_3O^+ and OH^-. However, in the undiluted solution, 1.0 mol of each of these buffer components is available.
(b) Because only 0.10 mole of NO_2^- is available to neutralize added acid, the addition of 0.11 mol of strong acid will exceed the diluted *buffer's capacity* to neutralize acid by 0.01 moles and thus result in the pH of the diluted buffer decreasing significantly. The undiluted buffer, however, has 1.0 mole of NO_2^- available and can easily neutralize the added acid. The pH of the undiluted buffer solution will therefore not drop appreciably.
3. a) The combination of 0.10 M HI and 0.10 M NaI does not qualify as a buffer because although the HI is capable of neutralizing added base, the iodide ion is the conjugate base of a strong acid. This means that I^- cannot neutralize added acid because it cannot accept protons.
b) The combination of 0.50 M NaF and 0.50 M NaCN does not qualify as a buffer because although sufficient quantities of weak base (F^- and CN^-) are available to neutralize added acid, no weak acid is present in the solution. This means that the solution has no ability to neutralize added base.
c) The combination of 1.0 M $K_2C_2O_4$ / 1.0 M KHC_2O_4 does qualify as a buffer because this solution has appreciable (and in this case equal) quantities of both a weak acid ($HC_2O_4^-$) and its conjugate base ($C_2O_4^{2-}$). Therefore, both added acid and base can be neutralized by this solution.
d) The combination of 0.20 M HF and 0.20 M HCN does not qualify as a buffer because although sufficient quantities of weak acid (HF and HCN) are available to neutralize added base, no weak base is present in the solution. This means that the solution has no ability to neutralize added acid.

Page 356, Practice Problems
1.

	Weak Base	Added Compound
a)	1.0 M CH_3NH_2	1.0 M CH_3NH_3Cl
b)	0.80 M N_2H_4	0.80 M $N_2H_5NO_3$
c)	0.20 M $(CH_3)_2NH$	0.20 M $(CH_3)_2NH_2Br$

(Note that in the above table, the anions present in the added compounds are the conjugate bases of strong acids. This ensures their role as spectator ions in the solution.)
2.

Net Ionic Equation When Acid Added	Net Ionic Equation When Base Added
a) $CH_3NH_2(aq) + H_3O^+(aq) \rightarrow CH_3NH_3^+(aq) + H_2O(l)$	a) $CH_3NH_3^+(aq) + OH^-(aq) \rightarrow CH_3NH_2(aq) + H_2O(l)$
b) $N_2H_4(aq) + H_3O^+(aq) \rightarrow N_2H_5^+(aq) + H_2O(l)$	b) $N_2H_5^+(aq) + OH^-(aq) \rightarrow N_2H_4(aq) + H_2O(l)$
c) $(CH_3)_2NH(aq) + H_3O^+(aq) \rightarrow (CH_3)_2NH^+(aq) + H_2O(l)$	c) $(CH_3)_2NH^+(aq) + OH^-(aq) \rightarrow (CH_3)_2NH(aq) + H_2O(l)$

Page 359, Practice Problems

1. The four buffer solutions ranked in order from lowest to highest capacity are:

b < d < a < c

2. Because the $[A^-]/[HA]$ ratio should be no less than 0.1 and no more than 10 for a buffer to be effective, the Henderson-Hasselbalch equation shows us that buffers have a usable range within ± 1 pH unit of the pK_a of the acid component as shown by the following:

$$pH = pK_a + \log\left[\frac{[A^-]}{[HA]}\right]$$

$$pH = pK_a + \log\left[\frac{1}{10}\right] = pK_a - 1 \quad \text{and} \quad pH = pK_a + \log\left[\frac{10}{1}\right] = pK_a + 1$$

$$\text{Buffer pH range} = pK_a \pm 1$$

3.

Desired pH	Weak Acid	Weak Acid pK_a	Salt of Conjugate Base
4.00	**benzoic**	**4.19**	**NaC_6H_5COO**
7.00	**bisulfphite ion**	**7.00**	**Na_2SO_3**
10.00	**phenol**	**9.89**	**NaC_6H_5O**

Page 360 Quick Check

1. a) $HPO_4^{2-}(aq) + H_3O^+(aq) \rightarrow H_2PO_4^-(aq) + H_2O(l)$
   b) $H_2PO_4^-(aq) + OH^-(aq) \rightarrow HPO_4^{2-}(aq) + H_2O(l)$
2.
   a) If the concentration of dissolved carbon dioxide in the blood is too low, the above equilibrium will shift to the left and so the concentration of hydrogen (hydronium) ions in the blood will drop. This will raise the blood pH level.
   (If the blood pH level gets too high, the $[HBO_2^-]$ will get too high to allow for adequate release of molecular oxygen from hemoglobin. This condition is called *alkalosis*.)
   b) Breathing into a paper bag means that exhaled breath containing CO_2 in continually re-inhaled. This raises the concentration of dissolved carbon dioxide in the blood which shifts the equilibrium described in 2(a) above to the right. This in turn increases the $[H^+]$ in the blood and thus lowers the blood pH level.

Page 363, 6.2 Review Questions

1. The purpose of a buffer is to resist significant pH changes following the addition of relatively small amounts of strong acid or strong base.
2. The components of a buffer solution are normally a conjugate acid-base pair because these components will not react with each other.
3. A buffer must be able to resist pH changes following the addition of either an acid or a base. Although HNO_3 is certainly capable of neutralizing added OH^- ions, its conjugate base, NO_3^-, cannot neutralize added acid. This is because the nitrate ion is the conjugate base of a strong acid and is thus incapable of accepting protons.
4. C_6H_5COOH / KC_6H_5COO
   $CH_3NH_3NO_3 / CH_3NH_2$ $K_2SO_3 / KHSO_3$
   KIO_3 / HIO_3 $NaHS / H_2S$ HF / LiF
   $H_2O_2 / RbHO_2$
5. a) As $[HCN] = [CN^-]$, then $[H_3O^+] = K_a$ for $HCN = 4.9 \times 10^{-10}$ M
   b) This solution considered to be a basic buffer because it buffers the solution in the basic region of the pH scale.
   c) $CN^-(aq) + H_3O^+(aq) \rightarrow HCN(aq) + H_2O(l)$
   Following the addition of a small amount of HCl, the pH of the buffer solution will decrease slightly.
   d) $HCN(aq) + OH^-(aq) \rightarrow CN^-(aq) + H_2O(l)$
   Following the addition of a small amount of NaOH, the pH of the buffer solution will increase slightly.
6.

Stress Applied	Net Ionic Equation	How $[HA]/[A^-]$ Changes	How pH Changes
H_3O^+ added	$A^-(aq) + H_3O^+(aq) \rightarrow HA(aq) + H_2O(l)$	$[HA]/[A^-]$ ratio increases	pH decreases slightly
OH^- added	$HA(aq) + OH^-(aq) \rightarrow A^-(aq) + H_2O(l)$	$[HA]/[A^-]$ ratio decreases	pH increases slightly

7. The buffer solutions listed in order from lowest $[H_3O^+]$ to highest $[H_3O^+]$ are:
   b < a < c < d
8. Buffer Capacity is defined as the amount of acid or base a buffer can neutralize before its pH changes appreciably. Buffer Capacity depends on the absolute concentrations of the buffer components. A more concentrated, or *high-capacity* buffer will experience less of a pH change following the addition of a given amount of strong acid or strong base than a less concentrated or *low-capacity* buffer will. Therefore, buffer solution "d" listed above would have the highest capacity.
9. The buffer solutions listed in order from highest to lowest capacity are:
   d > b > a > c
10. Buffer range is defined as the pH range over which a buffer acts effectively. That pH range is normally from 1 pH unit below the pK_a value for the weak acid component of a buffer solution to 1 pH above the pK_a value.
11. When the concentration of dissolved carbon dioxide in the blood decreases, the concentration of hydrogen (hydronium) ions in the blood also decreases. This raises the blood pH level.
12. Alkalosis occurs when the blood pH level gets too high. This causes the $[HbO_2^-]$ to increase to the point where the release of O_2 from hemoglobin molecules is compromised. In short, the hemoglobin will not release the oxygen molecules to which it has attached.
13. Acidosis occurs when the blood pH level gets too low. This causes the $[HbO_2^-]$ to decrease to the point where hemoglobin's affinity for oxygen is reduced. In short, hemoglobin and oxygen will no longer bind together.
14. By considering the net ionic equation for the neutralization of a strong base by the acidic component of a buffer, the answer to this question becomes clear. In this case, when NaOH is added to a solution of HNO_2, the following represents the net ionic equation:
    $HNO_2(aq) + OH^-(aq) \rightarrow NO_2^-(aq) + H_2O(l)$
    This shows us that if we add 0.50 mol NaOH to 1.0 L of 1.0 M HNO_2, the 0.50 mol NaOH will be totally consumed and in the process stoichiometrically convert 0.50 mol HNO_2 into 0.50 mol NO_2^-. We will therefore have a buffer solution containing equal concentrations of the weak acid HNO_2 and its conjugate base, NO_2^-.
15. The Henderson-Hasselbalch equation shows us that if the buffer component concentrations are equal, then the pH of the buffer solution simply equals the pK_a of the acid present in the buffer.

As $pH = pK_a + \log\left[\frac{[A^-]}{[HA]}\right]$

If $[A^-] = [HA]$, then $pH = pK_a$

   a) $pH = pK_a$ for $HNO_2 = -\log(4.6 \times 10^{-4}) = 3.34$
   b) $pH = pK_a$ for $CH_3COOH = -\log(1.8 \times 10^{-5}) = 4.74$
   c) $pH = pK_a$ for $NH_4^+ = -\log(5.6 \times 10^{-10}) = 9.25$
   d) $pH = pK_a$ for $HF = -\log(3.5 \times 10^{-4}) = 3.46$

16.

a) The solution must be buffered to pH = 10.00 using CO_3^{2-} and HCO_3^-.
Therefore:

$$10.00 = pK_a \text{ for } HCO_3^- + \log\left[\frac{[CO_3^{2-}]}{[HCO_3^-]}\right]$$

Because the $[HCO_3^-] = 0.20$ M, the above equation is written as the following:

$$10.00 = 10.25 + \log\left[\frac{[CO_3^{2-}]}{0.20}\right] \quad \text{so:} \quad \log\left[\frac{[CO_3^{2-}]}{(0.20)}\right] = -0.25$$

$$\frac{[CO_3^{2-}]}{(0.20)} = 10^{-0.25} = 0.562$$

so: $[CO_3^{2-}] = (0.20)(0.562) = 0.112$ M

$$[CO_3^{2-}] = [Na_2CO_3] = \frac{0.112 \text{ mol}}{\text{L}} \times \frac{106.0 \text{ g } Na_2CO_3}{\text{mol}} \times 1.0 \text{ L} = 12 \text{ g}$$

b) 9.99

17. a) pH = 4.92
    b) pH = 9.13
18. a) pH = 4.74
    b) pH = 4.64
    c) pH = 4.85
19. pH = 3.42
20. 6.2 to 1 (6.2:1)
21. 0.80 mol/L
22. a) pH = 4.79
    b) (i) 4.1×10^{-2} mol/L
    (ii) 0.200 mol/L

Page 370, Quick Check

1. To ensure that an acid-base titration reaction goes to completion, at least one of the two reacting species must be strong.
2. An "endpoint" or "transition point" in an acid-base titration is the point at which an indicator changes colour and is only dependent upon the chemical nature of the acid-base indicator.
   The "equivalence point" or "stoichiometric point" in an acid-base titration is the point at which the total number of moles of H_3O^+ from the acid equals the total number of moles of OH^- from the base. The equivalence point is only dependent upon the chemical nature of the reacting species.
3. The table shows that the volume from trial 1does not agree to within 0.1 mL of the volumes from either trial 2 or trial 3. Trial 1is therefore discarded and the volumes from trials 1 and 3 are averaged to obtain the correct volume of standard solution recorded by the student.

Titration Trial	Volume of Std. Solution
1	23.88 mL
2	23.67 mL
3	23.59 mL

Average volume of standard solution

$$= \frac{23.67 \text{ mL} + 23.59 \text{ mL}}{2} = 23.63 \text{ mL}$$

Page 371, Quick Check

1. A 4.00 g sample of NaOH will contain less than 0.100 mol of the compound. A portion of the sample's mass will be due to absorbed water and also Na_2CO_3 produced from the reaction of the NaOH with atmospheric CO_2.
2. a) A volumetric pipette ensures the accurate and precise measurement of the volume of the solution being analyzed in the reaction flask.
   b) Standardizing the titrant against a primary standard ensures the accurate and precise determination of the titrant's concentration.
   c) A burette ensures the accurate and precise measurement of the volume of titrant required in the titration.
   d) An appropriate indicator signals the correct determination of the equivalence point during the titration.

Page 372, Practice Problems

1. 0.121 M NaOH
2. 0.1259 M HNO_3

Page 373, Practice Problems

1. 0.0603 M
2. 0.206 M
3. 0.101 M

Page 375, Practice Problems

1. 24.1 mL
2. 38.5 mL
3. 27.2 mL

Page 377, Practice Problems

1. 88.1 g /mol
2. 94.9 g/mol
3. 285 g/mol

Page 379, Practice Problems

1. 93.40 %
2. 92.5 %
3. 94.9 %

Page 382, 6.3 Review Questions

1. Disagree. Because a titration reaction goes to completion, the volume of standard solution required is only dependent upon the stoichiometry of the reaction and the moles of each species (acid or base) that it must neutralize. *It is not dependent upon the strength of those species.* Thus each acid solution will require approximately the same volume of standard NaOH solution to reach the equivalence point.
2. Agree. The volume of solution to be analyzed has been recorded and thus the number of reactant moles has been specified. Adding water to the reaction flask will not change the number of moles of reactant present and will thus not affect the volume standard solution required to reach the equivalence point.
3. Agree. A 25.0 mL of approximately 0.2 M acetic acid contains approximately 0.005 mol of acid as given by the following:
   $$0.0250 \text{ L} \times \frac{0.2 \text{ mol } CH_3COOH}{\text{L}} = 0.005 \text{ mol } CH_3COOH$$
   A 50.0 mL burette filled to capacity with 0.0650 M NaOH contains only 0.00325 mol NaOH as given by the following:
   $$0.0500 \text{ L} \times \frac{0.0650 \text{ mol NaOH}}{\text{L}} = 0.00325 \text{ mol NaOH}$$
   Thus there is insufficient standard solution available in the burette to reach the equivalence point.
4. Agree. NaOH is normally only 95 – 98 % pure and rapidly both absorbs water and reacts with CO_2 from the atmosphere. Therefore, any amount of NaOH will contain impurities and thus less than the measured mass of NaOH. This means that the calculated [NaOH] will be too high.
5. 0.162 M
6. 0.170 g
7. 28.3 mL
8. 27.5 mL
9. 122 g/mol
10. 104 g/mol
11. 91.6 %
12. 95.6 %
13. 89.5 %
14. The "analysis" process is always based on the volume of solution added from the burette. This determines the number of moles of one reagent required to reach the equivalence point and all subsequent calculations proceed from that data.

Page 389, Practice Problems

1. 3.8; $K_a = 2 \times 10^{-4}$
In a 1.8×10^{-4} M HCl solution:
$[H_3O^+] = [HCl] = 1.8 \times 10^{-4}$ M (This equals the approximate K_a of bromphenol blue.)
And $pH = -\log(1.8 \times 10^{-4}) = 3.74$
Because the solution pH corresponds to the transition point pH for bromphenol blue, an intermediate green colour will be seen.
2. $[H_3O^+] \approx 10^{-8.1} \approx 8 \times 10^{-9}$ M (1 sig. digit)
3. an intermediate orange colour is seen.
4. $K_{a1} = 4 \times 10^{-7}$
$K_{a2} = 2 \times 10^{-12}$
5. Solution A has a pH ≥ 10. This must be the Na_2CO_3 solution. The carbonate anion is a relatively strong weak base and the cation dos not hydrolyze.

   Solution B has a pH ≈ 7. This must be the NH_4CH_3COO solution. Both the cation and the anion of salt hydrolyze, but because the K_a of the cation = K_b of the anion, the solution will be neutral.

   Solution C has a pH between 4.4 and 7.0. This must be the NaH_2PO_4 solution. The cation of the salt does not hydrolyze, and the K_a of the amphiprotic anion (6.2×10^{-8}) is greater than its K_b (1.3×10^{-12}). Therefore the solution will be slightly acidic.

   Solution D has a pH ≤ 3.2. This must be the $NaHSO_4$ solution. The cation does not hydrolyze and the anion (which can only donate protons to water) is a stronger weak acid than any ion present in the other salts. This solution will therefore be the most acidic.

Page 394, Quick Check

1. $H_3O^+(aq) + OH^-(aq) \rightarrow 2H_2O(l)$
2. Phenolphthalein is often chosen because the appearance of a pink colour in a colourless solution at the transition point is much easier to detect than a change in colour from one colour to another.
3. The pH at the equivalence point of a strong acid – strong base titration is equal to 7 because neither of the dissociated ions from the salt that exists at the equivalence point will undergo hydrolysis.

Page 395, Practice Problems

1. 4
2. 10
3. The solution at the equivalence point will be slightly basic. Although the cation (Na^+) of the dissociated salt will not hydrolyze, the anion (SO_4^{2-}) of the salt the conjugate base of a weak acid and will thus hydrolyze by accepting protons from water producing OH^- ions.

Page 402, Quick Check

1. The "buffer region" of a weak acid – strong base titration curve is so-named because during this part of the titration, appreciable quantities of both a weak acid and its conjugate base exist in the reaction flask.
2. The pH at the equivalence point of a weak acid – strong base titration is higher than 7 because the cation of the product salt will not hydrolyze, but the anion of the product salt is a weak base. Thus, the anion will accept protons from water producing OH^- ions.
3. Beyond the equivalence point, the contribution the acetate ion makes to the $[OH^-]$ is insignificant because excess NaOH is present in the solution.

Sodium hydroxide is a *strong base* and the excess hydroxide ions from this base suppress the hydrolysis of the weakly basic acetate ion by forcing that equilibrium further to the left as shown below:

$CH_3COO^- + H_2O \quad CH_3COOH + OH^-$

4.

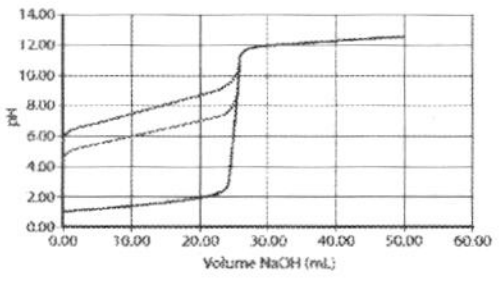

Page 402, Practice Problems

1. a) 3.66
   b) 8.37
2. The weak acid being titrated is benzoic acid.
3. a) 4.6×10^{-4} M
   b) 8.36

Page 408, Practice Problems

1. 9.22
2. Once the titration curve is drawn for the titration of a weak base by a strong acid, the pH, and thus the pOH, of the solution halfway to the equivalence point can be determined from the curve. The pOH of the solution halfway to the equivalence point equals the pK_b of the weak base being titrated. From that pK_b value, we can determine the K_b of the weak base.
3. 1.637; This calculated pH value does agree with the titration curve.

Page 408, Quick Check

1. The pH of a weak base – strong acid titration is lower than 7 because the anion of the product salt will not hydrolyze, but the cation of the product salt is a weak acid. Thus, the cation will donate protons to water producing H_3O^+ ions.
2. Phenolphthalein would be a poor choice for an indicator because as the strong acid is added to the weak base in the reaction flask, the indicator's pink colour will disappear at pH 8.2. This is in the basic range of the pH scale and well above the equivalence point pH which is below 7 in the acidic range of the pH scale. The result would be an incorrectly low volume recorded for an equivalence point and thus a calculation of too few moles of acid.
3. Beyond the equivalence point, the contribution the ammonium ion makes to the $[H_3O^+]$ is insignificant because excess HCl is present in the solution. The excess HCl is a *strong acid* and the increasing $[H_3O^+]$ from that acid forces the weak acid hydrolysis equilibrium even further to the left as shown below:

$$NH_4^+(aq) + H_2O(l) \rightleftharpoons NH_3(aq) + H_3O^+(aq)$$

The result is that we can safely ignore any contribution to the $[H_3O^+]$ in the flask by the ammonium ion.

Page 411, 5.4 Review Questions

1. Given that: $\frac{K_a}{[H_3O^+]} = \frac{[In^-]}{[HIn]}$ and $K_a = 1.0 \times 10^{-7}$

Then:

Solution	[In⁻] / [HIn] Ratio in Solution	Solution Colour
0.0010 M HCl	$\frac{1.0 \times 10^{-7}}{1.0 \times 10^{-3}} = \frac{[In^-]}{[HIn]} = 1.0 \times 10^{-4}$	Yellow
Pure Water	$\frac{1.0 \times 10^{-7}}{1.0 \times 10^{-7}} = \frac{[In^-]}{[HIn]} = 1.0$	Green
0.0010 M NaOH	$\frac{1.0 \times 10^{-7}}{1.0 \times 10^{-11}} = \frac{[In^-]}{[HIn]} = 1.0 \times 10^{4}$	Blue

2. a) Because the yellow form of the indicator is seen in the presence of HA1, then HIn is a stronger acid than HA1.
   b) Because the red form of the indicator is seen in the presence of HA2, then HIn is a weaker acid than HA2.
   Thus: HA1 < HIn < HA2

3.

Solution →	0.10 M HCl	0.10 M NaOH	0.10 M $FeCl_3$	0.10 M NaCN
Indicator 1: methyl violet	*yellow/green*	blue	blue	blue
Indicator 2: bromthymol blue	yellow	blue	*yellow*	blue
Indicator 3: indigo carmine	blue	*yellow*	blue	*blue*

4.

	HNO_3 + KOH	NaOH + HCOOH	HBr + NH_3
pH at Equivalence Pt.	7	above 7	below 7
Indicator	phenolphthalein	phenolphthalein	methyl red

5. a) The K_a for bromcresol purple is slightly less than the K_a for acetic acid and so bromcresol purple is a slightly weaker acid than acetic acid.
   b) Because the two weak acids are so close in strength, when both are present in a solution, the position of the equilibrium will not favour one side appreciably more than the other. This means that approximately equal [HIn] and $[In^-]$ will exist in the solution resulting in an intermediate colour between yellow and purple. Thus, bromcresol purple would not be an ideal indicator to show that acetic acid is acidic.

6.

Solution A	Solution B	Solution C	Solution D	Solution E
HIO_3	**NaCl**	**K_3PO_4**	**CH_3COOH**	**LiHCOO**

7.

Indicator	pK_a	K_a	Colour in Pure Water	Colour Displayed in 0.010 M NaOH	Colour Displayed in 0.010 M HCl
Phenol Red	7.3	5×10^{-8}	yellow/orange	red	yellow
Methyl Orange	3.8	2×10^{-4}	yellow	yellow	red
Alizarin Yellow	11.1	9×10^{-12}	yellow	red	yellow

8. a) In a weak acid – strong base titration, the weaker the acid being titrated, the or higher the initial pH of the solution will be, and the higher the pH at the equivalence point will be.
   b) In a weak base – strong acid titration, the weaker the base being titrated, the lower the initial pH of the solution will be, and the lower the pH at the equivalence point will be.

9.

	Calculating pH Halfway to the Equivalence Point (Chemistry of Buffers)	Calculating pH at the Equivalence Point (Hydrolysis of Salts)
Titration of a Weak Acid by a Strong Base	A buffer solution exists at this point in the titration such that [weak acid] = [conjugate base] in the reaction flask. Thus, the $[H_3O^+] = K_a$ for the weak acid and $pH = pK_a$.	At the equivalence point for this type of titration, the anion of the salt that exists at the equivalence point is the conjugate base of a weak acid. Being a weak base, it will thus hydrolyze by accepting protons from water producing OH^-.
Titration of a Weak Base by a Strong Acid	A buffer solution exists at this point in the titration such that [weak base] = [conjugate acid] in the reaction flask. Thus, the $[H_3O^+] = K_a$ for the conjugate acid and $pH = pK_a$.	At the equivalence point for this type of titration, the cation of the salt that exists at the equivalence point is the conjugate acid of a weak acid. Being a weak acid, it will thus hydrolyze by donating protons to water producing H_3O^+.

10. For each type of titration described in question 8 above:

    Step 1 in calculating the equivalence point pH involves calculating the final concentrations of the reacting species resulting from the titration reaction which goes to completion. This is most conveniently done by employing an *ICF* table in the solution process.

    Step 2 then involves using the concentrations calculated in step 1 above as the initial concentrations in either a weak base pH calculation (due to anionic hydrolysis in #8. (a)) or a weak acid pH calculation (due to cationic hydrolysis in #8. (b)). This is most conveniently done by employing an *ICE* table in the solution process.

11. a) 3.74
    b) 25.0 mL
    c) 8.40
12. Thus pK_a for weak acid = 3.456 and so $K_a = 10^{-3.456} = 3.50 \times 10^{-4}$; This matches the K_a for hydrofluoric acid.
13. Thus pK_b for weak base = 14.00 - 9.50 = 4.50 and so $K_b = 10^{-4.50} = 3.2 \times 10^{-5}$
14.

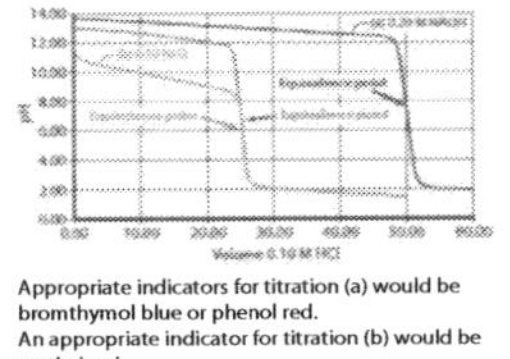

Appropriate indicators for titration (a) would be bromthymol blue or phenol red.
An appropriate indicator for titration (b) would be methyl red.

15. a)

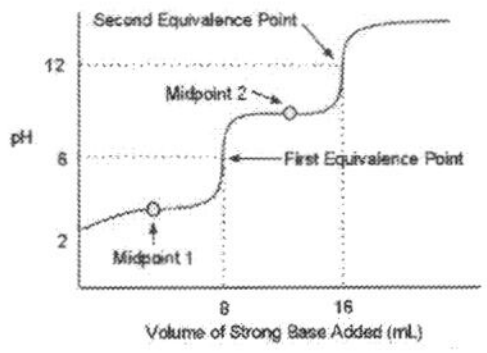

(b) Selecting a diprotic indicator with pK_{a1} and pK_{a2} values close to the first and second equivalence point pH values respectively would be appropriate. Alternatively, monitoring the pH during the titration with a pH meter would be advisable.

Page 417, Quick Check

1. For a metal oxide to react with water to produce a basic solution and thus be considered a basic anhydride, the metal oxide must be both highly ionic and soluble.
2. The elements in Groups 1 and 2 (except beryllium) are the metals that satisfy these criteria.
3. The calcium oxide in the cement is a basic anhydride that will react with moisture on the skin to produce hydroxide ions. This strong base is corrosive and will cause irritation to the skin.

Page 418, Quick Check

1. The exhaled breath contains CO_2 which reacts with the water in the beaker to form H_3O^+ions. This lowers the pH of the solution causing the universal indicator to change colour.
2. No hydroxide ions are formed when covalent oxides react with water because no oxide ions are released into water during the hydrolysis.

Page 419, Practice Problems

1. a) $K_2O(s) + H_2O(l) \rightarrow 2KOH(aq)$
   b) $MgO(s) + H_2O(l) \rightarrow Mg(OH)_2(aq)$
2. a) $Al_2O_3 < SiO_2 < P_4O_{10} < SO_3 < Cl_2O_7$
   b) $Cl_2O_7(aq) + H_2O(l) \rightarrow 2HClO_4(aq)$
   $SO_3(aq) + H_2O(l) \rightarrow H_2SO_4(aq)$
3. a) In general, *ionic oxides* react with water to produce ionic bases.
   b) In general, *molecular oxides* that react with water produce acids. Acids are molecular compounds.

Page 421, Quick Check

1. NO_2, SO_2, and SO_3.
2. The combustion of impure coal containing pyrite produces SO_2 according to the following reaction:
   $4FeS_2(s) + 11O_2(g) \rightarrow 2Fe_2O_3(s) + 8SO_2(g)$
3. In polluted air containing *ozone*, O_3, and *fine dust particles* (especially in the presence of *sunlight*), oxygen and ozone will oxidize some of the SO_2 to SO_3:

   $2SO_2(g) + O_2(g) \rightarrow 2SO_3(g)$

   $SO_2(g) + O_3(g) \rightarrow SO_3(g) + O_2(g)$

   Sulphur trioxide now reacts with water to form the *strong acid* sulphuric acid:

   $SO_3(g) + H_2O(l) \rightarrow H_2SO_4(aq)$

Page 424, Practice Problems

1. $2SO_2(g) + O_2(g) \rightarrow 2SO_3(g)$
   $SO_3(g) + H_2O(l) \rightarrow H_2SO_4(aq)$
   $2NO_2(g) + H_2O(l) \rightarrow HNO_3(aq) + HNO_2(aq)$
2. In water, hydrated aluminum ions function as weak acids according to the following:
   $Al(H_2O)_6^{3+}(aq) + H_2O(l) \rightleftharpoons Al(H_2O)_5OH^{2+}(aq) + H_3O^+(aq)$.
   Thus aluminum ions entering aquatic ecosystems lower pH levels and threaten aquatic life.
3. Scrubbing involves first blowing powdered limestone ($CaCO_3$) into the combustion chamber where heat decomposes it to CaO and CO_2 according to the following:

   $CaCO_3(s) \rightarrow CaO(s) + CO_2(g)$

   The calcium oxide (lime) then combines with the sulphur dioxide gas to produce solid calcium sulphite:

   $CaO(s) + SO_2(g) \rightarrow CaSO_3(s)$

   As a second step, to remove the $CaSO_3$ and any unreacted SO_2, an aqueous suspension of CaO is then sprayed into the exhaust gases before they reach the smokestack to produce a thick suspension of $CaSO_3$ called a slurry.

Page 427, 6.5 Review Questions

1. a) $Rb_2O(s) + H_2O(l) \rightarrow 2RbOH(aq)$
   b) $SrO(s) + H_2O(l) \rightarrow Sr(OH)_2(aq)$
   c) $SeO_2(s) + H_2O(l) \rightarrow H_2SeO_3(aq)$
   d) $N_2O_5(g) + H_2O(l) \rightarrow 2HNO_3(aq)$
2. $CaO(s) + H_2O(l) \rightarrow Ca(OH)_2(aq)$
   "Sweetening" the soil refers to increasing the alkalinity (the pH) of the soil. Moss thrives in acidic or "sour" soil, but doesn't grow as well in alkaline soil.
3. $P_4O_{10}(s) + 6H_2O(l) \rightarrow 4H_3PO_4(aq)$
4. Oxygen gas and nitrogen gas will not react with each other under normal conditions of temperature and pressure because the activation energy for the reaction is far too high.
5. Several serious problems associated with acid precipitation are:
   - Aquatic ecosystems are harmed because most species of fish will perish at pH levels below 5.
   - Terrestrial plants are damaged and weakened when exposed to acidic precipitation.
   - Acid precipitation contaminates the water supplies that human populations depend upon.
   - The soils in many areas contain aluminum salts that are nearly insoluble in normal groundwater, but begin to dissolve in more acidic solutions. This dissolving soil releases the Al^{3+} ions into aquatic ecosystems where they lower the pH of the water and threaten fish.
   - The dissolving soil also leaches out many valuable nutrients that are lost in the runoff.
   - Many buildings, monuments, and even headstones contain $CaCO_3$ in the form of either marble or limestone. Carbonate salts dissolve in acids and long-term exposure to acid rain significantly degrades such structures.
6. a) $SO_3(g) + H_2O(l) \rightarrow H_2SO_4(aq)$
   b) $2NO_2(g) + H_2O(l) \rightarrow HNO_3(aq) + HNO_2(aq)$
7. The oxides of sulphur and nitrogen that cause acid precipitation are gases that are carried into the atmosphere. Prevailing atmospheric winds can push clouds containing these oxides great distances from where the nonmetal oxides are actually produced.
8. Some lakes in regions where acid precipitation occurs are naturally protected because they are bounded by soils rich in limestone. As the limestone dissolves, the hydronium ions from acid rain cause more bicarbonate ions to form according to the following:
   $CO_3^{2-}(aq) + H_3O^+(aq) \rightleftharpoons HCO_3^-(aq) + H_2O(l)$
   Over time, as the $[HCO_3^-]$ increases, the lakes become effective bicarbonate / carbonate buffer systems and maintain a relatively constant pH. If a lake's soil *does not* contain sufficient limestone, a temporary solution is to add $CaCO_3$ or CaO directly to the lake.
9. a) The purpose of "scrubbers" in coal-burning electrical power plants and smelters is to remove sulphur dioxide gas from the exhaust stream before the exhaust stream is released into the atmosphere.
   b) Two problems associated with the process of scrubbing are:
   i) The process is expensive and consumes a great deal of energy.
   ii) Because no use has yet been found for the $CaSO_3$, the great quantities of this compound

that are produced by the process are usually buried in landfills.

10. A catalytic converter significantly reduces the levels of nitrogen oxides released into the atmosphere by using catalytic materials such as transition metal oxides and palladium or platinum metals to convert gaseous nitrogen oxides in the exhaust stream to nitrogen and oxygen gas before it leaves the tailpipe. The catalyzed reaction can be represented as follows:

$$2NO_x(g) \rightarrow xO_2(g) + N_2(g)$$

(The value of "x" is either "1" or "2")

11. Gaseous ammonia can lower NO_x emissions when it is reacted with the hot stack gases to produce nitrogen and water vapour according to the following reaction:

$$4NO(g) + 4NH_3(g) + O_2(g) \rightarrow 4N_2(g) + 6H_2O(l)$$

Chapter 7

Page 433, Practice Problems

1. H = +1 O = -2
2. Cs = +1 O = -1
3. C = +4 O = -2
4. Na = +1 Cr = +6 O = -2
5. Ba = +2 H = -1
6. N = -3 H = +1
7. S = 0
8. Al = +3 S = +6 O = -2

Page 434, Quick Check

1. 6 e-
2. nothing (no e- transferred)

Page 435, Quick Check

1. You – oxidized (LEO)
   Partner - reduced (GER)
2. Which partner acted as an "oxidizing agent"? my partner (they got reduced)
   A "reducing agent"? me (I got oxidized)
3. What happened to your "oxidation state"? Increased (I was oxidized)
   What about your partner? Reduced – got smaller (they were reduced)

Page 436, Practice Problems

0 0 -4 +1
1. $C(s) + 2H_2(g) \rightarrow CH_4(g)$ O.A. = C(s)
   R.A. = $H_2(g)$

0 +3 -1 0 +2 -1
2. $3Sr(s) + 2FeBr_3(aq) \rightarrow 2Fe(s) + 3SrBr_2(aq)$
   O.A. = Fe^{3+} R.A. = Sr

+2 -2 +5 -2 +4 -2 0
3. $5CO(g) + Cl_2O_5(s) \rightarrow 5CO_2(g) + Cl_2(s)$
   O.A. = Cl_2O_5 R.A. = CO

-3 +1 0 0
4. $4PH_3(g) \rightarrow P_4(g) + 6H_2(g)$
   O.A. and R.A. = PH_3

0 +1 -2 +2 -2 +1 0
5. $Ba(s) + 2H_2O(l) \rightarrow Ba(OH)_2(s) + H_2(g)$
   O.A. = H_2O R.A. = Ba

Page 438, 7.1 Review Questions

1. Elements that get oxidized (act as reducing agents) for (a) + ions when they react. This means reducing agents are generally (b) metals. Reducing agents may also be (c) negatively charged ions. The most active reducing agents likely belong to the (d) alkali metal family on the periodic table. The most active oxidizing agents must belong to the (e) halogen family.

2. a) $\underline{Ca}I_2$ +2 b) $\underline{O}F_2$ +2 c) $\underline{C}_6H_{12}O_6$ 0 d) $Rb_2\underline{O}_2$ -1
   e) $\underline{S}_2O_3^{2-}$ +2 f) $Be\underline{H}_2$ -1 g) $\underline{Br}O^-$ +1 h) $\underline{Cl}_2$ 0

3. a) A species that gets reduced/causes other species to be oxidized/gains e-
   b) A species that gets oxidized/causes other species to be reduced/loses e-
   c) Increased electronegativity makes a stronger O.A. and a weaker R.A.

4. For each of the following reactions, indicate the species being oxidized and reduced and show the oxidation states above their symbols.

5.

+1 +5 -2 +1 -1 0
a) $2KBrO_3(s) \rightarrow 2KBr(s) + 3O_2(g)$
Oxidized: $KBrO_3$ Reduced: $KBrO_3$

0 +1 +5 -2 +2 +5 -2 0
b) $Sr(s) + 2CuNO_3(aq) \rightarrow Sr(NO_3)_2(aq) + 2Cu(s)$
Ox'd: Sr Red'd: Cu^+

0 0 +2 -1
c) $2F_2(g) + O_2(g) \rightarrow 2OF_2(g)$
Oxidized: O_2 Reduced: F_2

-3 +1+5 -2 +1 -2 +1 -2
d) $NH_4NO_3(s) \rightarrow N_2O(g) + 2H_2O(l)$
Ox'd: NH_4NO_3 Red'd: NH_4NO_3 (solid)

5. Determine the oxidizing and reducing agent in each of the following reactions. Then indicate the number of electrons transferred by one atom of the reducing agent.

0 0 +2 -2
a) $2Sn(s) + O_2(g) \rightarrow 2SnO(s)$
OA: O_2 RA: Sn No e: 2

0 0 +5 -1
b) $2V(s) + 5I_2(g) \rightarrow 2VI_5(s)$
OA: I_2 RA: V No e^-: 5

0 +1 -1 +2 -1 0
c) $Sr(s) + 2HCl(aq) \rightarrow SrCl_2(aq) + H_2(g)$
OA: H+ RA: Sr No e^-: 2

-8/3 +1 0 +4 -2 +1 -2
d) $C_3H_8(g) + 5O_2(g) \rightarrow 3CO_2(g) + 4H_2O(g)$
OA: O_2 RA: C_3H_8 No e^-: 6⅔

6. a) Write a balanced redox equation (in net ionic form) to show what has occurred in the beaker over time: $Fe(s) + Cu^{2+}(aq) \rightarrow Fe^{2+}(aq) + Cu(s)$
   b) What is the oxidizing agent? $Cu^{2+}(aq)$ The reducing agent? Fe(s)
   c) How many electrons were transferred in the equation? 2e-

7. Give the oxidation state of the underlined element in each species:
   a) $\underline{P}^{3-}$ -3 b) $(NH_4)_2\underline{Zr}(SO_4)_3$ +4 c) $Na_2\underline{C}_2O_4$ +3
   d) $\underline{N}_2H_5Cl$ -2 e) $\underline{Mn}O_4^{2-}$ +6

8.

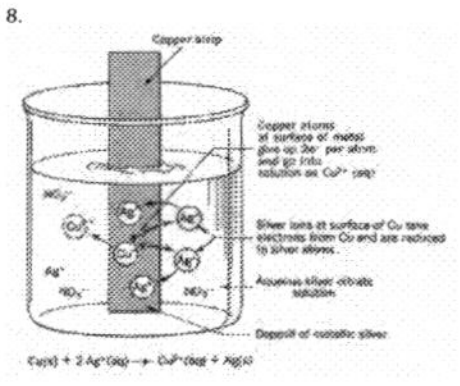

a) see above
b) Oxidized? Cu metal
Reduced? Ag^+ ion
c) Reducing agent? Cu metal
Oxidizing agent? Ag^+ ion
d) 2e-
   a) Alkali metal family (IA)
   b) Halogens (VIIA) or (17)

9. a) ClO_4^-, ClO_3^-, ClO_2^-
   b) Cl_2, Cl^-

Page 444, Practice Problems

1. $Sm \rightarrow Sm^{3+} + 3e^-$ *oxidation*
2. $8e^- + 10H^+ + NO_3^- \rightarrow NH_4^+ + 3H_2O$ *reduction*
3. $2e^- + H_2O + IO_4^- \rightarrow IO_3^- + 2OH^-$ *reduction*
4. $5H_2O + S_2O_3^{2-} \rightarrow 2SO_4^{2-} + 10H^+ + 8e^-$ *oxidation*
5. $10e^- + 6H_2O + 2BrO_3^- \rightarrow Br_2 + 12OH^-$ *reduction*

Page 447, Practice Problems

1. $4Zn + 8H^+ + H_3AsO_4 \rightarrow AsH_3 + 4H_2O + 4Zn^{2+}$

Species	Reactants	Products
Hydrogen	11	11
Zinc	4	4
Oxygen	4	4
Arsenic	1	1
Charge	+8	+8

2.
$4H^+ + 4NO_3^- + C_2H_5OH \rightarrow CH_3COOH + 2N_2O_4 + 3H_2O$

Species	Reactants	Products
Hydrogen	10	10
Nitrogen	4	4
Oxygen	13	13
Carbon	2	2
Charge	0	0

Page 449, Practice Problems 7.2.3

1. $2HXeO_4^- + 2OH^- \rightarrow XeO_6^{4-} + Xe + O_2 + 2H_2O$

Species	Reactants	Products
Hydrogen	4	4
Xenon	2	2
Oxygen	10	10
Charge	-4	-4

2. $6H_2O + 2BrO_3^- + 10Br^- \rightarrow 6Br_2 + 12OH^-$

Species	Reactants	Products
Hydrogen	12	12
Bromine	12	12
Oxygen	12	12
Charge	-12	-12

3. $2H_2O + 2CH_3COO^- \rightarrow 2CH_4 + 2CO_2 + 2OH^-$

Species	Reactants	Products
Hydrogen	10	10
Carbon	4	4
Oxygen	6	6
Charge	-2	-2

Page 452, 7.2 Review Questions

1.

	Reactants	Products	Add
e.g.	2+	3+	1 e^- to products
a.	3+	2-	5 e^- to reactants
b.	1-	3-	2 e^- to reactants
c.	2-	4+	6 e^- to products
d.	1+	5+	4 e^- to products

2.
a) $2e^- + 2NO_3^- + 2H_2O \rightarrow N_2O_4 + 4OH^-$ (reduction)
b) $2Cr^{3+} + 7H_2O \rightarrow Cr_2O_7^{2-} + 14H^+ + 6e^-$ (oxidation)
c) $8e^- + ClO_4^- + 4H_2O \rightarrow Cl^- + 8OH^-$ (reduction)
d) $S_2O_5^{2-} + 3H_2O \rightarrow 2SO_4^{2-} + 6H^+ + 4e^-$ (oxidation)

3. a) $14e^- + 16H^+ + 2ClO_4^- \rightarrow Cl_2 + 8H_2O$ (reduction)
   b) $H_2O + 2FeO \rightarrow Fe_2O_3 + 2H^+ + 2e^-$ (oxidation)
   c) $2H_2O + N_2O_4 \rightarrow 2NO_3^- + 4H^+ + 2e^-$ (oxidation)

4. a) $4H_2O + 4e^- + CrO_4^{2-} \rightarrow Cr(OH)_2 + 6OH^-$ (reduction)
   b) $2S_2O_3^{2-} \rightarrow S_4O_6^{2-} + 2e^-$ (oxidation)
   c) $4e^- + 3H_2O + IO_3^- + 2Cl^- \rightarrow ICl_2^- + 6OH^-$ (reduction)

5. a) $4H_2O + 2MnO_4^- + 3Sn^{2+} \rightarrow 3Sn^{4+} + 2MnO_2 + 8OH^-$
   b) $2H^+ + 2H_2SO_3 + 4V^{2+} \rightarrow 4V^{3+} + S_2O_3^{2-} + 3H_2O$
   c) $3H_2O + IO_3^- + 5I^- \rightarrow 3I_2 + 6OH^-$
   d) $3N_2H_4 + 4ClO_3^- \rightarrow 4Cl^- + 6NO + 6H_2O$
   e) $4H_2O + 2NO_3^- + 3Zn \rightarrow 3Zn^{2+} + 2NO + 8OH^-$
   f) $2H^+ + 11ClO_3^- \rightarrow 8ClO_4^- + Cl^- + Cl_2 + H_2O$
   g) $5H_2O + 3SnS_3O_3 + 16MnO_4^- \rightarrow 16MnO_2 + 10OH^- + 9SO_4^{2-} + 3Sn^{4+}$
   h) $2Mg_3(AsO_4)_2 + 6SiO_2 + 10C \rightarrow 10CO + As_4 + 6MgSiO_3$

6. a) $6H^+ + SeO_3^{2-} + 4F^- \rightarrow Se + 2F_2 + 3H_2O$
   b) $2H_2O + 4ReO_4^- + 3Sb_2O_3 \rightarrow 4ReO_2 + 3Sb_2O_5 + 4OH^-$
   c) $16H^+ + 4NO_3^- + 3Pd + 18I^- \rightarrow 3PdI_6^{2-} + 4NO + 8H_2O$
   d) $Pb(OH)_4^{2-} + BrO^- \rightarrow PbO_2 + Br^- + H_2O + 2OH^-$

7. a) $16HCl + 2K_2Cr_2O_7 + 3CH_3CH_2OH \rightarrow 3CH_3COOH + 4CrCl_3 + 11H_2O + 4KCl$
   b) $4NaCl + 2H_2SO_4 + MnO_2 \rightarrow 2Na_2SO_4 + MnCl_2 + 2H_2O + Cl_2$

Page 459, Practice Problems

1. yes; $2I^- + Br_2 \rightarrow 2Br^- + I_2$
2. no; both are oxidizing agents
3. yes; $2Ag^+ + Sn \rightarrow Sn^{2+} + 2Ag$
4. no; I_2 isn't a strong enough oxidizing agent to spontaneously react with Cl^-

Page 460, Practice Problems

1. no; I_2 isn't a strong enough oxidizing agent to spontaneously react with F^-
2. yes; $3Cu^{2+} + 2Al \rightarrow 2Al^{3+} + 3Cu$
3. yes; $Cl_2 + 2Br^- \rightarrow Br_2 + 2Cl^-$ (* Question revised from complimentary copy)
4. no; Al^{3+} isn't a strong enough oxidizing agent to spontaneously react with Sn

Page 462, Quick Check

1. Sr
2. Fe^{3+}
3. I^-
4. Sn^{2+}
5. B^-
6. +0.80 V
7. +2.87 V

Page 464, Practice Problems

1. $Sn^{4+} + Ni \rightarrow Sn^{2+} + Ni^{2+}$
2. $3Cu^{2+} + 2Al \rightarrow 2Al^{3+} + 3Cu$
3. $2Cu^+ \rightarrow Cu^{2+} + Cu$
4. $Cu + Br_2 \rightarrow 2Br^- + Cu^{2+}$

Page 465, Practice Problems

1. a) $Cr_2O_7^{2-} + 6Fe^{2+} + 14H^+ \rightarrow 2Cr^{3+} + 6Fe^{3+} + 7H_2O$
   b) 0.0900 M
2. 0.183 M
3. a) 1.97 M
   b) 11.5%

Page 467, 7.3 Review Questions

1. a) no
   b) yes
2. Either Fe^{3+}, Hg_2^{2+}, Ag^+, or Hg^{2+}
3. a) yes; $3Mg + 2Al^{3+} \rightarrow 3Mg^{2+} + 2Al$
   b) no
   c) yes; $Hg^{2+} + 2Ag \rightarrow Hg + 2Ag^+$

4.

Metals	Non-metals
bottom right of SRP Table	**top left of SRP Table**
tend to give electrons	tend to take electrons
give e^- to chemicals above them on the left	take e^- from chemicals below them on the right

5. a) yes; $Fe + Sn^{2+} \rightarrow Fe^{2+} + Sn$
   b) yes; $F_2 + 2Br^- \rightarrow Br_2 + 2F^-$
   c) no
6. a) $2I^- + 2Fe^{3+} \rightarrow I_2 + 2Fe^{2+}$
   b) $Br_2 + 2Fe^{2+} \rightarrow 2Br^- + 2Fe^{3+}$
7. $3Sn^{2+} + 2NO_3^- + 8H^+ \rightarrow 2NO + 4H_2O + 3Sn^{4+}$
8. No. The Fe^{3+} would oxidize and dissolve the Al container.
9. a) reverse
   b) forward
10. $Mg + 2H^+ \rightarrow Mg^{2+} + H_2$
11. The H^+ in acids is not a strong enough oxidizing agent to oxidize silver but the nitrate ion in nitric acid is.
12. $2Na + H_2O \rightarrow 2Na^+ + H_2 + OH^-$
    The OH^- turns the phenolphthalein pink. The H_2 is ignited by the energy released by the exothermic reaction.
13. a) Ag^+
    b) Mg
14. Ga^{3+}; Al is being oxidized by gallium ions therefore Ga^{3+} is a stronger oxidizing agent (higher on the left in the SRP table) than Al^{3+} and so Ga^{3+} has a greater reduction potential than Al^{3+}.
15. a) +1.09V
    b) +0.76V
16. a) $Fe + Co^{2+} \rightarrow Fe^{2+} + Co$
    b) $Cu^+ + Cr^{2+} \rightarrow Cr^{3+} + Cu$
    c) $Cu^{2+} + Sn^{2+} \rightarrow Sn^{4+} + Cu$
17. $Zn + 2Fe^{3+} \rightarrow 2Fe^{2+} + Zn^{2+}$
18. a) C^{3+}
    b) D
19. 2.62 M
20. 0.0179 M
21. a) $2Cr_2O_7^{2-} + C_2H_5OH + 16H^+ \rightarrow 4Cr^{3+} + 11H_2O + 2CO_2$
    b) 0.0700%. Legally impaired now, not before Sep. 2010.

Page 473, Quick Check

1. Cr
2. from right to left or from the Cr electrode to the Ag electrode
3. from right to left or from the Cr/Cr^{3+} half-cell to the Ag/Ag^+ half-cell
4. Ag

Page 475, Practice Problems

1. $Ni \rightarrow Ni^{2+} + 2e^-$ $E° = 0.26$ V
   $Br_2 + 2e^- \rightarrow 2Br^-$ $E° = 1.09$ V

   $Br_2 + Ni \rightarrow Ni^{2+} + 2Br^-$ $E° = 1.35$ V

2. $2Al \rightarrow 2Al^{3+} + 6e^-$ $E° = 1.66$ V
   $3Cu^{2+} + 6e^- \rightarrow 3Cu$ $E° = 0.34$ V

   $2Al + 3Cu^{2+} \rightarrow 2Al^{3+} + 3Cu$ $E° = 2.00$ V

3. $6I^- \rightarrow 3I_2 + 6e^-$ $E° = -0.54$ V
   $2Au^{3+} + 6e^- \rightarrow 2Au$ $E° = +1.50$ V

   $6I^- + 2Au^{3+} \rightarrow 3I_2 + 2Au$ $E° = +0.96$ V

Page 479, Practice Problems

1. $E°_{cell} = +0.19$ V;
   $K = 10^{6.4} = 3 \times 10^6$
   Prediction: If $[Fe^{2+}]$ decreases, Q decreases, log Q decreases, E increases. $E = +0.23\ V$
2. $E = 0.52\ V$
3. $Q = 3.07 \times 10^{11} = 10^{11}$
   $$[Cu^{2+}] = \frac{1.0\ M}{10^{11}} = 10^{-12}\ M$$

Page 482, Quick Check

1.

Type	Anode Material	Cathode Material	Electrolyte Medium	Use
Alkaline Cell	Zn powder packed around a brass pin	$MnO_2(s)$ and powdered C	a moist paste of KOH	e.g. portable electronics, toys, flashlights
Lead-acid Storage Battery	Pb alloy grids packed with spongy Pb	Pb alloy grids packed with PbO_2	$H_2SO_4(aq)$	automobiles
Fuel Cell	porous carbon	porous carbon	proton exchange membrane	e.g. electric vehicles, space travel,

Page 484, Quick Check

1. hydrated iron (III) oxide or iron(III) oxide monohydrate
2. $\frac{1}{2}O_2(g) + 2H^+ + 2e^- \rightarrow H_2O$ or $\frac{1}{2}O_2(g) + H_2O + 2e^- \rightarrow 2OH^-$
3. impurities or physical stresses or $[O_2]$ or [ions] or surface area
4. coating it with paint or grease or cathodic protection or galvanizing it.

Page 486, 7.4 Review Questions

1.

Anode	Cathode
oxidation occurs	reduction occurs
mass decreases	**mass increases**
attracts anions	attracts cations
electrons flow away	**electrons flow towards**

2. a) The diagram should show e^- flowing through the wire from the Fe/Fe^{2+} half-cell to the Ni/Ni^{2+} half-cell.
   b) Fe/Fe^{2+}
   c) $Fe \rightarrow Fe^{2+} + 2e^-$; $Ni^{2+} + 2e^- \rightarrow Ni$
   d) Fe labelled anode; Ni labelled cathode
   e) $E° = +0.19$ V

   f) NH_4^+ flow from the salt bridge into the Ni/Ni^{2+} half-cell
   NO_3^- flow through the salt bridge into the Fe/Fe^{2+} half-cell
   g) The Fe electrode loses mass. The Ni electrode gains mass.

3. For example:

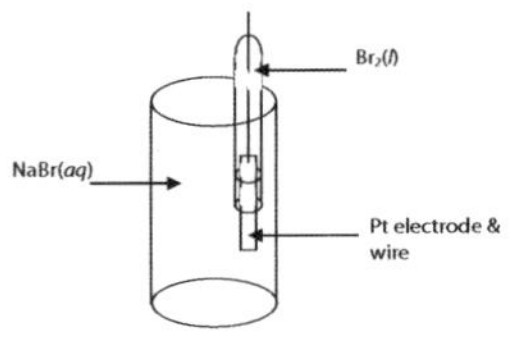

4. a) The diagram should show e^- flowing through the wire from the Cr/Cr^{3+} half-cell to the H_2/H^+ half-cell
   b) H_2/H^+
   c) $Cr \rightarrow Cr^{3+} + 3e^-$; $2H^+ + 2e^- \rightarrow H_2$
5. a) Cr labelled anode; Pt labelled cathode
   b) 0.74 V
   c) Cr^{3+} flow through the porous barrier into the H_2/H^+ half-cell
   Cl^- flow through the porous barrier into the Cr/Cr^{3+} half-cell
   d) The Cr electrode loses mass. The Pt electrode's mass is unchanged.

6.

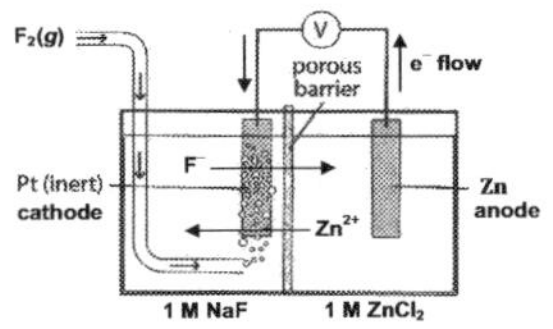

d) $Zn \rightarrow Zn^{2+} + 2e^-$ $E° = 0.76$ V
   $F_2 + 2e^- \rightarrow 2F^-$ $E° = 2.87$ V
   ---
e) $Zn + F_2 \rightarrow Zn^{2+} + 2F^-$ $E° = 3.63$ V

7. It allows ion migration that completes the circuit
8. $2Fe^{2+} \rightarrow 2Fe^{3+} + 2e^-$ $E° = -0.77$ V
   $Br_2 + 2e^- \rightarrow 2Br^-$ $E° = +1.09$ V

   $2Fe^{2+} + Br_2 \rightarrow 2Fe^{3+} + 2Br^-$ $E° = +0.32$ V
9. a) 2.07 V (the E° of $F_2 + 2e^- \rightarrow 2F^-$ is 2.07 V greater than the E° of $Ag^+ + e^- \rightarrow Ag$)
   b) −3.17 V (the E° of $Mg^{2+} + 2e^- \rightarrow Mg$ is 3.17 V less than the E° of $Ag^+ + e^- \rightarrow Ag$)
10. $Cr^{2+} + 2e^- \rightarrow Cr$ $E° = -0.56$ V
    $Sr \rightarrow Sr^{2+} + 2e^-$ $E° = +2.89$ V (from Table A7, p.487)
    $Cr^{2+} + 2e^- \rightarrow Cr$ $E° = -0.56$ V

    $Sr + Cr^{2+} \rightarrow Sr^{2+} + Cr$ $E° = +2.33$ V (provided by question)
11. a) 0.83 V
    $Cu \rightarrow Cu^{2+} + 2e^-$ $E° = -0.34$ V (from Table A7, p.487)
    $Pd^{2+} + 2e^- \rightarrow Pd$ $E° = +0.83$ V

    $Cu + Pd^{2+} \rightarrow Cu^{2+} + Pd$ $E° = +0.49$ V (provided by question)
    b) −1.90 V
    $2Np \rightarrow 2Np^{3+} + 6e^-$ $E° = 1.90$ V
    $3Pd^{2+} + 6e^- \rightarrow 3Pd$ $E° = 0.83$ V (answer to 10 a.)

    $2Np + 3Pd^{2+} \rightarrow 2Np^{3+} + 3Pd$ $E° = 2.73$ V (provided by question)
    1.90 V is the Standard Oxidation Potential (SOP) of Np therefore the Standard Reduction Potential (SRP) of Np^{3+} is −1.90 V.
12.

		Reduction Half-cell	
		$Cd^{2+} + 2e^- \rightarrow Cd$	$Pt^{2+} + 2e^- \rightarrow Pt$
Oxidation Half-cell	$Pt \rightarrow Pt^{2+} + 2e^-$	**− 1.60 V**	0 V
	$Ni \rightarrow Ni^{2+} + 2e^-$	− 0.17 V	+ 1.43 V
	$Ce \rightarrow Ce^{3+} + 3e^-$	+ 1.93 V	**+ 3.53 V**

Construct an SRP Table from the data provided:

$Pt^{2+} + 2e^- \rightleftharpoons Pt$ + 1.17 V (1.43 V above $Ni^{2+} + 2e^- \rightarrow Ni$)
$Ni^{2+} + 2e^- \rightleftharpoons Ni$ − 0.26 V (from Table A7, p.487)
$Cd^{2+} + 2e^- \rightleftharpoons Cd$ − 0.43 V (0.17 V below $Ni^{2+} + 2e^- \rightarrow Ni$)
$Ce^{3+} + 3e^- \rightleftharpoons Ce$ − 2.36 V (1.93 V below $Cd^{2+} + 2e^- \rightarrow Cd$)

13. a) increased voltage (The reactant concentrations are greater than 1 M so the cell's potential will be greater than the standard cell potential.)
    b) 0 V
    c) increased voltage (The product concentrations are less than 1 M because the S^{2-} ions precipitate out some Fe^{2+} so the cell's potential will be greater than the standard cell potential.)
    d) no effect
14. For e.g. Reactants biodegradable. Products are just CO_2 and H_2O. No metal or metal ion reactants or products.
15. Weld a zinc bar to the staircase preferably above the area exposed to ocean spray. The zinc is oxidized more readily than the steel (Fe). The zinc bar transfers electrons through the staircase to the oxidizing agents in the ocean spray thus leaving the staircase intact.
16. If the zinc is oxidized it forms zinc oxide. Zinc oxide forms a hard, impenetrable coating. Should the zinc or the zinc oxide coating be scratched off in some areas, the remaining zinc coating still provides cathodic protection.
17. The reactants in electrochemical cells react through electrical contact, via an action-at-a-distance force, without ever coming into physical contact, i.e. colliding.
18. The voltage changes by + 0.03 V each time the concentration changes by a factor of 10.
19. $E°_{cell} = -0.86$; $K = 10^{-150}$
20. a) $E°_{cell} = +2.20$ V; $K = 10^{223}$
    b) E is greater in these conditions than standard conditions. Mathematically, Q in standard conditions is 1 (molarities of each ion is 1.0 M) Thus the log of Q is 0. The change of these concentrations resulted in a greater E value. K does not change as there was no change in temperature. (Only changes in temperature can alter K values).

21. a) $E^{\circ}_{cell} = +0.76$ V
b) $7 \times 10^{-5}\ M$
c) $pH = 4.2$
22. a) $E = +0.26\ V$
b) $E^{\circ}_{ox} = +0.26$ V
c) Ni(s)

Page 494, Practice Problems

1. $2Ag \rightarrow 2Ag^{+} + 2e^{-}$ $E^{\circ} = -0.80$ V
$Ni^{2+} + 2e^{-} \rightarrow Ni$ $E^{\circ} = -0.26$ V
$2Ag + Ni^{2+} \rightarrow 2Ag^{+} + Ni$ $E^{\circ} = -1.06$ V

A voltage of at least 1.06 V would be required to operate this cell.

2. $2F^{-} \rightarrow F_2 + 2e^{-}$ $E^{\circ} = -2.87$ V
$Cu^{2+} + 2e^{-} \rightarrow Cu$ $E^{\circ} = +0.34$ V
$2F^{-} + Cu^{2+} \rightarrow F_2 + Cu$ $E^{\circ} = -2.53$ V

A voltage of at least 2.53 V would be required to operate this cell.

3. $3Sn \rightarrow 3Sn^{2+} + 6e^{-}$ $E^{\circ} = +0.14$ V
$2Al^{3+} + 6e^{-} \rightarrow 2Al$ $E^{\circ} = -1.66$ V
$3Sn + 2Al^{3+} \rightarrow 3Sn^{2+} + 2Al$ $E^{\circ} = -1.52$ V

A voltage of at least 1.52 V would be required to operate this cell.

Page 496, Quick Check

1. electrochemical cell
2. electrolytic cell
3. both
4. electrochemical cell
5. both
6. electrolytic cell
7. electrochemical cell

Page 499, Practice Problems

1. a) Type 1 $2I^{-} \rightarrow I_2 + 2e^{-}$
$Mg^{2+} + 2e^{-} \rightarrow Mg$
b) Type 2 $H_2O \rightarrow \frac{1}{2} O_2 + 2H^{+} + 2e^{-}$
$2H_2O + 2e^{-} \rightarrow H_2 + 2OH^{-}$
c) Type 3 $Fe \rightarrow Fe^{2+} + 2e^{-}$
$2H_2O + 2e^{-} \rightarrow H_2 + 2OH^{-}$

2. Anode $2Br^{-} \rightarrow Br_2 + 2e^{-}$ $E^{\circ} = -1.09$ V
Cathode $Ni^{2+} + 2e^{-} \rightarrow Ni$ $E^{\circ} = -0.26$ V
$E^{\circ} = -1.35$ V

A voltage of at least 1.35 V would be required to operate this cell.

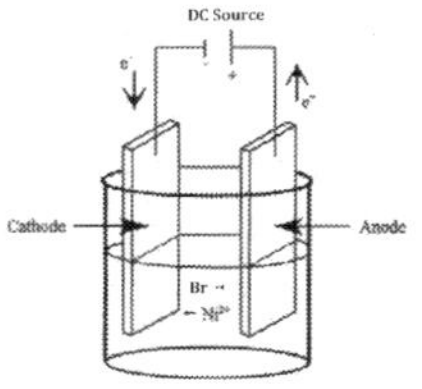

Page 501, Quick Check

1. the electrolytic recovery of a metal from a solution containing its ions.
2. aluminum oxide dissolves in molten cryolite ($Na_3AlF_6(l)$)
3. sodium hydroxide and chlorine
4. impressed current cathodic protection

Page 503, 7.5 Review Questions

1. citric acid (weak electrolyte), sodium chloride, sodium citrate, and potassium dihydrogen phosphate
2.

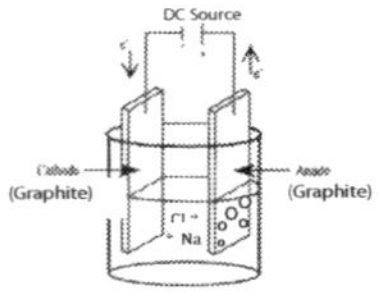

Anode $2Cl^{-} \rightarrow Cl_2 + 2e^{-}$ $E^{\circ} = -1.36$ V
Cathode $Na^{+} + e^{-} \rightarrow Na$ $E^{\circ} = -2.71$ V
$E^{\circ} = -4.07$ V

A voltage of at least 4.07 V would be required to operate this cell.

3. Because the products (Na and Cl_2) spontaneously react with each other
4.

	Cell Type (1,2,3)	Electrolyte	Anode/Cathode	Products	
				Anode	Cathode
a.	**1**	NaCl(*l*)	Pt / Pt	**Cl_2**	**Na**
b.	**2**	NaCl(*aq*)	Pt / C	**Cl_2**	**$H_2 + 2OH^{-}$**
c.	**2**	$CuBr_2$(*aq*)	C / C	**Br_2**	**Cu**
d.	**2**	AlF_3(*aq*)	C / C	**$\frac{1}{2}O_2 + 2H^{+}$**	**$H_2 + 2OH^{-}$**
e.	**3**	$CuCl_2$(*aq*)	Cu / Cu	**Cu^{2+}**	**Cu**

5. a) Anode $H_2O \rightarrow \frac{1}{2} O_2 + 2H^{+} + 2e^{-}$ $E^{\circ} = -1.37$ V (approximate)
Cathode $NO_3^{-} + 4H^{+} + 3e^{-} \rightarrow NO + 2H_2O$ $E^{\circ} = +0.96$ V
$E^{\circ} = -0.41$ V
b) A voltage of at least 0.41 V would be required to operate this cell.
6. $2H_2O + 2e^{-} \rightarrow H_2 + 2OH^{-}$
7. In electrorefining, the metallic ions reduced at the cathode are replaced by oxidizing an impure anode.
8. Uneconomical to electrolyze $Al_2O_3(l)$ because aluminum oxide has a high melting point. Impossible to produce Al by electrolyzing $Al_2O_3(aq)$ because water is a stronger oxidizing agent than Al^{3+}.
9. In impressed current cathodic protection the metal being protected acts as the cathode in an electrolytic cell (non-spontaneous redox reaction) whereas in galvanic cathodic protection the metal being protected acts as the cathode in an electrochemical cell (spontaneous redox reaction).
10.

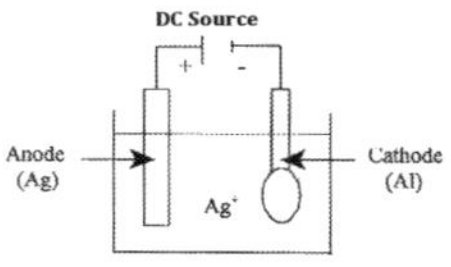

$Ag \rightarrow Ag^{+} + e^{-}$ $E^{\circ} = -0.80$ V
$Ag^{+} + e^{-} \rightarrow Ag$ $E^{\circ} = +0.80$ V
$E^{\circ} = 0.0$

In theory, it should require no voltage to operate this cell because no net reaction occurs. In practice, a small voltage is required to overcome the internal resistance of the cell.

11. a) Type 1 Cell. Only one chemical, water, can be oxidized or reduced. Water is molten H_2O.
b) Any salt containing ions which are weaker reducing agents and weaker oxidizing agents than water; for example, sodium sulphate.
12. 0.75 V
$2Br^{-} \rightarrow Br_2 + 2e^{-}$ $E^{\circ} = -1.09$ V
$Cu^{2+} + 2e^{-} \rightarrow Cu$ $E^{\circ} = +0.34$ V
$2Br^{-} + Cu^{2+} \rightarrow Br_2 + Cu$ $E^{\circ} = -0.75$ V

Page 506, Practice Problems

1. 121 g Al (s)
2. 1.5 A
3. a) This reaction takes place at the anode because species lose electrons at the anode resulting in oxidation. Sulfate is losing electrons in this half reaction.
b) 3.15 h

Page 509, Practice Problems

1. $\Delta G^{\circ} = -46\ kJ/mol_{rxn}$
2. − 0.40 V
3. a) − 2.19 V
b) $E^{\circ}_{ox} = -0.53$ V
$X_2 = I_2 =$ diatomic Iodine
If − 0.53 V is the oxidation potential, the reduction potential is + 0.53 V. The oxidation potential corresponds to the iodide ion.

Page 511, Review Questions

1. a) 0.44 g Cr (s)
b) 820 s or 7.3 h
c) 1.99 A
2. a) Placing a layer of tin against the steel, which is mainly composed of iron, protects the iron/steel can. Iron oxidizes spontaneously with water (and oxygen) where tin will not spontaneously react, thus becoming a protective barrier. Furthermore, if the iron were to oxidize at all, it would force electrons onto the tin keeping the tin in its reduced form. The first "layer" of protection is "barrier protection". The second is called "cathodic protection".
b) i) 6.92 g Sn (s)
ii) 3.69 M
3. 2080 s
4. a) 5.38 g Co (s)
b) 1.02 L O_2 (g)
c) Two methods to identify hat the gas is oxygen gas: 1 - relighting a glowing splint
2 - using an indicator to show the accompanying H^{+} ions
5. a) $E^{\circ}_{cell} = -1.23$ V, $\Delta G^{\circ} = 475\ kJ/mol_{rxn}$
b) $E^{\circ}_{cell} = +1.27$ V, $\Delta G^{\circ} = -490.\ kJ/mol_{rxn}$. (b) is spontaneous
6. a) $E^{\circ}_{red} = +0.34$ V, $E^{\circ}_{red} = +0.34$ V
b) $\Delta G^{\circ} = -213\ kJ/mol_{rxn}$
7. a) $\Delta G^{\circ} = -89\ kJ/mol_{rxn}$
b) − 0.17 V
8. $4.3\ g$
9. $E^{\circ} = +1.33\ V$
10. 9.30 V
11. a) $6\ AlOF_3^{2-} + 3\ C(s) \rightarrow 2\ AlF_6^{3-} + 3\ CO_2 + 4\ Al$
b) $\Delta G = 320\ kJ/mol_{rxn}$

Made in the USA
Middletown, DE
05 October 2022

11983168R10311